ALSO BY KEVIN BROWNLOW

The Parade's Gone By . . .
How It Happened Here
The War, the West and the Wilderness
Hollywood: The Pioneers
Napoleon: Abel Gance's Classic Film

BEHIND THE MASK OF INNOCENCE

Kevin Brownlow

BEHIND
THE MASK OF
INNOCENCE

University of California Press

Berkeley and Los Angeles

UNIVERSITY OF CALIFORNIA PRESS
Berkeley and Los Angeles, California

Library of Congress Cataloging-in-Publication Data
Brownlow, Kevin.
Behind the mask of innocence / Kevin Brownlow.
p. cm.
Reprint. Originally published : New York : Knopf, 1990.
Includes bibliographical references and index.
ISBN 0-520-07626-5 (pbk.)
1. Silent films—United States—History and criticism. 2. Social
problems in motion pictures. I. Title.
[PN 1995.75.B68 1990]
791.43'655'09041—DC20   91-23050
                                                                  CIP

Manufactured in the United States of America

1   2   3   4   5   6   7   8   9

The paper used in this publication meets the minimum requirements of American
National Standard for Information Sciences—Permanence of Paper
for Printed Library Materials, ANSI Z39.48–1984. ∞

Frontispiece: Ellis Island re-created in the studio for The Strong Man,
directed by Frank Capra, 1926.

For Virginia and Julia

"There is the same world for all of us, and good and evil, sin and innocence, go through it hand in hand. To shut one's eyes to half of life that one may live securely is as though one blinded oneself that one might walk with more safety in a land of pit and precipice."

OSCAR WILDE

"The motion picture industry is the greatest enemy of civilization, greater even than the liquor traffic. For a generation it has been the universal school of crime in all nations, creating the international ill-will of foreign peoples against the United States and seriously interfering with our commerce abroad."

CANON W. SHEAFE CHASE,
rector of Christ Church, Brooklyn, New York, ca. 1926

Contents

Acknowledgments

Academy of Motion Picture
    Arts & Sciences
Lars Ahlander
Edward Allatt
Richard Ariano
Geoffrey Bell
Walter Bernstein
Bob Birchard
Lenny Borger
Q. David Bowers
Eileen Bowser
David Bradley
British Film Institute Information
    Department
British Library
Peter Cowie
David Crippen, Edison Institute,
    Ford Museum
Bob Cushman
Ray Daum
Gustav Deak
Samson De Brier
Angela Doyle
William Drew
Hervé Dumont
Harold Dunham
Edison National Historic Site
Bernard Eisenschitz
William Ellington
William K. Everson
Leatrice Gilbert Fountain
George Geltzer
Bob Geoghegan
David Gill

Bob Gitt
Peter and Anne Gower
Kevin Green
Dr. Fritz Güttinger
Michael Henshaw
Steven Higgins
Derek Hill
Historical Health Film Collection,
    University of Michigan
Frank Holland
Jim Hoberman
J. B. Kaufman
David Kenten
Paul Killiam
Linda Kowall
Annette Kuhn
Jay Leyda
Lilly Library, University of Indiana
Lars Lindstrom
Jack Lodge
Bruce Long
Gloria Loomis
Patrick Loughney
Arthur Lubin
Sue McConachy
Gerald McKee
Richard Maltby
Anna-Maija Marttinen
William T. Murphy
Charles Musser
Herbert Nusbaum
Steve Oney
James Patterson
James Pepper

Martin Pernick
David Platt
George Pratt
Susan Ralston
Adam Reilly
Ira Resnick
David Robinson
Steven Ross
John Rylands Library,
    Manchester University
Mr. and Mrs. Donald Salinger
Markku Salmi
David Samuelson
Edith Schwartz
Daniel Selznick
David Shepard
Martin Short
Charles Silver
Joel Silver
Scott Simon
Jeff Smith
Martin Sopocy

Paul Spehr
Patrick Stanbury
Laura Starrett
Thames Television
Lawrence Copley Thaw, Jr.
David Thaxton
Frank Thompson
Yuri Tsivian
Charles Turner
George Turner
United States Library,
    University of London
Mia Vander Els
Alexander Walker
Marc Wanamaker
Charles Wenden
Wichita State University,
    Special Collections Department
William Wilson
Michael Yocum
Kyril Zinovieff
Albin Zwiazek

. . . and special gratitude to Gloria Loomis, who rescued the manuscript from a snowdrift of rejection slips, and to Susan Ralston, for her epic job of editing.

K. B.

Introduction

The silent era is celebrated for its innocence. The charming picture it presents of America in the early years of the century has led people to assume that life was quieter then, gentler and more civilized. But the silent era recorded another America. It revealed the corruption of city politics, the scandal of white slave rackets, the exploitation of immigrants. Gangsters, procurers, and loan sharks flashed across the same screen as Mary Pickford, but their images have mostly been destroyed, leaving us with an unbalanced portrait of an era.

This book is an attempt to set the record straight. I believe that one day, those films which give us an accurate impression of how people lived will be regarded as precious as the most imaginative flights of fiction.

Our view of the silent era is conditioned by the minuscule number of films in

Lois Weber exposes corruption in American politics with The Hypocrites, *1915. The grafting politician is paid off by the gangster, the cop, the saloonkeeper, the madam, and the drug dealer. (The madam is Jane Darwell, of* Grapes of Wrath *fame.) (National Film Archive)*

circulation—films which have selected themselves by virtue of their availability. This book will show the astonishing range of subjects dealt with in that period. While few of these films made history, all of them—if only for a few moments— recorded it.

The early films were made to a pattern which had proved its commercial value on the popular stage. Give the audience someone to identify with, bring in "heart interest," a pretty girl or an appealing child, and wind up with a happy ending. Into this you can mix whatever theme you want. Banal it may sound, but some remarkable films were made with this formula.

Some smothered their subject matter with glutinous sentimentality. They were old-fashioned in the worst sense. A critic of 1913 described them as exhibiting "a feeble-minded subservience for what may have served some past generation but which has no bearing on this one."[1] Other films adopted plain stories and a straightforward approach, which became the trademark for American films. Their very directness appealed to audiences, but often disturbed those in authority. Strong themes unimpaired by symbolism or sentimentality brought down upon the industry the wrath of clergy, reformers, and politicians alike.

If the subject of prostitution were to be shown, a parable set in Biblical times might (just) be acceptable to the bluenoses. Imagine their shock when upon the screen appeared modern settings, realistic playing, and equally realistic prostitutes! No matter that such films were animated by reforming zeal. What of their effect upon adolescent boys? They must be stopped.

Sadly, even these realistic films stopped short of attacking the system that led to prostitution. Melodramatic devices would place the police in the role of heroes; a love affair would end a corrupt regime in City Hall; an evil factory owner would be redeemed by a worker's child. Melodrama was an antidote to the sting of truth.

Nonetheless, that sting sometimes penetrated the hokum, to the discomfiture of those in authority.

They took their ideas from the newspapers. The stories of many one- and two-reelers, especially those of D. W. Griffith, were adapted from current issues. Many workers, illiterate and foreign-born, read no newspapers, and the nickelodeon was thus a source of astonishment. Nickelodeons were sometimes seen as breeding grounds for crime and sedition. Surveys had shown that almost three quarters of the audience of such places came from the working class.

As late as 1920, a member of the Canadian Parliament declared that pictures were an invitation to the people of the poorer classes to revolt. "They bring disorder into the country. Thank God there is not a moving picture show in any town or village in my constituency, and I hope that there will not be any for a long time."[2]

The movies were born into the era of reform, which (roughly) opened with the inauguration of President Theodore Roosevelt in 1901 and closed with the entry of the United States into the First World War in 1917. The optimism with which

"Mrs. Raymond (Julia Swayne Gordon) makes a secret visit to her gambling palace"— Vitagraph's The Sins of the Mothers, *1915, written by Elaine Sterne, winner of the $1,000* New York Evening Sun *Photoplay Contest. (Robert S. Birchard Collection)*

it began was still evident in 1916 when a clubwoman declared, "Motion pictures are going to save our civilization from the destruction which has successively overwhelmed every civilization of the past. They provide what every previous civilization has lacked—namely a means of relief, happiness and mental inspiration to the people at the bottom. Without happiness and inspiration being accessible to those upon whom the social burden rests most heavily, there can be no stable social system. Revolutions are born of misery and despair."[3]

If the movies never quite lived up to the reformers' expectations—either by preventing revolution or by causing it—they did eventually become the most powerful medium of communication in the world—a universal language. In order to outdo the rivalry of the press, they had to forego what a newspaper contained—hard news, preaching, and propaganda—and become a reliable source of entertainment. Soon, even newsreels were full of hokum, extolling flagpole squatters and stunt flyers, but avoiding industrial or political unrest. In the twenties, if a film set out to educate rather than to entertain, audiences knew, by some sixth sense, how to avoid it.

"Why in the world does anybody want to see life represented on the screen as it is?" asked a Florida fan. "How can they stand to see anything so monotonous? We all see these commonplace things every day of our lives and when we go to the theatre we want something unreal and beautiful to give us courage and hope to face the trials of this drab world of ours . . . So please, Mr. Directors, give us not life as it is but as we would like it to be. . . ."[4]

Countless social or message pictures had played on people's sense of outrage, and they had grown tired of feeling ashamed or indignant when they went to the movies. A producer's wisecrack—"If you want to send a message, send it Western Union"—summed up the desire to rid the movie theatre of the problem picture. As people stayed away from war films once the war was over, so they stayed away from social pictures once the era of reform was over.

The term "progressive" at the turn of the century referred to a breed unlike the left-winger of today. It meant a reformer, an enthusiast for moral uplift, and a campaigner for liberal reform. "Muckraking" journalism flourished at this period, exposing injustices and arousing the social conscience of the movement.

Progressives were particularly concerned with the problems of the city; most shared the old agrarian idea of the city as the heart of moral corruption. And the cities were expanding at a terrifying rate.

While most progressives were opposed to monopolies, political machines, and labor unions, they were no more united in aim than in politics and are as hard to generalize about as they were to categorize. Among their number were Eugene Debs, leader of the Socialist party, and Senator Tom Watson, a populist and a racist. While some were concerned and compassionate, like Jane Addams of Hull-House, the pioneering settlement in the slums of Chicago, others were little more than moral police. When they won control, they brought liberal reform to an end. As Robert Sklar wrote, they were anxious to control access to information so the lower classes should remain ignorant of the social system in which they lived.[5]

Mostly middle class, invariably Protestant, and the backbone of their communities, these moral police kept a stern eye on the leisure activities of the working class. Its fondness for drink was being dealt with. Now appeared a social disease quite as insidious in its effects as alcohol—"nickel madness." By 1910, 26 million people in the United States were frequenting the five-cent theatres every week.[6]

It was "the academy of the working man, his pulpit, his newspaper, his club."[7] Largely operated by the foreign-born, the craze threatened to undermine all the institutions Americans held dear. It had to be controlled by responsible people, and the most effective form of control was thought to be censorship.[8] "For all of their faith in the limitless capacity of mankind," wrote William Drew, "Progressive leaders were often quick to shield the public from ideas they considered harmful."[9]

Yet many were convinced that the amazing progress of science and technology would solve the problems of society—and involved in that progress was the moving picture. They felt it should be used for propaganda, which had not yet become a dirty word. Dr. H. E. Kleinschmidt of the Tuberculosis Association described good propaganda as "mental inoculation" whose goal was "*will control* . . . through education."[10]

The industry, seeing all reformers in the guise of censors, wanted nothing to do with them, even though films were made of many subjects close to the reformers' hearts, such as prohibition and child labor. D. W. Griffith was particularly contemptuous of them. In 1913, he made an extraordinary film called *The Reformers, or the Lost Art of Minding One's Business.* A candidate for mayor, with his wife, campaigns around town[11] on an antivice platform, closing saloons and theatres. Safe at home, their adolescent children read racy magazines and imbibe alcohol, and (by implication) the daughter is seduced by the local wastrel. Keeping children ignorant seldom keeps them innocent, says Griffith. And if you close the saloons, liquor will circulate in secret. Two of his reformers are obvious homosexuals, and Griffith goes so far as to show prostitutes, dressed as pious churchgoers, continuing to ply their trade. (Three years later, he struck reformers even harder with *Intolerance,* causing such shock and distress that on its reissue it had to be amended.) Yet Griffith, whether he liked it or not, was part of the progressive movement, and many writers have called him a reformer himself.

The relationship between reformers and the industry deteriorated to the point of open warfare. In 1921–1922, during the Fatty Arbuckle and William Desmond Taylor scandals, the moral police—particularly clubwomen and church groups— summoned such power that they made the industry fear for its survival. It was dependent on the family audience, so it had no alternative but to create a figurehead, a sort of Moses with a fresh list of commandments. But by that time, the political climate had changed and the movies reflected the new conservatism. Social films were fading away.

"As the poor became less important as the mainstay of the movies," wrote Lewis Jacobs, "the ideals and tribulations of the masses lost some of their importance as subject matter for the motion picture. Patrons of the better-class theatres had more critical standards, more security in life, and different interests. . . . Pictures began to be devoted almost exclusively to pleasing and mirroring the life of the more leisured and well-to-do citizenry."[12]

In all my years as a silent film historian and collector, I had found so few social problem films that when I contemplated this book, I wondered if there was enough material. But as I began to dig, and as my generous fellow historians William Drew, George Geltzer, J. B. Kaufman, and Q. David Bowers sent me material from America, I became overwhelmed by the sheer number of such films. I never dreamed they had been produced on such a scale or had taken so radical a viewpoint. While it proved frustrating to have to leave out so many fascinating films, the research has given me a new insight into, and a new enthusiasm for, the period.*

So many social films were made that a reviewer talked of a plot being "typically sociological."[13] (A large proportion were three- and four-reelers, which seem to have perished in greater numbers than one-reelers, or even features.)[14] Yet by

---

*I have not dealt with the longest of all, Erich von Stroheim's *Greed,* originally forty-two reels. For one thing, so much has been written about it; for another, in its cut version the social elements were largely honed away. I have kept my references to *Intolerance* and *The Birth of a Nation* to a minimum, since definitive studies exist on both, one written by William Drew. (*D. W. Griffith's Intolerance,* McFarland & Company, Inc., Box 611, Jefferson, North Carolina 28640.) I have been obliged to cut a section on films about blacks for reasons of length—but far better studies of the subject have been written by Thomas Cripps and Daniel J. Leab.

the late silent period, social films were almost unknown. On the rare occasion a writer tackled a problem drama, he could be sure that his brainchild would be unrecognizable if it failed to be slaughtered first.

Sam Ornitz[15] wrote a story about an unmarried mother for Josef von Sternberg; as he described it at the time, "She's been seduced and has a baby, which is the only thing she lives for. In fact, to provide for it she is at last driven to the streets. Then one of these interfering societies—America is lousy with them—steps in and has the baby taken from her. Says she isn't fit to bring it up. Why, they might as well tear the heart from her. The rest of the play shows the girl's attempts to drag herself back to social responsibility to get the child again."[16]

Von Sternberg's scenario writer, Jules Furthman, fresh from his triumph with *The Docks of New York* (about a sailor and a prostitute) wanted to change the story, which angered Ornitz.

"Look here, Sam," said Furthman, "We've just done a story with that kind of atmosphere in it; we can't do two, one after the other, exactly alike."

He and von Sternberg decided to set it in Vienna, in its prewar glory. And Furthman felt that the heroine could hardly be a streetwalker: "We'll just have to make it so she's poor and can't nourish the kid properly." Then came another creative bloodletting: "You know, old man, this unmarried-mother stuff won't go with the great American public, so we'll have to make it seem like she was seduced by the young man of the house. . . ." And so the realism was smoothed away, and the picture ended up artistically impressive but completely escapist. Never mind;

Esther Ralston in Josef von Sternberg's The Case of Lena Smith, *1929. (National Film Archive)*

The Case of Lena Smith was a success and Sam Ornitz was promised a thousand-dollar bonus. "So I have to keep my mouth shut," he said, disgustedly, "because I've got a wife and kids over here."[17]

By this period, the star system was in full swing, and a "star vehicle" was hardly the right conveyance for burning issues. In the early days, by contrast, a well-known player would often be happy to tackle a difficult subject, regarding it as a challenge.

The early social films often contained precious historical evidence. Some were shot in the slum districts of the big cities; others featured the very people at the storm center of controversy. They were not always popular with exhibitors or even audiences, but they were endured, for a while, as a child endures castor oil.

"I don't like such things," complained a reviewer of *In the Grip of Alcohol* (1912). "I don't believe the motion picture playhouse the place to see gruesome, heartbreaking tragedies. I wouldn't want my little boy to look at that set of films. But that it teaches a terrible lesson, and may perhaps be a terrific force for good, I am not prepared to deny."[18]

A film like *In the Grip of Alcohol* could only have been made in the early years. Once prohibition had taken effect, scenes of people drinking—indeed any violation of the Volstead Act—had to be treated with the utmost discretion. Those early years, before 1919, were the richest source for social films, which is one reason why there are fewer firsthand interviews in this book than I would wish. The pioneers of the social film have long since gone. Fortunately, some talked to the trade press, and one or two left memoirs. Occasionally, I was able to talk to those who had worked with them. But most left nothing, not even their films.*

The makers of the early social films—George Nichols, Barry O'Neil, Oscar Apfel—were not lionized as were popular directors of later years. Many were stage people, reaching the end of their careers. Few continued making films into the twenties.

Only one filmmaker in America devoted an entire career to making what were known as "thought films." That filmmaker was a woman, Lois Weber, who worked as a reformer within the industry. Born in Allegheny, Pennsylvania, and educated in Pittsburgh, her ambition was to cultivate her voice in New York. Her parents refused, so she ran away, with eight dollars, only to find her music instructor had gone abroad. Too proud to return home, she endured the kind of poverty she so vividly captured in her films. At one point she had to sing in the street for food. She spent two years as a social worker in the slums of Pittsburgh and New York and worked as a missionary among the prisoners on Blackwells Island.[20]

Eventually, she joined a musical comedy company, became an actress, and met her husband, Phillips Smalley.[21] But she never forgot the immigrants and their struggles. "I came suddenly to realize the blessings of a voiceless language to them," she said.[22] As a filmmaker she decided to make what she called "missionary

---

*Luckily, other voices from the past have much to say on their own account: the reviewers for the trade papers, fan magazines, and newspapers. Their opinions are less important than the attitudes they unwittingly display. Wherever possible, I have quoted verbatim both the review and the story of a film, the description of the time being so much more resonant than a paraphrase.[19]

Lois Weber, the "picture Missionary." (Kobal Collection)

pictures." Some of these she made with her husband (both were Christian Scientists), but she was always the dominant partner. "I like to direct," she said, "because I believe a woman, more or less intuitively, brings out many of the emotions that are rarely expressed on the screen. I may miss what some of the men get, but I will get other effects that they never thought of."[23]

The range of subjects Weber tackled was as astonishing as the speed with which she produced them. *Suspense* (1913) outdid Griffith in its technical wizardry.[24] *Civilized and Savage* (1913) had Smalley as a white man nursed to health by a black woman (Weber), who, her task complete, sets out to find his wife.[25] The Smalleys handled a story about Jews with great care, even calling in an advisory body of rabbis, who objected only to the title, *The Jew's Christmas* (1913).

In 1915, Weber created her first sensation, *The Hypocrites*. A four-reeler made the previous year for Bosworth, it was held back because of its inflammatory treatment. Using an allegorical style, with multiple exposures, to flay politics, big business, and the church, it further shocked the establishment by having a naked girl play the figure of Truth. Audiences flocked to see the nudity and were then obliged to sit through the moral lesson, upsetting to many of them. The nudity was filmed so innocently than few boards of censors could ban it. There were several attempts; the Catholic mayor of Boston demanded that Truth be draped, so clothes were allegedly painted, frame by frame, onto the film![26]

After making films about such subjects as families destroyed by scandal mongering, Weber and Smalley played together in *Hop, The Devil's Brew* (1916), a drama of opium smuggling.[27] *Where Are My Children?* (1916) was unique: a film attacking abortion which nonetheless defended birth control.

Curiously, Weber referred to such films as heavy dinners. "Anything that promises red lights will crowd the box office," she said in 1918. "I don't want to produce that type of play. I want to give the public light afternoon teas—that is what I term the light, artistic production, the one which charms the eye, leaves a pleasant fragrance behind it, and which is accompanied by music of just the proper sentiment."[28]

Fortunately, she had made several heavy dinners by that time, including *Shoes* (1916), a parable of poverty inspired by a paragraph in a Jane Addams book about a working girl who, after months of resistance, "sold out for a pair of shoes;"[29] *The People vs. John Doe* (1916), an anticapital punishment saga; *Even As You and I* (1917), which showed how a young couple resisted temptation—until drink dragged them down;[30] and *The Hand That Rocks the Cradle* (1917), a salute to Margaret Sanger and her birth-control campaign.[31]

Lois Weber continued to make social films well into the Jazz Age, when she suffered the rejection of audiences. She and Phillips Smalley were divorced in 1922—he had become an alcoholic—and her company failed. She made a few more pictures, one of which, *The Angel of Broadway* (1927), combined the cynicism of the twenties (nightclub parodies of the Salvation Army) with the commitment of the reform era (social work in the slums). It was her last silent film, and by 1930 she was managing an apartment building.[32]

She made a minor film in 1934 and died in 1939, the same year as Phillips Smalley. Both were forgotten. Neither talked, as far as is known, to any historian, nor did they leave their memoirs. So most of their memories have been lost, along with most of their films.

Some of those who made social films were unaware they were doing so. An example is Raoul Walsh, who made *Regeneration* for Fox in 1915. The story, based on fact, of an Irish gangster reformed by a girl from a settlement house, is one of the most effective social films of its era. Yet it is clear, both from Walsh's memoirs and from my own interview with the man, that he never thought of it as such, but as a strong story which he told with as much punch and realism as he could. It was the same with King Vidor. He did not regard *The Crowd* (1928), arguably the finest silent social film, as a work of social or political value at all. The theme fascinated him, and he persuaded MGM to let him go ahead and make it. "I didn't know it was a social film," he told me with an ironic smile, "until people like you told me."

Even Mrs. Wallace Reid, whose most significant social film was *Human Wreckage* (1923), a treatise against drug addiction, was uncertain of the term:

"I was making what they call . . . not problem pictures, but I mean pictures of that kind."

"Social films?"

"Yes, more or less, but I tried to do it with a plot which was interesting enough to hold people. And I tried to give them a message at the same time."[33]

I must admit that the term "social film" is imprecise and even misleading. (It is such a useful one, however, that I shall continue to employ it.) In Hollywood, with its painful memories of McCarthyism, the term is confused with "socialist." Willis Goldbeck grew angry when I used it. I hoped that as a screenwriter, journalist, and later director, he would give me an illuminating explanation of why so few social films were made in the twenties. But he bridled at the question. "We made entertainment until the liberal element came along," he snapped. And he wanted nothing more to do with anyone who could ask such a question.

One thinks of Hollywood people as frivolous and apolitical; some of them undoubtedly were. Colleen Moore told me there was very little interest in politics in the twenties: "We were only interested in Paramount, Universal, MGM—who was president of them, not who was president of the United States."[34] Yet when Judge Ben Lindsey visited Hollywood in the late twenties, he found the same interest in the great social and economic problems that he had met at the table of Jane Addams of Hull-House in Chicago.[35]

At that period, however, such problems were not the kind of thing anyone thought of making films about. With America in control of the film markets of the world, its product had to appeal to an international audience. American social problems like prohibition were of little interest to Europe, while wider issues— poverty, strikes—stirred up uncomfortable fears about Bolshevism and were therefore avoided.

Such films *were* made, however, if not always by the film industry. The most extreme—and extraordinary—example was *The Passaic Textile Strike* (1926), produced by the embattled strikers themselves and used to raise money to sustain the strike. It was the discovery of this film which finally led to the writing of this book. For years, I had regarded it as a book which I would write "one day." Without seeing *The Passaic Textile Strike*, I felt it was not worth starting. But when I visited New York's Museum of Modern Art in September 1983, curator Eileen Bowser told me that the film had been found in the collection of Tom Brandon. A few moments later, I was watching it, and a few weeks later I was talking to one of the organizers of the strike, who had also played a role in the film. Subsequently, Eileen Bowser and Charles Silver, Supervisor of the Film Study Center, made available many documents from the Brandon collection which proved invaluable.

I feel drawn to the subject of social films not only because I have been a film historian for so long, but because I have a degree of sympathy for everyone's point of view. When I was a filmmaker, I made what might be called social pictures. I saw for myself how hard it was to attract audiences. As a film-goer, I tended to betray my own aspirations and head for the enjoyable rather than the educational. This paradox may have something to do with my background. Although I was born in England, my father came from Southern Ireland, with its rich tradition of theatre and storytelling. But *his* father came from the Protestant North, with its puritan distaste for entertainment. Without knowing it, my father passed on both traditions to me. So I understand the censor and the prohibitionist, while sympathizing with the rebels who fought against them.

I am sometimes asked why I stick so rigidly to the silent film. Were no worthwhile social films produced in the thirties? Of course there were. But many books and articles and even documentary films have covered this area, whereas hardly

Mill girls on the picket line: The Passaic Textile Strike, *1926. (Museum of Modern Art)*

anything has been written about the silent social films, resulting in a dismissal of the period.* Thanks to recent revivals, the silent era has at last been accepted as a rich source of artistic innovation. But social films? "By and large," said one historian, " 'social issue' films did not make an appearance until the thirties."[36]

Historians can be forgiven for avoiding the period because so many of the films are "unavailable for study," i.e., lost. But I am also a film collector, and the first rule of the collector is never to give anything up as "lost." My book *The War, the West and the Wilderness* led to several of the "lost" films discussed in its pages coming to light. This book has already had a similar result, including the recovery of a Lois Weber film, recut for European release.

There are some films which I suspect would replace many of the accepted classics if only we could see them. Yet the most promising title—like the suffragist film *Eighty Million Women Want*—can nonplus the most devoted film scholar, while a commercial gangster film from the Fox studio can stand among the most impressive achievements of the entire period.

It would be cynical to say that a title has to appear in print before it is taken

*Kay Sloan has since written *The Loud Silents, Origins of the Social Problem Film* (Urbana: University of Illinois Press, 1988).

seriously, but often a description of the plot alerts the memory of an archivist. (If you know of any old films in their original state—35mm nitrate—I urge you to get in touch with me c/o the publisher.)

If more of these social films could be rediscovered, what a panoply of American history they would represent!

KEVIN BROWNLOW

Postscript

In *The War, the West and the Wilderness,* I made an attempt to list all those films I understood to be lost. Since then, I realize that this was a waste of time. Until all the archives of the world fulfill their obligation and publish lists of their holdings we will never know what survives and what doesn't. A partial list has been printed by the Federation of Film Archives (FIAF), but I am told it can only be consulted by "authorized" people. A number of archives refuse to reveal the contents of their vaults. We will never know what we have lost. Nineteen-ninety inaugurates the last decade of nitrate—much of it has lasted well beyond the fifty years predicted for it. It is not expected to last into the new century. Yet still many archives are nothing but vast depositories, lacking the finances to copy their fast-decomposing nitrate. Unless the archive movement can be properly funded to make the best possible copies of its precious original prints, posterity will judge us harshly.

K. B.

BEHIND
THE MASK OF
INNOCENCE

Making America Safe for Morons

Chapter One

CENSORSHIP

THE NATIONAL BOARD OF REVIEW

The patron saint of censorship in America was Anthony Comstock, special agent for the post office, a man who said he stood "at the sewer mouth of society."[1] The 1873 Comstock Law gave the post office the power to decide what was obscene. Mercifully, Comstock had little to do directly with the moving picture. In his day, the source of evil was "the half-dime novel and story paper" (and he told of a fourteen-year-old driven to murder by reading such sensation). However, Comstock's name, and more often his spirit, will recur in this narrative, for he had a baleful influence. By the time he retired in 1915, it was said that he had convicted enough people to fill a passenger train of sixty-one coaches.[2]

The scandal of the century—at least, its first decade—occurred in 1906. Stanford White, America's most celebrated architect, was shot by Harry K. Thaw on the roof of New York's Madison Square Garden, a building designed by White. Thaw, a wealthy young man from Pittsburgh, had discovered that his wife, actress Evelyn Nesbit, had been White's mistress before the marriage. The yellow press gave ordinary Americans a full account of the case, with intimate glimpses into the private lives of the privileged—the kind of people who formed uplift societies to raise the morals of the poor. The privileged were deeply disturbed.

In March 1907, the Chicago *Tribune* launched an attack on the nickelodeons, describing their influence as "wholly vicious."[3] Among the films to which they objected was *The Unwritten Law,* a reenactment by the Lubin Company of Philadelphia of the Thaw case. The film still exists and even today carries a prurient fascination. The sight of an actress portraying Miss Nesbit on the famous red velvet swing and the glimpse of the boudoir of a hundred mirrors suggest that White organized his private life like a DeMille fantasy.

The police soon stopped the showing of another film, *The Thaw-White Tragedy.* And in New York, in May 1907, the Children's Society had a nickelodeon proprietor arrested for showing yet another, *The Great Thaw Trial,* to a house packed largely with schoolchildren. (He was fined $100 for impairing their morals.[4]) This film, too, included all the elements of the saga—the mirrored boudoir, the swing, the murder. Superintendent Jenkins described it as "lewd and disgusting."[5] The Thaw films obliged the establishment to take a new interest in the moving picture; they realized it was capable of untold damage. Most obviously, it was eroding the lower classes' faith in authority. A survey of working-class amusements in New York, conducted by the People's Institute, an adult education center at Cooper Union, warned that the moving picture was "potentially too great an influence of popular attitudes to be left unsupervised."[6]

Censorship in the guise of moral vigilance was deemed essential. It began officially in November 1907, when Chicago set up a municipal censorship board. New York went further; Mayor George Brinton McClellan closed down all the moving picture theatres in 1908. Charles Sprague Smith, founder and director of the People's Institute, came to the public defense of the theatres, declaring there were other things in the city that needed cleaning up more than the picture shows. McClellan, the son of the famous Civil War general, was unmoved. His excuse was safety; his true concern, public morals.

Panic-stricken exhibitors organized an emergency meeting for Christmas Day— such was the finesse of McClellan's timing—and their attorney managed to obtain no less than four injunctions against the mayor's order.[7] The theatres opened again, but the city council had another shock in store, barring all children under sixteen unless accompanied by an adult.[8]

New York's showmen were now frightened enough to install censorship on their own volition. The New York Board of Censorship of Programs of Motion Picture Shows came into being early in 1909, a nonprofit organization with Charles Sprague Smith as director and John Collier* as his associate. Members of the Motion Picture Patents Company (General Film) paid three dollars a reel, while the independents were charged nothing, amazingly enough, as an inducement to use the board's services. Part of the board's work was also the inspection of New York's theatres. It adopted "National" status in May 1909 and became the National Board of Censorship.

Charles Sprague Smith, who died in 1910, was succeeded by the social reformer Frederic C. Howe. A supporter of women's suffrage and other ideas then considered radical, Howe had the kind of background in law and politics that made him acceptable to conservatives. The author of a famous book, *The City: The Hope of Democracy* (1905), he was deeply concerned with social issues and opposed to censorship, whether voluntary or not. He presided over an intentionally liberal period of the board's history, when it acted as an enlightened censor in the hope that the more vicious variety might be neutralized by its existence.

The General Committee of the board was composed of "persons of culture, judgement and discretion," most of them married women connected with civic organizations or child welfare groups and innocent of any connection with the picture business.[9] The board won the approval of the forces of reform.[10] On its Advisory Committee was Jacob Riis, master photographer and housing reformer; on the Executive Committee, a representative of the Society for the Prevention of Crime, headed by Comstock.[11]

The true purpose of the organization was to protect the motion picture "from any ill-advised efforts to hamper its growth or smother it, before it could confer its benefits on the American people,"[12] but its ostensible mandate was to protect the public against unclean pictures. Exhibitors could show a film rejected by the board, but they risked arousing the wrath of the local authority (thereby losing their license) or the exchange (losing their supply of films). On the whole, they toed the line, because the board was liberal—far too liberal for many people.

---

*Collier was later educational secretary and eventually general secretary of the board.

Agitation from what it called "narrow-minded clubwomen and bigoted reformers"[13] was building up across the country. These people—moral police to a man, or woman—accused the board of showing too much friendliness toward the industry, and in 1913 anti-motion picture legislation in many states threatened to become law. A South Dakota bill was introduced to make it unlawful to show any film "depicting any humorous or dramatic story or illustrating illicit love, resisting an officer or, in fact, anything but a scenic."[14]

Even those who favored the board's activities were dismayed at its lapses. W. Stephen Bush asked if a picture in which a hanging was shown "with disgusting realism" had been seen and passed. The reply was that it had been, together with another showing an electrocution. "The moral lesson conveyed by the execution," explained the board, "must outweigh any horrors at the gruesomeness of the details."[15]

This was not worthy of serious consideration, retorted Bush. Why not have all executions public? Instead of deterring potential murderers, public execution brutalized the whole community. "It sickens every friend of the motion picture to see fathers and mothers cover the faces of their children with their hands in order to shut out the sight of objectionable scenes in the films."[16]

The years up to 1914 were turbulent but successful, with 95 percent of all films passing the scrutiny of the board. Thereafter, the organization spent as much time defending itself from a barrage of criticism as doing its job.* The way it did its job was to assemble volunteers living in the New York area into a Review Committee that was then divided into sections which held twenty-five to thirty review meetings a week. The committee members had neither the corporate strength nor the political acumen to harass the manufacturers. Nor did they wish to. Many were devoted to the idea of art for art's sake,[17] a point which their opponents found thoroughly distasteful. After all, these people were supposed to be *censors!*

In 1914, the Commissioner of Licenses of the City of New York, George H. Bell, whose official task was the supervision of safety in theatres, set up a citizens' committee to deal with the small group of films that escaped the net of the National Board. His "small area" soon expanded, and he became, to all intents and purposes, the censor for New York before an official board was installed.[18]

In 1914, the industry also mounted a massive campaign against censorship, and, to the dismay of social workers, women's clubs, and church groups, the board supported the drive. These opponents of the movies then demanded state censorship—"censorship with teeth in it."[19]

The board rejected state censorship as unconstitutional and unnecessary;[20] to make the point clear, it changed its name, on March 29, 1916, to the National Board of Review of Motion Pictures,[21] with the slogan "Selection—not censorship—the Solution." It advocated the kind of self-regulation employed by newspaper editors and devoted itself to previewing films and categorizing them as a guide for the public and industry. Some members, disturbed by this change of policy, left the board.[22]

---

*Howe resigned in 1915 to devote more time to his work as commissioner of immigration of the Port of New York. Cranston Brenton, Director of the American Red Cross, replaced him.

Audrey Munson was the model for the figure on the memorial coin at the 1915 San Francisco Exposition. She was signed by the American Film Company for a picture entitled Purity, *1916, for which Clifford Howard was ordered to write a scenario. The idea was to show as much as possible of Miss Munson, and to arouse the audience, but not the censors. The result was a sensation. The artist is Alfred Hollingsworth. (Robert S. Birchard Collection)*

Two confirmed enemies of the moving picture, the Reverend William Chase, a supporter of the Ku Klux Klan,[23] and the Reverend Wilbur Crafts, were behind a bill introduced in Congress in 1914 to create a Federal Motion Picture Commission to supplant the board. The bill was defeated, but others followed. To combat such activity, the picture business formed the National Association of the Motion Picture Industry (NAMPI) in 1916. Four states had introduced censorship laws— Pennsylvania (1911), Ohio (1913), Kansas (1914), and Maryland (1916). More were in the offing. The war effort strengthened the legislators' zeal, for many had substituted patriotism for social concern. Yet the board, instead of tightening its hold, relaxed more and more of its strictures, becoming a joke to the industry.

"By 1919," wrote Robert Fisher, "the Board was passing films concerning such controversial subjects as birth control, capital punishment, nudity, prostitution, 'the single standard of morality' and socialism—so long as they were not depicted in 'a crass, crude and commercial manner.' "[24]

This further inflamed the opposition. "The camouflage of the National Board of Review . . . has become no nauseating that a person of average intelligence must protest at such attempts to dupe and delay," declared a pamphlet of the General Federation of Women's Clubs in 1919. "Their stream of literature and bulletins, pouring into every corner of our land, at enormous expense, is the motion picture industry's attempt to furnish well-intentioned, reform-bent ladies with harmless, busy work. . . . They persistently preach 'promote the good, the beautiful, smother the evil with good.' Meanwhile, the stream of filthy films flows for him to see—who may or will."[25]

The board never claimed that it had cleaned up the industry, but its opponents made the claim on its behalf, in order to demolish it: "If you want unmistakable evidence of the fact that the National Board of Review has not cleaned the industry," said Father Dineen of the Chicago Motion Picture Commission, "we can take you to the tenth floor of this City Hall building, where the censorship of pictures is conducted, and give you an exhibition that will make you blush for very shame that men in the business would be so degraded as to produce the pictures that have been suppressed there."[26]

It was pointed out that compared to the Pennsylvania state censors (among the most reactionary in the land), the board appeared almost willfully liberal. Out of 2,126 films containing scenes of "lust and indecency" from which the Pennsylvania censors had made 1,464 eliminations, the board had made only 47.[27] It was clearly in the pay of the industry and under orders to retain as much salacious material as the public would tolerate.[28]

For their part, the picture people were unhappy because they could not depend on the board to protect them from damaging legislation.[29] Its pronouncements fell far short of the stringent censorship the industry would have needed to forestall the establishment of the Hays Office, but the board carried on throughout the reign of Hays, the attitude of each being cool and distant.[30] It acted as a catch net for those films made by companies which did not belong to the Hays organization. By 1926, the board's secretary, Wilton A. Barrett, felt able to declare: "They may not be perfect, but I believe the pictures are essentially wholesome."[31]

STATE AND MUNICIPAL CENSORSHIP

Reading the trade papers of the time of the great censorship debates, one is struck by the declarations of purity. What we stand for, picture men repeat ad nauseam, is clean pictures. Universal conducted a survey of exhibitors, asking whether they preferred wholesome pictures or smutty ones, and Carl Laemmle published an editorial on the result: "Instead of discovering that 95% favored clean pictures, I discovered that at least half, and maybe 60%, wanted the pictures to be *risqué*, which is a French way of saying smutty. The whole thing is an eye-opener, so totally different from what I expected that I am stumped. The Universal Picture Company does not pose as a guardian of public morals or public taste. For that reason, it is quite possible that we may put out a picture that is off-color now and then as a feeler. We have no such picture yet, but it is quite easy to make them."[32]

It did not pay to be frank, even in the trade press. This editorial proved helpful to those campaigning for state censorship. The conflict between what was acceptable for general commercial purposes—like the Thaw films—and what was acceptable for small-town theatres was virtually impossible to solve. The very fact

The Three Fates

A cartoon from D. W. Griffith's pamphlet The Rise and Fall of Free Speech in America. *(National Film Archive)*

that the National Board of Review was national rendered it valueless to the small-town reform bodies, which wanted their films especially pruned for local needs and added their voices to the clamor for state censorship.

However, the censorship boards which had already been established in some states were arousing attention by their odd rulings. One of the first acts of the Ohio board was to cut shots of newborn babies from a film about Cambodia.[33] Pennsylvania was notorious, too, for its attitude toward childbirth: a mother could not even be shown making clothes for an unborn child. Most film people accepted this, along with other bewildering strictures; but when one of them questioned it, he received an astonishing answer: "The movies are patronized by thousands of children who believe that babies are brought by the stork, and it would be criminal to undeceive them."[34]

The state boards were a source of intense irritation to the picture business, because no two would agree on what should, or should not, appear in a film. Since producers could not anticipate one week what might be vulnerable the next, they issued instructions for directors to avoid a wide range of topics and a wider range of details. The result was a series of films tailored for censors rather than audiences. Said *Photoplay*: "The manufacturers, trying to make money . . . have decided to issue soothing serums which could not inflame the optics of a man suffering from pink eye. They want to get their pictures by without destruction. Therefore they have begun to make them so flaccid, soft and nerveless that they cannot offend even in Pennsylvania or Ohio, where lettuce blushes to see the salad dressing."[35]

To be a censor required a suspicious mind and an accusing eye. Playwright Channing Pollock appeared in court in Philadelphia in 1915 on behalf of the Lasky Company and its production of his *Secret Orchard* (directed by William de Mille). "To our intense surprise," he wrote, "the [Pennsylvania] censors discovered that the first scene took place in a bagnio. Agnes and Everton Castle had written the novel, I had written the play . . . a reputable company had photographed it, without suspecting . . . the awful truth.

" 'Do you mean to say,' the board's attorney thundered at me, 'that you do not recognize this as a brothel?'

" 'I admitted that I didn't.'

" 'The censors do,' said the attorney.

" 'Which only goes to prove,' I replied, 'that the censors know more about brothels than I do.' "[36]

Perhaps Pennsylvania's most willful act was its cutting of D. W. Griffith's *Way Down East* (1920), a melodrama so Victorian in its sentiment one might have thought it a censor's ideal. A young country girl (Lillian Gish) comes to the city and is tricked into a mock marriage by a charming rogue (Lowell Sherman). She has a baby, which she baptizes just before its death. The censors cut out the mock marriage; the honeymoon went, too, and all hints of maternity and childbirth were removed—a total of sixty cuts. "Imagine the surprise of Pennsylvania fans," said *Photoplay,* "when the baby, utterly unexplained, burst upon the scene just before its death!"[37]

No other picture had been so savagely treated, but perhaps the censors were taking revenge for a pamphlet Griffith published at his own expense, *The Rise and Fall of Free Speech in America* (1916). Employing a newspaper technique of headlines, cartoons, and quotes, Griffith lambasted censors, pointing out that the integrity of free speech had not been so seriously attacked since the sedition law expired in 1801. He argued for the constitutional right of every American to publish what he pleased—subject to his personal liability after publication. The trouble with censorship was that it exercised its ban before publication. One was denied one's day in court.

Fine Arts films, which emanated from the Griffith studio, carried this title: "Every state, city or town has laws for the arrest and trial of those responsible for immoral exhibitions or publication, and this includes motion pictures. Therefore, why censorship?"

Unfortunately, the anti-censorship movement had suffered a crushing defeat in 1915, when the U.S. Supreme Court ruled, in *Mutual Film Corporation* v. *Industrial Commission of Ohio,* that the First Amendment did not apply to motion pictures. They were "a business pure and simple, originated and conducted for profit, like other spectacles, not to be regarded . . . as part of the press of the country or as organs of public opinion."[38] (Not until 1952 was this ruling reversed.)

Meddling with movies became more and more prevalent. As William de Mille pointed out, censorship also meant political patronage; it was the ideal job in

Lowell Sherman as the charming seducer of Anna Moore (Lillian Gish) in D. W. Griffith's Way Down East, *1920. (Kobal Collection)*

which to bury the kind of man likely to make trouble closer to the party machine.[39]

In 1916, to help to head off censorship in New York State, D. W. Griffith made a one-reel film at his own expense. But five years later, censorship was imposed by Governor Miller. In 1921 it cost the state $250,000.[40] By 1925 that figure had increased to $480,000. The censors banned or cut 235 films in 1921; by 1924 the number had risen to 3,684.[41] And censorship continued, even when Alfred E. Smith was elected governor. He spoke out against it, but his energies were reserved for the repeal of prohibition. The censors, though accused of graft, sailed blithely on.

"We who made the pictures," wrote de Mille, "were sometimes led to wonder whether commercialized virtue might not be as unhealthy for the country as commercialized vice, while utterly lacking the latter's brighter side."[42]

Anti-censorship campaigns helped to keep state boards at bay, but there was a more widespread type of censorship, the municipal variety. More than a hundred cities established censorship boards, each one guided by a different set of rules. They proved a lasting irritant to the industry. By 1928 20 percent (some historians say 50 percent) of the film distribution territory was affected, and censorship was costing producers $3,500,000 a year in eliminated sequences.[43]

Even more than state boards, the municipal censors, whether the police department or a civilian committee, were accused of being provincial, narrow-minded, and inconsistent. No wonder some producers thought that federal censorship, with one set of rules, would be the lesser evil.[44] (And a Federal Motion Picture Commission was a distinct possibility, the Harding administration selecting Herbert Hoover to head one and—irony of ironies—naming D. W. Griffith as a member of the advisory committee.)

Censorship was intended to protect citizens from unwholesome influences and to ensure they remained law-abiding. Thus, the city with the strictest censorship should, by the rules of logic, have been blessed with the lowest crime rate. Unfortunately, that city was Chicago, which endured a level of violence only slightly below that of total war. It is instructive to examine the kind of scene that bothered the city's police: according to John Collier, in one month the Chicago censors cut "the application of the third degree by police; the bribing of a policeman; brutal handling of prisoners by police; prison guards failing to preserve order; bribing of a detective; theft of a police uniform; love scene between a married woman and an army officer."[45] And, in a city soon to be notorious for the Tommy gun and the automatic, the showing of firearms was forbidden on the movie screen. Special billboards had to be prepared during the war, showing soldiers going over the top without rifles. It was all rather embarrassing to advocates of American democracy, for police censorship was regarded as one of the chief attributes of autocratic governments—like that of Imperial Russia.

The chief censor was a former insurance agent, civilian Deputy Police Superintendent Major Metellus Lucullus Cicero Funkhouser. In 1913 he had arrested a woman for bathing in bloomers without a skirt, and he had demanded the removal of a nude statue in the Art Institute to a place where the eyes of Chicago youth would not encounter it.[46] Funkhouser believed that youthful malefactors were led to crime by cheap novels and motion pictures which ridiculed authority.[47] His reasons for banning pictures—when he bothered to explain them—were peculiar, to say the least. He prohibited a film about German torture, *The Spy* (1917), because, he said, the acting was too powerful and it made the sweat stand out on his brow.[48] He censored Griffith's *Hearts of the World* (1918) and a film based on Ambassador James Watson Gerard's best-seller, *My Four Years in Germany* (1918). Dismissed from the force after he was convicted of a variety of charges unrelated to censorship, Funkhouser was succeeded by others of his ilk. And years later, Chicago banned *Scarface* (1932), a picture based on the city's most celebrated citizen, Al Capone.[49]

WILL HAYS

In 1917, investigators reported that from the point of view of morals all was well in the film industry.[50] A couple of years later, however, it was hard to avoid the conclusion that the industry was headed for disaster. The harmless fluff which once filled movie columns was now so routine that editors refused to run it. The surest way of getting stars' names in print, in this heyday of the yellow press, was to reveal lurid details of their private lives. Press agents staged fake suicides and other hoaxes to "push" their stars and their pictures.[51] Again and again, people read of movie actresses being arrested. California vagrancy laws required transients to register their occupations; prostitutes often registered as film extras and called themselves movie actresses, but this was not explained to the public. It would have made little difference anyway, now that so many real stars were the center of controversy. But it all contributed to soaring circulation, rising disgust, and falling admissions.

Then there were the films themselves. Exhibitors and producers had been hit by a series of calamities—an infantile-paralysis epidemic in 1916, the imposition of a crippling war tax in 1917, and Spanish flu in 1918. Now they found themselves in much the same situation as the press agents—the harmless fluff was no longer saleable. For an audience reared on yellow journalism, pictures had to be more sensational. Independents grabbed at the most shocking subjects they could think of—venereal disease, prostitution, abortion. Although these areas had been dealt with for years, often by fly-by-night promoters, they now caused a tide of anger to rise against the entire industry. The demand for censorship became more vociferous.

A study for the General Federation of Women's Clubs said that of 1,765 films examined, 20 percent were "good," 21 percent "bad," and 59 percent "not worthwhile."[52] Religious organizations passed resolutions; editorials and articles in newspapers and magazines condemned the industry, which lacked the unity and commitment to fight back.

Admittedly, an effort to defeat censorship was organized in 1919 by the National Association of the Motion Picture Industry, its president, William Brady, insisting that only the filmmakers had the right to censor their product. Unfortunately, NAMPI soon became more of a liability than an asset.[53] And Brady proved an inept politician, letting drop remarks of great value to the opposition: "With two or three other men I control every foot of film shown in the United States; what we say goes."[54] According to him, the industry intended to become a factor in the election of every candidate from alderman to president, from assemblyman to United States senator.[55]

In 1920, Brady demanded that the industry be put on its word for just one year: "We will show you how to clean up the motion picture business."[56] He was asking for trouble. A series of scandals burst like depth charges in the very heart of the film world:

Mary Pickford secured a divorce from her first husband under such unusual

Pre-Hays nudity of the kind favored by director George Fitzmaurice: The Right to Love, *1920.*

circumstances that the attorney general of Nevada began proceedings against her for fraud, collusion, and untruthful testimony.[57]

Olive Thomas, on her long-delayed Paris honeymoon with Mary's brother Jack, was found dead of an "accidental" drug overdose.[58]

There were several suicides in the picture colony, including that of scenarist Zelda Crosby in 1920.

A "wild party" that had been given by several producers in 1917 came to light at this inopportune time (June 1921). Girls had been supplied, blackmail was involved, and it was all acutely embarrassing. This party had followed a dinner in honor of Roscoe "Fatty" Arbuckle—which could hardly have been more ironic, for another Arbuckle party, in San Francisco on Labor Day 1921, became notorious when Virginia Rappe died and Arbuckle was charged with manslaughter.

On top of all this, one of the trade papers ran a series exposing graft in the picture business.[59]

Just one of these scandals was enough to cause deep anxiety. The lot of them caused panic. They coincided with the postwar recession: box-office receipts had dropped dramatically. There had been a general strike in the studios. Bankers were refusing to invest in pictures. The industry was losing the support of those clubwomen and civic groups who had remained loyal. The demand for federal and state censorship increased to a roar. During 1921, nearly a hundred measures to control moving pictures were introduced in the legislatures of thirty-seven states.

In the style of President Woodrow Wilson's peace proposals, NAMPI had introduced thirteen points to help producers steer clear of the censor boards. And Famous Players–Lasky (around whom virtually all the scandals revolved) had gone one better with fourteen.[60] But none of this had the slightest discernible effect. It was like trying to smother a fire with a tea cozy.

When corruption had been exposed in baseball in 1919, Judge Kenesaw Mountain Landis had been wheeled in as a symbol of respectability. Industry heads searched for a similar figure—not a judge, few of whom were sympathetic toward movies, but a man with the supreme cachet of the president's cabinet.

Having organized the campaign to get Warren G. Harding into the White House, Will H. Hays, an Indiana politician, had been rewarded with the office of postmaster general. Something about that position appealed to the industry men. Was it the memory of Anthony Comstock?[61]

Hays had first become interested in movies when he saw how the Democrats used Thomas Ince's *Civilization* to help reelect Wilson in 1916. During the Harding campaign, he treated the newsreel men with unusual consideration and was rewarded with fuller coverage. Hays was a Presbyterian church elder with a reputation as a peacemaker. He might have had the face of a startled mouse, but his personality was engaging and he had a sense of humor.

He was asked to take control of the film industry in December 1921 at a salary of $100,000 a year—$25,000 more than the president was paid. Hays worried himself into the job. The governorship of his state was within his grasp, not to mention a seat in the Senate. But the administration he had helped put into power would soon be revealed as the most corrupt in American history; five cabinet officers would go to jail. He had already committed one or two irregularities himself,[62] so perhaps he welcomed the chance of stepping across to supervise the moral health of the movies. He accepted the job on January 14, 1922—just in time, for in February, with the Arbuckle case still on the front pages, director William Desmond Taylor was found dead in his Hollywood home, giving Hays his baptism of fire.

Hays's organization, called the Motion Picture Producers and Distributors of America, Inc. (MPPDA), replaced the late, unlamented NAMPI. Its goal was "to establish and maintain the highest possible moral and artistic standards of motion picture production and to develop the educational as well as the entertainment value and general usefulness of the motion picture."[63] Yet it was granted no legal standing. It was really in no stronger a position than the National Board.

Hays's first test was a Massachusetts censorship referendum. He threw the weight of this new organization into the fight against the measure. Thanks to his expert political management, censorship was defeated and Hays's methods applauded.[64] The victory turned the national tide; after 1922 no state passed censorship laws, although in the next five years most of them tried. "Censorship," said

ARBUCKLE JURY SPLIT, 8 TO 4

5 CENTS
San Francisco's First
Great Daily; Founded 1856

THE SAN FRANCISCO CALL

FINAL HOME EDITION

TWENTY-FOUR PAGES—SAN FRANCISCO, THURSDAY, FEBRUARY 2, 1922

Price 5 Cents

$300,000,000 YANK AID REVENUE MAPPED

SLAY FILM MAGNATE

Conclave on Pope Election Opens

JURY CALLS FOR RAPPE TESTIMONY RECORD

TOBACCO TAX, AUTO TAX, PLAN FOR VETERANS

FREE Bicycles FOR Boys AND

2 CARDINAL FACTIONS TO CLASH OVER SELECTION

William Desmond Taylor, film producer and director, who was slain under mysterious circumstances today in Los Angeles.

L. A. MOVIE DIRECTOR IS KILLED IN MYSTERY

By International News Service.
LOS ANGELES, Feb. 2.—Shot down while writing at a desk by a mysterious assassin, William Desmond Taylor, well known motion picture producer and director, was found dead today in his bungalow in the Westlake district.

NEWS DOWN TO THE LAST MINUTE

WARRANTS FOR L. A. DRY AGENTS
By Associated Press.
LOS ANGELES, Feb. 2.—Charges of brutality made to the Los Angeles County district attorney resulted today in the issuance of complaints against four federal prohibition enforcement agents, charging them with assault with intent to kill, in the office of a dry raid. The officials named were C. H. Wheeler, James Pierce, J. A. Boyle and Jos Krumbhaar.

BLUEBEARD LOSES APPEAL
By International News Service.
PARIS, Feb. 2.—The appeal of Henri Landru, so called "French Bluebeard," who was found guilty of murdering ten women and a boy, was rejected by the court today. Landru will be executed.

GOODCELL NOMINATION TO SENATE
WASHINGTON, Jan. 2.—Nominations of postmasters sent to the Senate today included Arthur M. Becker, at Visalia, Cal. Nominations sent to the Senate by the President...

The Taylor sensation breaks on top of the Arbuckle scandal, February 1922.

Will H. Hays. Picture people referred to him as "the czar of all the rushes." James Quirk, editor of Photoplay, called him "a mail order Moses."

Hays piously, "is unfair, unreasonable and impossible of operation."[65] Although nine companies had sponsored Hays's new position, others remained suspicious at what they saw as thinly disguised government intervention, resulting in what they feared would be Pollyanna pictures. Hays was a master of public relations, and he managed to win over most of them. He approached the industry, he said, "not merely with the viewpoint of men who had millions of dollars invested in the business, but with that of the parents who had millions of children invested in it."[66] Reformers and clubwomen responded warmly to this sort of talk, and many joined his Committee on Public Relations.

Hays assured the world it was possible to control the behavior of the movie employees as well as the films they produced. Accordingly, in April 1922 he banned Roscoe Arbuckle from the screen.*

Hays's first months were so successful, from the public relations point of view at least, that he felt able to give Arbuckle a little Christmas cheer by lifting the ban in December 1922. He was not thanked for his charity. The press and women's clubs attacked him. James Quirk referred to the act as "stupidity."[68] Hays had failed to consult his Committee on Public Relations, and some of the members resigned. Zukor insisted on upholding the ban. Was he rescuing Hays from an embarrassing situation? Opponents charged that he was only too anxious to keep Hays in office as "a shield for a cynical industry."[69] The ban was sustained.

As if Hays had not taken enough punishment, in January 1923 came the news of the death from drugs of one of the most popular stars in Hollywood, Wallace Reid. According to Hays, this "smashed his good works,"[70] yet the very existence of the Hays organization kept the story from becoming another circulation-boosting sensation. Some papers portrayed Reid as a hero, fighting a losing battle against morphine addiction; most of them dropped the story as soon as he died. Hays owed much to the dignified conduct of Reid's widow, whom he later permitted to produce a film on the proscribed subject of the drug peril.

Stars were soon obliged to accept morals clauses in their contracts. One read: "The Artist agrees to conduct himself with due regard to public conventions and morals, and agrees that he will not do or commit any act or thing that will tend to degrade him in society or bring him into public hatred, contempt, scorn or ridicule public morals or decency or prejudice the Producer or the motion picture industry in general."[71]

By restricting subject matter so that many of the vital topics of the day could not be touched upon, by rejecting scripts which were "too provocative," and by anesthetizing anything political, Hays ensured that American film stories would suffer from arrested development. Had he been in office a decade earlier, there might have been no *Birth of a Nation,* no *Intolerance.*

He also discouraged the film from attaining the intellectual level of the Broad-

---

*According to David Yallop, Hays was merely the front man for this decision. Arbuckle's employers, Zukor and Lasky, were responsible for the ban, even though it meant a loss of many million dollars.[67] But, to some extent, Hays owed his new job to the Arbuckle affair, and he could hardly have done otherwise and survived.

The DEVIL'S CAMERA

R·G·BURNETT & E·D·MARTELL

The cover of a British-published attack on the immorality of the screen.

way theatre or of popular literature by means of his Formula of February 1924, designed "to prevent the more or less prevalent type of novel and stage play from becoming the prevalent type of motion picture."[72]

In 1924, a pamphlet was surreptitiously sent to the Paramount mailing list that amounted to a vicious attack on the company, quoting statements from the studio's own advertising: "Betty Compson in *The Female* __ promises to show her more nearly nude than she has yet appeared on the screen." The pamphleteer added: "Every parent and teacher in this country should be up in arms. Are they willing to have the minds of their boys and girls defiled and their lives demoralized in order that __ picture producers may gratify their lust for gold?"[73] (The blanks stood for a racist adjective removed by the *Variety* reporter who published the story.) It was a Ku Klux Klan stunt, an onslaught on "the flood of Oriental [i.e., Jewish] and Papal debauchery which was flooding the country."

It would not have been gratifying for Hays to find his words and actions endorsed by the KKK. But his speech to advertising men a few days later had the same tone. "You had better mend your ways," he said. He spoke of *Three Weeks** and declared, "There was no excuse whatever for filming this book. On the face of it, the title was innocuous and much of the filth in the book was purged for screen presentation. But was the intent of the production an honest one when they filmed this book, realizing that libraries all over the country have refused to place it on their shelves because of its salacious details?" Producing books and plays which could not honestly and properly be made into films was only a form of cheating.[74]

Hays may have had an essentially advisory role, but producers fell into line because they feared further state censorship, and they appreciated the money he saved them with his advice. In some ways they even welcomed the discipline he imposed. Should some member of the MPPDA produce an outrageous but profitable sex picture, they were within their rights, indeed they were bound by this treaty, to cut the maverick off from his outlets and put him out of business— which saved all the trouble of having to produce a rival picture.

Such sexually explicit pictures as were made for public exhibition were produced by companies outside the Hays umbrella. In 1927, 510 features were made by members of the MPPDA and 159 by outsiders.[75] About fifty of these were the kind of pictures which would would have been shown on "the sex circuit" in downtown, big-city theatres which catered to transients, or at traveling road shows in the countryside.

And yet the major companies knew they could get away with it if they tried, as with *Three Weeks*. The Goldwyn Company released it in February 1924, before the Formula was officially announced. Reformers were furious. When challenged, the Hays Office, rather than admit its embarrassment, resorted to the politician's trick of the qualified lie: "It was made by a company that didn't care about anything, over which we had no moral or legal control whatever." Strictly speaking, the MPPDA had no moral or legal control over any of its members. But the Goldwyn Company, far from being an outsider, was one of the MPPDA's leading

---

*Elinor Glyn's sensational romance of 1907, filmed in 1924.

lights. And to show what he thought of it, Samuel Goldwyn followed *Three Weeks* with Joseph Hergesheimer's proscribed book *Cytherea.*

Over Hays's objection, Famous Players–Lasky released *West of the Water Tower,* which presented the very image of America he strove to suppress—portraying illegitimacy and robbery, a dissolute clergyman and petty small-town characters.[76] The National Congress of Parents and Teachers and the General Federation of Women's Clubs broke away from the Hays Office over its failure to restrain the studio.

In July 1924, the members of MPPDA adopted the Formula a second time. "Some members forgot the agreement after a while," admitted Hays ruefully.[77] They certainly did. Clubwomen, on a tour of the Lasky studios, were horrified to discover Pola Negri filming the forbidden story *Song of Songs.*[78] And Goldwyn, true to form, filmed the banned play *Tarnish.* Both pictures appeared in August 1924.

"The members of the Public Relations Committee," said Mrs. Robbins Gilman, "became conscious that they were engaged in inconsequential work, and, one after another, withdrew."[79] The committee was dissolved in 1925. Reformers now saw the Hays Office as a smoke screen, behind which the picture business was going from bad to worse.[80] And worse still was to come. Hays's Formula was to be breached by a number of clever filmmakers.

Raoul Walsh proved to be the champion bareback rider of the Formula. In *What Price Glory?* (1926), a war picture about the rivalry of two marines, he allowed the marines to swear authentically at each other and provided innocuous titles. Only lip readers were shocked, but the number of lip readers increased dramatically.

In October 1927, Hays issued a series of Don'ts and Be Carefuls. One of the Don'ts was a reference to *What Price Glory?*—"pointed profanity—by either title or lip." Hays said later that the matter of profanity was discussed far into the night, "incidentally, with plenty of profanity."[81] Also forbidden were scenes involving illegal drug traffic, sex perversion, white slavery, miscegenation, V.D., childbirth, children's sex organs, ridicule of the clergy, and willful offense to any nation, race, or creed. The Be Carefuls included everything from the use of the flag to attempted rape.

Observance was still optional. But to give a semblance of compulsion, the Hollywood Jury was established, a panel of producers—or, as they were better known, "the pinochle club."[82] Hays complained they were never objective: "Plagued by the same problems that confronted their fellow producers, or expecting to use the same device themselves next week, they hesitated to be impartial, and in most instances decided in favor of the next producer. . . . The so-called Hays Formula, as well as the Don'ts and Be Carefuls groaned under the weight of the next three years, until we got a Code."[83]

Hays admitted that the dozens of ways of injecting sex into films led to games of hide-and-seek. Directors, having to cope with Hays *and* the state boards, became adept at signaling to the audience over the heads of the censors. Of course, it depended on the censor; the type who saw sin in sandwiches would let nothing through. But others were more literal. A shot of a girl dusting foot powder into her shoes would indicate to them merely that she suffered from tired feet. A more

Gloria Swanson, as star-producer, won a victory of a sort over Hays with her Sadie Thompson, *1928, directed by Raoul Walsh.*

sophisticated audience, trained to watch for the smallest hint, would realize at once that the girl was a streetwalker.[84]

Hays was not entirely concerned with purifying the movies. His job was to sort out industrial problems as well, and in this area he could lay claim to more solid achievement. He hired the Burns Detective Agency to investigate the theft of films[85] and brought the abuses of extras by employment agencies to an end with the formation of Central Casting in 1926.[86] The old Studio Club, founded by the YWCA, was enlarged and reequipped. Hays laid down strict regulations for the treatment of children in pictures. And the MPPDA arranged for films to be shown in orphanages and prisons, as well as on steamships bringing immigrants to the United States.

Hays's Open Door policy acted as a punching bag for those dissatisfied with the industry and sometimes defused their anger before it exploded in print. Not only clubwomen complained: the Yellow Cab Company protested that in the movie criminals always escaped in cabs, the National Billiard Association objected to the number of low-grade poolrooms in pictures, and the American Hotel Association complained about scenes of people smoking in bed.[87]

But it is as a censor that Will Hays will be remembered. And the most notorious example of defiance he had to cope with was *Sadie Thompson* (1928), directed by Raoul Walsh. Frantic after the failure of her first independent production, Gloria Swanson asked Walsh for a challenging idea. Mischievously, Walsh suggested W. Somerset Maugham's *Rain,* knowing it was on the Hays list of banned plays. It dealt with the attempt by a fanatical minister in the South Seas to reform a prostitute. Instead of reforming her, he falls for her and commits suicide. "Filming *Rain* in 1927 was the maddest idea in the world, but every other idea suddenly seemed dull," wrote Swanson.[88]

Walsh and Swanson invited Will Hays to lunch. Swanson told him the story in the vaguest of terms and charmed from him his word of approval. Secretly, she and Joseph Schenck bought the rights to the play and the original story, but as soon as word leaked out, the combined force of all the members of the MPPDA was brought to bear on the project. They made the strongest possible protest to Schenck. But Swanson said she was the producer, not Schenck. She insisted she had Hays's approval, that she endorsed what the MPPDA stood for, that she would not make an unclean film, and that she had invested far too much money to stop now.

Of course, all the other producers wished they could make *Rain* and were furious at having been outwitted. When the picture was finished, the Hays Office

A Woman of Affairs, *1928, MGM's version of* The Green Hat. *Although everything was changed, including the title, director Clarence Brown managed to signal that Diana (Garbo) is in hospital following a miscarriage. Lewis Stone plays Dr. Hugh Trevelyan, an old family friend.*

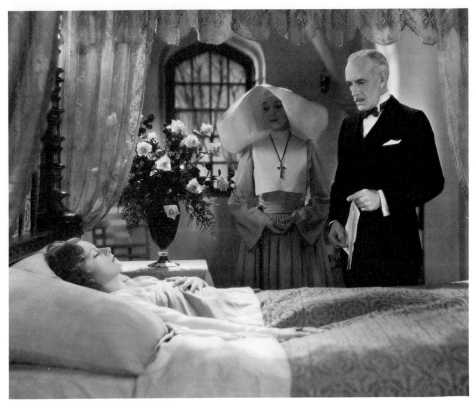

inspectors scrutinized its every inch and hired lip readers to ensure that Walsh had not repeated his *What Price Glory?* trick. They did not object to the fact that it rained in the picture, but they removed the word "rain" whenever it cropped up in the titles. "They drove the editors crazy," said Swanson, "and Raoul and I had to fight for every word and every foot of film."[89]

Wrote Welford Beaton: "Instead of the kind of director that [*Rain*] needed, one of fine instincts, culture and good taste, Raoul Walsh, whose obsession is that the public is degenerate, directed the picture and turned out one that the United Artists people had the greatest difficulty in cleansing sufficiently to make it fit to be released.

"A picture that had to be put through such a delousing process ... cannot emerge as a good example of screen art. In removing the filth it is not possible to avoid scraping off some of the healthy substance."[90]

Sadie Thompson was not the shocker it might have been without this treatment, but it was still a highly entertaining and daring picture. Its success further reduced Hays's credibility and encouraged MGM to sidestep the Formula and select another banned title, Michael Arlen's *The Green Hat,* for Greta Garbo.[91] Nevertheless, a year later, Gloria Swanson walked off the set of *Queen Kelly* when she realized that Erich von Stroheim was shooting scenes in a brothel which were censorable (and wildly over budget). So the Hays influence could hardly be discounted, even though the years 1927–1933 proved the most liberal of his reign.

Wrote Robert E. Sherwood: "If Mr. Hays were sincere in his attitude, even those who disagree with him could not seriously condemn him. But his whole policy is based on the theory that anything is all right if you can get away with it. He has been terrorized so completely by reformers that he himself is becoming a party to their fanaticism and hypocrisy.

"He countenances such a sickening example of vulgarity and bad taste as *The Callahans and the Murphys* [a film by MGM about Irish immigrants] and allows *Rain* to be filmed only on condition that all disparaging references to the clergy (in other words all the points of this fine, true play) be removed."[92]

The intervention of Will Harrison Hays may have been a disaster aesthetically, but it made financial sense. Along with self-censorship, Hays restored self-confidence. And he served as an instrument of unification. That he was successful in his control over the image of America cannot be denied, for it was partly due to him that the era became known as the Age of Innocence.

Chapter Two

MATTERS
OF SEX

Priscilla Dean and Ben Wilson in Lois
Weber's Even As You and I, 1917.

A T THE TURN of the century, there was a word shocking to many Americans. That word was "novel."[1] The novel and the film were fictional, and thus untrue, and they shared an obsession with romance. Romance, as Puritans knew only too well, was simply a cloak for naked sex.

In case you think only bigoted farmers in the rural South felt this way, let me quote from Edward A. Ross, the leading sociologist of the Progressive era. In 1926 he declared that "conscienceless film producers and negligent parents" had allowed to be committed against children "one of the worst crimes on record." Apart from the occasional sex film from which children were barred, as a publicity dodge to make adults anticipate something spicy, "children have been allowed to see everything which adults have had access to."[2]

Ross blamed on the movies the fact that young people were more "sex-wise, sex-excited and sex-absorbed" than any previous generation. "Thanks to their premature exposure to stimulating films, their sex instincts were stirred into life years sooner than used to be the case with boys and girls from good homes."

He accused producers of making hundreds of millions of dollars, yet of paying not the slightest concern to the effect of their films on children. "I fancy that if every juvenile movie habitué were to develop leprosy within ten years, most of the producers would still fight any movement to bar children from their shows. Never have we witnessed a more ruthless pursuit of gain."[3] (Now that the children have grown up and become grandparents themselves—often objecting strongly to what their grandchildren are watching—how many were corrupted?)

It is easy to laugh at the concern for the moral welfare of children in a distant era when the movies appear so harmless. But films then had a far stronger impact than they do today, when moving pictures are as available as tapwater. And parents had reasons for their concern, reasons which escape our eyes—partly because the films we see are often more heavily censored than the versions they saw at the time. Many have come down to us in 16mm prints prepared for home movie use by the Eastman Kodak Company, most were abridged from seven or more reels to five, and the cutting was done with an eye to the family audience. Anything remotely risqué was removed.

The most strenuous objections were made to *The Wanderer* (1925), an adaptation of the Old Testament story of the Prodigal Son, directed by Raoul Walsh. It was intended as a sequel to *The Ten Commandments* (1923), in which Cecil B. DeMille had used the Bible to provide censor-proof excuses for extremes of sex and violence.

At a hearing of the Committee on Education before the House of Representatives in 1926, Wilton Barrett, secretary to the National Board of Review, was asked if he approved of *The Wanderer*. Absolutely, he replied. His interrogator,

Greta Nissen as the seductress in The Wanderer, *1926. (National Film Archive)*

Mr. Fletcher, had just seen the picture: "Mrs. Fletcher and I were very much interested in the reaction of the young people, when the draperies were drawn and he was with the woman, nude except for a few flowers." (An exaggeration, of course!) "Their exclamations and observations were very interesting. And when he came out, fatigued, somewhat staggering, the next morning, after his experience with the woman through the night, their exclamations were again very interesting to observe; very audible were their exclamations. I was just wondering where you would begin to censor a picture of sex questionableness?"

Mr. Barrett fell back on a quotation from Dr. Lovejoy Elliott to the effect that you cannot divorce a motion picture from the environment and training of the person attending it. "And it would be hard to tell where the motion picture was the stimulating influence and where it was environment and heredity."[4]

Unusually, this moment survives in the otherwise heavily abridged 16mm version (nine reels to five), and while one can see what a mild bit of vamping it is by modern standards, one can also appreciate why it upset people at the time. A glamorous priestess, Tisha (Greta Nissen), ensnares the young man (William Collier, Jr.), and slave girls drape muslin around them. The film fades out on Tisha's inviting expression and fades in the next morning as the young man, obviously exhausted, takes his departure. One can imagine a college audience sending it up with hoots of merriment.

But the big sex scene—even so sober a critic as Pare Lorentz described it as "one of the most salacious scenes ever put into a film"[5]—was cut very short indeed: "The temptress, barely covered by a leopard skin, receives the prodigal on a rose-strewn couch in no mild manner. Yet because the hero was chastened, punished and repented (in one short reel) this movie was hardly touched by the hands of the godly."[6]

In any case, sex or no sex, *The Wanderer* was a flop with the public, and a sequel, *The Lady of the Harem,* made by the same team, lasted but a day at Loew's New York.[7]

To modern eyes, the sex in American silent films is unbelievably tame. So it is in Victorian paintings, until you become aware of the symbolism, or view an Alma-Tadema, the DeMille of his day. But while the sex content of most regular releases was kept to one tenth of 1 percent, stronger stuff was available. Not on the open market, of course, but through the agency of bootleggers. Soft-core pornography could be purchased in 100-foot rolls for home movie projectors in the 1920s. The films tend to look innocuous and rather charming when seen today.[8] In one, a girl in her bath sees a mouse, shrieks, and brings a man running in from the street. As she eyes him in alarm, he is transformed into a large version of the mouse that scared her. In another reel, schoolgirls play strip poker. The headmistress surprises the naked girls and announces, "Young ladies, may I remind you that this is a finishing school? And YOU ARE ALL FINISHED!"

The hard-core films were difficult to obtain then and difficult to see now. A few surviving examples going back to the birth of the cinema (and, I suspect, assisting at it) were included in a documentary called *Ain't Misbehaving* (1974) made by Peter Neal and Anthony Stern.

I came across a print of *A Free Ride* at a collectors' convention in Los Angeles. It was described, somewhat unfairly, as a pornographic Griffith Biograph of 1915! Judging by the fashions, the film was actually made around 1923. The three participants are disguised. The two girls wear wigs—one curled in Mary Pickford style—and the man wears a villain's mustache. (During the subsequent excitement it falls off, and as he sticks it back on he shields his face with his arm against possible recognition.) The locale is Southern California; two girls are picked up on a lonely road by a man in a Model T and driven to the desert, where they prove that sex in the twenties was conducted in precisely the same way as it is today, whatever the movies would have you believe. And pornographic films were as crudely made; when a girl's leg moves to the wrong position in a close-up, the cameraman's hand appears in frame to push it back.

In the industry, you will hear rumors that famous stars began their careers in such films, that professional technicians made them after hours, and that blackmailers became rich from them. None of the examples I have seen betrays the skill of a professional, nor have I recognized any of the participants. (In a film shown in *Ain't Misbehaving,* a man was dressed in an "Arab" headdress to resemble Rudolph Valentino in *The Sheik.*)

Pornographic films were known as "cooch reels" (after hoochie-coochie dancers), and they were astonishingly expensive. They sold for $100 to $200 per reel ($1,000 to $2,000 in today's money). The police conducted raids whenever they were tipped off that a theatre owner or distributor was trafficking in them, for they were not always shown in private. One proprietor was arrested for showing obscene films to 300 patrons after hours—although, admittedly, he had the doors locked.[9] Members of the Women's Viligant Committee witnessed the destruction of such films.[10]

Since the police might raid a theatre showing a perfectly innocent picture on the word of some reformer, their view of cooch reels was as all-embracing as their idea of "Reds." In 1919, a police captain marched into a theatre in Buffalo, New York, and ripped pictures of Annette Kellerman, the famous swimming star, from the walls, declaring that they were not fit to be exhibited.[11]

Much of the wrath directed at the movies was sparked off by the advertising displays which accompanied them. In some cases, attacks on movies were inspired by the billboards—which were detested anyway—the reformers not troubling to see the films they advertised. The titles alone were enough to cause apoplexy: *Passion Fruit, His Naughty Night, The Married Virgin, Don't Blame the Stork, Up in Betty's Bedroom, Sex, His Pajama Girl*. . . .[12]

Many of these titles were dreamed up to sell to exhibitors before the films were even made. Thus, the content was often at complete variance with the title. *The Night Club* (1925), a Raymond Griffith comedy about a man running away from women, contained no shot of a nightclub from start to finish. *The Bedroom Window* (1924) was advertised in the usual way—a face leering in at a bedroom—but it turned out to be a story of a middle-aged woman writer of detective stories without a hint of sex.

Producers lacked the daring to make their pictures actually indecent, suggested *Motion Picture Magazine,* so they injected enough suggestiveness into their titles to draw a crowd.[13] And the advertising copy in the newspapers often suggested a film far more lurid than the one on display: "She lured men. Her red lips and warm eyes enslaved a man of the world . . . and taught life to an innocent boy! Hot tropic nights fanning the flames of desire. She lived for love alone."[14] This habit harmed the industry. It was not eliminated even under Hays, who was supposed to control advertising.

The real immorality of the photoplay, according to the intelligentsia, lay in its lack of reality, its sugary sentimentality, its specious philosophy, its utterly false values. Happy endings were far more likely to corrupt the mind than love scenes.[15] One might have added, too, that melodrama encouraged people to regard their neighbors in terms of black and white—good or evil—a habit with potentially disastrous results politically. But as long as moral behavior was associated in the public mind exclusively with sex, such arguments were meaningless. The conflict was particularly harsh in the twenties, for Victorians and religious fundamentalists were living in the same communities with flappers and their sheiks. The industry had the impossible task of appealing to both extremes. The Victorians would attend the Biblical films, only to be shocked by the orgies. The flappers would flock to the sex films, to be maddened by the moralizing.

Before the war, a number of films featured nudity—such as *Purity* (1916), with Audrey Munson. But the censors clamped down on these, and picture men tried the "educational" ploy. The helping hand was more often outstretched for greed than guidance, but the films offered fascinating insights into the mores of the period.

THE VAMP

When Theda Bara initiated the vamp cycle, playing temptresses who lured men to their deaths, people began to identify vamps they knew in real life. One woman, accused of murdering her lover, called upon Theda Bara to testify to the mental attitude of a jilted vampire.[16] (Bara declined.) The vamp cycle was short-lived; before it passed, the Essanay Film Company tried to capitalize on it by making a film about a self-confessed vampire from Butte, Montana, called Mary MacLane.

Born in Winnipeg, Canada, in 1881, as a child MacLane had moved to Minnesota and later Montana. She found Butte the quintessence of ugliness and saw no romance in its mining camps or its desolate hills and gulches. Her life was an "empty, damned weariness,"[17] although she found a little fulfillment from writing. She wrote every day, and described herself as a genius—"although not of the literary kind." She completed *The Story of Mary MacLane* when she was nineteen, and it was published in Chicago (the home of Essanay) in 1902.

In her confessions she admitted to feelings of sexuality toward women, she longed for the devil to visit her, and she acknowledged that she was a liar and a thief. The book brought her "astounding notoriety," fueled by reports of girls who killed themselves after reading it. Any sign of revolt among young ladies was called "MacLaneism."[18]

A New York newspaper called the book "ridiculous rot," while a Winnipeg paper, at her death, said, "the wonderful thing about this book is not that it was written, but that this child of ignorance wrote it. Coming from this young girl, it should rather inspire a feeling of awe. You can no more explain Mary MacLane than you can explain Charlotte Brontë. Shut up there in a bleak and lonely moor, she is the genius she proclaims herself."[19]

She wrote three more books. The last, *I, Mary MacLane, a diary of human days*,[20] described her life in Boston and New York: "She was careless toward men in their crude sex rapacity in ways no 'regular' woman would dare or care to be. No man could wring one tear from her, nor cause a quickening of her foolish heart, nor any emotion in her save mirth."[21]

This sounded as good as Theda Bara, and Essanay had a brain wave. It offered the leading role not to a vamp actress, but to Mary MacLane herself. And even though she described herself as a "plain-featured, insignificant little animal,"[22] she accepted. Her book revealed that above virtually anything else, she longed for fame. She even wrote the script, for she was an ardent admirer of the motion picture.[23]

Men Who Have Made Love to Me was directed in the summer of 1917 by Arthur Berthelet and released early in 1918. The title was "as shocking as the reputation of its star" to the Chicago *Tribune*.[24] Yet it was not quite so startling then as it appears to our eyes, oddly enough. For the euphemism "making love" did not apply solely to coitus, as it does now, but referred to any romantic approach.* Nevertheless, Essanay intended it to be a thoroughly sensational production. The

---

*There was a 1917 series called *How the Great Stars Make Love*.

(Kobal Collection)

image of Mary smoking was used in the advertising; this was little more than a
decade since women had been arrested for smoking in the street, and the image
symbolized decadence throughout the silent era.

It was an episodic picture, an account of six affairs: a callow youth (Ralph
Graves), who quickly bores Mary; a self-obsessed literary man (R. Paul Harvey);
a depraved gentleman (Cliff Worman); a cave man (Alador Prince) she is forced
to give up; a bank clerk (Clarence Derwent) who wants a baby and a cottage but
loathes her smoking and drinking. The sixth is "the husband of another [Fred
Tiden] who gave her a thrill one night by breaking down the bedroom door, but
spoiled the ecstacy by having stale liquor on his breath."[25]

Wid Gunning, reviewer and publisher, admired the playing, the treatment,
and even Mary MacLane's qualities as an actress, but he noticed one great defect—
"it is absolutely cold."[26] Mary regarded each man as a specimen to be stuck on
pins and examined under a microscope.[27]

Variety was contemptuous of the whole thing: "The Butte brand of vampire is
nix. . . . The picture is replete with radical and ultra subtle subtitles which smack
of Mary's authorship."[28] The opening title was certainly hers: "God has made
many things less plausible than me. He has made the sharks in the ocean, and
people who hire children to work in their mills and mines, and poison ivy and
zebras."[29]

But James McQuade, in *Moving Picture World,* found the film utterly gripping and stressed its one indisputable asset: "It is the first time in my remembrance that I have seen on the screen author and actress concentrated in the same person, and that person acting over again love scenes in her own life with a matter of fact realism. . . . Mary MacLane never laid claim to being an actress and never before risked an appearance before the moving picture camera, yet in my opinion no other woman could take her place in these episodes . . . for the simple reason that the author appears as her very self. True Mary has no fine stage airs . . . and her stage walk shows . . . an inclination to what might be termed a waddle, yet we welcome these seeming defects because they are really part of herself."[30]

The picture was banned in censor-ridden states like Ohio. And on August 1, 1919, while Mary was entertaining a friend at her home in Chicago, two detectives arrived, armed with a warrant for her arrest. She was accused of stealing dresses by Madame Alla Ripley, the designer of the gowns for the picture. "Dressed in an embroidered Japanese kimono and a feathered hat, Mary was escorted to the Women's Detention Home, where she was forced to remain until her friends could raise bail—for although she was said to be living in 'surroundings of comfort and luxury' she had only 85¢ in her purse."[31]

This sad episode was typical of her last years. She was addicted to gambling, her books were no longer in demand, and she seemed unable to write more. In 1929, she was found dead in "a lonely room on the fringe of Chicago's poorest quarter. . . . No one was at her bedside when she died. Death was due to natural causes."[32] She was only forty-eight.

DIVORCE

Divorce was another word for disgrace. Yet by 1908, it ended one in ten marriages. Those who went through with it were either very desperate or very brave. Women, economically dependent upon their husbands, were often ruined, alimony or no alimony. They could be driven not only from their homes, but from the very districts in which they lived. As *The Social Leper* (1917) pointed out, a divorced man was also a social outcast. "As a result of our picturesque laws," said a reviewer, "[divorce] is always an exciting and dramatic theme."[33]

Newspapers were the acid in the wound of divorce. Upton Sinclair recalled what happened to him: "the newspapers invented statements, they set traps and betrayed confidences—and when they got through with their victim, they had turned his hair grey."[34]

In *The Woman's Side* (1922), a B. P. Schulberg production written and directed by J. A. Barry, a newspaper issues a threat to publish details of a divorce and a woman warns of suicide unless it is retracted. Divorce sometimes did lead to suicide, but then such deaths were understandable: "after all, she *was* divorced . . ."

The husband of a successful actress in Cecil B. DeMille's *What's His Name* (1914) finds himself being divorced, to his intense surprise, losing his home and his furniture, which were in his wife's name, and even his much-loved daughter (Cecilia de Mille, Cecil's daughter). His attempt at suicide only fails when the gas man disconnects the mains. And this was in a comedy!

Based on a Eugène Brieux story about the effect of divorce on a child, The Cradle, *1923, featured Charles Meredith as a doctor who falls for one of his patients and Mary Jane Irving as the child maltreated by that patient.*

Loss of affection was not legally recognized as sufficient reason for dissolving a marriage until the late twenties,[35] yet newspapers complained that divorce was becoming too easy. In some places, it did become less complicated. A divorced man in Indiana told Robert and Helen Lynd: "Anyone with $10 can get a divorce in ten minutes if it isn't contested. All you've got to do is show non-support or cruelty and it's a cinch."[36] But elsewhere, if couples made the mistake of agreeing that they wanted a divorce, the judge was likely to deny them a decree.[37] The entire system was described by Judge Ben Lindsey as "bungling, dishonest and putrid."[38]

A generation or two earlier, divorce had been virtually unknown. "Our great-grandmothers and fathers got along very well without divorce to a great extent," commented *Variety,* "contenting themselves with cheerfully throwing the china at each other. Divorce . . . does not flourish in the tenement districts because it is too expensive. But it thrives in elevator apartments with three or four baths and maids leashed to lap dogs."[39] (This was why most divorce scenarios dealt with the upper middle classes.)

Hollywood was depicted by the press as the divorce center of the nation. (It wasn't—that was in the Midwest.) In California, divorce was regarded as an evil, but not a stigma, which had to be tolerated, for so many resorted to it. Yet it seldom affected the popularity of the stars. "Who can ever again see Mary Pickford or Douglas Fairbanks," asked the Santa Ana *Daily Evening Register,* "without mentally recounting the destruction of family ties and ideals that lie back of their marriage?"[40] But seldom was a divorce so quickly forgotten, and Pickford and Fairbanks were soon the respected leaders of the motion picture community.

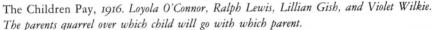

Divorce was an obviously commercial subject; the American Mutoscope and Bio-graph Company made what was probably the first essay on the subject with *Detected* (1903), an episode from *The Divorce* (a stage play): a wife becomes suspicious of her husband, hires a detective, and the two of them ambush the husband in a private dining room, where he is living it up so energetically with his girlfriend that the wife faints in horror.

But it took more than a decade for the subject to be treated with concern and its victims with compassion. *The Children Pay* was a Fine Arts production of 1916 starring Lillian Gish and directed by Lloyd Ingraham, from a story by Frank Woods. "Parents, consider your children before you enter the divorce court" was its message. It caught the poisonous atmosphere surrounding a family torn by divorce. Millicent (Lillian Gish) and Jean (Violet Wilky) are sisters placed in the care of a nurse in a small town, who are shunned by all the neighbors and their children, while they await the outcome of their parents' divorce action. Who will win custody of whom?

The mother wins Jean, the father Millicent. The father marries again; his new wife is a social butterfly. Millicent leaves home in the middle of her coming-out

The Children Pay, *1916. Loyola O'Connor, Ralph Lewis, Lillian Gish, and Violet Wilkie. The parents quarrel over which child will go with which parent.*

party and runs away with her sister. They turn for protection to their old nurse. An officer of the court discovers them and takes them back, and another custody battle ensues. The hero (Keith Armour), a young lawyer, solves the problem by marrying Millicent, who is then awarded custody of her younger sister.

"The entire theme is absolutely without foundation in law," protested *Variety,* "for if the court had jurisdiction over the older girl in the matter of her guardianship, then she was not of age and could not marry without the consent of her guardian or parents. As a picture it will get by . . . but the law students will have a good laugh."[41]

Julian Johnson in *Photoplay* considered the film "the sanest, most humanly interesting" feature of the month and praised Lillian Gish as a real, believable young woman. "There are those who say the final legal situation is impossible. I don't know. I do know that the body of the play is a page of life, of which the screen shows far too little."[42] According to Anthony Slide, the film is an impressive work, told in the simple style perfected by Griffith at Biograph.[43] Ironically, when the film was released in the 1920s for home movie use by Pathex in America, the story was altered; the divorce element was removed and the children became orphans.

"And they lived happily ever after."

Most Hollywood romances ended with that idea, if not that title. *The Hungry Heart* (1917), a five-reeler from a novel by David Graham Phillips, directed by Robert Vignola, began where such films usually ended. Pauline Frederick played the wife, left to her own devices by a husband who treats her as a child, despite her college degree. She asks to assist him with his work in chemistry, but he simply laughs at her. She has a child; the couple drift apart; she has an affair with one of his handsome colleagues. The husband sues for divorce and only then realizes how much she means to him. He admits to having neglected her and agrees to her working with him. The lover offers to marry her, but she goes back to her husband.[44]

In an era when a woman's adultery, on the screen, often had to be paid for by death or ruin, this was a refreshing treatment. *Variety,* however, could not stand it. "It is just an impossible hodge-podge, much tainted with the atmosphere of improbability."[45]

The paper preferred William Fox's *Blindness of Divorce* (1918,) written and directed by Frank Lloyd, which was designed to show divorce "as a work of the devil,"[46] echoing Theodore Roosevelt's declaration that easy divorce was "an evil thing for men and a still more hideous thing for women."[47]

Suffering from the producer's customary delusion that he had made the picture, Fox told the trade press, "I have aimed to show just what the 24-sheets [posters] represent—a fiend pushing apart a man and a woman whom God joined together. In my time I have seen a good many divorce cases, but I am convinced that there was not one in ten that was justified. Good people everywhere agree with me. Our clergy, our prominent thinkers, our judges are crying out against this shattering of family ties and sapping of our national life by the divorce de-

The Blindness of Divorce,
1918. Bertha Mann as the wife
who takes up gambling and
prostitution when her husband
(Charles Clary) divorces her.
The child is Nancy Caswell.
(Museum of Modern Art)

cree—a decree that is all too often lightly granted. Therefore I have produced this
picture in an effort to arouse the public against this curse to men, women and
innocent children.''[48]

In *Blindness of Divorce*, John Langdon (Charles Clary) prefers to spend his time
with friends at the club rather than with his wife and child. A young lawyer called
Merrill (Bertram Grassby) takes advantage of this neglect and forces his attentions
on the unwilling wife (Bertha Mann). Returning home unexpectedly, Langdon
catches his wife in Merrill's arms, and, despite her protestations of innocence,
divorce follows. Langdon wins custody of the child, and the disgraced mother is
scorned by society.

Fifteen years later, Langdon is living with his daughter, Florence (Rhea Mitchell), in another city. Florence marries a district attorney (Fred Church), who is
campaigning for a second term. Unknown to Langdon, his former wife runs a
notorious house of gambling and prostitution in the same city. An opponent of
the D.A. blackmails Florence, eventually sending her to see her mother's establishment for herself. The mother pretends not to know her, although her heart breaks.
That night, the police raid the place and Florence is rounded up with the others.
The D.A. fears the worst and sues for divorce. At the trial, however, the former
Mrs. Langdon makes an appearance, tells the whole story, and roundly accuses
''man-made'' laws. Florence and the D.A. are reunited.[49]

Photoplay described the film as an attempt to prove that divorce was a great
evil by showing a lot of stupid people doing a lot of stupid things. ''It is incomprehensible that Frank Lloyd, the one directorial genius in the Fox organization,
wrote and produced [i.e., directed] this hodge-podge.''[50]

Whatever its aesthetic drawbacks, *Blindness of Divorce* created a sensation in Brooklyn, where people recognized the story. It paralleled a divorce case which had occurred in the neighborhood a few years before: "The rumor that *Blindness of Divorce* was practically a picturization of this case, and even explained some of the mysteries connected with the subsequent careers of the principal parties, quickly spread all over the district and combined with the regular clientele to crowd the theatre to its utmost capacity for the four days shown. A repeat is likely."[51]

The divorce pictures did not develop into a cycle of sensation like, say, the white slave films; the subject was too close to that mainstay of regular releases, the love triangle. But during the twenties, about 200 features involving the subject of divorce were put into production,[52] and of them all, perhaps the strangest was *The Lonely Trail*.

THE LONELY TRAIL   The official attitude toward divorce was perhaps best crystallized in the furor which surrounded the release of this film. An incident celebrated as the Stillman case was exploited by an independent producer, who had the idea of casting the handsome corespondent, Fred K. Beauvais, in the lead. Beauvais worked as an "Indian guide" on camping trips, and he played the same role in the film. The trouble was that he had become famous—or infamous— as the Stillmans' Indian guide in the real divorce case.

The New York State Motion Picture Commission passed the film, which, by all accounts, was innocuous. But in December 1921, in the wake of the Arbuckle scandal, the picture business became nervous about such films. Members of the Motion Picture Theatre Owners Chamber of Commerce held a meeting and stated that they would not play it. The trade press wholeheartedly condemned the producers (whom they resolutely refused to identify). Eventually, the film was offered to Lewis J. Selznick for $1,500. They chose the wrong man, since he was currently negotiating to hire Will Hays away from the post office. Selznick turned it down, and it wound up opening at the Shubert Theatre—a vaudeville house—on New York's 44th Street. The Shuberts were not fussy about the content of pictures so long as they drew the customers.

Variety's reviewer "Fred" went to see it and reported that it had been cut to a mere forty minutes. "As a picture it is one of the saddest bits of screen production shown anywhere in a long, long time."[53] He added that curiosity about Fred Beauvais was pulling in money, but it would not entertain. And "The girl with bobbed hair must have been picked with an eye to resemblance to Mrs. Stillman, but it ends right there. As long as the program did not give her name it must remain a secret. . . ."[54] If left alone, he said, the picture would die before the week was out.

It was not left alone. It arrived in Washington, but the theatre owners refused to touch it, their inappropriately named spokesman, Sidney Lust, stating that as long as they could get clean plays, with respectable players, it would not be necessary to fall back upon persons who possess "absolutely no histrionic ability, but are featured solely because they have figured in a nauseous scandal."[55]

The New York State Motion Picture Commission justified having approved the film, saying that Beauvais's participation did not make the film immoral. It

Mrs. James Stillman interviewed by A. A. Brown with her new husband, Fowler McCormick, at their honeymoon bungalow, Southampton, Long Island. A shot taken in the early days of talkies: Dion di Titta using the Wall camera which was exceptionally quiet.

would be a different matter, said the chairman, if the advertising drew attention to the fact that the hero of the picture was involved in the Stillman scandal. Of course, the advertising did just that, so the commission was able to save a little face by ordering the removal of the name Stillman from all references to the film.[56]

"If Clara Hamon and Roscoe Arbuckle are barred by popular sentiment from the screen," declared William Brady of NAMPI, "the same holds good in the case of Fred Beauvais. . . . If one can become famous through murder, divorce or scandal, then encouragement only goes to spread the present wave of crime."[57] Clara Hamon* was accused of murder, Arbuckle of manslaughter; divorce was seen not as private grief, but as public crime, and bracketed with the most serious offenses it was possible to commit. The picture was banned in several states, and the incident culminated in a lawsuit, as the producers—at last revealed as the Primex Picture Corporation—sued the Shuberts in the U.S. Supreme Court for breach of contract.[58] The only people to gain from such a case were the lawyers— as in divorce.

---

*Clara Hamon was accused of the murder of her husband—she even admitted to it—but was acquitted. She made a film called *Fate* (1921). See pages 153–55.

WHY CHANGE YOUR WIFE?   To describe a divorce case as entertaining is perhaps unfortunate, but in the hands of William and Cecil DeMille it invariably was. *Why Change Your Wife?*, probably the best of the DeMille marital pictures, was shot in 1919 and released the following year. Written by William de Mille,[59] it was graced with witty and elegant titles and a story packed with incident, and Cecil's direction, although lacking the same elegance, conveyed his enthusiasm for the subject.

It would be a mistake, however, to regard it as a faithful portrayal of its time. Admittedly, DeMille directed it like a social historian, showing us details of perfume bottles, liquor decanters, razor sharpeners, shimmying dolls, and phonograph records. But he and his art director, Wilfred Buckland, created a land of the imagination, where a girl like Gloria Swanson could wear a bathing costume slashed to the thigh at the swimming pool of a big hotel, where the men clustering around her could include an aviator in leather coat and flying helmet.

Thomas Meighan plays Robert Gordon and Swanson plays Beth, his wife, "whose virtues are her only vices and who willingly gave up her husband's liberty when she married him." Like so many husbands, Robert is puzzled by the difference between his wife and the girl he married: "Molten lead poured on the skin is soothing compared to a wife's constant disapproval." Beth, whose pince-nez symbolize her frigidity, criticizes Robert ceaselessly, particularly his attempts to lay down a wine cellar.

"How *can* you spend money for all this," she asks, "when you think of the starving millions in Europe?" Robert replies that they give constantly to the starving millions. "Why is it that anything I do for our personal pleasure robs people in Europe?"

He thinks a present might restore the smile to her face, but while buying a negligee in a fashionable store he meets his old friend Sally Clark (Bebe Daniels), "legally a widow and optically a pippin." She sets out to ensnare him, and Beth does her inadvertent best to throw them together. She rejects the negligee and turns down his offer of tickets to the Follies, anxious instead to attend a musical soiree.

"Then I'll dine at the club," says Robert. "I'm sick to death of hearing that wire-haired foreigner torturing a fiddle."

Sally calls, and they go to the theatre together. "When a husband has had his faults thoroughly and constantly explained to him at home, he listens more easily to an old friend tell him how wonderful he is."

At Sally's apartment afterward, he is invited in. "One *teeny* sandwich won't take a minute." An arm of her davenport hinges back to reveal a phonograph; the other contains a glittering decanter called Forbidden Fruit. (This was not a DeMille invention; it really existed.)[60]

This being a pre-Hays picture, DeMille manages to implant a genuine erotic charge into this scene, which is also very amusing. When Robert tries to light a match, Sally holds up her shoe, so he can strike it on the sole. She puts scent on her lips and his coat collar. Robert goes as far as a passionate kiss, but there he stops, to Sally's (and the audience's) disappointment.

Why Change Your Wife?, *1920. Bebe Daniels and Thomas
Meighan, who is providing a remedy for Bebe's headache in this
risqué scene, which is not in the final film. (Museum of Modern Art)*

He returns to his wife, who lies in bed, her book, *How to Improve the Mind,*
beside her. She looks at the clock—1:45 A.M.—and demands to know where he
has been. He shows her a ticket stub. Feminine intuition leads her to search his
pockets for the incriminating companion to that ticket. "A friend went with me,"
he says lamely. Beth is hurt and angry. He apologizes and calms her down, and
she lays her head on his shoulder. It is then that she smells Sally's perfume. This
time, he confesses that the "friend" was female. Beth leaps out of bed, puts on
her robe, and starts packing: "I don't use vulgar perfume. I don't wear indecent
clothes. As you have evidently found someone who does, I won't stand between
you and your ideal."

She is so implacable that Robert decides he should be the one to leave, and
with that, at least, Beth agrees. "So when morning comes at last, merciless virtue
proves stronger than love—and wrecks a home."

Some time later, Beth overhears one gossip point out an item in the paper to
another. "Oh look, Mrs. Robert Gordon has got her divorce. No wonder she lost
him—she just wouldn't play with him. Then she dressed as if she were his *aunt,*
not his wife. Still, I'm terribly sorry for her, poor thing."

"They pity me, do they?" sneers Beth. "Pity me because I've been fool enough
to think a man wants his wife modest and decent. Well, I'll show them!" Beth

goes berserk; she tears off her sedate clothes and demands the latest styles—"sleeveless, backless, transparent, indecent—I'll go the limit." And after the divorce, she flaunts herself at a big hotel in Atlantic Beach, where she encounters Robert and his new wife. "When a woman meets her ex-husband she realizes all she has lost. When she meets his wife she realizes all he has lost."

The story develops into a fight for possession of Robert. Injured in New York, he is taken home by Beth, and she and Sally fight for the door key like wildcats over his sickbed. Finally, Beth grabs a vial from a drawer and shouts, "Get away from that door, or I'll spoil your beauty with this so that no man will ever look at you." Sally cowers, and Beth wins custody of the invalid. But before she goes, Sally finds the vial and hurls the contents at Beth in a moment of vicious revenge. "It's all right, dear," Beth says to Robert. "It's only my eyewash."

Defeated in every way, Sally takes a roll of bills out of Robert's trousers and stalks out with the remark, "There's only one good thing about marriage and that's alimony."

Upstairs, the maid and butler reunite the twin beds, and a final title tells us, "And now you know what every husband knows; that a man would rather have his wife for a sweetheart than any other woman, but ladies, if you would be your husband's sweetheart you simply must learn when to forget that you're his wife."

The final scene from Why Change Your Wife? *The butler and maid reunite the twin beds and display the nightwear. This kind of touch would soon be associated exclusively with Lubitsch. (Museum of Modern Art)*

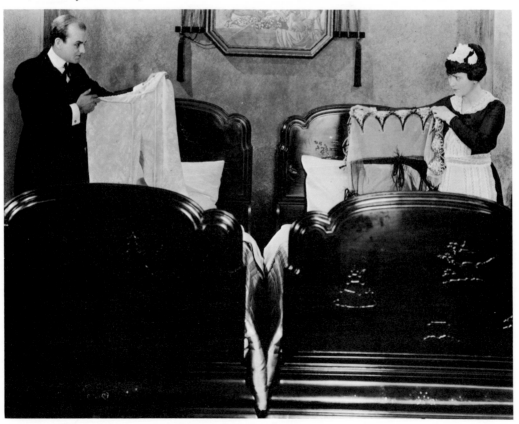

Feminists then, as now, would have disapproved thoroughly of the whole dubious tale. But the moviegoing public adored it: the picture cost $130,000 and earned $1 million.[61] If it was far-fetched, that was what they went to a DeMille picture for.

Charles Higham claims in his book on DeMille that the fight at the end was based on a quarrel between two of DeMille's mistresses, Julia Faye and Jeanie Macpherson. In this case, Jeanie threw not acid but ink.[62]

"DeMille caters for the sophisticated," said Herbert Howe in *Picture Play,* "and, judging by the crowds patronizing this picture, we are a sophisticated nation. *Why Change Your Wife?* is a rouged, gemmed, silk, and sensuous reflection of the artificial life."[63] "Sophisticated and searching is the photoplay of 1920," said Frederick James Smith. "Franker and franker does it become each month in dealing with that eternal theme—sex. The picture puritan may lift up his trembling hands in horror, but we see the photoplay as in its adolescent period."[64]

Burns Mantle in *Photoplay* issued a prescient warning. He had no doubt the picture would be a best-seller, that women's clubs would protest, and that the financiers would pay them no heed, but merely gloat over the night letters from exhibitors telling how they called the fire department to deal with the overflow mob. But sooner than we think, he said, we shall see a reaction against the society sex film: "Mr. DeMille and his studio associates know that the 'moral' they have tacked on to this picture—that every married man prefers an extravagant playmate-wife, dressed like a harlot, to a fussy little home body who has achieved horn-rimmed spectacles and a reading lamp—is not true of normal husbands anywhere in the world, however true it may be of motion picture directors. But there is enough hidden truth contained in it to make a lot of husbands and wives unhappy, and a lot of fathers and mothers uneasy. From which centers of observation the return kick is likely to start, and gather such momentum as it proceeds that when it lands the recipient will be surprised."[65]

How right he was!

ARE PARENTS PEOPLE?   One of the most sympathetic films about divorce was Mal St. Clair's *Are Parents People?* (1925), based on a story by Alice Duer Miller, published in 1924. The story was radically different from the film, its attitude to divorce conveyed through clever dialogue. The charm of the film is that so much is conveyed visually.

The opening sequence gently observes the end of a marriage: love letters are torn up and thrown away. In a close-up of Mrs. Hazlitt (Florence Vidor), her eyes carry a hint of tears.

Next door, women's slippers are emptied from a drawer by Mr. Hazlitt (Adolphe Menjou). His butler watches dolefully.

Mrs. Hazlitt opens a book and reads the inscription, "To my darling wife—may your love endure as long as mine." She takes it next door, places it open on the table, and leaves without a word.

Hazlitt examines the inscription, grins ironically, and takes it back to his wife. He returns to his room and is followed by the book, which comes flying across the hall.

"I won't need the car," Hazlitt tells the butler. "I've decided to have dinner—alone."

He spots a framed portrait of his wife which the butler has sneaked into his suitcase. Assuming his wife has placed it there, he enters her room and puts his own picture into her suitcase.

The maid sees this, and, thinking her mistress has packed it, is silently delighted. Hazlitt picks up the book, reads the inscription, and grins again. Mrs. Hazlitt, watching his every move, sees the grin and angrily slams her door. Hazlitt throws the book at the door. She opens it and slams it again. Cut to close-up of the exhaust pipe of the car. As the vehicle departs, Mrs. Hazlitt assumes her husband has left. "I've changed my mind," she announces. "I'm going to have dinner alone."

Hazlitt and his wife open their doors simultaneously and face one another, startled. Slam . . . slam. Hazlitt peers through his keyhole, then creeps out and turns the key in his wife's door. Then, with a self-righteous nod of his head, he goes down to the dining room. Where he sees his wife, beginning her first course . . .

The film is concerned with the effect of the divorce on the Hazlitts' daughter, Lita (Betty Bronson). "There's nothing wrong," her father tells her, "except your mother and I can't agree. It's what the lawyers call incompatibility." Lita becomes a "grass orphan," her only home a boarding school. When she is expelled, her parents meet and quarrel. "If you can't cooperate about me, why bother about me at all?" demands the girl.

Lita has read in a book on divorce that parents may quarrel over trifles, but let danger threaten their children and the gulf is bridged. She runs away to the house of Dr. Dacer (Lawrence Gray). He is out, so she curls up in his reception room and inadvertently spends the night there. Dr. Dacer is furious when he discovers her in the morning. "I suppose you know you've compromised me . . . ruined my practice, my reputation?" Angrily, he drags her over to her anxious parents and rounds on the Hazlitts: "The trouble with you both is that you're so busy being incompatible that you haven't time to look after your own child. You ought to be ashamed." The Hazlitts are abashed, the incident achieves the reconciliation Lita had hoped for, and the film ends with the suggestion that she will become Mrs. Dacer.

Are Parents People? appeared in the National Board of Review's 40 Best of 1925, and several critics placed it in their Best Ten. All the reviews welcomed it, *Picture Play* calling it "one of the few good pictures of married life."[66] None of them criticized its attitude toward divorce, even though it portrayed it in such human terms. Perhaps, as William K. Everson said, this was because it was sparkling light comedy, "wagging an admonishing yet friendly finger at the audience for being possessed of the same human foibles that motivate the story."[67]

Director Mal St. Clair managed to be warm and tender without waxing sentimental. To show the bond strengthening between the parents as they wait by the telephone for news of Lita, he has Hazlitt place his overcoat over his wife, who is half asleep on the couch. Mrs. Hazlitt touches it, then pulls it closer, smiling as she scents the familiar tobacco.

In an earlier scene, when both parents arrive at the school to take Lita on holiday, they are asked to wait in the anteroom. St. Clair builds up the tension with superbly played reaction shots, close-ups of Hazlitt's swinging foot and, in the denouement to the scene, Hazlitt picking up his umbrella and sending a vase crashing to the floor. The headmistress smiles icily and politely inquires, "Accident?" St. Clair uses the query again to end the picture. Hazlitt knocks over another vase, and his wife asks the same question—with a smile. The shared joke is all that is needed to end the hostility between them.

COMPANIONATE MARRIAGE

Judge Ben Lindsey had aroused furious controversy over his juvenile court decisions in Denver, Colorado (see pages 170–73). He aroused even more when he proposed something called "companionate marriage" in a book of that title, the sensation of 1927.[68] Everyone assumed he meant trial marriage, but that was not quite what he advocated. A companionate marriage was one not primarily devoted to producing children, allowing the use of birth control and divorce by mutual consent. "People may live in the 'companionate' relation without enforced celibacy until they are ready to have children."[69]

For this, he was beaten up in the Episcopal Cathedral of St. John the Divine, New York, by churchgoers aroused by an inflammatory, anti-Lindsey speech from

Companionate Marriage, *1928, based on Judge Ben Lindsey's notorious book, with Richard Walling and Betty Bronson. (National Film Archives)*

the pulpit.[70] They also tried to have him jailed. He was eventually thrown out of his court in Denver and lampooned on the vaudeville stage. A song written for Al Jolson had a young man serenading a girl beneath her bedroom window:

"Oh, my darling, oh, my dear, will you try me for a year?"

The window flies open and a man leans out: "Go away, you crazy freak. I'm on trial here for a week."[71]

Lindsey was treated more kindly by Hollywood. He admired the moving picture, considering it of great benefit to mankind. And it was inevitable that some company would buy the rights to his book and involve him in its production.

Companionate Marriage was a seven-reeler made in 1928, directed by Erle C. Kenton from a screenplay by Beatrice Van. It starred Betty Bronson, of *Are Parents People?,* and was made by a poverty row company called Gotham, although it was credited to the "C. M. Corp" (Companionate Marriage Corporation). Behind it were E. M. Asher, who had once been involved in *Last Night of the Barbary Coast* (see page 85), agent Edward Small, and Charles R. Rogers, in association with Sam Sax of Gotham.

Sally Williams (Bronson), the product of poverty and a broken home, works as a secretary for wealthy James Moore, whose son, Donald (Richard Walling), proposes to her. Embittered and cynical, Sally wants no part of marriage and turns him down. Ruth Moore (June Nash), Donald's sister, impulsively marries Tommy Van Cleve (Arthur Rankin) during a drunken party at a roadhouse and is herself quickly disillusioned. After the birth of a baby, Tommy deserts her and she commits suicide. Moved by Donald's grief and anger, Sally offers to marry him. He refuses until Judge Meredith (Alec B. Francis), a family friend, draws up a legal contract whereby if, at the end of a stipulated period, either party is dissatisfied, the marriage is legally abrogated. Several years pass, and Donald and Sally find nothing but happiness and joy together.[72]

Judge Lindsey appeared at the opening of the picture, and he was present during its production, but, according to *Photoplay*, he was not crazy over the results. Said *Photoplay*, "Neither are we."[73]

Erle C. Kenton made a film called *Trial Marriage* (1929), written by Sonya Levien, for Columbia. There were also several exploitation films which suggested that trial marriage was only a step from prostitution.

In *Marriage by Contract* (1928), a husband in a companionate marriage goes philandering on the first night after the honeymoon, and the wife finds that "no decent man of her class will marry her."[74] Patsy Ruth Miller played the wife; her gradual aging through the picture impressed the critics. According to Miss Miller, the studio bought the rights to an episode in Lindsey's book. The judge came out to Tiffany-Stahl to discuss the project; she met him and received a copy of his book. The material was then rewritten and retitled.[75] She was not aware that it ended up as an attack on his theories, but that's what happened. *Picture Play* called it "claptrap,"[76] but Irene Thiers gave it three stars for timeliness, for Miss Miller's splendid characterization, and, above all, for being a direct argument against Judge Lindsey.[77]

Trial Marriage, 1929, directed by Erle Kenton, from a Sonya Levien scenario. Sally Eilers and Thelma Todd auction themselves for a charity dance. (Museum of Modern Art)

BIRTH CONTROL

The very term "birth control" entered the language as a result of the work of Margaret Sanger. "I never could credit the power those simple words had of upsetting so many people," she wrote.[78] Her name is most closely associated with the subject, yet it is not generally known that she made a largely autobiographical film about her campaign and appeared in it herself.

Born Margaret Higgins, she was one of eleven children. Her father, an Irishman, was a supporter of women's suffrage *and* a socialist. Yet he opposed his daughter's crusade, as she was indeed bitterly opposed by Catholics generally. But she felt that happiness or unhappiness in childhood depended on whether one belonged to a small or a large family, not so much on the family's wealth or poverty.[79] While working as a nurse she became aware of the dilemma of working-class mothers, desperate to avoid having any more children. In many cases, their health depended upon it. "The first right of a child," she said, "is to be wanted."[80]

She met architect William Sanger and married him, and, despite her own ill health, had three children. Ordered to have no more, she returned to part-time district nursing, specializing in obstetrics. More and more of her calls came from the Lower East Side, where pregnancy was a chronic condition and abortion methods were either ineffectual or dangerous.

It was against the law in New York to give information on contraception to anyone for any reason. And yet wealthy people not only knew about it, they practiced it. "The doomed women implored me to reveal the 'secret' rich people had, offering to pay me extra to tell them; many really believed I was holding back information for money. They asked everybody and tried anything, but nothing did them any good. On Saturday nights I have seen groups of from fifty to one hundred with their shawls over their heads waiting outside the office of a five-dollar abortionist."[81]

Sanger was helpless. But one case changed her outlook. She saved the life of a twenty-eight-year-old woman dying of a self-induced abortion. The woman was overcome by depression, knowing that another baby would finish her. All the doctor would suggest was that her husband sleep on the roof. The woman pleaded with Sanger to tell her the secret, but, obedient to the law, the nurse declined to do so. Three months later, pregnant again, the woman killed herself. "No matter what it might cost," wrote Sanger, "I was resolved to seek out the root of the evil."[82]

She started a magazine, *The Woman Rebel,* and Anthony Comstock barred it from the mails, classifying a mention of contraception as pornography. Facing a trial for an article she didn't even write, Sanger slipped away to England. Comstock imprisoned her husband because of her activities, and although this case was dropped, she was arrested again and again. Charities were terrified of her, but at last, on October 16, 1916, she opened the first birth control clinic in America, in the Brownsville section of Brooklyn, New York. The vice squad promptly arrested her and her sister, Ethel (who was almost killed by forcible feeding).

Sanger became concerned for the other inmates and, once she was free, set herself the task of changing the law through education.

One attempt to educate the public was the production of a motion picture, *Birth Control* (1917). With her associate Frederick A. Blossom, she wrote a scenario: "Although I had long since lost faith in my abilities as an actress, I played the part of the nurse."[83]

Financed by an associate of Blossom's and produced by the Message Feature Film Corporation, *Birth Control* was advertised with the kind of sensitivity that exhibitors appreciated: "You Don't Have to Be a Film Buyer or Seller to Clean Up a Quick Profit on This. Everyone in the world will want to see it. It's the Safest, Surest State Right Proposition Since Big Film Features Began, and We'll Guarantee You It's Law Proof and Censor Proof. Five Reels of Stirring, Varied and Picturesque Exposition of the Vital and Dramatic Phases of the Crusade That Sent its Martyr Heroine to a Prison From Which She Has Just Been Freed."[84]

A statement by Sanger was included as a "certificate of genuineness": "This is the only picture on Birth Control in which I shall appear. Part of the profits go to extending our cause."[85]

Variety thought the title suggested a grim film with the atmosphere of a clinic: "The picture is anything but that. It is rather a combination of a New York travelog and the quite dramatic personal experiences of Mrs. Margaret Sanger, its heroine, who appears in almost every scene. The average observer is electrified with the intense convictions of the propagandist, taken hither and thither throughout New York's teeming child streets, to the almost childless precincts of the informed wealthy."[86]

One aspect of the film which struck the *Variety* reviewer was the pervasive sincerity of Sanger: "Playing a role that is herself, one looks for at least fleeting moments of artifice in the woman's efforts to repeat for the screen the emotions she lived while conceiving her crusade and fighting for it until she fought herself into jail. But there's no artifice in the Mrs. Sanger of the screen. She is the same placid, clear eyed, rather young and certainly attractive propagandist that swayed crowds at her meetings and defied the police both before and after her incarceration. And facts are given that if not making everyone who sees the picture a convert to her cause will certainly make everyone think twice before denouncing the movement."[87]

The picture opened with a double exposure contrasting the struggling mother of the poor, lacking the money to buy the knowledge which would lessen her burden, and a middle-class woman with a small family. An interview with Sanger was illustrated by images of the weak and crippled children of exhausted, poverty-stricken mothers. There followed the story of the suicide of her patient, the persecution of Sanger by the authorities, scenes shot at her Brownsville clinic, and the trial. The film ended with shots of Sanger behind bars, with the subtitle "No matter what happens, the work must go on."[88]

Birth Control was submitted to the National Board of Review, which passed it with the comment that it had been "handled with such a deft touch and intelligence" that there was no need to remove so much as a subtitle.[89] It was this which encouraged the promoters to guarantee it as censor-proof. But just in case, they

Right: Margaret Sanger, 1916. Below: Margaret Sanger, in Birth Control, *1917. (Sophia Smith Collection, Smith College)*

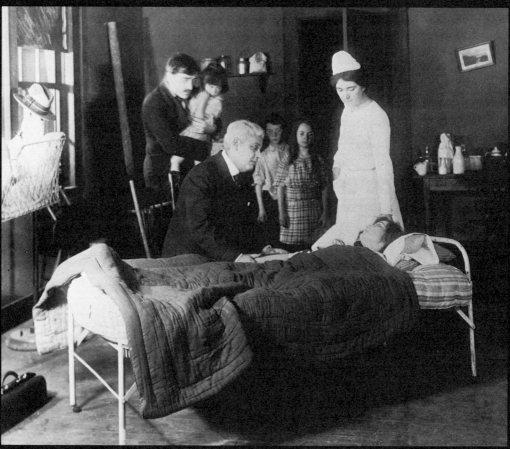

provided an alternative title, *The New World,* and issued alternative posters and advertising material.

The day before the opening at the Park Theatre at Columbus Circle, New York City License Commissioner George H. Bell informed the licensee that the film was "immoral, indecent, and directly contrary to public welfare." If it were shown, action would be taken. When the Park Theatre had exhibited *The Inside of the White Slave Traffic,* the police had arrested most of the employees, so the opening of *Birth Control* was cancelled.

Sanger staged a flamboyant coup twenty-four hours after the ban. She held a special showing of the film for newspapermen, so that they could decide whether or not it was "morally objectionable." The distributors also applied for an injunction and Sanger sued the commissioner, to make him personally liable for damages suffered from the stigma placed upon the production and from the loss of receipts.[90]

Along with the press, 200 people came to the show, many of them concerned with social welfare. The entire audience voted emphatically in favor of the film, and they signed a letter to this effect.[91]

At the hearing, Bell held that the film should be suppressed because "it tends to ridicule the public authorities" and the state law. It also raised a class issue by "setting before the public the squalor, poverty and ignorance of the poor" compared to the luxury of the rich with their small families "[and] depicts the wealthy as contributing funds for the prosecution of those who attempt to enlighten the poor with respect to birth control and for the avowed purpose of maintaining the poor as the servant and laboring classes."[92] He added that it was going rather far to classify a birth control film as theatrical entertainment.[93]

Judge Nathan Bijur ruled that the commissioner's action violated the constitutional right of free speech, but the Appellate Division of the New York State Supreme Court overturned this decision, citing the by now famous Mutual Film Corporation ruling that the business was not protected by the First Amendment.[94]

Sanger said that exhibitors, "fearful lest the breath of censure wither their profits," were too timid to show the film,[95] and it was only seen by those who attended her lectures. It would have been illegal to show the film in public until 1965, when the U.S. Supreme Court finally overturned state laws making the spread of birth control information a crime[96]—by which time the film had long since turned to dust.

WHERE ARE MY CHILDREN?

"The scavengers of the screen," said *Photoplay* in April 1917, "availing themselves of every fetid air which sweeps up from the sewers of thought, have successfully sailed the sea of maudlin popularity in the rotten bottoms of impossible adventure, white slavery, morbid romance and nakedness for its own sake. The present conveyance is birth control, for and against, under a variety of tissue guises and prurient titles of the *She Didn't Know It Was Loaded* order. Lois Weber, with her very fine and sweet play *Where Are My Children?* opened the door to the filthy host of nasty-minded imitators, who announce obscenities and present bromides."

Where Are My Children? (1916),[97] however else you described it, could hardly be called "sweet." It was an unpleasant but extraordinary film—expressing support for birth control, but abhorrence for abortion. The impact of the picture is strong enough today; what it must have been like in the age of innocence one shudders to think. Its strength derives not so much from its filmic qualities—it is no better made than many other dramas of its day—but from its subject matter.

There are two prints in existence, both incomplete, but complementing each other, the American version and the European version. Because the film was made while the war was on, but before America had entered it, there are distinct differences between the two.

The American version opens with this exposition, missing from the European:

The question of birth control is now being generally discussed. All intelligent people know that birth control is a subject of serious public interest. Newspapers, magazines and books have treated different phases of this question. Can a subject thus dealt with on the printed page be denied careful dramatization on the motion picture screen? The Universal Film Manufacturing Company believes not.

The Universal Film Manufacturing Company does believe, however, that the question of birth control should not be presented before children. In producing this picture, the intention is to place a serious drama before adult audiences, to whom no suggestion of a fact of which they are ignorant is conveyed. It believes that children should not be admitted to see this unaccompanied by adults, but if you bring them it will do them an immeasurable amount of good.[98]

Variety urged Universal to cut this long and muddled title.

It was not often that controversy began at the very opening titles of a film. The first sequence shows swirling clouds and massive gates opening. This special effect, which recurs frequently, is shabbily done, even for 1916, with smoke standing in for clouds and gates, columns, and celestial figures all looking as though they have been cut out of a book of Victorian lithographs.

"Behind the great portals of Eternity, the souls of little children waited to be born." The souls are represented by the faces of infants, with cherublike wings. Among the souls are "chance children," who descend to earth in large numbers, "unwanted souls," who are constantly sent back, marked as morally or physically defective and bearing the sign of the serpent.

"And then, in the secret place of the Most High were those souls, fine and strong, that were sent forth only on prayer. They were marked with the approval of the Almighty." Surmounting the smoke and the little faces with wings, a single bright cross appears. Then the story proper begins: Richard Walton (Tyrone Power), a district attorney, is a great believer in eugenics. Standing at the door of a court as a working-class couple is led out, he tells his assistant, "Those poor souls are ill-born. If the mystery of birth were understood, crime would be wiped out."

It is a great disappointment to Walton that his wife (Helen Riaume) is childless. "Never dreaming that it was her fault, the husband concealed his disappointment." Whenever his sister visits to show off her new baby, he is careful to conceal his delight in case his wife feels upset.

A case comes to trial that greatly interests Walton. Young Doctor Homer (C. Norman Hammond) is accused of distributing indecent literature advocating birth regulation. Walton reads passages from his book, which are shown on the screen:

"When only those children who are wanted are born, the race will conquer the evils that weigh it down."

"Let us stop the slaughter of the unborn and save the lives of unwilling mothers."

Dr. Homer describes to the jury the slum conditions that prove to him "the necessity of worldwide enlightenment on the subject of birth control." Nonetheless, he is convicted.

Intercut with the trial we see Mrs. Walton guiding her best friend, Mrs. William Brandt (Marie Walcamp), to her own obliging Dr. Malfit (Juan de la Cruz), a villainous-looking foreigner in a piratical beard (although one suspects the producers were just trying to make him as unlike any other doctor as they could). Mrs. Brandt is ushered into the examining room; next we see a soul ascending to heaven, and the portals closing.

"One of the 'unwanted' ones returns, and a social butterfly is again ready for house parties."

Mrs. Walton's rakish brother, Roger (A. D. Blake), seduces the housekeeper's beautiful daughter Lillian (René Rogers). The onset of pregnancy is conveyed by a child's face, framed by wings, superimposed on Lillian's shoulder. Roger seeks help from his sister, who recommends Dr. Malfit. But this time, the obliging doctor bungles the operation. Just before Lillian dies, she confesses to her grief-stricken mother, who begs forgiveness for not having told her what she needed to know.

Walton institutes proceedings against Dr. Malfit, whose defense is that he worked for the improvement of mankind by "preventing motherhood for vain, pleasure-seeking women and degenerates." Malfit is sentenced to fifteen years hard labor. As he is dragged away, he shouts at Walton that before he sits in judgment on other people he should see to his own household. Walton examines Malfit's account book. An invoice for fifty dollars to Mrs. Richard Walton leaps off the page. There are further bills for "services rendered": fifty dollars . . . seventy-five dollars . . . Walton is horrified. He drives home and interrupts his wife's tea party: "I have just learned why so many of you have no children. I should bring you to trial for manslaughter, but I shall content myself with asking you to leave my house."

As the women depart, protesting, he advances on his wife: "Where are my children?" She collapses. "I—an officer of the law—must shield a murderess!" He staggers out, and she faints.

She visits a church. "Prayerfully now, Mrs. Walton sought the blessing she had refused, but, having perverted Nature so often, she found herself physically unable to wear the diadem of motherhood."

The District Attorney (Tyrone Power, Sr.) ejects his wife's friends—"I should bring you to trial for manslaughter"—when he discovers the reason for their childlessness. From Lois Weber and Phillips Smalley's Where Are My Children?, *1916. (Museum of Modern Art)*

The picture ends with a shot of the Waltons seated before the fire. "Throughout the years, she must face the silent question—'Where are my children?'" Mrs. Walton sees in her imagination a little girl clamber into his lap. Then her husband grows old, and three grown-up children gather, smiling, behind his chair. The scene is beautifully lit, originally toned purple, and is surprisingly touching.

Although this film is very strong medicine, which one wants to like because of Lois Weber, one chokes on its disturbing sentimentality. The district attorney spends too much of his time kissing little children in the park—in a more modern film he would be an object of suspicion. At the same time, there is an implication that certain children are undesirable.

Nevertheless, it is handsomely shot, with a spaciousness and use of light appropriate to its upper-class milieu. The limousines are as beautiful and elegant as the women who ride in them. If the acting is on the heavy side, somewhat more theatrical than in Weber's later films, the subject needed an extra layer of seriousness to get it by the censors, for there is no happy ending. That alone contributed to its disturbing effect.

Universal was terrified of it. The National Board of Review rejected it for mixed audiences,[99] and the studio feared the local censorship boards. So Universal held it back from release and presented it in an exclusive engagement at the Globe Theatre in New York,[100] risking a ban by the license commissioner. The studio hoped to secure enough endorsements to protect the picture on its journey across the country. The risk proved worth taking; the film did record business. Four shows a day were not enough, and people were turned away in large numbers.[101]

Where Are My Children? received excellent reviews, although the name of Mrs. William Brandt had to be changed after a protest by a well-known New Yorker of that name. Titles in the print in the Library of Congress use the name Mrs. Carlo. The National Board of Review was obliged to look at the film again, and this time sixty out of eighty-one members of representative organizations approved it for adult showing.[102]

Adverse criticism concerned questions of fact. As *Moving Picture World* pointed out, physicians like Dr. Malfit were not patronized by women like Mrs. Walton and her friends: "Safe means of checking child-birth are not a problem for the well-to-do. They are taken as a matter of course. The whole purpose of a campaign of the kind being waged by Mrs. Sanger and Emma Goldman is to place the same means within the reach of the less fortunate."[103]

And why does the district attorney call his wife a murderess because she chooses to remain childless? "According to his reasoning she has committed a crime, yet in the first part of the picture he unmistakably favors the publishing of a book on birth control. Surely the principle involved is not affected by the methods adopted?"[104]

Released on a States' Rights basis, the film ignited fiery indignation all over the country, sparking off court actions from which, surprisingly, it usually emerged unscathed. One place it did not survive was Pennsylvania, whose censor, Dr. Ellis P. Oberholtzer, declared: "The picture is unspeakably vile. I would have permitted it to pass the board in this state only over my dead body. It is a mess of filth, and no revision, however drastic, could ever help it any. It is not fit for decent people to see."[105]

Catholics were placed in a quandary by the film, for while it was the strongest possible propaganda against abortion, it defended birth control—which was one of the reasons why the Catholic mayor of Boston, James Michael Curley, who also served as municipal censor, found himself the center of a scandal. His censorship commission virtually ignored the film; they were waiting, they said, for a "proper complaint."[106] The film had been running to enormous business in Boston for months, even though ex-mayor John F. Fitzgerald objected to it.[107] The turnaway on opening night was estimated at 2,000.[108]

At the height of the war, the film arrived in Great Britain, where the authorities were opposed to birth control, especially since the conflict had taken such a toll of the young men and the birth rate had dropped so dramatically. So the film was recut to eliminate the sequence of the defense of Dr. Homer, and these shots were inserted into the trial of Dr. Malfit. Dr. Homer was now apparently giving evidence against him, equipped with such titles as "All incurable mental defectives, drunks, criminals and suchlike must be prevented from propagating their defects in their descendants BUT NEVER BY UNLAWFUL MEANS."

Many other titles were altered, too. When Walton marches in to the tea party, he is made to say: "I have just learned why so many of you have no children. You avoid motherhood out of selfishness. You are a thousand times more evil than the poor girl who had to pay for her ignorance with her life."

This meddling gravely upset the drama and by depriving the opening sequences of variety converted the first reels into a series of comings and goings of limousines.[109]

Despite, or perhaps because of the recutting, the reaction of the English press was excellent. Said the *Pall Mall Gazette,* "How the obvious difficulties of presenting such a theme for public exhibition have been overcome is a wonder. People who are used to photographic dramas will agree, one believes, that *Where Are My Children?* is far and away the most perfect film that has yet been exhibited. The usual weak sentimentality is absent, and in its place a fine and natural poem of the emotions."[110]

Universal's representative in England, John D. Tippett, made a deal with the National Council of Public Morals limiting exhibition of the film to adults in special halls; in return, it could be advertised with the council's endorsement.[111] Thirty thousand people paid to see it in Preston, Lancashire, and 40,000 in Bradford, Yorkshire.[112] In Sydney, Australia, it played to 100,000 viewers in two weeks.[113]

In 1917, Lois Weber released another birth control picture, *The Hand That Rocks the Cradle,* perhaps because she realized the shortcomings of the first. The story was based on the imprisonment of Margaret Sanger and her sister's hunger strike. Weber and Smalley appeared in the leads, which makes it all the more frustrating that the film is lost. Said *Wid's,* "Both make their characters very impressive because they have poise, authority and repose."[114]

"Many of the scenes are exceedingly painful," said the New York *Dramatic Mirror,* "and a few seem to invade the privacy of domestic life with unnecessary frankness, but the production on the whole has been handled with the utmost delicacy and skill."[115]

The New York license commissioner, who had restrained himself over the earlier film, pounced on this one. Apparently, persons of high standing had reported that it was "contra bonos mores" (against good morals). Universal *did* manage to secure a temporary injunction and the picture was able to play out its engagement at the Broadway Theater, but the ban prevented it being shown anywhere else in New York. [116] The state supreme court later denied Universal a permanent injunction, the judge declaring: "If the ignorant and uninformed are to be educated by being told that laws which they do not like may be defied, and that lawbreakers deserve to be glorified as such, there would be a sorry future in store for human liberty."[117] And he referred to the precedent established in the case of the Mutual Film Corporation that moving pictures were a business, pure and simple, and were not to be regarded as part of the press.

Margaret Sanger's name was not used in *The Hand That Rocks the Cradle,* but most of the reviews drew attention to the plot's similarity to recent reports of her crusade. *Variety* accused the filmmakers of seizing the opportunity provided by the Sanger picture to make a quick dollar.[118] But the fact that Lois Weber herself played the role so closely identified with Margaret Sanger is sufficient testimony to her admiration for the crusader.

The Hand that Rocks the Cradle, 1917. *Lois Weber (center) plays a character based on Margaret Sanger, here being arrested on the platform. (Richard Koszarski)*

SOCIAL DISEASES

GHOSTS   At the pinnacle of the mountain of taboo subjects was what were euphemistically called "social diseases." When the editor of *Ladies' Home Journal* mentioned them in 1906, he lost 75,000 horrified readers.[119] The less they were spoken of, the more they proliferated, for the majority of young people knew nothing whatever of the dangers. The result was that venereal disease became an epidemic without the public being aware of the fact. The obvious preventative, sex education, was regarded by many people, particularly the highly religious, as a crime: "The more we put such ideas into their heads, the more they will think of them."[120]

In 1881, the great Norwegian playwright Henrik Ibsen published a play on the subject of hereditary syphilis, *Ghosts*. It was greeted with a torrent of abuse on the Continent and tight-lipped censorship in England, and that was before it had even been performed. (Chicago—of all cities—gave it that honor in 1882, albeit in Norwegian.)

When the Lubin Film Company stole the story and filmed it in America in 1911 as *The Sins of the Father, Moving Picture World* recognized its origin at once and printed what was probably the most vituperative editorial in its history: "If ever there was a case of perversion of genius it was Ibsen's writing of *The Ghosts* [*sic*]. The ordinary human being would just as soon think of making himself comfortable in an asylum for incurables as deriving any pleasure or moral from looking at such a play. The subject is disgusting at best and Ibsen has used his marvelous dramatic powers to make it horrible and revolting. To film such an atrocity is to sin both against art and decency. A mother telling her 'tainted son' of the vicious life of his deceased father; the son developing 'the taint' by his undue indulgence in drink and his mild assault on a woman servant and the finish of a son asking the mother to help him in committing suicide—these are things that should have no representation either on the silent or the speaking stage."[121]

D. W. Griffith's Reliance-Majestic company released a version in 1915 which was described as "hardly Ibsen's *Ghosts,* but a classic nonetheless."[122] Directed by George Nichols, and featuring Henry B. Walthall, this *Ghosts* omitted almost every reference to venereal disease. The play was so altered that denunciations of the film appeared in magazines like *Current Opinion.*[123] Vachel Lindsay said that whenever in the play there were "quiet voices like the slow drip of hydrochloric acid, in the film there were endless writhings and rushings about, done with a deal of skill, but destructive of the last remnants of Ibsen."[124]

Mary Alden and Henry B. Walthall in Ghosts, *1915. (John E. Allen)*

Ghosts may lack the shattering impact of Ibsen's play, but for anyone familiar with the subject it would have been disturbing enough. The visual emphasis is on Alving's drinking, but Oswald, his son, suffers from "an hereditary taint" leading to blinding headaches; a title identifies the cause as "Locomotor ataxia." He is only just prevented from marrying his half-sister. His mother has no part in his death in this version, but die he does, by suicide. The film is true to the spirit of Ibsen, even if the theme itself is a ghost.

DAMAGED GOODS   Eugène Brieux, a French playwright, caused a similar sensation with his *Damaged Goods (Les Avariés)* of 1902. It was first presented in America at the Fulton Theater in New York, on March 14, 1913, under the auspices of the *Medical Review of Reviews* and its Sociological Fund. The star was Richard Bennett, who had brought the play to America and who had a hard job finding actors who did not consider a play about venereal disease to be professional suicide. Six actresses were rehearsed for the part of the prostitute; all six vanished. The role was eventually played by Bennett's wife. "The effect of that single matinee performance was like a thunderbolt," wrote Joan Bennett. "The 'conspiracy of silence' surrounding an objectionable subject had been lifted at last."[125]

Bennett took the play on the road and had to fight the censors at every turn. He developed a curtain-call monologue which became famous. It concluded: "A respectable man will take his son and daughter to one of those grand music halls where they will hear things of the most loathsome description, but he won't let them hear a word spoken seriously on the great act of love. . . . Pornography, as much as you please—science, never!"[126]

When the film version of *Damaged Goods* came out in 1915, reviewers found it "a tremendous shocker."[127] It was produced in seven reels by the American Film Manufacturing Company, directed by Thomas Ricketts[128] and adapted by Harry Pollard.

Bennett regarded the picture business with a contempt fashionable among actors of the day: "Whenever you think there are movie scouts out front, let me know," he used to say, "and I'll stay home sick."[129] The chance to carry his crusade to millions more people, however, was irresistible. Joan Bennett credits him with writing the script and directing the film, and even though others are credited, he probably exercised a great deal of creative control. After all, no one but its author knew the play better than he.

"While the stage play was compelled to limit the intended lesson to a mere recital," said *Variety,* "the film carries the audience into deeper details, giving vivid visual illustrations and a close view of the disease in actual action. The camera even invaded the sacred interior of an Institution where it pictured patients suffering from the so-called tertiary stage and brought forth the paralyzed and twisted form for 'close-up' inspection. Withal its expose of what has hitherto been a medical and scientific secret, *Damaged Goods* carries a ray of hope for the syphilitic and teaches the absolute necessity of early treatment."[130]

The scenario followed the plot of the play. George Dupont (Bennett) graduates

Richard Bennett in Damaged Goods, *1915. (Wisconsin Center for Film and Theater Research.)*

from law school and returns home to a clutch of love affairs and an arranged marriage to a senator's daughter. At his bachelor dinner he gets drunk, goes to the apartment of a friend's mistress, and meets a girl with whom he spends the night. He finds he has contracted syphilis, and is about to commit suicide when he is stopped by the girl (Adrienne Morrison),[131] who tells him she deliberately infected him. She had been seduced, was refused treatment by hospitals, went half mad, and took revenge on the society which allowed such things. She sends George to the specialist who has regenerated (but apparently not cured) her. The doctor forbids him to marry for two years, but because his wedding is imminent, George goes to a quack who guarantees a cure in three months. The marriage takes place, a baby is born, and then comes the shock of learning that the infant has inherited syphilis. The senator comes to kill George, only to find that he has already committed suicide—walking into the sea, along the path of a moonbeam.[132]

The film, like the play, blamed nobody, showing sympathy even for the plight of the prostitute and demonstrating that the problem was a social one. In 1917, Bennett was asked by the War Department to appear with the film in training camps throughout the country. Secretary of the Navy Josephus Daniels, who had banned the play from Annapolis in 1913, was obliged, by the soaring incidence of venereal disease, to combine forces with Secretary of War Newton D. Baker and to show the film as widely as possible. Later, Bennett was offered a commission to accompany the film to France and to lecture with it. He replied that if he was asked to serve democracy, he would like to start at home, where American suffragists, who dared demand political freedom, were held in vile conditions.[133]

When the British production of the play opened at St. Martin's Theatre in London in 1917, with Ronald Colman in the lead, some of the scenes were considered "harrowing in the extreme."[134] The Samuelson film version of 1919, directed by the Canadian Alexander Butler, was praised for the opposite reason by the British trade press: "nothing has been introduced into this film that would be calculated to nauseate rather than instruct."[135]

The British film survives, while the American has disappeared—another example of the vagaries of film preservation. The British version faced harsher censorship. It could therefore risk nothing in the way of illustration and came dangerously close to being a series of subtitles, interrupted merely by shots of appropriate characters. The story resembled the play, except the girl (Vivian Rees) was a country orphan, who seeks a job at a fashion house and is raped by the proprietor (by implication). Befriended by a prostitute, she becomes one herself after the birth of her child, whom she hands over to a convent.

The subtitles were overlong, but fascinating for the attitudes they revealed. When Dupont asks the doctor if it is certain his wife will catch the disease, the doctor replies, "Come, come! You are a man of business. Marriage is a contract. If you marry without saying anything, you will be giving an implied warranty for goods which you know to be bad. It would be a fraud which ought to be punishable by law."

Toward the end of the film, the doctor's ironclad attitude softens and he entreats the wife's father (an M.P. in this version) to forgive Dupont: "Are you yourself without sin that you are so relentless to others?"

"I have never had any shameful disease, sir!"

"I was not asking that. I was asking you if you have never exposed yourself to one. Ah, you see! Then it was not virtue that saved you; it was luck."

In order to effect a happy ending, the script has the doctor guaranteeing that in two or three years, the M.P. will be a happy grandfather (something he insisted in an earlier scene could not be foreseen). And three years later, the suicide episode quietly removed, the family is happily united.

Following the American technique of winning the support of churchmen, reformers, and the press, the producers held a special screening of *Damaged Goods* at Terry's Theatre on December 16, 1919, followed by a luncheon at the Savoy Hotel. The main speaker was the Reverend Bernard John Vaughan, celebrated for his relief work among the poor and for his sermons attacking social evils. Unusually for a churchman, he supported the cinema. And he supported this film. "I want this wonderful film shown everywhere," he said, "because it is destructive of vice, and I want encouragement to be given by its means to people to live clean, strong and straight lives. . . ."[136]

The picture was never passed by the British Board of Film Censors. The board had no more legal power to prevent exhibition than the National Board of Review, but since the exhibitors had created it the censors could exact penalties of their own. Defying the censor was a risky practice. However, D. W. Griffith had presented *Intolerance* without a censor certificate and got away with it, and Watch Committees in the big towns sometimes allowed a film which the censor had banned. Samuelson apparently took advantage of this loophole, suggests historian Harold Dunham, for his research has shown that when the picture was banned in Belfast, the corporation was told that it had already been shown in every other large city in the United Kingdom.[137]

Films like this soon found it harder to find a home in England, where even the local authorities cracked down on "prurient so-called propaganda films"[138] which the censor refused to pass.

FIT TO WIN During the war, sexually transmitted disease rendered so many troops unfit for combat that propaganda films were ordered by the military authorities as a matter of urgency. The British had virtually ignored the problem until 1916. In the United States the following year, a major crusade was launched by attorney Raymond B. Fosdick, with full government approval, with the slogan "Fit to Fight"—the title of the first film produced for this campaign. Directed by Lieutenant Edward H. Griffith, it opened with a full reel illustrating the effects of venereal disease. The story concerned five young men; we see them first in civilian life, then in the army receiving instruction on V.D. All but one, Billy Hale, fall for the temptations of the town streetwalkers. Kid McCarthy resorts promptly to prophylactic treatment and escapes infection; the others contract diseases of varying unpleasantness. McCarthy accuses Hale of being a "mollycoddle." They fight; McCarthy is beaten and agrees to reform. These two are the only members of the group fit for service abroad. "Back in the hospital," concluded the synopsis, "are the 'useless slackers' who through weakness and disobedience of orders have made themselves a burden on the government by contracting venereal disease."[139] Many in the audience might have ruminated on the fact that unpleasant though the diseases might have been, a stretch in the hospital was preferable to an unspecified period of trench warfare.

Fit to Fight was revised after the armistice for civilian use and retitled *Fit to Win*. Extra scenes were shot at the Metro studios in New York. Kid McCarthy had died bravely at the front, and Billy, promoted to captain, brings his medal back for his sweetheart. He visits his old pals; now almost cured, they still have to face the shame of their parents. The picture ends with Billy and his fiancée at the altar.

The government entrusted the film to the Public Health Service for distribution to regular theatres. It was potential dynamite, for it dealt openly with the way the infection was spread; the titles spoke of seminal emissions, and the value of continence was discussed.[140] To forestall the anticipated fury, a letter signed by the Assistant Surgeon General was circulated to the trade papers: "The United States Public Health Service asks the co-operation of State and Municipal governments and requests the abrogation or suspension of such censorships as might impede this very essential missionary work."

Careful precautions were taken: the film could only be shown to segregated audiences—males one day, females the next—or the theatre had to be divided, with men in the balcony and women downstairs. No children were allowed. Solemn warnings were posted at the doors in case people wandered in casually to see a favorite actor (Raymond McKee played in this, as in *Fit to Fight.*)[141] Poor Edward H. Griffith, the director, despite praise from reviewers for a powerful production, found his name had been removed to avoid confusion with his more illustrious namesake: "It is always better never to mislead in the slightest degree."[142]

"No one but the Government could get away with it," warned Wid Gunning. He thought it splendid, however, that the government *had* done it, because anyone else would have been accused of exploitation.[143]

No sooner had the picture opened at Brooklyn's Grand Opera House than License Commissioner Gilchrist and the New York City Police Department threatened to revoke the theatre's license unless it was taken off at once. The Opera House secured a temporary injunction.[144]

After viewing the film, Judge Learned Hand decided that it was a proper subject to present to the public, providing two scenes were removed—"the bawdy house 'flashes' and those wherein police protection is alleged to shelter such dens."[145] He would then grant a permanent injunction against the license commissioner. But opposition came from another quarter—District Attorney Talley, who contended that the V.D. pictures, and *Fit to Win* in particular, were made dishonestly. A great deal of their footage had been obtained speciously, if not fraudulently. The consent of naval and military authorities had been secured by the government because it was understood the films were to be shown to service personnel only and that "posing for a picture" was "a patriotic duty."[146]

Talley ordered an investigation of the head of film distribution for the Public Health Service, Isaac Silverman. The sole distributor of *Fit to Win* when it was purely a government picture, Silverman had branched out as "a purveyor of social hygiene pictures for public consumption and private gain," with his company, Public Health Films. Silverman had an original retort: he charged that the district attorney's opposition to *Fit to Win* was the result of a move on the part of the "movie trust" to distract attention from the charges of graft made by the congressional committee.[147] In fact, a congressional committee was about to descend on the whole subject of the "social hygiene" films, and questions were asked about the American Social Hygiene Association, which had first financed *Fit to Win.* Severe criticism was directed at the film industry, which was both unwelcome and unjustified, considering it had had nothing to do with any of the pictures.

In July, a decision by the Second Circuit Court of Appeals reversed Judge Hand's judgment and the film was banned in New York City. "Revolting details caused a storm of protest against *Fit to Win,*" reported *Variety.*[148] The license commissioner had once more acted as unofficial censor.

In 1919, the federal government commissioned a report from the Psychological Laboratory of Johns Hopkins University to determine the effect of these V.D. films. Doctors Karl Lashley and John Watson showed *Fit to Win* to nearly 5,000 people. They discovered that the emotions aroused by the film—especially by the opening sequence—were horror and fear: "The fear of infection is the chief motivating agent to which the film appeals. The other possible incentives to continence which are touched upon in the film are given too brief space or too little dramatic value to impress any great number of men."[149]

The doctors encountered an antipathy to the film from the well-informed, who dismissed it as "tedious and maudlin." But they were struck by the value it had for more ignorant audiences. Twenty percent of the soldiers were either illiterate or could hardly speak English, and many men did not even understand the term "sexual intercourse" used in the titles. The film had the strongest appeal for blacks.

The doctors concluded that the film was "moderately efficient" in conveying information but that a lot of valuable footage was wasted by the drama. Only where the information was simple and clear did many of the men grasp it. Nevertheless, 70 percent gained a fairly accurate knowledge of the points made by the film. "We believe," wrote the doctors, "that the results speak very well for the effectiveness of the film in bringing home the lesson which it was designed to teach."[150]

But they believed the film exaggerated the dangers of venereal disease without giving accurate information about the cause or the possibility of a cure. "Some of those with whom we talked feel they have caught the authors of the film in a lie which shows that its purpose is to foist on them a moral code under the guise of hygiene."

No lasting effects were found, either positive or negative. The main facts were remembered for periods of up to five months; otherwise, the picture seemed forgotten as quickly as the average entertainment film. (But then five months was the extent of their investigation.)

WHATSOEVER A MAN SOWETH *Whatsoever a Man Soweth* was a feature made in England for the Canadian army. Joseph Best, who had edited Pathé News, was released from the British army in 1917 to make the film for the War Office. "I wrote the story in twenty-four hours," he recalled, "had it approved the next day, produced, did all the camera work, edited, made the titles, joined them in, and finally projected it myself to the Army Council—a one-man job if ever there was one. It was well liked, and some hundred copies were sent to all British and Allied fronts for showing to the troops. I made most of it at Richmond Park, using army huts, soldiers . . . hospitals etc."[151]

One has to admire Best's enthusiasm while acknowledging that the film is made with no skill whatever. As a social document, however, it is of exceptional value. Parts of the film are disturbing, even today, so its effect on soldiers seventy years ago must have been electrifying.

The majority of the five-reeler concerns the misadventures of a young Canadian soldier, Dick. Before he leaves home, his mother tells him, "You are going to fight for honour and principle . . . never forget it, dear, wherever you may be—do nothing of which you could be ashamed to tell your sister or your mother."

There were an estimated 60,000 prostitutes in the County of London in 1917, 40,000 of them refugees from France and Belgium.[152] One of them approaches Dick outside the National Gallery. A passing Canadian officer taps him on the

Whatsoever a Man Soweth, 1917. *Dick's encounter with a prostitute in Trafalgar Square is interrupted by an officer. (Bob Geoghegan)*

shoulder and interrupts the proposition: "Do you realise, young man, the risks you run in associating with such women?"

Dick shoos the girl away (and she walks off across Trafalgar Square, clutching her hat, which is flying off in the wind, and grinning broadly). The officer proffers him a card with the address of a doctor. Dick agrees to consult him and produces a photo of his fiancée. The officer declares, "Ah! I thought I had seen you somewhere before. Jane is my sister." This startling twist was evidently concocted by the title writer, for Dick does not react at all.

Dick keeps his promise and visits Dr. Burns. He is conducted around hospital wards and shown victims of venereal disease in every stage. Censorship being lifted for troops, close-ups of rotting legs and hands spare the audience nothing. At this point the film turns into a textbook, and the pages of the *Final Report of the Commission on Venereal Diseases* fill the screen. We learn that hereditary syphilis, generally acquired from the mother, leads at an early age to blindness and deafness. We are shown the germs of the disease, threadlike bodies seen under a microscope attacking healthy corpuscles, and then a syphilitic sore, seething with spirochetes.

Dr. Burns directs Dick to the nearest school for the blind for further facts about what the film coyly refers to as "wild oats." A title states that more than half the children contracted blindness because of hereditary venereal disease. The children are given the subtitle "Daddy took a chance." The close-ups of the boys in their Eton collars are heartbreaking.

"There is no such thing as a 'safe prostitute,'" says a title. "They are practically all diseased—some of them all the time and some of them some of the time. . . . A single exposure may mean a lifetime affliction.

"The man who carries disease to an innocent wife does worse than murder.

"FOR THE SAKE OF HEALTHY CHILDREN. Every child has a right to be born clean into this world, and that man is to be pitied whose own flesh and blood looks him in the face to say, 'Curse you, Dad, I was dirty born and you are the reason why!'"

When the war is over, Dick's brother, Tom, comes under scrutiny. We saw him consorting with prostitutes in London (and being robbed for good measure). Now he returns to Canada, and his wife falls ill with a strange malady. The doctor is called and reveals that she has been infected with syphilis. Tom confides in Dick, who urges him to undergo a cure. The cure is successful, and Tom returns from his "business trip" to see the baby born during his absence. But there is something wrong with the child—he is incurably blind. Tom is overcome with despair. The film ends with lines by Ella Wheeler Wilcox:

> *And the child she bore me was blind*
> *And stricken and weak and ill,*
> *And the mother was left a wreck*
> *It was they who paid the bill.*

Whatsoever a Man Soweth also showed the danger of treating V.D. with patent medicine. Tom tries a brand before he leaves for the front and it seems to work, but the disease returns.

THE SCARLET TRAIL   The sale of "quack" patent medicine was a lucrative racket which fed upon the victims of the white slave trade. John S. Lawrence wrote and directed a film about this problem, *The Scarlet Trail,* in 1918. He was inspired by a booklet—"Don't Take a Chance," by Charles Larned Robinson of the Social Hygiene Committee of the American Defense Society—2 million copies of which had already been distributed to the army and navy by the YMCA. Like the Canadian picture, this film showed the blind and crippled children who had resulted from the spread of venereal disease.

"Out and out preachment," said *Wid's,* "the entertainment value registers somewhere near the zero mark. . . . Everybody concerned in the somber tragedy is so apparently keen to point a moral that they don't get to you as real human beings."[153] But the review pointed to an intriguing aspect of the film; as in *Traffic in Souls,* the patent medicine racketeer had contacts in the reform movement. They help him frame the woman who exposed him by accusing her of endangering the morals of children to whom she teaches sex hygiene.

OPEN YOUR EYES   Backed by the state health authorities, Warner's *Open Your Eyes* (1919) attacked those who felt that V.D. should never be mentioned. "Silence is not golden," was its message, "it is criminal." It opened with a convention of medical men, one of those "talkie" sequences jammed with titles which were considered so necessary in these propaganda pictures. The titles declared that syphilis could be contracted through kissing, public towels, and drinking cups, that 10 percent of young men were syphilitic and had contracted the disease from prostitutes, and that 28 percent of the insane were victims of syphilis: "It is time for moralists to stand to one side and health officials to roll up their sleeves."[154]

The story by S. L. (Sam) Warner and C. L. Mintz was straightforward—and therefore shocking—and yet the director, Gilbert P. Hamilton, felt it necessary to impose coy visual euphemisms. When a mother explains the facts of life to her daughter, he cut to a hen hatching chicks. When the girl, Kitty Walton, reaches eighteen, she falls for a boy who is a "rounder* along Broadway." He had caught syphilis and consulted a quack instead of a proper doctor. He had also had an affair with a girl in the suburbs and had set her up in an apartment before she realized she had been infected.

Variety's laconic description of the film should be quoted verbatim: "The suburban kid finds herself in the dreaded ten percent class and she dramatically crabs the rounder's marriage with Kitty by exposing him as a syphilitic before the assembled wedding guests. In the end, the rounder goes to the nut factory while the girl victim (after being cured) marries a youth who had gone to the city and had been bitten by a prostitute who worked more rawly than the cops permit these days."[155]

The picture played in several cities before it opened in New York. Everyone invited to the opening received a testimonial from officials in the other cities, together with a speech from Louis Brownlow, President of the Board of Commissioners for the District of Columbia: "One little streetwalker will spread more disease, cause more misery, ruin more lives, bring about more deaths in the course of two or three years than all the lepers who have been in the District of Columbia since the foundation of the Government."[156]

END OF THE ROAD   Director Edward H. Griffith, who had made *Fit to Fight* and *Fit to Win,* also directed *End of the Road.* Taken from a story by Dr. Katherine Bement Davis, former commissioner of correction in New York,[157] it was based on actual cases and was aimed primarily at women. Scenes of infected women were filmed at Blackwells Island, New York City. The interiors were shot at the Famous Players studios in New York.

Helen Ferguson, who played an Irish servant, admitted she knew nothing of the subject. "If I'd had to ask my mother what V.D. was, she would have had to look it up in the dictionary. That was the age of innocence, genuine innocence.[158]

"The makeup man came over and put what looked like a great big fever blister on my mouth. Richard Bennett, playing the doctor, and Claire Adams were in that scene. Griffith came over and said, 'I don't think there's any sense in rehearsing this. I think I'll just keep the closeup camera on the kid here and let her take it from there. And you just tell her what's the matter with her.'

---

*A man who goes the rounds of the bars.

The End of the Road, *1919. Richard Bennett as the army doctor, Claire Adams as Mary Lee, the nurse, and Joyce Fair as a victim of syphilis. (Museum of Modern Art)*

"I was pretty doggone curious; what *could* be the matter that I would go to see a doctor because of a cold sore? Claire was playing the sympathetic friend and being very tender, and the doctor was very sweet and gentle, so something bad was obviously the matter with me. The doctor asked me where I'd been. I told him I'd taken this cab to Yaphank and the cab driver—that's how they protected the boys in the army from any connection with what was the matter with me— dragged me out of the cab and into the woods on the way to the camp. Then the doctor explained that the thing on my face—they'd done tests, and I had a very bad disease called syphilis. He put his arm round me very gently and told me also I was pregnant.

"Well, it didn't take an awful lot of acting, you know. I knew the camera was on me. But at the end, Griffith threw down his megaphone and jumped up and down and shouted 'Hooray' and some of the prop men started cheering and I knew I'd gotten through the scene all right. And I was a lot wiser than when I went into it. The tough studio manager came bursting through the door. 'What's going on here? We haven't had so much excitement round this studio since Pickford was a pup.' "[159]

The idea behind the film was to emphasize the importance of childhood character training on later life—one girl has a mother who instructs her truthfully; the other has an ambitious mother concerned only to find her a rich husband. The first girl becomes an army nurse, the second becomes a hospital case, affected by advanced syphilis.[160]

The reviewers thought the picture rambled, and, while it showed flashes of intelligence, lacked flair. Some details were "nauseating."

"I believe the government is making a mistake in trying to handle propaganda work of this sort through the medium of the regular film theatres," said Wid Gunning. "The government apparently believes in making these productions so frank that they will shock people into paying attention to their propaganda."[161]

The St. Paul Auditorium in Minneapolis was due to open at 7:00 P.M. Half an hour earlier, someone picked the lock. When state Board of Health officials arrived, they were astounded to find 2,000 people already in their seats. The rest of the house filled up at once, and by 7:30 officials had to lock the doors. Outside, another 4,000 people surged around, hoping for a second screening. Officials tried to oblige, but in vain. "The disappointed crowd became so insistent that police reserves were called to quell the riot. It required nearly two hours to clear the streets."[162]

As Public Health Films offered *End of the Road* to city after city, the local authorities became more and more nervous. The first "civilian" showing was supposed to have been in Syracuse, New York, even though it occurred after the Minneapolis affair. (Perhaps every city was offered the first "civilian" showing!) The Syracuse exhibitor took no chances and showed it first to a local "semicensoring" committee of churchmen, dramatic editors, and city officials. They all gave it their approval except Assistant Commissioner S. T. Fredericks, who wanted to think about it overnight. Next morning, he had made up his mind; the picture was unfit to be shown in public.

Edward H. Griffith had taken the precaution of accompanying the film as "War Department Representative," and he and the exhibitor organized a showing for society women and clubwomen. "There was a near riot as a result," said *Variety,* "but the picture came through with one hundred percent approval, including the hearty indorsement [*sic*] of Commissioner of Public Safety Walter W. Nicholson."[163]

With admission from 25 cents to one dollar, the picture continued on its highly profitable propaganda course. In Philadelphia, one theatre scooped $9,000 in the first week.[164] But at the start of the following week, with several hundred people lined up outside the Garrick Theatre, the police announced the film would not be shown. The state Board of Censors, assuming it was government property, had caught up with it a little late. The exhibitors insisted that since it was "educational," it did not need the endorsement of the censors. They threatened injunction proceedings against the board. After all, they had permission from the state Board of Health. Under a storm of criticism, including a letter from Archbishop Dougherty describing the film as "indecent and dangerous," the commissioner of the Board of Health ordered the picture to be taken off. The manager turned a blind eye to the order and continued to sell tickets until he received a personal note from the commissioner; then he obeyed out of fear of losing his license.

The task of returning everyone's money caused as much of a crush as the show itself. Ticket speculators—known as "specs" in the business—had made a killing, charging $1.50 for 25-cent tickets. But customers received only the face value of their tickets, and their anger at the specs was only slightly mollified later by the news of a police raid, which netted three of them.

The closing of *The End of the Road* was a great relief to those exhibitors showing regular entertainment pictures in Philadelphia.

Great Britain had even harsher censorship than Philadelphia, yet so serious was the postwar V.D. crisis that the Ministry of Health gave its approval and the picture was shown under the auspices of the National Council for Combating Venereal Diseases. The censor, however, refused to pass it, and that very fact brought enormous crowds to the Polytechnic Theatre, Regent Street, where Vivian Van Damm risked his livelihood by booking it.

"We had to cope with the fact that at each performance someone was almost certain to faint," wrote Van Damm. "The proportion of faints was ten men to one woman."[165]

Van Damm had the questionable habit of removing sequences from the print at one show and putting them back at another, sparking disputes and obliging people to see the film again to settle the argument.

A group of medical students from Middlesex Hospital told Van Damm that they resented him making V.D. a public spectacle: "We're going to stop you by smashing up the theatre." He calmed them down by promising to take it off if, once they'd seen it, they still felt it to be against the public interest. The police were tipped off, just in case. But when it was over, the students were clearly moved by what they had seen. They gravely thanked Van Damm and sent staff from the Middlesex to see it. Van Damm kept a doctor and two nurses on duty at every performance.

But the film encountered more vocal opposition. According to Dr. H. W. Bagley, president of the Society for the Prevention of Venereal Diseases: *"The End of the Road* is a terrible film which suggests that every man who indulges in irregular sexual intercourse will get venereal disease, will commit suicide, or get covered with sores, or end in a madhouse. . . . We are very much against it because it terrifies people. I myself know of several suicides which have occurred because the poor people had seen the film and thought there was nothing but the madhouse lying before them."[166]

In September 1919 the Public Health Service withdrew its endorsements of the venereal disease pictures. "This action had been taken," explained Surgeon General Blue, "in order that the educational, medical and legislative phase of the venereal disease program of the various states and municipal health organizations could be co-ordinated."[167] The vague verbiage of the bureaucrat camouflaged the intention of the Public Health Service to withdraw the films from commercial distribution and save itself a great deal of aggravation. By now, the National Catholic War Council had added their fuel to the fury.

Despite the terrifying numbers of troops returning with disease—one in four officers, for instance[168]—the government bowed to the forces of reaction and ended the campaign. Although *The End of the Road* was later reissued in an abridged form, and although the occasional warning was sounded (as in the film *T.N.T., The Naked Truth* [1924]), few people could expect to see them since their release was so restricted. Meanwhile, venereal disease continued to sweep through the population, in many cases unreported. By 1936 it was estimated that one American in twenty-two was a victim.

A theatre in Crookston, 1914. (Q. David Bowers)

THE WHITE SLAVE FILMS

"In every large city," wrote Jane Addams in 1912, "thousands of women are so set aside as outcasts from decent society that it is considered an impropriety to speak the very word which designates them."[169] Prostitutes were called "scarlet" or "sporting" women or, by the very fastidious, "midinettes." "White slavery" described coercive prostitution. (While it was a form of slavery, by no means were all the slaves white.) Procurers were "traffickers";[170] pimps were "cadets" (a shortened form is more familiar, "cad"); a brothel was known by a range of terms, from "resort" to "house."

Society used euphemisms to cloak these activities and segregation to camouflage their existence. Confining prostitutes to red-light districts in rundown parts of town meant that respectable people never needed to encounter them. Prostitutes served as a safety valve, keeping sensuality at a discreet distance from the community. Almost every major city had a red-light district; New York and Chicago had several.

In the 1890s, the Reverend Charles H. Parkhurst, minister of the Madison Square Presbyterian Church, investigated New York's brothels, saloons, and gambling houses and came to the conclusion that such places could not exist without the cooperation of the police.[171] Graft payments amounted to between $4 million and $5 million a year. This and other exposures of the Lexow Committee,[172] which studied the Parkhurst revelations, led to a rebellion against Tammany Hall, headquarters of the Democratic party. But Tammany, "corruption with consent"[173] as

Lincoln Steffens described it, survived a brief reform administration, and prostitution in New York was flourishing as profitably as ever.

Few women chose to become prostitutes, but many, trapped by desperate poverty, accepted the life, thus placing themselves beyond the law. Pimps could beat them up in broad daylight and no policeman would interfere, as was illustrated in *The Girl Who Went Astray* (1902).[174] A pimp attacks a prostitute on the street at the very moment that her aged parents find her. The father is knocked down, the girl dragged off, and the mother faints. A cop, casually tossing his nightstick, passes the melee and takes no notice whatsoever.

Any treatment of this subject was inflammatory, for political bosses had property interests in the red-light districts; police chiefs and judges, not to mention the man on the beat, were on the take, the liquor interests were implicated through the saloons, and even big corporations and banks were involved.[175] But Tammany boss Charles Murphy, forced to act after the 1912 Rosenthal murder,* began to move against New York's red-light district. And when Tammany was ousted in 1913, the white slave issue exploded. Indeed, 1913 proved a significant year in many respects. In March, the Eugène Brieux play *Damaged Goods* had opened in New York. This was so violently controversial that it filled the theatre for months, and ensured that other "frank revelations of vice" would follow, among them *The Lure, The Traffic, The Fight, The Battle,* and *The House of Bondage*.[176] Then the report of the Rockefeller Commission was released; it concluded that police corruption was the single most important factor in the operation of the traffic. "Prostitution," said Jane Addams, "was the unbreakable bank to which every corrupt politician repaired when in need of funds."[177]

It was into this volatile atmosphere that George Loane Tucker launched his sensational feature production *Traffic in Souls.*

TRAFFIC IN SOULS   George Loane Tucker (real name George S. Loane) was one of the most charismatic of the early directors. Born in Chicago in 1881, he had been a railroad clerk and freight agent before entering the theatre in 1904. Although strikingly handsome, he had an undistinguished career as an actor. He joined the picture business around 1908 and in 1911 began to direct. His most famous picture—*The Miracle Man*—would appear in 1919, but a career of exceptional promise was cut short by his early death in 1921.

Tucker is credited by Terry Ramsaye with the idea for *Traffic in Souls* (1913), the background of which Ramsaye described in his entertaining, but not always reliable, history of the industry, *A Million and One Nights*: "Tucker saw everything on Broadway including *The Lure* and *The Battle,* both of which were so highly colored that they brought police intervention. He was afire with inspiration. He would make a great revealing motion picture, dealing with the white slave traffic."[178]

Another vital figure in the drama was Jack Cohn. Brother of the soon-to-be-notorious Harry, and later vice president of Columbia Pictures himself, Jack was

---

*Rosenthal was a minor gambler who talked to the press about the police protection racket and was shot—allegedly on the orders of a police lieutenant. See page 185.

the chief cutter at Universal. His father, a cutter of a different sort, had been a tailor of police uniforms. As a boy, Jack had been fascinated by the police, and as soon as he was old enough he became a reservist, taking part in raids. Cohn was all for making the picture and, with his contacts, undoubtedly helped smooth the path for police cooperation. To proceed with the Ramsaye version: Tucker approached the head of Universal, Carl Laemmle, for authority to put the picture into production. It would be a feature-length picture—an idea Laemmle opposed. The prospect of spending $5,000 on a single film—an amount that would pay for ten one-reelers—was, to Laemmle, the height of stupidity. He rejected Tucker's proposal.

When Tucker reported his defeat, a conspiracy was born. A filmmaker's combine was set up, five investors putting up $1,000 each. If Laemmle was not impressed by the final film, they would pay the costs themselves and recoup from the anticipated profits. Apart from Tucker, the investors were director Herbert Brenon, actor King Baggot, Jack Cohn, and William Robert Daly, an actor-director.

Ramsaye says that the studio manager (Julius Stern) went abroad and that his replacement (Mark Dintenfass) was too involved with the internecine warfare at the Broadway headquarters to notice what was going on at the Fort Lee studio: "The boys at the studio were merrily engaged in photographing *Traffic in Souls,* a scene at a time in odd moments when opportunity permitted, keeping up meanwhile the continuous grind of one- and two-reel pictures."[179]

In four weeks the picture was photographed by Henry Alden Leach. It was ten reels long without titles. Tucker and Dintenfass had a row, and Tucker left the company and set sail for England.[180] Cohn cut the picture down to six reels, working at night and hiding the negative in his safe. Full of apprehension, he took it to Laemmle, who talked to his lieutenants all the way through and hardly noticed the picture. In desperation, Cohn visited Laemmle again that night and talked him into another showing. This time the boss was duly impressed. But what on earth was he going to do with it? Universal distributed one- and two-reelers; features had to go into legitimate theatres. His opponents accused him of squandering the company's money on "Tucker's Folly." Laemmle offered to take the picture off Universal's hands for $10,000. But "if you put up ten thousand, it must be worth a million," replied the studio, raising the ante to $25,000. The picture thus remained the property of Universal.[181]

Ramsaye wrote his account only a decade or so after the film was made, and he had the inestimable advantage of having talked to some of those involved—in particular Jack Cohn—while their memories were fresh. But he was a dyed-in-the-wool newspaperman, anxious to play up the drama in any story, and those who talked with him knew it. His tale was recounted in John Drinkwater's 1931 biography of Carl Laemmle, but this version made Laemmle the hero, fighting for the film against all opposition and seeing it triumph in New York.

Where did it triumph? At the Joe Weber Theatre, owned by the Shuberts, who had had a big success with *The Lure.* And, as Lee Shubert said, "We were in *Traffic in Souls* from the beginning."[182] Walter MacNamara, who not only wrote the film but also produced it, said that the picture was his idea and that *he* approached the Shuberts about distributing it.[183]

Traffic in Souls cost not $5,000, but $25,000. The chief investors were Lee Shubert; Joseph L. Rhinock, an officer of the Shubert Theatrical Company and a former senator; and a Cincinnati businessman, George B. Cox, a major backer of the Shubert interests. Each invested $5,000 privately, testing the waters, before becoming more involved in film production.[184] These investments appear to have been made after production began, so it is still possible that Ramsaye's filmmakers' combine initiated the project.

But Ramsaye, no filmmaker, did not realize that to produce a ten-reel picture in a mere four weeks one would have to work at the speed of a crew making a modern TV series. And *Traffic in Souls* was one of the most elaborate features so far produced by the American film industry—there were so many two- and three-reel vice films around that a big feature was required to scoop them all. Hardly anyone had done it before; even D. W. Griffith had progressed only as far as four reels.

Unfortunately, none of the technicians is alive to be consulted. I have questioned one of the players, Ethel Grandin, but her memories were too vague to be reliable. Ernest Palmer, cameraman for Tucker's later films, told Jack Lodge that he never heard any talk of the film being made without the knowledge of the front office.[185] The studio heads may indeed have been so involved in their political battles that they ignored the project. But to say that such a big film was made in secret is clearly absurd.

Documents and publications of the time give a different impression of how the film came about that is no less fascinating than Ramsaye's account.

Between 1907 and 1910, the United States Immigration Commission endeavored to find out the effects of the increasing wave of immigration on American life. The White Slave Traffic Act (later known as the Mann Act) was a result of this investigation; Congress passed it in 1910 to prohibit the transportation of women for immoral purposes from state to state or by foreign commerce.[186]

A congressional committee of enquiry, headed by Professor Jeremiah Jenks of Cornell University, concentrated on female immigrants and the fate of those who traveled alone. Its report[187] was a shock to politicians and public alike, for it revealed that thousands of young women never reached the end of their journeys. A few came with the intention of becoming prostitutes, but many were forcibly abducted. The traffickers would start their operation in Europe, becoming engaged to or even marrying young girls. The trafficker would leave for America, promising to send for his "bride." And sure enough, a ticket would arrive; the girl would travel to New York and be met and escorted to her new "home." Once inside the brothel she was deprived of her street clothes and money. Having no friends, not knowing the language, she could not escape. (Or the trafficker might pose as an immigrant on a ship, winning a girl's confidence during the voyage. Upon landing, he would spirit the girl away in a cab during a specially arranged diversion.)

To warn the immigrant girls, pamphlets and tracts were printed by the thousands, but they were of little help—even when printed in the appropriate language, they could hardly alert the many girls who could not read.[188] The president of the Immigrant Girls' Home in New York City, Mrs. S. M. Haggen, came up with a striking alternative—a moving picture—and sought the help of Walter Mac-Namara, "special photoplay writer" (scenario editor) at Universal.*

Among MacNamara's scenarios was a police story, *The Rise of Officer 174*,[190] which used the notion of detection via dictagraph. Several important court cases had recently hinged on evidence from dictagraphs,[191] and a couple of other recent pictures had exploited the invention.[192] For *Traffic in Souls*, MacNamara repeated the dictagraph idea but included a bugging device to give greater audience appeal to Mrs. Haggen's grim case histories. Since these centered around prostitution, he had the idea of approaching the Shuberts who had staged *The Lure* (it would be filmed by Alice Blaché in 1914) and discussed with them a feature with the same box-office potential. He shifted the emphasis from immigrants to white slavers, but this made the story more commercial. It also brought up the vexing matter of the police. Being an Irishman—and didn't every Irishman have a relative on the New York City force?—he would hardly have wished to make villains of the police. Nor would Jack Cohn. In any case, with the police able to shut theatres, such an attack would never have seen the light of day. But a story which left their pride unimpaired would have a flying start and would ensure cooperation for all the location shooting in the streets of New York.

The story of *Traffic in Souls* was so fast-moving and so packed with direct and veiled references to the vice trade that it is a wonder audiences could keep pace with it. Modern audiences are lost, submerged by a welter of detail from a forgotten era, unable to focus on one before being swept away by another. They assume they can follow so apparently simple a plot, but it is not so. I had to see it several times and study the background before I could understand the whole thing.

Of course, lost footage missing from the recently available (Blackhawk) version makes it all seem snatched and hurried. I have examined the English release version, at the National Film Archive, which is more complete, and the picture makes more sense. It is better paced, has a few more explanatory titles, some good domestic scenes with Mary and her father and some extra touches of humor—together with the complete ending. (The Blackhawk version ends two scenes before the original finale.)

The picture opens in the modest home of an invalid inventor (William Turner) who has two daughters. Mary (Jane Gail), "the head of the house," is enamored of a policeman, Officer Burke (Matt Moore). She keeps an eye on Lorna (Ethel Grandin), very pretty and very lazy. Lorna has been spotted by the local white slavers, who begin to close the net.

An impressive figure by the name of William Trubus (William Welsh) inhabits a luxurious mansion with liveried footmen and devotes his life to reform. He has a daughter (Irene Wallace), too, who has just become engaged to Bobby Kopfman, "the greatest society catch of the season."

---

*Born in Lismore, Ireland, in 1876, MacNamara began his working life as a blacksmith and later became a marine engineer.[189] One of the first vice presidents of the Gaelic League, a founder of the Fabian Society, he had been a war correspondent in South Africa and an actor on and playwright for the stage.

By contrast, we glimpse the denizens of a brothel—"They who traffic in souls," as a title puts it. And we meet a cadet, "the most infamous type of man," called Bill Bradshaw (William Cavanaugh).* The house has been made much bleaker than we know such places to have been; there is no sign of the plush furniture, the gilt mirrors, the piano. One woman tries to escape, and it takes the threat of brute force to keep her inside her "cell."

Traffic in Souls, 1913, frame enlargements by Gerald McKee. Arrival at the Battery from the Ellis Island ferry.

Trubus is revealed as the controller of the traffic. He operates from a private office with INTERNATIONAL PURITY AND REFORM LEAGUE on the door (a reference, perhaps to the International Reform Association, which was so hostile to the moving picture). Downstairs is a similar office where the Go-Between (Howard Crampton) receives the money from the brothels. He has all the latest equipment, such as a dictagraph, and even a sort of telegraphic pen by which he transmits the latest figures to "the man higher up."

Two Swedish girls are ensnared on board an immigrant ship by a trafficker disguised as a Friendly Old Swede. He shows them a communication from the "Swedish Employment Agency"—a couple of jobs have fallen free. They are only too eager to accept them, and he signals a colleague (Walter MacNamara), who alerts headquarters with a coded Marconi cable which he gives to the ship's wireless operator (George Loane Tucker).

An unsuspecting woman from the country is shadowed by a respectable looking pimp.

At the Ellis Island ferry dock, the immigrant girls are met by their brother. Waiting lookouts push and punch the brother, and when he tries to defend himself, the police arrest him. The Friendly Old Swede is kind enough to escort the girls to the Employment Agency. Once inside the building, the girls are set upon. But Officer Burke's suspicions are aroused by the Swedish Employment Agency sign which has suddenly appeared outside the house. He

Officer Burke (Matt Moore) suspects the sudden appearance of a "Swedish Employment Agency."

---

*Cavanaugh was a policeman from Venice, Calif., according to Swedish historian Bo Berglund.

The shootout in the brothel from Traffic in Souls, *1913. Matt Moore (center) with Ethel Grandin. This picture was posed; the film is more realistic. (National Film Archive)*

arrives at the door, and a cadet tries to bribe him. Burke laughs and sticks the money back in the man's pocket before smashing him over the head with his own signboard. A fight breaks out, and Burke, revolver drawn, escorts everyone to the precinct house, where the girls are reunited with their brother.[193]

Meanwhile Bradshaw makes off with Lorna, whom he drugs and delivers, semiconscious, to the brothel. When she recovers, she tries to escape and is roughed up.

Mary, desperately anxious about Lorna, asks that Burke be assigned to the search for her. Mary loses her job as a result of her sister's presumed disgrace and is immediately offered a position as a telephonist—in Trubus's office. Left alone while the reformers confer next door, she discovers a set of earphones and, putting them to her ear, recognizes the voice of the man who abducted her sister. She follows the wire to the fire escape and through a window below sees Bradshaw taking money from the Go-Between.

That night, Mary and Burke borrow her father's invention for intensifying sound waves and recording dictagraph sounds on phonographic cylinders. They break into the office and conceal the equipment. Next day, Mary hands over the incriminating cylinders to the police and a raiding party moves into action.

In the brothel, Lorna is being threatened with a whipping. Outside, the raiding party is poised, crowbars and axes at the ready. Burke climbs the fire escape and blows his whistle from the roof. Bradshaw, about to whip Lorna, looks up in alarm. The crowbars smash the front door and the police pour in. Burke descends from the roof and rescues Lorna. A gun battle rages. Burke chases Bradshaw to the roof and shoots him as he reaches the fire escape. He falls over the parapet to his death on the street below.

At "the proudest moment of his life," Trubus settles his daughter's betrothal arrangements and beams on the assembly when the police burst in and arrest him. The fiancé and his parents depart in horror.

The traffickers are locked up; Trubus is later released on bail. Outside the courthouse he is nearly lynched by an angry mob (one of the most convincing scenes in the picture). When he returns home he discovers that his wife, to escape his shame, has killed herself. His daughter, distraught, will have nothing to do with him. Overcome with remorse, he collapses by his wife's deathbed, and the picture slowly fades out.

As the National Film Archive version shows, however, this was not the original ending. We cut to a newspaper in a trash can:

TRUBUS A SUICIDE

His go-between and associates sentenced.

His mind unbalanced by the death of his wife, whose heart gave way under the shock of his exposure; his daughter insane from shame and grief and fearing to face his trial, he evidently determined to end everything. His go-between and the entire unsavory crew have had sentences meted out from five to twenty years.

Burke and Mary visit the police captain, and Burke asks for a leave of absence. The captain hesitates a moment, causing Mary some nervousness, then gives his warm assent, congratulating them both. As Burke goes out the door, he says, "We'll name the first after you." The captain throws his arms in the air and roars with laughter.

Traffic in Souls was a potential sensation. Universal proposed to set up a separate operation to handle it, spending $1,000 a week on a national advertising campaign[194] that was gleefully mendacious: "The sensational motion picture dramatization based on the John D. Rockefeller White Slavery Report and on the investigation of the Vice Trust by District Attorney Whitman—a $200,000 spectacle in 700 scenes with 800 players."[195]

None of these facts is correct. But official endorsements were essential for a film as risky as this, and Universal had none.[196] The publicity department went so far as to quote Rockefeller as saying that the scenes in the brothels, including that in which the kidnapped girl was beaten into submission, were exactly as witnesses had testified before his committee.[197] Rockefeller later issued a disclaimer, denying that this film, or any of those which followed it, was based on his commission's investigations and adding that in his judgment the films exercised an evil influence.[198]

This was not the opinion of the National Board of Censorship, which agonized over *Traffic in Souls* but eventually allowed it to be shown with only minor excisions.[199] The board had decided to pass films which presented the problem of prostitution in a sincere, dramatic manner.[200]

The film opened in New York at Joe Weber's Theatre on Twenty-ninth Street and Broadway on November 24, 1913, becoming the first film not taken from a novel or a play to receive a Broadway opening.[201] It was an immediate smash hit—

a thousand people were turned away the first night. Thirty thousand saw the film the first week, many of them girls of between sixteen and eighteen. "Fully two-thirds of the audience are women," said the *New York Times*.[202]

While *Moving Picture World* greeted the film with awe, *Variety* was less respect-ful: "There's a laugh on the Rockefeller investigators in the personality of one of the white slavers, a physical counterpart of John D. himself so striking as to make the observer wonder whether the granger of Pocantico Hills really came down to pose for Universal." The reviewer thought the film showed in motion picture terms what the newspapers printed from day to day of the barter of women: "Anthony Comstock will probably yell murder the first time he sees 'em, one particular turkey trotting boy and girl in a cabaret scene. Despite its choppy form, the drama moves along briskly, concluding with a fine piece of movie staging in a raid by a squad of cops on one of the vice dens."[203]

Traffic in Souls outraged such pillars of the theatrical establishment as Oscar Hammerstein, who sued that other pillar, David Belasco, for permitting it to be shown at the Republic Theatre, into which it moved on December 22, 1913. This theatre was contracted to produce only first-class performances, and Hammerstein charged Belasco with forfeiting its reputation. Belasco countered that he consid-ered the motion picture on a level with the stage; he did not therefore feel that the tone of the theatre had been lowered.[204] Hammerstein won in the first court, but lost on appeal.[205]

Within a month, twenty-eight theatres in the New York area were showing the film, although it was banned in such cities as Chicago. Business dropped to a trickle within a few weeks, however, as the public realized it had been fooled, that there was no sex in the film whatever, and it was merely an elaborate police drama. But by this time, Universal had made a great deal of money; the picture eventually grossed about $450,000.[206]

The most valuable aspects of the film today are its scenes of documentary realism, such as that at the ferry dock, shot while real immigrants were coming ashore. The cooperation of the police and immigration authorities enabled the players to mingle with the crowd. We are fortunate that an account of the filming survives:

"An unusually green looking immigrant, apparently a youth of twenty, came out of the Ellis Island ferry-house, escorting two pretty girls . . . He looked and acted so green that even the Battery Park loungers, used as they are to seeing every costume and every race of the world passing out of the little ferry-house, turned to stare in wonder and amusement!

"Suddenly, in full view of the crowd, a roughly clad man walked up and deliberately pushed the young immigrant, then struck him a violent blow. The act was so unprovoked, so outrageous, that the loungers jumped up from the benches and made for the scene. The immigrant and the man who had struck him were now fighting and scuffling, and a crowd began quickly to gather. At this point a third man stepped up, and, taking the two girls by the arms, tried to escort them off the scene. Cries of indignation arose from the crowd, the old game was so obvious. The two men who interfered with the immigrants were about to be roughly handled by the crowd, when someone on its outer fringe cried out:

'Let 'em alone; it's all right!'

"A roar of laughter arose. Even above the noise a peculiar rattling buzz could be heard. Then came another voice:

'Let 'em alone; it's the movies!'

"The crowd drew back, laughing and good natured. Then the immigrant boy and the other man continued their shuffle, and the third man walked off with the pretty girls. A policeman stood off to one side watching them, curling his mustache and grinning.

"Presently the two men stopped wrestling and walked off to an automobile, in the back seat of which the two girls were seated, laughing. The three men climbed in, followed by the operator and his machine, and the automobile shot away from the curb, up Broadway."[207]

Tucker clearly had such trouble with these crowds that he later restaged his fight scene on a deserted part of the New York waterfront, on the French Line pier.[208]

Seeing the film nearly eighty years after it was made, one is aware of its shortcomings: the painted interior scenery which clashes with the vivid reality of the exteriors, the imaginary inventions which make the factual quality of the story less convincing, the overacting of Ethel Grandin as she rolls around her bedroom in the last stages of despair. Most of the acting is naturalistic, however, and Tucker shows considerable flair in his direction, especially in the final assault on the brothel, which is pure cinema, edited by Jack Cohn as well as anything Griffith had achieved.

Traffic in Souls gives a fascinating glimpse into life in New York before the war. From this point of view, it is priceless. As an exposé, it is hollow. The Rockefeller Commission's revelations of police corruption were entirely suppressed.* And Tucker and MacNamara deliberately hurt the reform movement with their depiction of "the man higher up." (In this, they anticipated D. W. Griffith's *The Mother and the Law,* which was shot the following year and also included a portrayal apparently based on Rockefeller.) However hypocritical some may have been, no reformer is known to have run a vice ring. Many are known, however, to have harassed the police, who were involved up to their necks. The film, which so strongly attacks hypocrisy, is thus hypocritical itself.

Matt Moore, Ethel Grandin, and Jane Gail became stars overnight. (By 1916, their stardom was over,[209] although Matt Moore continued to play leads into the 1920s.) George Loane Tucker directed films in England, then faded from view, to make a triumphant return with *The Miracle Man* in 1919. Walter MacNamara had the satisfaction of seeing *Traffic in Souls* become the first film to be used as the basis of a novel.[210] He was promoted to director and made a child labor film.[211] He then left Universal, set up his own company, and made a sequel to *Traffic in Souls, The Heart of New York,*[212] which had none of the success of the original.

Although MacNamara had altered the emphasis of Mrs. Haggen's original idea, the immigration people were evidently gratified, for they later commissioned other films and showed them, as well as *Traffic in Souls,* on board steamers, at the

---

*It is a trifle ironic that Officer Burke should be offered a wad of bills by one of the pimps, even if he turns it down. The fact that such a scene could be included hinted at the real problem. Curiously, no reviewer drew attention to this whitewashing of the police.

quarantine station, and in the detention sheds of Ellis Island, where unaccompanied girls were held until claimed by their friends.[213]

But the sociological aspect was the least of the concerns of those who made the picture. And what must have been galling for all of them was the speed with which the imitations appeared—especially *The Inside of the White Slave Traffic,* which, by 1914, was beating the original film at the box office.

THE INSIDE OF THE WHITE SLAVE TRAFFIC   Of all the films sparked off by the white slave controversy, *The Inside of the White Slave Traffic* caused the greatest commotion. It opened in New York at the Park Theatre, Columbus Circle, in December 1913, and was soon taking in twice as much money as *Traffic in Souls.* The film was no better than its predecessor, but, as its title indicated, it went to the heart of the matter. As *Variety* said, "It goes in for the utmost fidelity in picturing the evil which has been its inspiration."[214]

The film was more documentary than melodrama and, although not nearly so well made as *Traffic in Souls,* it had impeccable credentials. It was written and produced by Samuel H. London, who headed the staff of the Rockefeller Commission.[215] Before that, he had been director of the Secret Service, the federal agency which combated vice.[216] London posed as the man solely responsible for the film, but it was actually directed by Frank V. Beal. Edwin Carewe (later a famous director) played the lead, with Virginia Mann, Jean Thomas, Ninita Bristow, and Elinor D. Peterson. It was filmed in New York, New Orleans, and Denver.[217]

To armor-plate his film against criticism and censorship, London opened it with a statement to the effect that it had been based on facts gathered during his intensive investigations of the white slave traffic, in close cooperation with the U.S. Department of Justice. A series of endorsements followed, including those of Eugène Brieux, author of *Damaged Goods;* Mrs. O. H. P. Belmont; and Inez Milholland Boissevain, socialist and suffragist.

As further protection, London called the company which made the picture The Moral Feature Film Company, and the distributor, Harry White, named his releasing outfit The Sociological Research Film Corporation. After such precautions, London might have been forgiven for thinking his film would have no trouble. He was wrong.

Looking at the film today, it is not too hard to see why it caused such a furor. Although only two chopped-up reels survive of the original four, and although the most controversial material has disappeared, what remains is startling enough.

Because of the missing footage, the story is hard to follow. It opens with a scene of George Fisher (Carewe), a procurer, climbing wearily out of bed and getting dressed. He makes a phone call, and a girl in street clothes walks in and hands him a wad of money. He examines it and snarls at her: too little. The girl, young and attractive, removes her hat, and we realize with a sense of shock that she is preparing to take over the very bed he has vacated.

George goes out and takes part in a game of "Stuss," the gangsters' favorite game, a New York version of faro.[218] He loses, with ill grace, the money he got from the girl. We see him walking through the crowded streets of lower Manhattan and calling at a cigar store. The owner is a friend. He telephones the girl in his room, and she goes to meet him, carrying yet more cash, which presumably she has earned in the interval.

The girl is later arrested and taken before the night court,[219] but this strand of the plot disappears with the missing footage. A new episode begins with the title "The innocent in danger." A girl visits the cigar store, and George asks his friend to identify her. Apparently, she's a sewing machine girl. To make her acquaintance, George arranges a fake fight on the street, from which he rescues her. (This episode is also missing.) He takes her to a restaurant and slips something into her drink. There is a direct cut, due to more missing footage, to the bedroom. The girl, Annie, is alone. She looks at the bed, and makes it obvious to the audience that she realizes what has happened.

"The home of yesterday. Parents, beware the 'out of my house' policy."

Annie is welcomed back by her mother, but when she relates what has befallen her, the mother is appalled. Annie's father, even more shocked, throws her out of the house. She has nowhere to go but to George. He agrees to marry her but, as the title says, "The marriage ceremony is seldom genuine."

George takes Annie to a fake parson, who responds understandingly to his wink.

"Two weeks later, the Trafficker tells Annie he is without funds, and must place her with friends until his next payment." He takes her to a brothel. "And in time the usual developments." Admittedly, there is footage missing, but the sight of Annie, in a lovely white dress, streetwalking on a sunlit New York thoroughfare, comes as a bit of a shock. *(Variety* even identified the street—Ninth Avenue near Thirty-fourth Street!)[220]

"The method employed by procuring Traffickers is the 'turnover.' " Annie is horrified to receive a note from George saying that he is leaving the city for good. She breaks down in tears. The messenger, Felix, offers her an alternative: "If you will come with me to New Orleans, I will have your marriage to Fisher annulled and I will marry you."

Annie agrees, and they shake hands on it. The turnover completed, we see Felix paying George $300.

They set out for New Orleans, which has the only district in the United States set aside by law for prostitution.[221] Here, further missing footage commits further offenses to the plot. We see a flash of Annie, wearing a kimono, about to be beaten, when suddenly a title says "Denver."

Annie has run away. There are some striking shots of her wandering the streets and being turned away by brothel keepers because news of her escape has filtered through the system. She pawns her last possession, her wedding ring, and travels to Houston, but the system is everywhere. She cannot even get a job in a saloon. She spends her last dollar on lodging.

Meanwhile, Felix uses the system to locate her. He walks straight into her room. At first scared, she then falls on his shoulder with relief and remorse. He merely laughs. They return to New Orleans, and she goes out slaving for him again.

After more missing footage, and fragments of a subplot concerning the fate of an immigrant girl, we find Annie working in a department store. She takes her pay home to Felix, trying to pass it off as money earned on the streets. Felix realizes her subterfuge and leaves her dreaming miserably of the life—and the children—she might have had.

"And in the end she was laid away, an outcast in Potter's Field."

This abrupt end is presumably due to further missing footage. We see a communal graveyard of wooden posts, all marked anonymously with a set of official numbers, and the story is over.

Variety—which called these films "patchouli and kimono pictures," after the scent and costume worn by the girls—warned that this one, like its predecessor, would lower the esteem in which film plays were held. But if it kept clear of trouble, it would do land-office business.[222]

They were right. On the second night at the Park Theatre, 2,000 people had to be turned away. Exhibitors who had no vice films to show were furious. They worded their protest to the trade press in the form of a legal document, each clause beginning with "Whereas."

"Whereas . . ." the police had stopped the stage plays *The Lure* and *The Fight* because of scenes set in bawdy houses, then those scenes were a violation of the penal code. If that was the case, then the same applied to the scenes in the white slave films "even to more extreme degrees of vicious exposure."[223]

A final "Whereas" betrayed the real cause of indignation, the fact that these highly profitable films were invariably booked into legitimate theatres rather than motion picture houses.

So successful was the New York run that the promoters booked *The Inside of the White Slave Traffic* into a second theatre, the Bijou, starting on December 22. But in January 1914, the picture suddenly disappeared and the employees of the Park Theatre found themselves under arrest, waiting to go before a particularly fierce magistrate.[224]

The last time the picture had been in court, this same judge had censured the film but had allowed the theatres to remain open. The Bijou had promptly doubled its admission price. But the legal problems gave the management second thoughts; they canceled the film and substituted a foreign picture which they renamed *The Exposure of the White Slave Traffic*.[225] It did them no good. The Bijou employees were also rounded up by the police, although all but the manager were later released.[226]

The state and municipal censors were no better disposed toward these vice pictures. In Chicago, Major Metellus Funkhouser showed *The Inside of the White Slave Traffic* to a committee of prominent people before he banned it. The committee had decided that it contained a moral lesson of great value to girls, so why ban it? Funkhouser said the effect on boys might be injurious.[227]

Samuel London countered with an impressive coup. He persuaded the Sociological Fund of the *Medical Review of Reviews,* the fund that had been behind the staging of *Damaged Goods,* to organize a private exhibition in Chicago. *Moving Picture World* sent along a reporter, James McQuade, who recorded the interchange that resulted:

"When the manager read from the stage a number of telegrams purporting to have been received from a distinguished Eastern sociologist, a bald-headed man in the audience exclaimed:

'That's a lie. No decent man would send such a telegram.'

'Put him out,' said an excited woman.

"An usher induced the man to refrain from further interruption.

'I think this motion play is too indecent to be shown even in this sort of private exhibition,' said Alderman James A. Kearns. 'Major Funkhouser performed a public service in prohibiting it.'

'There is nothing indecent so far as I can see,' said Mrs. Herman Landauer. 'Certain unsophisticated women ought to see it, but it ought not to be shown in theatres to all women.' "[228]

There is no record of it ever being shown in Chicago.

The very authenticity of his film caused trouble for London. The girls of the red-light district in El Paso, where scenes had been secretly photographed, protested to their mayor against the presentation of their pictures on the screens of New York. It was not the invasion of privacy which upset them; they were identified as denizens of the legal red-light district of New Orleans, and the ladies resented being connected with New Orleans even socially.[229]

Such revelations did nothing to help London and his beleaguered colleagues. In denying their application for a permanent injunction against the police in New York City, Judge Gavegan handed down the following opinion: "Some of the films [*sic*] depict scenes supposed to be enacted in a resort where women are subjected to involuntary degradation. As it is well known that to maintain such a place is of itself a criminal offense, I am unable to perceive why the public exhibition for money of scenes supposed to transpire therein should be entitled to the protection of a court of equity."[230]

A grand jury was shown the film, and soon afterward Samuel London, with his manager, the manager of the Bijou, and six others, appeared in court on a charge of holding an exhibition tending to corrupt morals.[231] London was convicted, but the jury recommended leniency. The judge said that what was really on trial were the vicious films, and these he consigned to oblivion. London and the others were released.[232]

Seeing the film today, one is struck by the matter-of-fact way it deals with its inflammatory subject. London set out to show the ramifications of the system "without exaggeration or fictional indulgence." In this respect, he was successful. It is oddly compelling to see characters who might have strayed from a Griffith Biograph film behaving as though caught by a cinéma vérité camera. Not all play realistically—the father, in particular, seems struck by a coronary when ordering his daughter out of his house. But perhaps the overemphasis was deliberate. London intended the picture to attack the "out of my house" policy of so many parents.[233]

London saw no lasting value to his film. In 1924 he sold the rights to his distributor, Harry White, who saw little value in it, either. White eventually sold the rights to James B. Leong for the sum of one dollar.

But as late as 1920, London was still paying for his film. A Mrs. Nettie Hechter sued him, charging that the film led one to believe that her husband's restaurant, which had been used as a location, was the headquarters of this traffic—coupled with the fact that she was also shown in the film. She won her case and was awarded $5,000.

THE HOUSE OF BONDAGE   Judge Gavegan, considering *The Inside of the White Slave Traffic,* declared that some people would pay to see the workings of a sewer. Such remarks proved mild when set against the reaction to *The House of Bondage.*

"It is impossible to describe the contents of this 'feature' without soiling the pages of a reputable journal," wrote W. Stephen Bush. "After seeing six reels of this vile and revolting stuff, I was glad to get out into the fresh air and any persistent attempt to recollect all the filthy details of the production might act as an emetic. How any human being can have the base effrontery to offer such a digest of dirt for public exhibition is utterly beyond my comprehension."[234]

Adapted from a book by Reginald W. Kauffman, and written and directed by Pierce Kingsley, the film was produced by the Photo Drama Motion Picture Company. The story concerned Mary Denbigh (Lottie Pickford, Mary's sister), a young girl rebelling against her tyrannical school, who yields to Max Crossman (Armand Cortez) and his promises to marry her. Crossman, a cadet, delivers Mary to a brothel run by Rose Legere (Sue Willis). Mary manages to escape with the help of a sympathetic client. She tries to get a regular job, but is pursued by her misfortune and is fired again and again. Her own parents throw her out. She returns to Rose Legere, who rejects her because of her physical condition.[235]

"To aid the reader to make an assay of the mental and moral calibre of the promoters of this infamy," wrote Stephen Bush, "I think it is well to set down an incident that occurred during the running of the 'feature.' The country girl, ruined by the procurer, is now walking the streets and she meets him and they go to a dive for a drink. The procurer is soon under the influence of the cheap alcohol and the girl says, via a title, 'Come on, Max, come to my room—you can sleep it off there.'

"One of the film men spoke to a colleague, 'Say, maybe this title is a bit raw.'

" 'Naw,' came the reply. 'That's all right.'

"Thus was the day saved for morality," concluded Mr. Bush. "If this sickening monstrosity is permitted to be publicly shown it will do more harm to the motion picture art than it is possible to calculate . . . whoever has charge of the screen where this mass of corruption was shown will do well to disinfect and fumigate the projection room . . . For the men whose 'avaricious enterprise' has made them lose sight of the commands of ordinary public decency we have as much contempt unmixed with pity. They really have brought reproach upon the human species."[236]

Far from deterring them, such remarks generally had a galvanizing effect on exhibitors. But *The House of Bondage* was a flop. The company had set much of the story in a brothel, and the courts had ruled that such scenes constituted an obscene exhibition, likely to corrupt the morals of the young.[237] So the picture had to be recut and "partly disinfected," and, to Bush's delight, it failed to elicit "the slightest response of encouragement" from the public.

Variety and *Moving Picture World* refused to advertise any more vice films after February 1914: "They are intended to stimulate and exploit the morbid interest in the harrowing details of a sickening and revolting aberration of the human soul."[238] The white slave cycle was about to take a new turn.

"I have been accustomed to seeing women exploited all my life," said settlement worker Mrs. Kate Waller Barrett, president of the National Florence Crittenton Mission, "and especially to seeing unfortunate girls exploited by unprincipled men and women and by greedy corporations; but in all this bloodsucking I have never seen anything to equal the exploitation of unfortunate girls by so-called philanthropic organizations and uplift movements, such as moving-picture shows, problem plays and so-called saviors of the white slave."[239]

VIRTUE TRIUMPHANT?

Streetwalking practically disappeared, wrote Benjamin Hampton, when five-cent shows spread across the United States in the thousands, "the girls finding in the movies amusement and recreation and a new outlook on life that propelled them away from the red-light districts and into homes of their own."[240]

It would be comforting to believe that the movies performed this astonishing feat—wiping out the oldest profession overnight—but the nickelodeons and the red-light districts passed into history at about the same time, being replaced by the neighborhood theatre and the question "Who's your neighbor?" Movies, and prostitution, had simply moved closer to home.

By bringing the vice problem to the attention of those who had been untouched by it, the white slave movies undoubtedly contributed to the drive to eliminate the red-light districts. But segregation disappeared primarily because of the vice commission reports and the resulting publicity. In 1913 alone, ten cities embarked on this program. One was San Francisco.

The city had been chosen as the site for the Panama-Pacific Exposition of 1915. To make it appear respectable enough for women and children to visit, the city fathers decided to close down the notorious Barbary Coast, even though the district had already changed, from a center of prostitution to a conglomeration of rowdy dance halls. "By 1910," wrote Herbert Asbury, "the City had gone dance crazy . . . There were three hundred saloons and dance halls crowded into six blocks centering on Pacific Street."[241]

A vice crusade was led by William Randolph Hearst's San Francisco *Examiner,* but the most significant campaign was the work of the Reverend Paul Smith, who declared that 25,000 people had a livelihood from vice in San Francisco—a figure embracing liquor trade employees as well as prostitutes, "and undoubtedly exaggerated for publicity purposes."[242]

The last night of the Barbary Coast was to be marked with a celebration. San Francisco film promoter Sol Lesser decided to make a film of the event and hired a young cameraman named Hal Mohr,[243] who later recalled: "I went to the Public Works department and got two of those street arc lamps. And I built a couple of things like hangman's scaffolds that I could hang these things on, and believe it or not, with these two arc lights down on Pacific Street, and down all these alleys

A film about juvenile delinquency, sponsored by a New York policewoman, Mary E. Hamilton, who was involved in the rehabilitation of wayward girls. Mrs. Hamilton played in the film, Lilies of the Streets, *1925, directed by Joseph Levering. This scene shows Virginia Lee Corbin as a wild young flapper brought to heel. (Museum of Modern Art)*

where the prostitutes' houses were, we'd haul these arcs and stand them up on their stands, and I'd run wires, connect them up somehow—I don't know where the hell I connected them to—but with these arc lights I photographed the last night of the Barbary Coast.''

Mohr was told there were about 10,000 prostitutes in the area, but according to Herbert Asbury, the number of girls employed in the dives ranged from 800 to 3,000: "Their principal duties were to dance and drink with the customers and to appear in the ensemble numbers of the shows. . . . It is doubtful if there were many prostitutes in the dance halls.''[244]

The prostitutes operated from the "fast houses." Said Mohr: "The main entrance was the parlor, where the girls displayed themselves, and then upstairs were the rooms where the work benches were, where they would take the men. And these fast houses operated, believe it or not, for a one-dollar fee. So for these shots, I went down on a Sunday morning, and I had photographed several shots of these streets, and had fellows going up the steps and ringing the bell and one thing and another. And finally, as if it were a cue, those upstairs windows of the places where I had the camera set up all opened and I was deluged by chamber pots being thrown at me to chase me out of there. So I picked up the camera and got the hell out of there in a hurry."[245]

The film was 1,400 feet long and sold for twelve cents a foot. The advertisements said that it had been made under police protection, but emphasized not so much the vice as the modern dances which had originated in the district: "See the famous Turkey Trot, Texas Tommy, Bunny Hug. See the negro dance halls with their own styles of dancing never before seen. Interior and exterior day and night scenes of the famous Midway Cafe where 500 dancing girls were employed. See Glimpses of Chinatown."[246]

The Last Night of the Barbary Coast was released by Lesser's Progressive Film Producing Company in November 1913. "Seldom has a two-reel feature aroused more interest among the critics," said *Moving Picture World*. "The distributor was greatly troubled about possible objections from a moral point of view. To ease his mind, he summoned the critics. They were on hand with rare but commendable promptness. Old and blasé critics who gossip and dally with cigarettes while an ordinary supply of pictorial art is being displayed on the screen, hung with mute and undivided attention to these two reels. It was only at the very last scene that they relaxed their moral vigilance and came to the conclusion that there was not an improper or illegitimate shock in the entire production—though some of the critics used very unparliamentary language in recording their opinion."[247]

The leading figure in the campaign to close the Barbary Coast, the Reverend Paul Smith, was a Methodist minister whose parish was close to the district. Four years after his success had been trumpeted across the nation in the newspapers, he found himself the author of a film called *The Finger of Justice* (1918), which purported to show why the Barbary Coast had to be closed down and how much good resulted.

Grace Marbury Sanderson, a scenario and short story writer, approached Smith and asked him and his church to produce it. According to Geoffrey Bell, the plot centered on "Crane Wilbur [the "Fighting Parson"], [who] sought to destroy a ring of vice operators whose aim was to exploit girls and drag them into the depths. Because of these efforts, the parson was framed by the vice boss. . . . The parson's zeal in exposing the vice ring was finally crowned by his marriage to a wealthy social worker, who had joined him in his cause."[248]

W. L. Shallenberger, who released the film through his Arrow Film Corporation, said that the picture, which was produced under Smith's direct supervision and directed by Louis W. Chaudet, contained not a foot of film that was offensive: "It depicts in a straightforward and dramatic manner incidents in the lives of the women who inhabited this vice district, events leading up to the vice raid; the part which corrupt politics played in the episode, and the tragic scenes following the ousting of hundreds of women who knew no other homes than the home of vice and corruption."[249]

The picture was promptly banned by the New York State board. Despite Smith's protests, the ban was not lifted for five years.[250]

The former lieutenant governor of Illinois, Barrett O'Hara, was largely responsible for *The Little Girl Next Door* (1916), which was based on a report by the Illinois Vice Commission.[251] *Moving Picture World* called it "a noxious effusion," exhibitors condemned it, and *Photoplay* called it "dirty flubdub paraded right by the censors wearing a sanctimonious false face called 'Vice Exposure.'" But it was so successful that O'Hara hired George Siegmann, an associate of D. W. Griffith's, to make not one but two more films, based on the same report.

It was the last straw for the National Board of Review, which announced that it would no longer pass white slave films. This failed to stop them. Pictures simply became more and more dependent on highly moralistic introductions (Katherine Karr calls them the "square-up"),[252] endorsements by respected figures of religion or medicine and, ideally, a presentation by an outstanding sociologist.

The Reverend Dr. Charles Parkhurst, whose investigations in the 1890s had created such a sensation, was placed in charge of the presentation of another 1916 film called *Is Any Girl Safe?* It was financed by Universal, hiding behind a company calling itself the Anti-Vice Motion Picture Corporation.[253] *Is Any Girl Safe?* was a five-reeler, written and directed by serial specialist Jacques Jaccard and featuring Raymond Nye and Mina Cunard. The most significant member of the cast was a self-confessed white slaver, Yusha Botwin, who was photographed making his confession in the district attorney's office.

"Botwin informed the District Attorney that a private plot in the Washington Cemetery, Brooklyn, was used by the New York Benevolent Association for the burial of the victims of the white slavers," said *Variety,* "and scenes of this are shown in the picture."[254]

Dr. Parkhurst and representatives of the New York *American,* who were behind the picture, were shown, in an opening sequence, discussing the vice racket. The story dealt with two cadets and revealed their system for trapping girls. One takes a girl to meet his mother, and drugs her. The other uses an accomplice to molest the girl on the street, so he can intervene and take her under his protection. The story develops into high melodrama when the first cadet interrupts the second to find his own sister being seduced. Both cadets subsequently realize how wrong they have been, and, after a full-scale battle in the brothel, broken up by the now statutory police raid, they marry their victims.

"It can't be done," said *Wid's,*[255] who found the film painfully slow and declared that were it not for the prestige given it by Dr. Parkhurst, it would have been passed over as a very ordinary picture.

A prostitute was the subject of *Who's Your Neighbor?,* a six-reeler of 1917. When her brothel is raided she moves into an apartment house and causes havoc in the lives of a young boy and his father. At the end she pleads to be put where she can do no more harm. Ben Grimm, in *Moving Picture World,* considered it "one of the most insidious, moral-destroying" films ever produced. "It will lower to the level of a bawdy house any theater in which it is shown. It reeks with a filthy sex element that struts across the screen in the sheep's clothing of alleged propaganda advocating the segregation of vice. It is good propaganda for procurers and their ilk, for it makes vice attractive."[256]

Directed by S. Rankin Drew, a promising young director who was killed while on active service in the war, *Who's Your Neighbor?* was written by Willard Mack. "The fact that the picture is well produced makes it even more harmful," said Grimm, "in the sense that a well dressed criminal is less likely to be suspected than a poorly dressed one."[257]

Like many others, Grimm was upset by the film's implication that the drives against the red-light districts had not eliminated vice. Prostitutes had merely scattered into tenements and apartment houses all over the cities, so the identity of one's neighbor was sometimes a suspicious mystery. The story, he admitted, was unusual and strong—"so strong that persons of refinement will turn away."[258] The New York *Dramatic Mirror* thought it "remarkably clever, powerful but cynical."[259]

Who's Your Neighbor? has the hallmarks of an important social film; let us hope this lost film will be rediscovered.

After the war, with the change in the political climate, vice films faded away. In routine dramatic films, it was usually possible to recognize a prostitute only by a coded signal—a girl placing a folded bill in her stocking[260] or an ambiguously phrased title, such as "A woman who has known no good man ... a man who has known no good woman."[261]

In the 1920s, the Hays Office kept any serious study of the subject at bay.[262] But one or two were made by brave, or unscrupulous, independent producers.

Lilies of the Streets (1925), written by Harry Chandlee and directed by Joseph Levering, was a return to the old days—and was even equipped with endorsements from prominent people. This story of a wild young flapper (Virginia Lee Corbin), mistaken for a prostitute, who ends up facing the death sentence, was sponsored by Mary E. Hamilton, a New York police matron with the rank of captain who was involved in the rehabilitation of what were then known as "wayward girls." Mrs. Hamilton supervised the writing of the scenario and played herself in the picture, saving the flapper from death by persuading the true culprit to confess.

"I got the Police Commissioner to lend me for this job, because there are evils which can only be remedied through publicity," she said. "I especially want to show up the wrong of mixing first offenders with hardened crooks in the detention pens, before they are brought to trial."[263]

Photoplay was more cynical. "Anyone who believes the film was made as an altruistic warning to keep good girls out of dance halls is entitled to free admission."[264]

THE RED KIMONO   One of the strangest attempts at a serious social study, *The Red Kimono* (1926), also had a strange history. It was made by Mrs. Wallace Reid. Having lost her husband under tragic circumstances (see pages 106–09), she embarked on a crusading film, *Human Wreckage* (1923), which made

The Red Kimono, *1925. A scene, missing from surviving prints, of Priscilla Bonner, as Gabrielle Darley, in jail. (National Film Archive)*

enough money to set her up as an independent producer. And she made *The Red Kimono* as part of her "Sins of the World" series.[265]

Why did she make it? An exposé of the curent prostitution racket might have fulfilled her purpose as a cinematic reformer. But an exposé of the white slave traffic as it had existed nearly a decade earlier was, to put it mildly, a curious exercise. The story was set in 1917, but no attempt was made to depict the period. The cars were current, the fashions those of the twenties.

In a 1976 interview, Mrs. Reid frequently referred to "dirty films"—or exploitation films—and while she did not admit to making any, she did say, "A lot of fancy business goes on. They sell a picture and they haven't left a thing with the audience. But that's beside the point. We're making entertainment—we have to be forgiven for some of that."[266]

The film was set in Storyville,* the red-light district of New Orleans that had been shut down in November 1917.[268] Was *The Red Kimono* a serious study of prostitution or a thinly disguised exploitation film?

The leading actress was Priscilla Bonner,[269] who said that Mrs. Reid had emerged from her tragedy with universal respect and admiration: "She had two small children to support and no money, but great strength of character and spiritual strength. She was a Davenport, and she had friends who came to her aid. One was Thomas Ince . . . [and] Adela Rogers St. Johns was a close friend. She had been a police reporter for Mr. Hearst. A few years before, there was a sensational murder trial. Mr. Hearst sent Adela to cover it.

"A young and lovely looking girl had shot her lover. She had no money and no high-powered attorney. She took the stand and told her story—the truth, as it happened. She was acquitted. Adela suggested they use this. It was another plea for compassion. Adela wrote the story. The truth was so dramatic it needed no changes. They told it as it happened. The only fiction was the chauffeur, whom the girl marries in the picture."[270]

Dorothy Arzner, a film editor soon to become a director, wrote the scenario. The director was a newcomer, Walter Lang (who later made *The King and I*). He co-directed with Mrs. Reid at the old Fine Arts studios, where Griffith had made his masterpieces.[271] They worked on a very low budget.

The Red Kimono opened, like a nickelodeon morality play, with a brief allegorical scene of Hades, the shades begging for mercy. Then we fade in to Mrs. Reid in what is supposed to be the file room of a daily newspaper, but whose book-lined walls are all too obviously painted.

In a rare camera movement, we track over her shoulder to a volume dated "1917." She opens it to reveal a headline about the Gabrielle Darley case. This true story is not unique, she explains, but is occurring even now to hundreds of unfortunate girls.

The film uses Gabrielle's court appearance to tell her story in flashback. The moralizing tone is reflected in Malcolm Stuart Boylan's titles, which are as pious as Victorian samplers. "Home is a place where a mother smiles at children. All others are guest houses. . . ." "Three little words—'I love you'—sometimes a sacred prayer, sometimes a cowardly lie."

As a young schoolteacher in a small southern town, Gabrielle Darley attracts the attention of Howard (Carl Miller[272]), a nattily dressed ladies' man. She accepts his offer of marriage and goes to live with him in New Orleans. The manner in which she is lured into white slavery in Storyville is not illustrated in the surviving version, which is incomplete. But after "two years of bondage, sorrowful, sordid," we find Gabrielle in her crib. She reacts with horror when the doorbell rings. She stands symbolically across the door, arms stretched against the threat, until, realizing the hopelessness of her situation, she removes her wedding ring and powders her nose.

Abandoned by Howard, Gabrielle follows him to Los Angeles and discovers him in a jewelry store, in the act of buying a wedding ring for someone else. She shoots him, and as he dies she reveals to us that she still loves him.[273]

---

*Named, to his disgust, for Alderman Story, who set the area aside for prostitution in 1897.[267]

The jury acquits her, but she refuses to return to New Orleans. The war is on, and she decides the only way to erase the past is through service to her country. She joins the Red Cross.

A wealthy society matron, Mrs. Fontaine (Virginia Pearson, the former vamp), befriends Gabrielle. She is interested only in her publicity value and invites her friends to meet her. Their questions are prurient: "Do you poor dears have to—?" (The titles are cautious.) Gabrielle's situation is symbolized by a dissolve to a kitten surrounded by hostile cats.

She forms a close relationship with the chauffeur, Frederick (Theodore von Eltz), but soon the society matron tires of her. "You lasted longer than most," she is told. "The bank robber only lasted a week." Gabrielle finds herself on the street again. Branded by her past—a huge "A" sizzles over her breast in one encounter[274]—she cannot get a job and decides to return to New Orleans. Fred races to the station to stop her, misses the train, and follows on the next. Gabrielle is now set to face her Gethsemane. No sooner has she arrived in New Orleans than a former client (George Siegmann) tries to rape her. Trying to escape, she is knocked down by a car and taken to the hospital. Fred searches the red-light district, but eventually abandons all hope and volunteers for the army.

Gabrielle recovers and becomes a cleaner at the hospital. The flu epidemic is raging, and Fred, now an ambulance driver, is detailed to take victims to the hospital. He and Gabrielle are reunited. But not before a last dose of morality. Having had sexual relations with countless men, Gabrielle now refuses to consummate her love for Fred until he returns from the war.

Mrs. Wallace Reid reappears and concludes the picture with a final plea for tolerance and education for wayward girls.

Historian Anthony Slide points out that not once is there any condemnation of Gabrielle or any suggestion that she might have chosen another life-style.[275] This is true; if only the treatment had been more skillful.

The picture suffers from a lack of realism, mainly in its art direction. It would have been a relatively simple matter to re-create the red-light district on location in a rundown part of town; instead, it is reproduced on an unconvincing set. Perhaps Mrs. Reid remembered the lawsuits that followed the first spate of white slave pictures, when owners of restaurants used as locations took companies to court and won. The trouble with this film is that all the other exteriors were shot on location, and this blatant artificiality destroys conviction.

The picture was not produced by a member of the MPPDA, so it bypassed Will Hays. It was savaged by the censors, however. It was subjected to no less than twenty-five cuts in Pennsylvania, where the censors changed the entire plot, for good measure, by ordering all the titles to be reshot.[276]

Although *Variety* thought the film rather well directed, it added that "Mrs. Reid . . . may believe she is doing something for the fallen women in turning out a picture of this sort. But the chances are that she will do tremendous harm to the picture business as a whole and herself in particular because she sponsors it by permitting it to continue."[277]

Said the *New York Times:* "There have been a number of wretched pictures on Broadway during the last year, but none seem to have quite reached the low level of *The Red Kimono,* a production evidently intended to cause weeping, wailing and gnashing of teeth. Possibly it might accomplish its purpose if the theatre doors were locked, but so long as one knows one can get out of the building, it is another matter."[278]

The most ill-advised action of the people involved in this picture was to retain the actual name of the leading character. Gabrielle Darley had recovered from her experiences and had remarried. One day she and her husband went to a movie—*The Red Kimono.* She sued Mrs. Reid, and she won.

"She took everything," said Priscilla Bonner, "including her home."[279]

Chapter Three

DRUGS

His Blind Power, *1913. A* Lubin
*production with Romaine Fielding
(right) as writer, director, and lead.
(Robert S. Birchard Collection)*

THE FOREWORD to the script for *Human Wreckage*, written in 1923, declared that habit-forming drugs were the gravest menace confronting America:

"Its victims, numbering hundreds of thousands, are scattered throughout the length and breadth of the land. They range from children to old men and women and embrace the entire social scale from the dock laborer to the bank president. Every profession, every walk of life, has contributed its quota to Dope and the sacrifice continues daily.

"Immense quantities of morphine, heroin and cocaine are yearly smuggled into America across the Canadian and Mexican borders. The dope traffic has grown alarmingly within the past ten years and is now of gigantic proportions."[1]

In 1900, if you wanted a stimulant or a painkiller, you simply went to your corner druggist and bought opium or its derivative, morphine; the cost was a few pennies.[2] During the Civil War, injured soldiers had been given morphine and found it so effective they continued using it after the war, recommending it to friends and relatives.[3] Addiction spread so rapidly it became known as "the American problem." Yet if you, like one out of every 400 Americans,[4] became an addict, few people noticed because your supply route was assured. You were no more of a social outcast than is a diabetic today.

No laws banned the sale of narcotics, and few people objected to their use on moral grounds. Opium joints were the object of curiosity and opprobrium because the dens were operated by the Chinese and the whole thing was so thoroughly un-American; nevertheless, tour guides included them in their itineraries, and several films were made about them, including *Chinese Opium Den* (1894), a Kinetoscope loop, and *Rube in an Opium Joint,* made for the Mutoscope in 1905, which showed a slumming tour visiting a Chinatown den. (Indeed, many were operated purely for tourists.) For patent medicine manufacturers (the largest single user of newspaper advertising space), addictive drugs were ideal ingredients, as they ensured that customers returned for more. It was only when muckraking journalists began to reveal, in 1904, that infants were being stunted or killed by the opium in patent medicines that some states passed laws to curb its distribution.

In 1898, a German researcher had produced a wonderful new substance called heroin from a morphine base. It was introduced under that name as a cough suppressant by Bayer & Company. Everyone believed it was nonaddictive, and it was even used to cure morphine addiction.[5] Doctors prescribed it for birth pains (the mother in Eugene O'Neill's *Long Day's Journey into Night* becomes addicted in this way). Not for years were its addictive properties suspected.

Coca-Cola, whose formula involved the use of both the coca leaf (source of

Agents burning opium in front of the San Francisco City Hall (under construction) in 1914. Frame enlargement from a newsreel in the Bay Area Archive. (Bert Gould)

cocaine) and the cola nut (which contains caffeine), was introduced in Georgia in 1886 as a headache remedy. In 1906, after the passage of the first Pure Food and Drug Act, the federal government investigated Coca-Cola; the manufacturers faced criminal charges for adulteration and misbranding.[6] The company eventually managed to outmaneuver the Supreme Court, and it was never proven that Coca-Cola contained cocaine. But if it had, it would not have stood alone. In 1909, thirty-nine soft drinks, available to children, were laced with the drug.[7]

And the case gave rise to one of the first films to show the danger of the drugs, D. W. Griffith's *For His Son* (Biograph, 1912): "A physician, through his love for his only son, whom he desires to see wealthy, is tempted to sacrifice his honor by concocting a soft drink containing cocaine, knowing how rapid and powerful is the hold obtained by cocaine. . . . The drink meets with tremendous success . . . but his son cultivates a liking for it. The father discovers his son's weakness too late, for he soon becomes a hopeless victim of the drug."[8]

Griffith and author Emmett Campbell Hall called the drink Dopokoke and gave it the slogan "For That Tired Feeling." The son (Charles West) eventually dies and the plight of the father (Charles Hill Mailes) is summed up in the closing title: "He did not care whom he victimized until he found the result of dishonor at his own door."

With the passage of the Opium Exclusion Act in 1909, opium smuggling became big business in the United States. In 1912, Selig made a film about it called *The Opium Smugglers,* describing the operations on the border between Montana and Canada. The Harrison Narcotics Act was passed in 1914. But it was 1913, the year of the white slave hysteria, which marked the beginning of the flood of drug pictures. A three-reeler called *Slaves of Morphine* was released that year by Leibow's Features (probably the Danish *Morfinisten* [1911]). And in San Francisco, the chief inspector for the State Board of Pharmacy broke up a morbid tableau. A China-town guide had rounded up a group of "derelict dope fiends" for a film to be made by a local picture concern. The addicts were each paid a dollar, supplied with "hop," and filmed injecting it into their arms. The scene was described as "very realistic—particularly so after the pharmacy official arrived."[9]

Ordinary moviegoers, few of whom were aware of the drug problem, were astonished by these pictures. But the trade press took exception to them. "While the police are lenient," said *Variety*, "and well known but weak-minded people will endorse 'vice pictures,' feature films like *The Cocaine Traffic* will be publicly exhibited for the prime purpose of making money for the promoters, while at the same time spreading an unhealthy education amongst the young."[10] A film like that, in a small town, would corrupt the morals of the entire place, *Variety* added.

The Cocaine Traffic (1914), better known as *The Drug Terror,* was directed for the Lubin Film Company by Harry Myers, who played the drunken millionaire in Chaplin's *City Lights.* It was written by Lawrence McCloskey "with the assistance and approval of the Director of Public Safety and the Police Department of the City of Philadelphia." The story was strong stuff: Spike Smith, a cocaine sniffer, induces his former boss, Andrews, to become a dealer on the side. Dealers were now regarded as worse than addicts: "Low as Spike Smith had sunk, Andrews had now fallen to a greater depth."[11] Spike's wife leaves him, and he becomes a drifter in the Tenderloin, where coke sellers are plentiful. When a police raid cuts off his source of supply, he returns to Andrews, now a wealthy cocaine king, whose daughter is about to marry Hastings, a society man. Spike acquires cocaine and for good measure hooks Hastings—who passes on the habit to his new wife. Andrews has to take his daughter into a sanitarium and watch her suffering. Hastings sinks to the level of derelict and visits Andrews one night in search of the drug. After a fight, he kills the cocaine king. The house burns down with both men in it.[12]

Variety called it six reels of misery: "When one sees the endorsements and reads the press stuff on these 'vice films' to 'save souls' it is almost laughable, when the self-same pictures are sending more souls to hell at 25 cents each at the box office than were ever captured by all cadets."[13]

These drug films needed an aura of respectability to get them past the censor boards. Medical people provided endorsements because they felt that any propaganda against drugs was worthwhile, but they did not always come cheap. For the use of his name in connection with *The Cocaine Traffic,* Dr. Frederick H. Robinson, president of the *Medical Review of Reviews,* was said to have been promised 5 percent of the gross.[14] When the picture opened in Detroit, its press agent announced that Dr. Robinson would make a personal appearance, but there was some dispute about his commission and he refused to come. A Detroit paper got wind of this and sent him a wire. Dr. Robinson wired back to stop the use of his name. The newspaper attacked the film, the police condemned it, and the effect of the row on the box office was a loss for the film of $2,175.[15]

The Drug Traffic, made by Eclair, was a 1914 two-reeler which reflected the change in the law regarding the sale of narcotics. The synopsis is an eye-opener:

"Johnson, a druggist, plies an illicit trade in cocaine and morphine, which he sells slyly over his drug counter to selected clientele. In his richly furnished office, the head of the Kurson Chemical Company (Alec B. Francis) counts the receipts from the Kurson Consumption Cure, a patent medicine which contains a large amount of morphine. He also sells morphine to Johnson."

Johnson's daughter, Lucille (Belle Adair), suffers severe headaches, and she and her fiancé, James Young (Stanley Walpole?), drop into the drugstore for a remedy. There they see morphine being sold to a young boy. They follow him to a hovel, where they find his mother struggling in agony on the floor. Beside her, Lucille sees a bottle of the Kurson Consumption Cure. When she sniffs the bottle she gets her first smell of the intoxicating drug. The police are called. The old woman, deprived of her source, dies, and Lucille and James take charge of the boy.

Lucille becomes an addict herself and sneaks out one night to her father's home to obtain morphine. The boy follows her and reports to James. Johnson is arrested, but nothing can be done for Lucille, who collapses in the street and dies at the police station. Distraught with grief, her fiancé swears to kill the man at whose door he can lay the crime.

At the prison, Johnson points to Kurson, who has been summoned by James, and says, "There is your man." The revolver falls from James's nervous hand, and he falls across the body of Lucille as they lead Kurson to a cell.[16]

The United States discovered that it had become the most drug-afflicted of all nations, and sweeping legislation was planned to stamp out cocaine once and for all. But while newspapers gave more space to drugs than virtually anything else, picture people were even more likely to exploit the situation. Herman Lieb, who had written and acted in a vaudeville sketch about drug addiction, adapted it as a six-reeler called *Dope*. It was criticized for its sensationalism and for its vice scenes—a middle-class mother forced by her cocaine habit to become a street-walker.

A husband becomes an addict by taking headache powders in *The Derelict* (1914), a Kalem two-reeler written by James Horne and directed by George Melford. The powders are administered by a false friend (Douglas Gerrard), who has his eye on the man's wife. The picture was unusual in that for once there was a happy ending—the false friend has a change of heart, the husband fights off the drug habit with the help of a sympathetic doctor, and his married life picks up where it broke off.

The Secret Sin (1915), written by Margaret Turnbull and directed by Frank Reicher for Famous Players, featured Blanche Sweet in a double role as twin sisters. Grace experiments in a Chinatown opium den and falls ill; when a doctor prescribes morphine she becomes addicted. Her sister tries to rehabilitate her, but Grace conceals her supply and even makes out Edith is the addict. Technically, the film shows no advance on the old Biographs, but it is full of startling facts. Fake prescriptions are provided by an uptown "resort." When it is raided, the prosperous clients are driven to slumming in Chinatown, where they must distinguish between the fake dens, set up for tourists, and the real thing.

The New York *Dramatic Mirror* thought *The Secret Sin* a good picture, even though it lacked suspense and the action was slow. The reviewer criticized one scene in particular: "It is doubtful whether the fake doctor's prescription calling for morphine would ever have passed the scrutiny of a reputable druggist."[17] Alas, the film did not have to resort to fiction; this kind of thing happened every day.

Once it became clear that drugs were a box-office draw, pictures which had nothing to do with the subject dropped dope into the plot in the hope of higher grosses. *Bondwomen* (1915), directed for George Kleine by Edwin August, was a study of the average American wife, showing the humiliation that may be caused by the lack of an independent bank account. "A secondary theme has been introduced showing the effects of cocaine, and much footage is used up in the exposition of a new cure for this soul-destroying habit—which is very fine, except that it has no basis of medical fact."[18]

These were the days when a director would see an article in the newspaper and sit down and write a script about it, as John Noble did when he read about the addiction of messenger boys to cocaine. The result was *Black Fear* (1916). Although he praised it as "a mighty good picture," the reviewer for the New York *Dramatic Mirror* called the story "exceedingly complicated." It opened with the statutory allegorical scene in Hell, then showed in detail how messenger boys doing night work are kept awake with small doses of cocaine; soon they are confirmed addicts and cannot live without the drug. The film also showed how boys were used to obtain the drugs and portrayed the manner in which they were forced to become "intimately acquainted with all forms of vice."[19]

The impact of these crusading pictures was diminished by luridly melodramatic drug films such as *The Devil's Profession* (1915), an English production in which a doctor runs a sanitarium whose patients are kept under the influence of drugs. One of his patients eventually turns on him and blinds him with vitriol.[20]

Originally called *Cosette, The Rise of Susan* (1916) was a World Film Production starring Clara Kimball Young. It was written by Frances Marion, impressively photographed by Hal Young, and adequately directed by S. E. V. Taylor. The surviving print has surprisingly little punch, despite its theme—perhaps because three reels are missing, but more probably because the acting by Young as Susan is uninspired. It is a story of a girl who poses as a countess, falls for a wealthy young man, and loses him to another girl, Ninon (Marguerite Skirwin), a drug addict. Nevertheless, it contains fascinating glimpses into this taboo subject: Ninon possesses a beautifully bound book which, when opened, proves to contain her hypodermic needles. When her mother is confronted with it, she insists it belongs to her physician and is deeply insulted by the suggestion that her daughter might be an addict. The film demonstrates that drugs lead to insanity. Susan becomes a nurse and looks after Ninon, who attacks her with a pair of scissors and flings herself out of the window. Susan is blinded, yet still wins the wealthy young man.[21]

The trade press detested it. *Wid's* described it as a hackneyed melodrama, the story "painfully ancient," with far too many titles, "the effect being at times of reading the plot rather than seeing someone trying to act it."[22]

Drug films became a glut on the market, and when *The Devil's Needle* came out in 1916, *Variety* greeted it glumly: "The drug story has been so often sheeted

Howard Gaye, Tully Marshall, Marguerite Marsh, and Norma Talmadge in
The Devil's Needle, *1916.*

there is nothing left for it.''[23] Yet this was a relatively sober and compelling story, showing how easy it was to become dependent on narcotics. Produced at Fine Arts, written by Chester Withey and Roy Somerville and directed by Withey (his first film), it starred Norma Talmadge and Tully Marshall, who was picked for this role because of his highly acclaimed portrayal of the dope fiend in Clyde Fitch's play *The City.* In *The Devil's Needle,* he plays John Minton, ''an artist of the modern school''—neurotic, chain-smoking, constantly dissatisfied. His model, Renée (Norma Talmadge), relieves the tedium of posing with an occasional injection. (When the film was reissued in 1923, a title explained her addiction as a habit contracted during wartime service as a nurse!)

When the artist sees what she is doing, he is fascinated and appalled. ''You don't know its advantages,'' she says. ''It kindles the fires of genius—it is inspiration ready-made.'' Against his better judgment, he tries it and finds he works with greater intensity. He falls for, and marries, another model, to Renée's dismay, but soon becomes an almost hopeless addict. Worse, he tries to addict his wife, and eventually attempts to kill her. He is taken for a cure in the country, where hard work and fresh air restore his health. His wife is captured by gangsters and Renée sacrifices herself that the couple may be reunited. *Wid's* thought this appropriate, since she hooked Minton in the first place.[24]

The underworld scenes, shot in the Plaza district, contain the most graphic coverage of the slums of Los Angeles of any surviving picture. But *Variety* had nothing but scorn for the idea that the artist could kick the habit with a trip to the country. "If it's true that hard manual labor will kill the taste for drugs, Chester Withey . . . deserves to have a niche in the film discovery hall."[25]

The Ohio board of censors rejected *The Devil's Needle* in its entirety on the grounds of its subject. Informed of its value as an agent of reform, the board confessed it had made a mistake. The picture was passed—in its entirety—and opened in Cleveland.[26] (Such occasions were extremely rare in the history of censorship!)

Fine Arts contributed another story to the drug saga, although they disowned it. *The Mystery of the Leaping Fish* (1916) has become a cult film because of the way it deals with cocaine. D. W. Griffith is supposed to have written the story, although the film credits it to Tod Browning.

Tod Browning sounds more likely; this is one of the most bizarre films ever produced. Perhaps if he had directed it, the result might have made more sense. What is surprising is to find Douglas Fairbanks in the lead. His costar was Bessie Love (who would later star in a more significant drug film, *Human Wreckage*). Alma Rubens, who became a drug addict in real life, also played in it. Intended as a parody of Sherlock Holmes, with Fairbanks playing a crackpot detective called Coke Ennyday, it resembled nothing so much as a home movie shot in the style of Mack Sennett. What makes it of interest today is the fact that anyone could find anything funny in the subject of drug addiction. Coke Ennyday injects himself

Mystery of the Leaping Fish, 1916. Gag shot with Douglas Fairbanks as Coke Ennyday, a cocaine-addicted parody of Sherlock Holmes, and Bessie Love. On the right, the McCarthy brothers, who devised the "flying fish."

frequently and literally vibrates with glee. Fairbanks was hyperactive anyway; D. W. Griffith thought him afflicted with St. Vitus's dance and felt he belonged at Keystone. This picture looks like some kind of awful revenge, for it was released as a two-reeler under the Keystone brand. Surprisingly, it was made twice—once by William Christy Cabanne, who was fired, and then by John Emerson, who reshot the entire picture with assistance from Tod Browning.[27] Anita Loos wrote the titles.

The story revolves around a plot to smuggle drugs into the country hidden inside inflatable rubber fish. The special-effects man, J. P. McCarthy, had invented six-foot-long fish with rubber fins which could be used by bathers for floating, sitting, or swimming. (The idea was decades ahead of its time—at least McCarthy and his brother had the foresight to patent it.)

Douglas Fairbanks disliked the picture so much he tried to have it withdrawn, and one can only sympathize with him.

"The film's basic idea is confused," wrote Arthur Lennig. "Ennyday (an addict) prevents illegal importation of the very thing which he is addicted to. If this inconsistency is supposed to be ironic or humorous, the effect does not succeed."[28]

Fine Arts was one apex of the Triangle Film Corporation; another was Kay-Bee, managed by Thomas Ince, whose contribution to the drug controversy was *The Dividend* (1916). Written by C. Gardner Sullivan and directed by Walter Edwards, it starred Charles Ray, revered for his performance in the Civil War drama *The Coward*. *Variety* thought his playing in *The Dividend* far superior and stamped it as the highest kind of screen art.

"John Steele (William H. Thompson) is head of a large realty corporation who squeezes his poor tenants and cuts wages in his factory. He is a widower with an only son (Charles Ray), but is too busy even to attend his boy's graduation. The boy comes home and asks his father for a job. Steele scoffs and offers him $3.00 a week to sweep out the office. The boy is serious-minded and argues that with his education he is entitled to a better opportunity. Steele hands him a check and laughingly tells him to go out and play. While out doing the town one night, the youngster visits an opium joint and becomes addicted. When Steele finds out, he throws his son out of the house.

" 'If you had been a real father to me I wouldn't have become a dope fiend. Did you ever give me any encouragement?' "[29]

The father, obsessed with his business, continues to accumulate wealth. But there comes a time when he yearns to see his son, and his wish is granted in the grimmest fashion—the boy is brought home after a street brawl, a hopeless wreck. He eventually dies.

"The scene between father and son as the boy regains consciousness and finds himself in his father's arms will bring a lump into the throat of a mummy," said *Variety*.[30]

Said the New York *Dramatic Mirror*: "The idea of the millionaire building a mission to salve his conscience, and his heavenly attitude when he is to speak at the opening of it, does much to give irony to the picture, and it has been so well directed that this and other big scenes of dramatic character at most eclipse the somewhat disgusting details of the gutter."[31]

Drugs produce hallucinations; perhaps the men who made films about them

Charles Ray and Ethel Ullman in The Dividend, *1916. (National Film Archive)*

should have tried some. Harry Pollard demonstrated a degree of cinematic flair in his *The Devil's Assistant* (1917), which featured his wife, Margarita Fischer, but when it came to the allegorical scenes his imagination deserted him. Written by J. Edward Hungerford, the film laid great store by its hallucinations, or visions as they were usually called in pictures. But instead of the bizarre and surreal landscape of dreams, Pollard evokes only stock-company scenery for his images of Hell.

It is night and a storm breaks out, the lightning achieved by the simple expedient of scratching on the negative. But now something fresh; a car bounces toward us, its headlights glaring, the rain streaming past the light in silver rivulets. As the car passes the camera, the heavy cable supplying the arc lights in the headlamps can be seen trailing behind it. Never mind; the next scene, in a wayside shack, is lit by the headlights. A black chauffeur watches the attempted seduction of Miss Fischer by an evil doctor (Monroe Salisbury), a drug pusher. When she realizes his intentions, she throws a candle at him. The darkness returns and the scene is lit by lightning flashes, and we can see the doctor advancing, the girl holding a chair—a fight—the flashing almost fast enough to induce hallucinations on its own. At length, a thunderbolt hits the shack and the roof collapses. A skeleton on horseback gathers up the girl and rides through the night sky. A bearded boatman rows them across the Styx, where stray souls struggle in the fog-shrouded water. Cerberus, the three-headed dog, guards the gates to Hades. "Out of the Abyss of Darkness comes the Promising Light of Hope," as the girl is rescued and she and her husband (Jack Mower) pose against the rising sun as they depart to start life anew.

"As soon as this thing started," wrote Wid Gunning, "it was painfully obvious that we were in for five reels of tortured heroine, and, believe me, we got it with all the frills." He warned that audiences were liable to find it excruciatingly funny, especially the director's conception of Hell. "Along with other weird things, he had a big dog with a couple of bum heads hung on either side of his real head, and—oh boy!—if they don't get a laugh it'll be because no one in your community has a sense of humor."[32]

Such films feared to tell the truth about the drug traffic. One film which made a valiant effort in this direction was *A Romance of the Underworld* (1918), Frank A. Keeney's first venture into production. It was essentially a melodrama about a girl fresh from the convent who joins her brother on the Lower East Side. A young reform lawyer opens an investigation which reveals that the brother is the lieutenant of a notorious drug trafficker. The story was based on a 1911 play by Paul Armstrong, who also wrote *The Escape*,[33] and the film was shot on location in the streets of the Lower East Side, in Chinatown, and at the Tombs prison with its Bridge of Sighs. It was directed by James Kirkwood.

The film was taken to Sing Sing and shown to the inmates, who applauded it warmly. A review written by a prisoner indicates how close this lost picture came to suggesting the involvement of municipal politicians in the drug traffic: "The two greatest evils in the world today are Prussian 'kultur' and the 'dope' habit, and although the former sooner or later will surely be crushed, the latter will continue to wreck the minds and bodies of men and kill their souls just as long as drugs can be obtained in an unlawful manner. The theme . . . portrays in a vivid manner the power of the ward 'Boss' that makes possible the existence of this horrible menace."

Frank Keeney said he valued this review more than any other. "If such an audience cannot size this picture up at its true worth, no audience can."[34]

The Devil's Assistant, *1917.*
Margarita Fischer as a woman
addicted to drugs after the loss
of her baby. (Wichita State
University Library)

The drug-film cycle came to an end about this time, when, with America at war, such critical subjects were felt to be unpatriotic. In 1918, narcotics clinics were opened to ensure addicts a steady supply under medical supervision and to wipe out drug peddling. In New York, on some days, the lines of addicts extended for several city blocks. Newspapers wrote sensational reports, public opinion was outraged, and the moral police rose up to seal the doom of the clinics.

In December 1914, President Woodrow Wilson had signed the Harrison Narcotic Act, which specified that everyone involved in narcotic transactions, except the customers, had to register with the government. In 1919, a Supreme Court decision exploded like a time bomb, revealing an aspect of the act few had taken seriously: the provision that unregistered persons could purchase drugs only upon a doctor's prescription and that that prescription had to be for legitimate medical use. The provision destroyed what peace of mind remained to most addicts, among whom were many casualties of war.

"As a direct consequence of [the act], the medical profession abandoned the drug addict," wrote Troy Duster.[35] Doctors who continued to prescribe were arrested, prosecuted, fined, or imprisoned. The addict, isolated from legal sources, was forced to turn to the underworld.

The same year, the Volstead Act outlawed drugs as well as alcohol. The narcotics clinics were closed between 1920 and 1922, and the number of arrests for narcotic offenses rose from 888 in 1918 to 10,297 in 1925.[36] In 1922, the Jones-Miller Act established a Narcotics Control Board and a five-year sentence for pushers.[37] And such drug films as reached the public screens were invariably condemned for "educating" an innocent public.[38] Heroin, easily prepared and transported, leaped into prominence on the black market. By 1929, it was estimated there were between 1 and 4 million addicts consuming $5 million worth of drugs annually.[39]

"The American problem" was now out of control. It had already begun to take its toll of the motion picture industry itself.

HUMAN WRECKAGE   Dedicated to the memory of "A MAN who fought the leering curse of powdered death and, dying, was victorious," *Human Wreckage* was made as a direct result of the Wallace Reid case.

Wallace Reid was the son of playwright and film director Hal Reid, who died less than three years before him. He was on the stage with his parents at the age of four, although he was later sent away to prep school. Good-looking, with an easy charm, he was talented in many areas. He was well-read, eager, and energetic. But he remained a dilettante; he painted in oils (adequately), he wrote poetry (which he showed to very few), he studied chemistry (for a while), and he played (quite well) a number of musical instruments. Acting was at the end of his list of accomplishments, and, while he enjoyed it, he was not particularly interested in it. He was far more enthusiastic about directing. In the early days, he was able to combine scriptwriting and directing with acting, but soon he was such a favorite with audiences that he was forced to concentrate on acting. "I'm looking forward to the day when I'm fat, forty and directing," he used to say.[40]

So popular was Reid as the jaunty, sporting young American that Famous Players–Lasky rushed him from picture to picture—many of them cheaply made—and he turned out more films in the last two years of his life than any other male star.[41] It was almost as if the front office knew the end was at hand.

Reid was the kind of young man immortalized by F. Scott Fitzgerald. He should have had a large house on Long Island and unlimited leisure. Yet when he first came into pictures, in 1910, he was known as the most industrious person on the lot, practicing with cameras, working on scripts, performing stunts, until he was as much of an all-rounder with film as on the sports field.

According to his friends, his greatest weakness was his unfailing good nature. He was unusually generous, giving away much of the money he had earned, helping people in trouble. He was essentially a child, fascinated by toys such as motorcars and forgetting appointments if he became involved in something more interesting. He was the life of the party, even if it meant staying up until five, with a hard day ahead, because he could not bring himself to ask his guests to leave.

"They would laugh at you if you told them I ever had a serious thought," Reid told Herbert Howe, "but just between you and me I'd like to do something worthwhile some day—give something to the world beside my face and figure."[42]

He liked motion picture work, but detested the parts he was assigned by Famous Players. He wanted something more demanding. According to cameraman Percy Hilburn, he grew bored and listless, neglecting his real talent;[43] but this may have been the effect of his addiction.

Precisely how Reid became addicted is hard to ascertain. Close friends remained guarded. "I shall not attempt," said one, "to tell when and why Wally started on his fatal journey. A number of circumstances brought about his trouble."[44] Later, an explanation surfaced which was so straightforward one wonders why it was not in circulation at the time of his death. On location in the High Sierras for *Valley of the Giants* (1919), the company train was wrecked and Reid was injured. Nevertheless, he assisted in the rescue operation and was the last to receive medical attention. Thereafter, he suffered from blinding headaches, and his back also hurt. A doctor gave him morphine. He was confined to bed for three months, the morphine continued, and he became an addict.

The only thing wrong with this story is the bit about Reid as hero. Alice Terry, who as Alice Taafe worked on the picture, remembered the accident and an account that appeared in such newspapers as the Los Angeles *Herald*.[45] It was nearly fatal—a caboose full of people somersaulted down an embankment—and a number of the cast and crew were injured. Reid was badly cut in the back of the neck. Said Alice Terry, "They gave him veronal in milk so he could sleep, because he was quite badly hurt and had a lot of stitches. After that picture, I heard he was still taking it, and then of course. . . ."[46]

Reid's wife acknowledged the accident and admitted that he had been given morphine, but she denied that he then became an addict. This did not occur, she said, until 1921, when he went to New York to make *Peter Ibbetson* (released as

Forever), the most difficult role of his career. He fell ill, and when he realized the extent to which he was delaying the production and adding to the cost, he became worried. "It was his grim determination and his good nature which prompted him on. To nerve him for his daily and arduous task, the New York physician gave him morphine."[47]

Mrs. Reid's insistence that he was given morphine not in Hollywood but in New York arouses one's suspicions. Was this something she agreed upon with Hays and the studio heads? Pinning the "blame" on an anonymous New York physician would deflect it from the studio doctor.

Karl Brown, a cameraman on other Reid vehicles, had no doubt of the studio's involvement: "The picture was nearly finished, but there was no way of shooting around Wally. He just had to be had. So the company, not wanting to lose the investment entirely, sent a doctor with an ample supply of morphine to the location, where he injected Wally to the extent that he could feel no pain whatsoever and he was able to finish the picture. But after the picture was over Wallace Reid was thoroughly hooked on morphine. Normally, he could have been sent to a sanitarium. But he was altogether too good box office, there was too much to be gotten out of Wallace Reid. So in order to keep the services of this most popular of popular leading men, the studio kept him supplied with more and more morphine."[48]

Brown explained the role of the studio doctor: "He goes where he's told, he does what he's told. At the moment he enters a studio, which is in effect a small principality with the vice president in charge of production being the prince, whatever is required of him he does. Now that means everything from an injection of a forbidden drug to an abortion and all things in between."[49]

Mrs. Reid's insistence that her husband's addiction did not begin until *Peter Ibbetson* fails to take into account the rumors that were already in print by the time of the film's release. *Variety,* in September 1921, reported that the wife of one of the most popular of the younger male stars had time and again had the peddlers of dope who were supplying her husband arrested, but she had been unable to get him to kick the habit.[50] A confidential report issued in 1921 by the Los Angeles County marshal stated that within a short time a whole new crop of picture favorites would be necessary because of the prevalence of drug addiction among the current stars.

According to his widow, Reid began to use liquor as a cover for the drugs. Eventually he confessed to her that he was a morphine addict. He was determined to fight it, but his easygoing personality had altered and he became more and more difficult. According to Douglas Whitton, he blackmailed directors into bribing him—sometimes a thousand dollars a day—to get him on the set.[51] He flaunted his habit, showing director James Cruze a trick golf club with a hypodermic syringe in the handle. (This would have intrigued Cruze, soon to be addicted himself.)

Wallace Reid pictures continued to be released, but the fans noticed that his eyes looked tired and that his old spontaneous manner had gone. They wrote letters about him to the fan magazines: "Snap out of it, Wally!" they demanded.[52]

During the making of *Thirty Days,* he collapsed. Famous Players–Lasky had survived the Arbuckle and Taylor scandals, although Arbuckle had cost them an estimated million dollars in lost revenue. Reid, the company's top star, would represent another two million down the drain if his films were banned by Hays. The studio presented Reid with an ultimatum: kick the habit or face the consequences.

Reid went into a sanitarium, telling Cecil B. DeMille, "I'll either come out cured or I won't come out."[53] By arrangement with Hays, Mrs. Reid helped to defuse the situation by holding a press conference at her home and taking the reporters into her confidence. They responded by treating the case with compassion. The Los Angeles *Examiner,* presumably on Mr. Hearst's orders, printed a special copy for delivery to Reid with the news of his struggle omitted. *Photoplay* told its readers that he was suffering from Klieg eyes and a serious nervous breakdown.[54]

Reid appeared to be winning his fight, but after he had reported back for work, an intestinal disturbance developed which baffled his doctors. Every test known to medical science was tried. "Needles half a dozen inches long were driven into his spine," said Mrs. Reid. "The pain he endured was terrible. . . . Not a single test showed a positive result."[55] On top of all this, the complete withdrawal of morphine had affected his metabolism. He caught influenza; like an AIDS victim of today, he had no resistance. He died on January 18, 1923, at the age of thirty-one.

As Reid's body lay in state, traffic was held up for blocks; thousands jostled for a final look. The streets were packed along the route of the funeral procession and the church was filled with flowers.

The papers dropped the matter, and *Variety* wondered why: "The exploitation of Reid's death would have been the best weapon Fate has ever put into the hands of publicists against the drug habit. The death of one of the most notable screen stars is a terrific object lesson. It will do more to break the drug traffic than all the warnings from pulpits or lecture platforms that could be delivered in a generation by reformers whose exposes are scarcely more free from self-interest than the newspapers."[56]

Mrs. Reid was grief-stricken and exhausted, and she simply wanted to retreat from the public eye. "I am very, very, very tired." she said. "For two years I have waged my own little battle against this thing alone and too often in the darkness of ignorance . . . But during these days since my husband's going, my home has been flooded with appeals to me to *do something.* 'They will listen to you. They loved Wally and they admired his brave fight and they hate the thing that killed him. Tell what you know for the good of humanity.' "[57]

Mrs. Reid, with Adela Rogers St. Johns, attended a conference on narcotics in Washington, and on her return to Hollywood set to work on a drug-propaganda film, in collaboration with Thomas H. Ince. It has been said that Ince produced the film out of kindness to Mrs. Reid, but producers are not noted for kindness. In any case, Mrs. Reid is on record as saying it was not her idea. Will Hays gave special dispensation for the film, which violated most censorship codes, to be produced under the sponsorship of the Los Angeles Anti-Narcotic League.

Mrs. Reid selected Bessie Love to play the suicidal addict, Mary. The actress

was not exactly thrilled at the prospect—her friends warned her she would be thought of as an addict herself. But Mrs. Reid talked her into it. Bessie Love was quoted at the time, in the stilted phraseology so beloved of publicity departments when striving for dignity: "To fully prepare myself for the role, which first of all entailed a thorough psychological understanding, I availed myself of the friendly offices of a physician. . . ."

Bessie Love did not talk, or write, like that. Over lunch one day in 1978 she told me of her experiences:

"We had a doctor as a technical adviser, and he suggested that he take us down to the jail to meet the real addicts—the women, anyway. I went thinking I must do my duty, all buttoned up. I never had so much fun in my life. Oh, I had a ball. There were a few really distressed women—but the others! They were such fun. One girl showed me how to do it. She took me behind a door—she was very modest—and she showed me how she was punctured all over. She'd run out of places to stick a needle.

"They thought I was a nurse; I wouldn't have been allowed in otherwise.

" 'Did Mrs. Reid go down?' I asked.

"Bless her heart, she didn't have to."[58]

Bessie Love received a letter in the early 1970s from a man who had played her baby in the picture. By an extraordinary coincidence, he had grown up to become a narcotics agent.

James Kirkwood, who played the doctor, resigned from the cast of the stage play *The Fool* in New York after being advised by clergymen that he would be accomplishing a bigger work were he to undertake the lead in the film.[59]

Something of what Mrs. Reid had gone through was incorporated into the story, and while MacFarland, the character played by Kirkwood is an older, more dedicated man than Reid, much that happened to Reid happens to him—although, as Mrs. Reid was at pains to point out, her husband never had to obtain his morphine from the underworld: "His source was neither illicit nor illegal—it didn't have to be. Wally could charm any doctor into giving him the tablets he wanted. He knew just enough about medicine to convince doctors that he knew exactly how many grams he could safely take every day."[60] And he had constant and unfettered access to the studio doctor at Famous Players–Lasky.

Whatever the merit of the final result, it was courageous of Mrs. Reid to work on the film in any capacity; to agree to act in it was positively heroic, for it brought her into direct contact with scenes which must have chilled her. Ironically, the character she plays overcomes her husband's addiction by a ruse—by her own skill as an actress—and the story ends with a victory to compensate for all the defeats.

D. H. L. Kirby, former executive secretary of the China Club in Seattle, who had just completed a national anti-narcotics crusade, assisted Mrs. Reid,[61] and the picture featured a number of prominent people: Mayor George B. Cryer of Los Angeles and Chief of Police Louis D. Oaks—both members of the Anti-Narcotic League—appeared in small roles, along with Dr. Rufus von Kleinsmid, President of the University of Southern California, and Judge Benjamin Bledsoe.[62]

Shooting the final sequence, the wild taxi ride in the streets of Los Angeles, required police cooperation. Cameras were set up on top of vehicles and on the back of a police car which went through the streets with its siren wide open. An event occurred which even at the time, *Photoplay* admitted, sounded like something from the fertile brain of a press agent: "As the whistles blew and the camera began to grind, a Chinaman started across the street, evidently quite unconscious of what was happening around him. Two policeman started toward him, anxious to get him out of the path of the taxi. But the Chinaman misunderstood. With a terrified glance at the two officers, he dropped something from the sleeve of his jacket and, slipping into the crowd of bystanders, disappeared. The scene was shot before one of the policemen noticed the little package the Chinaman had dropped. Picking it up he found that it was filled with little 'bindles' of cocaine."[63]

Human Wreckage is in the vanguard of the legion of lost films. It is therefore of particular importance to provide details of the story. My source is the script, by C. Gardner Sullivan, first entitled "Dope" and then "The Living Dead."

"The Dope Ring," declares the prologue, "one of the most powerful and vicious organizations in American history, is composed of rings within rings, the inner ring undoubtedly including men powerful in finance, politics and society. But the trail to the 'men higher up' is cunningly covered. No investigator has penetrated to the inner circle."

The picture fades in to an Indian poppy field. The poppies are nodding in the breeze, and the gray, wasted faces of addicts are faded into them. Mrs. Wallace Reid delivers a statement, in the company of her two children: "The drug evil is daily devastating more homes than the white plague [tuberculosis]. None of us can render a greater service to humanity."

A brief visual sketch of a great city gives way to a bird's-eye view over which is superimposed the symbol of the drug menace, a hyena.

"Ambitious, unafraid, seemingly unconquerable, but bleeding in secret from the fangs of THE BEAST."

Dope pushers are characterized not only as furtive men or flashy gangsters, but also as elegantly dressed women. Peddlers are shown to be particularly active around high schools, in the slums, and on the smuggling routes from Canada to Mexico.

Jimmy Brown (George Hackathorne), a frail, likable twenty-year-old, has been a heroin addict for a year. He sniffs a dose and gains the confidence to snatch a watch from a pawnshop. He runs straight into an old friend, Ginger (Lucille Ricksen), who grabs hold of him. She defends him against the police, but they haul him off.

His mother, Mrs. Brown (Claire McDowell),[64] a faded woman of forty-five, is visited by the police at her shabby tenement and told the news. A neighbor, Mother Finnegan (Victory Bateman), senses something is wrong. She lives with her daughter, Mary (Bessie Love), who has a baby of six months. Mother Finnegan tells Mrs. Brown not to cry: "I'll take you to see Mrs. Alan MacFarland."

Ethel MacFarland (Mrs. Wallace Reid), wife of a famous attorney, devotes much of her time to helping those less fortunate than herself. When Mrs. Brown is brought to her, she listens with sympathy and persuades her husband to take the case.

James Kirkwood stands with director John Griffith Wray on a set inspired by Caligari—*the view of a drug addict—for* Human Wreckage, *1923.*

Alan MacFarland (James Kirkwood) is shocked at the idea of a twenty-year-old addict: "It's a disgrace to the state," he says. At Jimmy's trial, MacFarland insists he is not guilty. "Why? Because he was under the influence of a powerful drug and was not morally responsible."

There is a cut to a grotesque street—"something on the order of Dr. Caligari's Cabinet" specified the script—with the houses set at insane angles. Down the street prowls the hyena.

MacFarland wins his case, and Jimmy is sent to the narcotics ward of the county hospital: "Great types to be picked here; we should get the real thing so far as possible." Jimmy is put through the first stage of the cure—deprivation. He suffers agony, but tries to take his punishment cheerfully. His mother is warned that the real danger lies ahead, when he leaves the hospital, becoming easy bait for the dope peddlers.

MacFarland, driving himself beyond endurance on another case, is offered something to keep him going by a fellow club member, Dr. Hillman (Robert McKim)—morphine. "No," says MacFarland in disgust. "The cure is worse than the disease."

"I use morphine at times," says Hillman mildly. "Do I look like a dope fiend?" MacFarland submits. "Once can't do me any harm." But once is not enough, and soon he awaits the regular visits of the drug peddler.

His wife, visiting the Browns, notices a curious thing: Mary Finnegan slips into her bedroom; the door does not quite shut, and, through a mirror, Ethel sees

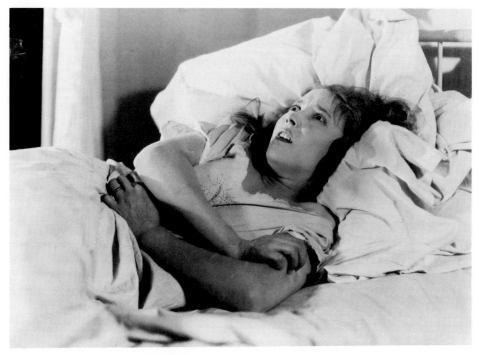

Bessie Love as the drug-addicted mother in Human Wreckage, *1923, produced by Mrs. Wallace Reid and directed by John Griffith Wray for Thomas Ince.*

Mary injecting herself. As if this were not shocking enough, she does something else.

"This scene," says the script, "will have to be taken with extreme care. The reflection of Mary includes her head and body down to her waist. Taking a small bit of morphine from the same bottle from which she filled the needle, she dilutes it in a glass of water. Opening her dress she dips her fingers into the weakened morphine solution and rubs it on her breast. Although this scene must be handled with extreme delicacy there should be no doubt as to what Mary is doing. She has gotten into the habit of rubbing morphine on her breasts to quiet the baby when he nurses."[65]

Ethel cries out, rushes across the room, and snatches the baby from Mary's arms. Remorse overwhelms the girl. The revulsion in Ethel's face is too much for her to bear, and, crying "I know I am worse than a murderess," she tries to kill herself by jumping from the window. Ethel seizes her and drags her back.

Mary is taken to a private hospital and separated from her child.

Mary's pusher, Harris (Otto Hoffman), is arrested by the Federal Narcotic Squad, and because he is high on cocaine himself, they manage to trick him into giving them the names of other drug peddlers. MacFarland's dealer, Steve Stone (Harry Northup), is the next to be picked up. But he has influence, as he is the supplier to all the best people. A title—"Higher up"—introduces the luxurious headquarters of a wealthy and powerful group. The men keep their backs to the camera, and we never see their faces. Orders are issued: "Furnish bail for Stone immediately—then have him see the best lawyer in the city."

The best lawyer is MacFarland. In no time at all, the newspapers proclaim:

STONE "NOT GUILTY" ON DOPE RING CHARGE. Jimmy Brown, now a taxi driver, tells his friends, "Every hophead in town knows that Stone handled dope." The title "Not guilty" is repeated like a tolling bell before a shot of Mary, suffering in the hospital and before a shot of a peddler selling dope to a girl of sixteen. Even in jail, the drugs circulate smoothly, thanks to the "underground," and Harris is kept fully supplied. He makes plans to escape.

A package is delivered to MacFarland, a present from a grateful Stone—a bottle of morphine. His battle with himself is now reaching a crisis. He does his best to suppress the craving, but once he has injected himself he feels a wonderful sense of relief.

Ethel discovers him in an unnatural sleep, and finds the needle and bottle. She is filled with despair.

Harris escapes, and an accomplice slips him a gun. He shoots a policeman and also a bystander by mistake before he is gunned down.

Ethel decides the only thing to do with MacFarland is to take him to a cottage on the seacoast where no drug peddler can reach him. MacFarland cooperates with Ethel in her struggle, but his desire is too strong. Denied a needle, he drinks the morphine right from the bottle. When Ethel discovers this, she gives up. MacFarland is shaken to discover that his wife has all the symptoms of addiction herself.

"I am so tired and I can't sleep," she says. "I envied you last night."

Her husband is appalled. "Ethel, dear, I am not worth saving, but *you* are."

In desperation, he searches for a bottle he knows she had hidden and at last experiences something of what he has put his wife through. He forces himself to destroy the morphine and to give up the habit once and for all.

The doctor arrives, and Ethel says, "Thank God, I don't think we will need you." And she explains how she tricked her husband: "He couldn't conquer for himself, but he has conquered for me!"

Now the city opens its war on the drug ring. As Ginger says, "It's about time, for the love of Mike!" Dr. Hillman, the dope doctor, is arrested. The men higher up put out the word to MacFarland to stop this crusade, and Stone calls to deliver the message: "Don't forget we can ruin you!"

MacFarland makes an idealistic statement: "The American public no longer regards the drug addict as a criminal, but as a sick person needing the best medical attention obtainable."

Jimmy Brown picks Stone up in his taxi and takes him on a wild, drug-induced ride through city traffic. "You're on your way to hell," he tells him, moments before he drives at full speed into a locomotive. Both are killed.

MacFarland writes another statement, which belies the first: "If we are to crush the drug evil, we must have a law which will *bite*. It cannot be too drastic."

And at the finale, Mrs. Wallace Reid reappears to ask: "Won't you help us?"

An epilogue was originally planned, to be set in the Federal Hospital for Drug Addicts at San Clemente, California. The script specified:

"An imaginary view of buildings and pleasant grounds.

ONE WAY OF HELPING THE DRUG ADDICTS—A GOVERNMENT HOSPITAL TO BE ESTABLISHED ON SAN CLEMENTE ISLAND OFF CATALINA,

WHERE ADDICTS COULD BE GIVEN THE PROPER ATTENTION AND
GUARDED AGAINST DOPE-PEDDLERS."

We were to be shown modern wards, and addicts on the road to recovery, looking
forward to a new and useful life.

The scene was deleted from the script, just as the scheme was scrapped in
reality. The island was used for target practice by the marines instead.

Much of the critical reaction to the film fulfilled Mrs. Reid's highest hopes. The
reviewers were a hard-bitten lot and would not have praised it out of mere sympathy for her plight. *Variety*'s man, Sime Silverman, certainly spared her nothing:
"*Human Wreckage* is strictly a commercially made drug expose film. Like many
others preceding it, there is no merit to any part, from story to acting. As an
educator for the purpose of suppressing the drug habit, *Human Wreckage* isn't. It
is more of an enlightener. The young can see here things they should not know."[66]

The other reviewers were almost unanimous in their praise. *Motion Picture
Classic* said: "*Human Wreckage* is a profoundly moving picture handled with dignity
and restraint. There is nothing cheap or sensational about it. Quite the contrary.
A tremendous and unmistakable sincerity animates everyone who had anything to
do with it. It is a grim, terrific, tragic indictment of stupidity and criminal indif-
ference toward these 'living dead' whose pitiable army is vaster than you or I ever
dreamed of."[67]

On the opening night in New York, June 1923, the entrance to the Lyric
Theatre was choked with people. One reporter admitted to being there out of
curiosity, doubting the motives, not to mention the taste, of the film. That reporter
became an instant convert: "No one could impugn the motives of Mrs. Reid if
they had seen her standing up in a box, after the picture, while flowers in gracious
tribute were laid at her feet; standing there white faced and weary-eyed, the tears
rolling down her cheeks, very near to collapse, a tragic, pitiful, inarticulate figure."[68]

In Los Angeles, crowds stormed the doors of the Rialto and hundreds had to
be turned away on the first night. The picture was one of the financial hits of the
year. The Los Angeles *Examiner,* engaged in the Hearst anti-drug campaign, called
it "the most important picture ever made."[69]

The film was not shown in England: "Few films the examiners have seen are
more dangerous than this."[70] But it made money for Thomas Ince, and enough to
enable Mrs. Reid to take care of her family, set up her own production company,
and further her work for the Wallace Reid Foundation Sanitarium in the Santa
Monica Mountains. She continued to make personal appearances with the picture
and to speak to women's clubs and other influential groups. She asked them not
to think of drug addicts as strange and curious beings but as sick people who
could be helped. And she urged that terms like "hophead" and "dope fiend" be
dropped.

Wallace Reid would have been proud of her. "If I had known a year ago what
I know today," she said, "my history might have been very different."[71]

THE GREATEST MENACE   Released before *Human Wreckage, The Greatest Menace* might prove equally important—if only it could be found. An independent production, written and directed by Al Rogell, it was not approved by the Hays Office. Rogell had read the many reports of drug cases in the papers, and he knew two addicts. "It was a popular subject," he said. "It was being discussed and yet it was kind of hushed up. It was a terrible thing which America recognized. I needed something to write, something to promote. I made it up as I went along."[72]

He wrote an outline and contacted Mrs. Angela C. Kaufman, a wealthy philanthropist deeply committed to the fight against addiction who was known as "the angel of the county jail." "She had gone down to the jail on behalf of the prisoners innumerable times," said Rogell. "She thought the picture was a wonderful idea. She got together her spiritualist group and agreed to put up the money—not very much for a picture, around $20,000."[73]

Rogell spent a lot of time with Mrs. Kaufman in the company of addicts at the county jail. And for three days he lived in a cell, dressed as a convict, observing two men who were trying to kick the habit. "They thought I was just another inmate," he recalls.

Angela Kaufman was credited with the story, in which Charles Wright, Jr. (Robert Gordon), the son of a district attorney, determines to write about life as it really is. He ignores the warnings of his lawyer sister, Velma (Ann Little), and visits the haunts of drug addicts. A girl who works for the drug ring encourages him to sample narcotics, and soon he is addicted himself. When the girl dies, Charles is arrested for her murder; unaware of his identity, Velma and her father intend to prosecute. But when she learns who he is, Velma defends him and wins the case, and Charles is reunited with his family.[74]

Rogell previewed the picture at the Ambassador Hotel on January 18, 1923. "They had a theatre there. I'll never forget coming out and newsboys were shouting that Wallace Reid had died. I was just getting into my car when a fellow came up and handed me a card and said, 'This man wants to see you.' The card said Louis B. Mayer. It turned out it wasn't Louis B. but Jerry G. Mayer, his brother, who had a little exchange downtown. He convinced me he knew all the angles.

"I also got a call from Thomas Ince. He wanted me to send the picture out. He didn't think I'd bring it myself; I was the producer. But I took it out myself, took it to the projection room and watched it. Ince and two or three of his cohorts were down below. And in those days, the sound of the projector didn't bother you; you could open up the trap. Between reels, Ince said, 'Hold it a minute.' So the operator stopped and I listened, and he was talking to the boys. His plan was to keep me interested and hold up my release—to get out a picture written by Wallace Reid's wife, Dorothy Davenport, who was also in the room. I didn't know what to do. I just grabbed the film and then I called this fellow, who was supposed to be Louis Mayer. He told me what a great man he was and what he could do, so we set off for New York—Mrs. Kaufman wouldn't let him take the picture without me. While we were on the train, Ince came out with the ads for the Mrs.

Wallace Reid Special. We were now second-best. Mayer turned the film over to a company called Asher, Small and Rogers, and they distributed the picture, states rights. It did fairly well and Mrs. Kaufman was pleased. They kept most of the money. We got back a few thousand, but not enough to cover the cost of production. And I didn't get paid—I had a piece of the picture instead."[75]

The film was released a month before *Human Wreckage,* in May 1923. No reviews appeared in *Variety* or *Photoplay.* "That could have had something to do with Ince," said Rogell. "He was a very powerful man. And I remember when I saw *Human Wreckage,* I was infuriated at the ideas he'd taken from me."[76]

THE PACE THAT KILLS   In the twenties, films about drug addiction had to be morality plays of Old Testament intensity to get by the censors. Yet *The Pace That Kills* (1928), for all its moralizing, is at times nearer to an instructional documentary. One sequence actually shows the preparation of the potions. Another portrays a method of peddling drugs. The ending is heavy with self-sacrifice and suicide, but for a few reels the place of drugs in society is vividly explained. Thus, *The Pace That Kills* is a social film of no mean value.

What mars it is the performance of the leading man. Owen Gorin was chosen for the part of Eddie presumably because of his weak but good-looking face. Once he has caked it in make-up, however, he acts as if his eyes were fried eggs. All sense of conviction flies out the window, as Gorin himself nearly does, so wildly do his arms gyrate. Virginia Roye, by contrast, is first-rate; as his girlfriend, she has something of the energy of Clara Bow.

Once again, the city is shown as a place of moral destruction, which has already sucked Eddie's sister into its maw. Eddie sets out to search for her, saying farewell to his simple country folks. The transition from farmland to town is managed with admirable economy: from the wheel of a car we dissolve to the pistons of a locomotive and to the bogies of a streetcar. Eddie gets a job in a department store, where Fanny (Roye), a sexy shopgirl, takes an instant fancy to him. Eddie's first busy day exhausts him, and he complains of a headache. Fanny has the remedy. Her expressive eyes dart from one side to the other, and, as the coast is clear, she pulls up her skirt and from beneath her rolled stocking discloses a small packet containing white powder. When Fanny shows him the technique of cocaine sniffing—exactly that used in an earlier century for snuff—she turns her back on the camera. But it is obvious what she is doing. And Eddie's sudden return to health must rank among the cinema's more embarrassing moments.

Fanny takes Eddie to a nightclub, he anxiously watching the taxi meter as the fare rises like the National Debt. In the cabaret (the one expensive set in the picture), Eddie discovers his sister is now a gangster's moll. She spurns him.

A few scenes later, Fanny takes Eddie to a party. Opening on the legs of girls dancing the Charleston, we mix to an establishing shot before cutting to the pianist. He is sluggish. The same condition affects many of the guests, but it is dispelled by the arrival of Snowy the Peddler ("Arch Fiend of Humanity"). The guests crush round him—"A bunch of 'Snow Birds' with their 'Happy Dust' and 'Joy Powder.' " The pianist feels much better, and the music begins again, hotter and faster to judge by the dancing. That drugs are a prologue to further licentiousness is indicated by couples going off by themselves to spacious sofas in dark corners, switching out the light. Fanny smokes a reefer, which she shares with Eddie.

"Soon, all sense of honor and decency lost, the addict will do anything to get dope." Both are fired for pilfering, and they move in together in a rundown boarding house. They need money to assuage the craving and their harridan of a landlady. In a mirror, we see Fanny taking a shot as a prelude to sex. A symbolic coffee pot boils over.

Next we see the various drugs and their method of preparation . . . morphine . . . opium, "which dulls the sharp ache of living for a while—rots the moral fiber" (the film lays the entire responsibility for opium on the Chinese population) . . . and finally heroin.

Now Fanny is forced to get money by the only method left open to her. She powders her face to hide the shadows under her eyes and takes up her position in a doorway. She returns to Eddie, shaken but successful. Eddie is not so far gone that he cannot guess where she's been.

To ease his incessant craving, Eddie moves to a Chinese opium den. In bursts his sister, desperate for relief. She is offered opium, but she needs something stronger—heroin. Eddie staggers over to her. "Oh, Eddie," she gasps, "has it got you too?" A newspaper headline conveniently reveals her plight. She has shot the gangster—we see the event in superimposition—and is on the run. The police burst in and arrest her.

Back at the lodgings, Eddie stares at a photo of his dear sister, who faces death one way or the other. "Eddie," says Fanny, "we've got to go straight, because . . ."

"God," says Eddie, "a baby born to a dope fiend and a—"

"Don't say it, Eddie, don't say it." Fanny gives him one last shot to calm his nerves and sits down to write a note. She kisses Eddie, goes down to the harbor, and ends it all. When Eddie hears the news, he staggers down to the pier and follows her into the next world.

The final title urges audiences to support the Porter Bill—"for the segregation and hospitalization of narcotic addicts—the greatest constructive measure ever offered for the abatement of the narcotic evil."

Like the lawyer in *Human Wreckage,* Representative Stephen G. Porter, sponsor of the bill, regarded drug addicts as sick people. "You can't cure a sick person by sending that person to jail," he declared. (The bill became law on July 1, 1930, four days after Porter's death.)[77] Originally, the film depicted Eddie's cure—months of misery in the hospital.[78]

Norton Parker, the director, had worked for Mrs. Wallace Reid as writer on *The Earth Woman* (1926), and he had recently made another "Awful Warning" picture, *The Road to Ruin* (see page pages 175–76). Made by a company outside the jurisdiction of Hays, *The Pace That Kills* reached the public in a number of states.

"If you can stand the sermon-length opening title," said *Photoplay,* "you can probably stand the rest of it. It's hot propaganda against the narcotic evil, authentic to the point of grotesqueness, and a scientific treatise for lecture rooms, not amusement houses. . . . Not the least bit entertaining."[79]

Parker's co-director, William O'Connor, remade the picture in 1936. This time, it was banned by Hays.

Chapter Four

PROHIBITION

Burning the Candle, *1917, directed by Harry Beaumont. Molly Carrington (Mary Charleson) pledges her hand to James Maxwell (Henry B. Walthall), who subsequently becomes an alcoholic. (George Eastman House)*

IN DECEMBER 1900, a stout lady in her midfifties, dressed in black, marched into the Carey Hotel bar in Wichita, Kansas, armed with two pieces of iron and some rocks. She swept the decanters from the bar. She hurled a billiard ball at the plate glass mirror behind the bar, and attacked a painting of Cleopatra at her bath, smashing the glass and almost destroying the picture. A policeman had a hard job stopping her and was subjected to a temperance lecture en route to the station. She was placed in the county jail.[1]

Carry A. Nation was president of the Barber County Women's Christian Temperance Union. She had bitter experience of the misery caused by alcohol, for her first husband had "filled a drunkard's grave." Since liquor was supposed to be illegal in Kansas, she felt she was within her rights to destroy saloons. (In later raids she adopted a hatchet.) She called herself Home Defender. Women were not served in saloons; such women as frequented them were invariably prostitutes, and this was another source of her rage.

In a film made by John B. Tackett, a photographer who owned a theatre in Coffeyville, Kansas, we see an actress playing Mrs. Nation purchase a hatchet at a hardware store. She marches into the Carey Hotel, and when asked to sign in she (incorrectly) flourishes the hatchet. Although the painting of Cleopatra was worth $300, this was too cheap for the film, which has her "destroying a $10,000 oil painting."

Primitive and crude, the film was probably made to commemorate Mrs. Nation's death in 1911, although it looks as if it had been made even earlier.[2] Photographed in Wichita, it contains some authentic exteriors, but the Carey bar was re-created with flimsy canvas scenery; Tackett could not afford to lose as much as Mrs. Nation destroyed. The film supports her; a title states she was "thrown in jail by an unjust law for destroying an evil vice."

Mrs. Nation was an active crusader against smoking, too. In the prison scene the men in the next cell insult her as she kneels in prayer by blowing cigarette smoke at her. She is released to attend church services, and in the street the local children taunt her. She disperses them rapidly enough. The final title might have been her rallying cry: "Let Him Who Is Without Sin Among You Cast the First Stone."

There were those who thought Mrs. Nation insane. Not even her second husband agreed with her methods. But the publicity she aroused was invaluable for the prohibitionist cause, although many temperance reformers were distressed by Mrs. Nation's high jinks, especially when she took to appearing in vaudeville. (When she worked for future film producer William Fox in vaudeville, she forced him to give up smoking.)[3] The Edison Company made two brief films in 1901 ridiculing her activities, *The Kansas Saloon Smashers* and *Why Mr. Nation Wants a Divorce,* which showed her husband being driven to drink.[4] Biograph made *Carrie Nation Smashing a Saloon* and Lubin brought out *Mrs. Nation and Her Hatchet Brigade,* also 1901.

Carry Nation prays in jail. (Wichita Public Library)

The drive toward Prohibition was not entirely in the hands of a single unhinged woman. Nor was it simply the concern of a cabal of fanatics. The Prohibition movement was propelled by middle-class men and women with a sense of mission. So powerful an influence did they wield that the Prohibition party became the leading reform party of the late nineteenth century.[5] By 1900, every state had a law requiring the teaching of temperance in the public schools.[6] But in 1912, Americans spent one and a quarter billion dollars a year on drink—eleven times more than they spent on education.[7] In one square mile of Chicago there were 400 saloons.[8]

The first great wave of prohibition swept the country in the 1850s, a second in the 1880s. The Anti-Saloon League won the leadership of the movement in 1905, and it was this group which set in action, in that crucial year of 1913, the drive which led to the adoption of the Eighteenth Amendment.[9]

Films which look back on Prohibition make the Volstead Act, as the amendment was known, seem violently unpopular, as though "the Noble Experiment" had been imposed upon the nation as Stalin imposed collectivization on Russia. Yet twenty-six states adopted Prohibition even before the passage of the Volstead Act.

Although a handful of theatres existed which were linked to bars, the moving picture theatre and the saloon were usually commercial rivals. Often, when a moving picture house was set up, the saloons on its right and left declared bankruptcy.[10] A show cost no more than a single drink, and a man could take his whole family to the pictures for the cost of an evening in the saloon.

Reformers objected to saloons not only because so many normally upright citizens had been laid low, but because crime and politics were run from them.[11] Saloon owners had to have political connections to protect their income. This came not so much from the legal sale of liquor but from what went on in back rooms and up the stairs: gambling and prostitution. Saloon power, said Thomas Dixon, ran every great city.[12]

The liquor interests loathed the moving picture, regarding it as having an even worse effect than the prohibitionists. In 1916, the National Retail Liquor Dealers' Association complained: "In the vast majority of displays of moving pictures, films portraying conditions surrounding the retail liquor trade have been preposterously and untruthfully magnified by those operators who are paid vast sums by the opposition to our business."[13] And one of the breweries approached a film company with the offer to provide the fixtures whenever a saloon scene was required— they wanted to fit up a barroom the way they thought it should look. The offer was refused.[14]

That same year, at a dinner given for President Woodrow Wilson by the Motion Picture Board of Trade in New York City, producer J. Stuart Blackton presented statistics concerning the effect of movies on the liquor business, taking the area around Wilkes-Barre, Pennsylvania, as an example. In that district there had been 10,000 saloons in 1906, but only 1,400 in 1916.[15] There were other factors Blackton did not touch upon, but the movies could legitimately claim to be the saloon's chief commercial enemy.

All the more ironic, then, that alcohol should prove the undoing of so many careers in the picture business. Among the outstanding personalities who became alcoholics was D. W. Griffith, who made thirteen pictures against the evils of drink at Biograph and whose career closed with another, *The Struggle* (1931).

The Little Colonel of *The Birth of a Nation,* Henry B. Walthall, was a victim who put his affliction to use. He specialized in roles which called for physical disintegration. In *The Outer Edge,* a three-reeler of 1915, he portrayed a surgeon who discovers a new procedure, the one cure for a rare disease. He is the only man able to perform it, but due to his drinking he bungles an operation on a child, and the child dies.[16]

Reviewers felt that *Burning the Candle,* an Essanay five-reeler directed by Harry Beaumont, was saved from the hazard common to all prohibition plays—that of making the audience laugh—by Walthall's acting skill: "Walthall can play this type of alcohol victim with a sincerity that makes it seem a chapter from the life of some unfortunate friend rather than a vaudeville sketch of the 'we-won't-get-home-till-morning' variety. He never overacts or tries to get a cheap effect through obvious comedy and his make-up in the gradual stages of his downfall is astonishingly realistic."[17]

This story of a young man with brilliant prospects who becomes a jolly good fellow once too often and sinks to the gutter—redeeming himself only when the shock of divorce brings him to his senses—contained a moment which might have destroyed conviction. "The scene in which the Southern colonel smashes up his wine cellar and literally swims about in rum dangerously suggests the end of a Keystone comedy. Here again Walthall saves the situation and gives the real horror of the drink evil just as it was degenerating into farce."[18]

Jack London is featured in the advertising for this 1914 adaptation of his novel. (Robert S. Birchard Collection)

The old fable of a duck who, when a flood came, drank up all the water in order to save the other ducks was used as an introduction to *The Girl Glory* (1917), directed by Roy William Neill. It featured Enid Bennett, who tries to free her grandfather of the liquor habit by a similar method. "There is plenty of humor but a great deal more pathos in the child experimenting with the raw whisky in order to find out what is 'in it' that has such a fatal attraction for her grandfather."[19] When she learns that the saloon cannot be shut down unless the bartender violates the law, she smuggles herself in, swallows a glass of redeye, and exposes the sale of liquor to minors. The saloon is closed, Grandfather signs the pledge, and the reviewers loved it. "An original and most picturesque solution of the liquor problem," said the New York *Dramatic Mirror,* although it added, "it is not to be recommended for general use on all occasions."[20]

"A compelling plea for Temperance," *John Barleycorn* was a six-reel feature of 1914; its scenario, written by Lois Weber, was based on the Jack London book. The previous year, London had severed his connection with the Balboa studios and signed an agreement with actor-director Hobart Bosworth and real estate operator Frank Garbutt to make pictures from his stories.[21] As authentication, a shot of Jack London sitting at his desk or posing against an appropriate landscape opened each film.

Bosworth was the kind of man London liked—he had run away to sea at twelve and had worked on a ranch in 1880, when the West was still wild.[22] Their

John Barleycorn, *1914. The young Jack London (Matty Roubert) refuses wine at an Italian-owned vineyard. (Robert S. Birchard Collection)*

first collaboration was *The Sea Wolf* (1913), which was both successful and thoroughly approved of by Jack London. He liked all the Bosworth films of his works, and it is a tragedy that only fragments survive.[23]

John Barleycorn was based on London's own experiences. The opening scenes were shot in Oakland, California, his former home.[24] Three actors played the leading character—called, simply, "Jack"—Matty Roubert, the child; Antrim Short, the adolescent; and Elmer Clifton, the youth.

The child, following his father at the plow, is sent for a pail of beer. Sampling it, he soon collapses in a drunken stupor. As an adolescent, working on an Italian-owned ranch, he is forced to drink red wine. And as a young married man, he has a wife to help him in his struggle against strong drink. He rejects alcohol on several occasions, but fails again and again in his resolve. The film, which was not so much a drama as a biography—as episodic as a diary[25]—was, according to *Moving Picture World,* the most powerful moral lesson ever conveyed in films: "When it comes to delineating the struggles of the soul, Jack London writes with an x-ray concealed in his pen."[26]

London published the book in 1913. By 1916 he was dead. He took poison, his friend Upton Sinclair said, "to escape the claws of John Barleycorn."[27]

Liquor interests, anxious about the film's impact on prohibition referenda, tried to bribe Bosworth into holding back the film until after the elections in six states. Bosworth refused.[28]

Curiously enough, the chief censor of that fanatical board of Pennsylvania,

J. Louis Breitinger, was so bitter in his opposition to the film that he threatened the Paramount man, William E. Smith, with arrest if he dared to show it, even to the YMCA. Smith showed it to the YMCA, at a free performance, and the audience pronounced it "a strong moral lesson."[29] Breitinger was not concerned with the opinion of the YMCA or even churchmen: "All those ministers, church workers and temperance people are biased, anyway, against the other side." But he restrained his power of arrest. The picture people began to wonder which side he was on. "He insisted that nearly every scene in which booze is shown in its hideous features shall be eliminated or softened," said Smith, "and that an extra 500 feet of pleasant domestic life be added to rob the picture of its dramatic climax."[30]

William Smith defied Breitinger's threats and put the picture on at the Garrick Theatre, Philadelphia. Paramount and Bosworth people turned up, half hoping to be thrown into patrol wagons. They even had a camera ready to record their arrest, but they were denied their martyrdom. A man from police headquarters arrived, but only to order two tickets. Even Breitinger's cousin was there. But Breitinger, embarrassed and compromised, stayed away. The press revealed his connections with the liquor interests, but he insisted he was a total abstainer. Surprisingly, he took no action, and although the film was showing at twenty-five cents admission instead of the five and ten cents more normal in the city, it attracted huge crowds.

Drunkenness, as the most visible of the day's evils, was dealt with in innumerable films, many of them depicting how alcohol could kill. The most elaborate was the six-reel melodrama *Prohibition* (1915), made by James Halleck Reid, the father of Wallace Reid. A newspaperman who became "the father of American Melodrama"[31] with plays like *The Confession* and *Human Hearts,* he made the occasional campaigning motion picture, each as melodramatic as his stage plays.

Prohibition was immediately adopted by several anti-saloon organizations as political propaganda.[32] The prologue featured the champions of the movement: Secretary of State William Jennings Bryan, Secretary of the Navy Josephus Daniels, and a clutch of United States senators. To ask such prominent men to endorse a propaganda film was one thing, but to persuade them to appear in it quite another, an indication not only of the urgency of the problem but of the reputation of Hal Reid.

The story concerned two brothers who love the same girl. One is accepted on condition he never drinks. The other takes revenge by awakening his brother's latent desire for whiskey. "Whereupon the director carries his audience through a series of scenes depicting the misery inflicted upon the innocent wife, etc., climaxing his tale with the justifiable murder of the schemer and the vindication of the brother."[33]

Variety thought one good feature of the direction was the absence of "weepy scenes." But their description suggests Hal Reid, as author and director, had a curious idea of the hereditary aspect of alcoholism: "The wife of the principal victim earnestly centers her thoughts upon a waterfall in order to protect her unborn babe from the prenatal influence of whiskey."[34]

Reid used allegorical figures—Mephistopheles, the Demon Rum, and the Drink Octopus sapping the blood of its groveling victims, although the Angels of Prohibition and Intelligence prove the stronger powers for good.[35] Reviews were enthusiastic, despite the lurid melodrama: "It looks like another *Traffic in Souls*," said *Motion Picture News*.[36] Made by the Photo Drama Company, for the Prohibition Film Corporation, the film was given a lavish advertising campaign, including a huge bottle, with the sinister Demon Rum leering from its mouth, hauled through the New England states by E. W. Lynch Enterprises.

The president of the Prohibition Film Corporation was Robert T. Kane, later an important producer associated with First National and Famous Players. He staged a bizarre publicity stunt, attending Salvation Army meetings to announce a hundred-dollar prize for the best story of the film "written by one of the derelicts who came to the meetings in hope of finding a better way."[37]

To enable them to see the film without paying, Mr. Kane organized a special screening at a Broadway theatre at 2:00 A.M. to which were invited "inebriates only." The theatre was filled, and 1,200 entries were submitted. The winner was one Donald Hobart French, a former Australian newspaperman "who had lost his grip when he found himself unable to keep his foot off the brass rail." Mr. Kane had a chat with French, who said that with the hundred dollars he would try again. "Mr. Kane added another hundred dollars to give him two tries."[38]

In D. W. Griffith's *Intolerance* (1916), reformers close saloons and brothels, leaving the field clear for the gangsters—which was precisely what happened when Prohibition came in. As William Drew has shown, *Intolerance* was used as anti-Prohibition propaganda. Two Prohibition amendments were before the voters as the film was released, and the United California industries, representing the vine-yard interests of the state, exploited the film in their advertising: "See D. W. Griffith's *Intolerance* and learn through the story of the ages how Intolerance and Prohibition has disrupted the states, brought suffering to innocent people and invaded the privacy of homes. Learn from this picture how you should vote on Amendments 1 and 2 at the November election."[39]

The amendments were duly defeated.

In January 1919, with the Eighteenth Amendment due to go into effect in a year, many liquor store owners and saloon keepers, hardly recovered from the war, decided to quit the business. And to what business did they decide to switch? The moving picture business, of course. Accustomed as they were to dealing with the public, many chose to become exhibitors; the spate of theatre buying resulted in one of the greatest booms the entertainment business had ever experienced.[40]

Whatever their private thoughts, the leaders of the film industry publicly welcomed Prohibition. The closing of saloons, they felt, could only work to their advantage.[41] "It has been noted that the man even slightly under the influence of intoxicants does not patronize the picture theatre."[42] Showmen from dry states warned that Prohibition would have no effect on business, but others were sure that men denied the saloon would bring their families to the theatres twice a week.[43] "Don't chortle too soon," said D. W. Griffith, warning that reformers released from Prohibition would soon be busy on other "improvements," such as censorship.[44] After the first year of Prohibition, exhibitors claimed a 30 percent increase in attendance. (It did not last; a slump was just around the corner.) "Strangely enough," said J. Stuart Blackton, "Prohibition has brought about the unique situation of reminiscent and heart-felt applause from the audience whenever a man is seen to take a drink on the screen."[45]

"Result of prohibition is bad," said director Allan Dwan. "Too many actors growing wall-eyed staying up nights working in their private stills."[46]

Exhibitor Jules Mastbaum said that before Prohibition it was unusual to see whole families attending picture houses. Now, especially in the neighborhood theatres, it was a common sight. "This I regard as one of the most glorious results of the arid condition that now exists."[47]

The reformers found new ammunition with which to attack the picture business. R. G. Burnett and E. D. Martell, British authors of *The Devil's Camera,* writing in 1932, argued that the motion picture had no right to claim to be anti-liquor. "People, after all, do not normally go to the cinema more than once or twice a week. There are plenty of other nights for drinking. And can it be said that what they see on the screen is likely to create in them a desire to give up intoxicants?"

The annals of Prohibition are full enough of hypocrisy and absurdity, but a footnote should be reserved for the story of an anti-alcohol epic called *Throughout the Ages,* which was to have starred William Jennings Bryan and which was almost financed by a liquor concern. The project started in 1917 when George R. Dalton, an actor and scenario writer, approached "The Great Commoner" with the idea for a movie.

"At that time," Bryan explained, "Prohibition was an issue and I declined to have any financial interest in the play, but, for the benefit of the cause, I was willing to contribute arguments which were to be illustrated by the picture."

When the amendment was ratified, the script was altered to show Bryan making speeches in favor of total abstinence—speeches to be illustrated in lavish style with Oriental feasts and Biblical reenactments. Footage of the 1912 Democratic National Convention was to be included; this was owned by the National Film Company of St. Louis, which had inherited it after the collapse of a scheme by one Edward F. Goltra to make a film about the event. Goltra, a boyhood friend of Bryan's, was a prominent St. Louis politician and a member of the Democratic National Committee.

Bryan now decided he would like 20 percent of the proceeds—a demand he later increased to 37 percent—and suggested Goltra as an investor. To Dalton's surprise, Goltra offered not merely to invest, but to finance the whole project. He was related by marriage to the Hostetter Bitters Company of Pittsburgh, wholesale liquor dealers and medicine manufacturers who had just been fined $160,000 for revenue violations, having produced a medicine which was actually cheap whiskey. Goltra called on prominent members of the Wilson administration with whom he was on close terms and offered a deal—if the money were returned (and even federal lawyers thought it should be), he would invest it in an anti-alcohol propaganda film which would feature the great William Jennings Bryan.

When the Hostetter Company was reimbursed, Goltra gave the green light to the National Film Company. The celebrated producer of *Battle Cry of Peace,* J. Stuart Blackton, agreed to direct. Blackton cared little for the theme, but he knew Bryan's box-office value. Dalton's script he rejected as worthless and rewrote it with Stanley Olmstead and an Anti-Saloon Leaguer called Dr. E. C. Dinwiddie.

Blackton proceeded on the promise that Bryan would take part. He had completed everything but Bryan's sequences when the project collapsed. Was it due to a report that the government had reopened the case and was demanding its money back? No one knew for sure, but Bryan refused to cooperate. Blackton lost a lot of money, Dinwiddie resigned, and other heads rolled as well. The film was regarded as a "might-have-been."

Yet the picture *was* completed, albeit without its famous star. Blackton dropped the propaganda and simply made alcohol the theme of the film, which was released as *The Moonshine Trail* (1919), starring Sylvia Breamer. *Variety* said, "The Prohibition Party should strongly endorse this feature. . . . There is not a single subtitle that savors of sermonizing. . . . It just speaks for itself."[48]

Dalton tried to sue William Jennings Bryan, but the lack of further press reports suggest that he failed.[49]

Hollywood owed a great deal to the prohibitionists. In 1887 Harvey Henderson Wilcox, a prohibitionist from Kansas, subdivided a ranch his wife had named Hollywood. Two years later, a couple named Blondeau bought six acres at the corner of Sunset and Gower and built the Cahuenga House. Threatened with closure if liquor was served, the place remained circumspect until well after Wilcox's death. But when the city fathers imposed prohibition, the Blondeau roadhouse, suffering from terminal drought, went on the market. In 1911, the vacant building was acquired by some picture people from the East and became the first studio in Hollywood.

Even after the Volstead Act there were few speakeasies in Hollywood. (An actor was murdered in one of them, the Crescent Tea Rooms at 1440 North Cherokee.) So long as you could afford the services of a bootlegger[50] you were assured of a supply.[51] But if there were few speakeasies in Hollywood, there were something like 30,000 in New York.[52] The most famous were lavish nightclubs run by a former taxi driver called Larry Fay and his partner, Texas Guinan.

Born on a ranch in Waco, Texas, and christened Mary Louise Cecilia, Texas Guinan had held a variety of jobs from Sunday School teacher to circus bronco rider. On the screen she won a certain following as a sort of female William S. Hart. Her films tended to be disliked by censor boards for being "saturated with crime" and her series was canceled.[53] By 1921 she was also a little old for the part, and after a couple of program pictures and some lawsuits she turned to the real thing. She was arrested on charges of passing a bad check[54] and then for car theft. She attempted to return to the New York stage, but found fame and wealth in company with Larry Fay.

At his El Fey club, Texas was the center of attention, dressed to dazzle with diamonds and sequins, sporting a clapper and a police whistle and welcoming customers with a cry which for many summed up Prohibition: "Hello, sucker!" Lloyd Morris thought she was a disillusioned sentimentalist with "a strong tincture of puritan moralism in her contempt for the public."[55]

Texas Guinan and the El Fey Club were featured in Allan Dwan's *Night Life of New York* (1925).[56] But despite her fame, or because of it, she and Fay were

Texas Guinan in Queen of the Night Clubs, *1929. (Museum of Modern Art)*

harassed by Prohibition agents. When she and Fay finally split, Texas returned to Hollywood to appear in talkies. She was typically caustic at the way some people in Hollywood turned up their noses at her attempt to reestablish herself: "In this little old town they don't know how to *play*. People pay $100,000 for my entertainments in New York, but when I come out here and want to give them something for nothing, they don't like it and then fight like cats. Some people are so narrow-minded their ears overlap."[57]

Texas starred in *Queen of the Nightclubs* (1929)—the name by which she was known. Her acting style was similar to that of Mae West. She died shortly after completing *Broadway Through a Keyhole* (1933).

There were surprisingly few films about Prohibition made during the silent era— Will Hays saw to that. One of the first on the subject was *The Midnight Girl,* a two-reeler written and directed by Adolf Philipp, who also played the lead, a wealthy man-about-town who has "a lovely voice for drinking." He is in despair at the loss of the saloon—"How he yearned for the mahogany bar, the little brass rail and the wild women"—and tries to shoot himself. His butler obligingly supplies him with a vast range of cocktails, but not until he discovers Cabaret Bohème, "a dive where a ginger ale highball still retains its kick," does he spring to life. A sign says "TEA 3 STARS."

The remarkable thing about this comedy, which is not remarkable in itself (too many titles and all rather inconclusive), is the fact that it was released in September 1919, presumably a result of the onset of "wartime" prohibition on July 1 of that year. It proves that the conditions we associate exclusively with the Roaring Twenties were already all too familiar to deprived drinkers.

The National Federation of Settlements partly financed a study of Prohibition and concluded that between 1920 and 1923 the experiment had worked. It had not abolished drinking, but it had cut down on alcoholism and improved life in the tenement areas. But as enforcement failed and bootlegging flourished, the situation changed.[58]

The moving picture reflected it in many curious ways. Will Hays issued a ukase ordering picture people not to mock the Volstead Act and to treat drinking scenes with great care. He even forbade stills to be published which showed bottles.[59] Directors went to great lengths to obey Hays and yet remain true to their subjects. Clarence Brown's *The Goose Woman* (1925) was a character study of an alcoholic old woman (Louise Dresser), once an opera star. When she takes a swig from the gin bottle, she turns her back to the camera and expresses her pleasure with a shudder. William Seiter, directing *The Mad Whirl* (1924) for Universal, opened his picture at "Bromo-Seltzer time in the Herrington household," when butlers and maid simultaneously carry their trays to the respective bedrooms of hungover father, mother, and son. When the son (Jack Mulhall) is shown drinking and driving, the camera shoots from the back of his car, so we see merely the

A once-great opera star, brought low by alcohol, played by Louise Dresser in Clarence Brown's The Goose Woman, *1925. (National Film Archive)*

movements of his straw hat. W. C. Fields took no such precautions and exploited the lust for alcohol in films like *It's the Old Army Game* (1926).

William Wellman went too far in *The Boob* (1926), a comedy in which Joan Crawford played a Prohibition agent. One scene was set in "The Booklovers Club," a library-cum-tearoom where the books have unusual titles; *Old Crow: Stories of Bird Life, Gunga Gin, Three Plays by Brew*. The books are equipped with stoppers, and their contents poured into coffee percolators. There is even a floor show. It begins sedately enough, with the girls carrying parasols and wearing hoop skirts, but their costumes are attached to wires; at a signal a stagehand pulls a series of levers and whips them off, and the girls break into a Charleston.[60]

Wellman was fired by MGM after this film, and having seen the picture, I would have done the same to him myself. The only excuse was that he was drunk while he was making it. George Geltzer told me that it lasted just one day on Broadway. Apart from the inventive club sequence, the picture uses alcohol for a series of gags which would have embarrassed even Mack Sennett. It is impossible to believe that this director would make *Wings* the following year. (In any case, Wellman was in good company. MGM fired Josef von Sternberg the same week.)[61]

The fact that Prohibition was a failure meant that propaganda films were still necessary. A short called *Episodes in the Life of a Gin Bottle* (ca. 1926) might have been made at the height of Prohibition agitation except for its sophisticated technique.

Rex Lease plays the Spirit of the Gin Bottle. A couple are drinking and necking in the back of the car. The girl gets out, and we see her in a stage dressing room where miserably she makes up and drinks directly from the bottle. The show folds, and the bottle passes to a gambling joint, where it is refilled with hooch. A bootlegger delivers it to a girl who uses it to enliven a date. (The Spirit appears occasionally to encourage the drinker.) The boyfriend lurches into the street and throws the bottle away. A garbage cart rolls up and loads it aboard, and eventually the bottle falls into the hands of a tramp. God knows what goes into it, but an old derelict, who takes a swig, goes blind. The Spirit in the bottle turns into the symbol of death.

THOSE WHO DANCE   Made on closed sets at the Thomas H. Ince studios in Culver City in 1924, *Those Who Dance* has all the signs of being the most significant film about bootlegging to be made in the twenties. But we are unlikely to know for sure, for the picture has not been seen for decades.[62]

Directed by Lambert Hillyer, a former newspaperman who had been William S. Hart's director, it starred Blanche Sweet, Bessie Love, and Warner Baxter. "Almost the best cast of the year," thought *Photoplay*,[63] which chose the film as one of the six best of the month. The main source for Hillyer's script was *Prohibition Inside Out* (1923) by Roy A. Haynes and William Pickett Helm, Jr. Haynes was the federal Prohibition commissioner, and thus government cooperation was assured.[64]

Bob Kane (Baxter) becomes an implacable enemy of bootleggers when his young sister (Lucille Ricksen) dies in a car crash because her date is blinded by

Those Who Dance, *1924. Bessie Love and Matthew Betz.*

drinking wood alcohol. Bob is sworn into the Prohibition force. Since he is un-
known to the liquor peddlers, Chief Monahan (John Sainpolis) details him to
shadow an enforcement officer he suspects of being hand-in-glove with the liquor
ring: Slip Blainey (Frank Campeau). Bob soon establishes that Slip is working with
"Joe the Greek" Anargas (Matthew Betz), a master New York bootlegger. Matt
Carney (Robert Agnew) is a well-meaning but weak youth who drives a truck for
Anargas. His mother, sensing something is wrong, sends his sister, Rose (Blanche
Sweet), to visit Matt. Rose finds him living with Joe Anargas and his wife, Veda
(Bessie Love), of whom she is instantly suspicious.

"Everybody breaks the liquor laws," says Matt. "Some of the best people are
on our books." He refuses to break with the gang, so Rose pretends to fall in with
the underworld. Chief Monahan sets a trap for the Anargas gang. Escaping, Anargas kills an officer, but Slip plants the gun on Matt, who is convicted and
sentenced to death.

Veda, angered by her husband's brutality, blurts out the story to Rose, who
hurries with it to Chief Monahan. The chief works out a plan by which Bob Kane
can get the truth from Anargas. Bob makes up as "Scar" Henry, a Chicago gangster, and Rose takes him to Anargas's apartment as her new sweetheart. Bob uses
a dictagraph to record a conversation which will convict Anargas. At the gangsters'
ball, however, Anargas traps him and he is only rescued by a clever ruse by Rose;
Blainey shoots Anargas and is promptly arrested. Matt is freed and Rose and Bob
decide they will work together under the name of Kane and Kane.[65]

Those Who Dance features a character seldom seen in later Prohibition dramas—the hijacker—and identified the chief gangster as a Greek. Presumably it
was felt that Greece was less likely to take commercial revenge than Italy, but

someone overlooked the fact that a surprising proportion of American exhibitors were of Greek origin. Joe Anargas later gained a new identity.

The film originally featured "the filthy holes" where liquor was manufactured from wood alcohol and showed how the process worked.[66] This was against the rulings of the Hays Office. Ince had received dispensation for *Human Wreckage,* and again for *Anna Christie,* his prestigious adaptation of Eugene O'Neill's play about a prostitute. He evidently took too much license with *Those Who Dance* and had to overhaul it completely.

Even so, the revised version, reviewed in July 1924, caused *Variety* to warn that state censor boards may cause trouble "because of the way the stuff is made, which may be something of an expose, although seemingly exaggerated."[67] (It wasn't.) They mentioned, too, shots of a young couple getting booze at a soda fountain and a scene of Rose and Bob Kane in bed together, which was intended to confirm their relationship to Anargas but which was strictly forbidden by Hays.

On top of this, the Ince Corporation received a letter from an attorney representing the Rose Room Dance Hall, complaining that in the scene of a dance attended by bootleggers and criminals, the entrance to that establishment was shown on the screen—complete with name. The dance hall was then shown being raided by the police, giving the public the impression that the Rose Room "is a place of ill repute . . . and has actually been raided by the police." The hall's patronage had been nearly destroyed, dropping by nearly 50 percent in the past two weeks.

The Ince people had, in fact, paid the Rose Room for use of the hall. Moreover, Pinkerton detectives reported a substantial flow of business during the two weeks in question. The Rose Room settled out of court for $375, and the Ince Corporation agreed to eliminate the name of the hall from the film.[68]

The reviews were good. Only one critic dismissed the film as "dime novel stuff," and even he thought it carried a kick as forceful as a "white mule."[69] *Picture Play* thought it had "a few neat lessons for those who buy their stuff direct from the ships," but added that it tried to preach no lessons—it was good, straight entertainment with "more suspense than I have seen in any picture in a long time."[70] Everyone thought Bessie Love exceptional as Veda. *Motion Picture Magazine* said that Blanche Sweet, as Rose, gave a performance comparable to the one she gave in *Anna Christie* and thought the sequence in which she foists a federal officer on the bootleg king and lives with him in the gangster's home "is just about as daring as well as dramatic as we've seen on the shadow stage in a long, long while."[71]

The total direct cost of *Those Who Dance* was $256,894.95. The film showed a deficit of $44,929.75. The failure was explained thus: "It was a good picture with an excellent cast and should have made a very considerable profit, but the exhibitors seem to be against a picture that carries any propaganda even tho [*sic*] it is a propaganda which everyone recognizes as a good cause."[72]

Shortly after the picture opened, its director, Lambert Hillyer, and his wife and chauffeur were arrested and charged with possession of ten quarts of liquor and concealed weapons after a wild automobile ride near Fullerton, California. The Hillyers objected strenuously to the arrest, which was hardly surprising since three revolvers were found in the car. Mrs. Hillyer said she needed the protection;

she was wearing $24,000 worth of jewelry, and one of the rings alone was valued at $6,000. As bail, the Fullerton judge took all the cash they had on them—$350. Hillyer's lawyer complained that his absence from the set was costing $5,000 a day—the payroll for his current production, *Idle Tongues.*[73] The Hillyers were eventually fined $1,000.[74]

TWELVE MILES OUT   When Pathé News showed rumrunners, "taken without bias or without motive save to enlighten the public," bootlegging could be seen as an activity with a dash of romance. Pathé News's own methods were nothing if not swashbuckling. Editor Emanuel Cohen and a group of cameramen chartered a fishing schooner and sailed fifteen miles off the coast of Massachusetts. They were all in disguise, wearing oil slickers and hip boots like the crew of their vessel, and the cameramen were hidden under tarpaulins.

They approached the rumrunning ships at anchor without arousing any suspicion and filmed the unloading of 1,200 cases of liquor from one vessel, 10,000 from another. They also managed to film the pursuit of a rumrunner by a Treasury cutter and the jettisoning of the cargo. Pathé also covered rumrunning in Canada, the Bahamas, Cuba, and Florida, as well as on the links of Scotland. A few years later, when Metro-Goldwyn-Mayer made a film about these smugglers, they made the chief bootlegger not a vicious gangster but a glamorous daredevil, played by John Gilbert.

MGM had established itself as the studio preeminent in well-made, entertaining, and intelligent films. From its headquarters in Culver City had come the epic of war, *The Big Parade,* starring Gilbert. When *Twelve Miles Out* was suggested, Gilbert was enthusiastic, for he felt that it could be the epic of Prohibition. It was based on a play by William Anthony McGuire[75] which had opened in New York in 1925; the scenario was by A. P. Younger. The script was too restricted, and Gilbert, who had been a scriptwriter himself, contributed a sequence showing the background of the bootlegger as a daredevil motorcyclist in an amusement park. His girlfriend in this section was played by Betty Compson.

In 1927, there was a change of leadership in MGM's parent company, Loew's Inc. Economy measures were imposed on such films as *Anna Karenina* (released as *Love*), to their detriment. The director assigned to *Twelve Miles Out,* Jack Conway, was an easygoing man; MGM was a producers' studio where the director was expected to obey orders. And the orders were to turn out this bootlegging drama as speedily and cheaply as possible.

The film was freely adapted from the play. The bootlegger is named Jerry Fay—a reference to Larry—and the picture shows his liquor schooner and a freighter making a rendezvous "twelve miles out" (the search limit was an hour's steaming distance from the seacoast).[76] Just outside the three-mile limit, the cargo is transferred again, to a speedy motorboat capable of eluding the Coast Guard and Treasury cutters. When the motorboat is caught in the beam of a searchlight and machine guns open up, the crew takes shelter in a Long Island cove. Nearby is a beach house, which the smugglers seize at gunpoint.

Inside the beach house are a young girl, Jane (Joan Crawford), with her wealthy but weak fiancé, John Burton (Edward Earle). Burton declares with distaste that

Three machineguns aboard the rum-runner in Twelve Miles Out, 1927. Tom O'Brien at helm, Joan Crawford and Edward Earle in background, John Gilbert in command. (Museum of Modern Art)

Twelve Miles Out. Joan Crawford, John Gilbert, and Ernest Torrence. (National Film Archive)

Fay must be a bootlegger. Fay takes Burton's glass, sniffs, and points out that without bootleggers people like him would be unable to violate the law. When Burton tells Jane to remember the face for court identification, Fay takes them prisoner aboard his ship. Jane regards him with loathing and calls him a braggart and a coward. Stung by her insults, Fay gives Burton a loaded gun and turns his back. As he expects, Jane stops Burton from firing.

That night, the ship is caught by a Coast Guard cutter, and Fay has no alternative but to surrender. When the crew swarms aboard, he is relieved to recognize the captain as his old rival Red McCue (Ernest Torrence) in disguise. The hijackers seize control of the ship and McCue tries to seize control of Jane, but Fay challenges him to an alcoholic duel, which he wins by subterfuge. Fay alerts the Coast Guard. When McCue recovers consciousness, he insists on the *droit de seigneur,* and he and Fay indulge in hand-to-hand combat, which is incredibly brutal and vicious, but which both obviously glory in. When genuine Coast Guard men board the ship, they demand to know the owner. The two men, torn and bleeding, lie exhausted on the deck. "It's mine," says Fay. "He's a cock-eyed liar," says McCue, "it's mine," and collapses. Fay asks Jane for a kiss, just to prove she doesn't despise him too much. Jane now loves him, but she no sooner delivers the kiss than he dies.

The unhappy ending staggered the critics. Robert E. Sherwood thought it must be the first time in film history that an unhappy ending had been substituted for a happy one.[77] But it was the only way MGM could get the story past the Hays Office, for *Twelve Miles Out* was more of a love story than an epic of Prohibition— a love story with sadomasochistic overtones.

There was little evidence in the film of those documentary glimpses of bootlegging which would have made such a story so fascinating. Yet a former hijacker and bootlegger was employed as technical adviser at the studios and shown— masked—in publicity stills![78] (He was known around the studio as Mr. X.) And the boat used in the film, equipped with special hatches and "grab hooks" for handling liquor cargoes and dumping them rapidly into the sea in case the boat was overtaken, was a close replica of a rumrunner captured in New York. Research taken from police records and prohibition agencies was used in preparing the rumrunning scene, publicized as "the first authentic exposé on the screen."[79]

Jerry Fay was characterized as a flamboyant and glamorous figure, slightly mad, but irresistible to women. Yet John Gilbert was bitterly disappointed by the film. It was made so economically, he charged, that the theme was ruined. He had a furious row with Louis B. Mayer during the course of production—and relations with the producer of the film, Hunt Stromberg, were cool.

"We go around glaring at each other like a lot of spoiled children," he said. "I don't like the management I've had lately and I've told them so. . . . I haven't seen the picture and did not even go to the preview. It is not a good picture. We didn't have the proper story to work with. One thing that makes me furious is that there is a good story in the bootlegging industry. There is an epic tale there and some day someone is coming along to do it."[80]

When this interview appeared in the Los Angeles *Times,* the story caused "volcanic eruptions" at the studio and Gilbert was forced to apologize publicly. What must have added salt to his wound was that his amusement park sequence survived only the first preview. With it went all traces of Betty Compson's role. Scenes with Paulette Duval and Gwen Lee were substituted. Despite this, the picture did very well. It opened at the Capitol, New York, to a capacity house and took in $59,000 the first week. The reviews confounded all Gilbert's pessimism.

Welford Beaton said Jack Gilbert was a poor critic. It was not a great picture, but it was highly entertaining: "I think it is quite delightful to have a picture about bootlegging and highjacking [*sic*]. Highjacking is a splendid way to get one's liquor; one gets it by the thousand cases and has some exquisite sport thrown in for good measure. Bootleggers play such an intimate part in the lives of all of us that we have a personal interest in the worries that beset them."[81]

Said *Photoplay:* "Here is a fine picture in which John Gilbert gives one of the soundest performances of his career. The moral is that the wages of bootlegging is death or the hoosegow or maybe both. They call it 'the epic of rum-running.' "[82]

Said the *New York Times:* "It's gory, it's gruesome, but both men shoot with such fierce abandon, with such mad joy in the thing, even when they are hit, that it all fairly fascinated the spectator, jerking him into another world of savagery and blood. . . . It's not pretty, that's true. But it's not pap. That's great!"[83]

MGM defied Hays in releasing *Twelve Miles Out,* yet Louis B. Mayer issued a resolution calling upon producers to eliminate from the screen nudity, robbery, ridicule of race and creeds, and all the rest. The inference was that other producers were committing these crimes, said James Quirk, but that he was innocent of them.

"Every time the poor motion picture is accused of anything, someone like Louis B. Mayer notifies the newspapers, then rushes to the district attorney, breaks down and confesses on behalf of the industry and promises to go straight.

"Mr. Mayer is holier than none. No hotter screening of 100 percent sex than *Flesh and the Devil* has appeared in years. . . . *Twelve Miles Out* violated so many of the rules he so smugly set up for the other producers and offended theater patrons to the extent that many exhibitors regretted showing it.

"There is one screen crime that Mr. Mayer ignored—the highest crime of all—bad taste. I recommend it to his personal attention. It was reported recently that the gentleman's salary is $800,000 a year. That makes Mr. Mayer the highest priced actor in motion pictures."[84]

By 1926 illegal liquor was a $3.6 billion business.[85] Al Capone had the highest gross income ever enjoyed by a private American citizen—$105 million a year, which was $35 million more than Henry Ford at his best.[86]

Prohibition bred a contempt for the law from which America never recovered. And it failed to serve the very purpose for which it had been created. By 1929, admitted Mrs. Mabel Walker Willebrandt, the former assistant attorney general of the United States in charge of Prohibition prosecutions, liquor could be bought "at almost any hour of the day or night, either in rural districts, the smaller towns or the cities."[87]

As Carry Nation put it:

"100,000 drunkards die every year.
BUT NOT BY MY VOTE."

Chapter Five

CRIME

The City of Darkness, *1914*.
(*John E. Allen*)

SCANDAL AND NOTORIETY

PUBLIC OPINION   Trial by newspaper is not a recent phenomenon. It was so common in the early part of the century that a film, *Public Opinion* (1916), was made on the subject by the Jesse L. Lasky Feature Play Company. Margaret Turnbull wrote the scenario, which was directed by Frank Reicher.[1]

The opening title read: "In law, the accused is held innocent until proven guilty, but when public opinion is poisoned by yellow journalism, it condemns the accused before the trial begins." A nurse, Hazel Gray (Blanche Sweet), is employed by a wealthy philanthropist, Mrs. Carson Morgan (Edythe Chapman), whose husband is a doctor (Earle Foxe). This doctor, who had a brief affair with Hazel, is now after his wife's money. He poisons her and manages to throw the blame on the nurse. The yellow press splashes the case across the front pages, and the girl is condemned before the trial has begun.

One young juryman (Elliott Dexter) is convinced of her innocence and succeeds in persuading the rest to deliver a verdict of not guilty. But public opinion is far from satisfied. The crowd outside the court is convinced she has got away with it because of her good looks. And although the girl is released, the newspapers make her life a misery, and she is ostracized, a fate "almost more terrible than capital punishment."[2]

A dope addict shoots the doctor when he refuses him drugs, and the doctor makes a dying confession, which exonerates Hazel. She marries the young juryman, a conventional end to a far from conventional picture.

The strangest comment came from *Photoplay,* which called the jury "pumpkin headed" for letting the girl off. "Though the woman is innocent, material evidence is against her." They blamed it on the male jury's traditional chivalry to the pretty thing, as though "material evidence" was all that counted.[3]

"While the story of *Public Opinion* may not be based upon a recent New York murder case," said the *New York Dramatic Mirror,* "the resemblance is apparent."[4] Lasky publicity asserted that the big courtroom scene was "an exact replica of that in which the trial was held [and] upon which the story is based."

Historian J. B. Kaufman has discovered that in September 1915, Dr. Arthur W. Waite of New York married Clara Peck, the daughter of a millionaire drug manufacturer in Michigan. Within six months, he had poisoned both his in-laws and had attempted to murder his wife in the same way. When the police came to arrest him, they found him in a drug-induced stupor. There was no parallel in this case to the Blanche Sweet character. "The closest thing to it was a black maid who testified that she saw Waite put some 'medicine' into the father-in-law's food, and that he tried to bribe her to keep quiet."[5]

What is remarkable about the case is that it occurred *after* Margaret Turnbull's

Earle Foxe as the guilty doctor in Public Opinion, *1916, directed by Frank Reicher.*
(Museum of Modern Art)

story was bought by Lasky. It is almost certainly the case referred to by the New York *Dramatic Mirror* and exploited by the publicity department, but Kaufman can find nothing similar that might have inspired Margaret Turnbull.

Curiously enough, for so intriguing a film, Blanche Sweet had not the slightest memory of having played in it and had to look it up before she could be persuaded that she had.

EVELYN NESBIT   America's most distinguished architect, Stanford White, was shot by millionaire playboy Harry K. Thaw in 1906. This event has a fascination which sets it apart from most *crimes passionnels,* a fascination revolving around the girl in the case, Evelyn Nesbit. She was only sixteen when raped by Stanford White, "a great man," in her view, however "perverse and decadent."[6] And she was only twenty when she became involved in "the Crime of the Century."

The story has so many ramifications into the world of cinema that an entire book could be devoted to them. One of White's studios, at 540 West Twenty-first Street, New York City, became the headquarters of the Reliance Film Company. Above White's offices was the workshop of his friend Peter Cooper-Hewitt, whose mercury-vapor lights were so crucial to the motion picture studios. Evelyn—then Florence—Nesbit was sent by White to the DeMille School at Pompton, New

Evelyn Nesbit in 1902, before the scandal broke. (Ira Resnick)

Jersey, run by the mother of the future directors. (William was in residence at the time, writing his play *Strongheart*.) Nesbit was courted by John Barrymore. Thaw's prosecutor, New York district attorney William Travers Jerome, later raised funds for the Technicolor Corporation. Thaw tried to become a producer in the 1920s and introduced Anita Page to Hollywood.

The case itself had great significance for motion picture history, for it contributed to the beginning of censorship (see page 4). And it provided a career for Evelyn Nesbit, thanks less to her talent than to her notoriety.

Evelyn was born at Tarentum, outside Pittsburgh. As a young girl she became an artists' model and then went on the stage, joining the *Floradora* company and concealing her true age. When she met Stanford White, a much older man (he was fifty-three when he died), she was touched by his kindly, fatherly interest. He impressed both Evelyn and her mother as someone absolutely safe. On one occasion, her mother went out of town, leaving her in White's sole guardianship. He gave her champagne, probably drugged, and she felt dizzy and faint. When she came to, she was in bed, naked. "It's all over," said White. "Now you belong to me."[7]

Harry K. Thaw, a wealthy young man from Pittsburgh, saw her on the stage and bombarded her with letters. When she met him, she was both attracted and repelled. She soon learned that he was a drug addict, an accomplished sadist, and mentally unbalanced. Nevertheless, she felt sorry for him and agreed to marry him. (He was, after all, extremely rich.) When he demanded assurance that she was a virgin, she broke down and told him about Stanford White, a man he hated anyway. Now it was his turn to break down.

Harry and Evelyn were married. On June 25, 1906, they visited *Mlle. Champagne* at the dining theatre on the Madison Square Garden roof. They thought the show "putrid" and decided to leave. They had reached the elevators when suddenly Thaw ran back, shot Stanford White at point-blank range, and killed him outright. Incarcerated in the Tombs, he explained that his wife had been White's "sex slave"—that was how the newspapers put it. Thaw made the "unwritten law" plea world famous.

Evelyn Nesbit played her role carefully in the witness box to ensure that Thaw was not sentenced to death. She knew, however, that to avoid a scandal in which they would all be exposed, "the inner circle" had persuaded district attorney William Travers Jerome to have Thaw locked up in an asylum. (They were all members of the conservative Union Club.)

Thaw's lawyer, Delphin Delmas, persuaded the jury that his client suffered from "dementia Americana" at the moment he shot White—a neurosis, invented for the occasion, for Americans who believed every man's wife is sacred. After a retrial, the jury obligingly returned a verdict of not guilty on grounds of insanity—and Thaw was sent to Matteawan, the New York State Asylum for the Criminally Insane.[8]

First to benefit financially from the murder, after the yellow press, was Madison Square Garden itself. The building had been designed by Stanford White, and the roof garden restaurant became more popular than ever as people flocked to stare at the scene of the crime.

To permit people to stare in larger numbers, the subject was hastily put on film. It was ideally suited to satisfy the audience's scornful curiosity about "the idle rich." At least one of these films still survives: *The Unwritten Law* (1907), made by the Philadelphia company, Lubin.[9] It is a vivid reenactment, or, as *Variety* unkindly called it, "a fake." Harry Thaw leaves the court a free man, which proved the film had been made in a hurry and suggested, too, that audiences expected the verdict to be fixed.

This little picture is as good as a Griffith Biograph in terms of technique and has similar marks of imagination—the vision in the prison, for instance. Painted interiors aside, there is no artifice to spoil the enjoyment. Perhaps Stanford White (here called Black) dies overdramatically, but otherwise the playing is as naturalistic as a documentary. The suggestiveness of the red velvet swing and "the boudoir of a hundred mirrors" must have been potent images for audiences from cold-water flats.

The red velvet swing became so notorious that the phrase passed into the language. (A film about Evelyn Nesbit, on which she served as consultant, was made in 1955 as *The Girl in the Red Velvet Swing*.) Evelyn testified at the trial that when she was sixteen, she and a friend visited White's studio on Twenty-fourth Street—the most gorgeous place she had ever seen—and he gave them a tour of the rooms upstairs. In one was a large velvet chair hanging from two ropes: "He would push us until we would swing to the ceiling. There was a big Japanese umbrella on the ceiling, so when he pushed us our feet would crash through."[10]

In *The Unwritten Law,* slightly more sedately, White fastens a parasol to the door, and encourages Evelyn to swing until her feet touch it. (The other girl does not appear.) Later, Evelyn performed the trick in the nude, but of course the film does not hint at that. Instead, it proceeds to the next thrill, the Boudoir of a

Hundred Mirrors. In an elaborately painted rococo set, White gives Evelyn the fatal drink. She becomes dizzy, and he places a screen around her. That is all we see. But those familiar with the yellow press could fill in the rest.

In the scene at the Tombs, Evelyn and her mother try to console Thaw. When they leave, he suffers alone, and a vision of the murder appears in the window above him. Actually, Thaw managed to maintain his way of life in prison; his meals came from Delmonico's, whiskey was smuggled to him, and he continued to play the stock market.[11]

The print in the National Film Archive is cataloged as featuring Evelyn Nesbit herself, but the girl who appears in it does not resemble her, being a different shape and lacking her beauty. Miss Nesbit was also said to have made her screen debut in *The Great Thaw Trial* (1907), which, like the Lubin film, covered the main events, but she was not in this one, either. At this stage, she said, she had an aversion to trading on her association with Thaw.[12] But Thaw, behind bars, must have been permitted to see the film, because he sent his attorney to the court where a proprietor of a theatre had been charged with imperiling the morals of young boys by showing it. "Mr. Thaw has requested me to inform the court," the attorney said, "that the moving pictures which have just been under consideration are not what they are purported to be. He wants it distinctly understood that the picture of his wife is not a good one and that the other pictures do not show the marriage ceremony as it occurred, nor the principals in it. The same applies to the tragedy of the roof garden."[13]

The Thaw film attracted twice as many spectators as *The Life of Christ*.[14]

Evelyn Thaw gave birth to a son, Russell. She declared he was Harry's child, even though Harry had been locked up for several years. Filing for support, she explained that Harry had bribed a guard at Matteawan to allow her to spend "a heavenly and fruitful night" with him.[15] Harry hotly denied this, and Evelyn eventually admitted another prominent man was the father, but she would take the secret of his identity to her grave.[16]

Evelyn appeared in vaudeville in 1913 at the astonishing salary of $3,500 a week and broke box-office records.[17] Harry Thaw helped her box office by escaping from Matteawan, and Evelyn capitalized on that by telling the press of his death list, with her name at the top. Harry was captured in Canada, which guaranteed Evelyn Canadian bookings, and he was then deported to the U.S.

Hal Reid, who produced *Harry K. Thaw's Fight for Freedom* (1913), had written and produced a play in which Thaw was portrayed sympathetically. He went to Sherbrooke, Canada, and New Hampshire and talked to Thaw in his cell. The prisoner agreed to be filmed, and Reid photographed 500 feet of him eating, looking out of his cell window, and talking. The promoters, the Canadian-American Feature Company, wanted $1,500 a week for the reel. Several other Thaw films appeared on the market, including one called *Harry Thaw's Escape from Matteawan*,[18] so Thaw had obligingly sent Reid a telegram from Quebec, which was used in the advertising:

THE ONLY MOVING PICTURE TAKEN OF ME IN MY CELL AT SHER-
BROOKE OR ANYWHERE UP TO DATE WERE TAKEN BY YOU. I AU-

(Ira Resnick)

THORIZE YOU IF YOU SO DESIRE WITHOUT COST OR PREJUDICE TO ME
TO LEGALLY PUNISH OR ENJOIN ANY AND ALL PERSONS WHO SHOW
ANY MOVING PICTURES CLAIMING THEY ARE OF ME INSIDE ANY
PRISON.[19]

Reid's film was shown on the Keith and Orpheum circuits, although in some cities, such as Spokane, Washington, the censor refused to pass it. And a five-reel feature about Thaw was so badly mauled by the Detroit censor that only the last two reels survived. All the early scenes—the Red Velvet Swing, the murder—were cut.

"The real interest around Thaw," said Commissioner Gillespie, who ordered the cuts, "is his escape. I think the masses are now in sympathy with him. I can see no objection to pictures of his escape, but nothing previous to that."[20] The newsreels were able to run items on Thaw unmolested.

Hal Reid's film, elaborated into *Escape from the Asylum*, "converted many people to the belief that Thaw had been sufficiently punished and that he deserved sympathy."[21]

By May 1914, the public's curiosity having been satisfied, the Evelyn Nesbit

Thaw vaudeville show closed. She announced that hereafter she wanted to be known as Evelyn Nesbit, and she formed her own company.[22] She went to Paris, where, just before the outbreak of war, she made her first motion picture appearance (newsreels apart), when footage was shot with Fred Mace and Marguerite Marsh in and around the Cluny Museum.[23]

The Threads of Destiny (1914), a five-reeler directed by Joseph Smiley, was shot at the Lubin estate, Betzwood, and featured not only Evelyn but her young son, Russell Thaw, and her future husband, Jack Clifford.

In 1915, Thaw was pronounced sane by a New York court and he was released. He divorced Evelyn in Pittsburgh in 1916. The following year, she began her motion picture career in earnest. It must be admitted, however, that while she regarded her vaudeville career as something of enormous importance, her films did not mean much to her. She accords them a mere passing mention in her autobiography: "I made two pictures for Joseph Schenck then six for Fox at Fort Lee."[24]

She starred in *Redemption* for Triumph in 1917, which *Variety* called "the best thing she has ever done upon the stage or screen."[25] Written by John Stanton, produced by Julius Steger, and directed by Steger and Joseph A. Golden, it showed a mother forced to confess to her grown son a mistake of her youth. (Evelyn was still only thirty-one!) *"Redemption* is continually suggesting it may be a revamp in part at least of her life's history." She played an actress who gained notoriety when young but who renounces the life at her marriage. Among the ghosts from her past is a wealthy architect! When she rejects him, he seeks a revenge which leads indirectly to the death of her husband and her own financial ruin.

Her son, Russell, again played in the picture. Wid admitted she screened well, but charged the picture with being a justification of Evelyn Nesbit's errors. He advised exhibitors not to book it merely because of the star's notoriety.[26] The picture turned out to be a "terrific draw"[27] and broke records. It guaranteed a film career for both Evelyn and her small son.

"Redemption is an illustration of the fact that those upon whom we look with averted eyes," said *Motion Picture Magazine,* "may be more sinned against than sinning."[28]

When the picture came to England, as *Shadows on My Life,* controversy broke out anew, and even though it was made clear that there was nothing sordid, gruesome, or repellent about it, the Cinematograph Exhibitors' Association's General Council passed the resolution: "THAT ANY FILM EXPLOITING THE NOTO-RIETY OF EVELYN THAW IS PREJUDICIAL TO THE BEST INTERESTS OF THE INDUSTRY."[29]

The British Board of Film Censors had passed the film without comment (probably oblivious of Evelyn Nesbit's identity). One exhibitor believed he was correct in saying that not one member of the General Council had seen the picture.

It was not the film, said a member of the General Council, but the exploitation of Evelyn Thaw's notoriety to which the council objected. The thought of a young girl turning to her parent and asking "Who is Evelyn Thaw?" pained the chairman. They had been fighting to keep the screen pure, and it was absolutely wrong to show this film, owing to its publicity matter.

Evelyn Nesbit and Irving Cummings in The Woman Who Gave,
1918, directed by Kenean Buel. (National Film Archive)

After all the fuss, the (private) trade show was invaded by a large crowd of
uninvited members of the public. The reviewers in the press were disappointed
that all the objectionable features of the Thaw case had been sponged away. "It
would not raise a blush on the cheek of your maiden aunt," said the Glasgow
Bulletin.

Nesbit's contract with Fox led to a series of features, the first of which was
The Woman Who Gave (1918), directed by Kenean Buel. The story included a scene
of Evelyn posing, as she did in real life, for such celebrated artists as Charles Dana
Gibson, and the brutal Thaw was symbolized by an even more brutal Bulgarian
nobleman. Fox reported that bookings on the Nesbit pictures had broken all
records.[30] Her name was advertised thus: EVELYN NESBIT!

I Want to Forget (1918) was a German spy drama written and directed by James
Kirkwood, which teamed Nesbit with Henry Clive, an artist of some distinction
himself. Her acting was praised—"she becomes more of an actress as her screen
experience broadens," said Wid,[31] but the story was not worth bothering about.

Kenean Buel's *Woman! Woman!* (1919) was greeted by Julian Johnson in
Photoplay[32] as the sort of picture which made censorship inevitable. "If we are to

have slime of this sort dragged through our projectors, we shall soon have our photoplays in the hands of a Russian secret police system—with no one but ourselves to blame. William Fox is handing the complacent Evelyn Nesbit scenarios the like of which Theda Bara in her boldest days never attempted." He added that "the filthy story" would not bear synopsizing. *Variety* was more accommodating: a country girl, Alice, comes to the city and gets mixed up with the Greenwich Village "free love" crowd. She marries a young engineer (Clifford Bruce). His employer, a multimillionaire (William H. Tooker), offers gold and jewels for the chance to make her his mistress. When her husband falls ill in the tropics she takes up the offer, thus earning the money to save her husband's life. But when her husband comes home and learns the truth he throws her out, together with her child, whom the millionaire claims as his. After the divorce, she returns to the country, but her reputation precedes her and she is ostracized. Her husband eventually apologizes; she tells him she made the greatest sacrifice a woman can make, and he failed to appreciate it. The millionaire proposes, but she turns him down and remarries her young engineer.[33]

My Little Sister (1919), also directed by Kenean Buel, was based on a novel by Elizabeth Robins, which caused something of a furor when it came out in 1913. It was the story of two country girls removed to London and trapped in a brothel patronized by the wealthy. "Sensational and brutally unpleasant," said Wid, although he admired Nesbit's acting: "She plays the part of the elder sister more effectively than it probably would have been played by many an actress possessing more technical accomplishments."[34]

This was her last film for Fox, although not the last to be released. Her contract expired, and she returned to vaudeville, where she faced a lawsuit from the tax authorities and a divorce suit from Jack Clifford.

She made a picture called *The Hidden Woman* for Joseph Schenck which was directed by Allan Dwan. It was released in 1922, probably some time after it was made. Dwan found her a pleasant, ordinary woman: "She was a rough sort underneath, and tried to be dignified—but she was a nut."[35]

In the film, Nesbit played a frivolous society girl who loses her fortune on the stock market and retires to the Adirondacks, where she incurs the wrath of local reformers.

"The murder didn't make Evelyn Nesbit a big actress to me," said Dwan, "just a dame that got into trouble. So I met her and saw she had limitations; she was squawking because she wanted to go to the country for the summer. She had a little place up in [Lake Chateaugay] New York, a cottage beside a lake, so I said fine, we'll do it there so you can have a vacation and make some money. She thought that was fine. She was bedded down with a man who was a boxer. One day she says, 'Won't you do me a favor and come over tonight and referee a party I'm having?' I said, 'What do you mean?' She said, 'Come over and I'll show you.'

"That night I went over with my assistant, I didn't want to go in alone, and she was loaded up with these strange hangers-on, New York people, strange crowd, mostly pugilists, and they were having an ether party. I had never heard of an ether party; what they had to be careful of was that nobody had too much ether, or they would pass out and swallow their tongue. The referee's job was to look them over and shake them up if they were too far gone. They started getting cock-eyed drunk on ether and my assistant and I were pretty busy until three in the morning waking up these people and tossing them out in the lake to sober them up. That pretty near turned me off."[36]

Dwan telephoned Joe Schenck and told him the situation; Schenck came up and persuaded Evelyn to abandon her ether parties until the picture was finished. Dwan did not see her again until he met her in Atlantic City: "She was running a nightclub, but was doing well, making money, based entirely on the notoriety she'd got from the murder case."[37]

Dwan did not know that her experiments with ether were an attempt to break away from cocaine and morphine, to which she had become addicted. She suffered from agonizing neuralgia and even tried suicide.[38]

Author Samson De Brier knew Evelyn Nesbit in Atlantic City and considered her a remarkable woman: "In those hypocritical years, when scandal both shocked and titillated the public, Evelyn wore her notoriety with forbidding dignity. And she was shrewd enough not to reveal the whole truth. Thus she negated her past and, perhaps, any guilt she may have felt.

"She had a dichotomous attitude towards her position in the affair. She resented being considered only as a 'succès de scandale,' but her questionable publicity did afford the opportunity to provide a living for herself and her son.

"She had great presence and an assured manner and she could never become an obscure housewife. Curiously, she never again made a 'brilliant' marriage or alliance. Yet her beauty was only more striking as she matured.

"She did not talk about the 'case,' as I was in my teens when I first knew her and did not have the skill to draw her out. I just enjoyed knowing her as a fascinating and beautiful woman. She often had me to dinner at her tiny and sparsely furnished apartment in Atlantic City. Her son was living with her there— a quiet boy.

"Years later, when I was in the position to offer her an interview on a New York radio station, she refused. She was sick and tired of going through the old story again. And years after that, when we had both moved to California, she was apprehensive about Joan Collins playing her part [in *Girl on the Red Velvet Swing*], because she did not know of her. She thought she would be portrayed by a famous movie star. Of course, none of them were young enough. After she met Joan Collins, she was pleased. And she was glad to get the money—her final chance to get a sizeable sum for her declining years. If only she had collaborated with a 'ghost' she could have made a fortune. But by that time she was plagued by ill-health. She moved to a little hotel way out on Figueroa Street, a location where no one here would ever think of going. I never saw her again. I was settling in to a very busy social life, and she lived so far away. I shall always regret not making more of an effort to see her."[39]

BEULAH BINFORD   Beulah Binford was a seventeen-year-old girl who became notorious after the arrest of Henry Clay Beattie, Jr., for the murder of his wife in Richmond, Virginia, in 1911. Although she was repudiated by Beattie on the witness stand, she testified that her association with him had begun when she was thirteen.

The president of the Levi Company, Isaac Levi, signed a contract with Binford and filmed her brief life at his Staten Island studio. The New York *Evening World* appealed to public sentiment to prevent the exploitation of this girl on film or stage. At the behest of Mayor William Gaynor, the commissioner of licenses informed Levi that under no circumstances would the film be approved. Levi said the film was intended to carry a moral lesson and a warning to other girls "to shun the temptation to which she had succumbed."[40]

Leon Rubinstein, in charge of the picture and probably its director, too, had taken Beulah into his own house. He arranged a meeting for the girl and the members of the National Board and showed them the film. He was furious when they still refused to endorse it; he declared that Beulah was being robbed of her one chance to make an honest living. He would fight the ban. The Reverend Madison C. Peters declared that the picture was no more harmful than the play *Way Down East:* "The girl should have a helping hand extended to her. It is a blot upon the Christian ministry . . . that she had received no offers of aid or sympathy." Surely, he said, she should not be held responsible for mistakes committed when she was thirteen. "Her story, instead of being one to damn her, is an indictment against a society that enables such things to be."[41]

The film showed Beulah as a baby, left in the care of a grandmother while her mother played the horses. She grows up a tomboy and is seen taking automobile rides with a man, presumably Beattie. "Another picture shows her tear-stained and weary. It is labeled 'Realization,' " said *Moving Picture News.* She tries to get work, but is harassed by men. The film ended with the murder and the third degree and scenes of the girl in prison. The picture was entitled *The Wages of Sin.*

The Board of Censors thought the film's only appeal was to morbid curiosity: "The picture intrinsically fails to teach any lesson except one of sentimental toleration for the girl who takes easy opportunities to 'go wrong.' "[42]

Rubinstein wrote to the trade press saying that his film sounded the warning of the dangers of parental neglect and pointed to phases of the social system that needed correction: "Have moving pictures ever before been devoted to such serious work?"[43]

Mayor Gaynor may have barred the film in New York, the Board of Censors may have condemned it for the rest of the country, but it was shown just the same. The publicity of the Beattie case aroused a tremendous demand, and the Special Feature Film Company announced in September 1911 that 116 towns— including New York—had shown it to 684,164 people.[44]

Two months later, Henry Beattie was executed and Binford, having achieved only a small role in a Richmond stage play, was living in seclusion in the Bronx.[45]

THE DE SAULLES CASE   So common had it become to feature the central character of a famous or infamous event in a film that it was inevitable some producer would merely pretend to do so. When William Fox set up a film about the De Saulles murder, *The Woman and the Law* (1918), he gave the job of direction to Raoul Walsh. He had his eye on Miriam Cooper, Walsh's wife, who resembled Bianca De Saulles.

"I'd go into a store or a restaurant," said Miriam Cooper, "and hear people whispering behind my back, "There's Bianca De Saulles!""[46]

Miriam Cooper fell ill; but Fox executive Winfield Sheehan wanted to produce the film while the story was hot, so the role went to a society girl. Sheehan soon called on Mrs. Walsh and told her the girl was lousy and, ill or not, she was needed for the lead. She gave in.

Exteriors were shot in Miami Beach, then just a long strip of sand, a few beach cottages, and a couple of big hotels. The co-respondent (based on dancer Joan Sawyer) was played by Follies girl Peggy Hopkins, later one of the most celebrated courtesans of the twenties as Peggy Hopkins Joyce.

The name De Saulles was changed to La Salle, but Fox had the brainstorm of omitting Miriam Cooper's name from the credits, so an intriguing blank would appear opposite "Mrs. Jack La Salle." Cooper said she would not tolerate that,[47] but evidently she had no option. *Variety* recognized Miriam Cooper, at least in the second half. The film carried the title "Based on the sensational Jack De Saulles case," which *Variety* thought made the whole thing utterly morbid and mercenary. "The story of the De Saulles case—a young wife is divorced from her husband, with her little boy allotted to each parent for certain portions of each year. The child goes to visit his father and the mother is taunted with the declaration he won't be returning to her. She goes to the father and shoots him, the jury acquitting her."[48]

Walsh's direction was exceedingly classy, thought *Variety,* but the scenario was cheap and the situations obvious.

Fox might have employed a principal witness while he was at it and perhaps created a further sensation. His name was Rodolpho Guglielmi, an Italian immigrant who had played a few screen roles as Rodolpho di Valentino. (He had testified against his dancing partner, Joan Sawyer, in the divorce suit, but left New York when the murder took place—a journey which eventually took him to Hollywood.)[49]

THE CLARA HAMON CASE   "No man or woman with the least trace of self respect would attend again a theater that slapped public decency in the face by defiling its screen with it."[50]

James Quirk was referring to a film called *Fate* (1921), which aroused so much anger one might be forgiven for assuming it to be openly pornographic or an apologia for Bolshevism. In fact it was, like so many other films, a murder story. The only difference was that the alleged murderess played the leading role, and, to all intents and purposes, produced the picture.

It is important to realize that in real life Clara Hamon was acquitted. There was no doubt, however, that she did shoot her husband; she admitted it when she gave herself up. So whatever the provocation, and whatever the sentiment in her favor, she was a killer. It was this unpalatable fact that caused her so much difficulty when she came to make her picture.

The plot of the film, as related in the AFI catalogue, was the story of Clara's relationship in Oklahoma with middle-aged Jacob Hamon (played by John Ince).[51]

Clara is an innocent high school girl when she meets Hamon, who offers to help pay for her education and employs her as his confidential secretary. Although Hamon is married, they become lovers. Hamon arranges a marriage of convenience between Clara and his nephew, F. L. Hamon, which enables them to travel together as Mr. and Mrs. Hamon. Jake Hamon strikes oil and rises to influence in politics and business, but his excessive drinking results in increased debauchery and brutality. On one occasion, he is particularly violent to Clara and she shoots him. He dies a few days later, and Clara flees first to Texas, then Mexico. She later surrenders, returns to Oklahoma, and is tried for murder, but is acquitted, to the joy of the courtroom audience.[52]

The promoter of the picture, W. C. Weathers, found the backing largely from men in the oil business who had been associated with Hamon. When Clara Hamon and he arrived in Hollywood, however, they had enormous difficulty persuading technicians to work on the film. The industry had apparently placed a ban on it. Such men as René Guissart, cameraman, and James P. Hogan, director, turned them down. And André Barlatier, who accepted $500 a week as cameraman, was drummed out of the American Society of Cinematographers as a result. The ASC was opposed to its members working on films in which people involved in public scandals were prominent. The group had specifically pledged that no member would be concerned in a picture exploiting the Hamon case. Barlatier took the job after this pledge had been made.[53]

The making of the film was clouded by rumor and counterrumor. Apparently, a member of the technical staff hired two thugs to beat up a young man who refused a job on the film and revealed all he knew about it around Hollywood. (He was uninjured only because he turned out to be a skillful amateur boxer).[54]

The film, which cost $200,000, was shot at the Warner Bros.' small studio on Sunset Boulevard. When all the directors turned it down, declining a huge fee, John W. Gorman accepted $75,000 to make the picture. No one in Hollywood seemed to have heard of him. Born in Boston, he had been an actor on the stage, both legitimate and vaudeville, and claimed to be the author of six plays and 150 vaudeville acts. He started his film career with the Liberty Motion Picture Company and Pioneer, before setting up John Gorman Productions, for which he produced a handful of low-budget features.[55]

Gorman also wrote the scenario, being careful to subdue the sordid side and emphasize the moral. During the making of the film, a romance developed between the director and the leading lady, and in August 1921 Clara Hamon became Mrs. John Gorman.[56]

The picture had the desired effect. Once it was shown in Ardmore, Oklahoma, where the events occurred, sentiment toward Clara changed. A number of women subscribed for stock in the enterprise.[57] Although production was complete, money was still needed to distribute the film.

When *Fate* opened in San Francisco, W. C. Weathers, the promoter, was arrested on a charge of violating the ordinance forbidding the display of censored films. It was the wrong town in which to open. The Arbuckle case had aroused deep feeling against the entire motion picture profession.[58] District Attorney Matthew Brady announced that he was starting an inquiry into several prior affairs in which Hollywood people had taken part. An "unknown woman" was supplying the police with acres of information about such orgies.

Brady, encouraged by a local newspaper campaign, had banned *Fate,* which had been booked into the College Theatre on Market Street for an indefinite run. Branding the picture "thoroughly offensive," a way for Clara Hamon (he referred to her as "Miss" Hamon) "to coin into money the blood of the man she murdered," Brady promised legal action to prevent the showing of the picture following a private review by himself and police officials.[59] This suggested that he had not actually seen it, "thoroughly offensive" or no.

Weathers asked for a jury trial, and the jury acquitted him in ten minutes on the grounds that no crime had been committed in the presentation of the film. It returned to the College Theatre, but business was poor, largely because the local press refused to advertise it—both editors and theatre managers felt the picture should not have been shown at all. (One suspects they didn't see it either.)

James Quirk agreed with them: "Despite the clearly voiced opinion of the country that Clara Hamon . . . should not try to capitalize her disgusting notoriety on the screen, she proceeded to make a picture. The National Association of the Motion Picture Industry is fighting to exclude it from the theatres. No decent distributor would handle it {and] any exhibitor that showed it in his theater should be run out of town."[60]

Other cities followed San Francisco's example. Kansas City's censors refused even to look at it. Undoubtedly a strong press campaign would have put the picture over, whether it was good or bad, but exhibitors dared not risk outraging the forces of reform so soon after the Arbuckle revelations. Clara Hamon's sole plunge into the picture business was a disaster. But the press made play of that very fact: "Its reception has justified those people who maintain that pictures are daily growing better and cleaner—that the standard of production is far higher than it used to be. And that the public is still clinging to the right sort of ethics and ideas."[61]

THE OBENCHAIN CASE When the murder first hit the Los Angeles headlines, it was more properly called the Kennedy Case. J. Belton Kennedy was a handsome, well-to-do young man, the sort of character who appeared in many a silent picture. His girlfriend was ideally cast, too. Madalynne Obenchain was a product of the new consumer society; obsessed with fashion, etiquette, and her own appearance, she was attractive enough to carry her narcissism with style.

To complete the melodrama, there was a villain, a character of uncertain origin called Arthur Burch. He was the first to be arrested, which was a trifle odd. But there was something odd about the whole affair.

It began when Madalynne fell for young Kennedy. She was still married to Ralph Obenchain. Evidently she felt more for Kennedy than he for her, for when she divorced Ralph, Kennedy tried to give her the slip. She pestered him with phone calls until his mother put a stop to it. Then she inveigled him into giving her a farewell drive in his roadster and begged him to call at the little cabin he owned in Beverly Glen, and there she . . . or someone . . . shot him.

Arthur Burch had a gun of the same caliber as the murder weapon, so the police picked him up. Madalynne was later charged as his accomplice. He stood trial alone, but the jury could not come to a verdict and he had to endure a second one. Meanwhile Madalynne went on trial herself, watched by members of the movie colony such as Leatrice Joy (who based part of her performance in *Manslaughter* on her). Madalynne spun a scenario so implausible no movie producer would have touched it: she had lost her memory from the moment she heard the shot until she had "woken up" much later. Ralph Obenchain had rushed to the court from Chicago to act as a character witness, convinced of Madalynne's innocence and offering to marry her again if she were willing. He became the hero of the case, creating an extraordinarily favorable impression. Everyone sympathized as he covered his head with his hand, a picture of misery, listening to her love letters being read out in court.

The letters proved the great attraction of this melodrama. They were full of purple prose and betrayed the influence of movie subtitles: "Some day we will go down to the ocean together, and all this pain will have been forgotten, as we watch the great image of eternity and listen to the mournful music of the waves."[62]

In the trials of both Burch and Madalynne, implausible stories were backed up by equally implausible yet curiously convincing witnesses. The story became more and more confusing, and then a second batch of letters, to another lover, were read out—in almost the identical phraseology. It must have been hell for Ralph.

But Ralph was not giving in to his misery. He was starring in a film, playing himself. *A Man in a Million* was a three-reeler, produced by an independent producer-director, Charles R. Seeling, who probably photographed it as well, as he was a former cameraman and specialized in making films as cheaply as possible.

According to *Variety, A Man in a Million* covered the early romance of the Obenchains at Northwestern University and showed Ralph's youth, his entry into the army, "and numerous other events prior to Mrs. Obenchain's arrest."[63] *Variety* warned that since Ralph has had no stage experience, "the film will have to make a stand before being booked." Seeling arranged for Ralph to make personal appearances whenever the picture played a big city. Ralph, man in a million to the end, insisted that the profits would go toward the defense of his former wife.

That lady was meanwhile causing havoc at the county jail, where the other inmates resented the privileges she was receiving—a maid and a regular supply of candy and bottled water. Neither she nor Burch was ever convicted. Their defense, preposterous as it was, could not be satisfactorily challenged, and after a couple of trials each and a year in prison they were released.

"Considering that they were almost certainly guilty of a very cowardly murder," wrote Veronica and Paul King in *Problems of Modern American Crime*, "they got off very lightly." Mrs. Obenchain, perhaps encouraged by the fact that Ralph had made a film, began to study the art of acting. But she had chosen the wrong time to exploit her notoriety. Will Hays was now in charge, and she had less chance of breaking into the movies than of remarrying Ralph. It was just as well. As the Kings put it, "The United States public is rather tired of bad women who are worse actresses."

THE POLICE

In 1907, a photographer from the San Francisco company of Miles Brothers filmed the crowd outside the boxers' training ring in Long Beach, California. When the film was shown in Chicago, three detectives recognized one of the men in the crowd and set out at once for Long Beach, where they arrested a wanted man called Rudolph Blumenthal.[64]

A great many films, however, served as vinegar in the wound of the collective pride of the police. As early as 1902, a Mutoscope loop called *A Legal Holdup* showed an encounter between a silk-hatted drunk and a policeman. The cop snatches his cigar, robs him of watch and wallet, pushes him onto a park bench with his nightstick, and strolls off. It was intended to shock, and it still does so. Yet the policeman as criminal was an insistent theme for muckraking journalists.

The association between moving pictures and crime has long fascinated audiences, bothered censors, and (usually) maddened the police. Being portrayed as a hero did not aid the policeman's job when crime victims expected miracles. Being depicted as a buffoon was humiliating to him and a source of satisfaction to his opponents. (The police were particularly upset by the Keystone Cops.)[65]

Picture men learned to make films that would please the police because they were dependent on police cooperation. Filming in the streets, unless carried out by hidden cameras, often attracted vast crowds, impossible to control without the police. One wonders whether some of the early films were not a kind of gratuity on celluloid for favors past!

Stage people also found it essential to curry favor. Al Jolson's first film was not *The Jazz Singer,* but a Vitagraph picture about traffic cops made in 1918 for the police benevolent fund and shown at a special benefit performance of Jolson's *Sinbad* at the Winter Garden Theatre, New York.[66]

Irrefutable proof of police corruption came with the revelations of the Rosenthal case (see page 185). Thanhouser released *One of the Honor Squad* (1912), a portrayal of a heroic policeman, and had to justify it somehow. So their advertisement read: "While the country is agog over the 'crooked' policeman and his connivance at gambling and murder, we spring this story of the Honest Copper. . . . Take your mind off Police Corruption and think, for a change, of Police Heroism. This picture points the way."[67]

*The Line-Up at Police Headquarters** (1914), coming out after the flood of vice pictures, had to be advertised as "Not a White Slave Picture . . . Not a Sex Problem . . ."[68] It was a six-reeler, said to have been based on police records. Certainly, the police cooperated in the production. Former Deputy Commissioner George S. Dougherty appeared in it and undoubtedly wished he had not, for he was injured when a property bomb exploded during filming at the Ruby studios.[69] The film depicted "the Official (Inside) Workings of the New York City Police Headquarters," which, enthralling as it must have been, did not quite justify the

---

*Rediscovered by UCLA Film Archives. The film was directed by Frank Beal.

OUR CINEMATOGRAPHIC CARTOONS. NO. 58.

THE AMERICAN POLICEMAN: HIS FUNNY LITTLE WAYS.

AS SEEN ON THE SCREEN AND TRANSFERRED TO PAPER BY FRANK R. GREY.

description bestowed upon it in its advertising: "The Sort of Story that has Thrilled Mankind Since the Creation of the World."[70]

In an era when female suffrage was a headline topic, people were intrigued by the idea of policewomen. To offset the illusion that they were used merely for a little light dusting, Balboa made *The Policewoman,* written by Frank M. Wilter-mood, in 1914, and hired for the lead Mrs. Alice Stebbins Wells, said to be the world's first regular policewoman.[71]

Policewoman Alice Clements resigned from the Chicago force to accompany a motion picture in which she appeared on a lecture tour. Chief Garrity appeared in it, too, so it had the blessing of the department. But not the entire department. The film, entitled *Dregs of a Large City,* was supposed to be an educational depiction of life in the old Levee, the red-light district of a decade earlier, but when it came before the Chicago censors, they banned it.[72] The Levee summoned up sickening memories for older members of the force. In this Wild West–style frontier town, a morals squad officer had been accidentally killed by another detective, and the closing down of the brothels was accompanied by a battle royal between the two squads of police.[73]

What was unmentionable in drama was, oddly enough, acceptable in comedy. *When the Girls Joined the Force,* a Nestor comedy of 1914, directed by Al Christie, featured Miss Laura Oakley, the only woman police chief in the world, who was chief of Universal City.

In the film, a police chief is dismissed because of graft in his department, and the whole force is accused. Women take over, with Mrs. Van Allen (Laura Oakley) appointed to succeed the old chief. The entire police force of Universal City appeared in the film. Al Christie secured permission from the mayor of Los Angeles (not to mention the police!) to march the Universal City force through the city streets, headed by a band and followed by a line of political women. *Moving Picture World* wrote, "This incident, humorous for the dismay and disturbance it caused among the business sections of Los Angeles, is cleverly incorporated in the picture. Then we have scenes in the police station after the women come into power. What the women do not do to make the station a sublime dwelling place for the men isn't worth doing."[74]

The number of pictures about honest policemen who withstand the lures of politicians indicates how wide was the spread of graft. A typical example was a three-reel Selig picture of 1915, *How Callahan Cleaned Up Little Hell,* directed by Tom Santschi from an I. K. Friedman story. Santschi himself played John Calla-han, an honest police captain, in a documentary-style drama entirely without love interest. "A cast with more tough looking men would be hard to assemble," said *Variety.*[75]

Callahan refuses to release a pickpocket who is the crony of a ward heeler and is transferred to "Little Hell," the worst district in the city. When the local political bosses set out to buy him, they find him incorruptible. But Callahan is in financial trouble—his daughter is ill and he cannot pay his mortgage—and the grafters make another offer. In real life, Callahan's resistance would crumble at this point, or he would be beaten up or killed; in the movie, his detective colleagues come to the rescue. Callahan cleans up Little Hell, and he and the leading gangster become friends, the crook joining him in his fight against vice.[76]

Few dramas of the twenties dared to deal with police corruption, but the comedies gave the game away. *Paths to Paradise* (1925), a Raymond Griffith feature, opens with a police raid on a gambling joint. A detective passes among the patrons with a hat—soon brimful with dollar bills. The raid turns out to be a stunt by rival crooks, but the point is inescapable.

The police used censorship to control the depiction of crime on the screen—particularly their own. In 1913, Royal A. Baker, censor of amusements for Detroit's police department, drew up a list of the activities producers should avoid showing:

- The wrongs committed by the agents of the law . . . must never be shown in films
- Pictures must contain a moral ending
- Don't show suicide (ever)
- Never show strikers rioting, destroying property, or committing depredation or violence
- Avoid tricks educational to crime, including:
  a) taking impressions of keys on wax, putty, etc.
  b) cutting telephone or telegraph wires
  c) turning railroad switches
  d) criminals using autos as an instrument to assist depredation, escape
  e) picking locks, blowing safes, using a "jimmy" or a "pinch" bar
  f) badger game, white slavery, street soliciting, and "vulgar flirtation"

Detroit would not have permitted the outstanding *Detective Burton* series of two-reelers produced by Reliance the following year, which went into remarkable detail about the methods of both criminals and police. *Detective Burton's Triumph* is reminiscent in style of *The Musketeers of Pig Alley,* but it displays the more advanced technique of 1914 with bold close-ups and smoother editing. It shows how "yeggmen" (safecrackers) operated, cooking dynamite in order to extract the nitroglycerine, then straining this "soup" through a scarf and pouring it into bottles. We see how explosive is affixed to a safe and how that safe is blown. We see how the criminals are identified from the Rogues' Gallery and watch the police close in on them in a saloon, using a barely noticeable system of coded gestures.

Broken Nose Bailey (1914), another in the same series, shows police using the Bertillon system of identification, measuring every inch of a criminal (played by Eugene Pallette), particularly his broken nose. Introduced from France in 1887, this method used the photographic mug shot together with precise anthropometric measurements which together added up to an individual's unique portrait—the dimensions of the head, the length of the right ear or left foot.

In 1911 Captain Joseph Francis Faurot, known as the "thumbprint expert," appeared in a film called *The Thumb Print* about this new method of identification recently adopted by the New York criminal courts. A wife is about to be convicted of the murder of her husband, when Faurot shows the court the difference between the wife's thumbprint and that of a man who had left his mark on a pair of shears—the murder weapon.[77]

Faurot, now an inspector and head of the NYPD Detective Bureau, worked with Vitagraph again in 1916 on *The Human Cauldron,* directed by Harry Lambart. The three-reeler had documentary sequences woven into a fictitious story about two gangsters and their girls caught by the police. One man is sent to Hart Island and a girl to Bedford Reformatory. Both these institutions were shown, as Commissioner Katherine Bement Davis led a tour of inspection. A number of other policemen also took part in the film, and Vitagraph player William Dunn was cast as a police applicant, among dozens of real ones.[78]

All of which may give the impression that the police were the friends of the moving picture. It was not so. They were often hard on companies working on location, insisting that they display their permits when filming. "Any time you made a scene in Los Angeles," said Hal Roach, "you were compelled to have two policemen to see you didn't break any law."[79] Confronted by cameras at scenes of serious accidents, the police would often stop the filming by arresting the photographers or smashing their equipment. The newsreel men covering the Passaic strike of 1926 were indiscriminately clubbed by police and had their cameras destroyed. (Next day, the newsreel men returned in armored cars!)

The police blamed the movies for the increase in juvenile crime and for giving the public an unflattering picture of their work. There had been much speculation about the "Third Degree" thanks to films like *The Burglar's Dilemma* (1912), directed by D. W. Griffith for Biograph, from a scenario by George Hennessy. A murder is blamed on a young burglar (Bobby Harron). The police open their interrogation in brutal fashion, ramming the burglar's face against that of the corpse. Then, in a naive and obvious manner, Griffith presents the hot-and-cold treatment of the third degree. An unpleasant cop threatens and intimidates the burglar, then a pleasant cop takes over and calms him down. Eventually, the corpse (Lionel Barrymore) recovers and the cops let the young burglar go—reluctantly.

In the antigambling picture *The Wages of Sin* (1913), a Mafioso is arrested; at the psychological moment, the blinds are raised and the corpse of a man he is accused of murdering is revealed outside the window. The Italian breaks down and confesses.[80]

The Third Degree, a Broadway stage success by Charles Klein, was made into a film in 1913 by Barry O'Neil, for the Lubin Company. No one had any illusions about the subject; the picture was described as "the secrets of the modern torture chamber" and "the real story of the police method of torturing a confession out of a victim."[81] There was even an unscrupulous police captain (Bartley McCullum), determined to wring a confession out of his victim at any price. The confession is finally obtained through hypnotism, which stirred up a great deal of controversy in the newspapers.[82] The picture was as huge a success as the stage play.

The viciousness of the third degree could hardly be exaggerated. Searching for the ringleaders of a riot of 1913, detectives pointed a loaded revolver at the head of a young worker and threatened to shoot unless he confessed; when he still refused, they pistol-whipped him. A detective on another case was sentenced to a year in jail for cruelty.[83]

Police brutality was almost eradicated from the screen under Hays, but the occasional independent film obliquely referred to it. Edward Sloman's *The Last*

Hour (1923) showed a private detective leading a squad of policemen and committing a cold-blooded murder. Despite the presence of the law, he receives not so much as a reprimand. But by 1923, audiences would have regarded that as a flaw in the story, not the system.

From Moving Picture World, *March 29, 1913.*

THE SENSATIONAL MASTERPIECE
OF MOTION PICTURE PRODUCTION

Detective William J. Burns in
"THE EXPOSURE OF THE LAND SWINDLERS"
IN THREE PARTS

KALEM   KALEM

To Be Released Tuesday, April 1st, 1913

THROUGH THE GENERAL FILM COMPANY
EXCLUSIVELY

Detective Burns personally appears in the production which vividly portrays the scientific methods of criminal investigation that have made him the greatest sleuth of all time. The story is based on actual experiences in his career. Miss Alice Joyce, Kalem's celebrated leading lady, heads the supporting company.

Beg It, Borrow It or Steal It—But Above All Get It!

THE GREAT DETECTIVES

When it was common practice for films to be reprinted—or duped—and illegally exhibited, a company called Monopol hired the William J. Burns National Detective Agency to prevent infringement of a valuable Italian film. It was little more than a publicity stunt (by Frank Winch, former press agent to Buffalo Bill), but it was an impressive one. Perhaps it awakened a producer to the possibilities of using William J. Burns in a film, for a year later he appeared as a central figure in a Kalem three-reeler about political fraud, *The Exposure of the Land Swindlers* (1913), with Alice Joyce. The trade advertisements, true to the spirit of a company upholding the law, urged exhibitors "Beg It—Borrow It or Steal It But Above All Get It!"[84] The enthusiasm was understandable, for Burns was regarded as "the greatest sleuth of all time."*[85]

Moving Picture World said the film "shines in the unwonted gloss of novelty." The introduction of William J. Burns as a detective who investigates a land fraud using a dictagraph and other modern techniques[87] was carried out with "telling and sensational effect."[88]

Burns returned to the screen in 1914 with *The $5,000,000 Counterfeiting Plot*, a six-reeler, released by the Dramascope Company, written by George G. Nathan and directed by Bertram Harrison. The picture was produced under Burns's supervision with the help of Clifford Saum and William Cavanaugh, and he appeared in nearly every shot, together with former members of the Secret Service.[89]

It was based on one of Burns's most celebrated cases, the Philadelphia-Lancaster counterfeiting mystery. Scenes were shot at the Treasury Department, Washington; Moyamensing Prison, Philadelphia; Lancaster, Pennsylvania; and New York City. Burns showed on the screen how bogus Monroe-head hundred-dollar silver certificates were made. These counterfeits were so remarkable that the Secretary of the Treasury had to recall the entire issue of that currency, amounting to over $27 million.[90]

Burns was hailed in the advertisements as "the greatest living detective," and to give his reputation an even more Holmesian touch, he was brought together in the last scene with Sir Arthur Conan Doyle, who congratulated him on his many successes. He was also given credit for directing the film, which might not have pleased him had he read the scathing review in *Variety,* which reported his speech before the opening night in New York, when, apart from declaring that Leo Frank of Atlanta was innocent (see pages 378–379), he said the picture people had taken "picture license" in making the film.

"The picture people didn't take a 'picture license' alone," said *Variety.* "It was an all-night license covering everything." *Variety* criticized details: a counterfeiter pulling a proof from a half-tone plate—"when you can pull a proof from

---

*Burns began his career as a detective in Columbus, Ohio, in 1886, worked for the U.S. Secret Service for fourteen years, and in 1905 started the Burns and Sheridan International Detective Agency. In 1909 he bought out his partner to operate under his own name,[86] and he later became head of the U.S. Department of Justice's Bureau of Investigation—even later known as the FBI.

The Great Detective William J. Burns assists director Raoul Walsh with his version of the Paul Armstrong–Wilson Mizner play The Deep Purple, *1920. (National Film Archive)*

copper with bare hands you are going some." Burns in Washington leaving his cab without paying—"if Washington's that easy, let's move there"—and the building in Lancaster being blown up to destroy the evidence, even though that same evidence had been shown being burned in an earlier scene. "Badly padded and fails to convince,"[91] was their conclusion. Said *Moving Picture World:* "Not one foot of noticeable padding. . . . The camera might have been on the job at the start and 'got its story' while the original players were not actors nor acting."[92] Burns came across as an accomplished actor. "He is as much of a professional as anyone in the picture. His facial expression gave one of its best touches of humor and made the only loud ripple of laughter at the first performance."[93]

But the picture was involved in some unseemly squabbles over distribution and wound up in court.[94]

Burns did not have a high opinion of the new medium as entertainment. He thought most plots were so implausible they did nothing but harm. Crimes were committed with such ease on the screen that a potential wrongdoer could take in the technique at a glance, try it out for himself, and, before he was aware of it, be embarked on a criminal career.[95]

This was not enough to keep Burns out of pictures. He cooperated on several silent detective dramas, including Raoul Walsh's *The Deep Purple* (1920). In 1930, he was tempted back by the production of twenty-six shorts dramatizing the crimes he and his coworkers had solved. One was *The McNamara Outrage,* about the dynamiting of the Los Angeles *Times* building; another was *The Philadelphia-Lancaster Counterfeiters.* All were produced by Educational Pictures.

Burns revealed that for years his men had watched movies, not only for entertainment but to catch fugitives: "When Lon Chaney made *The Hunchback of Notre Dame,* I remember, one of my men spotted an extra in a mob scene who was wanted for forgery. A wire to the Hollywood police did the trick and he's still serving time."[96]

Even more famous than Burns was William J. Flynn, the former chief of the U.S. Secret Service. During the war he had enjoyed great acclaim for his serial of sabotage and espionage, *The Eagle's Eye.*[97] In 1920, he decided once again "to tell all" for the motion picture screen.

J. Gordon Cooper directed the Chief Flynn stories, with Herbert Rawlinson in the lead. The official records of the Secret Service provided the basic plots, but the scenarios were written by Wilson Mizner. A celebrated humorist, Mizner could have given each episode a rare degree of authenticity, for he knew the underworld and was a gambling crony of the gangster Arnold Rothstein, who virtually ran New York City.[98] Instead, he smothered them in hokum.

Photoplay wrote, "The first three pictures in the series are *The Silkless Banknote, Outlaws of the Deep* and *The Five Dollar Plate.* There is enough material in each of them for a five-reel picture. For terseness of action and for human interest, they rank with the O. Henry series ... The 'crook stuff' is lightened with plenty of comedy and many scenes of unpretentious pathos."[99]

INTO THE NET Richard E. Enright, Police Commissioner of New York for eight eventful years, wrote a story about a heroic detective that was picked up by Malcolm Strauss, a producer. Frank Leon Smith was assigned to write the screenplay. "The story that became *Into the Net* (1924) was hard to write because of an embarrassment of riches," said Smith. "When I asked Malcolm Strauss what good the Enright tie-up was to us, with some irritation he said: 'Well, what do you want?' In desperation I exclaimed: 'The Brooklyn Bridge!' To my amazement he asked, 'When, and for how long?'

"It was as easy as that! The cops roped off the Brooklyn Bridge for us and George Seitz, the director, staged some good fights at mid-day in the middle of the bridge. Chase scenes up and down busy Manhattan streets became common and ritualized. First Enright's official car and his personal aide ran interference; second, the car with the villains; third, the car with the heroic element; fourth, the camera car, with the director. Traffic cops had no advance notice. When they saw Enright's car, they leapt aside, blew their whistles, and along we sped.

"We had good luck throughout the production—except once. Seitz was staging a street fight in Harlem between heroes and heavies when a plainclothes cop, not in on the act, ran up, and, reaching over the crowd, rapped one of our guys on the head with a blackjack.

"During the weeks *Into the Net* was in production, the newspapers seemed unaware that the Police Department was being used by a movie company. New York cops were even taken to Fort Lee to appear in interiors (they got $5 a day as extras, in addition, of course, to their city pay).

"As for Police Commissioner Enright, none of us ever saw him—until after the serial was finished."[100]

When it was over, Smith was taken to police headquarters to meet the com-

Into the Net, 1924, in production on Brooklyn Bridge. Jack Mulhall, right, is in danger of being hurled off. George B. Seitz right of camera, Edna Murphy center, Spencer Gordon Bennet pointing, and no sign of Police Commissioner Enright. (Note second camera lashed to girders, extreme right.)

missioner: "I was introduced as 'the young man who wrote the scenario' and I put out my hand. Enright took my hand, pulled me forward a little; big smile— and I thought he was going to say something. Nuts. Not a word for the guy who'd ghosted a 15 episode serial for him. He was pulling me ahead and out of the way so he could greet Miss Edna Murphy, who was in line behind me."[101]

But not only was the picture advertised as "Written by Police Commissioner Richard Enright of New York," a poster contrived to suggest that he had directed it, too.[102]

Photoplay thought *Into the Net* sustained interest throughout and credited George Seitz for his exceptionally good direction. (The leading players included Jack Mulhall, Edna Murphy, and Constance Bennett.) The English were more critical: "However prominently the police may figure in their assistance to the hero, it says little for the Detective Force which could allow an exponent of the White Slave Traffic to carry on so elaborate an organisation in the centre of Long Island until it is brought to the notice of the police by means of a private detective."[103]

As Frank Leon Smith pointed out, every serial involved the kidnapping of girls; these beautiful victims were the descendants of the "disappearing women" of the white slave films.

While I was writing this book, *Into the Net* was discovered in the vaults of the Cinémathèque Française—a total jumble, restored and retitled by Renée Lichtig.

It was a version of the serial cut down to feature length in the twenties. As such, it has astonishing similarities to *Traffic in Souls* and was clearly an attempt to cash in on the same subject. This being the twenties, the white slave racket is run not by a reformer but by the obligatory Evil Oriental of so many serials. A police raid on a gambling den is directed in an identical fashion to the climactic police raid in *Traffic in Souls;* some shots might almost have been borrowed from Tucker's film. Documentary authenticity is undermined by the use of interior sets—although there is location shooting at a night court. But the exteriors are exceptional in every way. Very well shot—they include high angles, rare at the time—they form a valuable record of old New York. One wild chase sequence contains shots racing down Broadway from above Times Square, past the Flatiron Building down to Washington Square. The final race to the rescue is beyond parody; not only are there powerful police cars and motorcycles, but columns of police horses, so Seitz can shoot it like *The Birth of a Nation,* and even motorboats so the Oriental, escaping aboard a steam yacht with a heroine, can be apprehended at sea. (He dives overboard, presumably to reappear in a future serial.)

Richard Enright was later responsible for organizing a special squad of policemen to cope with the crowds at movie premieres in New York City.[104]

Publicity for Into the Net, *1924. From* Photoplay, *November 1924.*

Police Commissioner of New York City and author of "Into the Net," Richard E. Enright, examines "rushes" of the picture which shows the police of the metropolis at work in a thriller

JUVENILE DELINQUENCY

The fear that films about criminals would create criminals began, appropriately enough, with *The Great Train Robbery* (1903)—the famous Edwin S. Porter "Western." In 1912, the Philadelphia *Record* carried this headline:

BOY IS TO HANG FOR PICTURE PLAY ACT

Young Bishie's Express Robbery Tragedy
an Exact Reproduction from "Movies"
Slew Trusting Friend
Waited for Whistle at Long Curve So the Shot
Would Not Be Heard[105]

The paper stated that at the time of the crime, December 1911, *The Great Train Robbery* was being shown in a Scranton theatre. *Moving Picture World* disputed this charge, pointing out that *The Great Train Robbery* could not have been seen in Scranton or anywhere else in December 1911 since "the age and physical condition of the film forbade its going through a moving picture machine." The film survived to be copied, and dupes are still being shown more than eighty years later, so that ends that argument. The boy could not have learned from the film to wait for the whistle so the shot would not be heard, but otherwise the facts fitted, so why not blame the film? Citing the moving picture as the inspiration for one's evil deeds had already become such a common practice that reformers looked upon the medium as wicked and deplorable, a perverter of youth and a breeder of crime. Those who studied children were, for the most part, convinced that moving pictures had a great deal to answer for. Asked what proportion of disciplinary cases were attributable to the movies, a Chicago superintendent of child study replied, "I should almost say they all were."[106]

But in a survey of forty-two probation officers, conducted by the National Board of Review, five called motion pictures responsible for much juvenile delinquency, ten thought they contributed, and twenty-seven maintained they were not directly responsible to any appreciable extent.[107] And in his 1926 book *The Young Delinquent,* Cyril Burt wrote that only mental defectives took the movies seriously enough to imitate their criminal exploits.

Yet the movies were the main source of excitement and moral education for city children.[108] As early as 1909, Jane Addams wrote of the impact of the five-cent theatres on young minds: "Nothing is more touching than [to] encounter a group of children and young people who are emerging from a theater with the magic of the play still thick upon them. They look up and down the familiar street scarcely recognizing it and quite unable to determine the direction of home. From a tangle of 'make believe' they gravely scrutinize the real world which they are so reluctant to re-enter, reminding one of the absorbed gaze of a child who is groping his way back from fairy-land whither the story has completely transported him."[109]

Youthful revellers stage a car fight—charging each other's vehicles until one is wrecked—at a roadhouse. From Walking Back, *1928, directed by Rupert Julian, although this sequence may have been directed by Cecil B. DeMille.*

While realizing that "the drama and the drama alone performs for them the office of art," Adams added: "An eminent alienist of Chicago states that he has had a number of patients among neurotic children whose emotional natures have been so over-wrought by the crude appeal to which they have been so constantly subjected in the theaters, that they have become victims of hallucination and mental disorder."[110] She was also convinced that for every child driven distraught, a hundred permanently injure their eyes watching the moving films, and hundreds more seriously model their conduct upon the standards set before them.[111]

A survey of the effects of the cinema on children was carried out in Britain during the war. The Report of the Cinema Commission of Inquiry, instituted by the National Council of Public Morals, was published in 1917.[112]

One probation officer said he regularly took his charges to the pictures "with beneficial results."[113] If cinemas were closed down, there would be an immediate and immense increase in hooliganism, shoplifting, and street misdemeanors: "Fifteen years ago, street hooligan gangs were a real menace. Now such gangs are unknown in my district."[114]

"Just imagine," said a social worker, "what the cinema means to tens of thousands of poor kiddies herded together in one room—to families living in one house, six or eight families under the same roof. For a few hours at the picture house at the corner, they can find breathing space, warmth, music (the more the better) and the pictures, where they can have a real laugh, a cheer and sometimes a shout. Who can measure the effect on their spirits and body?"[115]

The commission was shocked by the revelation that the least desirable picture house was a better place for children than their homes or the streets and that no alternative entertainment was provided for them. "Except," as one schoolmaster said, "the appalling entertainments provided by the Churches in the way of bands of hope and mission rooms. They are absolutely dreadful."[116]

A magistrate was more complacent. "If the child is in the cinema seeing horrors, that child will not be in the streets stealing things off a barrow."[117]

When the National Board of Review asked the chief probation officers of the principal American cities for their views on juvenile delinquency and the movies, the response was strikingly similar to the English report. Of forty-five who replied, only five indicted motion pictures as an important cause of delinquency—and two of those were in states with strict censorship, Ohio and Pennsylvania.

But religious groups responded as though it were still 1649. "Most of the pictures glorify crime," said the *Christian Advocate* in 1925, "or depict the rotten trail of sensuality. It is sought to justify their exhibition by the explanation that they point a moral. As sensible would it be to drag a child through flames so that later he might feel the soothing effect of salve! Sear the mind of a child with rottenness, and no moral will ever produce relief, much less a cure."[118]

The unconventional Mayor House of Topeka, Kansas, put it more succinctly: "If you have a boy who can be corrupted by the ordinary run of moving picture films you might as well kill him now and save trouble."[119]

SAVED BY THE JUDGE   Thanks to the liberal legal requirements of the time, Ben Lindsey was already an experienced lawyer when he was admitted to the Colorado bar in 1894, at the age of twenty-four. He became a judge in 1901 and discharged his responsibilities conventionally until a remarkable moment in his courtroom. He had just sentenced a young boy convicted of larceny when an appalling cry rang out. It came from the boy's mother, crouched among the benches at the back.

"I was a judge, judging 'cases' according to the 'Law' till the cave-dweller's mother-cry startled me into humanity. It was an awful cry, a terrible sight, and I was stunned," recalled Lindsey.[120] He adjourned the court and retreated to his chambers.

The boy was guilty, but should he go to prison when he had a mother and a home? The only course was for Lindsey to accept personal responsibility for the lad. He had no idea what he was going to do, except visit his charge, but probation proved so much more successful than prison that it transformed Lindsey's outlook. "The old process is changed," he wrote. "Instead of coming to destroy, we come to rescue. Instead of coming to punish, we come to uplift. Instead of coming to hate, we come to love."[121]

"The criminal court for child-offenders," wrote Lindsey, "is based on the doctrine of fear, degradation and punishment. It was, and is, absurd. The Juvenile Court was founded on the principle of love. We assume that the child has committed, not a crime, but a mistake, and that he deserves correction, not punishment. Of course, there is a firmness and justice, for without these there would be danger in leniency. But there is no justice without love."[122]

Lindsey's idea of trying youthful offenders in a special court spread across the nation. But he enraged those to whom property was more important than people.

Crime was the result not of character, but of environment, he asserted. What determined the environment? Ruthless private greed, flowering in an irresponsible capitalism. The true enemies of society were not the delinquents, but respected men in private life.[123] "I sometimes felt like suggesting," he said, "that we empty the jails altogether in celebration of the fact that the bandits who robbed almost everybody never got in them at all."[124]

In retaliation, city officials and businessmen declared war on Lindsey. He was insulted and humiliated. Prostitutes were bribed to name him as a customer. The Democrats tried to drop him from their ticket, but he formed his own party and was elected unanimously.[125] He caused 151 new laws to be passed,[126] and delegations from many countries came to observe his methods. The Japanese even sent a photographer so the courtroom furniture could be accurately reproduced in Tokyo.[127]

Damned for his sympathy with the criminal, Lindsey received little official praise for his successes—the hundreds of delinquents who passed through his hands to become good citizens. He found an unexpected ally, however, in George Creel, a journalist appointed Denver's police commissioner, who was to find fame during the war as chairman of the Committee on Public Information. Otis B. Thayer, a former Selig man, persuaded Creel to write a scenario about the Lindsey method for a three-reeler called *Saved by the Juvenile Court* (1913), or *Fighting Crime.* The story was in two parts. In one, fourteen-year-old Bob is arrested for picking coal in a railroad yard to save his poor family from freezing. In prison, Bob finds himself in the company of hardened criminals and becomes one himself. Released, he robs a bank and is killed in a gunfight with his pursuers.

In a contrasting story, Charles, a street waif, is arrested for attempted robbery. He is taken before Judge Lindsey, who gives him commitment papers and trusts him to make his own way to the Industrial School at Golden, Colorado, for training.[128] Meanwhile, Alta, the boy's sister, has been frequenting low dance halls. She is picked up by a policeman just as she is about to take her first drink, and Lindsey commits her to the girls' school at Morrison, Colorado, where she receives an education. When the children return from school, they find that their widowed mother, under Lindsey's influence, has opened a bakery shop and Charles has joined the motorcycle brigade of a large department store. One day, he stops the runaway horse of a banker's daughter, and his heroism is rewarded with a job in the bank. He falls in love with the banker's daughter, Beatrice. Alta assists her mother in the bakery and meets the man she wants to marry. Judge Lindsey is eventually called upon to officiate at a double wedding.[129]

Terry Ramsaye describes how this picture was pepped up with footage shot at the Cheyenne rodeo, and, after Creel's drive against the red-light district, retitled

*Judge Ben Lindsey (right) puts the case of the boy (Lewis Sargent) to Patrolman Jones
(Russ Powell), in a scene from William Desmond Taylor's* Soul of Youth, *1920, written by Julia
Crawford Ivers. (Museum of Modern Art)*

Denver's Underworld.[130] The director, Otis Thayer, should have had a talk with the
judge, for apparently he skipped the state owing a lot of money.[131]

The Columbine Film Company received many letters from child-betterment
organizations pleased at having the work of Judge Lindsey introduced by means
of the motion picture.[132] Thus encouraged, Lindsey let it be known that he was
considering directing features on the child labor question, following a series of
articles he had written for the popular magazines.[133] Sadly, nothing came of it.

In 1920, William Desmond Taylor followed the success of his *Huckleberry Finn*
with *The Soul of Youth,* written by Julia Crawford Ivers. In this pre-Hays period,
Taylor was at liberty to portray an orphanage in muckraking style, as a sordid
dump, full of wretched boys who fought each other at the slightest opportunity.
The most troublesome youngster (Lewis Sargent) escapes and lives rough on the
streets until he is arrested during a burglary. He is brought before Judge Lindsey,
who plays not merely a cameo but a proper role, with close-ups, titles, and reaction
shots. (In one scene, he appears with his wife.) The judge comes across with
warmth and sympathy, and the film itself is exceptional. The odd touch of sentimentality is offset by the realism of the orphanage scenes, the beautiful photography (by James Van Trees), and the atmospheric art direction of Wilfred
Buckland.[134]

Lindsey testified before the Committee on Education of the House of Representatives in 1926, saying that he had yet to find a single case of crime among

youth that could fairly be traced to the movies: "But I do know thousands of children who have been elevated, inspired and made happier because of the movies; who have been kept off the streets, out of the alleys. . . . If we did not have any motion pictures at all we would have far more crime than we have. Nothing in the last fifty years of the most eventful history of all time has done more to reduce sin and crime and add to the happiness, education and progress of the human race than the motion picture. And it is going to do more and more in this regard in the years to come."[135]

Judge Willis Brown was a man of the Lindsey type. He came to fame with the scheme of "Boy City," on the lines of Father Flanagan's Boys Town, immortalized in the Spencer Tracy film. He first established "Boy Cities" in Charlevoix, Michigan, and Gary, Indiana, in the 1900s. (Selig made a one-reeler about these operations.)

Brown then presided over the juvenile court of Salt Lake City. Invited by the editor of the *Publishers' Guide* to comment on motion pictures, he wrote, "If I owned a motion picture house, I would show children the pleasing, helpful things of life. I would make it possible for all parents to send their children to my house."[136]

The editor challenged him to write a scenario which would meet his requirements yet still be a draw to the public. The judge did so and took it to the editor, who showed it to several producers. The result was that the judge himself directed a five-reeler about an immigrant lad who benefited from "Boy City." The actual boy, Willie Eckstein, and the judge each played himself in the film, which was called *A Boy and the Law* (1914).

The Chicago *Herald* made arrangements for all children under sixteen to see the film free at special matinees. Willie Eckstein traveled with the picture and delivered a running commentary while it was shown.

Judge Brown either had too little time, or too little faith in his ability as a director. For his later films, he hired the young King Vidor first to write, then to direct his scripts. Brown rented a group of buildings in Culver City, California, where he hoped to establish a studio-cum-"Boy City." He called it the Boy City Film Corporation. Vidor described how he would pick up newsboys to play in these pictures, offering them a two-dollar cash advance:[137] "The films invariably started with a group of boys seated around a large conference table with Judge Brown. The parents of some unruly boy would present a seemingly insoluble problem of an erring son. Judge Brown would always prescribe some unorthodox but deeply human remedy. The main film story would concern itself with the manner in which these intensely human problems worked themselves out. I deeply believed in these films and I put my heart and soul into making them."[138]

BROKEN LAWS   During her personal appearance tour in connection with *Human Wreckage,* Mrs. Wallace Reid visited hospitals, prisons, and reformatories and saw a phase of life she had never encountered before: the plight of the juvenile offender. The fault, she was convinced, lay not so much with the young

*Broken Laws, 1924. Arthur Rankin as Bobby Allen—"at sixteen, arrogant and lawless"
—with Mrs. Wallace Reid as his mother. (National Film Archive)*

people as with their parents; firm discipline was the only way to stop children
from becoming criminals.

Under the Thomas H. Ince banner once again, she starred in a drama written
by her friend Adela Rogers St. Johns, adapted by Marion Jackson and Bradley
King. It was directed by Roy William Neill.

Bobby Allen is spoiled as a child by his indulgent mother (Mrs. Reid), who
never resorts to corporal punishment. Bobby causes trouble at school and grows
up arrogant and lawless. When his mother buys him a Stutz Bearcat he begins to
lead a wild life. One night, returning from a "disreputable roadhouse" (roadhouses
which served liquor were notorious for prostitution), his car crashes into a wagon
and kills an old woman. He is convicted of manslaughter in the first degree. His
mother pleads with the judge to allow her to serve his term, acknowledging that
she is responsible for his conduct. The mother wakes up, and, realizing that she
has just had a nightmare, gives Bobby—still aged eight—a good spanking and
makes him return to school to apologize for his poor conduct.[139]

Said *Picture Play:* "There is something so sincere and so steadfast in Mrs.
Wallace Reid's picture, that before the first reel is over you are completely won
by it. People who have a 'message' are usually great bores. But *Broken Laws* isn't
a bore; it is an excellent study of family life as waged in the Great American
Home. . . . I hope you see *Broken Laws* because I want you to feel that Wallace
Reid's widow can do braver things than *Human Wreckage.*"[140]

Despite such reviews, and despite all that press agents could do, neither *Broken
Laws,* nor Mrs. Reid's personal appearances, were as successful as before.[141]

Mrs. Reid was a reformer at heart, but she had a showman's outlook. Brought up in the theatre, and a pioneer in Hollywood, she believed that the primary mission of the screen was to entertain.[142] Combining propaganda with entertainment was a difficult exercise in an industry ruled on one side by Hays and on the other by exhibitors, and it was not surprising that her later pictures—such as *The Red Kimono*—veered toward exploitation. And those involved with her, as if learning how to do it, made "propaganda pictures" on their own which proved to be pure exploitation films. The most startling of these were directed by Norton S. Parker.

THE ROAD TO RUIN   Norton S. Parker's *The Road to Ruin* (1928) was a cheap exploitation picture, shot in ten days, which held some kind of record for its box-office success. It cost a mere $2,500—*Variety* claimed it grossed more than $2,500,000.[143]

It holds another sort of distinction, too. In the American Film Institute's catalogue of feature films of 1921–1930, it has the synopsis which has drawn the most attention. It is impossible to parody or even to paraphrase, so here it is in full: "Lack of parental guidance leads Sally Canfield down the ruinous road. Exposed to liquor and cigarettes, she succumbs to their effects and drifts through a series of love affairs with older, worldlier men. Apprehended by the police one evening during a strip poker game, Sally is reprimanded and sent home. She discovers several weeks later that she is pregnant, submits to an illegal abortion, and dies of shock the next evening after unwillingly being paired off with her father in a bawdy house"[144] (The AFI catalogue lists the subjects included in this film as Parenthood, Adolescence, Abortion, Alcoholism, Incest, Smoking, Whorehouses.)

This would hardly have received the blessing of the Hays Office. Produced by Cliff Broughton Productions, distributed by True Life Photoplays, it was the sort of thing one would expect to see in the company of tramps, seeking shelter from the cold. Yet it was sponsored by the juvenile authorities as an exposure of juvenile delinquency and was shown by them in the high schools.[145] "It is a sensational portrayal of a deplorable social evil, with all Ts crossed and all Is dotted," said *Photoplay*.[146]

The Road to Ruin was banned in a number of cities,[147] and it is safe to assume that state censors, regarding it as a catalogue of all they objected to, would have burned at the stake rather than let it be shown in the area under their jurisdiction. It was popular, however, on the road-show circuit.

The picture survives, and makes doleful viewing. Even though it was photographed by the pioneer Henry Cronjager (who shot *Tol'able David*), it has a lackluster look to it. The action moves agonizingly slowly because it was shot intentionally fast—perhaps even more than twenty-four frames per second—to fill the reels as quickly as possible.

I managed to contact someone who remembered the film. "I saw it when I was only thirteen in Salt Lake City," she wrote. "I suppose it would be considered an X-rated movie by today's standards, and it was advertised with lurid billboards emphasizing 'No one under 16 admitted.' My girlfriend and I were so intrigued with all this that we 'borrowed' our mothers' lipsticks and hats and high heels and managed to get by the ticket taker at the old Rialto Theater. And there we sat in the darkened movie house, our eyes as big as saucers as we watched Helen Foster's virtue being destroyed by Grant Withers."[148]

My correspondent subsequently married the director of *The Road to Ruin*, Norton S. Parker:

"He told me Helen Foster was a lovely, innocent, blue-eyed brunette and he used to have to keep a case of gin on the set and keep her half smashed so she would take off her clothes in the famous strip-poker scene.[149]

"Also, the picture could not be released unless it had a *moral*. So at the end where Helen lay dying after an abortion, Norton conceived the brilliant idea of having letters of fire appear over the bed as though forged by the hand of God, 'THE WAGES OF SIN IS DEATH.' "[150]

Mrs. Parker assured me that the picture was a collaboration with Mrs. Wallace Reid, but I have found no evidence to support this and her name is not on the credits. However, Mrs. Reid was kind enough to write a letter of endorsement, as did Kate H. Brusstar, Superintendent of the Detention House of Camden County, who described the film as the most gripping she had seen for years: "Among the guests who saw the picture was a clergyman. He called to see me this morning and said he could not get the picture out of his mind. I think you deserve the highest commendation for putting out this picture and you have portrayed in a wonderfully artistic manner a very unpleasant subject."[151]

I am astonished that such a picture won the support of the authorities. To indicate the high-minded nature of Willis Kent, the man behind the picture (who also wrote the story), here is his statement to exhibitors: "MAN, MAN, what a box office picture and what a really worthwhile story. Oratory couldn't sell these seasoned picture men, high pressure wouldn't move them; they are impervious to 'bull' but THE ROAD TO RUIN sold itself and adorable little Helen Foster won a permanent place in every heart."[152] Or, as the posters put it, "The Mantle of False Modesty Torn Ruthlessly Aside!"

THE GODLESS GIRL   What Judges Lindsey and Brown were trying to save children from were reformatories.[153] One would not, perhaps, place Cecil B. DeMille in the same evangelical class, but he, too, produced a remarkable indictment of these institutions—*The Godless Girl* (1928). Because DeMille tended to revel in sadism, one is tempted to dismiss his depiction of the savagery of reform school life as merely a Jazz Age version of the Inquisition.

And yet there was more to the film than at first seemed apparent. A journalist, Dorothy Donnell, was permitted to examine the research material at the DeMille studios, research which had allegedly cost $200,000 and consumed eight months. It was carried out, according to Miss Donnell, by a private detective. Eddie Quillan, who played in the film, said that DeMille had smuggled a young man into a boys' reform school, and a young woman into the girls.' They were not only observed but experienced many of the vicious punishments.[154] Stored in two immense books at the DeMille studios were sworn affidavits from paroled inmates. "I have seen these books," said Dorothy Donnell, "and read in them things so revolting that they will probably never be printed."[155]

Authentic-looking reformatory re-created on the backlot by art director Mitchell Leisen for Cecil B. DeMille's The Godless Girl, *1928. From* Picture Play, *July 1928.*

DeMille was thus able to base every incident in the film on fact. In one scene George Duryea[156] filled a hand barrow with 200 pounds of rock, staggered a thousand feet across a yard to empty it, and then repeated the process. This form of punishment was used in a Midwest reform school and was guaranteed to break a boy's spirit within a few hours. The bloodhounds used in the film were a feature of several state reformatories.[157]

Dorothy Donnell was convinced that DeMille undertook this project in the same spirit that led Dickens to write *Little Dorrit* and close the debtors' prisons of England forever or Thomas Mott Osborne to fight for a reformed Sing Sing. Seeing the film today, one cannot entirely share her faith, for the film has an element of exploitation about it. But one cannot deny, either, its remarkable power.

The idea of the picture was welcomed by prison reformers, said DeMille in his autobiography.[158] His researchers acquired as props an armory of implements: leg chains, manacles (as used in fifteen state institutions), human restraint gloves, straitjackets, adhesive tape to seal mouths, and a photograph of seventeenth-century–style stocks, still in use in a Southern reform school. Although a title was inserted in the picture to point to the existence of excellent reform schools, far too many were medieval institutions where a girl of fourteen might be left hanging by her thumbs for three hours for the offense of speaking to another girl in "the silence" . . . where twin thieves aged three were confined for stealing candy . . . where the instruments of torture were so sophisticated they were operated by electric motors.[159]

Original caption: " 'NO CORPORAL PUNISHMENTS!' SAY WOMAN'S PRISON BOARD AFTER
DEMILLE REVELATIONS. *Members of California Commission shocked by treatment of girls in worst
type of institutions, which they observe reproduced from signed descriptions of eye witnesses, in
Reformatory sequences of Cecil B. DeMille's* The Godless Girl. *Later some of the reconstructed
punishments are filmed for them by Patricia Kelly and Kate Price . . . while the following members
of the Commission study the demonstration: Mrs. Ernest Wallace of Alhambra, chairman; Mrs.
John Buwalda of Pasadena, secretary; Mrs. Ingram B. Slocum, of San Francisco, chairman, prison
relations committee. Tying up the girl in the form of torture known as the Thumb School. The cord
is stretched until the victim is on her tiptoes and part of the weight of her body is suspended from the*

Right: Lina Basquette as Judy, lashed to her cell as fire breaks out, reveals the marks of electrocution on her hand. From The Godless Girl, *1928. (Museum of Modern Art) Below: The electrified fence which separates girls from boys. (Robert S. Birchard Collection)*

The film is seldom shown today, which is a pity, for it is one of the few silent films with a built-in appeal for modern audiences. It is exceptionally violent, and one cannot wonder that it appealed so little to American audiences of the time that it became a financial disaster. The brutality is startling, even today. The picture is a true forerunner of *I Am a Fugitive from a Chain Gang* (1931), although it lacks the integrity of that film. It employs more melodrama than Mervyn LeRoy's masterpiece, which was almost documentary in its approach. But the parallels are close; the film is authentic, exciting, and shocking. It also led to reforms.

Brilliantly directed—the film is one of DeMille's best works—it betrays itself only in a couple of weak romantic interludes, and in the overwrought playing, particularly of Noah Beery as the sadistic head guard. J. Peverell Marley's photography is magnificent, if seen in original prints, and the reform school sets are so convincing it is impossible to believe they were all constructed, by art director Mitchell Leisen, on the "Forty Acres" back lot at the DeMille-PDC studios, Culver City.

Technically elaborate, with a *Seventh Heaven* elevator for the stairwell tragedy, and the kind of dynamic editing and camera placement one associates more with DeMille's second-unit directors than with DeMille himself, *The Godless Girl* rewards repeated viewings. It opens at a high school, where Judy (Lina Basquette) addresses a meeting of the Godless Society. Judy's love for Bob Hathaway (George Duryea), a "son of the gospel," does not protect her when he leads a storm troop to break up the meeting. Her pal "Goat" (Eddie Quillan) is beaten up, and a girl is killed when she falls from the top floor.

"DeMille had a factual basis for all this," said Eddie Quillan. "Even in Hollywood High School they were passing pamphlets about atheism like the ones in the film. They had a Godless Society right in the school here."[160] It was not, however, met with such ferocious violence as DeMille depicts.

Judy, Bob, and "Goat" are charged with complicity and sent to reform school, where we see them being processed. "What's the big idea?" asks "Goat" as they take mug shots of him. "I'm not a criminal."

"No," comes the reply. "But it won't be long now."

Both boys and girls have their hair shorn, and when the girls protest they are warned that every word they say will mean one day added to their sentence. The haircutting scene could be shot only once; Eddie Quillan recalled DeMille using at least ten cameras.

The boys are issued trousers marked with a stripe—to make a strong target, they are told, for the warden's rifles. And the girls have shoes with specially marked soles, to leave clear tracks in the event of escape.

When Bob steps out of line in the washroom, he discovers how swift and brutal punishment can be. The head guard turns a fire hose on him at full blast. Quillan recalled that the scene could not be faked, nor could Duryea be doubled. The hose proved very painful. When Quillan went to play his own part in the scene, remonstrating with Beery and being knocked down, he bounced straight off the water-soaked floor. It transpired that electric cables for the lights were lying in the water, and he had received a violent shock.

Electrocution provided the most savage moment in the film. Bob and Judy are assigned to garbage detail on opposite sides of the fence dividing the male compound from the female. Bob calls Judy over and tries to pass her an old glove to make her task slightly less revolting. The head guard sees them together, hands outstretched, about to kiss through the wire. He runs up to a watchtower, throws a switch, and watches their bodies gyrate, their fingertips smoke.

Even this was based on fact, although DeMille admitted it was a feature of only two institutions, where the electricity was switched off most of the time. But it was not simply an idea of Jeanie Macpherson, the scriptwriter.

With the current off, their flesh scorched, Bob and Judy find themselves in solitary, on bread and water, a punishment feared more than the whip.

In a well-organized escape, Bob and Judy get clear of the prison, but the guards set bloodhounds on them and soon they are back in their cells, manacled for safety. They are thus in appalling danger when fire breaks out.

"I did get burned in that fire scene," recalled Lina Basquette. "They put asbestos on our clothes and fireproofed the set." (Mitchell Leisen even flameproofed their hair.) "We had some kind of thing we spread on our bodies. But my eyelashes and eyebrows were singed. Thank God my eyelashes came back, but my eyebrows never grew back properly. And I had an effect like horrible sunburn—painful, though nothing like third degree burns. DeMille admired my guts because when the fire got too hot, George Duryea became scared and took off and DeMille yelled at me, 'Stay there, Judy!' and the cameras were grinding and I was screaming and carrying on and DeMille was very impressed with that kind of guts. He put poor George Duryea through such hell. DeMille was a typical tyrant—if he thought he could intimidate somebody and terrify them, God help them. But I kind of showed spirit and stood up to him right from the beginning and he loved that."[161]

After astounding scenes of panic and amid the inferno of the prison, the three are released, and there is an ending which suggests that Judy, the atheist, has been taught to believe.

Photoplay said that no one who likes an extraordinarily good show should miss it: "If it sticks a knife into existing abuses—that's just an extra for which parents, school-teachers and juvenile court judges will owe DeMille a prayerful vote of thanks."[162] But *Picture Play* regarded it as an example of judgment gone awry and values askew, rejecting the horror and declaring it as unreal "as life on an imaginary planet."[163]

Sound was in by the time the film was released, and talking scenes were added to the final reel. By this time, DeMille had left PDC and joined MGM, and Fritz Feld directed the sound sequences. The sound did not help. The film had cost $722,000; it grossed only $400,000.[164] And yet it was very popular in Germany and Austria.

"I received a fan letter written from Austria in 1929," said Lina Basquette, "from Adolf Hitler. The name meant absolutely nothing—it came to mind only later when he became famous. It said I was his favorite American movie star."[165] She received confirmation of this when she was invited to Germany in the late 1930s, to be considered for UFA stardom and met the Führer.

The Godless Girl shows how little distinguished certain prisons and reform schools in the United States from the early concentration camps of the Third Reich. How easily, as Sinclair Lewis warned, it could have happened here!

DeMille was not merely taking a religious stand with the early scenes of the film; behind this atheism he saw the specter of Bolshevism. He told John Hampton, many years later, that Communist Youth Societies began as Societies of the Godless, preaching Darwinism and atheism: "He then said that he had expected Russia would ban this film as they had *The King of Kings* and to his amazement he was told that it was being shown all over Soviet territory."[166]

When DeMille visited Russia in 1931, he found the film so popular that he was made to feel a national hero for producing it. The story of a girl's redemption by gaining faith in God did not seem the kind of thing the Communists would embrace. "It was not until near the end of my trip," he wrote, "that someone enlightened me. The Russians simply did not screen the redeeming reel, but played the rest of the picture as a document of American police brutality and the glorious spreading of atheism among American youth."[167]

The Soviet version still survives. It ends with the capture of the couple and their return to jail. The proper ending, with its religious message was eliminated—along with the essential fire scene.

Variety[168] insisted that reform school stuff had been done much better before, and one must take the journal's word for it. But with so many vital films missing, this stands among the most exceptional prison pictures ever made.

GANGSTERS

The Gas House Gang ... the Plug Uglies ... the Hudson Dusters ... The nineteenth-century gangs of New York with the colorful names were mostly Irish. Silent films, often made by directors of Irish descent, took a nostalgic view when they dealt with the gangs, portraying them as raucous and rough but basically warm-hearted and funny. Even *Lights of Old Broadway* (1925), which showed the authorities using fire hoses on the mob, placed the accent on humor.

In reality, the gangs were murderous. Gouging out eyes and stamping on the injured with hobnail boots were the least of it. Unspeakable tortures were inflicted on the Negroes, soldiers, and policemen captured by the mob during the anti-Draft riots of the Civil War, and Gatling guns and howitzers had to be used to restore order. In one riot, thirteen acres of New York City were laid waste.[169]

All of which was an embarrassment to Tammany Hall, the Democratic party machine that ruled Manhattan. The politicians, who owned saloons, gambling houses, and brothels, looked to the gang members as a private army. On Election Day they would turn out en masse to vote early and often (they were known as repeaters), to blackjack those who sought to vote differently, to stuff or steal ballot boxes, and occasionally to murder opponents. In return, the politicians provided the gangs with meeting places and boltholes and kept the police off their backs.[170]

By the turn of the century, and the advent of the moving picture, big gangs such as the Five Pointers could field 1,500 men; smaller outfits such as the Gas

Street fighting on Avenue A. Production still from Allan Dwan's Big Brother, *1923.*

House Gang numbered about 200. Jewish and Italian gangs added to the misery of the districts which they claimed as their own. Moving pictures could not reflect the scale of this gang warfare; they dealt with more modest aspects of criminal behavior—yeggmen, kidnappers, or burglars.

The first gangster film of any importance to survive is a D. W. Griffith one-reeler called *The Musketeers of Pig Alley,* made in 1912 for the Biograph Company. The Biograph studio was an old brownstone at 11 East Fourteenth Street, not far from "the nerve center of gangsterism," Tammany Hall. The street even had its own gang under the leadership of Al Rooney. While the Biograph studio ground out dramas of crime and poverty, historic events were taking place nearby. In December 1911, gangster Julie Morrell was shot by Big Jack Zelig in a Fourteenth Street saloon.[171] A month before *Musketeers* was released, Zelig himself was killed on a Second Avenue trolley car at Thirteenth Street.[172] A famous gangster of a later date, Lucky Luciano, grew up on Fourteenth Street, and since he was fifteen in 1912, one has an image of him with the other kids, drawn as if by a magnet to where the exterior shots of *Musketeers* were made and staring with admiration at the Gish sisters.

Musketeers is an impressive film in which the gangster clichés seem freshly

Lillian Gish and Elmer Booth in D. W. Griffith's The Musketeers of Pig Alley, *1912. (Museum of Modern Art)*

minted. Biograph claimed that real gangsters took part in it and went so far as to name them ("Kid" Broad and "Harlem Tom" Evans*).[173] One should distrust publicity claims on principle, but there is no reason why this should not be true. Biograph, in common with most picture companies, employed bouncers for protection when on location in the streets, and such men would of necessity belong to a gang. They were a protected species. If Jacob Riis could photograph them, why not D. W. Griffith?

This little picture even has its own James Cagney; Elmer Booth's characterization of the Snapper Kid has Cagney's looks, his humor, and his viciousness. The consciousness of the gangster as a social evil, the importance of territory, and the corruption of the police were all strongly suggested in this film.

It would be a mistake to make too much of the film merely because it survives. Biograph themselves acknowledged that the film "does not run very strong as to plot."[174] It was simply intended to show "vividly the doings of the gangster type of people." I saw the film at least a dozen times without being able to follow the plot; I thought the shots were in the wrong order. Not until I read Carlos Clarens's graphic description in his book *Crime Movies* did I notice the almost imperceptible

---

*But the leading gangsters are played by actors. "Kid" Broad was an East Side prizefighter. He also appeared in *A Romance of the Underworld* (1918).

movement of a gangster putting knockout drops into Lillian Gish's drink and causing the confrontation between the two gangs. Griffith's audience would have spotted that instantly, having read about it in the yellow press and seen it in the many white slave and gangster pictures made before his.

The street scenes, shot on West Twelfth Street,[175] are unusually evocative. The scene with the elderly Jew, which so resembles a Riis photograph, was as staged as any of the interiors. Griffith had noticed, in actuality shots, that people tended to stare at the camera. By placing a girl at the center of the shot and instructing her to do just that, he makes the scene seem utterly authentic, even though the "old man" discarded his whiskers as soon as Mr. Griffith called "Cut."[176]

The sensation of 1912 was the murder of Herman Rosenthal, who had opened several gambling houses, had failed with all of them, and blamed the New York Police Department. A trio of gamblers, Bald Jack Rose, Bridgey Webber, and Harry Vallon, hired four gunmen, who shot Rosenthal on the sidewalk outside the Hotel Metropole on West Forty-third Street. Police Lieutenant Charles Becker, corrupt head of the anti-gambling squad, was made the scapegoat in a vast cover-up. Rose, Webber, Vallon, and Sam Schepps (who had paid off the gunmen) were

Advertisement for Wages of Sin, *the film that exploited the Rosenthal sensation. From* Moving Picture World, *May 31, 1913.*

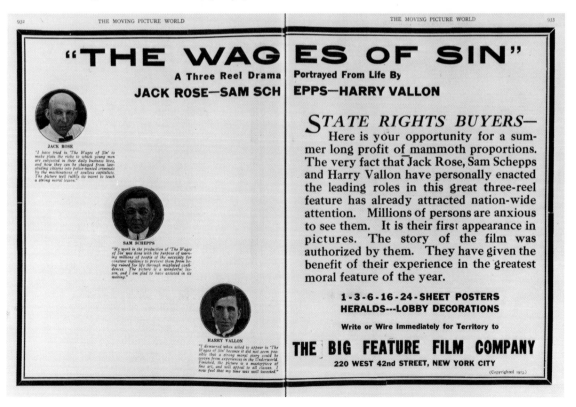

JACK ROSE

"I have tried in 'The Wages of Sin' to make plain the risks to which young men are subjected in their daily business lives, and how they can be changed from law-abiding citizens into police-hunted criminals by the machinations of soulless capitalists. The picture well fulfills its intent to teach a strong moral lesson."

A real gangster in a crime film; Bald Jack Rose is given high-minded sentiments by the press agent. From Moving Picture World, *May 31, 1913.*

only too pleased to cooperate with the district attorney. They were freed; Becker and the gunmen went to the electric chair.

The case mesmerized New York, the newspapers gave it more coverage than any crime story in their history, and the participants became household names. Sam Schepps invested in a motion picture called *The Wages of Sin,* about the perils of gambling. It did not touch upon the Rosenthal case, and there was nothing exceptional about it beyond the fact that the leading roles were played by Bald Jack Rose, Harry Vallon, and himself. (Bridgey Webber, sick with remorse, refused to take part.)

"A Disgusting Film," declaimed two editorials in *Moving Picture News,* which pleaded with exhibitors to ostracize *The Wages of Sin:* "All the worst elements in the youth in our cities will flock to see this film . . . All the moral, clean, upright, thinking people will once more refer to the degrading and disgusting condition of Cinematography."[177]

The National Board of Censorship initially rejected it, but the general committee overruled the board and passed the film, leading to a demand for the removal of the board. The chairman, Dr. Frederic C. Howe, explained that as far as he could see, the picture was just a harmless melodrama. There was nothing to suggest crime or to degrade moral standards. "All mention whatever of Messrs. Rose, Vallon and Schepps was eliminated from the main title and subtitles before the Board approved the film," he said. "The Board did not consider that it had any right to prohibit these men from going on the film stage, but it had a right to prevent the morbid exploitation of these men's reputations." Rose, Vallon, and

Schepps had not been convicted of a crime, but even if they had been, and had been sent to the penitentiary, the board would not have felt justified in forbidding them to appear in a film. "The Board is concerned with the moral effect of motion pictures, not with the moral character of the people who produce motion pictures or who act in them."[178]

The film was a three-reeler produced by David Horsley from a story by F. E. Farnsworth. "There is a realistic scene showing a table in a gambling house," said George Blaisdell in *Moving Picture World.* "It is said to be authentic as to detail. Certainly it should be."[179] The picture included references to the Mafia and the third degree. And since it was entirely concerned with thievery, blackmail, and murder, Dr. Howe's comments about the absence of crime are baffling.

Said *Moving Picture World:* "Of course, the motive behind the making of this melodrama is simply to exploit three men whose names—and photographs, like-wise—during the past year have been much in the public prints. . . . The three men under discussion are at liberty. Their friends will say they served the state. Their enemies and the friends of the five men under sentence of death at Sing Sing partly by reason of their testimony will use other language."[180]

The National Board of Censorship had no jurisdiction over posters, so while the names may have been expunged from the film, the picture was advertised as "The Three-Reel Moral Picture Enacted by Jack Rose, Sam Schepps and Harry Vallon."[181]

In 1914, Bald Jack Rose wrote the story for *Are They Born or Made?*, directed by Lawrence McGill, which not only drew attention to the role of environment in the creation of criminals, but also blew the gaff on the link between gangsters and politicians. Intriguingly, it was one of the early films distributed by Warner's, whose later gangster films are more famous.

But as long as most moving pictures hesitated to link the gangster with the politician,* some explanation had to be found for their antisocial behavior, for the gangsters of the early movies lived in a vacuum. Until Prohibition gave them a purpose, they were ordinary criminals. In *The Musketeers of Pig Alley,* the hoodlums are shown removing a man's wallet, the kind of thing an East Side street kid could do in a flash. In *Regeneration* (1915), they hang around gambling and looking threatening, but committing no offense until one of them knifes a cop. Even as late as 1927, in von Sternberg's *Underworld,* the gang leader, who in real life would have been running his team like the boss of a large corporation, is shown robbing a bank and a jewelry store *on his own!*

The Gangsters of New York,[182] a Reliance four-reeler directed by James Kirkwood, hinted at the link between government and crime by blaming the existence of criminals on "the saloon of disreputable character"—the saloon being a center of machine politics. "The tough resort is depicted exactly as it is, a nuisance, a caterer to all that is low in man's nature, blunting his moral sense and perpetuating organized crime."[183]

The only misdeed the gangster considers worthy of punishment is squealing,

---

*Griffith's *Intolerance* (1916) had a gangster using political influence—"The man higher up"—to frame the boy when he tries to go straight.

which was why, the film suggested, the police found it so hard to prove crimes. (It would be a brave film that suggested anything else.)

Variety criticized a sequence reminiscent of *The Musketeers of Pig Alley,* the two gangs prowling the streets looking for one another, "peeking round corners with their guns drawn, mostly repetition."[184] Yet the story was bolder than the Griffith film. The Dugan gang breaks up the annual ball of a rival gang, and in the shootout the rival gang leader is killed. The Dugan brothers are framed and convicted, and the elder brother is executed. When the younger brother gets out of jail he sets out for vengeance and corners the man who squealed. But the influence of a girl persuades him to let the man go.

The picture was largely shot in powerful close-ups; *Variety* praised the "unusually good photography, a point this film appears to make being the close range of the camera in which eye expression may be plainly observed."[185] The amount of publicity given to gunmen in the papers will make this a draw, they added. The acting of Henry B. Walthall and Jack Dillon was highly praised. And *Variety* pointed to an unusual subtitle, which apologized for the morbid scenes, such as the execution.

"The film cries out loud to the spectator in its agonizing appeal for a better understanding of conditions of crime," said the New York *Dramatic Mirror,* which thought its power and its "wonderful handling" beggared description.[186]

The majority of these early gangster pictures were shot in New York, some-

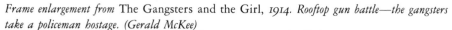

Frame enlargement from The Gangsters and the Girl, *1914. Rooftop gun battle—the gangsters take a policeman hostage. (Gerald McKee)*

times in the very slums where the gangs operated. In 1914, Thomas Ince produced a two-reeler which was so carefully made, its locations so well chosen, that historians assume it was also filmed in New York.[187] But *The Gangsters and the Girl* (1914) was directed by Scott Sidney, from a Richard Spencer scenario, in California. The commercial district of Venice, a relatively quiet town on the coast near Santa Monica, was used for the scene of the pickpocket, and the hijacking of the police car took place in the Los Angeles Plaza district, near the Southern Pacific railroad yards, which also figure in the story.

The rooftop battle was filmed in the Los Angeles business district, where the tall buildings resembled those of New York, and the steel skeleton of a brand-new block completed the impression of a city of skyscrapers. (A sign in the background of another building reads, "WE SELL UPRIGHT PIANOS"—they would not find many customers in the Five Points or the Bowery!)

Molly Ashley (Elizabeth Burbridge), whose sweetheart, Jim Tracy (Arthur Jarrett), is leader of the neighborhood gang, is wrongfully convicted of being a pickpocket. Tracy's gang hijack the police car transporting her to prison and take Molly back to their lair.

"Yuh couldn't live straight now if yuh wanted to," Tracy tells her. "Why, dere ain't a 'Harness Bull' in de district but would pinch yuh at sight."

Detective John Stone (Charles Ray) infiltrates the gang, bursting into their saloon and pretending the "bulls" are after him. One of the gang squeals to the police, who raid prematurely, before Stone has his evidence. The raid is a fiasco, but Stone's identity is discovered by Molly, who has fallen in love with him. Tracy accuses her of squealing, and Stone is forced to kill him to protect her. The picture ends with Molly installed at business college, receiving flowers from John Stone, who will certainly be her future husband.

The Gangsters and the Girl, made a mere eighteen months after *The Musketeers of Pig Alley,* shows how proficient the Americans had become with crime-and-police pictures, spurred by competition from French serials. It is of particular value today in its crystallization of the public's view of the New York gangsters, vintage 1914. Dressed like those in the photographs of Jacob Riis, they look convincing if you don't examine them too closely. (The scruffy gang leader looks out of place in a Los Angeles park.) The film depicts the hoodlums as reassuringly disorganized, under constant attack from vigilant cops, liable to turn informer at any moment, their criminal activities restricted to a little mild burglary. Too poor to own automobiles, they can drive them nevertheless, a skill they will need in a few years when their world will revolve around rumrunning trucks and armor-plated sedans, when the amateurish crooks of this film will appear to belong to a long vanished era.

REGENERATION   Owen Kildare was a Bowery gang leader of the 1890s. At thirty he could neither read nor write; at thirty-eight he was earning his living as an author. This transformation was brought about by a schoolteacher, Marie R. Deering, with whom he had fallen in love. His autobiography was named for her—*My Mamie Rose.*[188]

Kildare, half Irish and half French, ran away from an abusive foster father at the age of seven and joined a gang of newsboys led by Big Tim Sullivan. He developed into a strong fighter, boxed in the innumerable sporting houses in the Bowery, and worked as a bouncer. Society people who enjoyed "slumming" would hire him for a guided tour of the dives.

By the time these places closed (temporarily), Kildare was leader of his own gang. Outside Mike Callahan's saloon on Chatham Square (which the film re-creates), he met the schoolteacher who was to transform his life. Unlike the ravishing Swedish blonde who plays her in the film, she was somewhat dowdy. Marie, or Mamie as Kildare preferred to call her, not only taught him to read and write, she reformed him. Almost every night they went to Cooper Union—he often fell asleep, he admitted, in the more difficult lectures. Caught one night in a rainstorm, Marie developed "a trifling cold" and died a month before they were to be married. It took Kildare a long time to recover from her death, but eventually he entered a newspaper contest for a "True Love Story" and won. He became a staff writer on the New York *Daily News,* the paper he had sold as a boy thirty years before.

His book, which Hall Caine called the most remarkable ever written, was turned into a play by Kildare and Walter Hackett and became a Broadway success, with Arnold Daly. It was bought by William Fox (who had himself grown up on the East Side) and in 1915 was made into a film. The script, based more on the play than the book,[189] was credited to Raoul Walsh and Carl Harbaugh (his half brother), who was given a fictitious role as a district attorney.

But an uncredited influence is that of Rex Ingram, who joined Fox in May 1915, and wrote such scenarios as *Yellow and White,* released as *Broken Fetters,* about New York's Chinese gangsters. (He quarreled with Fox and moved to Universal as a director before the year was over.) Ingram had a fascination with bizarre types, who are well represented in *Regeneration.* There is even a scene of a drunk staring at a goldfish in his glass, which Ingram repeated in *The Four Horsemen.* And the picture has the qualities of stylized naturalism, which quickly became his trademark.

Walsh does not acknowledge Ingram in his 1974 autobiography, *Each Man in His Time,* but he forgot that he was supposed to have written the script himself. "After I read the script of *Regeneration,*" he wrote, "the first picture I was to make for Fox, I was interested in the latitude the story offered."

Rockcliffe Fellowes, from the New York stage, was cast as Owen Kildare— here called Conway—whom he resembled quite strikingly. The cameraman was a brilliant Frenchman, Georges Benoit. Together, they produced a film of such vigor, inventiveness and sheer filmmaking skill, despite all the changes made to the original story, that it is hard to believe it was made as early as 1915. In its bold technique, creation of atmosphere, use of locations and selection of players, it surpasses *The Mother and the Law,* the modern story of *Intolerance,* which Walsh's mentor, D. W. Griffith, had begun the year before.

Regeneration gains immeasurably from being shot on the Bowery and using local people. The streets have a distinctly seedy look, impossible to re-create in California. Some of the faces Walsh selected are astonishing and some repulsive (such as a man whose nose has proliferated in a series of molehills, a combined result, presumably, of syphilis and alcohol).

There were more gangs in New York at the end of 1913 than at any other period,[190] and it was likely that many of them wound up playing extras. It certainly looks like it; the secondary gangsters are obviously nonactors. And *Variety* referred to the film using "several hundred Bowery dive supers."[191] Raoul Walsh told me he used to round up characters by going through the saloons and dives.[192] Walsh was a great storyteller in the Irish tradition; he dressed up all his experiences like five-reelers, and how he really assembled these people is hard to tell. In his book, he says he went to Hell's Kitchen (some distance from the Bowery) and found a pair of "typical hooligans" to help find extras for the boat scene. "Using basic English, I managed to get it through their heads that I needed a hundred or so men and about fifty women for passengers: "Don't bring anyone who can't swim. They'll be paid five dollars and you'll each get ten finder's fee."[193]

The men showed up at the pier with a large crowd. "Some of the women were obviously hookers, many of the men looked as though they should have been on Death Row for every crime in the book,"[194] recalled Walsh. From journalistic color, Walsh's story leaps into fantasy when he describes the scene of the fire aboard the boat, the women jumping into the river, their skirts ballooning up to reveal they were wearing nothing underneath. Faced with disaster, he hired a man to retouch every frame to provide the women with undergarments. Unfortunately, the film shows plenty of men jumping from the boat, but no women (a couple swarm decorously down ropes); no skirts balloon, no retouching needed.

He also claims to have been arrested for staging the scene (on charges of arson, indecent exposure, and malicious mischief!)[195] and summons William Fox's secretary, Winfield Sheehan, to the rescue. Sheehan, later to become a producer, was the key to all this. For he had recently been secretary to Police Commissioner Rhinelander Waldo. A former *Evening World* reporter, Sheehan was one of the unofficial three-man committee that supervised gambling in Manhattan, allocating protection money by a method known as The Great Divide, to police and politicians. He figured in the background of the Rosenthal-Becker case (see page 185) and was involved in several cases of police graft, but was never indicted, despite his mysterious wealth.[196] He was forced to resign in 1914 when a madam named him as "the Man Higher Up."[197]

As a former Tammany Hall man,[198] he would have had no trouble in organizing the gangs for picture purposes—and there would have been no reason for an arrest at the end of it. As secretary to Fox, he would have arranged for money to pass hands in the customary manner. As Walsh said, "He knew every cop in Manhattan and pulled a lot of weight."[199] Sheehan first met Fox when the producer was fighting the Patents Trust. He organized Fox's private army and joined up full-time in 1914. He maintained cordial relations with both the police and the underworld.[200]

Regeneration starts with ten-year-old Owen (John McCann) watching from the window of a filthy tenement as the wicker coffin containing his mother's body is pushed into a hearse and driven away. An old couple across the hall take him under their wing, but they are drunken and violent and the boy's life becomes a nightmare. He takes to the streets and sleeps at night on the warm grating of a bakery.

At seventeen, Owen (H. McCoy) finds work as a longshoreman and proves

Frame enlargements from Raoul Walsh's Regeneration, 1915: Owen's mother's body is carried away. (Gerald McKee)

Owen's new guardian, the ferocious Mrs. Conway, played by Maggie Weston.

John McCann as Owen aged ten, sleeping on the streets.

himself a first-class fighter. At twenty-five, Owen (Rockcliffe Fellowes) is leader of a gang opposed by District Attorney Ames (Carl Harbaugh). The D.A. is a frequent visitor to the home of the wealthy Deerings, whose daughter, Marie (Anna Q. Nilsson), leads a butterfly existence, "hiding, even from herself, her finer qualities." The film contrasts the Deerings' refined dinner party with a replica of McGuirk's Suicide Hall in the Bowery, here called Grogan's. Ames agrees to take Marie slumming, but his publicity precedes him and Owen's gang makes it hot for him. His party scurries out of the hall, Marie silently pleading with Owen to intercede. Struck by her beauty, he escorts the party to safety.

Outside, a socialist speaker holds forth, pointing an accusing finger at the high-society slummers. His words strike deep; they awaken Marie's social conscience. She becomes a social worker and helps to organize the settlement house's annual outing—a river excursion—which ends in catastrophe. Fire breaks out aboard the steamer and the passengers panic, scrambling for the lifeboats and jumping overboard.*[201]

Owen helps Marie restore a child to its mother at the settlement house. She persuades him that the settlement house needs him more than the gang does and teaches him to read and write. He makes splendid progress. But his old loyalty obliges him to help a vicious criminal, Skinny the Rat (William Sheer). When Marie goes to find Owen at the gang's headquarters, she is set upon by Skinny. Owen bursts in, and a tremendous fight breaks out. The police arrive, and in the confusion Owen races upstairs and smashes into Skinny's lair. Skinny, escaping through the window, fires once and hits Marie, wounding her.

Owen carries her back to the settlement house, but she dies. He sets out for revenge and is only prevented from strangling Skinny

---

*An event based on a 1904 excursion-boat disaster. See note 201.

by a vision of Marie and a memory of her preaching. Skinny tries to escape by swinging hand over hand along a clothesline, four stories up, but Owen's friend shoots him. The last we see of Skinny is a horrifying flash of staring eyes on the blood-soaked cobbles.

The film ends with Marie's burial. "She lies here, this girl o'mine, but her soul, the noblest and purest thing I ever knew, lives on in me. It was she, my Mamie Rose, who taught me that within me was a mind and a God-given heart. She made of my life a changed thing and never can it be the same again."

Fire aboard the pleasure ship.

Walsh's memory of the film was very dim when he wrote his book, so he made up an ending: "the heroine kneeling at her slain lover's grave and strewing it with fresh flowers ... I wrote the epitaph for the tombstone: 'To Lefty, a sinner who found peace.' I had the camera move in for a closeup in best Billy Bitzer style. Anna's beautiful face was wet with tears when I told her to look at the camera. It was so harrowing that I almost bawled with her."[202]

As Walsh's wife, Miriam Cooper, put it, "Raoul never bored you with the truth."[203]

Walsh should have had more pride in his film; he should at least have kept a print of it. But it was a feature of the industry that its output was ephemeral. For sixty years the film was lost, and not until the late 1970s was it discovered by David Shepard and copied by the Museum of Modern Art just before it decomposed entirely. It is marred by mottled patches and blotches, but they do not completely erase Benoit's magnificent photography, with its sophisticated tracking shots. The use of locations and the appearances by assorted bums, winos, prostitutes, and heavies make it the most authentic-looking gangster film surviving from the entire silent period.

What is remarkable for a film of 1915 is the emphasis placed on environment. (One title says, "And so the days pass in the only

This bit player was almost certainly a real gangster.

A cop questions the gang—William Sheer, right.

environment he knows.'') Of course, the controversy over whether environment or heredity formed the criminal mind was in full swing, yet how few films ever tackled it! The titles of *The Mother and the Law* refer to it a couple of times, but the look of *Regeneration* makes one appreciate how much is missing from the Griffith film.

Owen's environment is the Bowery and the Lower East Side, its streets choked with people and pushcarts. He is surrounded by squalor, drunkenness, and brutality. As a boy, he is sent to the saloon for beer. Too young to be allowed in, he squats at the entrance and passes the pail (''growler'') underneath the swinging doors. On the way home, he drinks some of the beer—the way so many slum children were introduced to alcohol. Yet when the adult Owen is shown drinking a glass of beer, a quick mix to him eating ice cream as a child indicates how harmless it is, a rare example of an anti-Prohibition comment in an early film.

That Walsh did not set the film in period proved an advantage, for he could turn his camera on the slums with the freedom of a documentary filmmaker. *Traffic*

Fool's Highway, 1924. A remarkable re-creation of a Bowery bar for a remake of
Regeneration. *(Museum of Modern Art)*

in Souls captured the life of New York as a background, but Walsh brings it up to the foreground: we see one of the city's old flower women, selling a bunch and spitting on the money, and other close shots of picturesque inhabitants are dropped into the action throughout the film.

Regeneration has its faults. Anna Q. Nilsson, later an actress of considerable charm and talent, registers blankly in this, as though Walsh had no interest in her role.[204] The interior set of Chicory Hall is too obviously painted, as are the backdrops outside the windows of the tenement. The interior of Grogan's saloon is lit by direct sunlight, and the editing is sometimes too snatched, although it usually gives the picture terrific pace.

Regeneration received excellent reviews and in 1916 was selected as one of the great American films, along with Ince's *The Wrath of the Gods* and Griffith's *The Birth of a Nation*.[205] Walsh fulfilled the promise of the film and became an important director whose gangster pictures were among the best ever made—*Me, Gangster* (1928), *The Roaring Twenties* (1939), and *White Heat* (1949).

The film was remade in 1924 by Irving Cummings, the star of so many social films and by then a director. Although it was set in its correct period, 1892, this time it was just a "routine melodrama."[206] The difference between the two versions sums up the gulf between the Reform Era and the Age of Hays: the remake was entitled *Fool's Highway* after Kildare's definition of the Bowery as the "Highway of the Foolish." This time the schoolteacher (Mary Philbin) has become a seamstress in a secondhand clothing shop, not concerned about the environment or her lover's lack of education but simply fascinated by his brute strength. ("Mike" Kildare was played by Pat O'Malley.) And once he reforms, Kildare joins the police force![207]

THE PENALTY   A combination of gangster film, parable, and chilling melodrama, *The Penalty* (1920) is a remarkable piece of work, suggesting the direction such films might have taken had it not been for Hays. It also shows Wallace Worsley's promise as a director brilliantly fulfilled—it is a far more cinematic film than his handsome but stately *The Hunchback of Notre Dame* (1923).

Adapted from a novel by Gouverneur Morris and scripted by Charles Kenyon and Philip Lonergan, it depends upon symbolism, handled in such a way that the very symbols are entertaining. The theme of a gangster planning to take over a city could be seen as prescient, considering that "Scarface" Al Capone was, that very year, making his first big kill and inheriting an empire. The original story had appeared in *Cosmopolitan* magazine in 1912–1913; the situation in the film owed something to the Red Scare of 1919.

The Penalty is not the kind of picture one associates with the age of innocence. It equates Reds and immigrant workers with criminals and shows a killer who is never caught, a dope addict who carries out the gang leader's dirty work.

It tells of a boy, a victim of city traffic, who is operated on by the inexperienced Dr. Ferris. The child recovers consciousness in time to overhear Dr. Ferris being reprimanded for amputating both his legs and mangling his patient's life for no reason.

Blizzard (Lon Chaney), a gangster whose legs were amputated in childhood, takes his revenge on society in The Penalty, *1920.*

"Twenty-seven years later, San Francisco is the richest city in the western world. She has one hideous blemish—the Barbary Coast."

The place is still swarming with prostitutes and saloons, according to this freewheeling story, which is nonetheless given a contemporary setting. A prostitute is murdered and the killer sheltered by a cripple, Blizzard (Lon Chaney)—the injured boy grown up, the most vicious criminal the city has ever known. The Secret Service puts Rose (Ethel Grey Terry), its most daring operative, on the case. "We could get him for theft, arson, murder—but his criminal machine would still grind on," says the chief. "Through the Master I must reach his slaves—the underground powers of the Reds."

Blizzard runs a mysterious factory, where Barbary Coast dance-hall girls turn out hundreds of straw hats—all so innocent it *must* be sinister. Blizzard runs the sweatshop with an iron hand. Rose is warned that whoever enters that den risks worse than death, but she shrugs: "That's all in a day's work." (Considering the implication, this was not the sort of response of which the censors would have approved.)

Meanwhile, Dr. Ferris has prospered. His daughter, Barbara (Claire Adams), a sculptress, advertises for a model for "Satan After the Fall," and Blizzard applies for the job. Barbara and he develop a strange relationship which arouses the jealousy of Dr. Wilmot (Kenneth Harlàn), Ferris's assistant, who expects to marry Barbara.

Rose quickly becomes Blizzard's favorite and grows very fond of him. Yet duty first—whenever he leaves to pose for Barbara, she searches the place. She soon discovers concealed switches and subterranean passages, but her most astonishing discovery is of a fully equipped operating theatre and a weapons cache.

Blizzard's behavior disgusts Dr. Wilmot, who remarks, "That monster ought to be chloroformed and put out of the way." Dr. Ferris finally tells his daughter the full tragic story. "If you have made him what he is, it is all the more our duty to help him," says Barbara.

As Blizzard reveals his plans at last to his chief lieutenant, O'Hagan, so we see them in action. Blizzard has organized thousands of disgruntled foreign laborers. They all wear the distinctive straw hats, and he issues them rifles and pistols. He plans to take over San Francisco. Ten thousand foreign malcontents will infiltrate the city in small detachments. At the signal, an explosion, the men will open

One of the scenes that upset the censors: Claire Adams as the sculptress, with Cesare Gravina and Kenneth Harlan in The Penalty, *1920, directed by Wallace Worsley.*

GOLDWYN PICTURES

fire on the police, stage riots and burn buildings, and slowly draw police and military out to the suburbs, leaving the city undefended and at Blizzard's mercy.

O'Hagan is shocked. "You talk as if you had legs. By God, you've gone mad!"

But Blizzard plans to have legs. He intends to kidnap Dr. Wilmot and force Dr. Ferris to amputate his legs and graft them on to his. "You've played the trick with apes," he tells Dr. Ferris. "Now I'm putting human beings at your service."

Dr. Ferris agrees to conduct the operation. But when Blizzard wakes up he is a changed man. Ferris has operated on his brain, removed a tumor, and restored him to mental health.

"The tyrant's hand relaxed—the whirlwind breaks."

The gangsters realize that unless they finish him, he will finish them.

Blizzard and Rose are happily married, but he is shot through a window. Dying, he says, "Fate chained me to Evil—for that I must pay the penalty."

This was Lon Chaney's seventh release since his triumph as the cripple in *The Miracle Man* (1919). The production had been hard on him: his legs were strapped back, and the straps had to be removed every ten minutes and his legs massaged as they grew numb. He was in bed for weeks afterward and suffered a permanent muscle injury to his knees.[208] "The nervous strain was terrific," said Chaney.[209]

Burns Mantle in *Photoplay* thought the film about as cheerful as a hanging. "But for all its gruesome detail you are quite certain to be interested in it."[210] He described a final shot, missing from surviving prints, in which Chaney appeared with his legs attached and took a bow (to tremendous applause).[211]

The death of Blizzard could not offset the fact that the film was a compendium of all the scenes most loathed by censors—a naked model posing in a studio, a shivering drug addict being teased with a special dope kit (shown in close-up), a prostitute picking up a drunk outside a saloon, another prostitute being knifed in a dance hall—the real Thalia dance hall on the Barbary Coast[212]—a female agent prostituting herself for her job and falling in love with a gangster. The story had been printed as a serial in the Hearst magazines, then compiled in book form, neither of which caused any kind of disturbance. The film, however, came under strong attack. *Motion Picture Classic* called it "an orgy of unpleasantness. We do not mind constructive unpleasantness, but this is clap-trap magazine thriller goo."[213]

Early in 1921, the journalist Frederick Boyd Stevenson mounted an attack against *The Penalty* in the Brooklyn *Daily Eagle*. Proposing to view crime in the movies with "an unprejudiced mind," Stevenson based his remarks almost entirely on this one film, in his opinion, the strongest example of the current crop of "nefarious" crime and sex pictures: "It pretends to have a moral, but it has none . . . its only excuse is crime portrayed by a disgusting human beast. The whole thing was nauseating. The only motive is crime and an appeal to the worst sides of human nature—the licentious and the beast in man. You may imagine its effect upon young girls and young boys and even upon people of middle age in certain walks of life—the very people who attend motion picture theaters."[214]

Stevenson interviewed a member of the Review Committee of the National Board of Review. This exchange between a relentless interrogator and a moral guardian obliged to defend the board's action captures with great immediacy the floundering of the censors that rendered them so unsatisfactory to both hard-liners and liberals.

Stevenson asks if the lady objected to anything in the film:

" 'No,' she said. 'I saw nothing at all in it that was objectionable.'

"I reached into my bookcase and brought out a picture of Blizzard, the disgusting beast of a half-man sitting on a chair with the stumps of his legs sticking out straight and across them drawn the frail form of a pretty young woman, whom he was kissing.

" 'This picture,' I said, 'was, of course, much more sensual and revolting on the moving screen than it appears here. Did you see that picture on the reel of *The Penalty*?'

" 'Yes, I saw it,' said she.

" 'What did you think of it?'

" 'I thought it was just part of the play.'

" 'Did you object to it?' I asked.

" 'No,' said she.

" 'Why?'

" 'I didn't see anything objectionable in it,' she replied.

" 'Have you a daughter?'

" 'I have.'

" 'Would you care to have your daughter see that picture?' I asked.

" 'I would not have any objection to have her see it,' she replied. 'I think she would be so disgusted that it would not have any effect upon her.'

" 'Why, because the man has no legs?'

" 'Well, because of the general character of the play.'

" 'But if he had two legs—then you might object—'

" 'Oh, I've seen worse kissing than that in the movies.'

" 'Did you object to it?'

" 'I don't know that I did. There are worse scenes than that in *The Penalty*.'

" 'For instance?'

" 'Well, in the scene where Blizzard is in the studio of the surgeon's daughter. I thought it very improper for a young lady to receive such a man there alone.'

" 'Did you object to it?'

" 'No.'

" 'Why not, if it were improper? You were there to review it—were you not?'

" 'Oh, well, you can't cut out everything in life. You see we have no power of censorship, anyhow.'

" 'What is the use of having a Board of Review, then?'

" 'Well, we can make suggestions.'

" 'But you didn't make even a suggestion in *The Penalty*?'

" 'No, I didn't see any reason to.'

" 'Did you favor a real Board of Censors backed up by the law?'

" 'No, what's the use? It wouldn't censor.'

" 'What's the use, then, of a Review Board?'

" 'It can make suggestions.'

" 'To motion picture producers that pay fees of $6.25 per reel?'

" 'Well, that is legitimate. But you will never get anywhere with motion picture reform.' "[215]

The theme of revenge on society deserved a more realistic rendition, but this melodrama has a sadistic madness about it which admirably suits its subject. It was, alas, to be the last thoroughly vicious portrait of a hoodlum until the grand epoch of the gangster film, in the 1930s and 1940s.

Although the Hays Office would have preferred a moratorium on underworld pictures (as crime statistics rocketed), they remained enormously popular. But now that the industry was consolidated around studios, mostly in California, the realistic backgrounds of the big cities tended to be replaced by sets. This was so even in New York, where it was clearly more sensible to construct a slum at the Astoria studios than to take a film crew into the streets teeming with people, pushcarts, and other schedule-delaying obstructions. These sets were often so skillfully built that they were indistinguishable from the real thing and were usually peopled by ghetto residents. Nonetheless, *something* was missing. And when a director had the nerve to insist on filming on location, the difference was so apparent that reviewers drew attention to it.

Just such a film was *Big Brother* (1923), directed by Allan Dwan. By all accounts, this would have been a classic had Paramount permitted it to survive. Its vivid portrait of the tenement districts of New York might have made it one of the most treasured of all silent films.

James Quirk of *Photoplay* thought so much of it that he hailed it in an editorial: "Right on top of Pike's Peak, with the thermometer below zero, I would take off my hat and make a low obeisance to Allan Dwan for his production of *Big Brother*. He has made a truly great picture. In my opinion it ranks with *The Miracle Man*. What Chaplin did for Jackie Coogan, Dwan has done for seven-year-old Mickey Bennett."[216]

The Rex Beach story (adapted by Paul Sloane) concerned a gang leader, Jimmy Donovan (Tom Moore), whose lieutenant, Big Ben Murray (Joe King), is shot in a gang war. Dying, he commits his son, Midge (Bennett) into his boss's care with a plea to save him from his environment of crime and poverty. To keep the boy, Donovan finds that he must himself "go straight," but in spite of his attempt the little fellow is taken by the juvenile court and placed in an orphanage. Donovan is accused of a holdup, is arrested, escapes, and goes out to get the gang that committed the crime so that he may vindicate himself, for if he ever hopes to get the boy back he has to keep his record clean.[217]

Adele Whitely Fletcher of *Motion Picture Magazine* recognized that the film was propaganda for the Big Brother movement,[218] but it was so accurate a slice of New York gangster life that it aroused instant attention from the first scene.[219]

Variety's man was obviously *au fait* with the ways of the gangs, judging by his review: "One little detail will suffice to illustrate the knowledge of gangdom by the author and director. The leader of the rival gang arrives with his 'moll.' He wanders inside and is promptly 'fanned' for his 'rod' by the bouncers. He is 'clean' for he had previously slipped the gat to the dame. She had it planted conveniently in her handbag. Even in gangdom it is unethical to search a lady.

Big Brother. *Director Allan Dwan (right, by camera) shoots a meeting of the Car Barn Gang against the background of the Manhattan Bridge and South Ferry Terminal. Hal Rosson at camera. (American Museum of the Moving Image)*

"A stick-up by four auto bandits was just as intelligently handled. The much abused 'cokie' was rejuvenated by the character work of Raymond Hatton. His dope fiend is a sterling bit of character acting and another of the many details which make this picture stand out among underworld shots like the Woolworth Building in a Los Angeles suburb."[220]

Allan Dwan wanted realism in this picture. The great days of the New York gangs were over, but Dwan sent out his assistants to enlist the remnants to work in the film. "They agreed," he said, "because it was five dollars a day for each man. I was going to stage fights with them, but ones that I could blow a whistle on and stop. We engaged a big dance hall and put on a gangsters' dance. The way the story was written, this was presumably a dance held by the Hudson Dusters and their girlfriends, but the Gas House Gang butted in and made a shambles of it all."

The heavies assembled at the dance hall, agreeing to maintain a truce.

"While we were preparing, the Strong Arm Squad, as it was called in New

*Gangster Jimmy Donovan (Tom Moore) foster-father for Midge (Mickey Bennett)
in* Big Brother, *1923, directed by Allan Dwan. (George Eastman House)*

York—the toughest gang of policemen in the world—turned up. A tipoff had been
given that I had these two gangs up there and they knew that that wouldn't be
peaceful under any conditions, so they came in car loads, armed with billy clubs
and brass knuckles, everything that's necessary to subdue a crowd."

Dwan assured them there wouldn't be any trouble, and to reassure them (and
himself), he went up to the balcony and made a speech, making everyone swear
on their sacred word of honor that they would not start trouble unless he gave the
order. "If I tell you to do anything, or any of my men tell you to do something,
consider it an order and don't do anything else." They agreed. When they got a
look at the Strong Arm Squad beginning to crowd in the doorways, they decided
they'd better be good.

"We had to light this big place with Klieg lights—they were called broadsides,
and they were double arc lights, and we dropped a scrim in front of them to
subdue them. Those were called silks.

"The cameraman, Hal Rosson, took a look at the lighting and it looked fine
except in spots it wasn't enough. As the band was about to start up for the dance,
and the men were all in position with their girls, ready to start waltzing, he
hollered to his chief gaffer, 'Take the silks off the broads.'

"The order was immediately obeyed, every girl was ripped almost nude by the
obedient gangsters. The girls started to shriek and holler and that got the guys
fighting. The Strong Arm Squad went to work and in no time there was real panic.

"All I could do was holler 'Keep grinding!' to the cameras and we got great
shots of the mayhem. But when I wanted to release the picture I was stopped cold

by the censors, not because it was rough but because the girls were over-exposed. So that spoiled one of the greatest shots I ever saw come out of a camera."[221]

Historians have to be wary of Irish raconteurs, even Canadian-born ones like Dwan; this splendid story is too good to be true, especially when he admits it was cut out of the film. But perhaps there is some substance in it; perhaps some of the scene survived, for *Variety* said: "A gang fight which started at the annual ball of the Pastime A.C. was another triumph of direction and technique."[222]

One of the rare gangster films to link politicians and criminals was an unpretentious six-reeler from Preferred Pictures, B. P. Schulberg's company, entitled *Exclusive Rights*. The title of the original story by Jerome Wilson was better: *Invisible Government*. Directed by Frank O'Connor in 1926, it hovers on the edge of resembling a typical Warner Bros. picture of the early thirties.[223]

A corrupt political boss, Allen Morris (Charles Hill Mailes), schemes to break the new governor, war hero Stanley Wharton (Gayne Whitman), who intends to execute one of Morris's henchmen, Bickel (Sheldon Lewis), unless he reveals his employer. Boss Morris collaborates with Wharton's fiancée (Lillian Rich) in championing a new bill for the abolition of capital punishment; together they frame a wartime friend of the governor's, Mack Miller (Raymond McKee), with a murder. The governor's resolve is not shaken, and when Miller is led to the chair, Bickel finally breaks and implicates Morris.

The Boss is constantly surrounded by bodyguards and gangsters of the new breed—sleek, well-dressed men-about-town with automatics in their jackets who never take their hats off. Although bootlegging is not mentioned, much of the action is set in the boss's hangout, a nightclub called The Elite, with Grace Cunard, another veteran movie star, playing a Texas Guinan character. *Variety*'s man—who ought to know—thought all this was well-managed "with good pictorial shots of the semi-nude girls, the hard-boiled hostess and the specialty people, notably an eccentric dance by Jimmy Savo.... For some reason the producer does not exploit these night club bits in his billing matter, thereby missing a good bet. Instead, the billing emphasizes the death house angle and the political phase, which doesn't mean a thing."[224]

When the Boss orders the frame-up of Miller, we see another henchman, Flash (Gaston Glass), shooting a man (with a silencer) at the nightclub and tossing the gun on the body. Miller stumbles upon it, and a cabaret girl accuses him. When Miller is arrested, the Boss orders his men to get rid of Flash—he knows too much. In an imaginatively handled sequence, we see Flash preparing for a bath. The closet door slowly opens and a gunman emerges and tiptoes into the bathroom. Flash is now in the bath, and helpless, but he sees his jacket with a gun butt just visible in the pocket. He asks the man to pass it so he can get a cigarette. The gunman gives him one of his. Then the gunman lunges forward, and we see Flash's bare arm trying to grab his throat, then slowly relaxing and falling away. The gunman eventually straightens up and dries his arm. Fade-out.

Although *Variety* thought it skillfully done, the acting "extraordinarily convincing for a melodrama,"[225] *Photoplay* was surprisingly contemptuous: "Even if you are given free passes, don't waste your time."[226]

Many historians give the impression that *Underworld* (1927), directed by Josef von Sternberg, marked the start of the gangster cycle. Although it was adapted from a Ben Hecht treatment about the Cicero and South Side mob of Chicago—and although Hecht was a Chicago journalist who had witnessed the rise of the racketeers—the film was essentially a product of von Sternberg's imagination. The incidents, cleverly elaborated in Charles Furthman's story and Robert N. Lee's scenario, would have made an outstanding social film; as it was, von Sternberg turned them into a brilliant and almost poetic melodrama about the ethics of loyalty. A drunk who was once a lawyer (Clive Brook) is picked up by gang boss Bull Weed (George Bancroft) and put to work for him. The boss's girlfriend (Evelyn Brent) is magnetically attractive, but the lawyer keeps his distance until Bull is sent to prison. He then faces the choice: to run away with her or to rescue him. He chooses the latter course, but the gangster hears through the grapevine that the lawyer is meddling with his girl. He breaks out, returns to his hideout, and withstands a police siege. The lawyer and the girl risk their lives to rescue him, and, with proof of their loyalty, he gives himself up to the police and goes to his death.

"Jacob Kern, former State's Attorney of Chicago, was pressed into service as technical adviser on scenes for Ben Hecht's crime story Underworld.*" This original caption was typical press agent stuff, making the best of a brief visit by a prominent person.* Underworld, *1928, had little to do with the gangsters in the Chicago of the twenties—but was a brilliant picture, nonetheless. Fred Kohler (left), George Bancroft and Clive Brook (right). (National Film Archive)*

The City Gone Wild, *1927. James Cruze's gangster picture with Thomas Meighan as lawyer John Phelan, here calling on the gunmen to surrender. (Museum of Modern Art)*

George Pratt, who points out that the siege sequence was derived from Ben Hecht's story "The Man Hunt," thinks that the script reflected far more of Hecht's experience as a reporter than anything von Sternberg could add.[227] But the world of the gangster, with which we were to grow more and more familiar in sound films, is barely sketched in *Underworld*. True, Bancroft makes a magnificent twenties-style crook, well dressed, with a fashionable moll, but he is shown in 1927 behaving like a thug of the old days—robbing a bank and a jewelry store. Bootlegging does not come into it. The rivalry of the gangsters is merely an elaborate version of *The Musketeers of Pig Alley*. And although Hans Dreier's art direction is outstanding, the whole film was shot in the studio and Chicago is never mentioned (even though the film was entitled *Nuits de Chicago* in France).

Bull Weed's rival, Buck Mulligan (Fred Kohler), was based on Dion O'Banion, who was shot in a flower shop in similar circumstances to those in the film. This would make Bull a kind of Al Capone—but that would indeed be stretching a point.

According to von Sternberg, Hecht's contribution was a treatment eighteen pages long—"full of moody Sandburgian sentences."[228] Von Sternberg wrote: "It had a good title and dealt with the escapades of a gangster. It was untried material, as no film had as yet been made of this deplorable phase of our culture."[229] Von Sternberg was not expected to stay the course as director, and Hecht was hostile to his being assigned to it, as he had worked with Arthur Rosson. Von Sternberg provided what Hecht derisively termed "half a dozen sentimental touches"[230]—the gangster feeding a hungry kitten, for instance. Actually, von Sternberg used the film as "an experiment in photographic violence and montage,"[231] and the result was a magnificent piece of filmcraft. And while it had a superficial connection to topical events, it had very little to do with reality. When Hecht saw it for the first time, he declared, "I must rush home at once. I think it's mal de mer."[232] But von Sternberg cared nothing for authenticity: "When I made *Underworld* I was not a gangster, nor did I know anything about gangsters."[233]

The picture was an enormous hit; Ben Hecht won an Academy Award, and von Sternberg's career received a tremendous boost. The gangster picture was established as top box-office material; within three or four years, *Little Caesar, Scarface,* and *The Public Enemy* would all appear.

There was an irony about *Underworld* which no reviewer picked up. Bull Weed is arrested for murder, and, more ironic still, executed. Since 1922, not a single murderer from the ranks of the racketeers had been executed.[234]

Faced with the success of *Underworld,* Paramount put another gangster film into production as a vehicle for Thomas Meighan. His career had been on the wane for some time, and not even an excellent film like *The Canadian* (1926) had revived it. They gave him Louise Brooks (in a minor role) and James Cruze, of *Covered Wagon* fame, as director. The picture was called *First Degree Murder,* later changed to *The City Gone Wild* (1927). The story was by Jules and Charles Furthman and the titles by Herman Mankiewicz. Cruze had entertained Al Capone at his home, so he had a certain knowledge of gangsters.

The plot verged on the revolutionary, for its hero is a gangster's lawyer, John Phelan (Meighan), who always secures his client's acquittal on some technicality. His clients are currently staging a violent gang war, and he manages to impose a truce while his friend, D.A. Franklin Ames (Wyndham Standing), investigates. Nada (Marietta Millner) loves both men. She is the daughter of a powerful businessman whom Ames discovers is "the man higher up." Ames now knows too much, and he is killed. Phelan steps into his job to avenge his death.

The link between the criminals, politicians, and big business nearly popped into the open in this picture, which nonetheless blew the gaff on crooked lawyers. Unhappily, James Cruze shot in a hurry as a windup to his contract with Paramount. *Variety* said it was roughly handled by West Coast theatres; in San Francisco, Meighan's name was blocked out on the billboards. *Variety* thought it quite good, however: "The gang stuff is a la *Underworld*—machine guns and plenty tough. The two main yeggs each have a moll carrying their gat in the pocketbook. Very authentic in these little details is the picture."[235]

But it did nothing for Meighan's career, and Paramount sold his contract to Howard Hughes. By doing so, it inadvertently contributed to a remarkable gangster film, one which finally told the truth.

Prohibition had changed the structure of the underworld. "A new type of gang came into being," wrote Leo Katcher. "It had discipline and order. It possessed a chain of command. And, most important, it was financially independent."[236]

The Irish and the Jews were replaced by the Italians, and the old gangs, who controlled a few blocks, gave way to organizations controlling cities and states. "No law enforcement agency would remain uncorrupted."[237]

Only one silent film reflected this. There had been stories like *Flash* (1923), in which a police chief tries to clean up a city and arouses the anger of the gambling and political element,[238] and *The Last Edition* (1925), in which a bootlegger is protected by an assistant district attorney. But these were low-budget independent films, of a kind usually made outside Hays's jurisdiction. In the mainstream of American cinema only one film had the courage to tackle the new kind of gangster—a task not without danger.

Significantly, it was made from a play. Even more significantly, it was produced by Howard Hughes, who was independently wealthy himself, although his Caddo Company was a member of the MPPA.

THE RACKET Bartlett Cormack, a society reporter on the Chicago *Daily News* and a friend of Ben Hecht's, wrote the play *The Racket*. The film version was, by all accounts, the most important gangster picture of the silent era. It was directed by Lewis Milestone. Cormack did his own adaptation, and the scenario was written by Harry Behn[239] and Del Andrews. If it survives in the Hughes vault, no one will reveal.

It was important not because it was unusually well directed, as most critics agreed it was, but because at long last a film dealt head-on with the link between gangsters, police, and politicians—a link, incidentally, which was so thoroughly American it went back to Colonial times.[240]

The play was set in Chicago, and true to that city's tradition of fearless concern for the truth it was kept well away from there, for it included unmistakable references to Chicago's City Hall and its crooked mayor, Big Bill Thompson, who had been mayor from 1915 to 1923, when a reform candidate was elected. When he ran again in 1927 his victory was assured; Al Capone offered his full support and $260,000 for campaign expenses.[241] The play referred to Thompson not by name but as "the Old Man" and at one point accused him of having a man "accidentally" killed.

When Cormack published the play in 1928, he took the precaution of denying any resemblance to living persons.[242] Most people believed he had based the character of the gangster, Nick Scarsi, on Capone (the stage role had been played by Edward G. Robinson). In February 1928, the Illinois state attorney announced he was considering ways to keep *The Racket* from touring Chicago. "While the play actually can't be barred," said *Variety,* "theatre managers know that any house taking it will have a tough time; also, that the house will lose caste considerably with city officials."[243]

Leaving Chicago to be entertained by the real thing, *The Racket* went instead to Los Angeles, where it had a successful run. Robinson was rediscovered for the

The Racket, *1928. Thomas Meighan as Captain McQuigg and Louis Wolheim as gangster Nick Scarsi. (Museum of Modern Art)*

movies, although not for this one. Lewis Milestone cast Louis Wolheim (who had played in his *Two Arabian Knights* in 1927 and would play in his *All Quiet on the Western Front* in 1930) as Nick Scarsi.

"Scarsi is the first modern mobster leader of either stage or screen," wrote Gerald Peary. "He controls not only his own organization but extends his influence into all segments of the ostensibly non-criminal world."[244] Scarsi is an Italian immigrant, and Capone was born to Italian parents in Brooklyn. Scarsi is older than Capone, who, in 1928, was a mere twenty-nine. In real life, Wolheim had been a professor of mathematics at Cornell University and had acquired his distinctive broken nose on the sports field, but he looked squat, brutal, and neolithic, which was why he had been cast as O'Neill's Hairy Ape. He was a brilliant actor, but one wishes Robinson had repeated the role, for Wolheim resembled the old-style gangster. As a reporter in *The Racket* puts it, "In the old days, crooks were hard all right, but they were dumb, and you kind o' liked 'em. Now they're smart, and you don't like 'em."

While many of the new gangsters started out in the traditional way—and Capone received his basic training with the old Five Points gang in New York— they soon acquired such vast sums of money that they became the bosses of the politicians who had once bossed them.[245]

Playing the obstinate Irish police captain McQuigg was Thomas Meighan, whose contract Hughes had acquired from Paramount.[246] Meighan and Milestone had been associated on a picture about the Florida real estate boom, *The New Klondike* (1926), which had won him a new contract. It was Meighan who saw *The Racket* on the stage and brought the idea to Milestone. Meighan had once known the heights of stardom, but *The City Gone Wild* had not been the success he had hoped, and he was all set to leave pictures if *The Racket* was not a hit.[247]

It was greeted with admiration and enthusiasm. *Variety*'s language suited the subject: "Nick Scarsi tries to make McQuigg, in the usual ways, but the copper won't turn. Scarsi's political connections are of the strongest through his control of votes and repeaters. He has the captain transferred to a section where the goats are the only traffic problems. Two district men on a daily, looking for news, complicate matters here by ribbing McQuigg about Scarsi. The Cap tells them he was switched, not because he was afraid of Scarsi, but because Scarsi was afraid of him. He tells them to tell that to Nick. They proceed to do just that, finding Nick attending the funeral of a rival he has croaked. A touch of humor here is Scarsi's objections to a street calliope profaning the obsequies.

"Scarsi's brother is picked up by one of McQuigg's men (C. Pat Collins) as a hit and run driver. The kid brother has a yen for Helen Hayes (Marie Prevost), an entertainer. She's poison to Nick, as are all broads. Nick has incurred her enmity at a birthday party he gave the kid brother. At the party, Helen, doing a Helen Morgan on top of a piano, is cooing to the kid brother at Scarsi's table when the gorilla kicks the piano across the room. The gal flies back at him and bawls him plenty. Then she determines to make a play for the kid, just to burn Nick up. They are out in the kid's roadster, prior to the pinch. She leaves him flat when he develops hand trouble, and a police auto passing, stops as she steps out of the car. The kid screws, with the copper chasing. During the flight a spectator is hit, but Joe continues stepping on it until he runs the car into a fence and is nailed . . .

"How Nick avenges his kid brother and how McQuigg finally wins out when the district attorney double-crosses Nick and has him shot as he attempts to escape, complete the thrilling yarn."

The result, added *Variety,* was as nearly perfect a slice of screen entertainment as had run the gauntlet in months.[248]

Picture Play was equally impressed: "It has policemen who look like policemen, reporters who act like reporters, and crooks who look like crooks. Moreover, the policemen act like coppers, and not like Knights of the Round Table; the reporters are not handsome young men who solve the mystery that is baffling Scotland Yard, and the crooks perform as Chicago dispatches indicate they do. All of which is an excellent indicator of what a good director can do when he is not harassed by a supervisor.

"Lewis Milestone directed it, and, I was told, was given highly valuable assistance by the producer, Howard Hughes, in that he let him alone."[249]

Photoplay thought it gave Meighan his best role since *The Miracle Man,* Wolheim's interpretation was "a masterpiece," and the film was a classic. "The role of Nick Scarsi is one of contemptible villainy, but Louis Wolheim imbues it, through his incomparable touch, with that subtle sympathy and fascination which, since time immemorial, have given glamor to the bad man."[250]

According to Dunham Thorp, Milestone wanted some firsthand technical advice. He turned to a friend, "the biggest bootlegger in Hollywood" (probably Frank Orsatti, who had connections in Chicago), and asked for his help. "Eight genuine Chicago racketeers who, for various good reasons, were 'on the lam' and temporarily going straight in Los Angeles, were rounded up and induced to work in this crook melodrama. They were led to believe it was 'just one of those things'; no hint was dropped at all that this was to be the real stuff."[251]

The group included five bootleggers, a safecracker, a drug peddler, and a forger. What difference did they make? Dunham Thorp said quite a lot. "This picture has been judged as altogether too realistic by the very men it tells of. Their testimonials have come in what is perhaps the most unique form in screen history. The very types of men it deals with have done their best to stop its showing."[252]

Thomas Meighan, as the star, was regarded by the gangsters as the most responsible. He received death-threat phone calls, as did the manager of the Metropolitan Theatre (where the picture had its Los Angeles premiere), Hughes, Wolheim, and the leader of the eight fugitive gangsters. At first everybody thought it a great publicity stunt, including the chief jailer, Frank Dewar, but he changed his mind the minute he laid eyes on the chief crook: "I knew that guy well; and I also recognized other members of the cast as Chicago racketeers. If the friends or enemies of them babies had sent these letters, I knew it meant business."[253] He appointed himself Meighan's bodyguard and advised him to change hotels at once. Meighan took every precaution and checked his car for bombs. (On one occasion, his chauffeur pressed the starter. Nothing. He tried again. No result. Meighan leaped from the car and fled.)[254]

Nothing happened. After all, once the picture was out, there was little point in shooting the men who made it—that would merely arouse the newspapers to give it massive publicity. The only sensible course was to get it banned via the politicians. This proved more successful.

The picture was banned in such cities as Chicago (surprise!), Dallas, and Portland, Oregon, where a newspaper said, "This was apparently a political decision, the chief reason offered being that the film showed city officials as being crooks. Pure minded Portland must never see an official on the screen who was not honest. It might begin suspecting the home folks."[255]

The Hollywood *Citizen* editorialized: "Trouble is being experienced by the author and producers of *The Racket* . . . They find that in some cities the picture is barred while in others it is viciously censored . . . Crooked politicians do not like the picture at all . . . So political censors have in certain instances sought to destroy the effect of the production in getting over the message of political despoliation. That's one argument against censorship that is hard to meet ... If the metropolitan newspapers will not keep the public informed as to the actual conditions, a few plays and motion pictures, such as *The Racket,* are greatly needed."[256]

The New York and Pennsylvania censors did not ban the picture because it was so clearly set in Chicago. They merely slashed it to ribbons.

The critics were unusually enthusiastic. "This is one of those movies that comes along once in a Transatlantic flight," said Pare Lorentz.[257] Lines three deep formed outside the Paramount Theatre on the hottest day of the year.[258] It was transferred to the Rialto Theatre for an extended run.[259]

One fan, however, wrote to *Picture Play* with the complaint, "We don't want reality; we crave entertainment ... Who wants to spend two hours watching a typical, honest policeman fight crooked politicians and bootleggers? Give us more pictures like *The Singing Fool.*"[260]

Only in Los Angeles Could This Happen

HOW THE CHIEF EXECUTIVE OF SCREENLAND'S CAPITAL BECAME A FILM ACTOR

A YEAR ago Charles E. Sebastian was the chief executive of Los Angeles, one of the ten biggest cities in the United States and the largest in area and population in the West.

Now in the same city he may be seen daily with make-up on his face and his hair reddened to give it the proper shade on the screen.

Whether he will remain in the movies will depend largely on the reception accorded his first actorial effort, which is described as a picturized history of his public career as policeman, chief of police and mayor.

The film is entitled "The Downfall of a Mayor" and it is qualified with such sub-captions as "Exposing Chemically Pure Los Angeles" and "The Invisible Government." Sebastian was really ousted as mayor a few months ago, although his resignation was ascribed to ill health.

According to the advance notices, Hero Sebastian has plenty of opportunities to hero in the seven or eight reels comprising the film. He saves beautiful maidens from Chinese dens and white slave rings and other well-known birds of prey, who finally get together and put the intrepid cop out of business after he has matriculated to the mayor's chair.

Charles E. Sebastian, recent Mayor of Los Angeles.

Chapter Six

POLITICAL
CORRUPTION

"IT IS STRANGE with what matter-of-factness the pictures take it for granted that our politicians are corrupt," said the New York *Dramatic Mirror* in 1914.[1]

The ordinary neighborhood politician was the only hope for the poor. In exchange for their vote, he provided services which often amounted to favors— finding a job, releasing a relative from jail, chasing a landlord to carry out repairs.[2] No one was too poor to be helped. "But as the politicians grew rich and power- ful," wrote Lincoln Steffens, "the kindness went from their charity. They sacrificed the children in the schools, let the Health Department neglect the tenements and planted vice in the neighborhood and homes of the poor."[3]

THE LIFE OF BIG TIM SULLIVAN   New York City's elec- tion districts were divided into wards whose bosses had privileged access to Tam- many Hall, the Democratic party's headquarters.[4] From 1892 to 1912, Tammany was identified with Big Tim Sullivan, even though Boss Croker or Charley Murphy held the top job. Sullivan had run an East Side saloon that was the hangout of the Whyo gang, the most vicious of the Irish street gangs. The ward went over to Tammany with a little help from the Whyos, and Sullivan became as powerful as any European monarch. While state senator and later United States congressman, he controlled gambling and prize fighting in Manhattan and raked in millions from saloons, brothels, hotels, and theatres[5] on the East Side and eventually, the Tenderloin (the area around Times Square).

His mysterious death in 1913 was commemorated by a four-reeler, *The Life of Big Tim Sullivan* (1914). The film was divided into four parts, beginning with the arrival of Irish immigrants in New York, where Sullivan was born in 1863. He becomes a newsboy, ready with his fists, but ready, too, with help and sympathy for those who need them. "Pugnacity and heart feeling are the two things brought out in strong relief all through the picture."[6]

The second part covers Big Tim's youth and first political success, when the Whyo gang stampeded the nominating convention and made him assemblyman by every vote in the district bar four. (Sullivan remarked that the other side got one more vote than he expected, "But I'll find the fellow.")[7]

"The picture of an old-time voting booth will amuse," wrote *Moving Picture World.* "It has the honesty of being absolutely outrageous. A vote bought is a vote gained; but 'If it's true'—so they said in those days—'what of it' ?"[8] The role of Sullivan at this period of his life was taken by his distant relative, Joe Sullivan. Reviewers noted the actor's physical similarity to the great politician.

"The third period shows Tim at the time of his greatest power, which is truthfully shown and will startle, even though it is well known . . . Tim had almost as much power to open prison doors, when a friend was in trouble, as Nero. The film closes with an accurate and impressive picture of a requiem mass for the repose of Tim's soul. Last of all, it shows the Christmas dinner that he always gave to the Bowery derelicts, followed by the shoe party at which each poor hobo got a pair of shoes and a pair of socks."

These scenes were apparently strikingly authentic; derelicts were "enticed into the studio by the promise of a good meal and a few cents. 'We are told that the studio smelt strong at that time. We get a good view of the faces nearby, and then are shown an actual picture of the crowds coming from the Big Tim Sullivan Association's headquarters, 259 Bowery, with the shoe boxes under arm.' "

The origin of the shoe ceremony went back to Sullivan's childhood, when a teacher sent him to the brother of a Tammany leader for a new pair of shoes. "I needed them shoes then," recalled Sullivan, "and I thought, if I ever got any money, I would give shoes to people who needed them and I'm going to buy shoes for people as long as I live."[9]

The idea for the film came from Sullivan's long-serving secretary Harry Apelbaum. It was probably directed by the ever-resourceful Leon J. Rubinstein, who made several of these documentary-style dramas for his Gotham Film Company, and produced by Benjamin R. Tolmas.[10]

Biography was new to the cinema, and *Moving Picture World* thought that notice should be taken of that very fact: "Sincerity is written all over the picture; it was plainly made for love of the man and there isn't a touch of commercialism in it . . . Affection seems to be the sole cause and mainspring of it. There is no politics in it; no taint of scenario writer's conceit or producer's conceit. It is human."[11]

"Marcus Loew grabbed this one quick and put it right into his best House, the Broadway Theatre, New York," proclaimed Rubinstein's ads, with surprise. "Does Marcus Loew know pictures? Would he run anything in that jim-dandy theatre of his if it were not the best he could get? Why—that theatre uses only the pick of Famous Players' productions, yet right there squarely between Frohman and Belasco genius, Loew puts on our corking four-reeler. Have you seen how he advertises it all over Broadway? He's spending a mint on it."[12]

After its first showing at the Broadway, the picture went down to the Bowery, to the Delancey Street Theater and the Avenue B Theater. Many of the exteriors had been shot in the surrounding area, and hundreds of local people, including many who knew Sullivan and had worked with him, had appeared in the film.[13]

Tammany was the most colorful example, but city halls across the nation were run by men intent on improving their financial standing at public expense. The early movies spread the word. In 1913 the London *Daily Mail* commented: "There is no need for us to follow the language on the American screen and describe bribery as 'graft.'"[14]

Reliance made a film called *The Grafters* in 1913, directed by Frederick Sullivan, about a contractor, John Hascom (Henry Koser), whose business is in a bad way. His bookkeeper, Alva (Edna Cunningham), sees an advertisement for a large con-

Edna Cunningham and Henry Koser in the 1913 Reliance production of The Grafters. *From* Moving Picture World, *April 5, 1913.*

tract for street work. Only political friends of the administration will be considered, Hascom tells her, but Alva persuades him to file a bid anyway. The office boy who delivers the bid is told that the deadline has already passed and the contract has been awarded, but Alva knows otherwise. She braves the supervisors and demands a reading of her bid. They try to ignore her, but one old man, noted for his adherence to clean politics, supports her, and she is allowed to read her bid. The great discrepancy in the price starts a crusade for cleaner government, enabling men like Hascom to share in the city's work and Alva to share his life.[15]

Sullivan followed it with a remarkably similar film for Reliance, *The Big Boss* (1913), with a slight change of the contractor's name. Bascom (Augustus Balfour) is in financial straits, and he applies to the political boss, Morgan (George Siegmann), for help. Morgan offers to throw the aqueduct contract his way if Bascom will persuade his young daughter, Nell (Muriel Ostriche), to marry Morgan. Nell's fiancé, Dick (Irving Cummings), is a reporter investigating the graft scandals alarming the city. Dick uses a dictagraph to eavesdrop on the bosses, but the machine is discovered and Dick is nearly beaten to death. Bascom rescues him; Dick writes his article, then the boss has a change of heart and gives the contract to Bascom. Nell thanks him, and for her sake Dick flings his story on the fire.[16]

The "happy" ending is unintentionally realistic: the graft story killed by further graft, the boss untouched by the law, the system continuing unchecked.

Graft (1915) was the title of a Universal serial which had the distinction of being inspired by eighteen[17] of the most famous American authors, Universal having purchased *Crack O' Doom,* an anthology by such writers as Irvin Cobb, Nina Wilcox Putnam, James Oppenheim, Zane Grey, Rupert Hughes, and Louis Joseph Vance. The stories were turned into scenarios by Hugh Weir, Joe Brandt (Universal's general manager, whose idea it was), and Walter Woods and directed by Richard Stanton and George A. Lessey in twenty episodes. The titles make one wish the serial had survived: The Tenement House Evil . . . The Traction Grab . . . The Railroad Monopoly . . . The Illegal Bucket Shops . . . The Milk Battle . . . The Patent Medicine Danger . . . The Photo Badger Game. In the cast were Hobart Henley, the future director, Jane Novak, Harry Carey, and Richard Stanton himself. The idea was to tell a lively, exciting story and to accomplish something for the public welfare, too.[18] The stories were uncompromising: the first episode, *Liquor and the Law,* had a district attorney murdered by order of a graft syndicate known as "The Fifteen" and his son taking up the fight against them.[19]

The natural enemy of the grafter was the reform politician. In a two-reel Kalem film of 1914, *The County Seat War,* directed by J. P. McGowan, a reform district attorney is elected. The boss summons his gangsters, and together they attack the courthouse, seize the records, and burn the place down. A soldier is killed, and the militia sets out in pursuit. The men are cornered in a barn, and a full-scale gunfight takes place. The gangsters, outgunned, surrender. Some children, meanwhile, playing in the ruins of the courthouse, find a book. Scribbled on its pages are the soldier's last words, accusing the boss of his murder. The film ends with the boss about to face his execution.[20]

Nowhere did the critics suggest that this was a wild exaggeration and an affront to political bosses; they merely praised its maelstrom of action. But this was undoubtedly the era's harshest cinematic portrayal of the political boss.

A more human study of the phenomenon was *Canavan, the Man Who Had His Way,* written in 1918 by Rupert Hughes and made into a film in 1921 by E. Mason Hopper as *Hold Your Horses.* Irish-born Tom Moore played Canavan.

"Imagine a photoplay in which the hero begins as a street cleaner!" said *Motion Picture Classic.*[21] Canavan is humiliated to find that the only job he seems suited for is as a whitewing in New York. His life is made all the more miserable by his battle-ax of a wife (Sylvia Ashton). One day, Canavan is knocked down by the high-stepping team of the aristocratic Miss Newness (Naomi Childers). He recovers from the accident with only the imprint of a horseshoe on his chest as a sign of good luck. He lands a job with an excavating gang, detailed to halt Fifth Avenue traffic with his red flag whenever blasting begins. The feeling of authority is a powerful tonic to his self-respect. After bullying coachmen and chauffeurs, he thrashes his employer. The ward boss sees this and hires him as a lieutenant. "Now that I've got a good start," Canavan says to himself, "I think I'll go home and lick the 'ould woman.' "

He becomes boss of the city and uses his new power to free Beatrice Newness's husband from the penitentiary out of gratitude for the horseshoe incident. And

Tom Moore as Canavan, the immigrant from Ireland, who rises to the top in machine politics in Hold Your Horses, *1921. (John E. Allen)*

when both are free, he takes as his wife the woman whose horses once trampled him.[22]

The picture reached the screen just in time, for the following year Hays took office, and such social criticism, even in a comedy, would have been firmly discouraged. As it was, *Photoplay* was startled by its boldness, for once he tastes authority, Canavan departs from the usual type of movie hero: "As a boss he is frankly something of a grafter, selling his favors where they will do most good and accepting whatever comes his way . . . Returning from a yachting trip abroad to find his political power waning, he re-establishes himself by walking into his club and knocking the first enemy he meets flat on his back . . . Canavan is not one of those snow-white reformers who combat wrong everywhere, but a dishonest and crooked leader who has the district attorney under his thumb, and who smiles upon dangerous tenements when a friend owns them. Indeed, *Hold Your Horses* violates all the moral canons of the photoplay—and gets away with it."[23]

Lincoln Steffens, in his book *The Shame of the Cities,* saw behind political corruption the big businessman: "I found him buying boodlers in St. Louis, defending grafters in Minneapolis, originating corruption in Pittsburgh, sharing with bosses in Philadelphia, deploring reform in Chicago and beating good government in New York. He is a self-righteous fraud, this big business man. He is the chief source of corruption, and it were a boon if he would neglect politics."[24]

Heir to the robber barons of the nineteenth century, the railroad magnates, and the coal-mine kings, the big businessman was pilloried in many early films. The Edison Company's *The Reform Candidate* (1911) portrayed an electric-railway financier called Curtis Greer (Robert Brower) who makes a habit of using minor political machinery for business purposes because he knows every politician has his price. He attempts to fix Mayor McNamara (Charles Ogle), a saloonkeeper who runs the town. A reform candidate, Bryce (Harold Shaw), sets out to stop the valuable electric-railway franchise being given to men who don't give a damn for the welfare of the public. A girl reporter (Miriam Nesbitt) haunts McNamara's saloon posing as a prostitute in order to find proof of his collusion with Greer.[25] The film showed how the businessman had replaced the gangster as the source of finance for the political machine.

Films on crooked politicians and callous corporations flowed from the studios. But none dared attack a real company, or expose a real politician, as the muck-raking magazines were able to do. In 1913, however, a remarkable event took place. A politician, hounded by Tammany Hall, turned to the moving picture as a court of last appeal.

GOVERNOR SULZER'S BATTLE WITH TAMMANY HALL

They called him "Plain Bill" Sulzer, this remarkable politician who seemed destined for the presidency of the United States. He was born in Elizabeth, New Jersey, in 1863, of a German father and a mother of Scots-Irish origin. His early life was spent on a farm, but while he was still a boy, his family moved to New York's Lower East Side. Intending to become a Presbyterian minister, Sulzer attended night classes at Cooper Union, where his talents as a speaker were recognized. A Tammany leader, John Reilly, advised him to study law. He was admitted to the bar at twenty-one, but his fascination with politics caused him to become known on the East Side as "Reilly's boy spellbinder."[26]

Sulzer was only twenty-seven when he was elected by a large majority to the State Assembly. A wholehearted Tammany man, loyal to the then leader, Richard "Boss" Croker, he cultivated a theatrical style despite the scorn of the newspapers, who regarded him as "very much of an ass."[27] And he wrapped himself in the guise of a reformer, a statesman of the people. He won votes by espousing the Jewish cause, denouncing Russia for its outrages (the Sulzer campaign slogan was "Non-Jewish but pro-Jewish"); he also supported the Boers of South Africa against the British, which helped with the Irish vote. He took a firm stand for labor, introducing a bill in Congress to establish an eight-hour working day. But however many good causes he endorsed, he remained a Tammany man—which made it all

Former governor of the state of New York, William Sulzer, playing himself in The Governor's
Boss, *1915. (Museum of Modern Art)*

the more surprising that when he was nominated for governor (by Tammany boss
Charles F. Murphy), he announced, "William Sulzer never had a boss, and his
only master is himself."[28]

A split in the Republican ranks gave Sulzer the governorship of New York.
His inauguration was in contrast to the usual ceremony: "The People's Governor"
wore an ordinary business suit and fedora rather than the customary high hat and
frock coat and he walked to the Capitol instead of traveling by carriage. The crowd
loved it and cheered him when he declared, "The hour has struck and the task of
administrative reform is mine . . . No influence controls me but the dictates of
my conscience."[29]

By asserting his independence from Tammany Hall, Sulzer laid dynamite beneath his own feet. By repeating it on every possible occasion, he lit the fuse.

When he began dismissing people for incompetence or graft, relations with Murphy became volatile.

Sulzer had some strong supporters—penologist Thomas Mott Osborne, Assistant Secretary of the Navy Franklin Delano Roosevelt, Henry Morgenthau, head of the Finance Committee of the Democratic National Committee, and even former President Theodore Roosevelt. But he had some equally powerful opponents. He had angered the railroads by making secret pledges to the Brotherhood of Railroad Trainmen, which were revealed in the press. To the end of his life, he was convinced that the railroads had spent vast sums to destroy his political career.

He further helped his own downfall by fighting to secure the enactment of a statewide primary law, which drew his battle with the Democratic organization into the open. The defeat of the bill made Sulzer more paranoid than ever and led to what Jacob Friedman called "the desperate war of extermination" between the governor and the Tammany leaders, which ended in his impeachment trial in 1913.

Accused of a startling range of offenses, from misappropriating funds to corrupt stock transactions, Sulzer refused to utter a single word during the legislative inquiry and would not even take the stand during the impeachment trial. This was construed as a confession of guilt, even though Sulzer issued all-embracing denials to the press. His behavior dismayed even his most ardent supporters, but, although he was found guilty, many ordinary voters thought his conviction was the result of his stand against Tammany corruption.

"It was a political lynching," said Sulzer. "A horse thief, in frontier days, would have received a squarer deal."[30]

With all these troubles on his shoulders, with all the problems he had to face, Sulzer apparently found time to play the lead in a motion picture which was released in November: *The Shame of the Empire State.* In the absence of the film it is hard to judge the veracity of its claims. Did Leon Rubinstein do his usual trick and catch a few shots of Sulzer at open-air meetings and splice them into a melodrama? Or did Sulzer, desperate to cling to popular support, see a moving picture role as manna from heaven? As far as the working people were concerned, he need not have worried. Even after his impeachment, his popularity was remarkable, his return to New York City a triumph. The New York election cost Tammany four years' control of the government (John Purroy Mitchel swept into the mayoralty, carrying every borough), and Murphy had cause to regret his support for Sulzer's impeachment.

Rubinstein scooped the industry with the announcement: "The Whole Country Wondered—Meanwhile, WE DID IT! *The Shame of the Empire State,* with Governor William Sulzer Himself, GENUINE, PERSONALLY!

"The biggest moving picture interests in the world offered fabulous sums for the services of this man who for another year will be the central figure in the Nation's politics; his fate is the most absorbing topic in the country's affairs; his series of one hundred lectures will keep his name on the front page of every newspaper in the country, and his exposures of political corruption, even as electrifying as they are now, are only a small part of the story he is *yet to tell.*"[31]

Even if so sensational a figure as an impeached governor of the first state in the country were not appearing in it, the story would still be a powerful feature, continued the Ruby Feature Film Company ad.

"BUT HE IS! Not a fake, not an impersonation, but the real living Mr. Sulzer himself. We know it sounds too big to be true, but we always have dealt in big ones. The film is four reels, with a number of fights and riots and scraps and enough wallop to make you sit up."[32]

The very same month, the Fair Feature Sales Company offered *Making a Mayor,* in which Sulzer appeared (together with former district attorney Charles Whitman) in a documentary about the city's elections.[33]

In November, Sulzer was returned in triumph to the New York Assembly as an Independent. But thereafter he attracted little attention in this subsidiary role, beyond his familiar rantings against Tammany. By now he had lost most of his prominent supporters, including Theodore Roosevelt. In 1914 he stood again for governor, on a Prohibition ticket, and was defeated.[34]

In 1915, he appeared in another film, and this time there was no doubt that he played the lead. *The Governor's Boss,* originally a novel written by Sulzer's friend James S. Barcus, a former U.S. senator from Indiana, spluttered briefly as a play on Broadway earlier that year. Charles E. Davenport, who also adapted the scenario, made a film of it for a company calling itself The Governor's Boss Photoplay Company. This was backed by some of the most prominent citizens of Freeport, Long Island. The picture was largely shot in Freeport, with well-known local residents taking minor parts. The story was built around Sulzer's experiences at Albany, his fight against Boss Murphy, and his impeachment. "The former executive declares that he does not seek gold or fame as a movie actor, but merely wishes to show the public how his fall was brought about by crooked politicians and to win vindication in public opinion."[35]

Variety thought it melodramatic in the extreme, which is probably how Sulzer regarded the events in real life. "All of the modern expose devices are brought into play. There is the Dictophone, the dictagraph, the motion picture machine, etc."[36] As for Sulzer's performance, *Variety* commented that if given the chance he might have made a better governor of the Empire State than he ever would a motion picture actor. The picture was cheaply produced; some scenes were out of focus. Rape, blackmail, forgery, the stuffing of ballot boxes, and the bribing of state politicians all played a part in the saga.[37] It appears to have given free rein to Sulzer's paranoia, despite the fact that it had a happy ending, with the defeat of Tammany Hall.

Although the film did not follow the story of the actual impeachment, said *Moving Picture World,* there was enough election material to lend it lasting value as a recorder of events: "It is the punches which Director Davenport has injected into the scenario, which give the audience an insight into affairs with which it never comes in contact . . . and has no means of knowing anything about. It depicts just how candidates are 'nominated' and made to obey the will of the 'power behind the throne' and how the 'invisible government' puts across the 'work.' "[38]

Sulzer's political career ended not with a bang but a whimper. He was asked to run in the 1916 presidential election by the American party, formed by his supporters and independent Democrats. (The party was dedicated to "God, the people, and the overthrow of the political bosses.")[39] He declined the honor and returned to what must, for him, have been a very unwelcome obscurity. (His career was the inspiration for the Preston Sturges film *The Great McGinty* [1940].)[40]

"In the disgrace of William Sulzer," wrote Jacob Friedman, "future statesmen will find at least one useful lesson—that no man can afford to pit himself against a powerful political organization unless his own record is above reproach."[41]

Chapter Seven

WOMEN'S SUFFRAGE

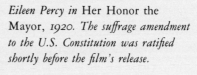

Eileen Percy in Her Honor the
Mayor, *1920. The suffrage amendment
to the U.S. Constitution was ratified
shortly before the film's release.*

ONCE WOMEN won the vote they would make a clean sweep of corruption. This plank of the female suffrage platform was also a hope expressed in films like Thanhouser's *The Woman in Politics* (1916), directed by W. Eugene Moore. Mignon Anderson played Dr. Beatrice Barlow, a city health inspector. She writes a report condemning a tenement owned by the mayor (Arthur Bauer) and is promptly discharged. With more revelations up her sleeve, she threatens the downfall of the city's entire political machine. The mayor tries to jail her. When this fails, she is lured to a sanitarium and kept prisoner. She is rescued, of course, and the mayor imprisoned, but the story paid eloquent tribute to the growing power of women—even before they won the vote.[1]

The National Woman Suffrage Association was started by Susan B. Anthony in 1869, but for many years female suffrage was not a burning issue. People thought it an excellent idea, but they did nothing about it.

"The suffrage movement was completely in a rut in New York state at the opening of the twentieth century," wrote Harriot Stanton Blatch. "It bored its adherents and repelled its opponents. Most of the ammunition was being wasted on its supporters in private drawing rooms and in public halls where friends . . . heard the same old arguments."[2] The years 1896–1910 came to be known as "the doldrums." But if the suffragists made no progress, their opponents were active, not least in the film business. Most of the pictures about suffragettes laughed at the whole idea of votes for women as raucously as any bystander at a suffragist parade.

A typical example was released by Pathé in 1908. *A Day in the Life of a Suffragette* was just a split-reel cops-and-suffragettes comedy, but the synopsis illustrates the attitude women had to fight: "Women are as good as men, they are often better than men: why should they stand the cruel oppression of the stronger sex? Thus a crowd of common women are making speeches and drunk with their own words and getting up to battle pitch, they start forth into the street armed with banners rapidly made and screaming revolutionary songs. They march against a police patrol, who are endeavoring to bar the way. The female onslaught is so powerful that the poor policemen fall sprawling on the ground, and as the female wave sweeps over their prostrate bodies they have reason to regret their rash attempt. Encouraged by their first success, our suffragettes go on their way, their numbers getting bigger at every street turn, until things take an alarming aspect; the militia is called out, and after a comic struggle between women and soldiers, the whole female force is marched into custody and locked up for the night. The next morning, the subdued women are seen coming out of jail and meekly following their husbands on their way back to their domestic duties."[3]

The guffaws this sort of thing attracted came not only from men. Many women were implacably opposed to their own enfranchisement. "Sensible and responsible women do not want to vote," wrote Mrs. Grover Cleveland in the *Ladies' Home Journal*. "The relative positions to be assumed by men and women in the working out of our civilization were assigned long ago by a higher intelligence than ours."[4]

The American suffrage movement emerged from its paralysis with victories in Washington state in November 1910 and California in 1911, but then was split by crippling disagreements. Two leaders held the various factions together—the veteran Carrie Chapman Catt and Harriot Stanton Blatch, daughter of the great pioneer Elizabeth Cady Stanton. They had organized the Women's Political Union in 1907.

Both had spent time in England, but had left before witnessing the British suffragettes' exploitation of violence.[5] Impatient with conventional methods, the British women had begun provoking police reprisals to embarrass politicians and to force them to take action on the suffrage question.

The approach in America was peaceful. Slide shows and dramatic sketches had helped to win California. There was even a stage play, *How the Vote Was Won*. Mrs. Blatch organized parades, and the 1912 New York City parade was filmed by the new newsreel companies and distributed around the country.

"Women who usually see Fifth Avenue through the polished windows of their limousines . . . strode steadily side by side with pale-faced, thin-bodied girls from the sweltering sweat shops of the East Side," reported the Baltimore *American*. "The sight of the impressive column of women striding five abreast up the middle of the street stifled all thoughts of ridicule . . . all marched with an intensity and purpose that astonished the crowd that lined the streets."[6]

The following month there appeared the first important suffrage film, *Votes for Women*, directed by Hal Reid. The headline "ANNA SHAW AND JANE ADDAMS IN PICTURES" told the industry that the leading figures of the National Woman Suffrage Association were cooperating on a film at the Reliance studios. Reliance had put the idea to the suffragists, and their first reaction was that a moving picture might injure the dignity of their cause. But Hal Reid was a good salesman, and they soon realized that it could prove powerful propaganda. The idea appears to have been with the ladies for a year before they finally made up their minds.[7]

Among the other suffrage leaders who took part in this long-lost picture were Inez Milholland, Harriet May Mills, president of the New York State League, Mrs. Mary Beard, and Mrs. L. H. Ozedam.[8] Max Eastman also assisted. The story was written by Mary Ware Dennett, secretary of the New York State League, Mrs. Harriet Laidlaw, and Mrs. Frances Bjorkman, all of whom played in the film, together with Florence Maule Cooley, who would write the next suffrage production.

"It opens with a scene showing the visit of the suffrage workers to a miserable family in a filthy tenement house," said *Moving Picture World*. "The tenement house belongs to a haughty senator who will not listen to the arguments of the cause. They learn that he is engaged to marry an estimable lady and they think that by enlisting her with the cause that they can eventually win him over to their way of thinking. In this idea they are correct, for the senator's fiancee succeeds in converting him and in making him an enthusiastic advocate of their principles. . . . The picture ends with the enormous suffrage parade, which recently took place on Fifth Avenue."[9]

The film was released as a regular Reliance two-reeler; moreover, the State Leagues of the NAWSA planned to use it in their campaign. "One of the significant facts in connection with this picture, is that some of the ladies who appear in it, at one time were to be classed as antagonistic to the moving picture."[10]

Moving Picture World commended the suffragists with only a hint of patronage. "They are not at all amateurish, as one might expect, but to the contrary they play their parts in a thoroughly natural manner."[11]

Kay Sloan has recorded the success of the film: "In New Jersey, the Women's Political Union brought *Votes for Women* into the state and secured its exhibition in many moving picture shows. In the Midwest, the Des Moines, Iowa, suffrage club showed the film in a small river front park near a bandstand where nightly concerts were given during Fair Week. Literally thousands of people saw the picture . . . Shown in nickelodeons, fairs and churches, the movement's first melodrama impressed suffragists with its versatility and its ability to reach wide audiences."[12]

It is a cultural crime that a film as important as this to American social history has been allowed to disappear.

The Edison Company made a Kinetophone talking picture under the auspices of the National Woman Suffrage Association in 1913, but it was taken off the screen by the suffragists themselves. Presented at the Colonial Theatre in New York in April 1913, it aroused derision from the men and shocked comment from the women. Mrs. Frances Maule Bjorkman: "Never shall I forget my emotions when that talking-picture abomination began to work. As the different women got up to speak they went up and up till they looked about twenty feet tall. My! I don't wonder the men jeered. And now they'll probably go to their graves thinking that suffragists really look like that."[13]

EIGHTY MILLION WOMEN WANT   A 1913 film about female suffrage, *Eighty Million Women Want*—produced by the Uneek [*sic*] Film Company, featuring Emmeline Pankhurst and Harriot Stanton Blatch—sounds like the fantasy of an overenthusiastic social historian. Yet in the 1970s, I heard that just such a film was available on 16mm from a Los Angeles rental company called Film Classic Exchange. I spent an inordinate sum of money purchasing a copy and having it shipped to my home in England. When the package arrived, I eagerly tore the film out of its wrapping and projected it. I have seldom been more disappointed. The entire thing was incomprehensible. (Politics in England have always been so different from those in America!) It was invisible, too—a pale dupe, which maddened me since the original 35mm had obviously been of excellent quality. But worse than the quality was the content. What looked like a routine thriller had been given a suffragist aura merely by the inclusion of Votes for

Mrs. Emmeline Pankhurst confronts Boss Kelly in Eighty Million Women Want, 1913.

Women sashes and a soundless address by Emmeline Pankhurst[14] (from which the titles had been removed). I put it away and forgot about it.

I researched all the other chapters of this book—political corruption, gangsterism, immigration—before returning to female suffrage. Then I looked at the film again. Suddenly, it made sense. It had no more cinematic virtue than before, but as a document of its time it was remarkable.

The film became known as *What Eighty Million Women Want.*[15] The story was credited to suffragist Florence Maule Cooley. I wrote to Pat Loughney at the Library of Congress to see if anything had been deposited for copyright purposes, and he discovered the original shooting script and was kind enough to send me a photocopy. What an excellent piece of work, I thought; the product of a seasoned professional. And then I recalled an interview I had conducted in 1966 with Mrs. Ad Schulberg, the widow of B. P. Schulberg, one of the most prominent producers of the silent era. I remembered her mentioning a film her husband had written for the suffragettes; could this be the one? I hunted through the trade papers, but could find no confirmation. Finally, I did the obvious thing and replayed the interview tape. Mrs. Schulberg had even mentioned the title of the film.

"He was making $35 a week as a cub reporter," she said. "Then he met the man [P. S. Harrison] who edited a little paper called *Film Reports.* B. P. became the assistant editor. Mrs. Pankhurst approached him and he did the scenario for *Eighty Million Women Want.* I think he got $50 a reel, and it meant a great deal to us."[16]

The plot is essentially a detective story, exposing the system of machine politics. The sleuth is female, and the remedy is votes for women.

A young lawyer, Travers (Ronald Everett), finds everything about his fiancée, Mabel (Ethel Jewett), irresistible, except for her politics. Boss Kelly (George Henry) decides to put Travers on his payroll. And though the young lawyer is sorely tempted, he puts his integrity first and denounces the boss.

Now we meet Ruth, whose boyfriend, Arthur, is injured by the district leader's automobile. Ruth brings the case to Travers, who assures Arthur he will win. But the boss intercedes with the judge, who owes his position to the boss and who rules in favor of the district leader. Arthur is shattered.

Mabel offers her services to the Suffragist Cause and is presented with a sash by Harriot Stanton Blatch, president of the Women's Political Union. The suffragists are denounced in the press by Boss Kelly. Their great English leader, Mrs. Pankhurst, on a lecture tour of the United States, pays the boss a call. When he refuses to listen she gives him such a tongue-lashing one can almost hear her.

The suffragists plant a spy as Kelly's secretary, and Mabel learns that Travers is secretly on Kelly's payroll after all. She is livid. Realizing the only way to win her back is to go straight, Travers has a row with Kelly—witnessed, through a keyhole, by the caretaker.

While his henchmen are diverted at the window by the spectacle of the grand suffragist parade, Kelly works alone—and is shot and wounded by Arthur. The caretaker implicates Travers, who finds himself in jail. Kelly is not seriously hurt and is soon back in action, issuing the names of absent voters to his gangsters. Mabel creeps to his office door, armed with a camera, and takes close-range photographs of the fingerprints in the thick dust of the door panels. Securing thumb prints of all the suspects, she identifies Arthur as the culprit and takes her evidence to the only straight politician in the picture, the district attorney. Travers is released; Arthur takes his place. His girlfriend, Ruth, weeps and takes off her Votes for Women sash. Mabel stops her, saying, "We must fight for right." (Schulberg's script added "and accept justice," but this was dropped.)

Travers foils the gangsters in their attempt to vote, and Kelly is confronted with evidence of his misconduct. He grins—he's been through all this before—and produces his checkbook. But this is, as a title puts it, "the District Attorney the Boss couldn't buy," and Kelly is arrested.

Election day; at Kelly's headquarters, the gangsters are dismayed by his defeat. But at suffrage headquarters, victory after victory—"Erie County, 10,000 for the amendment," "New York 21st Assembly District, 3,000 for the amendment." Joy is unconfined.

Kelly is brought before the judge—the same judge he fixed the last time—and is found guilty.

Mabel at last accepts Travers's proposal of marriage. They are about to kiss when they turn to the camera, stare in astonishment, and burst into laughter. Fade-out.

The film is a workmanlike production for 1913. It verges on the improbable only in its scene of Mabel photographing close-ups of thumb prints à la Faurot with a snapshot camera—a difficult task even today. Otherwise it is an absorbing, well-acted, and illuminating production. It moves rapidly from place to place, often without any continuity shots. When Mabel offers to track down the men whose names are on the blotter, we see her leaving suffrage headquarters and walking straight into Travers's office without intervening titles, or shots of her traveling in a limousine or walking up stairs, as was the practice in 1913. One suspects that this was because director Will Lewis forgot to shoot them—he was trained on Imp one-reelers—rather than because there was any particular daring in the editing.

The sets are a trifle crude; the ambience of Kelly's campaign headquarters is suggested with a few American flags, a desk, and a picture. But look further and some intriguing flourishes become apparent. Boss Kelly has a sleek Negro as an aide, with stovepipe hat and tail coat, who vets all his phone calls and keeps a wary eye on the gangsters. He did not appear in Schulberg's script. Kay Sloan, in an article in *American Quarterly*,[17] suggests that this was a racist touch, reminding audiences that while black men had the vote, white women did not.

At the first screening of the film at the Bryant Theatre, New York, the print arrived two hours late, giving many reviewers an excuse to creep out. Harriot Stanton Blatch amused the audience with her remarks, apologizing for "the non-arrival of the man-made film which was supposed to have started for the showing in a man-made taxi some short time previous." Accidents, she added, happen at times even to men, at which, reported *Motography*, "the back row lost its last male occupants."[18]

W. Stephen Bush, in *Moving Picture World*, gave the film an enthusiastic welcome, even though he assumed the scenario to have been the work of a woman: "This feature is not only a most effective means of propaganda for the cause of Woman Suffrage, but it would, I am sure, be welcomed by any man who wants to give his patrons a high class offering with plenty of pathos and humor ... Those who have looked upon the Votes-for-Women movement as the last refuge for old maids and cranks are due for a most pleasant and agreeable disillusionment. The heroine of the story, though a staunch enough suffragette, is womanly from top to toe."[19]

Suffragist leaders Rose Winslow and Helen Todd appeared at the opening presentation on December 10, 1913, at Marcus Loew's Circle Theatre, New York, and spoke after each show. For this was how the suffragists intended to use the film—to arouse interest in the struggle and then to explain it in detail afterward.[20]

No surviving film of this period is so outspoken about political corruption, and one must be grateful that at least this one survives—more or less intact.

The Germans stole a march on both British and Americans with a five-reel feature on the British movement, *Die Suffragette* (September 1913), written and directed by the Danish Urban Gad and featuring his wife, Asta Nielsen. Although shot in the conventional style of 1913, the film is distinguished by a vivid acting style most obviously from Nielsen. She plays the role realistically, yet with the extra strength required to convey her thoughts.

Nelly becomes infatuated with a handsome stranger on a boating lake. After a furious row with her father, she flees to her mother, Mrs. Panburne, leader of the suffragettes, who shows her the poverty and oppression of the slums and wins her to the cause.

Lord Ascue (Max Landa) proposes a law in Parliament ordering the mass arrest of suffragettes. One of the women has some old love letters from Ascue. Mrs. Panburne sends Nelly with these to persuade Ascue to withdraw the bill. In case she fails, she equips her with a bomb concealed in a bag. Nelly discovers

Ascue is her mysterious stranger. She pleads with him to no avail and dutifully plants the bomb. But she cannot kill the man she loves, and she returns to warn him. This time, the servants refuse to let her in and the bomb goes off—just after Ascue leaves the room. In an ending that must have been as hard to accept then as it is now, Ascue introduces Nelly to his ministers not as a suffragette but as his fiancée, and after the title "the hand that guides the cradle guides the world" (note the subtle difference in the wording), we see the happy couple with a healthy crop of children.

As this is a German film, it has none of the documentary detail one might have expected from an English film. But judging from stills and reviews, the film showed a great deal of violence—window smashing, hunger-striking, and force-feeding. All this is missing from the surviving print, together with an anti-Semitic subplot in which Nelly is pursued by a man called Levy. What's left is a bizarre tale in which the suffragettes are portrayed as though by caricaturists. Even Lord Ascue looks more like a Prussian officer than a British prime minister.

A German reviewer—female—who considered the suffragette movement "a historic blunder" nonetheless felt the film would be regarded as a cultural document by later generations. "The psychologically interesting point is the influence of the mother on the daughter, the drifting into a kind of trance, from the harmless, half-innocent, childlike state of her soul into political criminality, furthered through mass suggestion."[21] The drama, she added, was not successful in the provinces: "The German bourgeoisie does not read enough to be interested in the suffragette movement."

The film was retitled *The Militant Suffragette* for America, and there was some trepidation that women might attack theatres showing it. But suffragettes dismissed it as "entirely harmless."

I can find no record of the film having been shown in England, perhaps because, unlike America, suffragettes there had a record of violence. They carved up a cricket pitch; they might well demolish a theatre. But there is another possibility. The censors might have been anxious to avoid offending the distinguished Prime Minister, Lord Asquith.

The fear of violence inspired the Imp three-reeler *The Militant* (1914), which was also set in England. While it did not attack the right of women to vote, it declared that the destruction of property, of homes, and of lives was the wrong way to achieve it.[22]

"Naturally there is much spectacularism in the picture with the crowds, the destruction of railroad tracks, the dynamiting of buildings and the raids on the meetings by police."[23]

The film, directed by William Robert Daly, was partly shot in the Hell's Kitchen area of New York, which stood in for the East End of London.

Meanwhile, the anti-suffragist comedies continued. The Edison Company, which had made both pro- and anti-suffragist films in England in 1912 *(How They Got the Vote; A Suffragette in Spite of Himself)*, released a two-reeler in 1914 called *When the Men Left Town*, written by Mark Swan and directed by C. Jay Williams. In this film the women win every office in the town election; they stop everyone smoking and drinking, and the men decide to leave them to it. The women are forced to remove garbage, deliver express packages, run the trolley system—only the trolley system refuses to operate. The women ask the men to return, and when they do, amidst great rejoicing, the women resign their offices.[24]

The irony was that in England, a few months after this film came out, women would be doing just these jobs while the men went to war. And when the same thing happened in America, many women worked so successfully on the trolley system that they were filmed on the job for the benefit of the suffrage movement.

In 1912 the Women's Political Union collaborated with the Eclair company in producing a comedy of their own, *Suffrage Wins Herbert* (released as *Suffrage and the Man),* from a story by novelist and playwright Dorothy Steele, a member of the WPU. Mrs. Harriot Stanton Blatch appeared, together with many volunteers from the WPU and their male supporters.[25]

In 1912, Theodore Roosevelt adopted women's suffrage as a plank in his election platform. Woodrow Wilson did not, and he won, even though nearly a million women in six suffrage states had the vote. The day before Wilson's inauguration in March 1913, a suffragist parade in Washington was subjected to brutal verbal and physical abuse when bystanders turned into assailants.

What is one to make of the Colonial Film Company's one-reel special *Suffragette Pageant and Tableau*? It was released in March 1913, very soon after the event. The Colonial's advertisement showed a photograph of the tableau on the south steps of the U.S. Treasury Building. It was very dignified and very pretty. But it was a bit like showing the troops at Gettysburg drilling and leaving out the battle.

"The women," said a newspaper report, "had to fight their way from the start and took more than one hour in making the first ten blocks. Many of the women were in tears under the jibes and insults of those who lined the route." Troops of cavalry were rushed into the city to bring under control what was very close to a riot. All this was filmed by newsreels and almost certainly by the Colonial Film Company, based in Washington. But it was tastefully removed, despite a public outcry over the disturbances which cost the police chief of Washington his job.[26]

YOUR GIRL AND MINE   Under conditions of secrecy, *Your Girl and Mine,* the first large-scale suffragist film, went into production at the Selig Studio in Chicago. William N. Selig had signed Giles Warren, who had made pictures at Imp and Lubin, to direct, and then left for Europe for the summer, thus demonstrating how little the studio heads had to do with actual production.

Selig asked the trade press to maintain silence about the picture, but James McQuade of *Moving Picture World* leaked the news in September 1914. The film was made in collaboration with the Congressional Committee of the National American Woman Suffrage Association, of which Mrs. Medill McCormick was chairman. Mrs. McCormick, daughter of Senator Mark Hanna, proved to be the leading spirit for motion picture propaganda. "Ever since work was begun," reported McQuade, "she has given her strong personal interest to the production. She personally engaged some of the leading members of the cast, bringing them on from New York and elsewhere. She is tireless in her work to make the big suffrage photoplay a success, and can be found almost daily at the Selig studio in conference with Director Warren."[27]

Mrs. McCormick selected Olive Wyndham for the leading role, with John

Charles as leading man; both were from the New York stage. Katherine Kaelred played a woman lawyer, and Grace Darmond played an allegorical role as Equal Suffrage.

The script, which was written by Gilson Willetts, was scrutinized by the Congressional Committee, which included Jane Addams and Dr. Anna Shaw, and they praised it highly. Dr. Shaw played in several scenes herself.[28]

"Realizing that the suffragists, like all other propaganda organizations," said Mrs. McCormick, "spend most of their time in talking to themselves in public, I felt it was necessary to try and originate a means of really reaching the public. There is no opposition to woman's suffrage in this country, because there is no argument of moment against it. The difficulty lies in not being able to reach the actual voters and to have them understand the reasons why women are working to be enfranchised. With this purpose in view I consulted with one of the greatest moving picture men in the country, and together we have worked out and produced one of the largest photoplays yet presented to the public. . . ." She added that it would be the *Uncle Tom's Cabin* of the suffrage movement.[29]

It seems curious now that the suffragists should have agreed to a man writing the scenario. But Gilson Willetts had had an enormous success with *The Adventures of Kathlyn* earlier in 1914, and the fact that this was a favorite serial of many suffragists perhaps guided the choice. He had experience, too, as a political writer. He ensured that the film would not preach, but would absorb every member of the audience, whether or not they knew anything about the suffrage question.

Rosalind Fairlie is a wealthy heiress who marries what the synopsis described as "a spendthrift and a man of loose morals." Just after the honeymoon, an aggressive creditor forces his way into their home and demands immediate payment. Ben Austin, the husband, turns to his wife and says, "Sorry, my dear, but you must pay my bills or they will seize your property"—for the law states that a woman's possessions are controlled by her husband. Thus, Austin almost reduces his wife to beggary: "The law is on my side; I am absolute master here!"

Rosalind eventually attempts to flee her drunken spouse, taking her two small daughters, but the law orders them "returned to the roof of the father" and she is compelled by mother love to accompany them. She tries again when Austin dies and bequeaths the guardianship of the children to his unprincipled father, but she is arrested at the state line. A female lawyer, Eleanor Holbrook (Kaelred), takes her case.

"During the trial the subtitles are veritable bombs," wrote James McQuade, "every one of them hitting the bull's eye. Here are a few of them taken from the plea made before judge and jury by Eleanor Holbrook: "My client is charged with the crime of abduction, and the prosecution asks you to send her to the penitentiary because she has attempted to get back the children whom she bore, and whom her husband willed away without her consent. . . . If this mother's act was a crime, then all mothers are potential criminals."[30]

The jury returns a verdict of "not guilty," and the judge finds the children's grandfather unfit to be their guardian.

In Lois Weber (or Griffith) style, there were allegorical scenes, which McQuade thought incompatible with the dramatic sequences. But he declared that moving pictures like this one would accomplish more for the cause than all that eloquent tongues had done since the movement began.[31]

The New York premiere at the old Casino Theatre was a glittering occasion. "Silken banners of National Suffrage parties adorned the balconies, interwoven with American flags, and from every box scintillated the brains of the local organizations . . . while the orchestra seats, commendably crowded, held the army whose leaders sat in review."[32]

Your Girl and Mine had its premiere in Chicago at the Auditorium on October 14, 1914. Just before the show, Major Funkhouser decided one of the scenes would have to go.

"Censorship as an institution," declared Mrs. McCormick, furiously, "is medieval and undemocratic. As Major Funkhouser has exercised his power in this particular case, it is preposterous and officious of him to have cut the film. The scene which he has assumed [*sic*] to censure was a representation of the most convincing and realistic fight which I have ever seen staged. It showed a woman struggling with a man in the interest of her right. It was a splendid piece of acting, too—none of your stage claptrap about it."[33]

The film was greeted by waves of applause every time it scored a propaganda point. The reviews were excellent, and Lewis J. Selznick arranged to have the picture distributed by the World Film Corporation. His ads placed his picture alongside that of Mrs. McCormick and by heading it "The Brains of Two Big Enterprises Have Combined" contrived to eliminate Selig and Giles Warren, who actually made it.[34]

Sadly, the picture was not a financial success. "The failure of *Your Girl and Mine* probably discouraged the suffragists," wrote Kay Sloan. "While they continued to use theatres for their slide shows, the suffragists apparently made no other films."[35]

In a sense, the film industry itself took up the cause. Herbert Brenon's pacifist drama *War Brides* (1916) was propaganda for the suffrage movement. "It has as its very basis," said *Motion Picture News,* "the demand of women for equal voting rights in national government whereby they can approve or veto the plunging of their country into war."[36]

EVERY WOMAN'S PROBLEM   In 1917, Mrs. Wallace Reid appeared in a kind of vision of the future—what might happen when women won the vote and achieved positions of prominence. She played in *Mothers of Men* along with the director Willis Robards (who would play De Treville in Douglas Fairbanks's *The Three Musketeers* [1921]), and Hal Reid. The story was conceived in Hal Reid's favorite style of overwrought melodrama and was written by him and the director. Considering his stand against capital punishment, it was a curious tale: the wife of a prominent lawyer is elected judge of the criminal court and has to sentence a man convicted of murder purely by circumstantial evidence. She does her duty; the man is hanged. She is elected governor, at which point her husband, a lawyer, is also convicted of murder on circumstantial evidence. "Torn between love and duty—to copy the language of the subtitle," said *Moving*

Frame enlargements from Every Woman's
Problem, *1921—original version 1917.*
Mrs. Wallace Reid at home . . .

. . . and as a judge.

The public execution from Every Woman's
Problem. *(National Film Archive)*

Picture World, "and admonished to stand
firm for the good of the cause and show the
world that the new brand of womanhood
does not intend to be swayed by its heart in
place of its head, the wife and governor refuses her husband a pardon and he is only
saved from the rope by the confession of the
real murderer."[37]

The film was remade once women had
the vote (and the situation was slightly more
plausible), under the title *Every Woman's
Problem* (1921). It survives in the National
Film Archive in London, and I have seldom
seen a more obvious example of title writers' tyranny; in the first reel hardly a shot
runs its full course without titles leaping in
to advance the plot with elegant lettering
and hamfisted prose (by M. G. Cohn and J.
F. Natteford). The reason for the surfeit becomes apparent on close inspection of the
action; a great deal, if not all, comes from
the 1917 original. Since certain scenes had to
be scrapped, the titles made up the shortfall.
The man responsible for the mélange was
Nat Levine, who began his career by distributing this picture.[38]

The Woman's Party of a Western city
offers a brilliant young lawyer, Clara Madison, the nomination for judge of the superior court, which she wins, against the
opposition of a yellow press editor (Hal
Reid) and the city's machine boss. When
she marries a lawyer, Grant Williams (Robards), they implicate him in a bomb outrage.

Clara decides to resign, but her suffragist friends urge her to do her duty: "You
must not give up your chance of being the
first woman governor." Even though she is
pregnant, Clara agrees to struggle on. Popular indignation demands death for her husband as well as for two Italian bootleggers,
and another judge duly passes the sentence.

Clara is not opposed to the death penalty—she rejected an appeal from a common criminal, despite his children and

dying mother, and sentenced him to be hanged. But she is devastated by this dilemma. She carries on with her campaign, however, solemnly assuring the voters that if elected, she will not interfere with the course of justice. So, for the first time in history, a woman rules in the governor's chair.

Clara allows a stay of execution and is attacked by the yellow press. The Woman's Party urges her to stand firm. The application for a new trial is denied, and she must proceed with her task, even though her child is due.

A mob assembles at the prison gates, convinced the governor will break faith with the people and turn her husband loose. The sheriff decides to placate them by holding the execution in public.

These scenes are very striking, for the film people have assembled hundreds of workers, all looking shabby and down-at-the-heel, to pour into the prison yard, giving the scene a grim authenticity. Public executions must have looked exactly like this.* The Italian who made and threw the bomb confesses to a priest, but the priest cannot break faith any more than Clara. The plot takes a convulsive twist, as another priest holds up the ritual and climbs the scaffold to make one last appeal. The culprit breaks down, and Williams is free. (The crowd's jubilation is very half-hearted.)

Williams is driven through streets packed with cheering people. The governor's car drives up, and husband and wife embrace to the delight of the crowd. (Meanwhile, although the film does not tell us, they are presumably hanging the two Italians.)

And the film ends with a final example of its title writers' art: "When the wounds of the heart are healed, its reward is the hours of peace and love that make life a thing of lasting beauty."

By suggesting that women would do their duty just as pitilessly as men, the film made a better case for the abolition of capital punishment than for women as politicians. The propaganda, however, was anesthetized by the machine-gun titles.

Yet despite its flaws, *Every Woman's Problem* has some worthwhile documentary scenes. Its exteriors were filmed in Oakland, California; Clara's political rally is actually a wartime parade involving the Oakland National Guard and Young Ladies Institute![39] The wartime references were studiously ignored for the "remake," in which the dates of letters, etc., are all 1921.

The main trouble with the film is that it isn't a film; for the first half, it seems to show little but suffering people seated at desks. It grows more interesting when it moves out into the streets, but by no stretch of the imagination could any of it be called well made. The sad thing is that as one of the few surviving suffrage films, it is likely to become one of the most viewed.

---

*According to *Newsweek* (April 1, 1991, p. 44) the last public execution was held at Galena, Missouri on May 21, 1937.

Chapter Eight

PRISONS

*The second film with Thomas Meighan
to be shot "up the river" at Sing Sing:
The Man Who Found Himself,
1925, directed by Alfred E. Green from
a Booth Tarkington story. Its working
title was* Up the River. *(American
Museum of the Moving Image)*

"THE JAILS of the United States are unbelievably vile. They are almost without exception filthy beyond description, swarming with roaches and body vermin. They are giant crucibles of crime." These are the words not of a reformer, but of a federal inspector of prisons.[1]

If prisons were designed to deter crime, those in the United States should have ended it once and for all. Five hundred thousand people were incarcerated; 1,500 died each year.[2] Prison conditions were low on the scale of priorities, even in the age of reform, but there was a movement for change, and it was opposed to the idea that severity of punishment was in itself a deterrent to crime.

The moving picture came late to this movement; in any case, it was primarily concerned with sensation. It was a scoop for the early filmmakers to be allowed to film inside a prison, where normally it was forbidden even to take photographs.

In 1912 appeared *Convict Life in the Ohio Penitentiary,* a three-reeler made by America's Feature Film Company of Chicago, by special permission of Warden T. H. B. Jones. "The only moving pictures ever taken behind prison walls"[3] depicted the Bertillon room and the convict barbershop where heads were shaved, and it pointed out the difference between prisons in Ohio and in other states. Warden Jones believed in educating and elevating the convict, and the film showed the night school, the post office, and the modern cell house contrasted with the 1861 cell block where Confederate prisoners had been confined in the Civil War. The film claimed that in no other prison were the inmates treated with such humane consideration.[4]

The following year, a film came out advertised as "Absolutely guaranteed the first, original and authentic motion picture ever produced within Prison Walls. Every foot taken inside the Arizona State Prison."[5] *Life in a Western Penitentiary* was no plea for prison reform, but a revelation of the fate that awaited transgressors of the law: "See the place, 645 convicts, in real life. . . . Snake Hole Dungeon, Life Termers, Ball and Chain Men, Cells of Death Watch, Condemned Prisoners, Death Trap and Black Cap, Convict Burial, Prison Grave Yard, everything boiling with intense interest."[6]

Yet prison reform was a subject treated honorably by many films.

In the West, where proper roads were urgently needed, the overcrowded prisons were an obvious source of labor. In 1906, Warden Cleghorn of Canon City, Colorado, put a group of men into a road camp, promised them parole within a few months, and gave them one unarmed guard as supervisor. This "honor system" worked until the following year, when twenty men escaped. Thomas J. Tynan, who took over as warden, revitalized the idea. His convicts were only too keen to earn the parole and the money, and soon there were 200 working in the "honor camps" all the year round.

From Moving Picture World, *December 27, 1913.*

Like his friend Judge Lindsey, Tynan was a supporter of the moving picture. He arranged for films to be made at his prison, even though press agents abused his trust with wild stories of actors being shot at by trigger-happy guards.[7] He appeared in Selig's one-reel *Circumstantial Evidence* (1912), directed by Otis Thayer. Thayer also appeared in it, along with William Duncan and Lester Cuneo.[8]

Tynan installed projection equipment in the prison. "We found," he said, "that it helped keep better discipline, for the reason that men who violated rules were excluded from the picture exhibitions for three to six months."[9] In the first two years, his reports showed a drop of 400 in such violations.[10]

In 1914, Tynan received a visit from Edward A. Morrell of San Francisco, a representative of the California Anti-Capital Punishment League, together with Victor L. Duhem, a motion picture man (of Duhem and Harter), and Miss M. Ewing, a student of sociology at the University of California, Berkeley. Their purpose was to study Tynan's methods. Duhem filmed the "honor men" at work on the public roads in order to arouse support for Tynan's humane methods.[11]

While Tynan was leading the country in prison reform, Thomas Mott Osborne was about to accept an appointment from New York governor William Sulzer as chairman of a State Prison Reform Commission. To find out about conditions, he had himself locked into the Auburn penitentiary for a week as an ordinary convict. This won him derision from the press but the respect and confidence of many of the convicts.

Osborne then introduced what became the first Mutual Welfare League in any prison; the prisoners drafted their own regulations and organized the programs of entertainment in the chapel. He became warden at Sing Sing in 1914. "But under the intense glare of external publicity several disciplinary problems acquired a lurid character and because of a shift in state politics prompted an investigation of the Osborne administration."[12] In 1915, a grand jury indicted him on six counts including perjury, neglect of duty, and sodomy. But the trial was dismissed even before the judge had heard what Osborne had to say. He was cleared of all charges and reinstated in July 1916.[13] (He resigned the following October and became openly critical of prisons.)

Osborne was anxious to find employment for convicts who had served their term without a blemish on their records. In 1915, two such men were hired by Carl Laemmle of Universal Pictures. They were given new names, and their past records were forgotten.[14]

In 1919, in collaboration with Osborne, Edward MacManus produced *The Gray Brother*. It was directed by Sidney Olcott and written by Basil Dickey. The picture contrasted the old method of treating prisoners with those advocated by the Mutual Welfare League. A poor boy (Sidney D'Albrook) is sent to a traditional jail, with its brutal regime of lock step, prison labor, silence, and torture. A rich boy (Joseph Marquis) is sent to the same prison after its adoption of a humane regime. The two become friends, and when a third friend faces execution, they escape and find the evidence to clear him. For once, the race to the rescue comes too late— an innocent man is executed. The boys, however, are paroled.[15]

Osborne, now commander of the naval prison at Portsmouth, New Hampshire, visited Chicago in December 1919 and declared that the penitentiary at Joliet was an infamous institution with a cruel and brutal system of management. Ironically, a film of 1914 had presented Joliet as a model prison. A four-reel documentary made by the Industrial Moving Picture Company of Chicago, *The Modern Prison*, showed the routine and the industry—shoes, chairs, brooms—with emphasis on the "cleanliness" and "humanity."[16] The improvements were said to be entirely the work of Warden Allen, the reform administrator who supervised the film, and his deputy, Warden Walsh.[17]

Impressed by the example of Warden Tynan and the other officials who used moving pictures to entertain prisoners, the Minnesota State Penitentiary set aside Wednesday evenings for this purpose. The programs corresponded to the releases at the local theatre, except for one or two items Warden Reed did not allow: "We

Drawn by Norman Anthony

On Parole

From Photoplay, *May 1927.*

eliminate sickly-sentimental stuff, beer-drinking, saloon-brawling, woman-beating, safe-robbing and blood-and-thunder films in general, and in their place substitute wholesome dramas, interesting travel and educational films, and clean comedies. Shakespearean and other costume plays are very popular."[18]

But nothing matched the courage of Sheriff O'Leary at the Livingston County Jail in Geneseo, New York, "Pat O'Leary's Hotel" as it was affectionately known. He was an admirer of the motion picture and felt that a night out at a movie theatre would do a lot more good for a man than cramped cells and barred windows. All the men who wanted to work could do so, and earn money, returning to the "hotel" for an evening meal, after which O'Leary encouraged them to go to the movies—on their honor. The sheriff had been operating on a similarly relaxed principle for thirty-five years, and had never lost a man: "No, they never run away. I guess the movies help. It makes them keep good, otherwise they would not get out, and that would be punishment to some who are following a serial."[19]

Louis Victor Eytinge, a lifer who ran the film program at the Arizona State Penitentiary in Florence, confirmed the extraordinary effect the films had on discipline. One night, during a screening, all the lights went out. Four hundred inmates had to feel their way back to the cells through total darkness, and yet no one tried to escape, no one tried to settle an old score. Eytinge felt the reason for their exemplary behavior was because the picture programs represented the greatest positive influence in their lives. He had been astonished at the reaction to *The Miracle Man*, that story of the regeneration of crooks: "If you had seen the men march out of the Assembly Hall, with heads thrown back, moist but exalted eyes, with backbone bulwarked, you would have understood how pictures might accomplish more than all the religious services I've ever studied in my twenty years of prison experience!"[20]

Sing Sing, a mere twenty-five miles from New York City, at Ossining, New York, was a focus of fascination for filmmakers. When Charlie Chaplin visited the prison in 1921, he had the good fortune to travel with Frank Harris, the celebrated author, who wrote a detailed description of the place: "There it lay in the autumn sunshine with the beautiful river and the heights beyond, all bathed in glory; there it lay like a vile plague spot; a great bare, yellow exercise yard; a dozen buildings, the nearest a gray stone building with narrow slits of windows for eyes and bars, bars everywhere. The heart shrank before it."[21]

The prison doctor explained that 60 percent of all prisoners had venereal disease of some sort. "We can cure all the diseased here except the dope fiends," said the doctor, "and we can cure them while they are here, but dope long continued seems to break the will power and once they get out again we find that the addicts go back."

As they continued their tour, Warden McInerny pointed down to the yard and announced, "The next for the Chair." Chaplin was greatly affected by the sight of the man's face: "Tragic, appalling!"

The death house was a bare room with a plain yellow wooden armchair, equipped with bands to hold the arms and feet. The doctor described how he tried to give the signal when the lungs of the prisoner were as empty as possible, to ensure instantaneous death. They put Chaplin in the chair and showed him how everything worked. But Chaplin was haunted by the face of the condemned man: "I shall see that till I die."

As they walked from building to building, Chaplin was applauded and cheered. An old black man called out, "I'll be out in 1932. Mind you have a new picture ready, Charlie."

Chaplin performed tricks with his hat and did his funny walk, and the visit was over. On the journey back, Chaplin remarked, "Someone has said that prisons and graveyards are always in beautiful places."[22]

Slapstick was in great demand, but when Dunham Thorp interviewed Sing Sing inmates about their taste in pictures, he found that the most side-splitting of all to them were the supposedly realistic dramas of prison and the underworld. As an example, he cited a Tommy Meighan picture, the interiors of which had been made at Sing Sing itself.[23] That picture was *The City of Silent Men* (1921). It was pure hokum, and yet it was selected by the New York Institute of Photography as one of the best-directed films "because it raises crook melodrama to the level of high art."[24]

In the
Death-House
at Sing Sing

SEVENTEEN men —some of them almost counting the minutes until the little black door should open for them into eternity; cheering wildly, for the first time in the history of that place of doom. They were cheering the gift of a motion picture projection machine presented by Thomas Meighan and his director Tom Forman, who went to Sing Sing to take scenes for "The Quarry."

"It got me," said Meighan. "I tell you I appreciated the possibilities of pictures. They aren't just punishing men there—they're saving them! As a prisoner said, 'These entertainments are possible as concrete proof that the prisoners of the State, though deprived of liberty for faults committed, are in all other respects as other men.' The chairman of Sing Sing's entertainment committee, himself a prisoner, replied when I asked him what we could give the men, 'Meighan, I want a projection machine for the Death House worse than anything. They don't get to see our regular run.' And when those men saw it and realized what it was, they cheered until the walls shook."

Promotion for The Quarry—*retitled* The City of Silent Men. *From* Photoplay, *June 1921.*

An adaptation of John A. Morosco's story *The Quarry*, it was scripted by Frank Condon and directed by Tom Forman. Jim Montgomery (Meighan) is given a life sentence for a murder he did not commit. Hearing of his mother's illness, he escapes and after the funeral starts a new life in California. A detective catches up with him, and to avoid identification Jim deliberately shatters his hands in machinery. The detective is so astonished by this heroism that he lets him go. And Jim is eventually cleared.[25]

The New York *Herald* admired the film's documentary quality: "It shows in greater detail than the screen has ever exposed before the process of matriculation at Sing Sing, so that any spectator who later finds himself inducted at Ossining will know precisely the etiquette of the place."[26]

While Meighan was filming at Sing Sing, he met the former city editor of the

New York *Evening World,* Charles Chapin, who had shot his wife and been sentenced to twenty years. He had been given the task of editing the prison newspaper, which made him miserable, so he was moved to the garden in the prison yard, which delighted him. He became known as "The Rose Man of Sing Sing."[27] Chapin was proud to meet Meighan, for when his *Miracle Man* had been shown at the prison, Chapin declared it the best picture he had ever seen.[28]

At the end of the production, Meighan asked the chairman of the Entertainments Committee what he could give the men. "Meighan," he replied, "I want a projection machine for the Death House more than anything. They don't get to see our regular run." When the machine arrived and the men realized what it was, "they cheered until the walls shook."[29]

Sing Sing came first in the prison picture league by showing films—even if mostly educational—every night.[30] "I cannot see how we could do half the work that is done without them," wrote an inmate.[31] Some of the more lurid melodramas were booked just for the fun the men derived from kidding them. This could lead to embarrassment. Norma Talmadge's crook drama *Within the Law* (1923) was given a preview at Sing Sing, in the company of prominent picture people. A magazine editor reported: "It was odd, the things they laughed at. They laughed when a demented woman trampled upon a flower growing within prison walls . . . at 'retirement' describing a prison term . . . at Mary Turner who, having married young Gilder, taunted his father with: 'You took away my name and gave me a number when you sent me up. Now I've got *your* name.'

"The prison laughter! It impressed and depressed us most. Somewhere we remember having read a poem about its hollow sound. It is that . . . and barren of any ripple of mirth; rather a sudden empty boom, then silence."[32]

PRISON LABOR

To deprive a man of his liberty was punishment enough; to deprive him of productive activity was inhuman. So felt the reformers who supported the convict labor schemes, but the American Federation of Labor objected strongly to the unfair competition. Convict labor put its members out of work.

The controversy led to several films. *Life in the Ohio Penitentiary* (1912) included shots of the "antiquated bolt shop in which the unfair contract labor was in vogue."[33]

The Edison Company's *For the Commonwealth* (1912) told a simple tale: "An unskilled laborer applies at a shoe factory for employment and is told that he will not do, as men with brains rather than muscle are needed. He returns home, where poverty of the direst sort reigns. His wife berates him for his inability to obtain food for herself and child, whereupon he leaves the house in a rage and does not return. Days afterward the poor woman sees her husband on the street and points him out to the police. The policeman attempts to arrest him, but he snatches the officer's baton and beats him over the head. At this juncture, another officer rushes up and the man is arrested and later sent to prison for assaulting an officer."[34]

Unprotected, 1916. Directed by James Young from a story by Beatrice C. de Mille (mother of the de Mille boys) and inspired by New York Governor Whitman's criticism of the shipping of prisoners to privately owned farms. Lasky publicity claimed a genuine Southern turpentine farm was used, but it seems more likely it was shot at the Lasky ranch. (Robert S. Birchard Collection)

The wife takes a low-paying job in a shirtwaist factory; meanwhile, her husband and the other inmates are led into a new workshop where they are taught to make shirtwaists on sewing machines. The wife is laid off and is compelled to seek refuge with her child in the poorhouse.

The shirtwaist-makers appeal to the governor, who "realizes that his efforts to ameliorate the condition of the state's wards has resulted in the impoverishment of its free citizens." On a visit to the poorhouse, the governor finds inmates who lack shoes and learns that the authorities cannot afford to provide them. This gives him the idea of producing only what the state itself requires. The prisoners are taught shoemaking, and when the husband is released, his newfound skill wins him a job at once, and the picture ends with his reunion with his wife and child.[35]

For the Commonwealth was valuable propaganda for the National Committee on Prison Labor, at whose instigation it was made. A few years earlier, the Boot and Shoe Workers' Union had protested against the employment of 4,000 convicts in shoe factories in twelve prisons, dumping 25,000 low-priced shoes on the market every day.[36]

THE EXPOSURE OF THE
Delaware Whipping Post
A Remarkable 3 Reel Drama

A defense of the lash as a crime preventive and a defiance to the Sentimentalists who would abolish it. The State of Delaware is the only State in the Union that whips its criminals at public whipping posts, and also pilliories them.

It has done this ever since it became a State. There have been periodical waves of agitation throughout the Nation for the abolition of these forms of punishment. The most violent wave of this kind culminated recently in a demand before Congress for Federal action compelling Delaware to discontinue its whipping post.

Very attractive line of advertising matter. One, three and six sheets; heralds, photos, slides, etc. Don't delay to procure this money-making feature. Ready for immediate shipment.

FEATURE PHOTOPLAY CO.
220 West 42nd St., Candler Bldg.   New York City
PHONE BRYANT, 8486

From Moving Picture World, *May 16, 1914. (Academy of Motion Picture Arts and Sciences)*

Several states passed laws banning the importation of prison-made goods from other states, though to little effect. Other laws required state governments to order their supplies from prison industries. These regulations were never adequate, either.

Another Edison picture, written by Melvin H. Winstock, a distributor from Portland, Oregon, was based on Oregon's parole system, which broke up "a particularly obnoxious system of contract labor." *The Convict's Parole* (1912), which featured Marc MacDermott and Mary Fuller,[37] opened in the workshop of a state prison, where the convicts are being worked to a frenzy by supervisors. The contractor and the warden are in collusion, but the governor, unhappy about the condition of the men, changes the system to that of parole. The contractors try to force him to change his mind; failing this, they set out to make the prisoners violate their parole. A stool pigeon, sent after the parolees, manages to get three of them arrested and brought back. But one of the convicts overhears the plot and exposes the crooked warden, who is dismissed. The prisoners are released.[38]

Legislation helped the situation in the North; in the South, the exploitation of prisoners continued unabated.

The Fight for Right (1913), a Reliance two-reeler written by James Oppenheim, a prison labor reform agitator, and directed by Oscar Apfel, was set in a Southern mill town. A knitting company is forced to shut down because its owner, Durland, contracts with a prison to install a knitting plant. John and his brother, Joe, are thrown out of work. Desperate for medicine for their sick mother, Joe tries to rob Durland, but is caught and sent to prison—and put to work on Durland's knitting machine.[39]

Prison conditions in the South took a turn for the worse at this period, when convicts were put to work on the roads in chain gangs[40] (an abuse which inspired a masterpiece of the early thirties, *I Am a Fugitive from a Chain Gang*). Edward Sloman's *The Convict King* (1915), a three-reeler written by Dudley Glass and made for Lubin, highlighted this evil. It was about two highway contractors, Jared Austin (Melvin Mayo) and Ben Gray (Jay Morley), both of whom use convict labor. A bill is introduced to abolish the system, and Gray assures Austin he will speak against it. A train wreck mutilates Austin's face beyond recognition, and a convict changes clothes with him. Austin then experiences the horrors of the convict camp at first hand.[41]

While the majority of prison films supported reform, the Feature Photoplay Company of New York balanced the argument with a three-reeler called *The Exposure of the Delaware Whipping Post* (1914). "Exposure" was as emotive a word then as now, thanks to the muckraking journalists, but this film was, as an advertisement explained, "a defense of the lash as a crime preventive and a defiance to the Sentimentalists who would abolish it. The State of Delaware is the only State in the Union that whips its criminals at public whipping posts and also pillories them."[42]

Delaware had done this from its foundation as a state. Violent protests culminated in a demand to Congress for federal action to compel Delaware to abolish its whipping post. Hence the film. "Very attractive line of advertising matter," said the film company, showing a photograph of a guard about to lash the naked back of a prisoner.

Delaware did not abolish its whipping post until 1972.

The Whipping Boss (1924) survives in a private collection in England—some of it badly decomposed, but what remains is an astonishing exposé of the convict leasing system. Directed by J. P. McGowan and written by Jack Boyle and Anthony Coldewey, it was copyrighted in 1923, but evidently found some difficulty in getting a release.

McGowan, an Australian, was the husband of Helen Holmes, and the creator of such full-blooded serial melodramas as *The Hazards of Helen* (1914–17). He was a more than proficient director and while this story is told within the confines of a program picture, it still packs considerable punch. "This picture should do a lot of good," said *Photoplay*, "but it isn't easy to watch. . . . The story is taken, almost intact, from an actual occurrence."[43]

The story was set in Oregon, and the film equates the state's convict leasing system to slavery. A young drifter, Jim Fairfax (Eddie Phillips), trying to get home to his mother, falls in with hoboes, ignoring advice not to ride the rails through Woodward—"it's the gateway to the chain gang." Jim is duly arrested and transported to the Woodward Lumber Co. The state governor has prohibited the use of the lash, but the whipping boss (Wade Boteler) has a new superintendent (J. P. McGowan) who tells him, "You're not working for the Governor, you're working for me. Go ahead and use the lash." The scenes of brutality are mostly missing from this print. But the appalling conditions in the cypress swamps are portrayed with documentary realism. Working up to their waists in water, the convicts are victims of disease as well as the lash. They are observed by Dick Forrest (Lloyd Hughes), head of the local American Legion post, who is so shocked he mobilizes his men. To destroy the evidence of abuse, the lumber camp owner orders the place to be burned down—with the convicts chained to their bunks. The American Legion arrives in time to rescue the convicts who then try to lynch the prison guards. "The American Legion stands for law and order," warns Forrest, "not the tyranny of the mob."

It was an ironic line even then—a couple of years earlier, the American Legion had turned out to demonstrate against the showing of the German film, *The Cabinet of Dr. Caligari*, at its American premiere in Los Angeles. The Legion was a symbol of conservatism, and a surprising participant in one of the rare social dramas of the twenties.

THE HONOR SYSTEM   Two films of this title, produced within four years of each other, demonstrate the growth in power and sophistication of the social film in America. The first, made by Kalem in 1913, featured Carlyle Blackwell in a study of the effects on a prisoner of brutal treatment and the changes that result from humane conditions. How good it was we shall never know. The picture came and went, submerged in the flood of ordinary nickelodeon fare, and has never resurfaced.

The 1917 version has never resurfaced either, and from what we know about the film, the loss is one of the major tragedies of film history. The *New York Times* called it "the motion picture pretty nearly at its best,"[44] an opinion shared by *Variety*, which said, "The photography and direction are well nigh flawless."[45]

The difference between the two was the difference between a simple piano piece and a full-scale symphony. Of the second version, the New York *Dramatic Mirror* wrote, "*The Honor System* is undoubtedly the most powerful philippic against the prison system under which prisoners are held as wild beasts, rather than humans, that has ever been produced. If reform propaganda has a place on the screen, then assuredly this picture deserved first rank."[46]

The New York *American* went as far as it was possible to go: "*The Birth of a Nation* at last eclipsed."[47]

The Honor System, *1917, directed by Raoul Walsh: Milton Sills (center) and Gladys Brockwell.*

Written by Henry Christeen Warnack, editorial writer on the Los Angeles *Times*, and directed by Raoul Walsh, it featured Milton Sills as Joseph Stanton, a New England inventor who develops a scheme to revolutionize wireless telegraphy. Needing money to advance his project, he travels west to a job in the border town of Howling Dog. Mexicans raid the town, backed by Charles Harrington (Charles Clary), an attorney who pulls the strings for certain financial interests. Stanton grabs a horse and sets out for the nearest cavalry post, riding back with them to witness a spectacular cavalry charge.

A prostitute called Trixie (Gladys Brockwell) sets out to ensnare Stanton. During a fight at a dance hall, Stanton is attacked with a knife by her pimp. Defending himself, Stanton kills him. He is arrested, and during the trial, Harrington testifies that the dead man was unarmed. Stanton gets life.

He begins his sentence under the old-fashioned system, which turns convicts into permanent enemies of society. Floggings are administered daily, and the victims are then dragged into verminous, subterranean cells to remain in solitary confinement. Some men go blind; others, unable to bear the torture, kill themselves.

"Serves 'em right," says the warden (P. J. Cannon). Under his regime, no letters or newspapers are permitted, the food is unspeakable, absolute silence is imperative, and work means hard labor.

The prisoners attempt a breakout. The guards open fire, kill half a dozen, and subdue the rest, but Stanton and his pal Frenchy get away. Stanton delivers a note to the sheriff to hand to the governor:

"For God's sake, go and see for yourself the horrors of your state prison.

"I escaped from that hell, but I killed a man, and I feel in honor bound to return and serve my term. Imprisonment is just, but I implore you go and end the torture that takes the manhood from the unfortunates."

When Governor Hunter (James Marcus)[48] receives the note, he goes straight to the prison and asks to see Stanton. The brutal warden looks frightened. Stanton had received a flogging to celebrate his return and was then flung into an underground cell. Having lain there for months, he is now a physical wreck. The warden produces a Negro instead.

The governor insists. And Stanton is at last led out, a shockingly emaciated figure, and blind.

Governor Hunter fires the warden and his guards and brings the honor system to the penitentiary. The amazing difference is effected by a single speech in the senate: "Our penitentiary is a disgrace to the State, a disgrace to humanity." And Hunter produces his exhibit—Stanton, his eyes covered with a bandage.

Stanton works on his invention with the encouragement of the governor. He asks for parole to visit a radio station to test it. The crooked lawyer, Harrington, now chairman of the Board of Pardons, objects. "I'll stake my life on his return," laughs the governor. "Will you stake the honor system?" "Done," says the governor. "If he doesn't return I'll move for the ousting of the honor system and the return of the old order of discipline."

Harrington orders his thugs to trail Stanton, steal his wireless, and prevent his return. They lure him to an address in the slums, where they beat him and lock him up. Frenchy reappears, finds the former warden among the thugs, kills him, and releases Stanton.

Now Stanton races to the station to catch the train on which he had promised to return. But one of Harrington's gangsters attacks him, and there is a battle royal on the roof of the freight train. Stanton is flung off and stunned. When he recovers consciousness, he has to continue on foot. All night long he staggers onward, determined to vindicate the worth of the honor system. At the prison, the warden is informed that Stanton acted in self-defense at the dance-hall fight and will receive a pardon. But the train arrives with no sight of Stanton. The warden and his daughter, Edith (Miriam Cooper), wait through the night. Not until the early hours does he arrive, in the last stages of exhaustion. He has kept faith with the honor system, but at the cost of his life.

"The death of Stanton revolutionized the prison system, however, and put it on a new basis, where revenge was discarded and love, justice and honor took its place,"[49] noted *Picture Play*.

Although the scenario depended upon melodrama, with a Griffith-style race against time, it was far more significant than the entertainment it was designed for.

In his outline of the story, Henry Christeen Warnack included this foreword: "The Governor of Arizona has earnestly endeavored to bring about sane prison reform in the penitentiaries of his state. Many of the words attributed to him in this story are really from his tongue, and if this should be put on as a picture by a company that wanted to go to Arizona, Governor Hunt would give permission to make views, both in the dismantled prison at Yuma and in the new prison at Florence. He would be willing himself to appear at the meeting of the Board of Pardons and has in mind a worthy man who might be pardoned in conjunction with the climax of this photo-play."[50]

Raoul Walsh went to see Governor Hunt and asked to be put in jail for three days to add color to the script. In interviews, this became three weeks[51] and he witnesses a hanging for good measure. In his book, he misremembers the story of the film and has Gladys Brockwell playing the warden's daughter, not Miriam Cooper—an odd lapse, since Miriam Cooper was his wife.[52]

In her account, Cooper recalled that the picture was shot at both the old and the new penitentiaries in Arizona. The old prison at Yuma had been a horrifying place. As the film showed, prisoners were tied to stakes and flogged, kept in solitary confinement with snakes, rats, and scorpions for company, and treated with the greatest severity.[53] But she describes the conditions as though they existed at the time of filming, which did Governor Hunt less than justice; the old Yuma Territorial Prison had already been closed.

The new prison at Florence was in the desert. Fox put up a tent city outside the walls for cast and crew, and Cooper stayed with the warden. It was here that the spectacular Mexican raid was staged. It had absolutely nothing to do with prison reform, but Walsh was enthralled by Mexico and Pancho Villa had recently raided Columbus, New Mexico. Real convicts were used in the jail scenes.

Walsh told me this was the toughest picture he had made in the entire silent period. While in production, Fox sensed something special about it and instructed him to increase it from five to seven or eight reels, which was probably why the Mexicans were thrown in. A late telegram said, "Make it ten."

One of the most glowing endorsements for the film came from Louis Victor Eytinge, who had been incarcerated at Yuma, and was currently in somewhat happier conditions at Florence. It was also much admired by John Ford.[54]

Governor Hunt was only too happy to endorse the film. In a letter to William Fox, he wrote, "Everyone in the United States should see your production. . . . It contrasts the old prison conditions with its inhuman terrorism—its beatings, starvings, murders, suicides—with the modern method which recognizes that *every convict has a human soul worthy of redemption.*"[55]

The picture opened at the Lyric Theatre, New York, in February 1917 with a specially composed score and an orchestra of fifty. The *New York Times* thought it magnificent, but as an indictment of the prison system compared it unfavorably to Galsworthy's *Justice,* in which the prisoner was guilty and the administrators of the prison that crushed him were ordinary, decent men. "But *The Honor System* is an arresting reminder of the medievalism that survives in some of our prisons and will probably not suffer much as propaganda because of the hair-raising melodramatics."[56]

At the premiere, the audience applauded titles pleading for the improvement of the prison system.[57]

Like so many silent pictures, *The Honor System* began its career with a tragic ending, Stanton dying after returning to the prison. But Fox quickly substituted a happier finale, with Edith nursing him back to health.[58] Fox's publicity men dreamed up a novel ploy: they used one of Henry Ford's own tricks—the advertising of ideas in newspapers—and made him the butt. Their ad read:

Henry Ford:

With Your Millions

Why Do You Do It?

Starting with praise for Ford's genius, the ad continued, "In the face of so many fine accomplishments, it seems so wrong that you should leave yourself open to the charge of heartlessness—for no man without a heart could have taken such an interest in all of his fellow men.

"Come to New York *now*, Mr. Ford, and make public repentance. Bring some of your wealth with you, gather around you, as you did for your peace trip, some of the biggest minds in our nation and say: 'We failed to end the European horrors, but *now we will end the greatest of all horrors here at home.*'

"As soon as you have arrived take your party at once to the Lyric Theatre and see the greatest crime of modern society that can be charged up against you and all other wealthy, brainy and influential men and women . . .

"When you have witnessed this condition we do not believe you will ever again be content and peaceful of heart until you have started some great movement that provides a remedy."[59]

One hundred thousand people saw the film during its six-week run, some of them two or three times. Fox had as potentially sensational a film as had Griffith, yet his press agents could not resist the usual publicity nonsense; according to them Governor Hunt reprieved several murderers so they would not be hanged until they had seen themselves on the screen! "All of which," said *Photoplay,* "speaks well for the humanitarianism of the Arizona executive and the Fox typewriter soloist."[60]

Milton Sills confessed that he had failed to take the movies seriously until he came out to make *The Honor System:* "That experience convinced me that interesting and artistic things could be done in pictures."[61] Louis Devon, in a 1971 article on Sills, said that he worked with Walsh on the script. The picture still carried a strong memory for Devon: "I was quite young when I saw it and I still remember the impression made upon my young mind by a close-up of maggots crawling on the bread one of the prisoners was given to eat. I think Eisenstein must have been impressed by that close-up too."[62] (A touch of black comedy in the film showed the prisoners sending tiny messages to each other on the backs of cockroaches.)

If Walsh's astonishing grasp of technique, which he displayed in *Regeneration,* was as pronounced in *The Honor System*—and contemporary reviews suggest it was—then the tragedy of its loss is all the greater. But technique was of far less importance in this case than content. As Frederick James Smith put it, "This indeed is the first real attempt of the movies to enlist in a great humanitarian movement. Consequently, *The Honor System* can be said to have the biggest theme of any screen production thus far."[63]

Shortly after this, William Fox altered his policy. Instead of elaborate and costly films on challenging themes, he decided to concentrate on cheaper pictures with more profitable subjects. And for a decade, the company's name all but disappears from the history of the social film.

CAPITAL PUNISHMENT

Among the horrors in Electric Vaudeville, or amusement arcades, was a series of films depicting in loving detail each stage of the execution of a woman. To see them all, you had to move from one peep-show machine to another. When projectors were developed, the separate scenes were joined together to produce a film which, to the audiences of the time, looked distressingly authentic.

Adolph Zukor recalled that another of the early films showed the hanging of a Negro in a Southern jail, omitting no ghastly detail. "For years this piece of tainted celluloid dodged through the country just ahead of the sheriff and the police."[64]

And the Law Says, 1916. A law student (Richard Bennett) has an affair which results in an illegitimate child. He runs away from his responsibility. Eventually, he becomes a judge and one day, not realizing his own son stands before him, he sentences him to death. Here, the innocent son (Allan Forrest) awaits execution. (Robert S. Birchard Collection)

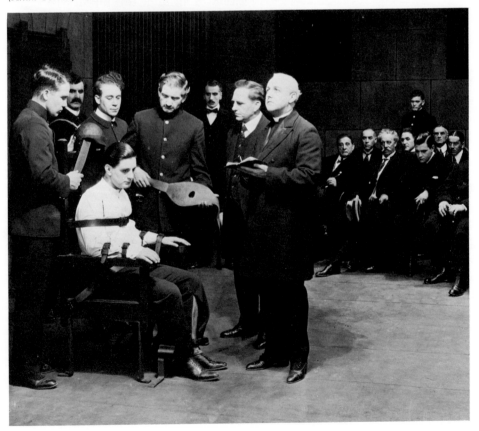

Such films were made for their shock value and their commercial potential, and execution scenes flourished long after the censorship which was supposed to abolish them.

"Pictures showing the harrowing details of an execution by hanging ought never to be passed by a board of censorship," said W. Stephen Bush. "It is no excuse to say that the execution was part of a dream. To the audience it is frightfully real, nevertheless. It is bad enough to flash a view of a gibbet before the eyes of an audience and to indicate, however dimly, that a human being is about to be done to death. To revel in such details and to stretch them out with painstaking care and an evident morbid relish, is an intolerable offense. What excuse can an exhibitor make to the outraged parents of boys and girls who are shocked and sickened by such exhibitions?"[65]

One fervent opponent of capital punishment was Hal Reid. His one-reel Vitagraph drama *Thou Shalt Not Kill* (1913) had a twist calculated to disturb every woman in the audience. It opened with a strikingly lit scene in which a mother (Julia Swayne Gordon) defends herself and her child against her husband: "If you ever treat me like that again I'll kill you." The child remembers this when the husband is accidentally shot while out hunting, and her innocent testimony puts the mother in the death house. But she is pregnant, and the governor rules that the state cannot take two lives for one. The child is allowed to be born, and during the delay the shooting mystery is cleared up.

Two years later, Reid made a five-reeler with the same title for his own Circle Film Corporation. Its publicity exploited the Leo Frank case (see pages 378–79), but it was actually a story of a boy in the Kentucky hills, the son of a judge, who is arrested for killing a deputy. A confession from the real killer reaches the boy's father just after his execution.[66]

The Gangsters of New York (1914) was also intended to evoke anti-capital punishment sympathy. While Biff Dugan (Jack Dillon) walks to the electric chair at Sing Sing, the sister of the chief gangster dies of consumption and a broken heart. "The actual death of the convict by the electrical current is not shown," said *Variety*, "but it goes as near to it as the prison warden dropping the handkerchief, which leaves little surmise." Yet *Variety* said that the film "points a finger at capital punishment as the possible end to more crime."[67]

A proprietor showing this film set up a mock "electric chair" complete with model victim outside his theatre and employed a barker to urge people to see the film. A crowd gathered, and the proprietor was arrested for disorderly conduct. "We doubt whether half a dozen men in the business could be found willing to stoop so low, but of course even one is enough to harm the whole industry."[68]

A two-reel melodrama called *The City of Darkness* (1914) was made for Thomas Ince by Walter Edwards, who also played the lead as the governor. Formerly a district attorney, the governor has made a deadly enemy of a ward boss (Herschel Mayall) by sending his son to the chair for murder. The ward boss seizes the chance for revenge by framing the governor's brother (Charles Ray). He is found guilty and sentenced to death. The ward boss visits the governor to extract the last ounce of pleasure from his predicament and makes him suffer more by telling him his brother is innocent. The governor struggles with the boss and then tries to prevent the execution.

"The innocent man is shown making his final preparations for death, while the governor is speeding to a form of rescue that has suggested itself to his acute intelligence. The boy is led into the death chamber and placed in the chair. The governor dashes into a tremendous building filled with machinery—it is possible to shut off the power that lights the city . . .

"Views are flashed of varied action in high and low society as the whole city is plunged into darkness. The suspense is all the more drawn out because the telephone lines to the prison are cut off to prevent a flood of morbid messages. But the boy is saved and justice is done in the end."[69]

The race to the rescue was already a standard feature of such films. It would make fascinating comparison to Griffith's in *The Mother and the Law*, which eventually formed the modern story of *Intolerance* (1916), his epic of injustice through the ages. *The Mother and the Law* was also melodrama, but the story was propaganda against capital punishment. For once there was no doubt that it was intended as such.

Griffith undertook research trips to prisons, with cameraman Billy Bitzer and his assistant Karl Brown. At San Quentin the party was shown a room where ropes were stretched with 150-pound sandbags before being used on the gallows next door.

"I was all prepared for what I was to see," wrote Brown, "because everyone knows that gallows are painted black and that there are thirteen steps.

"To my astonished disbelief the gallows was painted a baby blue. It was much bigger and higher than I had expected, all of twenty feet from the floor to the top crossbeams."[70]

The warden took them underneath to explain the mechanism. "See these four cords? They're heavy, hundred-pound-test-fishline and they run through a pulley to this fifty-pound sandbag. Cut the cords from above, the sandbag drops, and here—I'll show you."

"He pulled the cord by hand. The latch released the trap, which was made of heavy, laminated wood. This let the trap swing heavily to the opposite side, where it clanged loudly into another spring latch. That sound, in the bare, echoing room, was ghastly. I had never heard death proclaim itself in such a loud, definitive way."[71]

Of the four strings, which were accompanied by razor-sharp knives, only one was connected to the trip weight. Four men operated the knives, but they could not see the prisoner and they never knew which cord sprung the trap. It was the equivalent of the blank cartridge for the firing squad.

Griffith asked about a last-second reprieve: "I didn't see any phone on that gallows."

"You didn't because there isn't any. We wouldn't take a chance on not hearing a phone ring at a time like that. We have a direct line held open to the governor's mansion all during that last twenty-four hours; the instant a call comes through, the switchboard hits a big alarm bell that sounds all through the prison. The instant that bell sounds everything stops."[72]

Griffith does not ignore the telephone, but because it would have ruined his race to the rescue, he has the warden reject the message and proceed with the execution. His scaffold was built under the supervision of Martin Aguerre, for

Frame enlargement from Intolerance, *1916. A last minute rescue. The scaffold was constructed under the direction of a former prison official.*

twenty years warden at San Quentin. Since he had officiated at numerous executions, he supervised this one, too.[73] Griffith was criticized for his race to the rescue; despite the fact that it became one of the most highly praised sequences in film history, critics dismissed it as mere melodrama.

He justified it by referring to the recent Stielow case. "Stielow was convicted of a murder and sentenced to die," said Griffith. "Four times he was prepared for the chair, four times he and his family suffered every agony save the final swish of the current.

"What saved him was exactly what saved 'The Boy' in my picture; the murderer confessed, the final reprieve arrived just as the man was ready to be placed in the chair, his trousers' leg already slit for the electrode."[74]

Since the boy in the film is a gangster to begin with, his near execution is not so obvious a case of intolerance as it might have been had Griffith taken the Leo Frank case as a model. But then this story began life under another title *(The Mother and the Law)*. To make it more relevant to the new title, Griffith calls the prison "a sometimes House of Intolerance" and has the boy "intolerated away for a term."

"Griffith's realization of ritualized death in the finished film remains to this day as powerful as any such sequence ever done in the movies," wrote Richard Schickel, "precisely because the detailing is so lavish, so profoundly felt."[75]

The People vs. John Doe (1916), made by Lois Weber, was described by the *New York Times* as "the most effective propaganda in film form ever seen here."[76]

The story was actually a combination of several murder trials, with the essentials taken from the Stielow case.* A protest against capital punishment, the film was also a protest against the system that permitted the state to sentence a man to death on circumstantial evidence. "The horrors of the third degree are vividly portrayed and it is shown how it is possible that alleged confessions can be tortured from a man who is really innocent but will swear to anything so as to be let alone."[77]

The film had the backing of the Humanitarian Cult, whose founder, Mischa Appelbaum, gave a speech at the end of it emphasizing the theme. *Variety* said the exhibitor who could not secure local endorsements on this film had better go out of business.[78]

Under the title *God's Law,* the film was shown to Pennsylvania's House of Representatives as the state legislators debated the abolition of capital punishment.[79]

Even supporters of capital punishment were disturbed by the use of the electric chair, not for any moral reason, but because it was possible for the victim to survive even so massive a surge of electricity. In *The Return of Maurice Donnelly* (1914), a Vitagraph three-reeler directed by William Humphrey, a convicted man is electrocuted. The film shows a dead rabbit being resurrected through an electric shock. "Then the corpse is brought back from the electric chamber, quite dead and cold, and by the tremendous voltage likewise brought back. . . . This is without doubt the best part of the play, for good lighting effects make the intense spark, the bare torso and the more or less breathless expectation, the one really great moment of the play."[80]

Dorothy Davenport (Mrs. Wallace Reid) appeared in *The Girl and the Crisis* (1917), a five-reel Universal, written and directed by William V. Mong. A governor is shot and the murderer apprehended and sentenced to death. The young lieutenant governor, now in the governor's chair, is assailed by both sides and eventually commutes the sentence at the expense of his own political future.[81] But he does so too late—the condemned man's agony causes him to die of a stroke.

One ardent opponent of capital punishment was Maibelle Heikes Justice, a short-story author and screenwriter who worked for many picture companies including Selig, Lubin, Metro, and Essanay and who was the daughter of a well-known judge.[82] She wrote *Who Shall Take My Life?*, which was made in 1917 by Selig's leading director, Colin Campbell. Once again, it was the story of a man convicted by circumstantial evidence. After the execution is carried out, the warden receives word that the victim has been found alive, working as a prostitute in a Western city.[83]

The subject of capital punishment became merely a device to conclude thrillers during the twenties. There were so many races to the rescue in the style of *Intolerance* that they became parodies of themselves. *The Last Hour* (1923) was given this

---

*Its working title was *The Celebrated Stielow Case.*

B. P. Schulberg's Capital Punishment, *1925. Clara Bow and George Hackathorne as the innocent man condemned to death. (George Eastman House)*

dismissal by *Photoplay:* "Saved at the eleventh hour. From the hangman's noose. With the entire audience applauding the hangman, and cursing the automobile that makes such good time on the roads."[84]

At least one commercial film did set out to preach against capital punishment. In 1925 B. P. Schulberg's Preferred Pictures produced *Capital Punishment,* which had the advantage of two of the silent cinema's most seductive actresses, Clara Bow and Margaret Livingston, and a story by Schulberg himself.

The picture was inspired by the Leopold-Loeb trial.[85] In May 1924, eighteen-year-old Nathan Leopold and Richard Loeb, seventeen, two brilliant college students who were the sons of millionaires, committed the "perfect" (and motiveless) murder, killing a boy of fourteen and attributing it to kidnappers. When the body was discovered, Leopold's glasses were found nearby and Loeb cast suspicion upon himself by his remarks. At the trial their lawyer, Clarence Darrow, pleaded for life sentences rather than execution and succeeded.[86]

In the film, welfare worker Gordon Harrington (Elliott Dexter) bets his friend Harry Phillips (Robert Ellis) $10,000 that he can have an innocent man convicted of murder. He arranges with Dan O'Connor (George Hackathorne) to take the blame for a murder that will never occur. At the right moment the hoax will be disclosed and capital punishment will be discredited. He sends Phillips on a cruise and makes it appear that he has been murdered by O'Connor. O'Connor is convicted and sentenced to death. Phillips returns unexpectedly and, in an argument, Harrington accidentally kills him. His fiancée persuades him not to report the killing to the police. O'Connor is about to be executed when the girl changes her mind and turns Harrington in.[87]

B.P.'s son, Budd, in his book *Moving Pictures,* recalled a reprieve coming too late. According to him, when exhibitors pleaded for a happy ending, B.P. said, "If you're going to make a movie attacking capital punishment, then goddamn it, *attack it!*"[88] This scene was not the ending, however, but a prologue.[89]

The release coincided with a campaign by Bernarr MacFadden's newspaper, the *New York Graphic,* for the abolition of capital punishment in New York.[90] Given the title, *Picture Play* thought any expert fan would be able to tell the story: "There is the innocent boy who is sent to the electric chair; there are the trusting friends, the staunch girl and the surly influences. And, if you will credit it, there is the old race with death with the pardon arriving just as— But oh! my goodness, when will these governors learn to use the telephone?"[91]

Warden Lawes arranged a showing at Sing Sing, and a woman journalist from *Picture Play* went with the party: "They showed the film in the prison chapel, and the men seemed to love it. All the comedy scenes went over wonderfully, but when there was a serious title—'May God have mercy on our souls'—just after the warden had allowed an innocent man to be electrocuted, the convicts roared with laughter."[92]

Chapter Nine

POVERTY

*Agnes de Mille, the future
choreographer, as a street waif in her
father, William de Mille's, first film as
a director, The Ragamuffin, 1916.*

THE MOVING PICTURE documented nothing so thoroughly as the poverty in the big cities, partly because it was picturesque and partly because the urban poor lay at the heart of the reform movement. The early filmmakers, many of whom had come from precisely this background, believed they wielded a powerful influence for change.

The poor were referred to as "the submerged tenth." But figures available now suggest they constituted an eighth to a quarter of the population—15 to 20 million people.[1] Most seemed to be crammed into slum tenements, and most were foreign-born. A frequent visitor to New York's Lower East Side, Margaret Sanger, was seized with a deep depression whenever she approached: "All these dwellings were pervaded by the foul smell of poverty, that moldy, indefinable, indescribable smell which cannot be fumigated out, sickening to me but apparently unnoticed by those who lived there."[2]

Films did their best to dramatize the plight of the poor, but they stopped short of showing the details.[3] It was hard to tell the whole truth when the words needed to tell it could not be spoken in polite society.[4] Some focused on what they saw as oases in the vast deserts of poverty—the settlement houses.

The first of these was Hull-House, opened in the South Halsted Street slums of Chicago in 1889 by social workers Jane Addams and Ellen Gates Starr. Hull-House developed into a complex organization. "Situated in the very center of Chicago's vice, criminal and poverty-stricken district, surrounded by a large foreign population, the great institution stands forth as a lighthouse in the midst of a troubled sea."[5] So wrote *Motion Picture Story Magazine* upon the release of *Life at Hull-House* in 1911 from the Essanay Company of Chicago. It portrayed the benefits which the settlement had brought to the slums: the low-priced cafeteria; the delivery of hot soup and sandwiches to factories; the boys' club, carpentry shop, electrical classes, brass foundry; the "roughhouse room" where kids could do what they liked and make as much noise as they wanted to; the girls' cooking club; day nursery and kindergarten; an open-air school on the roof for tubercular children; a labor museum whose looms produced rugs, towels, and blankets; concerts, lectures, and, above all, plays—Greek plays, Italian plays, Yiddish plays. "Plays at Hull-House, once seen, are never forgotten."[6]

Settlements were a staple ingredient of the films about poverty because they gave the audience the reassuring feeling that something was being done—and the person doing it was invariably a golden-haired beauty like Blanche Sweet or Anna Q. Nilsson.

When the settlement workers associated themselves with the films, something

ACCOMMODATION DE LUXE.

WHEN THE ENTRANCE IS SO PALATIAL—

THE FOOTMEN SO SPECTACULAR—

THE LOUNGES SO IMPOSING—

THE DECORATIONS SO PRODIGAL—

THE SERVICE SO OVERWHELMING—

THE ATTENDANTS SO CAPTIVATING—

AND THE SEATING ARRANGEMENTS SO
LUXURIOUS—

IT'S RATHER A SHOCK TO BE FACED WITH
THIS SORT OF THING.

usually *did* get done. In 1914, Vitagraph produced a three-reeler called *The Silent Plea for a Widowed Mother's Allowance,* later known as *A Silent Plea*, in cooperation with the East Side Protective Association. It was written by E. Mae Koch and directed by stage actor Lionel Belmore, in collaboration with Sophie Irene Loeb, who was running the campaign for public assistance to enable widowed mothers to stay at home with their children.

The film made the point that while there is no substitute for a mother's influence in forming the character of a child, far too many mothers were forced to neglect their youngsters because they had to go to work. A husband is killed in a traffic accident, and his wife (Edith Storey) and two children are left penniless. "Her trials, during the years that she gets along as best she can on the scant wages earned in a factory, are visualized with much detail."[7] The camera watches the children, left to amuse themselves on the streets; "they adopt the manner and morals of street urchins."[8] The authorities decide the mother is no longer capable of looking after her offspring, and they are committed to a home, "a barren place, void of sympathy and affection. Every woman will understand the feelings of the mother when she goes to the institution on visiting days and finds herself less and less in touch with her children."[9]

Eventually, the boy turns to bank robbery and the girl starts out "on a dangerous path, the end of which is not shown in the picture."[10]

The story was told in flashback, as the mother tells it to an old friend who has become a state senator (Harry Morey). He is so moved he delivers a powerful speech in favor of the Mother's Pension Bill.

"Let us hope that in the near future some bona fide senator will do the same and effect its passage," said *Motion Picture News*.[11]

A Silent Plea was followed by Pathé's *The Pardon* (1915), directed by Donald MacKenzie, which followed a remarkably similar plot, but which again subordinated everything to the propaganda, asking the question, "Is it better to pay a mother to care for her child or to pay an institution to care for it for her?"[12]

With her campaign given a flood of publicity by these films, Sophie Irene Loeb did indeed succeed in establishing a New York State Widows' Pension Law.

TUBERCULOSIS

Settlement workers were also involved in the fight against tuberculosis, a cause to which the Edison Company was particularly devoted. "The white plague" swept through the slums like the Black Death. As early as 1882, the year Robert Koch discovered the tuberculosis germ, half the population of New York City had been crammed into the Lower East Side, suffering 70 percent of the city's deaths.[13] (Into one city block alone were packed 3,000 people.) Thanks to the immense publicity given the disease, it soon became known that the spread of TB could be prevented. In 1903, John D. Rockefeller put up $7 million to fight it. In 1904, the National Association for the Study and Prevention of Tuberculosis (now the Lung Association) was founded, and in 1910 the Edison Company collaborated with the association and the American National Red Cross to produce films to help the sale of Red Cross Christmas Seals.

SCENE FROM

THE RED CROSS SEAL

FILM No. 6722

When the Edison TB films began to appear, first *The Man Who Learned* (1910),* dealing with the pure milk question, then *The Red Cross Seal* (1910),† *Moving Picture World* said they had stemmed the tide of hostile criticism. Newspapers had been attacking the moving picture, charging that no film had contributed anything to the sum of human knowledge. In less than a year, these Edison films had "forced the recognition of the motion picture by the press, university, state, church and laity as the greatest educational agency since the discovery of the art of printing."[14]

According to Martin S. Pernick, some of the health films of this period reached audiences of several million. They were shown in schools, army camps, factories, county fairs, and churches, and Pernick has found several old men who remembered them vividly from military training in World War I.[15] The films may have been prompted as much by the need for first aid for the battered reputation of the industry as for the Red Cross, but their release was a social service.

The Awakening of John Bond (1911) was a one-reeler directed by Charles Brabin,

---

*Produced in cooperation with the New York Milk Committee.

†Produced in cooperation with the National Association for the Study and Prevention of Tuberculosis.

EDISON FILMS

To be released on April 17th, 20th, 24th *&* 27th, 1912

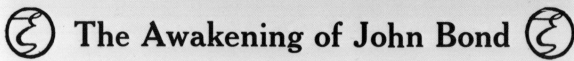

The Awakening of John Bond

Produced in Co-operation with the American National Association for the Study and Prevention of Tuberculosis

The Awakening of John Bond, *1911. An advertisement from the London edition of the* Edison Kinetogram, *April 1, 1912. The boy is the future cameraman Philip Tannura. (David Robinson)*

featuring Bigelow Cooper, Miriam Nesbitt, Mary Fuller, Harold Shaw, and Phil Tannura.[16] In the story, John Bond (Cooper) is a wealthy politician who ignores a tenement inspector's warning to improve his property. He also refuses to support the Tuberculosis Committee's campaign for legislation to aid sufferers. In one of his tenements live a family, all of whom suffer from the disease. When Bond marries and takes his bride (Nesbitt) for a honeymoon cruise, one of the boys from this family (Shaw) is among the crew, and from him Bond's wife contracts TB. Bond is forced to apply for aid to the Tuberculosis Committee and finds no space in the public hospital because he voted against it. He begins to realize the good being done by the association. His awakening is complete when he examines one of his tenements, and he writes out a substantial check. Mrs. Bond recovers; Bond is accepted as a candidate supporting the crusade against tuberculosis.[17]

One of the most vicious results of the TB scare was the sale of fake cures. Edison produced a film about this as well, *The Price of Human Lives* (1913), a one-reeler written by Epes Winthrop Sargent and directed by Richard Ridgely.[18]

The Toll of Mammon (1914), directed by Harry Handworth for the Excelsior Feature Film Company, was probably inspired by the visit to the United States of a German physician who claimed he had discovered a cure for tuberculosis. (He had not.) It was the frightening story of a poor doctor, John Wright (Gordon De Maine), whose wife craves luxuries far beyond his income. He makes a discovery that brings him fame but not much money, and when a company marketing a fake TB cure offers him $5,000 for an endorsement, his initial anger is curbed by thoughts of his and his wife's extravagance. The Wright sanitarium is founded, "and in pathetic scenes we see scores of poor dupes . . . submitting to treatment."

After a number of deaths, Wright offers $50,000 if the sanitarium will only take his name off the place; the owners refuse, and he is held captive to prevent him from exposing the fraud. Wright's little daughter contracts consumption, as tuberculosis was then called, and he eventually serves thirty years in the penitentiary, where he, too, succumbs to the disease. "Pardoned before the expiration of his term, he goes to an Adirondack sanatorium to take the only authentic treatment for the disease—fresh air and good food."[19]

Tenements were not the only breeding grounds for TB; factories could be equally squalid. In Edison's *The Temple of Moloch* (1914), written by Mary Mechtold Rider and directed by Langdon West, a worker contracts the disease from a pottery factory. (This is one of the few TB films to survive.)

A doctor (Harold Vosburgh) visits the family and warns the father (Carlton King) against spitting. The son must not drink from an unwashed glass. Mother must stop sweeping round the baby. And, opening the window, he tells them that fresh air is vital. (The moment he leaves, they shut it again.) The baby dies, but the father hears that the son of the owner has also succumbed. His pottery factory lacks ventilation, and the children working there catch the disease and pass it on.

In a theatrically staged scene, with all the characters squeezed in front of the camera, the father accuses the factory owner, who at last realizes he has obligations toward his workers. He promises to clean up his property and, as in *John Bond,* writes out a check.

Those who lived in the country were free of the disease. That, at least, is what a bank president (George Lessey) thinks in Edison's *Hope* (1912),* as he rejects the idea of a sanitarium in his rural town. When his fiancée, Edith (Gertrude McCoy), contracts the disease, she leaves the rural town and goes in desperation to the Bellevue Hospital in New York, "a remarkable demonstration," says Martin Pernick, "of the power of medical technology to compensate for the health dangers of an urban environment."[20] When she refuses to return to the country town, where there is no place to be cured, the banker rouses the townspeople to hold a fund-raising rally, the sanitarium is built, and he marries its first patient, Edith. This was simple, obvious stuff, but it provided the hope of its title to victims convinced there was no cure.

When filmmakers of this period treated social themes, they tended to lose concern for those qualities we would now term cinematic. But there can be no

---

*Produced in cooperation with the National Association for the Study and Prevention of Tuberculosis. Other Edison TB films were *A Curable Disease* (1912) and *The Lone Game* (1915). Selig made *On the Trail of the Germ* (1912).

The townspeople hold a fund-raising rally for a sanatorium in Hope, *1912. (Killiam Shows)*

doubt that the message was conveyed to the nickelodeon audiences, even if the impression was only fleeting. And a few of the films were beautiful to look at, as well as being valuable records of their time.

Directed by J. Searle Dawley and written by Dorothy Shore, *Land Beyond the Sunset* (1912) was made in collaboration with the Children's Fresh Air Fund, which sponsored excursions to the country for city youngsters in the hope that regular exposure to fresh air would save them from tuberculosis. A newsboy is taken on such an outing and glimpses the world beyond the slums. The children are told a fairy story which inspires their desire to escape (not quite what the fund had in mind, one suspects). When the others return to the city, this little boy finds a boat and pushes it out, drifting to the Land Beyond the Sunset in a superb shot of setting sun and sparkling sea.

The independents also did their bit for the cause. In 1911, Republic made *A New Lease on Life* about the work of the Ray Brook Sanatorium in the Adirondacks, the world's largest center for the treatment of TB.

In 1914, under the reform administration of Mayor John Purroy Mitchel,[21] the New York Department of Health began a massive cleanup. Eight hundred exhibitors cooperated with the board by projecting slides in English, Yiddish, and Italian with messages like "Dirt Breeds Flies. Flies Carry Disease. Disease Means Doctors' Bills. Avoid Disease and Doctors' Bills by Cleaning Up." During the hot summer nights, free moving picture exhibitions were held in parks and on recreation piers, with four films, *The Story of a Consumptive, The Production and Handling of Milk, The City Beautiful,* and *The Little Cripple.* "The audience watched each performance with unbroken attention, enjoying every minute, while the intended lesson was subtly but surely brought home to them.''²² The board received an anonymous gift of a complete set of motion picture equipment. And a few exhibitors offered the use of their theatres free from ten to twelve every morning. On the Lower East Side, audiences packed vacant lots at night to watch the films being projected on the side walls of their tenements.²³

Motion picture shows were not confined to crowded urban areas. This was the age of the traveling showman. In Vermont, the state Board of Health followed his example and employed a covered wagon, drawn by horses, carrying projector and generating machine, to reach isolated communities. The anti-tuberculosis associations of Maryland and Wisconsin used motorcars for the same purpose, as did the state Board of Health of North Carolina. In the mountain region, the shows were such a novelty that some inhabitants traveled as far as twenty miles to see them, their first experience of moving pictures.²⁴

So widespread was the publicity won by such campaigns that the interest of other moving picture concerns was aroused. Films like *For Those Unborn* (1914), which featured Blanche Sweet as a consumptive who forces her lover to end their engagement "for those unborn," upset people by portraying the disease as hereditary.

The Great Truth (1916), a two-reeler designed to prove that TB was not hereditary but could only be communicated by contact, was made for the National

Frame enlargement from The Land Beyond the Sunset, *1912. The newsboy is given a glimpse of the world beyond the slums. (Killiam Shows)*

Original caption: "Nellie Linn (Bliss Milford), a tenement house girl, who is taking 'Concura' for her cold, advises her lover to try the great remedy." The Price of Human Lives, *1913, produced in cooperation with the National Association for the Study and Prevention of Tuberculosis, was an indictment of quack patent medicines. (Robert S. Birchard Collection)*

Association by Plimpton Epic Pictures from a scenario by Elise Williamson Phifer. It was designed for the nontheatrical circuit—YMCAs, churches, and schools.

The White Terror (1915), by contrast, was, as its title suggests, a thoroughly commercial film. Made for Universal by Stuart Paton, it attacked the patent medicine merchants. So important did the National Association consider it that their assistant secretary, Philip P. Jacobs, worked on the picture with script writer Raymond L. Schrock. Perhaps that was why the film contained fierce attacks on child labor, bad housing and factory conditions, crooked politicians, and the excesses of the idle rich. The story dealt with a clash between the press and a magnate. A rich young man, in love with the daughter of a patent medicine manufacturer, buys out a newspaper in order to print the truth—the rotten conditions in the mills and the lethal nature of the medicine. The manufacturer's faithful partner blows up the newspaper office, with himself in it.[25] The daughter catches tuberculosis, and her father offers her his compound of opium and arsenic. Fortunately, a doctor intervenes, and the film shows sanitariums, open-air schools, and the latest methods for curing consumption. The story ends happily, with the magnate transformed into a philanthropist, making a gift of a TB sanitarium to the city to celebrate his daughter's recovery.

That same year, 1915, a fascinating contemporary reaction to *The White Terror* appeared in *The New Republic,* written by the radical young journalist Randolph Bourne.[26] He longed to believe passionately in the movies, but his faith could not surmount preposterous exhibitions like *The White Terror.* He realized that the public did not take kindly to pure "education" and had to have the pill liberally coated with drama. And he admitted that the drama was exciting. But the climax of the film came with a hopeful quotation from Pasteur: "It is possible to banish from the earth all such parasitic germ diseases within a generation." When they saw this, Bourne and his social worker friends had burst into peals of laughter. No one else joined in, and Bourne realized that the audience was taking it all perfectly seriously. He wouldn't have minded if the film had been pure melodrama, but it lacked even that virtue: "Melodrama was not quackery, but this current rubbish is. It catches the social cant of the day."

According to Bourne, the acting was wooden, the actors merely rolling their eyes; he found, however, the children appealing, especially "as they ran to their mother, lying dead from too much devotion to 'Saco-Ozone, Nature's Only Cure for Consumption.' " He described elaborate effects, white lines of skeletons superimposed over the magnate's patent medicine advertisements, and serried rows of gravestones, each marking the effect of a bottle of his poison. None of this appealed to Bourne, yet: "I have to take *The White Terror* seriously because it is as scientific a record as a statistical graph. Like the popular novel, it marks the norm of what happy and hearty America is attending to."[27]

The odd thing about *The White Terror* is that it appears to have been plagiarized from Samuel Hopkins Adams's novel *The Clarion.* When this was made into a film the following year, the story line was strangely familiar: "Surtaine (Carlyle Blackwell) is the son of a man who has made millions through a doped patent medicine. Given a large sum of money by his father (Howard Hall), Surtaine buys *The Clarion,* a paper which has incessantly attacked the false business. Surtaine prints nothing but the truth . . . (he) discovers that his father's medicine is all wrong and he breaks with him. Pursuing his activities further, he discovers an epidemic of fatal disease in the poorer quarter. One of the property owners is his fiancée (Marion Bentler), but he goes on with the attack and opens her eyes. The quarter is quarantined, and deprived of work, the men break loose and attack the *Clarion* office, blowing it up. Surtaine's fiancée then instigates improvements in her filthy quarter, his father at last sees the light and closes his patent medicine establishment."[28]

Directed in five reels by James Durkin, *The Clarion* was criticized for subordinating its exposé of patent medicines to scenes of squalor and misery. But *Motion Picture News* admitted that the film was strikingly realistic. "The filth depicted in the poor quarter is real filth, the mob scenes are good and the newspaper office a fine replica."[29]

By 1916, the crusade against TB had grown to a nationwide movement, with 3,500 agencies working with the National Association, which now supervised a five-reel feature, *The Invisible Enemy* (E-K-O). This was another exposé of fake medicines and appalling living conditions, produced by Emma K. Oswald, who played a leading role, directed by William Stormer, and supervised by Miss Tate,

Cassidy, 1917, with Dick Rosson: "The last hours of a human derelict suffering from tubercular lungs." (Robert S. Birchard Collection)

secretary of the association. A tenement house owner, James Haggerty (William Parsons), is anxious to marry the daughter (Oswald) of his business associate, Governor Webster (Frederick Vroom). Through political influence, Haggerty is allowed to leave his tenements in an unsatisfactory and neglected state, and only a chance visit to one of the buildings by Webster's son, Jack (Jack Cummings), reveals the true conditions. Faith (Lucille Young), a young laundress, is overcome on the street from sheer exhaustion and is taken home by young Webster. Her mother has died from the use of patent medicines, and the unsanitary conditions in the house now cause the death of Faith's young sister. Jack takes pity on the girl and marries her. Dr. De La Roche (Leon Kent), a TB authority, befriends them, but Jack's father disowns him. Haggerty's neglect of his property is exposed in a newspaper, and Governor Webster is forced to support the improvement society and make the tenements habitable.[30]

Variety gave faint praise to Miss Oswald, whose own company produced the picture: "One must laud the intent in making the feature. But that is just about as far as one can go. *The Invisible Enemy* is about as poorly written, wretchedly produced and horribly cut a feature as has been shown in years. No house manager would be foolish enough to accept it even if it were free."[31] In fairness to Miss Oswald, it should also be recorded that *Motion Picture News* thought it well acted, had perfect photography, and was ably directed.[32]

Cassidy (1917), produced by Triangle, written by Larry Evans, and directed by

Arthur Rosson, was devoted to the last hours "of a human derelict suffering from tubercular lungs." Desperate to get back to New York, his beloved city, to die, he resorts to burglary. The man who catches him turns out to be the local district attorney (Frank Currier), who befriends him instead of jailing him. Cassidy returns the favor by rescuing the D.A.'s daughter (Pauline Curley) from a band of white slavers operating from the local saloon. He is shot in the process and later dies alone in the railroad yards.

Dick Rosson, Arthur's brother and a future director, played Cassidy; the trade press thought it a brilliant and moving performance.[33] *Variety* wondered whether it was in good taste to have a central character suffering from so dread a disease "even though an attempt is made to keep the film free of picturing a phase of consumption that may be revolting. . . . Justification may be found in the fact that it is life."[34]

Picture people were not afraid of tragedy at this experimental period; by the twenties, hardly anyone could expire of tuberculosis except Camille.

LOAN SHARKING

Usury may have been the proper word for it, but lending money at extortionate rates was commonly known as "loan sharking." The activity received unwelcome publicity in 1912–1913 thanks to campaigns by city governments and an investigation by the Russell Sage Foundation.[35] Thanks to their experience with the "white plague" films, Edison was asked to cooperate with the Remedial Loan Division of the foundation.[36] The result was a film written by Theodora Huntington called *The Usurer's Grip* (1912), directed by Bannister Merwin. It was about a young man, hopelessly in debt, who appeals to the foundation and triggers off a citywide drive against usurers by the district attorney.

Thanhouser made another film to exploit the Russell Sage investigation; *The Snare of Fate* (1913) by Lloyd Lonergan had James Cruze as a usurer whose wife is so appalled by his brutal methods that she leaves him, taking their child lest he grow up to emulate his father. Meanwhile, as the usurer calls on a family to supervise their eviction, he suffers a stroke which leaves him paralyzed and deprived of the power of speech. He is treated kindly by the poor family, but the evicters mistake him for a tenant and he is dumped into the street with the furniture.[37]

Louis Reeves Harrison called it "superior in motive to any release I have ever seen from that company—and if carried a little further it might easily have ranked among the masterpieces of the day."[38]

Some cities adopted a fixed rate of interest to foil the loan sharks, but their trade somehow flourished. The racket was again exposed in a Reliance three-reeler called *The Bawlerout* (1913), directed by Oscar Apfel. Written by Forrest Halsey, it featured Irving Cummings, Muriel Ostriche, and Edgena de Lespine as "the bawlerout," a girl employed as a collector.* The picture had a bank president secretly

---

*Those who fail in their payments are visited at their place of employment by the girl, who literally "bawls 'em out," causing untold embarrassment.

conducting a loan shark business,[39] and it caused loan companies intense irritation. When it reached Evansville, Indiana, the local lenders took large newspaper advertisements to denounce the picture. No one quite knew what they intended to accomplish, but they provided gratifying publicity for the film.[40]

The most graphic surviving depiction of the methods of the loan sharks was made before any of the others. D. W. Griffith's *The Usurer* (1910) had strong affiliations to his *A Corner in Wheat* of the previous year. Intercutting the poor of the slums with the rich usurer squandering the money he squeezes out of them, it begins with his collectors warning the debtors while the usurer (George Nichols) embarks on a riotous evening. "The Blood-distilled wine" introduces a banquet, identical to the one in *A Corner in Wheat*.

In the slums, a mother (Kate Bruce) weeps at her daughter's bedside. The collectors call upon her with their warning. Next morning, the mother visits the usurer to beg for time; he is brutally rude to her. The collectors move against the slum dwellers, taking furniture from the families. In a scene which still carries shock value, the collectors force the mother to take her invalid child from its bed, while they close it up and remove it. An impoverished widower kills himself.

The usurer enters his strongroom. The mother calls, collapses from exhaustion, and accidentally shuts the strongroom door. A cleaner fails to notice. The usurer is trapped, "At the Mercy of the Time Lock." The old mother is helped home by a courteous cop, while we see the usurer in agony from lack of oxygen, his money suddenly valueless. By the time he is discovered, it is too late.

The film is overacted, but its strong story carries it triumphantly through the melodrama. The usurer's strong-arm men, ashamed of what they have done to the mother, return her child's bed, and the policeman returns her money. The usurer is dismissed with the title: "We have brought nothing into this world. And it is certain that we can carry nothing out."

"ONE LAW FOR THE RICH . . ."

In the earliest days of projection, when films lasted barely a minute, showmen stumbled upon the art of editing for social comment. Following a film of the fashionable Easter Parade on Fifth Avenue with one on the squalid streets of the Lower East Side, they made, without realizing it, the most powerful impact on their audience.

Edwin S. Porter's *The Kleptomaniac* (1905), while not as skillful as his *The Great Train Robbery* (1903), took this technique one stage further. A wealthy woman is arrested for shoplifting. She is given the deference due to her class; she is permitted to drive to jail in her own carriage, and the magistrate politely offers her his chair. Naturally, she is acquitted.

A poor woman with two starving children steals a loaf of bread (shades of *Les Misérables*). The police manhandle her into a patrol wagon, and she is arraigned before the same magistrate, who sends her to jail. In an epilogue, the figure of justice, blindfolded, holds up scales; on one side is a loaf of bread, on the other a bag of money. The scales move in favor of money. Then the blindfold is removed to reveal one glittering eye, fixed on the gold.

Lois Wilson as Miss Lulu
Bett, *1921, in Zona Gale's
story directed by William
de Mille. The trials of a girl
expected to act as a drudge
for her family. (Museum
of Modern Art)*

One law for the rich and another for the poor—this was the bluntly delivered
message of D. W. Griffith's one-reeler *One is Business, the Other Crime* by George
Hennessy, made early in 1912. Impoverished newlyweds move into a shabby apartment, warned by the landlord's agent, a man built like a steam engine, of the
consequences if they fall behind on the rent.

A wealthy young politician, also recently married, lives in connubial bliss. A
visitor brings a windfall—an envelope containing $1,000 and the promise of an-
other $4,000 if the politician will give a contract to a certain transportation com-
pany. He is slightly disturbed, but only slightly, and squirrels the money into his
desk, unaware that the poor young man (Charles West) has spotted him through
the window. That night West returns and attempts to break into the desk. He has
his hands on the money when the politician's bride (Blanche Sweet) marches in,
flourishing a revolver. The burglar pleads for mercy, declaring that his past life
has been honorable.

When the wife reads the letter that accompanied the bribe, she is shocked.
And when her husband comes home and finds her with the burglar, she tells him,
"Let him go. He is no worse than you."

The young politician admits it, and the poor boy is released, to return to his
ailing wife. The politician writes to the transportation company promising his vote
only if their project will benefit the community. Eventually, the project gets under
way, and he comes to the poor boy's neighborhood in search of labor, hiring the
man whose criminal action brought him to his senses and prevented him from
committing a crime of his own.

The rich man's repentance and his joining forces with the poor man is typical of the approach of so many of these populist pictures. Most begin with a situation which could start a revolution, but they end like *Elsie Dinsmore*.

One historian, Leslie Wood, has suggested that to talk of Griffith as a social reformer is misleading. Certainly many of his films dealt with the hardships of the poor. But in this period, Wood points out, the sufferings of the poor were common currency in literature and on the stage. There was still a hangover from the late Victorian period of sentimentality. To go slumming was still a popular pastime. "Just as Charles Dickens used the sufferings of the poor as good 'copy' without, in private life, doing anything to ameliorate their position, so Griffith, prompted by his sentimentality, used them as a popular screen subject."[41]

Dickens did enough for the poor merely by illuminating their wretchedness in his books. He was the social reformer par excellence. So was Griffith. To suggest that he merely exploited these situations is like accusing Tolstoy of exploiting the peasants. In one sense it is true, but common sense tells us the accusation is absurd.

For Biograph, Griffith made *A Child of the Ghetto* (1910) about a Jewish girl, Ruth (Dorothy West), whose mother dies and leaves her to face life alone. As so often with these early films, the action quickly moves out into the streets, and we see what the Lower East Side, in this case Rivington Street, looked like eighty years ago. Ruth searches for employment and, frightened and insecure, is all too easily rebuffed. But she persists and is rewarded with a bundle of work from a shirt factory. She returns with the completed shirts at the very moment the owner's son is imploring his father for money. Rejected, he steals some bills from his father's wallet. The loss is discovered, and to avoid detection the boy contrives to have Ruth blamed by placing the notes in her bundle. Officer Quinn (George Nichols) is sent for, but Ruth escapes to her room. The policeman follows, and Ruth runs down the fire escape and vanishes into the teeming crowds of Rivington Street.

She travels to the country by trolley and is taken in by a farming family. Gradually she recovers from her fear, and the boy of the house (Henry B. Walthall) falls in love with her. But a couple of men come to the house on a fishing expedition, and one proves to be Officer Quinn. He recognizes the girl, but when he tries to arrest her she begs so pitifully for her freedom that he lets her go. The boy asks her to marry him, and Quinn looks back at them from his fishing pool with a fatherly smile.

The picture is gripping in its simple storytelling, despite the occasional crudeness. And it was obviously designed for local consumption—the Lower East Side audiences would love it. But as more and more of these tales of the oppressed emerged from the studios, observers wondered whether any good could result from their constant emphasis on social division. "Subjects of this character are calculated to arouse class prejudice unless treated in the most delicate manner."[42]

Nothing was more liable to arouse prejudice than the actions of the unscrupulous slum landlord. He appeared in many early films, none of which pointed out that among the biggest slum landlords were distinguished seats of learning such as Columbia University, which refused to improve the slum property it owned,[43] and religious institutions such as Trinity Church.

Griffith made pictures on this subject, too. In *The Lily of the Tenements* (1911),

Poster for The Virtue of Rags, *1912. (National Film Archive)*

an impoverished girl (Dorothy West) is faced with an offer from her landlord (George Nichols) to become his mistress and so relieve the family's poverty. She resists until the scheme is foiled by the landlord's son (Arthur Johnson).[44]

Edison managed to make a comedy out of the subject, with a split reel called *How the Landlord Collected His Rent* (1909). A landlord called Grimes decides that his agents are utterly incompetent and takes on their job himself. He is ejected by a washerwoman, struck dumb by a prize fighter, assumed to be insane by a tailor, and almost seduced by a pretty girl. On his last call he determines to make up for his failures, but he encounters poverty so severe that his kindly nature takes over. "We then suddenly forget that his experiences up to this time have been productive of laughter, and tears unconsciously spring to our eyes as we see him slip a roll of bills to one of the poor women's children and gently steal from the scene."[45]

Theodore Wharton had a bright idea when he wrote and directed *The Virtue of Rags* for Essanay in 1912. A kind-hearted rent collector (Bryant Washburn) cannot bring himself to force a poor widow (Helen Dunbar) to pay up, and he is fired. The landlord (Francis X. Bushman) drives to the tenement himself and turns the widow out. He then visits his club, where the members have been told of his callous act. They dose him with a drink laced with sleeping powder, dress him in old clothes, and leave him on a park bench. A patrolman wakes him in the customary manner and orders him to move on. Refused admittance to his own home, he ends up in the cells. His friends carry him back to the club. When he awakes, imagining it all a dream, he changes his attitude to the poor. He gives the widow back her room, installs new furniture, and gives her some money to make up for her years of misery.[46]

Edward Sloman made a three-reeler for Lubin called *The Law's Injustice* (1916), from a Julian Lamothe scenario. It featured Helen Wolcott as Nina, an Italian girl working in the factory of Ashton Morris (George Routh). Her wages are not high enough to provide for her sick brother, Tony (Milton Flynn), and soon she is in the clutches of a loan shark. Her debt grows steadily. In desperation she goes to see Morris. He tells her there is nothing he can do—it is the law. But he suggests an easier way out. Nina spurns his advances.

The landlord's rent collector gives her no receipt and forces her to pay twice, using money that should have gone for medicine for little Tony. She appeals to Morris, but again he tells her it is the law. Seeing that she is not ready to consent yet, he places temptation in her way by giving her work to do at home. When Tony is taken worse, Nina sells the materials entrusted to her to buy medicine, but the child dies. As Nina sits at home in grief, the police come for her. Morris gives her a last chance, thinking she will surely yield, but the girl surprises him with a fierce denunciation. She is sentenced to three years in prison.

When she comes out, she has her revenge by causing political disaster for Morris, when he runs for governor, and imprisonment for his son, who is managing his campaign. But she realizes that her vengeance is not worth the remorse she feels.[47]

Taking the example recently set by the mayor of Indianapolis, Ulysses Davis directed *The Merchant Mayor* for Champion in 1912. Apparently, the mayor was so incensed by the squalor and privation reported to him that he decided to challenge the city's merchants. He bought up potatoes and sold them at cost. The people were amazed—they never dreamed the profit margin was so high—and the angry merchants were forced to meet his price. He did the same with poultry and other foodstuffs, alleviating a crushing pressure on many of his poor constituents.[48]

Edison's *The Wedding Bell* (1911) was another in their admirable series of sociological films. If the surviving examples seem pedestrian, this one, to judge from the synopsis, was extraordinary, the kind of film that brings a period alive as nothing else can.

A lecturer to a Young Women's Progressive League declares that Culture Clubs are a drug on the market: "The causes of poverty exist in the very homes and families of those, who, from a safe distance, scan the horizon with field glasses to discover the mote in their neighbor's eye." Taken aback by this charge, the members organize a trip through the East Side tenement district.

Clara Gray, the president, wishes to see the neighborhood from a secure vantage point, and so she has herself driven slowly through the streets in her limousine. "In its wake came the rising generation, very friendly, very loquacious, very

SCENE FROM
THE WEDDING BELL
FILM No. 6766

The Fenelosi family have turned their home into a factory for producing artificial flowers —and the flowers prove to be agents for the transmission of typhoid in Edison's The Wedding Bell, *1911. (David Robinson)*

numerous.'' To the kids, the grand lady emerging from her car is as entertaining as a moving picture show. They flock about her, and when they find she intends to visit a family—the Fenelosi—they all offer themselves eagerly as guides. Inside the tenement, Clara is overcome by the smell.

The Fenelosi mother, though young, is worn from exhaustion. Her small children toil away making artificial flowers for which they earn forty-two cents a day. Mrs. Fenelosi earned more in a shirtwaist factory, but now she must stay home to care for her sick mother. In a bed in the corner lies an emaciated woman too weak to sit up. Clara declares they ought to have better air.

"Oh, it's awful, lady. It makes us all sick. Sometimes I get so dizzy I can't see the flowers." She points out the cause of the smell—the sink is blocked. The agent does nothing but demand rent and evict tenants if he fails to get it. How can the landlord make improvements, asks the agent, if his tenants do not pay? The Fenelosi family faces eviction, but if they could produce enough flowers to fill Clara's generous order of 300 for her wedding, they would be saved. The whole family—

including the invalid mother—work as hard as they can and deliver the flowers on time.

A doctor points out the risk Clara runs using articles made by people in ill health, and, sure enough, Clara collapses with typhoid fever just as the ceremony is over. The doctor finds the fatal germs well distributed throughout the wedding bell of artificial flowers. He visits the tenement and finds young Mrs. Fenelosi dying of the same disease. In a fury he forces the agent to tell him the name of the owner and confronts him in his elegant home. The landlord, John Gray, replies that if the illness was caused by those dirty Italian flowers, then he would use every influence he possesses to restrict immigration. The doctor tells him the germs were contracted in his own tenement and escorts him on a tour of his property. Gray is filled with shame when he sees the place. The sick woman is taken to the hospital, the entire tenantry transferred. Construction crews begin work on improvements.

And six months later, the Fenelosi live in a model tenement. With health restored to the young mother and to Clara, they meet again, and John Gray is not ashamed to be there, too. He changes his mind about immigration and is proud to declare himself an enthusiastic member of the Society for the Improvement of the Condition of the Poor.[49]

THE ESCAPE   D. W. Griffith's contribution to the debate was *The Escape* (1914), freely adapted from the play by Paul Armstrong; it is one of Griffith's lost films.

While Griffith was shooting the picture, Blanche Sweet, who was playing the lead, fell ill with scarlet fever. "It was a tragedy," said Sweet, "not the fact of my having scarlet fever, but it was at a very crucial time in Griffith's career. He had left the Biograph company and formed a company of his own. We didn't have too much money and it was all sunk in *The Escape*. We worked Christmas Eve [1913] to finish some scenes and I went home. I broke out in spots, and I was shipped to the only hospital that would take me in the State of New York. So it was really a catastrophe. It was all my fault and everybody hated me in the studio."[50]

Griffith switched to another film on the subject of marriage, *The Battle of the Sexes,* from *The Single Standard* by Dr. Daniel Carson Goodman, who had an important role to play in *The Escape* when it was finally completed.

Dr. Goodman was the author of *Hagar Revelly*, a book considered so shocking it all but caused the demise of Anthony Comstock, but which was cleared of obscenity charges by a court in 1914. Griffith brought in Dr. Goodman to work at the Mutual studio on Union Square and to provide a scientific prologue to *The Escape.* He gave it the best part of a reel. The lowest form of life, the amoeba, gradually develops until it turns into the human body. Goodman made the point that while animals are bred with the greatest care, humans seem to lack all concern for the health of their mates.[51]

Variety could not see the connection of the prologue with the rest of the film, and, although the moral of *The Escape* was "the mis-mating of humans," thought it "badly selected."[52]

The Escape, 1914. D. W. Griffith's drama of the New York slums. Dr. von Eiden (Owen Moore) treats Larry (Robert Harron) for venereal disease. He has seen how Larry's brutal father transforms him from a dreamer into a sadist who will happily wring a kitten's neck. The doctor advises May (Blanche Sweet) to leave. Eventually, Larry is given back his sanity, thanks to an operation, and May and the doctor are married. (George Eastman House)

The main story concerned a tenement family: father, son, and two daughters, May (Blanche Sweet) and Jennie (Mae Marsh). The son, Larry, has a venereal disease. May leaves home for a "house" uptown and becomes the mistress of a wealthy man. Jennie marries a gang leader, "Bull" McGee, played by Donald Crisp in a dress rehearsal for Battling Burrows in Griffith's *Broken Blossoms* (1919). When he injures his baby, and the infant dies in his wife's arms, the drunken McGee slaps her. "Perhaps he gained a little sympathy, despite his brutal actions toward his wife, but none remained when he turned away from his wife's deathbed with a laugh."[53]

Variety had no sympathy for the film, either. "The tale is hung upon one of those all-wrong families on the East Side (and elsewhere) where the all-wrongness runs from the father down to the dog, if there is one." It complained that no one in the family had any means of support except the older daughter, and she had to leave home to get it. And it was foolish for the Mutual to let Mr. Griffith waste his time on such a scenario; there was no material for him to work on in the first place. "And if there had been, previous 'vice' or 'misery' films would have ruined any chance for this one. . . . And why, oh why, push so much misery on the screen when no one is looking for it?"[54]

On the other hand, *Moving Picture World* thought the picture "unsurpassable," that each scene was a marvel in itself, the most thrilling being the police raid on a red-light dive.[55]

Griffith made several versions of each questionable scene; "the one chosen for final use will be above the criticism of the strictest censor."[56]

"Until our slums are peopled with eugenic husbands and wives," said the New York *Dramatic Mirror,* "we must expect such a pitiable waste of life as is found here."[57]

Surprisingly, this epic of poverty was shown in a legitimate theatre, where to sit in the orchestra seats cost a dollar.[58]

THE BRIDGE OF SIGHS   Jeff Davis, the "King of the Hoboes," was famous for founding the Hotel de Gink on the Lower East Side. This refuge served as a combined flophouse and employment agency and, since hoboes seldom stayed in one place for long, it was quickly duplicated. Members of the West Coast

The Street of Forgotten Men, *1925, exposed the "beggar racket" in New York City. Director Herbert Brenon (right) with technical adviser John D. Godfrey. (American Museum of the Moving Image)*

branch of the International Hoboes of America contributed part of their tiny earnings to found a Hotel de Gink in Seattle, which housed and fed some 2,000 men at a time.[59]

"De Gink's management stressed cleanliness and discipline," wrote Graham Adams, Jr. "It insisted that all lodgers retire by 10:30 p.m. When auditors scrutinized the books they found the hotel self-supporting without a penny misappropriated."[60]

In 1915, the Broadway Film Company produced a four-reeler called *The Bridge of Sighs,* which featured Jeff Davis. New York's Bridge of Sighs was the stone bridge linking the Criminal Court with the Tombs prison, the picture being more concerned with the underworld than with hoboes. Nevertheless, it contained footage of the hotel.

"One expecting this feature to be slipshod and loosely put together is in for a mild little surprise," said *Variety.* The film was expertly photographed and directed, and Jeff Davis made a good actor: "The picture shows Jeff in a heavy coat and carrying a branch of a tree as a walking cane and handy weapon. He encounters a bo just thrown from a train and about to pump the brakeman full of lead and, of course, Davis stops him and takes his gun away from him for the time. A sort of master crook and dope fiend hangs out in a saloon and tries to induce the young bo to help him pull off a job. Davis again interferes. Meanwhile the girl enters. She tries time and time again to get work but fails. An invalid mother, presumably in the last throes of consumption, has no medicine nor rent money and she's about to be evicted. The girl falls into the hands of the crook. . . ."[61] It was that kind of story, but filmed on location in the streets of New York, it probably had a realism and vigor that would make it of immense historical value had it survived.

Variety thought that like Davis himself, the film would probably do better on the road than in the metropolis.

KINDLING   Cecil B. DeMille, who could never have been accused of socialist leanings, nevertheless made a socialist tract in 1915 which protested violently against conditions in the slums. It was called *Kindling,* a reference to the children who "burned up like kindling." Adapted by DeMille himself from the book[62] and the 1911 play by Charles Kenyon, it was one of those pictures the trade press described as "extremely morbid," which DeMille favored before he turned to social comedy.

DeMille was never interested in the documentary approach, and rather than take his cameras to a real slum, as Reginald Barker did for *The Italian* (1915), he had art director Wilfred Buckland build one at the Lasky studio in Hollywood. Lit by Alvin Wyckoff with "Lasky lighting," one street set, moody, atmospheric, peopled by petty crooks and streetwalkers, resembles a scene from a German film of a decade later. A slum interior is so filthy, more so than anything one would see today, that one has to assume the existence of such places. In it, a baby dies, surrounded by flies, his bottle containing only gin. (The baby was borrowed from a poor Mexican family and clearly shows signs of malnutrition.)[63]

The death is reported to the poor immigrant couple upstairs, Maggie (Charlotte Walker) and "Honest" Heinie Schultz (Thomas Meighan). (They became Maggie and John Smith when the film reached England, since audiences would have thrown refuse at a picture of Germans.) Maggie is pregnant but conceals the fact from her husband, for he refuses to bring a child into such conditions.

"All the kids born down here don't die," declares Maggie, defiantly.

"The health officer says that half of them die," replies Heinie. "The rest grow up to be crooks."

There is a haunting sequence in which they tour the streets, seeing a child steal from a sleeping man, an old drunk forcing a child to drink from his "growler," and two kids fighting over garbage.

"I'd rather kill a child of mine the day it was born," says Heinie, "than send it up against a game like that."

Variety found this scene hard to stomach. "While adding naught to the artistic value, it is revolting and should be eliminated. It shows two children of the tenements fighting like groveling scavengers over the carrion contents of a can of refuse in front of one of the Hell's Kitchen hovels that are termed homes. This scene is so strong that it is enough to cause one to become ill in viewing it."[64]

Maggie determines to travel west, where it is safe to bring up a family and establish a homestead on the government plan. But how can she find the necessary $100? It so happens that her hovel is owned by a wealthy dowager, Mrs. Burke-Smith (Lillian Langdon), whose social worker niece (Florence Dagmar) invites her to inspect the property. Surveying the Schultzes' home, Mrs. Burke-Smith remarks, "I am glad to see you have no children. They are an economic error in the tenements."

She offers Maggie five dollars a week to come and sew for her. Heinie reacts to the idea with fury: "Do you know if we had a kid, she'd send it coughin' and spittin' to hell?" But Maggie works out a plan to rob her "benefactress" and to get her hands on that precious $100. The scheme goes wrong, and the crime is discovered. "It is the plea she makes here for her unborn child that saves the day for her," said *Variety*, "and for *Kindling* as a feature film." Maggie's tragic outburst is also well acted: "I lied—I fought—I stole to keep my baby from being born in this rathole of yours—and now he's going to be born in jail."

The dowager is shamed into dropping the charges and paying for the Schultzes' journey west.

Charlotte Walker has some excellent scenes in the film, but she tends to strike its one false note. Her ingratiating grin in the early part of the film is unacceptable, even by the all-embracing standards of 1915. The rest of the cast, especially Raymond Hatton as a crook, is first-rate.

Yet *Variety* felt Charlotte Walker rescued what might otherwise have been exceedingly ordinary and at times repulsive. The New York *Dramatic Mirror,* however, thought it a picture of exceptional worth, with masterful handling of suspense. It pointed out that the story had lost every vestige of its origin as a play, "proof that the picture is a good one."[65]

The relish with which DeMille handles the material suggests he must have identified with socialism, at least fleetingly. And so must the public. The picture cost $10,039.52 and grossed $66,036.42.[66]

It was this film that led to the celebrated comment by the Pennsylvania censors: the movies were patronized by children who thought babies were brought by the stork, "and it would be criminal to undeceive them."[67]

THE CUP OF LIFE   Perhaps the most astonishing spurt in the cinema's creative development took place between 1911 and 1915, the years which saw the birth of the feature film—the years, too, in which most of the social films were made.

In 1911 Griffith released *The Two Paths,* in which he traced the lives of two sisters from a slum background. The elder plods along at the sewing machine, marrying a humble carpenter and ending up poor but happy. The younger dreams of the gilded life, has a wild time, and comes to the usual sticky end: in a dramatically lit shot, she is shown to a room where a symbolic kimono lies on a table. Her death follows.

In 1915, Thomas Ince produced *The Cup of Life,* an identical story of two sisters by C. Gardner Sullivan. Directed by Raymond West, it exists at the Library of Congress only in a faint replica as a paper print. Yet it comes across today with infinitely more power than *The Two Paths;* ten years rather than four might have separated them

Ince gave *The Cup of Life* an impressive cast. Besides Bessie Barriscale and Enid Markey as the sisters, the picture boasts Louise Glaum and a group of young men soon to become directors: Charles Ray (a star and director), Jerome Storm, Howard Hickman,[68] Arthur Maude, and Frank Borzage.

The picture is shot in a relaxed yet accomplished way, using bold close-ups and atmospheric long shots, and the players, acting in the naturalistic style, come across as human beings. The plot has been repeated a thousand times in soap opera, but the realistic settings, and the feeling the director conveys that he is telling the story for the first time, set the film apart. The first section, set in the slums, is brilliant, and Sullivan's titles do not intrude so much as in the later reels, when his moralizing prose strives too hard for poetry.

The picture opens at a dry goods store. Helen Fiske (Barriscale) is shown in close-up, making-up in a hand mirror. Such vanity was frowned upon by a puritanical society, when full make-up was worn only by actresses and prostitutes. The film industry is here commenting on a habit it will soon transform into an obsession.

Outside the store, Helen and her sister Ruth (Markey) meet Dick Ralston (Borzage) "of the other world," after almost being run down by his automobile.

In a nearby saloon, John Ward (Ray) and his lowlife pal Sam Dugan (Storm) fortify themselves for the evening. John is a devoted admirer of Ruth's, and he is slightly worried about his pal's crude behavior. "Don't eat onions, you boob. I'm going to introduce you to a pretty girl tonight."

The evening is not a great success. John and Ruth are as close as ever, but Helen is repelled by Sam Dugan; he is not merely crude, he has *dirty fingernails!* When the party breaks up, Ruth shows off the ring John has given her. Helen takes her to the window and points to her future—babies sleeping out on the fire escape. "You are pretty now, but wait until you've ground out your very soul for a husband who couldn't appreciate and understand you if he wanted to. For babies that will grow up to hate you for bringing them into poverty."

Across the yard, a large family is crammed into one squalid room. "When your youth, health and beauty are gone and you are old and weary before your time with the horror of it all, what will you have to show in return? Ashes—ashes of regret!"

By now, both girls are crying. "What does it matter?" asks Ruth simply. "I love him, I love him." Slowly, she pulls the blind down.

The wedding separates the sisters, and Helen encourages Dick Ralston again. A few nights later, a neighbor tells a shocked Ruth that Helen failed to sleep in her flat, a censor-proof signal that Helen has become Ralston's mistress. We enter a new world of smart shops, fashionable restaurants, and, always in the wings, wealthy predators.

The sisters meet again. Ruth begs Helen to come and live with her and her husband, but Helen disappears once more.

Months, years elapse. Helen is fought over by society men, while Ruth gives birth to her first child—"the one priceless treasure granted by poverty" in Sullivan's startling title. Helen goes abroad with her paramour and "finds the wine of folly is not all sparkle" when he rejects her. (Her reaction is one of her few moments of overacting.) Other men are waiting, but they, too, react against "the pathetic striving of a woman old before her time to keep her feet amid the tottering world of her own creation."

She returns to America and tracks down Ruth and her family. Touched by their welcome, she is moved to learn they have named their little girl after her. She keeps a rendezvous with an old flame, but the pattern continues—she spots the old lecher eyeing the maid. When he has gone she stares at herself in the mirror, and there is an astonishing dissolve from "the painted husk" to the fresh-faced young girl. She lights a reefer and pours a drink, and in a poignant flashback we see Helen and Ruth merrily making breakfast in their tenement flat. Helen lies back wearily in her chair.

Photoplay said Bessie Barriscale's portrait of the feminine adventurer "has never been surpassed on the screen. . . . As the last fadeaway dims to nothingness you see her reaching for that needle which is the assassin of yesterday and the abortionist of tomorrow."[69]

Tragic endings were as much a hallmark of Ince pictures as happy endings elsewhere. But to avoid depressing the audience too much, the picture fades back in again to a curtain rising, revealing Bessie Barriscale, acknowledging the audience and looking her lovely young self again.

The New York *Dramatic Mirror* called it "a story that will live in the archives of screen production, one that will take its place among the classics of filmdom."[70]

The film must have influenced Cecil B. DeMille in his marital pictures. What one regrets is that Ince abandoned this compellingly realistic style when he moved from Inceville to Culver City to concentrate on society dramas. In 1921 he made another film called *The Cup of Life*—it was escapist entertainment, a sea story about smuggling in Shanghai.

THE FOOD GAMBLERS   The price of food escalated when America joined the war. The effects were particularly serious in the poor districts of the big cities, where food riots took place.

Films blamed the high price of food on speculators, and they argued for state control to do away with the profiteering of the middlemen. *The Public Be Damned* came out in July 1917, a five-reeler produced by the Public Rights Film Corporation, written and directed by Stanner E. V. Taylor, a veteran who had worked with Griffith. Featuring Charles Richman and Mary Fuller, it was described as "an intense and moving appeal for food control, which has been endorsed by Herbert C. Hoover, Food Administrator of the United States."[71] Hoover charged that food barons were cheating the public of millions of dollars every day.[72]

The plot dealt with the struggle of a farmer's public-spirited wife against the Food Trust, which is buying the farmers' produce at a ridiculously small price and selling to the dealers at an exorbitant rate that brings the poor still closer to starvation. Her fight for justice is handicapped by a vacillating husband and an old admirer, who is now head of the trust.

"It would be difficult to imagine a more timely and at the same time a more dramatic theme," said the New York *Dramatic Mirror*. "In this play it is forcibly presented with the power that comes from absolute sincerity. No attempt has been made to elaborate the facts; indeed the facts are so dramatic in themselves that no such elaboration has been necessary and the result is a genuine and masterly piece of work."[73]

Variety agreed and described a series of "absorbingly interesting episodes showing the machinations of the trust, their methods of stifling competition, their control of legislation, and the ultimate winning over of the food baron through his love for the woman and his realization of the iniquitous methods of doing business." *Variety* summed up its enthusiasm with the remark: "It certainly strikes home much more forcibly than the European war thousands of miles away across the water."[74]

The Food Gamblers (1917) by Robert Shirley was directed by Albert S. Parker[75] for Triangle. "It gives a graphic picture of the suffering in the slums where starvation has driven the inmates of the tenements to desperation."[76]

A romance was inevitably woven into the story. A young newspaperwoman (Elda Millar) writes an article exposing the methods of the chief (Wilfred Lucas) of the ring of food speculators who are oppressing the poor. Attempting first to bribe her, then to discredit her, he finds himself falling in love instead. Her influence induces him to reform and to help her dismantle the corporation.

"All the situations have their basis in fact, and were suggested by the words of Food Commissioner Dillon, who appears on the screen in person."[77]

Although the New York *Dramatic Mirror* was enthusiastic—"the types of characters in the slums were exceedingly realistic and brought home the message of the play with unaffected pathos"[78]—*Photoplay* thought it "mediocre," although it admitted, "It was propaganda stuff that strikes a cord of public sympathy."[79] And *Variety* said, "No matter what the shortcomings the film may have on its production end the theme sure makes a strong, vigorous appeal for the common people to rise up in their wrath and swat the high cost of living a body blow that will mean a sweeping reduction in food prices. In fact at the close of the film there is an earnest and direct entreaty for 'you' to get busy and write to your local congressman or senator . . ."[80]

When the film arrived in England, *The Bioscope* thought some of the scenes, such as the rioting of the angry mothers and their children, and the pitiful spectacle of the starved children in the hospital, "unforgettable." It called it "a production of great and undeniable merit."[81]

The wartime boom in the economy was followed by a recession in 1921 after which the gross national product—$70 billion in 1921—rose to $103 billion in 1929. Nevertheless, the Brookings Institution estimated that the poor made up three fifths of the nation.[82]

The film industry took little account of them. The 1920s was the age of the picture palace, and these theaters already had difficulty finding the right kind of film. How could social problem pictures be shown in one of those places, with symphony orchestra and scented air? Picture palaces were designed to take people out of their mundane lives, not push them back in.

The poor were shown less and less during the twenties. When Gloria Swanson remade the 1919 Clara Kimball Young success *Eyes of Youth* as *The Love of Sunya* in 1926 (both, incidentally, directed by Albert Parker), she cut the sequence which showed her as a prematurely aged schoolteacher, scrubbing the floor of her classroom. If slums appeared, they did so in a fleeting and often stylized manner. *Irene* (1926) was advertised thus: "She laughed her way out of a shanty and into a mansion."[83] When slum interiors were shown, they were as spacious as a ballroom. Foreigners got the impression that in America even the poor were rich. No wonder they had to close the gates to immigration.

Yet there were some surprising exceptions. The opening sequence of Monta Bell's *Man, Woman and Sin* (1927) shows a ragged boy picking lumps of coal from the railroad track. As a train passes, guards hurl rocks at him and a rich boy on the observation platform says, "Mother, look at that dirty little boy!"

"Don't point, dear," she replies.

Said future President Herbert Hoover in 1928: "We in America today are nearer the final triumph over poverty than ever before in the history of any land. . . . The slogan of progress is changing from the full dinner pail to the full garage. A chicken in every pot and two cars in every garage."[84]

THE BLOT Poverty was the lot not only of those at the bottom, but of many skilled professionals. This was vividly portrayed in Lois Weber's *The Blot* (1921), a film animated by her sense of outrage on behalf of dedicated but underpaid clergymen and educators. Inadvertently, the exposure of genteel poverty impinges on a wider political issue, and *The Blot* begins to look rather like a socialist's view of America. The wealthy son of a college trustee is shown at a banquet, consuming expensive food and squirming with embarrassment as he thinks of the girl he loves all but starving. But at heart, the film is anything but radical.

The picture opens in a college hall, where Professor Griggs (Philip Hubbard) is faced by bored and obstreperous students. One of them, wealthy Phil West (Louis Calhern), is far more interested in the Professor's daughter Amelia (Claire Windsor), who works in the town library. He haunts the place in the hope of speaking to her. She, cool and distant, is merely puzzled by his interest in literature.

Amelia's mother (Margaret McWade), well born and ill equipped for poverty, resents the prosperity of her next-door neighbors. Hans Olsen, foreign-born, makes the kind of shoes "that ruin the feet of the wealthy women who wear them." Mrs. Griggs's shoes are worn, her carpets threadbare.

When Amelia falls ill, the doctor instructs her mother to prepare the proper food—preferably chicken. But how can she afford it? The food store refuses credit. Driven to the limit, she looks across at the Olsens' kitchen and sees several chickens being prepared. Overcome by the sight, she dashes over and grabs one. A second later, aware of what she has done, she replaces it. But Amelia fails to see this part of the incident. She has recoiled in horror from her bedroom window, convinced only that her mother is a thief.

When a chicken arrives as a gift from Phil, Amelia cannot eat it—she thinks it is stolen property. Ill as she is, she gets up next morning and goes to see the Olsens and offers to pay. Mrs. Olsen is overcome, but says nothing was taken. Amelia has to be carried home, where she and her mother embrace in a silent flood of emotion.

"The blot on our present civilization— that we engage the finest mental talent in the country for less than we pay the common laborer."

Frame enlargements from The Blot, *1921: The mother (Margaret McWade).*

The wealthy young man, Phil West (Louis Calhern).

The daughter, Amelia (Claire Windsor). (Gerald McKee)

Even if one did not know that *The Blot* was the work of a woman, one would be intrigued by the source of such feminine touches as a chair leg catching in a worn carpet, a garbage can being used as a symbol of reconciliation.

Weber's technique is reminiscent of William de Mille's, with its quietness, its use of detail, and its emphasis on naturalism. Weber used the same method of direction, too, filming in continuity.

Her naturalism did not appeal to many audiences or reviewers. *Photoplay* dismissed the message of the film: *"The Blot—or Do Schoolteachers Eat?* Apparently not, according to Lois Weber, who here pictures a starving professor, his wife and daughter, in a series of pathetic episodes. Luckily the rich young college lad, Louis Calhern, appears just in time with roast chicken and a wedding ring. Typical Weber exaggeration and rather tiresome. Censor proof."[85]

The film was almost aggressively noncommercial, and yet *Variety* predicted a profitable future for it, saying it "should clean up a tidy sum of money. It touches the heart. It is sensibly and intelligently put together, points a worthwhile moral without offensive preaching and is on a live topic . . . A good market bet."[86] Alas, it was a commercial failure. Distributed by the F. B. Warren Corporation, it vanished after its run and was rediscovered by the American Film Institute in 1975. Bob Gitt reconstituted it from an incomplete negative and an incomplete print.

Lois Weber, who undoubtedly experienced exactly the kind of genteel poverty she so vividly depicts, took a full-page advertisement in the 1921 *Wid's Year Book* to proclaim: "I am proud of the two productions *The Blot* and *What Do Men Want?* They were made as I wanted to make them, not 'Under Orders.' " She considered them better than most of her past successes.

The Blot is the ideal film to show to those who did not live through them what the twenties were like in small-town America. Thanks to a lighting technique invented by her old cameraman Dal Clawson, Weber was able to shoot in real houses, so for the first time one can see what living spaces were really like, not what art directors imposed on them—and what people really wore, not what fashion designers invented for them. The atmosphere is enhanced by some superb photography by Philip du Bois and Gordon Jennings; they are not afraid to let a face go dark on one side, or to show gloomy interiors as ill lit as they should be. One objects to the shot of Phil and Amelia through the windshield of the car as they drive in a storm (where is the rain?), but elsewhere the décor is absolutely authentic. (The college scenes were shot at the University of California campus on Vermont Avenue, Los Angeles.)[87]

The casting is very good, and many of the small parts—the butcher, a tailor— seem to have been cast from nonprofessionals. The professor, with his pince-nez and resigned patience, is rather a stereotyped character. The mother also plays her anguish on one level. But Louis Calhern[88] is outstanding; with his easy manner, his expensive sweaters and gleaming car, he is straight out of Scott Fitzgerald. Claire Windsor, whose real name was Ola or Viola Cronk, carries the difficult role of a frail and haughty spinster with elegant ease, but while she is neat enough for the part, with her delicate feet and hands arousing feelings of protectiveness from the audience, her face is just *too* beautiful. And it is odd, for a woman's film, how little characterization she is given. Her performance is cool and aloof until the emotional scenes at the end, which are poignant.

The film is about pride, and one can sense Lois Weber's pride for her class in one of her titles: "Here she was, the real thing—a gentlewoman, unbeatable!"[89]

THE CROWD   Lines of men struggle toward the employment office of a large factory. A young derelict fights his way forward. "I've got to get a job," he says. "I've got a wife and kids." The men elbow him away pitilessly: "So have lots of us."

The Crowd (1928) came out just before the advent of talkies; it is one of the most eloquent of all silent pictures. It came out, too, just before the Depression, and yet it might have been made in the thick of it so poignant is its picture of unemployment.

Johnny Sims (James Murray) is the hero of the film (and he is no hero at all). He grows up with faith in the American dream; he is going to be somebody big— all he needs is the opportunity. But life settles into its usual rut; he marries, has two children, gets an eight-dollar raise. He writes advertising slogans in his spare time. One wins a prize, but this leads to tragedy: his small daughter is hit by a truck as she runs to get her presents. John goes to pieces; he loses job after job and considers suicide, but fails even in that. His wife decides to leave him, but when he gets a meager job she decides not to go—not just yet. They celebrate at a vaudeville show and forget their troubles by laughing with the crowd.

That's all it is; the film is almost plotless. And yet each incident is so brilliantly directed and acted that the film blazes to life. John and his wife, Mary (Eleanor Boardman, Vidor's wife at the time), are getting up one morning in their poky little flat overlooking the elevated railway. The lavatory cistern jams. "Why didn't you tell me this was busted?" asks John. The bathroom door has always been defective, but he adds this to his catalogue of her crimes: "You've got this on the blink, too." The folding bed won't fit into its cupboard. "Will you please have that darn thing fixed today?" At breakfast, he stares at her, witheringly, "Your hair looks like Kelcy's cat." She adjusts it and tries to continue eating, but his remarks wear her down and she leaves the table: "I'm getting sick and tired of you always criticizing me."

"Forget it, Mary, I'll overlook your faults."

His heavy humor merely inflames her, and he becomes more annoyed himself. He reaches for a milk bottle. As he opens it the milk squirts him in the face. He turns on her again: "Why can't you tell me when things are full?"

Most directors would be satisfied to leave the scene there, but where most directors stop, the director of this film, King Vidor, is just beginning. Mary has taken all she can from John and declares that she's leaving. John seems glad. "Take it from me," he says, as he storms out. "Marriage isn't a word—it's a sentence." The door slams. Mary stares after him, full of self-pity and remorse. Vidor holds the shot of her without interruption, and it is one of the most brilliant examples of pure film acting in all cinema. Mary begins to cry; what *is* she going to do? Where will she go? As if for security, she clasps her arms across her stomach, and

Clockwise from above: A scene eliminated from The Crowd: *a holdup in a cigar store. James Murray as Johnny Sims (left). (National Film Archive). One of the scrapped endings of* The Crowd: *Johnny and Mary Sims in old age. (National Film Archive). Frame enlargement from* The Crowd, *1928. The insurance office where Johnny becomes "one of the crowd." (Kobal Collection). "Your hair looks like Kelcy's cat." Eleanor Boardman and James Murray.*

this gesture reminds her of something terribly important. We can see the realization flash across her face; she forgot to tell him! After an agonizing delay, she runs to the window and calls out. John, seen from above, stands in the street, unwilling to return, but she gently persuades him. The only title in the scene occurs when John runs upstairs and stands before her: "I didn't get a chance to tell you." She pulls him closer and does up one of his coat buttons. We can lip-read her saying she is pregnant, but there is no title. John's mood changes; he slowly embraces her, then suddenly becomes ridiculously considerate, sitting her down, putting the milk in her coffee, carefully wiping the plates. "From now on, I'm going to treat you differently, dearest." He goes to the door, and in contrast to the last time he left, he keeps popping back, grinning and miming the forthcoming event by cradling his hat.

"MGM was pretty liberal about letting me do the film," said Vidor. But it was only because of his amazing commercial success—his *The Big Parade* was the company's highest-grossing picture—that the company looked indulgently on the idea. Said the head of production, Irving Thalberg, "I can certainly afford a few experimental projects. It will do something for the studio, it will do something for the whole industry."

The idea had developed at a meeting with Thalberg, who had remarked that it was going to be hard for Vidor to top *The Big Parade.* Vidor said there must be other interesting environments which are dramatic for the average man.

"Such as what?"

Vidor had no idea worked out, but something sprang into his head.

"Well, I suppose the average fellow walks through life and sees quite a lot of drama taking place around him. Objectively, life is like a battle, isn't it?"

Thalberg was taken with the thought and asked for a title. "Perhaps *One of the Mob.*"

Thalberg liked it and gave instructions for Vidor to begin. With the writer of *The Big Parade,* Harry Behn, Vidor made a list of important things that happen to the average man: birth, school, job, girl, marriage, baby . . .

Three days later, they met in Thalberg's office. He was delighted with the story outline but concerned about the title. "Mob" sounded too much like a capital-labor conflict.

"Then how about *One of the Crowd?*"

"*The Crowd,*" said Thalberg. "That's it. *The Crowd.*"[90]

Vidor felt that a famous name in the lead would make it impossible for the audience to believe in an ordinary man losing his identity in the crowd. The story could carry conviction only with an unknown actor. He began to look around him—in drugstores, on streetcars. . . . One day, as he was chatting with a friend on the lot, a group of extras passed by and one of them stopped. "He jumped between us, did a little dance step which called my attention to him, and I knew he was the fellow I'd been looking for."[91]

Vidor followed him out of the studio and chased him on to a bus on Washington Boulevard. He asked him to come to the studio the next day, but the man failed to show up. By now, Vidor had forgotten the fellow's name; he had to go to the casting office and hunt through the list until he recognized it: James Murray. Murray was offered a day's pay to show up at Vidor's office, and this time he came. But he was offhand and refused to do a test unless he was paid for it. "I didn't believe you back there," he said. "I thought it was a gag or something."

Murray was twenty-six; he had been a dishwasher, art student, florist, model, clerk, and even a hobo. Vidor and Thalberg recognized in him one of the best natural actors they had ever had the good luck to encounter. En route to New York to shoot locations, Murray pointed out railroad stations along the way; he had washed dishes at one, shoveled coal at another.

"In *The Crowd*," said Murray, "we had a story that tells of life as I know it. The things that I was asked to do were things that I knew were real. There were many, I don't know *how* many scenes in it that left me absolutely washed out and trembling at their finish. But without that preliminary batting around looking for something to hang on to I couldn't have tackled it at all. I just couldn't have known what it was all about."[92]

Murray gave such an outstanding performance that he was cast by MGM in other pictures. Unhappily, like the character he played in *The Crowd*, he was already hooked on alcohol.

"I didn't know about this problem," said Vidor. "He kept it pretty well covered. I began to hear all these stories as soon as *The Crowd* was over. But I cast him in *Show People* and we waited and looked. We couldn't find him. He didn't show up. Do you know where we found him? Actually in a gutter. Where was the gutter? Right on the MGM lot. I found him all by myself. We waited three days and then we gave up and used Billy Haines."[93]

In a sense, *The Crowd* was even more ambitious than Vidor's war epic *The Big Parade*, for, unlike that picture, it had no more dramatic conflict than one can find in ordinary life. It was therefore a much more difficult kind of picture to make.

"*The Big Parade* had a lot of success with the details of soldiers fighting during the war," said Vidor, "and with this picture I was thinking about details of American life. The leaky toilet, the kids going to the bathroom on the beach. That was the mood of the picture; the challenge was to see if you could observe it enough."[94]

The style is naturalistic, but Vidor was fascinated by the German experiments and he (and his art director A. Arnold Gillespie) often stepped boldly into the realm of expressionism. They were making a realistic picture, but they were not afraid to heighten the mood. When the boy's father dies, the staircase to the bedroom is remarkably long and indistinct, making the child seem smaller and more lonely as he approaches the burden of responsibility.

The trigger for the scene came from Vidor's own childhood: "I went back to my home town," he said, "and went to the house where I was born, went up the stairs and looked down—and there was the stairway, the door and the automobile out in front at the curb. The whole thing was right there."[95]

However impressed Vidor may have been by the Germans, he strove above all for simplicity. The astonishing moments of technical virtuosity do not disturb the flow of the story. An audience of 1928 would hardly have noticed them as anything unusual; audiences of today are only surprised because they expect so little from a silent film. As Charles Silver has written, "It has become a commonplace that the film contains some of the most memorable and accomplished sequences in all cinema. *The Crowd* has been used as a textbook for filmmakers from Hollywood to Moscow. Yet its uniqueness is attributable more to its simple naturalism and pure humanism than to its accumulation of brilliant moments."[96]

There can have been no other film which combines the extreme artifice of the German film—involving scale models of skyscrapers and overhead wire trolleys for smooth tracking shots—with shots snatched in the streets of New York. For these, Vidor and cameraman Henry Sharp designed a rubber-tire pushcart, filled with packing cases. Inside was the camera.

"We cut a hole in the side of one of the boxes for the lens and shot real people along the street. It looked as if there were four packing cases piled on top of the cart, but we were able to fit the cameraman and his camera in there. There are some other shots we were able to get on location with a delivery truck. We used all sorts of signals and chalk marks to get these candid shots. We worked out a system of rehearsing without anyone knowing it. Between the shots I'd lean against the truck and talk to the cameraman inside. We were also beginning to work without a lot of make-up, so the actors weren't that noticeable."[97]

Curiously, far more of these scenes were shot than were used. Several exteriors were shot on the studio back lot. For the atmosphere of an industrial town, Vidor used the Los Angeles railroad yards, where he shot the scene on the railroad bridge so reminiscent of de Sica's *The Bicycle Thief*. ("I went to Italy last year," Vidor told Nancy Dowd in 1970, "and de Sica threw his arms around me and said, 'Oh, *The Crowd, The Crowd*! That was what inspired me for *Bicycle Thief*.' ")[98]

What distinguishes *The Crowd* from the majority of dramatic films of the time is the lack of melodrama. "You know," said Vidor, "villains are few and far between. The drama of life is not dependent on villains. Divorce, tragedy, illness are not dependent on villains. I never had any villains in my life and they're something I wouldn't know too much about. If you have villains, you have melodrama. If you have melodrama, you don't believe it too much."[99]

In most other films, the beautifully directed scene of John Sims returning home drunk on Christmas Eve would have developed into a full-scale fight. But John's wife simply says of her family, whose presence sparked the problem, "They don't understand you, but that doesn't matter."

"Do you understand me?" asks John.

She nods.

"I pulled that right out of my own experience with Eleanor," said Vidor. "I think she said that to me once, and I wanted to communicate it or preserve it."[100]

Yet Eleanor Boardman admitted she did not care about ordinary people: "I thought when you went into the movies that you wore curls and beautiful hats and gorgeous clothes. Suddenly I was cast in this downtrodden Mary-Doe-meets-John-Doe type of story—a boy and girl going through life with no education, no money, no knowledge of what they were doing. It was a job I had to do. I didn't like to be so drab and unattractive. My hair was hanging down, there was no make-up . . . I didn't object to it. I mean inwardly I did, but I made no objection about it. I had confidence in Vidor. He knew what he was doing."[101]

Vidor had to bear the Hays Office constantly in mind and have Mary Sims indicate she was pregnant without actually saying so. "I don't remember where I first saw an actress touch her stomach in relation to pregnancy," said Vidor. "It might have been on the New York stage. I remember thinking that one day I would use that gesture in a film. It was a way of caressing the womb."[102]

The Crowd was a confusing picture for Boardman: "First of all, I was supposed to be pregnant and I wasn't. King took me to the wardrobe department and had all my clothes padded, which I hated, thinking I was going to be glamorous in the movie. But it had to be done if this was going to be realism with a capital R.

"Then, when I really was pregnant, I wasn't supposed to be in the story. So they shot me behind a piano to hide my shape. I was pregnant when we did the scene at Coney Island" (actually shot at Ocean Park) "and I had to come down the shoot-the-chute, and then we had to get on a thing where we were flung out by centrifugal force—I was frightened to death for my child.

"The scene where I tell him I'm pregnant? It was the first thing in the morning at nine o'clock, and it was the most dramatic thing that I had ever done. You don't feel particularly dramatic at nine in the morning. You have to warm up to things like that. We set it up, and we played it through. 'We'll take it once again'—when I really got into it and that was it. I was lucky, and I was so happy it was over with."[103]

However sympathetic MGM may have been toward the picture (Louis B. Mayer hated it), the front office did not like the ironic and ambiguous ending showing the family at a vaudeville show, the camera pulling back until they are swallowed up once more by the crowd. The company had had bad experiences with realistic or tragic endings. The exhibitors, outside the first-run houses, often refused to accept them, and they had to be reshot. Poor King Vidor! Having produced what he felt convinced was his masterpiece, he was ordered to shoot a scene totally against the spirit of the picture. It was set in a mansion and showed John and Mary kneeling beside a glittering Christmas tree, exulting in the success that John's advertising slogans had brought them. And it ended with Mary's title, "Honest, Johnny, way down deep in my heart, I never lost faith in you for a minute."

The trade magazine *The Film Spectator* protested this banality. "We actually made seven endings and tried them out," said Vidor. "Seven different previews—and I finally came up with the ending where he's lost again in the crowd. But they still didn't want to buy that semi-cynical ending and they made me send the picture out with a happy ending also. The exhibitor had the right to choose one or the other. But I never heard of it being shown—it was so false, so ridiculous that I'm sure no exhibitor with an ounce of intelligence would ever run it. But it was there, if he thought the other was too downbeat."[104] Some critical reaction was excellent. "No picture is perfect," said *Photoplay*, "but this comes as near to reproducing reality as anything you have ever witnessed."[105] *Variety*, however, whose enthusiasm for social films was less now than it had been in their heyday, called *The Crowd* "a drab, actionless story of ungodly length and apparently telling nothing."[106]

Although the film has gained a reputation as a financial failure, it actually made a profit of $69,000.[107]

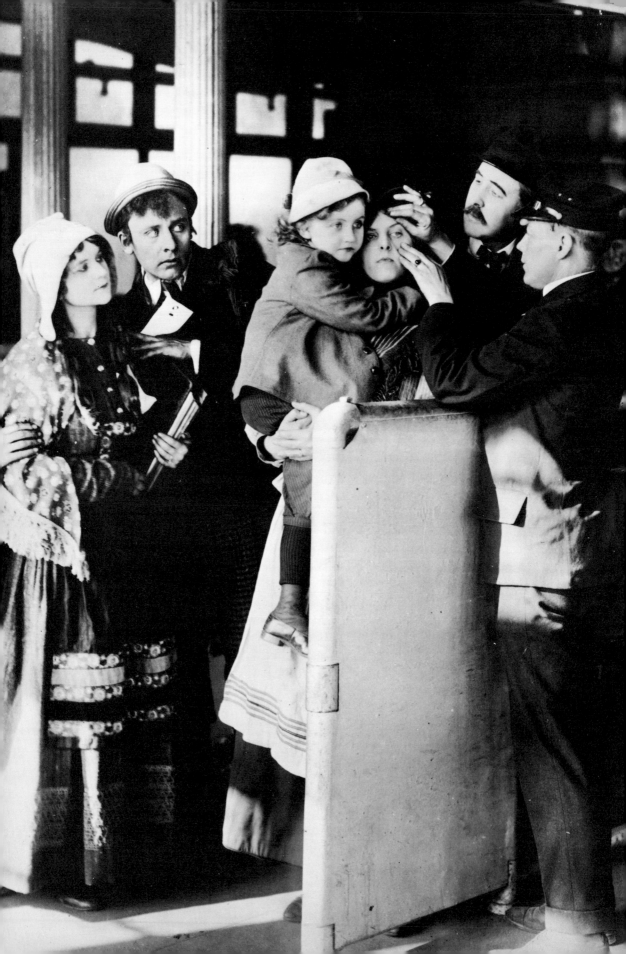

Chapter Ten

THE
FOREIGNERS

*Immigration officials at Ellis Island
inspect a mother's eyes—a scene from
a U.S. Government film,* The
Immigrant, *directed by Edwin L.
Hollywood and filmed at the
Examination Hall, Ellis Island.
(Museum of Modern Art)*

THE LARGEST human migration in recorded history they called it—with 35 million people sailing to the United States between 1815 and 1920.[1]

Since emigration was often an escape from overcrowding, it was curious how the newcomers clustered together in the big cities of the North. They wanted to stay where people spoke a familiar language; it was difficult to survive in rural areas without a knowledge of English. And the excitement and novelty of city life was as attractive to immigrants as it was to natives.[2] They were not all poor; the destitute could not afford the passage, and American poor laws kept them at bay. Yet immigrants were regarded as a threat; it was well known that they would work for low wages, thus undermining what American workers had struggled to achieve. They had brought cholera to the United States in the nineteenth century.[3] So their welcome was anything but cordial. They were treated with coldness and blamed for everything from the existence of slums to the rising crime rate.

A tract written in 1914 by the prominent sociologist Edward A. Ross held that immigration was good for the rich employers but disastrous for the American worker. Immigrants were dirty and drunken, illiterate and often mentally unbalanced; they fostered crime and bad morals; they were the ones who read the yellow press, who wrecked the educational system with parochial schools, who caused the proliferation of cities, who, by selling their votes for protection and favors, aided the grip of the bosses on city politics. They threatened to overwhelm "American blood."[4]

Several attempts were made at restricting immigration, but a constant supply of cheap labor was what an expanding country depended upon. Apart from the Oriental Exclusion Acts, not until 1907 was an act passed to exclude "undesirables," for America was happy to receive every year an army of able-bodied laborers as a free gift from the nations of Europe.[5]

Few immigrants realized, once they had endured the appalling voyage, what awaited them at the end of it. Ellis Island, the receiving station from 1892 on, was where the undesirables were weeded out. Thousands were sent back, either because they were too poor, a potential burden to the community; because they had an infectious disease such as trachoma; or because they were suspected of anarchist tendencies.

Ellis Island had a reputation for brutality and corruption which the New York press sustained with frequent exposés. In 1900, it was poorly administered, the officials resorting to "roughness, cursing, intimidation and a mild form of blackmail."[6] But officials were not the only guilty parties; the concessionaires were pirates, the lawyers crooks, and even the railroad companies would send immigrants to their destination along the most circuitous route. From the moment he arrived on American soil, the immigrant became aware of the power of the dollar.

Winifred Greenwood in A Citizen in the Making, *1912. (Academy of Motion Picture Arts and Sciences)*

Ellis Island was hell on earth, according to a German-language daily in New York, "where only the knout was lacking to make it a Czarist prison camp."[7] William Randolph Hearst, whose newspapers posed as the champions of the foreign-born (except Orientals!) called it "the Isle of Tears" and persuaded Governor William Sulzer to take up the crusade.[8]

Frederic C. Howe, the celebrated municipal reformer, even during his sojourn at the National Board of Censorship, did much to humanize Ellis Island in his role as commissioner. It was, he said, "a storehouse of sob stories for the press; deportation, dismembered families, unnecessary cruelties made it one of the tragic places of the world."[9] With enthusiasm, he wrought miracles. And in the winter of 1914–1915, a time of serious unemployment, he opened up the island to the homeless and unemployed.[10]

A number of factual films were made about Ellis Island, such as *Gateway to America* (1912), produced by Champion, probably in the course of filming immigrant scenes for its Russian pictures. It included shots of the medical staff, the boarding houses, and hospital, together with scenes of immigrant types.[11]

But the most fascinating films about immigrants came from the studios, most of which were situated in New York or New Jersey. It was no great distance to the Battery, where the Ellis Island ferries disembarked, and these films often contained footage of real immigrants.

Alice Guy Blaché, an immigrant herself, albeit a prosperous one, had been a director in France. She ran the Solax studios at Fort Lee, New Jersey. One of the films turned out there, *Making an American Citizen* (1912), was almost certainly directed by her (though there is no proof of this), for it was based on an incident which occurred at her own arrival. She watched a policeman stop a couple of immigrants, remove the baggage from the arms of the woman, and hand it over to the husband—"a lesson in American courtesy toward women,"[12] as she described it. The film elaborated that moment.

A husband (Lee Beggs) and wife (Blanche Cornwall) who "belong to the most ignorant and lowest classes of peasantry"[13] emigrate to the United States. On leaving the Ellis Island ferry, the husband loads a huge bundle on the back of his wife, attracting a crowd. Some laugh, others are indignant. A tall American pushes his way through the crowd, relieves the woman of her burden, puts the bundle on his own back, and orders them to march on.

"This is the husband's first lesson in Americanism. Other lessons follow . . . until after he has been arrested and sent to jail for beating his wife, he becomes thoroughly convinced that old world methods will not do in this strange new world. A transformation is also worked in the character of the wife. Her animal-like patience and servile docility gradually give place to a spirit of independence, until at last she vigorously resents the brutality of her husband and asserts her rights as an American woman. The scenario closes with husband and wife working harmoniously together."[14]

The immigrants' nightmare was to arrive in America and find no one to meet them. (This happened frequently.) In *Adrift in a Great City,* a 1914 Thanhouser film, an immigrant has saved enough to bring over his wife and daughter and arranges to meet them at the pier. On the way, he is injured in an accident and taken unconscious to the hospital. The women are stranded. In reality, they would have been deported, or they might have been escorted to an Immigrant Aid Society. But here, the women are simply cast adrift and reduced to begging in the street. It was an unlikely tale, enlivened by coincidences of Dickensian proportions, but reaching a happy conclusion.[15]

Not all the films thought the New World's methods were the best. *A Leech of Industry,* a 1914 three-reel Pathé drama directed by Oscar Apfel, was a study of Russian immigrants trying to earn a living in America. The parents retain the habits of their homeland, but the children rapidly become more American than Russian, picking up fast habits and wild ways.[16] Films like these seemed to have an underlying motive; when shown abroad, they would have discouraged potential immigrants. Was that the idea?

Such discouragement would have been welcomed by Sweden's National Society Against Emigration, for emigration from that country had reached a peak in 1909–1910 due to grim economic conditions. Swedish immigrants were looked upon with favor by the Americans, who far preferred them to those from Southern or Middle Europe, and it was felt that films should be made to discourage people from going.

Emigranten (1910), made by the AB Svenska Biografteatern in Kristianstad, was a one-reeler with amateur players designed to show how awful things were in America, and how farming folk should not abandon their responsibilities. The

Emigranten, 1910. At the travel agent's, the emigrants purchase tickets to America. (Lars Lindstrom)

Emigranten. The film emigrants travel with these real emigrants. (Lars Lindstrom)

Swedish idea of a low-class saloon in New York. Amuletten, *1910, was another film made to discourage emigration to the United States. (Lars Lindstrom)*

central characters are not young people but a middle-aged farmer and his wife. Working for them is an old couple and their son.[17] The farmer sees an advertisement for sailings to America. With startling speed he decides to go. "What will become of us?" ask his workers. No time to bother with that; the farmer and his wife set off on the long journey to Gothenburg to buy their tickets and board the ship.

The departure of the ship is well photographed, and particularly poignant, as the people lining the deck and waving handkerchiefs are real emigrants. It is raining and the people on the dock have put up umbrellas, and they wave their handkerchiefs beneath them. There are excellent shots of the passengers on board, none of whom look poor.

The passengers disembark at "New York." Lars Lindstrom, the former curator of the Kristianstad Film Museum, has tracked down the fact that the steamer in the film was the S.S. *Ariosto,* sailing on April 22, 1910, not to New York but to Hull. This was the usual route from Sweden; emigrants took the train from Hull to Liverpool and a transatlantic ship from there. But the filmmakers pretend that Hull is New York. A wall plastered with advertisements symbolizes the city. CITY V MEXBORO looked American to a Swedish eye, even if it did refer to Midland

League football. The man goes into a "farm agent's office" and puts down a payment on a farm. The scene shifts to the Swedish idea of wide-open spaces—a local park where rocks symbolize barren land. The farmer drops his ax in disgust when he surveys the terrain. He returns to his cabin to find his wife in anguish. He agrees the place is impossible, and they both pack up and return home, where their farm hands are delighted and give them a celebration.

Ironically, the film was written, directed, and photographed by Robert Olsson, eventually to emigrate to the United States himself.

Another film made by the same company, called *Amuletten* (1910), did not even go so far afield as Hull to re-create America. The picture was shot entirely in the Kristianstad studio and the streets of Stockholm. It was a reflection of dime novels and sensational American films. We see a disreputable saloon, peopled by prostitutes and thieves, into which a young man is inveigled. He is doped, robbed, and dumped unceremoniously into an alley. The police are surprisingly helpful and even arrange a job for him, but he fails, becomes a derelict, and expires. A friend returns to Sweden and visits the young man's mother. Instead of returning the amulet she gave her son, he shows her his own solid gold watch to show how well her son is doing in America. The old woman dies in peace.

The film warned those left behind that even when emigrants sent home evidence of success, they might still be experiencing disaster.

Lindstrom is certain these films never reached the public screen—they may have been used on lecture tours—but the Swedes made other anti-emigration films, at least three of which contained footage shot in the United States in 1911 as well as scenes shot aboard the *Lusitania*.[18]

The American company Kalem traveled to Europe in 1910, and director Sidney Olcott made a number of films in Ireland, at Beaufort, near Killarney. One of them, *The Lad from Old Ireland,* had such a success with the Irish emigrés in America that Kalem returned the following year (probably passing the Swedish troupe en route). On its first trip, Kalem also visited Germany and made a film about a German girl emigrating to America, *The Little Spreewald Mädchen.*[19]

A frequent hazard for girls traveling alone was posed by ship's officers, although, despite penalties, no officer was ever charged with assault. Valeska Suratt[20] starred for the Lasky Company as a Russian girl in *The Immigrant,* written by Marion Fairfax and directed by George Melford. Masha, traveling steerage, attracts the attention of one of the officers, who tries to seduce her. A young American engineer (Thomas Meighan) protects her and secures a berth for her in second class, paying the difference himself. A political boss, traveling first class, tries to take her over, and the rest of the film is concerned with her romantic adventures.

"The opening scenes of the play are particularly good," said *Moving Picture World.* "The contrasts between first and second cabin and steerage are brought out very cleverly."[21] But the New York *Dramatic Mirror* complained it was artificial: "The star appeared as an immigrant in the steerage, garbed in a dress that would not have been out of place on Fifth Avenue!"[22]

Charlie Chaplin made a comedy with the same title. It was his most beautifully constructed two-reeler, and yet an examination of the rushes, for the "Unknown Chaplin" television series,[23] showed that it began as a completely different film.

The original idea was a kind of skit on *Trilby,* set in the bohemian quarter of Paris. Then it became a series of mildly amusing gags set in a café. While he was working on this part of the film, Chaplin needed to know where his leading lady (Edna Purviance) came from. He made her an immigrant, set scenes aboard a boat, and came up with a comedy which has been shown more or less continuously since its release in 1917, not as an antique, but for its undying value as entertainment.

Chaplin himself was not an immigrant in the usual sense—he had come over with the Fred Karno troupe—but he had experienced something of what the immigrants had gone through. Judging from the film, his most vivid memory was the movement of the ship. He put the camera on a special tripod head which enabled it to rock from side to side. The interior of the dining saloon was shot at the studio, the whole set mounted on rockers. These boat scenes allowed Chaplin to indulge in every seasick gag he could think of.

He did not use the film to comment on the experience of immigration until the sighting of the Statue of Liberty. Then he included a sharp and savage little moment which historians have seen as political comment. I doubt that it was; Chaplin said he included nothing political in his pictures. It was the reaction of a comedy director: a title says "Arrival in the Land of Liberty," so the officers rope the passengers together like cattle. Chaplin was aware, however, that the scene could be open to misinterpretation.

Carlyle Robinson, Chaplin's press secretary, joined the studio on the very morning that the rushes of this sequence were being shown. Chaplin asked what he thought of them.

"Very funny and very realistic," Robinson replied.

"Do you find anything shocking in it?"

"Not that I can recall."

Evidently, the point had been raised by one of Chaplin's associates and Robinson's reply satisfied Chaplin. As Robinson said, "The scene was kept in the final version of the film and there was never the least complaint."[24]

In the 1890s, the vast majority of immigrants were Italians, Slavs, and Russian Jews. The native Americans and older immigrants regarded them as "educationally deficient, socially backward, and bizarre in appearance" and disliked them on sight.[25] Dislike combined with insecurity to produce fear, and racial theories were developed to strengthen the call for a firm restriction on immigration.[26]

The Knights of Labor complained about the deteriorating standard of immigrants; Hungarians and Lithuanians who "herded together like animals and lived like beasts" were crowding Americans out of the coal fields of Pennsylvania.[27] A flood of Italians on top of a lingering depression led to mass deportation in 1896 and encouraged the Immigration Restriction League to urge a literacy test to reduce this "unwanted" influx. The bill was passed the following year, but President Cleveland vetoed it, pointing out that the same things were said about immigrants who, with their descendants, "were now among our best citizens."[28]

*Enrico Caruso: newsreel men
U. K. Whipple and Emmanuel
"Jack" Cohn persuaded him
to crank Whipple's camera
on the legion of cameramen
photographing the great Italian
opera star—for Universal
Animated Weekly. From*
Moving Picture World,
March 13, 1915.

THE ITALIANS

The most recent wave of immigrants were always the most despised; the Italians were the most despised of all. They were at the bottom of the social scale, paid less than any other worker, black or white.

The Irish-Americans, establishing political power in the nineteenth century, needed scapegoats for the violence for which they were so often responsible. The Italians were therefore characterized as lawless. One newspaper charged that the Italian government made a regular practice of sending its criminals to the United States. Horror stories of the Mafia and the Black Hand gathered momentum. The Italians and the Irish, once joined in friendship by their religion, clashed violently in industrial warfare. The victims of the worst lynching in American history were not blacks, but Italians.[29]

Such treatment failed to stem the flood of migration, for conditions in Italy were grim. More than 80 percent of the people worked on the land, living in medieval conditions. Wages were absurdly low, and food cost the peasant 85 percent of all he earned.[30] Returning emigrants made a deep impression with their smart clothes, full wallets, and colorful stories. Another deep impression was made by the flow of money back home; the fact that a man could earn enough to live on and still send something to his family was enough to spur others to America.

When they arrived, the immigrants were at the mercy of a *padrone* (master), an Italian labor boss. A one-man employment agency, he advanced fares and served as interpreter, but his terms were extortionate, and the conditions to which he consigned the newcomers were often those of slave labor.[31]

"To an extraordinary degree," wrote Maldwyn Jones, "Italian immigrants duplicated the experience of the Irish half a century earlier. They settled in the same parts of the United States, dominated the same unskilled occupations, occupied the same overcrowded slums."[32]

Early films about Italians portrayed them as hot-blooded and violent, but the stereotypes were no more offensive than those for any other nationality. In Griffith's 1911 Biograph *Italian Blood,* a wife senses her husband's affection is cooling so she tries to arouse his love through jealousy. The plan misfires, the husband is driven into a frenzy, and he only comes to his senses as he is about to kill his own children.[33]

More sympathetic was *The Immigrant's Violin* (1912), an Imp one-reeler directed by Otis Turner. An immigrant girl (Vivian Prescott) is separated from her parents. As she is a violinist of ability, a society woman arranges a public appearance for her. On a concert tour she encounters her parents and is on the point of passing them by, for she now has a rich young lover. But her strong sense of family obliges her to acknowledge them, and the family is reunited.[34]

The Italians formed a large proportion of any audience and could not be ignored. When Vitagraph made a film of the Tripolitan War between Italy and Turkey, showing Italian atrocities, the Italians created such an outcry the film was withdrawn as a "fake."[35] Furthermore, there was a flourishing film industry in Italy, which happened to be superior to the American. Many Italian films were imported, and the Americans began making their own Italian stories more authentic in the hope of a favorable reception in Italy. But then came the outbreak of war, and the source was cut off.

There was an Italian colony in San Francisco, where Hal Mohr had the idea of setting up Itala-American Films in 1914 to make Italian subjects in America. He put his own money, and that of his father, into it; his main supporter was Johnny DiMaria, who owned most of the real estate on the old Barbary Coast.

"I had a little Italian sweetheart whom I made the leading lady," said Hal Mohr. "There was a jeweler by the name of Remy Taffuri, a little Italian fellow who was a natural-born actor, and I went to a theatrical agency and hired two or three of the local hams to play leading parts in the thing. It was made in the pure Italian style—the sets were Italian, the actors were all made to look like Italians. The idea was to compete, and it would have been a good idea if it had worked."[36]

Mohr took the film to New York to sell it, but failed, and the company was dissolved while he was there. While the biggest American manufacturers produced Italian subjects, there was no need for a specialized company. The only problem was that their films were invariably about crime.

It was significant that one of the first films made about the Italian community had the title *The Black Hand.* Made by the American Mutoscope and Biograph Company in 1906, it was photographed by Billy Bitzer. Its opening title proclaimed, "True story of a recent occurrence in the Italian quarter of New York."

Hal Mohr, second from the left, the future cameraman, creates Itala-American Films at Berkeley, California, in 1914. Remy Taffuri, seated, with moustache.

There was nothing true about the interiors; the cellar where the Black Hand members write their threatening letter is crudely painted.

The letter is shown in close-up: "Bewar! We are desperut! Mister Angelo we must have $1,000.00, give it to us or we will take your Maria and Blow up your Shop. BLACK HAND."

Maria is the small daughter of the butcher, whose shop is an elaborate set (lamb is twelve cents a pound) equipped with a cold store. When the butcher gets the letter he is furious, yells for his wife and daughter, and produces a pistol.

Once the picture leaves the artifice of the studio, it bursts into life. Bitzer has set his camera on Seventh Avenue to film a horse-drawn cab pulling up and the crooks jumping out and abducting the girl. But the action takes longer than he bargained for, and incidents occur quite unconnected with the film. A policeman strides past with an old derelict under arrest (they look as if they have blundered in from another film). People stare at the camera.

When the kidnappers come to collect the ransom, the police trap them by hiding in the cold store. This is described as "a clever arrest. Actually as made by

New York detectives." One gathers from the film that these two crooks are amateurs, operating on their own and using the name "Black Hand" to frighten their
victim into a prompt response.

As Martin Short points out, the Black Hand was not a single organization:
"The threats usually came from freelance hoodlums who found it easier to shelter
behind the symbols of a feared if mythical society than to invent a new one. . . .
For quick payoffs no emblem was more effective."[37]

Al Capone's father was the victim of Black Hand extortion; Capone found out
who the villains were and killed them.[38] When he moved to Chicago, he rid the
city of Black Handers (in order to substitute his own racketeers), which some
people still think was his greatest service to the Italian community.[39]

At the height of the Black Hand scare, however, Francis D. Culkin, a district
attorney who had spent his political life among immigrant groups, declared, "There
are no more law-abiding people in the country than those from sunny Italy."[40]
But the Black Hand provided sensational copy, and newspapers exploited it as
they had the Mafia and Comorra a few years earlier.[41]

Even so innocuous a title as *The Organ Grinder* (Kalem, 1909) turned out to
involve the Black Hand. "Renegade Italians concoct a 'blackhand' plot. They
abduct a child and bring her back to a hovel. The organ grinder happens to catch
sight of the child and informs her parents. Through his information she is restored
and the organ grinder receives the reward of his service. The views are startlingly
correct in the smallest detail and make a capital bit of film work."[42]

Kalem also produced *The Detectives of the Italian Bureau* in 1909. The company's
comments were enlightening: "For years it was found almost impossible to cope
with a certain class of Italian criminals because the detectives had little or no
knowledge of the Italian language and were not sufficiently familiar with the methods employed by the blackmailers and kidnappers who come to our shores from
the dregs of Italy. But now things are greatly changed. Every big city has a distinct
section of the detective force made up of courageous and honest men of Italian
birth, and these men are devoting their whole time to rounding up and punishing
Italian criminals. And so successful have they been that Black Hand crimes have
been practically blotted out in all of our large centers."[43]

The Kalem picture was in eight scenes. Nine-year-old Rosa is captured by the
Black Handers after the premature explosion of a bomb. She escapes and alerts
the Italian Bureau detectives, who round up the kidnappers and return Rosa to
her parents.[44]

The picture was well timed. The head of New York's "Italian Squad," Lieutenant Joseph Petrosino, had carried out a one-man campaign against the Mafia
and Comorra, identifying criminals as they arrived and deporting them and tack-
ling gangs single-handed. (He declared that as a large organization, the Black Hand
did not exist.) Police Commissioner Theodore Bingham sent Petrosino to Italy in
1909 to establish relations with the Italian police "so that the Comorra and the
Mafia may be watched on both sides of the ocean." His journey was supposed to
be a secret, but the New York papers provided full details and in March 1909 he
was shot dead in Palermo. "His assassins had definitely murdered the right man,"
wrote Martin Short. "With Petrosino dead American law enforcement lost sight
of the Mafia for almost fifty years."[45]

The movies maintained their interest. In Mary Pickford's *Poor Little Peppina* (1916), a member of the Mafia commits murder and kidnaps a child, who grows up in Italy. She escapes an overattentive *padrone* by stowing away to America, where she becomes involved in a counterfeiting gang run by the same Mafia man.

In *The Criminals* (1913), the Black Handers kidnap a little Italian child, and when the father refuses to pay the ransom they kill the youngster. The father is mistaken by the police for one of the criminals and imprisoned—the kind of irony which often appeared in films about Italian immigrants. Produced by Mecca, "the sets, acting and photography are commendable,"[46] wrote *Moving Picture World*.

Criminals were again offset by innocents in *The Padrone's Ward* (1914), a two-reeler from the Powers Company. The *padrone*, leader of an East Side gang of thieves and blackmailers, is the guardian of a girl who is rescued by an Italian-American banker. The banker becomes the target of the Black Hand, but he refuses to respond to the threatening letters and seeks the aid of the protective association. The blackmailers decide to kill him, but the man assigned to the job is the girl's sweetheart, a cripple. He tries to carry out the killing, but fails and finally warns the girl. The banker escapes death, and the blackmailers are rounded up.[47]

Many criminals who were not Italian at all used the symbol of the Black Hand. This formed the basis of a vaudeville sketch, written and performed by George Beban, which became known as "the sketch that never failed." So famous did it become that Klaw and Erlanger produced it as a four-act play on Broadway. Thomas Ince turned this into a film and as a *coup de théâtre* had Beban appear onstage and carry the story to its conclusion. This "Combination of Silent and Spoken Drama" was nine reels and one act and was entitled *The Alien* (1915). Raymond West directed (and turned his own camera, with Bob Newhard on second).[48]

Beban's aim was to introduce the real Italian to the screen instead of "the individual with a long black mustache and a bandana handkerchief, armed with a stiletto."[49]

A rich ne'er-do-well called Phil Griswold (Jack Nelson), in desperate need of money, turns to his elder brother, William (Hayward Ginn), for help. He is refused, so he kidnaps William's daughter, Dorothy (Thelma Salter), and writes "Black Hand" letters demanding a heavy ransom. He had noticed the child's fear when Pietro (Beban) delivered a Christmas tree. William instantly thinks of Pietro and sets off for Little Italy. En route, his automobile runs down little Rosa, Pietro's daughter. After taking her to her home and realizing she is dead, William escapes from the angry mob ("a scene that was unusually well handled," wrote the New York *Dramatic Mirror*).[50]

On Christmas morning, Dorothy's mother receives a ransom demand for $10,000, to be delivered to the flower shop and given to a man she will know "by the sign of the rose." Meanwhile, William has taken the case to the police, who are on hand waiting for the kidnapper. As the trap is set, the picture fades, the screen rises, along with the curtains, and a duplicate of the flower shop is revealed, with the characters in the same positions. Reviewers thought the players, excellent on the screen, were not strong enough for the stage and that there was too much unnecessary exposition. But when Beban appeared, the sketch caught light: "He never played the role with greater fire and sincerity."[51]

Few films showed what the immigrants went through on the voyage across. Camille Ankewich (better known later as Marcia Manon) played the Italian immigrant wife, with May Giraci as her daughter, in One More American, *1918. (Museum of Modern Art)*

The moment the immigrants dreaded: The Ellis Island doctor rejects Luigi's child. One More American, *1918, directed by William de Mille. (Museum of Modern Art)*

Half crazed, Beban buys a rose for his child's grave—convincing the police that he is one of the kidnappers.

"The demonstration is a surprisingly strong argument for the photoplay," said *Photoplay*. "Beban's facial emotion, magnified to intense proportions in the close-ups of the picture, is infinitely more convincing than the patently false illumination, confined settings and more or less distant figures of the theatrical stage. The duration of the play is so brief, however, its emotion so strong, that its vitality balances what is lost by the departure of Ince's splendid camera work."[52]

Motion Picture Magazine voted it one of the classics of the screen, along with *The Birth of a Nation* and *Cabiria*: "The acme of simplicity, appeal and beauty. Strong heart-interest story, fine characterization, plot a bit of real life. Well cast, ably directed and beautifully photographed and produced."[53]

George Beban did more for the Italian on the screen, let alone the stage, than anyone else, including Rudolph Valentino (who hardly ever played Italians). Perhaps Beban's greatest contributions were two fine immigration films, first *The Italian* (1915) for Thomas Ince, then *One More American* (1918) for Lasky.

A superb title, *One More American* was by all accounts a superb film. It was adapted from a playlet, *The Land of the Free*, by William de Mille, who also directed it. The scenario was written by Olga Printzlau, and the technical staff included Charles Rosher, already revealing himself as one of the finest craftsmen of the era, and Wilfred Buckland, revolutionizing the art of film design.

Beban played Luigi Riccardo, who operates a marionette theatre in the Mulberry Bend district of New York. For a long time he has worked to bring his wife and daughter from Italy. Now they are coming, and Luigi excitedly awaits their arrival. He reckons without Regan (H. B. Carpenter), a ward boss who wants his vote. Luigi regards him as a grafter and will not cooperate. But Regan, who has many followers in the neighborhood, decides to bring Luigi into line. He uses his influence to prevent Luigi getting his final naturalization papers. And then, through a physician (Hector Dion) whom he has appointed at Ellis Island, he has Luigi's daughter refused entry.[54]

This sequence impressed Wid Gunning so much that he described it in detail: "The doctor is examining Luigi's family. He begins with the wife (Camille Ankewich), finding her an admirable specimen of womanhood. He knows that he has promised Regan to find something wrong to hold them up; but for the moment his conscience overpowers him and he checks the woman's tag to signify her admittance to the country. A load off his mind with this act, he turns to the child (May Giraci) with the intention of passing her, too, when he sees Regan standing in the doorway. It is enough. He tricks the child into an appearance of imbecility and marks her tag with a cross."[55]

Wild with rage and grief, Luigi sets out to kill the ward boss. It so happens that Luigi has one friend who understands Regan's tricks—Sam Potts (Jack Holt), a reporter who has long been trying to get something on the man. He goes after the physician, secures a confession, and obliges him to pass Luigi's wife and child.[56]

Wid thought it a real box-office winner: "Heart interest just oozes out of it."[57] *Motion Picture Magazine* thought it "exquisitely rendered" and considered that Beban displayed a masterly hand in his treatment of grief and paternal love: "Beban never rose to higher ranks of pure emotionalism than when he literally throws himself against the wire screen that separates him from his dear ones and tries to tear the heart-breaking barrier down.

"One More American is a photoplay that sinks deeply into the heart."[58]

THE ITALIAN   Originally titled *The Dago,* filmed in 1914, and released early the following year, *The Italian* is one of the rediscovered masterpieces of the early years and the best of all the surviving immigrant pictures by far. Written by C. Gardner Sullivan, who helped himself to de Mille's playlet *The Land of the Free* and to a 1913 Imp picture called *The Wop,*[59] it was directed by Reginald Barker.

George Beban is shown in a prologue and epilogue in a library. The camera tracks forward as he pulls a book from the shelves and settles down to read it. The book is called *The Italian* by Thomas Ince and C. Gardner Sullivan. Beban is thus shown to be a man of education, just in case we think his peasant performance too convincing.

The first reel or so, set in Italy, is picturesque but theatrical. Posed scenes in the vineyards (filmed at a California mission) and some comedy with gondolas in Venice (filmed at Venice, California)[60] are the only relief in a long-winded introduction. Once Beppo departs for America, the film changes gear. It becomes serious, concerned, and emotionally involving. We no longer have to endure the make-up of stage Italians; now we are among real people. (The Italians reinvented this style of filmmaking after World War II, when it was called neo-realism.)

Beppo is shown on board the steamship as the Statue of Liberty heaves into view. The Ellis Island experience is left out, a grave omission in a film about an immigrant.[61] And suddenly Beppo is shuffling on to a street full of life and dirt and movement.

As soon as he gets his bearings, Beppo becomes a bootblack. One day, he is propositioned by the local ward boss, Big Bill Corrigan (Charles K. French): "Here's a little present for you. Have your wop friends vote for this guy." And he hands him a campaign flyer for Alderman Casey.

In Italy, Annette receives an invitation to join Beppo.[62] Her steamship arrives at the docks, but Beppo goes to the wrong pier. That night, he and Annette are married; the ceremony is performed by his "friend," Alderman Casey. "A year later; the dawn of a new life." Fade in on Annette and newly born baby. Beppo leaves a customer in midpolish, runs past a derelict scrabbling in a garbage can (the film is full of such details), and cannons into a passer-by who falls over a barrow, infuriating the old Jew who is pushing it. The hail of images comes to a halt as Beppo sees his baby. He slowly moves forward and kisses it. Outside, a crowd gathers and Beppo leads them all to the saloon to celebrate. Beppo whispers the good news to the barkeep and explains how the baby was sleeping, just like him, with his hand under his chin. The barkeep signals for the help to wake up all the drunks.

George Beban in the title role of The Italian, *1915, directed by Reginald Barker from a C. Gardner Sullivan scenario. Neighbors help Beppo celebrate the birth of his baby. (Anthony Slide)*

Months later, midsummer scorches the slums. A superb series of documentary shots shows crowds of children running after the water wagon and getting sprayed at the fireplug. Although the streets[63] do not look like New York, washing has been slung across them in a rough approximation of Mulberry Bend.

"Little Tony, one of the thousands of heat victims, grows alarmingly worse."

The doctor asks to see the milk—Annette produces a pail covered in flies. The doctor sniffs and shakes his head: "The heat and impure food are wearing him out. You must get him pasteurized milk."

The heat wave reaches its peak; the baby is still ill, and the supply of pasteurized milk has run out. Beppo gets a message that the baby must have more. Foolishly, he asks two men to watch his stand. They pursue him and beat him up in an alley and rob him. Beppo lies stunned in a dusty archway, his face partially lit by a shaft of sunlight. When he recovers and finds his money gone, he sits slumped on a garbage can, musing over his misfortune. The two men emerge from a saloon. He accosts them, pleads with them: "I must get-a-de milk or my babee is die" (there are few dialogue titles, but they tend to be in this style). A fight breaks out, and Beppo is arrested. He suddenly sights Corrigan.

"Knowing Corrigan to be the boss of the slums whose word is law, Beppo appeals to him for mercy." Beppo throws the cop to the sidewalk and leaps after Corrigan's car, even though it drags him along the road. Corrigan kicks him in the face, and Beppo is nearly killed as he falls before a streetcar.[64] Fighting all the way, Beppo is dragged to jail. Corrigan returns to his cool suburban home, to be welcomed by wife and daughter.

Beppo asks a warder to write a note and send it to his wife. Once out of sight, the warder tears the note up.

"A week later." We see an undertaker carrying a small coffin, followed by a weeping Annette. Beppo is finally released, and as he climbs his stairs he passes a neighbor who realizes he doesn't yet know the awful news and regards him with horror. He pushes open the door, and Annette cries out to him. They embrace. "Beppo, our poor little Antonio—he's—." Slowly, Beppo turns and walks toward the blanket-covered cradle. He pulls the blanket back, and, when he sees the emptiness, staggers slightly, then falls across the cradle. Annette tries to comfort him.

A month later, Beppo learns that Corrigan's child is near death. He steals into his house, determined to avenge himself by killing Corrigan's child. But as he advances on the bed, the child moves in its sleep and places its hand under its chin—"the gesture that was little Tony's." Beppo gasps, and all his resolve flows out of him.

"At the eternal bedside of his baby, where hate, revenge and bitterness melt to nothing in the crucible of sorrow," Beppo kneels at the graveside. We return to a brief scene of Beban finishing the book, and the curtain descends.

The Italian is a genuinely moving film, a description which, for all their energy and proficiency, can be applied to only a handful of the early features. Directors had not yet grasped the ability to sustain a scene. Perhaps because Beban's acting demanded it, *The Italian* shows the value of contrasting moods; after a hectic chase, Barker allows Beban to play a tragic sequence in slow motion. Although most of the other scenes are short, and the narrative is advanced in gulps, mostly with time-lapse titles—"A Year Later"—the mood is sustained from the moment Beppo climbs aboard the immigrant ship for America.

Thomas H. Ince was what would now be called a superpatriot, and so, to judge by the rest of his work, was C. Gardner Sullivan. If the unrelenting viciousness of the Americans encountered by Beppo comes as a surprise, one should remember that this sympathetic portrait of the Italian immigrant may well have been animated by anti-immigrant sentiment. Apart from a woman neighbor and a kindly old Jew, there is not a sympathetic character in all the New York sequences. Nothing is shown, apart from the ward boss's home, which could possibly entice anyone to leave their own country. Nor is there much sentimentality. The little gesture that was Tony's may seem corny by today's standards, but the fact that a gesture was selected as the climax of the picture is indicative of the subtlety and lack of melodrama in the rest of the American scenes.

Beban himself is stylized but convincing; once the opening cuteness is out of the way, his elaborate gesticulation seems appropriate to an Italian crippled by lack of English. (Ince claimed that Beban found his costume by buying it direct from an Italian immigrant at the Battery—the complete outfit, headgear and footwear, for ten dollars.)[65] The small parts are played well, as if they had been caught by a hidden camera. It is only when one sees the film several times that one begins to notice the discrepancies: the streets do not belong to New York, the lack of an Ellis Island scene, the suburban home so plainly in California. But although the background is not truly documentary, the atmosphere is—and the atmosphere is what provides conviction for an audience.

Those who interviewed George Beban described him as a powerhouse of a man. Ray Frohman of the Los Angeles *Herald* called him "an active volcano," compared to whom even Douglas Fairbanks was a snail. "He does not merely beat you about the head and body with those Latin hands of his to bring home his conversational points. EVERY PORTION OF HIS FAMOUS PHYSIOGNOMY IS WORKING WHEN HE TALKS . . ."[66]

Despite his Italian roles, and his many years of doing French parts, Beban was Northern Irish by birth. "I was dragged into pictures by the back of my neck," he said, "struggling against my will."[67]

Thomas Ince read the scenario for *The Dago* and realized that if Beppo could be played by someone of the caliber of George Beban, it would make one of the greatest pictures on the screen. Beban was then starring in *The Sign of the Rose* on Broadway, and Ince set out for New York, determined to sign him up. He had hardly been in the city two hours when he spotted Beban in the street. He introduced himself, but Beban resented his offer. It was a crime for an actor to go into pictures; taking the dramatic art and throwing it into the street depreciated the profession. Ince employed the most colorful rhetoric to win him over.

Beban recalled, "He pictured for me every imaginable luxury I would have if I would make just one five-reeler for him as my vacation at his expense, and then go on with my dramatic career as if nothing had happened—ocean view from my dressing room, sets built for me in the mountains, luncheon served by a stream, glorious sunsets on the Pacific. . . . (All of these were rather difficult to avoid at Inceville, but he threw in a fine horse and groom.)

"Then, after the matinee, with me in the shadows and himself under the light, reversing Belasco's tactics, Ince told me, without dialect, the story of that picture he wanted me for. He was all worked up to convince, crying like a baby . . . never in his career did he play a part like he played that! From beginning to end I was spellbound. . . . All I was able to say was three words: 'I'll do it!' "[68]

Beban insisted that the title be changed to *The Italian* and that it be a special and not a cheap program picture. Ince offered him $7,000 plus a percentage and all expenses paid. "He guaranteed that I'd make more money than I did all season in New York and the previous season—and by golly, I did!"[69]

The Italian was highly praised. Vachel Lindsay selected it for his book *The Art of the Moving Picture,* and, while he disliked the sequence in Corrigan's house, he called it "a strong piece of work."[70] It survived as a paper print in the Library of Congress and was used to guide Francis Ford Coppola in re-creating turn-of-the-century New York for The *Godfather, Part II* (1974).[71] And yet it was never shown in Italy.[72] The film made little impression in America at a time when immigrant dramas were not uncommon; the prejudice against Italians may also have had something to do with this. Although Beban played a French farmer the following year, he made several more films about Italian immigrants, often directing them himself. None of them survive. It is a miracle this one does, and it is reassuring to know that the Library of Congress has acquired an original print and will reprint it to enhance the quality.

For *The Italian*—at least for the most part—stands head and shoulders above any surviving attempt from this period to portray the lot of the underprivileged in a hostile world.

THE CHINESE

Drama is exploration; melodrama is exploitation. Since the majority of feature films were melodramas, requiring far-fetched situations and exotic villainy, it is hardly surprising that Orientals figured so prominently, for the Chinese were regarded in America not only as a mystery, but as a threat—far more of a threat than even the Italians. They kept to themselves, spoke their own languages, wore their own clothes, and, despite a vast weight of discrimination, they seemed to prosper.

Chinese history had impinged upon America in terms of horror—"Opium wars," "Boxer rising," "Chinese torture," and "Tong wars" were familiar subjects to newspaper readers, whose image of Oriental culture was a confusion of severed heads, temple bells, and screaming mobs. Yet were the Chinese not calm, stoic, philosophical? It was all very confusing. No wonder the great nations were constantly dispatching not merely missionaries to save the souls of these heathens but gunboats to protect their own interests.

The Chinese first came to the Americas as servants aboard Spanish galleons. The discovery of gold in California in 1848 attracted Chinese, who were among the first to stake their claims, only to be set upon by other miners. Many were given "women's work" in the mining camps—cooking and cleaning. Yet they were the major contributors to the building of the Central Pacific Railroad. (Some of the old Chinese workers were brought out of retirement to play in John Ford's 1924 reconstruction of those days, *The Iron Horse.)* When the project was completed, the laborers settled in railroad towns throughout the Southwest, although some tried to find work in the industrial towns of the East. Riots led to many Chinese being killed, and although they added up to a mere 1 percent of the entire immigrant population, labor unions agitated to stop more Oriental labor from reaching the United States.

In 1882, the Chinese became the first immigrant group to be barred, with the passing of the Chinese Exclusion Act, which excluded laborers for ten years, although officials, teachers, and merchants were still permitted. The act was renewed in 1892, and again in 1902, and in 1904 the Deficiency Act banned Chinese laborers permanently.[73]

The Exclusion Acts did little to reduce anti-Chinese prejudice. "The Yellow Peril" was a sweeping term covering all Orientals; it would have been better applied to the Hearst press, whose favorite topic it was. The motion picture industry as a rule followed the popular line. The Chinese tended to be portrayed as friendly but idiotic laundrymen, the subtitles leplesenting their lemarks thus, or sinister opium fiends, masterminding operations of unspeakable evil. The very word "wily" seemed to have been coined for these characters.

China was usually portrayed as a land of screaming mobs, temple bells, and torture. From The Vermilion Pencil, *1922, with Bessie Love. The mandarin is played by Thomas Jefferson.*

Yet films occasionally portrayed the Chinese with sympathy and understanding. *The War of the Tongs,* made by Universal in 1917, sounds like the usual melodramatic hokum, but titles can be misleading. This was the work of a Chinese writer (and possibly director), with a cast led by members of the Imperial Chinese players. The five-reel picture set out to expose the Chinese lottery system and the methods of the tongs.

These organizations—the name comes from the Cantonese pronunciation of t'ang, meaning "brotherhood"—were organizations exclusive to the Chinese in America. They sheltered behind respectable façades, as did regular gangsters, but they were synonymous with white slave trafficking, drug peddling, murders by "hatchetmen," and blackmail. *The War of the Tongs* revealed that the victims of the tongs were mainly the Chinese themselves. But it was not just a gangster film. It also served to spotlight the positive aspects of the community. "The Chinese are noted for their honesty in business transactions and this phase of their lives is carefully brought out in the development of the story, as some of the action takes place in a large Chinese mercantile house."[74]

Wid Gunning could not have cared less about Chinese honesty: "In the course of this wild career I am following—looking at about fifteen features a week—it becomes necessary for me to see some weird productions. Of all the poor, impossible offerings I've ever seen, however, presented seriously as entertainment, I believe this is the worst."[75]

The tong wars became as much a part of American life as the old gang wars. And movies melodramatized them. In 1921, the Chinese in Los Angeles approached Tod Browning (a director best known for his Lon Chaney productions) to make a propaganda film to bring the factions together and prevent further bloodshed. Browning's *Outside the Law* (1921) had a Chinese sympathetically presented (albeit played by E. A. Warren), who endeavors to reform a couple of crooks. But although Browning continued to make exotic and bizarre pictures, sometimes with Chinese backgrounds (*Drifting* [1923] featured Anna May Wong), he never made the film for the Chinese of Los Angeles. More's the pity.[76]

Chinese stories, which so often dealt with the forbidden, held a strong fascination for American audiences. In San Francisco around 1912, T. Kimmwood Peters made a series called *The Adventures of Boe Kung,* a Chinese Sherlock Holmes,[77] anticipating Charlie Chan by a couple of decades. In the same city, a company called Rice and Berkeley produced a four-reeler called *The Chinese Lily* (1914), with an entirely Chinese cast, under the direction of Arthur W. Rice. "An entirely new phase of Chinese life is presented without the usual odiferous opium and obnoxious white slave scenes," said *Moving Picture World.*[78]

A number of films were made with Chinese casts for the Chinese theatres in San Francisco, but according to Geoffrey Bell these were termed " 'inscrutable' . . . that is, only distributed to Chinese movie houses, not in regular distribution."[79]

The Exclusion Acts encouraged the smuggling of Chinese immigrants, and this was the theme of *The Yellow Traffic* (1914), a four-reeler produced and directed by Herbert Blaché (husband of Alice Guy). The advertisements referred to "the cargo of 'pig-tails' " and omitted the names of the Chinese. They listed the white players, who, they said, were "supplemented by a large number of Chinese actors."[80]

City of Dim Faces (1918) was a story of San Francisco's Chinatown written by Frances Marion and directed by George Melford. The Japanese actor Sessue Hayakawa played Jang Lung, the son of a rich Chinese importer and a white woman who falls in love with a girl whose cousin breaks up the affair "by disgusting her with Jang's race."[81] Jang's love turns to hatred, and he behaves in true movie-melodrama style, finally repenting and losing her—to a white man—before losing his life at the fade-out. Among the Chinese in the cast were James Wang, and, among the other Japanese, Togo Yama. (The future director James Cruze also appeared.)

The Japanese actor Jack Abbe starred as a Chinese in *Mystic Faces* (1918) with another Japanese, Martha Taka. The film was directed by E. Mason Hopper for Triangle; reviewers found it "refreshing."[82] The aim was to show that the Chinese was a greatly misrepresented person, and for once a Chinese character was allowed to play the hero, rescuing the heroine from the clutches of pro-Germans. *Variety* thought it full of quaint comedy, and "a thrill a minute."[83]

The spate of Oriental films at this period was largely due to the success of a play called *East Is West* (later filmed by Sidney Franklin).[84] The biggest Chinese production was *The Red Lantern* (1919) with Alla Nazimova, which brought Metro to the fore. A story of the Boxer Rebellion, it was directed by Albert Capellani from the novel by Edith Wherry. Scripted by Capellani and June Mathis, it told of an illegitimate Chinese girl, adopted by an American missionary, who falls for a young American. He has an affair with her (white) half sister. Said *Motion Picture Magazine,* "The Chinese girl, bitterly resenting the unfairness of a people who educate yet never accept socially one of the yellow race, joins in a Boxer uprising, portraying the part of the Goddess of the Red Lantern."[85]

Among those Orientals taking prominent roles were Yukio Ao Yamo, a Japanese, and Anna May Wong, soon to be a star.

These pictures may have convinced Western audiences, but the Chinese had a very different view of them. "In the Old Country," wrote Su Ah Hui, from Regina, Saskatchewan, Canada, "I have seven sisters who are also fans and when they see these strange dramas, with fine and authentic Chinese background *but white people playing Chinese,* they laugh heartily, thinking them comedies." They were equally amused by actresses, playing Chinese women, who take little mincing steps when they walk, and men of high degree who always stand with their hands folded over their stomachs. "As for that invariable hint of the subtle and treacherous which your producers incorporate into Chinese drama that is but a half-truth. You will find more throat-cutting and knifing-in-the-back among other races I could name. But try giving us real Chinese players and they will demonstrate correctly our character and behavior."[86]

He might have mentioned another drawback. However sympathetic the approach, there were only two possible endings to love stories: the Chinese either turns out to be white—or dies.

Although he failed to use a Chinese in the lead, D. W. Griffith made what one historian has called "the single compassionate dramatization on the silent American screen of love between white and Oriental races."[87] In *Broken Blossoms* (1919), the outcome was unusual, to say the least. All the principals die.

BROKEN BLOSSOMS　"A sordid and horrible story, if ever there was one," wrote Frances Taylor Patterson of Thomas Burke's short story "The Chink and the Child." "Mr. Griffith made the story over into a surpassingly beautiful play. But the play was somewhat of a commercial failure for all its marvelous technique. It had no message—unless the rather revolting example of the triumph of the religion of Confucius over that of Christ."[88]

The Burke story appeared in a book called *Limehouse Nights* published in 1916 by Grant Richards of London. It is the tale, admirable in its atmosphere if somewhat purple in its prose, of a poetic Chinese who falls for a girl of twelve in the slums of Limehouse. The girl, Lucy, would now be called a battered child. She is frequently beaten by her father, a boxer called Battling Burrows. She seeks refuge in an opium den, enticed there by a prostitute who hopes to make money out of her. She is rescued by the Chinese, who takes her to his home, and she responds to his kindness and gentleness. But her disappearance has been noted and her protector spotted. Burrows sets out in pursuit. The child is retrieved; her rescuer's home is utterly destroyed. When he discovers what has happened, he suffers terribly. He prepares a love-gift, for it is the custom that the dying shall present love-gifts to their enemies, and sets out for Burrows's home. Here he finds the girl beaten to death, but no sign of Burrows. He carries Lucy back, crouches beside her, and kills himself with a knife. Burrows appears to get away with his behavior until the last paragraph. In a twist worthy of O. Henry, Burrows returns home drunk, flops on his bed, and is bitten by the love-gift, an eighteen-inch snake.

Had the film been made by anyone other than Griffith—say, Thomas Ince—a powerful and brutal picture might have resulted, along the lines of *The Cheat* (1915). Marshall Neilan made just such a film, *Bits of Life* (1921), several years later. But Griffith transformed the story. *The Cheat* portrayed a vicious Oriental; why not make a film in which the white man is the brute and the Oriental the apotheosis of gentleness?

He made the Chinese, Cheng Huan (Richard Barthelmess), into a student priest, who leaves his country to bring the message of Buddha to the warring nations. He did not censor the lairs of the prostitutes, but he dropped the episode in which Lucy (Lillian Gish) is brought into the opium den. Instead, he has her stumble blindly into the streets after a beating and collapse against Cheng Huan's half-open door.

Griffith knew that his audience would expect *The Cheat* treatment as soon as it laid eyes on the Oriental, so he gave them an alarming moment where Cheng Huan advances on Lucy with obvious intent. And then he defuses the tension with a title: "His love remains a pure and holy thing. Even his worst foe says this."

And Griffith alters the ending. Cheng is a pacifist, so one might have expected a pacifist finale, with Cheng killing himself by Lucy's dead body, leaving Battling Burrows (Donald Crisp) to face the consequences of his actions. But this is an American film. Cheng arms himself not with a poisonous snake, which implies that he is a slimy and treacherous individual, but with a gleaming revolver, which he fires point-blank at Battling Burrows. One can almost hear the applause.

Whether the changes improved the story or not, Griffith produced a film hailed instantly as a classic, as the most beautiful production ever made. It was not the financial success it should have been, but it made money and was far from the commercial failure some historians have alleged.

The fact that *Broken Blossoms* was shot as World War I came to an end had a bearing on the treatment. Had Griffith made the film at any other time, his Chinese might have been far less sympathetic. When he adapted two more tales from *Limehouse Nights* for *Dream Street* in 1921, the Chinese characterization followed Thomas Burke more closely: an evil Chinese "vice-lord" is handed over to the police and warned: "After this, you leave white girls alone."

But in 1918, with the war almost won, the Hun-hatred and drum beating was giving way to a sense of idealism. America, which had saved the world for democracy, now showed the way with the League of Nations. Griffith abandoned his pacifism when he made *Hearts of the World* (1918). Now he returned to it, foreshadowing the popular mood which would sweep the world after the war to end all wars.

He could not decide on an actor to play Cheng Huan. First he asked George

Richard Barthelmess on location in Los Angeles' Chinatown for D. W. Griffith's Broken
Blossoms, *1919. (National Film Archive)*

Fawcett, who usually played flint-hearted fathers and was then working in Griffith's production for Artcraft, *A Romance of Happy Valley*. But eventually Griffith
borrowed Richard Barthelmess from Dorothy Gish Productions, where he was
making comedies. Barthelmess said, "With all modesty, I can state that after
having watched Fawcett rehearse . . . I merely went into rehearsals myself and
copied every mannerism that Fawcett had given the part."[89]

To give him a feeling for the role, Griffith took Barthelmess to Los Angeles's
Chinatown, where they visited the restaurants, shops, and temples. "I absorbed a
lot of Chinese atmosphere and ever since that day I have been a firm believer in
getting to know what to put into a characterization."[90] Instead of wearing make-
up, Barthelmess achieved the narrow eyes by wearing a tight rubber band underneath his Chinese skullcap. (The Chinese-American cameraman James Wong Howe
used to call whites in Chinese roles "adhesive tape actors.")

Rehearsals took place at night while Griffith shot *A Romance of Happy Valley*
during the day. They concentrated on the character of Cheng Huan because Lillian
Gish, who was to play Lucy, was having problems. Griffith had seen "The Chink
and the Child" as ideal for her, but when she read the story, she disagreed: "Dick
Barthelmess wasn't more than five feet six or seven, and I'm five feet six without
shoes on, and how could I bend my knees and get down to a twelve-year-old child?
I said to Mr. Griffith, 'I'll help any little girl, I'll be with her night and day if you
just won't make me play it.' He said, 'Don't be silly, you know a child can't play
those emotional scenes.' "[91]

Lillian Gish as Lucy in D. W. Griffith's Broken Blossoms.

Griffith did raise the age of the girl to fifteen, but he almost lost Gish. She was struck by the Spanish flu, and rehearsals had to continue without her. Her recovery speeded by many messages of affection, she returned to work too soon. The epidemic was still raging. "They were dying so fast in California that they couldn't build caskets, and they were burying the victims in one grave."[92] Griffith, who had a neurotic fear of germs at the best of times, insisted that Gish wear a face mask whenever possible.

The Chinese technical adviser was Moon Kwan. Griffith had a curious policy about whom he would credit and whom he would not: whereas Kwan gets a credit, James Wang, who played the High Priest in the temple, did not, nor did another assistant and interpreter, Leong But-jung (James B. Leong).

Griffith had a curious attitude to casting, too: most of the background characters are Chinese, but a role such as Evil Eye, which required acting talent, was entrusted to Edward Piel, who was all too obviously Caucasian. In the opium den scene,[93] a lascar seaman is clearly a white man with a coat of dark make-up.

In a further lapse of authenticity, Griffith confuses Chinese and Japanese customs and has Cheng Huan commit hara-kiri.*

The Chink and the Child had undergone a title change to *White Blossom and the Chink.* Griffith had to attend to the launch of *The Greatest Thing in Life,* as well as the formation of United Artists, and he neglected his new film. Jimmy Smith complained that he couldn't get the Boss to look at it.

Lillian Gish asked Griffith why.

"I can't look at the damn thing; it depresses me so," he said. "Why did I ever do a story like that? It will drive the audience out of the theater, providing you can persuade them to come in and look. I was a fool to do such a story."[94]

This was a natural reaction to a period of intense hard work. When he forced himself to attend to the details of editing, titling, and scoring, his love for his new child was restored.

One man, however, did not share his affection for the film, and that was Adolph Zukor. One of the shrewdest and most ruthless men in the business, he had financed Griffith since *Hearts of the World,* and planned to distribute the new film through his prestigious Artcraft releasing arm. When he saw the film, he saw box-office poison—a tragedy in which the girl wears rags and the handsome leading man is disfigured with Oriental make-up. He had made a lot of money from *The Cheat,* with an Oriental villain, but this was going beyond the pale. Zukor was probably angry with Griffith because of his negotiations to form United Artists, of which, secret or not, Zukor would undoubtedly have been aware.

According to Lillian Gish, Zukor said, "You bring me a picture like this and want money for it? You may as well put your hand in my pocket and steal it. Everybody in it dies. It isn't commercial."[95]

Griffith's response is not known, but apparently he returned a few days later and gave back Zukor's money. Tino Balio says that the picture had cost $88,000,

---

*The film was a success in Japan, perhaps because of its respect for Buddhism (William Drew).

and Zukor made no secret of the fact that he wanted to get rid of it. But guessing United Artists' plight—they urgently needed new releases—Zukor struck a hard bargain and insisted on $250,000—a fairly reasonable figure when compared against the average takings of a major film. UA had no alternative but to advance the money to Griffith in return for distribution rights. The film grossed $600,000 in the United States alone and made an eventual profit of $700,000.[96]

When Griffith "tried it on the dog" at Pomona, California, the commercial men's prediction followed Zukor's: "No big stuff, only three people in the cast and everyone killed off—can't be done."

That preview was so successful that Griffith began to think perhaps he had another hit on his hands. The title was still *White Blossom and the Chink,* which clearly had to go. The new title came from Burke's story: "Thereafter the spirit of poetry broke her blossoms all about his odorous chamber."[97]

In May 1919 Griffith went to New York, where he had engaged a legitimate theatre, the George M. Cohan, and arranged a repertory season of his films, opening with *Broken Blossoms.* He had the theatre decorated in Chinese style and offered a prologue to put the audience in the mood for tragedy: *The Dance of Life and Death.*

This prologue was filmed, and it was when Griffith was running the footage at the theatre with the stage lights accidentally left on that he saw the remarkable, vibrant, almost magical effect produced by diffused blue and gold lights projected obliquely on the screen. He immediately decided to use lights to enhance the presentation, and he went so far as to patent the idea for a period of seventeen years.[98]

Karl Brown, who saw the effect at Clune's later that year, described it in his book, *Adventures with D. W. Griffith:* "The houselights dimmed, but not entirely so. Instead of darkness, the entire auditorium was suffused with a strange, unearthly blue that seemed to come from everywhere—from the chandelier, from spots ranged along the balconies, from the footlights. There was something eerily supernatural about it. . . . The big curtain whispered upward, revealing the screen which was not at all white but bathed in that strange, all-suffusing blue coming from spots arranged around the inside of the proscenium arch."[99]

The lights, the music, and the decoration of the theatre were all designed to encourage the audience to lose themselves in what was not simply a tragedy but a fantasy. From the start of production, every effort, including the attempt to find "Chinese lighting," had been bent to remove the film from reality. No Chinese was so gentle, no Cockney waif so beautiful, no boxer so violent . . .

"For it *was* a fantasy," wrote Brown, "a dream, a vision of archetypical beings out of the long inherited memory of the human race. No such people as we saw on the screen were ever alive in the workaday world of today or any other day. They were, as Griffith had explained to me in that dark projection room, misty, misty. . . . They were the creatures of a poetic imagination that had at very long last found its outlet in its own way in its own terms. It was a parable in poetry, timeless and eternally true because it touched the deepest recesses of all who were there."[100]

Because the emotions it aroused were genuine, people mistook *Broken Blossoms*

Broken Blossoms. *A Limehouse opium den. (National Film Archive)*

for realism. When it opened in Paris, it was whistled at and booed. Battling Burrows· was "too realistic," and the Chinese poet was played by an American. In England, there were protests that Griffith's idea of Limehouse, of Cockneys, and of London police stations was all wrong.[101] But *Broken Blossoms*—one can almost scent the incense—was the escapist film par excellence, and with a stroke of good fortune that had eluded Griffith with *Intolerance,* it arrived at the perfect moment. The war had ended, and audiences wanted to escape not only from the present but from the immediate past. A film which takes place in limbo, which is idealistic and high-minded, where admirable behavior is offset by the sight of characters carrying on in a despicable manner, its eroticism hidden from sight but not from the subconscious, framed in an exquisite shimmer of light, color, and scent—this greatly appealed to the big-city audiences, despite an admission price of three dollars. The reviews were all outstanding.

Griffith chose San Francisco for the West Coast premiere, not only because of its large Chinese population but because it had given an excellent reception to David Belasco's production of *The First Born* (by Francis Powers), a Chinese story which Griffith considered the most artistic one-act play ever written in America.[102]

And then he brought it home, to Clune's Auditorium in Los Angeles. It was a grand farewell gesture, for while Griffith had not officially announced it, Hollywood knew that he and his company were moving east. As Karl Brown wrote: "The reaction of that crowded house was the ultimate in applause—a stunned silence of the deeply moved. This lasted a moment, and then came a spontaneous roar of sound, people on their feet shattering the air, hands smiting hands, voices crying 'Bravo, Bravo' and the walls loud with echoed uproar."[103]

The film became an instant classic. But, as Brown pointed out, when the picture went into the cold bleak world, to be shown in a regular picture house with no color projection (release prints were tinted, however), no special orchestras to help it out, "It was a sad, sad story. They walked out on it. The farmers who had cranked up the old flivver and driven into town to see a rattling good thriller like Griffith is famous for, couldn't quite dope out what it was about, so they went across the street to see some other picture that, like as not, the reviewers had tramped all over."[104]

A wave of features and serials followed *Broken Blossoms* with stories set in the Orient or Chinatown—*Crooked Streets* (Paul Powell), *The Yellow Typhoon* (Edward José) with Anita Stewart, the serial *The Invisible Hand* (William J. Bowman) with Antonio Moreno. Chinese extras were paid 50 percent more than their white counterparts ($7.50 per day as opposed to five dollars). And it was not advisable for casting directors to try to make do with Japanese extras; there was intense rivalry between the Chinese and Japanese and while the latter might have worked for five dollars, they would not put on Chinese costume.[105]

This did not apply to Sessue Hayakawa, who frequently played Chinese roles. In 1921 he filmed the tragic play *The First Born,* which had so impressed Griffith, working with an almost entirely Chinese cast. The play, however, was not written by an Oriental. And few of these films did anything to dispel the popular misconceptions about the Chinese. "I do not like pictures about Chinese," said a child, "because they are frightening."[106]

To combat the bad image of the Chinese purveyed by the motion picture, James B. Leong Productions (also known as the Wah Ming Motion Picture Company) was set up in Los Angeles, financed by Chinese businessmen. Its aim was to make Chinese stories with Chinese casts. Sadly, it was a short-lived experiment, for it appears to have made but one film. George Yohalem wrote a scenario for *The Lotus Flower* from an original story by James Leong.

Leong was born in Shanghai in 1889 and came to America in 1913. He went to college in Muncie, Indiana, and entered films about 1918, serving as interpreter and assistant director on *Broken Blossoms*.[107]

His story was an adaptation of an old legend of a girl who gave her life that the sacred bell might be sweet-toned and so saved her father's reputation as an artisan.[108] The cast, headed by Lady Tsen Mei,* included James Wang (who had played the Buddhist priest in *Broken Blossoms*), Goro Kino, and Chow Young. Among the Westerners were Tully Marshall, made up as a Chinese, and Noah Beery as a Tartar chief.

---

*She played in *The Letter* (1929).

The Pagan God, 1919, *directed by Park Frame (center), with H. B. Warner (right). Interpreter is Leong But-Jung (James B. Leong); the cameraman is William C. Foster. (Robert S. Birchard Collection)*

A mixture of Oriental and Occidental players in Purple Dawn, 1923. *James B. Leong (left), Edward Peil (standing) as tong leader, and Bessie Love (far right).*

In *Picture Play,* the director was named as Leong But-jung (James B. Leong's Chinese name). The magazine described a preview for the Chinese consul, at which But-jung answered all the questions of the American distributors. Yet when the film was released (under the new title of *Lotus Blossum*), the direction was credited to Frank Grandon.

But-jung announced another film, based on an old Korean legend, but nothing came of it.

As James B. Leong, or Jimmy Leong, But-jung turned to acting and played Oriental roles in numerous pictures, among them *The Purple Dawn* with Bessie Love.

James Wang, who came to the United States in the 1880s, appeared in some of the earliest American films, made in Chicago and New York. Although he left the Baptist ministry to act in films, he was not offended to be offered villainous roles. As one of the technical advisers on *The Red Lantern,* he interpreted French director Albert Capellani's orders to the 500 Chinese extras storming the palace. James Wang was the major source for Chinese actors and extras and thus a valuable member of the picture business.[109]

Equally important was Tom Gubbins, an Englishman born in China, where his father was in the diplomatic service. Gubbins spent his first eight years in China; when he moved to Los Angeles as an adult, he found himself more at home in Chinatown than in Hollywood. He endeared himself to the locals by helping to organize a strike among those who worked in pictures when they protested against the lurid screen portrayals of the Chinese.

When producers approached Gubbins, he insisted upon knowing the story, and he refused to ask the Chinese to appear in scenes which were derogatory.[110] He had several successes in his casting: he gave Anna May Wong, born Wong Liu Tsong* of Chinese parents in 1907 in Los Angeles, her first work as an extra at the age of twelve. She had a role in *The Red Lantern* and was featured in the Technicolor "Madame Butterfly," *The Toll of the Sea* (1922), directed by Chester M. Franklin, becoming as a direct result the only Chinese-American to approach stardom after Douglas Fairbanks saw her and featured her in his *The Thief of Bagdad* (1924). She had become obsessed with the movies after seeing companies at work in Los Angeles's Chinatown, and she frequently played truant to watch them, becoming known to technicians and players as the Curious Chinese Child. Her parents opposed her career, and her father refused to watch her films. But she succeeded in America and became the darling of high society in England, from whence she returned with a pronounced English accent and the startling statement that there was no racial prejudice in Europe. She had even worked in France and Germany. Wong felt that Sessue Hayakawa's career had been damaged because he was never allowed to kiss the object of his love if she happened to be white. The same applied to her; she was never permitted to kiss a white man.

Anna May Wong's departure for Europe in 1928 was spurred by dismay at the parts she was offered in Hollywood. "Why is it that the screen Chinese is nearly always the villain of the piece," she said in a 1933 interview, "and so cruel a villain. . . . We are not like that.

---

*Frosted Yellow Willow.

Anna May Wong (center) with a group of Chinese-American actresses in Drifting, *1923, a Tod Browning picture about opium smuggling in China.*

"How should we be, with a civilization that's so many times older than that of the West? We have our own virtues. We have our rigid code of behavior, of honor. Why do they never show these on the screen? Why should we always scheme, rob, kill? I get so weary of it all—the scenarist's concept of Chinese characters."[111]

Yet the nightclub dancer she played in *Piccadilly* (1929) in England, for German director E. A. Dupont, was hardly a fresh departure, although she stole the picture from its star, Gilda Gray. She knew little of China and when she visited that country found herself rejected by the Chinese theatre for being too American.[112]

"My Chinese are trying hard—very hard—to win the respect of Americans," said Gubbins. "They do not like to appear in roles which in any way seem degrading. Honor and honesty are characteristics of their race. For example, when we were working in the William Fox production *Shame,* directed by Emmett Flynn, the script called for scenes in an opium den. The action revolved about some low-caste Chinese characters and led to one of those dives where, in fiction, white girls become slaves of a fearful drug and are ruined.

"Do you think the Chinese would appear in those scenes? Not on your life! They chattered among themselves, shook their heads, backed off. It looked like mutiny. Then I was called, and I had to take great pains to explain that though the scene showed an opium den, the action would teach a great moral lesson, and

Chinese-American James Wong Howe, already one of the world's greatest cameramen, filming Sorrell and Son, *1927, on the roof of the Savoy Hotel, London. H. B. Warner (left) and director Herbert Brenon. (National Film Archive)*

it was their duty to help teach this lesson. I had to tell the whole story to them, and it was only then that they would agree to go ahead. At that, they didn't like it and very plainly told me that they wanted no more of that kind.

"And they also let it be known that they would take part in no scenes which showed Chinese kidnapping white girls. You remember, back in the old days of serials, the spectacle of the heroine being snatched by villainous Orientals and dragged into a den of vice. It was quite common. The truth of the matter is that fewer white girls have been attacked by Chinese than by any other race of people."[113]

The situation got so bad that when a company arrived to film sequences for *Pied Piper Malone* (1924) in New York's Chinatown, they were met with a near riot. Young Chinese tore the Mandarin clothes from the extras (also Chinese), and the company was bombarded with milk bottles, bricks, and old vegetables. The film people took cover until the police arrived. The main complaint was against the movies showing the denizens of Chinatown smoking opium.[114]

But melodrama, however exaggerated, contains a modicum of truth. Opium dens did exist, and it is fascinating to see the way they are portrayed in early films. One of the most startling comments in pre-Hays American cinema was in DeMille's *The Whispering Chorus* (1918), when the dishonest clerk is watching the New Year celebrations in Chinatown. He wanders into a Chinese bar, where he is offered not only opium but women, too. A blind is slowly raised revealing a bed, occupied by a girl. DeMille intercuts the clerk's wife marrying a politician, thinking her husband dead, while the clerk (symbolically) makes love to the Oriental girl.

A 1917 picture with Edna Goodrich called *Queen X,* an exposé of the opium traffic, featured the Chinese actor George Gee. In 1918, Gee was murdered at his Brooklyn home.

"For many years, Gee has been an informant of the Government," said *Moving Picture World,* "and aided the revenue agents in trailing scores of traffickers in drugs, with the result that a price of $500 is said to have been placed on his head by tongs interested in the opium traffic.

"In the film Gee was portrayed as the managing director of the Government campaign against illicit dealers in drugs and the Government officials believe that agents of the tongs recognized him in the film and spotted him as the informant who was responsible for the numerous raids which resulted in the arrest and conviction of illicit drug dealers."[115]

Sam Goldwyn purchased a fantasy by Gouverneur Morris called *What Ho the Cook,* and in 1921 he handed it to director Rowland V. Lee. "I loved the story," Lee said, "and saw many possibilities of making it into a charming, unique piece of entertainment."[116]

The story concerned a Chinaman who makes a trip to America; when he

Jack Abbe in What Ho, the Cook, *with gangster (Harry Gribbon).*

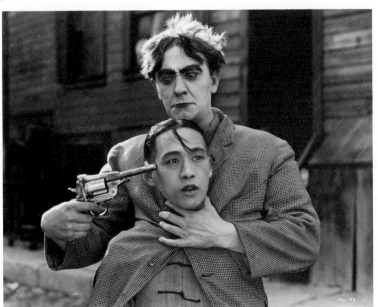

returns he tells the story of his adventures to his eight-year-old son. The attraction of the piece was its view of America through the imaginings of the boy. The hero, What Ho, is in love with a girl named Ting-a-Ling Wing, daughter of a laundry-man. Business is bad, and the laundryman decides to go to the United States, "where men wear starched collars every day." What Ho follows. After adventures with Mexican bandits, What Ho reaches the U.S. border, where a customs officer stands at a turntable. He sniffs the bottles that cross the line, seizing those containing liquor. The officer roars at What Ho, demanding a passport or a ten-dollar bill. What Ho has neither, but conceals himself in a grandfather clock. He arrives with a bang; the removal men drop the clock. Had they placed it carefully, it would have meant overtime. When he finds Ting-a-ling, she is much changed. She indulges in "flirting." This, she explains, is a custom by which a lady acts as if she doesn't like the man when in fact she does. Go-Hang, the Chinese owner of the local American Plan laundry, is angry at the competition offered by What Ho. "Don't I pay the aldermen for a monopoly?" he cries. "Send me the gangster and tell the cops to look the other way." What Ho manages to defeat the gangster, but not the policemen who support the gangster. Asked to obey the men in uniform, he even returns to give himself up to the customs officer, who offers a bargain bribe, $9.98. When What Ho hears he can leave the country without disobeying the men in uniform, he races back to Arcadia in time to break up the wedding of Go-Hang and Ting-a-ling and marry the girl himself.[117]

Rowland V. Lee and Cedric Gibbons indulged themselves with elaborate and amusing sets including Go-Hang's laundry, which featured a monstrous machine called The Button Remover. Their approach was to make the film resemble the illustrations in a children's book.

Jack Abbe was given the lead opposite an Oriental girl called Winter Blossom, and the title was changed to *Whims of the Gods.* Chaplin watched the rushes for several nights and was full of admiration.

It would be tempting to see the hand of Will Hays crushing the life out of this diverting little picture, with its cynical view of America, and certainly its non-appearance coincides with his acceptance of his new post. But according to Rowland V. Lee, the culprit was Goldwyn himself: "When the picture was cut, Goldwyn said it stank and had it put on the shelf. Long after I had left the studio an effort was made to salvage the film. A wise-cracking title writer was engaged. Result: disaster. The film was never released and I still think it was one of the best things I ever did."[118]

The official reason? The American public did not care for fantasy. Douglas Fairbanks made *The Thief of Bagdad* a few years later, and the American public embraced it wholeheartedly.

SHADOWS   One of the strongest influences of *Broken Blossoms* was not its tolerance but its violence. *Bits of Life* was made by Marshall Neilan in 1921. (A title in *Broken Blossoms* read: "Broken bits of his life in his new home.") It was a feature made up of four short stories and an artistic experiment in itself. Sadly, the film has been lost, but it made a stir in the business at the time because it seemed such a brave effort and proved such a financial flop.

Lon Chaney in Shadows, *1922, directed by Tom Forman. (National Film Archive)*

All the stories but the last ended grimly. The third, "Hop," by Hugh Wiley, featured Lon Chaney (in one of his remarkable make-ups, as a Chinese vice-lord) and Anna May Wong. As a boy in China, Chin Gow was taught that girl infants were undesirable. When he rises to overlord of the San Francisco opium dens and his wife produces a girl, he beats the wife and vows to kill the child.[119] A friend gives the wife a crucifix; as she hammers it into the wall, the nail penetrates the skull of Chin Gow, lying on a bunk on the other side, and kills him.[120]

Photoplay selected it as one of the eight best pictures of the year, but the censors took such exception to it that some states did not see it at all. In any case, the public stayed away. An exhibitor commented, "I tell you that Chink stuff of that kind won't do if we expect to stay in the game."[121]

The picture did nothing to improve the lot of the Chinese in America. Lon Chaney, however, had the distinction of starring in *Shadows,* produced in 1922 by B. P. Schulberg's studio. This was in many respects a routine low-budget melodrama, but what made it unique was that it dealt openly with racial prejudice and small-town hypocrisy, and its hero was an unattractive, opium-smoking Chinese laundryman. "Portraying the Oriental," said Lon Chaney, "is to my mind an art."[122]

The picture opened with the title "To every people, in every age, there comes a measure of God to man—through man.

"Even today, wisdom may dwell among us in humble guise, unknown, despised, until, its mission fulfilled, it slips back into the mystery from whence it came."

"Pray—or get out!" says the pillar of the church, Nate Snow (John Sainpolis) to the shipwrecked Chinese (Lon Chaney). A scene from Shadows, *1922. (Museum of Modern Art)*

In the little New England seaport of Urkey, a violent storm wrecks several boats and Dan Gibbs (Walter Long), the much-disliked "Admiral" of the fishing fleet, is lost. When a man is washed up on the shore, the townspeople are dismayed to find that he (Lon Chaney) is Chinese. They pray for the souls of the lost, but he fails to join them. "Pray—or get out!" says a pillar of the church, Nate Snow (John Sainpolis). "We are all believers in Urkey. We want no heathens."

But Yen Sin elects to stay. He sets up a laundry and keeps to himself. A young pastor, John Malden (Harrison Ford), comes to Urkey, "heartsore," as the title puts it, "because he had not been called to the 'Field' of the Far East." While the townspeople welcome him, their children beat up Yen Sin and Malden has to rescue the man. He and Sympathy Gibbs (Marguerite de la Motte), Dan Gibbs's widow, fall in love, marry, and have a child.

Malden receives a letter, purporting to come from Dan Gibbs, demanding $500. His quiet life becomes a nightmare. He takes Nate Snow into his confidence, and Nate lends him the blackmail money. But Malden is haunted by the possibility that Gibbs is alive, making him a bigamist. When this fear causes him to collapse in the pulpit, he resigns from the church.

"It seemed that all the purpose of Malden's life was now directed to the one channel left open to him"—he attempts to convert Yen Sin. Malden is shunned by the villagers; only Nate Snow stands by him. When the old Chinese falls ill and asks for the minister, Snow arrives and asks him to repent and believe.

Yen Sin says he will confess if Snow confesses too. Obligingly, Snow catalogues some minor offenses. But Yen Sin turns the tables on him and reveals him as the blackmailer. Malden, who has arrived together with some of the townspeople, is shocked. But his reaction is unexpected. "I have suffered," he says, "but you, Nate, you must have suffered a thousand times more to do the thing you did."

Yen Sin is so moved by this that he touches Malden's sleeve: "If you forgive, then Yen Sin believe!"

In the final scene, another storm springs up. Yen Sin, alone again on his old scow, cuts the mooring line, and the wind carries the boat into the darkness.

"The storm brought him," says Malden, "and the storm is taking him away— but the peace he found us is awaiting him in the harbor."

This touching story was directed with such sincerity that the melodramatic style only added to the poignancy. Adapted from the story "Ching, Ching, Chinaman" by Wilbur Daniel Steele, the script was written by Eve Unsell and Hope Loring. Tom Forman directed and Al Lichtman produced. The camerawork was by Harry Perry.

"Filming *Shadows* was a joy," wrote Harry Perry. "The exteriors were found not far from Monterey in west central California. Tom Forman took our troupe to a perfect substitute for a Massachusetts town. There, in spite of the worst weather conditions imaginable, I was able to photograph some of the most re-markable scenic effects I have ever recorded on film."[123]

The critical reaction was mixed. *Picture Play* considered it "a curiously dull transcription of an excellent story of New England people. Lon Chaney lifts it from mediocrity."[124]

Photoplay said, "An idea of delicacy and charm has been translated with great care to the screen. Tom Forman's direction is as inspired as possible in view of the fact that there are censors."[125]

Photoplay also revealed that those who objected to the title change should not blame the producers. Schulberg and Lichtman wanted to use *Ching, Ching, China-man* and wrote to exhibitors, asking for their opinion. Two thirds thought it a dreadful title.[126] Schulberg knew the risk he was taking by making the picture in the first place; there was no point in arousing further antipathy from exhibitors. He changed the title to *Shadows,* which meant very little and had to be justified by a title in the confrontation scene, when Malden says, "Then all my fears have been just—shadows?" Schulberg regarded this as his one concession to the box office.[127]

Thanks to Lon Chaney's drawing power—he had become a star with *The Miracle Man* in 1919, the year of *Broken Blossoms*—exhibitors reported excellent business in many parts of the country. One 4,000-seat theatre in Cleveland re-ported S.R.O. all day one Monday, when the opposition included a Wallace Reid picture and *When Knighthood Was in Flower* with Marion Davies. And several Mid-west theatres, whose patrons might have been offended by the story, reported excellent runs, with the public well pleased.

Louis F. Gottschalk wrote the score for the film, as he had for *Broken Blossoms.* And Robert E. Sherwood selected it for his book *The Best Motion Pictures of 1922– 1923.* Of the grave problems faced by such brave independent productions, he

Shadows *in production. Left to right, Lon Chaney; Eve Unsell, scenarist; B. P. Schulberg, producer; Tom Forman, director; Harry Perry, cameraman. (Museum of Modern Art)*

wrote: "*Shadows* provides definite proof of the regrettable fact that the best pictures aren't always to be seen in the best theatres.

"It is an open secret that the great majority of first-run theatres in all parts of the country are controlled by four great producer-distributing corporations—Famous Players, First National, Fox and Metro with an additional number that are devoted largely to Universal, Goldwyn and Pathé. These huge companies, which are always at one another's throats, fight fiercely for control in each city. The poor little independent companies stand helplessly by—knowing that regardless of who wins the big tussle, they are pretty sure to lose. They find it almost impossible to get their pictures into important first-run theatres; and must content themselves with those meagre scraps that they are able to pick off this second string.

"*Shadows* ran into this difficulty. Mr. Schulberg and his associate, Al Lichtman, tried to place *Shadows* in one of the first-run theatres in New York (there are five of them)—but it was met with nothing but rebuffs.

"The National Board of Review, however, discovered *Shadows* and lifted it from the obscurity in which it had been submerged; it proved to be financially successful."[128]

Sherwood considered *Shadows* not only an unusually good story, but a forceful lesson in religious tolerance: "As such, it probably proved offensive to many ardent churchmen who believe that intolerance is a weapon entrusted to them, and them alone, by God. . . . Mr. Chaney's performance of the benevolent laundryman, Yen

Sin, was the finest impersonation of an Oriental character by an Occidental player that I have ever seen."[129]

Shadows came out in 1922, but failed to make the kind of impact for which Schulberg hoped. Lon Chaney went on to make *Mr. Wu,* directed by William Nigh, at MGM in 1929, a return to the violent melodrama of *Bits of Life:* despite his love for his daughter, a Chinese kills her when she plans to marry an Englishman instead of a Mandarin.

Hollywood found the sinister Oriental far more profitable than the gentle and humane one. One of the most racist films ever made in America appeared from Warner Bros. in 1927, from the pen of Darryl F. Zanuck: *Old San Francisco,* directed by Alan Crosland. A white man hides a hideous secret: he has Chinese blood . . . a girl who has been captured by the Chinese is about to be handed over to the white slavers when she is saved by the San Francisco earthquake. It is serial stuff, impeccably produced, but utterly absurd, suffused by the kind of religion best practiced by the Ku Klux Klan:

> *In the awful light of an outraged, wrathful*
> *Christian God, the heathen soul of the Mongol*
> *stood revealed.*

THE JAPANESE

Picture the Japanese immigrant arriving in America between the years 1890 and 1924 with just a blanket on his back and faced with an alien landscape and equally alien faces. He was subjected to brutal inspection by officials, not one word of whose language he could understand. Occasionally Nisei (first-generation Japanese-Americans) might be on hand to assist the Issei (Japanese-born). If not, he was on his own.

Unlike the Chinese, the Japanese were not excluded by the United States. At first barred from leaving Japan by their own government, when they were finally permitted to emigrate, Japanese people were welcomed in America. But large numbers began to arrive at the worst possible moment, when the United States had "solved" the Chinese problem with the Exclusion Act of 1882. The Japanese replaced the Chinese, working hard for low wages and seldom complaining about conditions. This impressed employers but did not endear the newcomers to the unions. Restricted to low-paid laboring jobs, they gravitated toward agriculture; the vast majority of Japanese immigrants became farmers or gardeners.[130]

Japan's 1905 victory over Russia appalled the Western world. Films were even made about a possible Japanese invasion of America. When Japan was rumored to be preparing for war in 1908, President Theodore Roosevelt negotiated a "gentleman's agreement" by which no further passports would be issued to laborers; this was expected to reduce immigration. The Japanese who were already in America were ostracized, and social ostracism was, to them, almost more unbearable than the death penalty.[131] Then, in 1924, the Johnson-Reed Immigration Act excluded the Japanese altogether, despite a warning by the Japanese ambassador of

(Will the Japanese never *cope with our technology?) Sessue Hayakawa in* Hashimura Togo, *1917, directed by William de Mille. (Museum of Modern Art)*

the grave consequences of abandoning the gentleman's agreement.[132] The act shocked and insulted Japan and strengthened the hands of the nationalists and militarists. Leonard Mosley, in his life of Hirohito, points to the act as an important link in the chain that eventually led to the Japanese attack on Pearl Harbor in 1941.

The act was followed by a boycott in Japan against all things American—especially motion pictures.

There was another Japan in American minds; the land of *Madame Butterfly,* orange blossom, geisha girls, ornamental gardens, bold samurai. To bring audiences a scent of authentic Japan, the Star Film Company, run by the Frenchman Gaston Méliès, went there as part of their world cruise in 1912. The group sailed from San Francisco aboard a Japanese steamer and began filming at once. The subjects they produced were either documentaries—*A Japanese Wedding, Japanese Shoemaker at Work*—or dramas of shame, slavery, and suicide.[133]

The Vitagraph Corporation of America followed a year later.[134] They also traveled aboard a Japanese steamer and were astonished to find it equipped with a motion picture theatre, enabling them to shoot pictures during the day and show them at night. Director James Young, far from expressing gratitude, muttered darkly about the vessel crossing the Pacific some day as a military transport "laden with yellow warriors to overrun the Louisiana Purchase and points East."[135]

When the ship put in at Yokohama, the Americans were soothed and charmed. "For exquisite scenery and immaculate cleanliness Japan is in a class by itself."[136] But wherever they went, they were shadowed by secret service men and allowed to take pictures only on condition that a copy of each scene be handed over for government inspection. Two films, *Osaka's Wrath*[137] and *Jack's Chrysanthemum*,[138] were shot in the Yokohama area.

In 1917, The Fuji Yama Film Company of Yokohama brought out director Frank A. Thorne to help make its pictures. He was accompanied by his wife, the actress Lizette Thorne; both had worked for the American Film Company. Thorne told *Moving Picture World:*

"I am directing an eight-reel feature, which the company is here to make, entitled *Nami-Ko.* The entire cast is composed of Japanese actors, and while it is very interesting to see these quaint people work before the camera it is nevertheless quite a task to handle them, as everything has to be done through an interpreter, and when night comes I am very weary from the work . . .

"Their studios are fine and their settings are very elaborate; their actors are very good, and in many ways they can teach us, but they don't understand construction and cutting for dramatic value, and most of their plays are tragic and much overacted. Naturalness seems foreign to them, and if they can be taught this simple art their products are destined to give the world at large very keen competition."[139]

In October 1914, the Japanese-American Film Company began operations in California, capitalized at $200,000 by Japanese businessmen. A stock company of forty players was brought over from Japan to make films with Japanese themes, treating native customs with absolute fidelity. The president of the corporation was K. Numamoto and the secretary J. Takata. The leading lady was Hisa Numa, who had made pictures in Japan. Tomi Morri, a Japanese stage veteran who joined the company, had worked in pictures with Ince; other players included Kohano Akashi and Jack Y. Abbe. Abbe became the only Japanese other than the Hayakawas to attain any kind of prominence as an actor, even though he tended to specialize in Chinese roles.[140] The company's first production, *The Oath of the Sword,* was made in California. One might have hoped for a fresh approach from Japanese filmmakers—particularly in view of the outstanding Japanese films which would be made before the end of the silent era. But it was the usual hokum—a young Japanese loves a girl from his own nation. He goes away to college. When he returns he finds his sweetheart has married an American, who has left his wife and child in the United States. "The ensuing dramatic scenes are most thrilling, and include a new handling of the Japanese custom of hara-kiri."[141]

The Japanese film in the United States received its greatest boost when Thomas H. Ince signed a Japanese stage actress called Tsuru Aoki in 1913—together with her company of twenty Japanese players.* Tsuru Aoki had come to America as a child in 1903 with her aunt, Sado Yacco, a celebrated dramatic dancer, and her uncle, the owner of the Imperial Theatre of Japan. While they went to Paris, Tsuru was

---

*The Japanese were easier to employ than the Chinese, said Ince, because they didn't suffer from the same fear of the camera; *Motion Picture News,* May 1919, pp. 113–115.

Sessue Hayakawa and his wife Tsuru Aoki in The Courageous Coward, *1919, directed by William Worthington for Haworth Pictures Corp.*

left in San Francisco in the care of another uncle, Hyosai Aoki, an artist who placed her in a convent. He died while she was there, and an American newspaper woman adopted her and brought her to Los Angeles. So American was her up-bringing that while she retained respect for Japanese culture, she had to exercise great patience with all the preliminaries necessary to be correctly dressed and made up for Japanese roles.

In Los Angeles, she organized a Japanese theatre and was succeeding so well she began to direct plays herself. Fred Mace, the comedian, tempted her into pictures. He argued that the film would accomplish more for Japan in a short space of time than the legitimate drama in a very long time.[142] Actually, Mace just wanted her for a series of split-reel comedies at Majestic. But at the Boyle Heights studio she formed a friendship with director Dell Henderson and his wife, and they thought her wasted in these roles. Henderson directed her in *The Oath of O Tsuru San,* written by William Nigh. (In it, she fell in love with and *married* an American.) Then came the Thomas Ince contract.

Tsuru Aoki was born in Tokyo, but this was too mundane for the Ince pub-licity department; they declared her to be a native of the island of Sakura, which had recently been devastated by the eruption of the volcano Sakurajima.

"Miss Aoki, having lost practically all her relatives in this eruption, was in-consolable and Mr. Ince thought he was due to lose her, that she would have to go back home. But in consoling her, he induced her to work in conjunction with him on a thrilling and powerful heart interest story, entitled *Wrath of the Gods . . .*

revolving around Japanese legends and depicting the scenes and actions of her countrymen during the eruption, so that she could show the world the sufferings of her people."[143]

Tsuru Aoki's future husband, Sessue Hayakawa, was described by David Warfield as "the screen's greatest dramatic actor."[144] Born Kintaro Hayakawa in the township of Nanaura, on the island of Honshu, on June 10, 1890, he came of Samurai stock.[145] He entered the navy, but suffered a broken ear drum in a diving prank. He was dismissed from the navy and attempted hara-kiri. His family sent him to the University of Chicago. He began acting for the Japanese community and eventually played in Los Angeles. It was here that he met Tsuru Aoki.

"I was very much interested," she said, "in his brave attempts to play Ibsen and Shakespeare in Japanese, at the Japanese theatre in Los Angeles, and I promised to help in any way I could. I told him about my cherished plan to return to Japan some day and go on reforming the theatre, as my uncle and aunt had been doing, and I found that our ideals were identical."[146]

Tsuru Aoki persuaded Ince to see a performance of Hayakawa's staging of Melchior Lengyel's murder-mystery play, *The Typhoon.* Ince was so impressed he bought the film rights and placed Hayakawa under contract, casting him immediately in *Wrath of the Gods,* which was produced in early 1914. In May of that year, Tsuru Aoki and Sessue Hayakawa were married.

The Wrath of the Gods, *1914, directed by Reginald Barker, with special effects by Raymond West. (National Film Archive)*

The Wrath of the Gods opened with a typhoon (unlike *The Typhoon*) and closed with the eruption of a volcano. Ince's most elaborate spectacle, it was nevertheless entirely a Japanese story. Curious that such a film should have been made in California, where anti-Japanese prejudice was endemic! What was the reason? Was Ince nostalgic because his father once specialized in Oriental roles? Was he capitalizing on the worldwide coverage given to the Japanese volcano, which erupted in January 1914? (The full title was *The Wrath of the Gods, or the Destruction of Sakura-Jima;* since the action took place several centuries earlier, the reference was dropped.) Whatever the reason, Ince caught the public at precisely the right moment. So great was the demand that Marcus Loew opened up the Brooklyn National League baseball ground (Ebbets Field), seating 20,000; 40,000 people tried to get in, and a riot broke out when 15,000 were turned away. Police reserves from three precincts had to be called out, and there were several casualties.[147]

The sequence in which the town is destroyed by the volcano is staggering, even today. Taken half a mile out to sea, a long shot of the entire shoreline smoking and what looks like thousands of extras rushing in panic along the seafront is unparalleled. (Ince was able to recruit extras from a Japanese fishing village a mile from the studio.) Director Reginald Barker, who made several Japanese subjects that year of 1914, handled most of the picture, while Raymond B. West coped with the special effects.

"I never saw an audience more plainly moved than the thousands that sat in the Strand watching the kaleidoscope of elemental rage," reported W. Stephen Bush, who felt the appeal was doubly effective because the main roles were played by Japanese "with an earnestness and power which are rarely witnessed in the average screen performer."[148]

The Typhoon was also directed by Reginald Barker; it, too, was regarded as an early classic. An all-too-faithful translation of a stage play, with a notable lack of physical action, it is not so impressive. Frank Borzage, who later excelled in the direction of actors, overacts alarmingly; Hayakawa is not much better. The only player who seems in control is Henry Kotani.[149]

Hayakawa played Tokorama, a Japanese diplomat living in Paris, who is working on a crucial military report. His French mistress grows petulant at his long absences. When he discovers she has another lover, he orders her out and she turns on him: "You yellow whining rat—and your Japan, a yellow blot on the ocean." For which he kills her. Tokorama is protected by his compatriots, for only he can complete the vital report. An underling takes the blame; after an elaborate trial scene he is taken out and guillotined by the French authorities. Tokorama is found dead, his report completed. The ambassador is forced to burn it as the police smash their way in.

"The one impression of the play is that Japanese patriotism is a peculiar and fearful thing," wrote Vachel Lindsay. "Sessue Hayakawa should give us Japanese tales more adapted to the films."[150]

Hayakawa would have been the first to agree. "Such roles are not true to our Japanese nature," he told Grace Kingsley in 1916. "They are false and give people

Typhoon, 1914. Hironari (Henry Kotani) is led to execution, sacrificing his life for his superior. (George Eastman House)

a wrong idea of us. I wish to make a characterization which shall reveal us as we really are."[151]

This was a curious comment, for it had been Hayakawa who had brought the play to Los Angeles. DeWitt Bodeen says that *The Typhoon* was a veritable dramatic thunderbolt, and it made Sessue Hayakawa an overnight star. This must have taken Ince by complete surprise because he had nothing with which to follow up *The Typhoon*.[152] Although he tried to keep Hayakawa, he failed to match what Jesse Lasky offered.

Hayakawa appeared as the drunken son of a Sioux chief in *Pride of Race* (1914) (or *The Last of the Line*), an excellent two-reeler but hardly of the stature of the other films. When his contract lapsed, he went over to the Jesse L. Lasky Feature Play Company, and, after making a few films, including *The Secret Sin* with Blanche Sweet, in which he played the drug overlord of San Francisco's Chinatown, he won his most famous role, as Hishuru Tori in Cecil B. DeMille's *The Cheat* (1915).

The Cheat was one of the most sensational films of the early cinema. Edith Hardy (Fannie Ward), a society woman addicted to gambling, loses charity funds at a card game and borrows money from Tori, a collector and art connoisseur. The service she is expected to provide in return is implied in the bargain. When her husband (Jack Dean) makes money in the stock market and she is able to re-pay the debt in cash, Tori insists that she carry out their agreement. She refuses; he tears the gown from her shoulder and brands her like an object in his collection.

Tori (Hayakawa) attempts to contact Edith's husband to reveal her vast debt—a scene from the 1915 version of The Cheat, *directed by Cecil B. DeMille. (Anthony Slide)*

She shoots and wounds him, but her husband takes the blame. In the trial scene, he is on the point of being convicted when she rises and, baring her shoulder, reveals the incriminating brand. Tori is protected with difficulty against the fury of the mob.

From Hector Turnbull's scenario, DeMille made a powerful film which still retains much of its original impact. Although the film is unashamedly racist (Stephen Bush referred in his review to "the beastliness in the Oriental nature"),[153] Hayakawa's performance gives it much of its explosive quality. According to DeWitt Bodeen, the branding scene produced screams from the audience and some women fainted. "The effect of Hayakawa on American women was even more electric than Valentino's," he wrote. "It involved fiercer tones of masochism as well as a latent female urge to experience sex with a beautiful but savage man of another race."[154]

Variety said: "Here certainly is one of the best yellow heavies that the screen has ever had. . . . Without the third point of the eternal triangle having been one of an alien race the role of Edith Hardy in this picture would have been one of the most unsympathetic that has ever been screened."[155]

Japanese associations in California protested the picture vigorously on the grounds that the branding scene would embitter people against Japan,[156] and DeMille received an official protest from the Japanese Embassy. As Japan was an ally of Great Britain and France, apologies were made, but not until the 1918 reissue (by which time the United States was in the war) were the titles changed, Hayakawa becoming Hara Arakau, a "Burmese" ivory merchant. (Hayakawa was unrepentant and felt the nationality of his character was immaterial.)

In Great Britain and Australia, the film was banned for fear of offending Japan. Although France should have followed the same diplomatic line, she failed to do so, and the film was an enormous hit—so much so that it became the first (and possibly only) motion picture to be turned into grand opera when Camille Erlanger's *Forfaiture* was presented in Paris in 1921.[157] (It was not a success.)[158]

The great French writer Colette reviewed *The Cheat* with admiration: "To the genius of an Oriental actor is added that of a director probably without equal," she wrote. "Let our aspiring cine-actors go to see how, when his face is mute, [Hayakawa's] hand carries on the flow of his thought. Let them take to heart the menace and disdain in a motion of his eyebrow and how, in the instant when he is wounded, he creates the impression that his life is running out with his blood, without shuddering, without convulsively grimacing, with merely the progressive petrifaction of his Buddha's mask and the ecstatic darkening of his eyes."[159]

The French were even more enthusiastic about the film than the Americans, although Louis Delluc said, "No one actually wanted to see anything in it except the Japanese. . . . Hardly anyone thought of its absolute cinematic newness."[160]

Harry Carr claimed that Sessue Hayakawa gained stardom with a single glance. When Fannie Ward realizes she has made a blunder and tries to win Tori back, he meets her advances with a flash of cold scorn. "It sounds like an exaggeration; but it is an actual fact that, with that glance, Hayakawa not only made himself famous, but actually started a new school of acting—the school of repression."[161]

Hayakawa explained that he had been brought up to follow the Samurai traditions: "I was always taught that it was disgraceful to show emotion. Consequently, in that scene, as in all other scenes, I purposely tried to show nothing by my face. But in my heart I thought, 'God how I hate you.' And of course it got over to the audience with far greater force than any facial expression could."[162]

Hayakawa never had another sensation to match *The Cheat,* but he maintained his status as a star, moving easily from hero to villain and back again. As Karl Brown put it, "Sessue Hayakawa was a particular personality in his own right, something categorically personal having nothing to do with his being Japanese. A Hayakawa with another name would be as forbiddingly fascinating and as unpredictable as this man of mystery."[163]

Hector Turnbull atoned for the racism of *The Cheat* with *Alien Souls* (1916), in which Hayakawa played another wealthy Japanese, but this time he was a noble character. At least it inspired one reviewer to write, "We are interested to learn here that the Japanese are not the peculiarly monstrous Mongolians of the arts in general, but, after all, just—people, although a bit strange of habit and custom."[164]

Hayakawa specialized in romances and mystery stories, like other stars of the time. The nearest he came to a social film was *The Honorable Friend* (1916), about "picture brides," Japanese women so called because they were selected from photographs. They arrived in America, married, then went to work, thus defeating the gentleman's agreement.[165] Hayakawa played the young manager of the Cherry Blossom Gardens and Nursery whose employer lends him the money to bring over his picture bride (Tsuru Aoki). Once he sees her he proves to be anything but an honorable friend. The Japanese were played by Japanese, with the exception of the employer, for whom Raymond Hatton concocted one of his spectacular make-ups.

Hayakawa was not always cast as a Japanese; he played Indian princes, Mex-

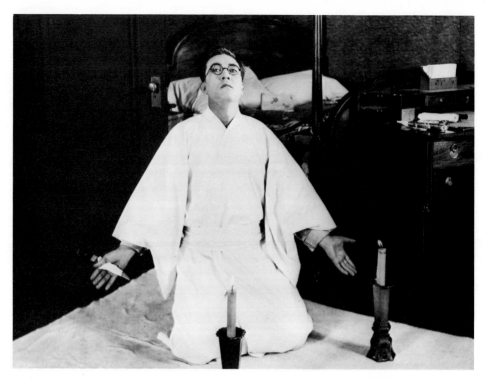

Sessue Hayakawa prepares to commit hara-kiri in Hashimura Togo, *1917. (Hayakawa had himself attempted hara-kiri when he was dismissed from the Japanese Navy.) (George Eastman House)*

ican bandits, Hawaiians, African chiefs, and, most significantly for a Japanese, he also played Chinese parts. He had only one major comedy role, in William de Mille's *Hashimura Togo* (1917), in which he costarred with Florence Vidor. She considered him "a great actor, very subtle, very concentrated, very honest: 'All I ever knew about acting I learned from Hayakawa.' "[166]

The first film Hayakawa made for his own company, Haworth,* *His Birthright* (1918), which was intended as a kind of sequel to *Madame Butterfly,* caused a flaming row. There had to be an American naval officer in such a story, but *Variety* was shocked that a rear admiral of the United States Navy should be placed in an "unenviable light" when confronted with an illegitimate son, the result of a long-ago affair with a Japanese girl. The character's name was Milton. At the New Orleans Navy Yard in 1918 there was a rear admiral named John B. Milton, whose friends saw the film and registered their protests. Naval intelligence officers raided the Palace Theatre and seized the film on the grounds that it reflected discredit on the U.S. Navy. It was sent to Washington for examination, where the harmless plot must have caused some amusement. Hayakawa was unlucky: Milton was on the retired list but had been recalled to active service.

"The scenario would have been in far better taste had it been built around an ordinary American citizen," said *Variety.*[167]

---

*Haworth (Hayakawa and director William Worthington) eventually took over the former Griffith-Fine Arts studios, where *Broken Blossoms* had been shot.

It became apparent around the end of 1919 that even though he was running his own company and helping to choose his own stories, Hayakawa was having difficulty with his subjects. (*A Heart in Pawn* [1919], had been based on his own play, *Shadows.*) The trade press commented on this when the overly artistic *The Dragon Painter* came out. At last he had made a pure Japanese film, but the public was not impressed, even though some critics were.* The following year he moved to Robertson-Cole.

The Hayakawas were among the social elite of Hollywood. Their home, Castle Glengarry, resembled a castellated Highland fortress, although it was actually built of wood. They entertained lavishly, sometimes welcoming as many as 600 guests. The racial problem was suppressed in their case, for their wealth engendered a degree of acceptance, yet it was ever-present nonetheless.

While making *The Swamp,* with Bessie Love, Hayakawa kept working despite an attack of appendicitis. Robertson-Cole executives warned that it would be financial disaster if he withdrew. He had just finished the film when his appendix burst, and he was rushed to the hospital.

Bessie Love also played with Hayakawa in *The Vermilion Pencil* (1922): "He wasn't just a semi-Japanese," she said, "he was the whole hog. A complete Japanese. And he didn't pretend to be anything else. If you didn't understand what he was talking about—and I never could—you were lost. Some people give you the gist, you get the drift, but not with him. He was so sweet.

"I was selling tickets for a function at the Hollywood Bowl and when I said I was starting work with Sessue Hayakawa, the organizing ladies looked askance and said, 'Don't sell one to him . . . we wouldn't want him sitting next to anyone.'

"Another time I was made up as a Chinese, with my hair pulled back. Somebody called me back to the set. "Oh, Miss Love, I understand you're invited to Hayakawa's home for dinner. I wouldn't do that if I were you.' "[168]

Legislation to prohibit Orientals from owning property was on the statute books in California, as anti-Japanese feeling increased. Yet press agents tried to give the impression that Hayakawa's father was American—making him only half Japanese.[169]

It was one of the mysteries of Hollywood that Hayakawa suddenly dropped out of the American picture business.[170] He went to Europe and appeared in French and British films, but Hollywood wondered what had happened. Interviewed in the January, 1929, *Motion Picture Magazine,* he blamed the standard of the stories he was given. But the interviewer, Winifred Eaton Reeve (Onoto Watanna), asked, "Surely you did not drop out of pictures because of that?"

"Oh, no," said Hayakawa hastily. "That was just one of many irritations." And he revealed another reason: "It was something deep. It *strike* me inside! It was something said to me that no true man should speak, and no true man can hear. Something that should not come out of the mouth. It was, you understand—not decent.

"I was associated with certain men in motion picture enterprise. They owe me

---

*The film convinced a modern critic, Fraser Macdonald, that it had actually been made in Japan; *Toronto Film Society Newsletter* (Winter 1987–1988), p. 17. Curiously, Hayakawa was not popular in Japan; his films were thought to show the bad side of the Japanese people. *The Cheat* was not forgiven. Tsuru was adored, in spite of everything (*Cinemagazine* 48, December 1, 1928, p. 298).

$90,000. I never ask for this money. I think there is plenty of time to pay. Perhaps it was that they think too much about this debt. They think it good to goad and humiliate me—to pick a quarrel.''

The quarrel he did not object to. But one of the men—the head of the company—grew very angry. "He called me a name. It is something that should not come out of the mouth. Something that is unpardonable insult to me and an affront to my nationality. No man can help where he is born—what is his blood. Only an ignorant coward throws up to a man that he does not like his race. I come of a proud people—a man of my quality could not endure an insult. Still I did not speak. I stare at this face, but I say nothing. He say then, 'People in this country have no use for Chinks.' I am not Chink. I am Japanese gentleman, and the word *Chink* is not fit to be spoke.''

Hayakawa said nothing to the man, but bowed and left the room. He dismissed his servants and went to Japan in May 1922. (The $90,000 was settled by the company that bought the assets of his production organization.) He stayed in Japan for a month, and then passed through the United States—avoiding Hollywood—to New York, where he appeared in an unsuccessful play. Then he received an offer from France to appear in a Russo-Japanese war drama, *Croix de Fer,* released as *La Bataille* (1923)—*The Danger Line* in America. He was allowed to wear the uniform of a captain in the French navy and received remarkable naval cooperation.[171]

Whether the insult was the true reason for his departure, we have no means of knowing. It may seem like a minor incident to us, but coming after years of prejudice it may have been the last straw. A more sinister story went the rounds that during the shooting of *The Vermilion Pencil,* a set was rigged to fall on Hayakawa. And it was this story, rather than the other, which he chose to tell in his (somewhat unreliable) ghostwritten memoirs, *Zen Showed Me the Way.* He claimed that overall, his films made a substantial profit. Figures do not survive to confirm this, but there is no doubt that Hayakawa's popularity was waning. His fans were satiated with stories with sad endings in which he was obliged to perish to leave the (white) lovers free. Although he felt that his acceptance in romantic roles by the public was a blow of sorts against racial intolerance, even if he *did* lose the girl in the last reel. He went on to make some talkies in Europe (and one in America, in 1933).

He was brought back to Hollywood for a Bogart vehicle, *Tokyo Joe* (1949), although his most famous role of later years was in David Lean's *The Bridge on the River Kwai* (1957). After Tsuru Aoki died in 1961, Hayakawa became a Zen Buddhist priest in Japan. He died in 1973 at the age of eighty-four.

The idea of the Japanese as aggressors was never laid to rest. Overt references appeared in *The Pride of Palomar* (1922), directed by Frank Borzage, in which the villain was a Japanese potato baron, Okada. His attitude toward the United States was symbolized by a shot of him striking a match across a bust of George Washington.[172] (Okada was played by Warner Oland, who, despite his Swedish origin, would specialize in Oriental roles.)

The threat of Japanese expansion caused William Fox to produce an educational feature, *Face to Face with Japan,* which appeared as part of Fox News. "So far as is humanly possible, it is said, this Fox production answers the query 'Does war threaten between United States and Japan?' " wrote *Exhibitors Herald.*[173]

Al Brick, the star cameraman of the New York office of Fox News, traveled 6,000 miles into areas "never before photographed or entered by civilized white men."[174] The documentary revealed the Japanese war machine and illustrated Japanese expansion since 1894. Brick also secured footage of the "camphor hells" on Formosa, where Japan controlled the world's output of camphor, used not only in mothballs but in explosives.

Yet at the same time, interest in the Japanese faded. In the decade from 1921 to 1930, the *American Film Institute Catalogue* lists just six fiction films (one of them the French production, *La Bataille*), which concern themselves with Japan. After December 1941, the American cinema corrected that oversight.

THE RUSSIANS

When the first moving pictures were made, Russia was undergoing a period of terrorism and repression that had started in 1881 with the assassination of Tsar Alexander by a nihilist. The 1905 revolution was preceded by another assassination in February, of the Grand Duke Sergius. Reverses in the war against Japan, particularly the disastrous naval defeat at Tsushima, led to mutinies in the Black Sea fleet, the most celebrated of which took place aboard the *Potemkin.* Twenty years before Eisenstein directed his masterly re-creation of the event, Pathé of France rushed out a reenactment which, however false the painted backcloths, nonetheless still carries impact with its scene of officers being thrown overboard.

"With the Japanese in the East hammering to pieces the armies of the Czar, with revolution fomenting throughout the empire, Russia demands the attention of the whole world," announced *The Biograph Bulletin,*[175] advertising their elaborate production of *The Nihilists* (1905). In the film, an aristocratic family in Russian Poland was torn apart by involvement in revolutionary politics. Grantwood, New Jersey, stood in for Warsaw.

In most of the early films about Russia, the nihilists resemble the French Resistance in World War II; in addition to blowing up oppressive officials and their mansions, they were often called in to get political suspects out of prison or across the border. Many of these films, however, were not political at all, but were merely an opportunity to put assaults on women and sadistic floggings on the screen. The leader of the nihilists, armed with gun or bomb, was invariably a girl who had suffered the death of her lover at the hands of the authorities.

Arthur Miller, the cameraman, recalled working on *Russia, Land of Oppression* (1910), made by Edwin S. Porter. The exteriors were shot on Staten Island and showed a Cossack raid on a Jewish village on the eve of Passover. Unfortunately, Porter could not afford to build the village. "The alarm shown by the peasants inside the cabins . . . was a trick used to avoid the necessity of building a cabin outside."[176]

Doors could be filmed bursting open or being smashed in from inside, and the Cossacks could beat the peasants and depart. "It was a horrifying subject for

The Sowers, *1916, William de Mille's film about Russian revolutionaries—made before the Revolution. Raymond Hatton as the peddler, on a set designed by Wilfred Buckland.*

a picture and the expectation that fast-riding Cossacks would create the same colorful excitement as cowboys and Indians did not materialize. Hence the picture had a disappointing lack of success."[177]

The trouble was the immigrant audiences often knew a great deal more about Russia than the people who made the films. Sets and scenery were often a cause for merriment.

The Girl Nihilist (1908) was described as "gripping" by *Variety*,[178] but the reviewer warned that the transition from Russian scenery to Ellis Island "may expose the locale of the country where the picture was taken." And *Lost in Siberia* (1909), a story of "Nihilist Intrigue, bomb throwing and banishment to Siberia," was criticized for the fact that "painted snow and calcimined rocks abound on every hand."[179] The street scene shown at the opening of *A Russian Heroine* (1910) was "the funniest looking village imaginable. If the peasants of Russia are willing to live in a village of that sort they should be oppressed."[180]

These early nihilist pictures would have horrified audiences had they been shown ten years later at the height of the Red Scare, for their sympathies lay firmly with the revolutionists, whatever ghastly crimes they may have committed. In *The*

Girl Nihilist lots are drawn for the execution of a governor. The heroine draws the fatal paper. She hurls a bomb beneath the governor at the railroad station and is caught by the guards. Instead of being shot, however, she is merely exiled to Siberia with her family.[181] Said *Variety:* "The brutality in the picture may be overlooked through the universal impression of the Russian. Following the striking down of the woman by the Tax Collector, everyone in the audience would have been delighted if the Russian Empire had been destroyed before their sight."[182]

Having committed their acts of revolutionary violence, the nihilists were usually only too keen to flee to the Land of Liberty. None of them seemed anxious to stay behind to continue the revolutionary struggle.

SOLD FOR MARRIAGE The guardians accompanying Marfa (Lillian Gish) in *Sold for Marriage* (1916) were immigrants of a less romantic kind. Obsessed with their plan to make money on their beautiful niece, Uncle Ivan (A. D. Sears) and Aunt Anna (Pearl Elmore) arrange a marriage. Marfa refuses to go through with it, for she has a secret lover, Jan (Frank Bennett), just back from America. When the local police chief (Walter Long) attempts to maul her, Marfa fights him off so violently she thinks she has killed him. The family has to flee, in an imaginative sequence (shot at Truckee, California), during a raging storm, with a furious wind and falling branches. They take the same boat to America as Jan, to Marfa's delight.

The film, written by William E. Wing, was evidently inspired by a newspaper report exposing the marriage market among Russian immigrants. In Los Angeles, Ivan meets his brother, Georg, identified as the leader of the Russian colony, who assures him that pretty girls bring high prices. Many scenes are set in what is described as the Russian quarter of Los Angeles. The crooks even have a contact in the police department who prevents the scheme from being cracked, and they are on the point of selling Marfa to an elderly suitor when Jan finds out, bursts in, and rescues her.

Sold for Marriage is a surprisingly gripping and colorful film to bear the name of Christy Cabanne—usually one of the dullest silent directors—but then it was made at Fine Arts, where the Griffith influence, although emanating almost entirely from *Intolerance,* still had some effect. A great deal of care was lavished on sets, costumes, and atmosphere, but *Variety* felt that the story justified none of it. Nevertheless, it casts an unusual light on the Russians in the period just before the Revolution. Or, as *Moving Picture World* put it, it affords "an interesting glimpse of the low status of Russian civilization."[183]

Now that the Russian archive has opened to us its amazing collection of pre-revolutionary dramas, we can see that Russian films were, on the whole, technically and artistically superior to the American product. But they dared not tackle political subjects, and concentrated instead on slow, meticulously staged psychological dramas with tragic endings. The political comment was there—sometimes the filmmaker's distaste with the hypocrisy of upper-class life betrayed his Menshevik leanings—but usually it was hidden.

Few Russian films were seen in America, whose film industry depended on

Sold for Marriage, *1916, directed by Christy Cabanne. The Cossacks pursue the fleeing family.*

emigrés to provide a veneer of authenticity for its Russian stories. The more enterprising directors realized that they would be seen by large numbers of Russians—those living in the United States. Thus, Russian immigrants with the right kind of experience were very much in demand by the early studios. It might have alarmed many residents of the Lower East Side to know there were Cossacks in the City of New York, but one such, a former officer called Daniel Makarenko, directed and appeared in *The Heart of a Cossack* for Reliance in 1912. For this costume drama, Makarenko had brought the clothing from Russia. He hoped to make a series of Russian pictures for Reliance, but there is no record of his having done so. He became an actor and technical adviser; fifteen years later he played the role of a Cossack in Edward Sloman's *Surrender!*

Nick Dunaew—or Nick the Dime-Bender as he was known[184]—was the leading man in two of Rex Ingram's films. He was born in Moscow in 1884; his father was a nobleman, and his mother, Fedosia Bagrova, came from a St. Petersburg literary family. He obtained a degree in literature, studied law, and made his stage debut in 1904. In America he played at Daly's Theatre and at Jacob Adler's Theatre, on the Lower East Side. He entered films when Blanche Walsh engaged him to assist with the décor and details of her production of *Resurrection* (1912).[185] He then became an actor at Vitagraph, where he met Ingram.

He also met the actor James Morrison, who told me that for *My Official Wife,*

Dunaew brought to the studio a Russian Jew by the name of Bronstein—who turns out to have been Leon Trotsky. This was confirmed by several other people who worked at the East Coast studios; furthermore, the story appeared in the trade press at the time[186] and passed into the annals of film history.[187] Photographic evidence to support this claim was published in 1932, when some old Vitagraph footage was being examined for a compilation film. Suddenly, the unmistakable image of Trotsky came on the screen in a scene with Clara Kimball Young. The photograph was syndicated to the newspapers and the leading man, Harry Morey, recalled the "shy, nervous" revolutionary.

The actor does look like Trotsky, but there is a problem: *My Official Wife* may have been reissued in 1917, the year Trotsky was in New York, but it had been made in 1914. Trotsky arrived in New York on January 13, 1917, and sailed on March 27, 1917;[188] did he work as a film extra in that time, perhaps appearing in retakes added to the story to take advantage of the February revolution? Perhaps, but there is little chance that he could have appeared with Clara Kimball Young, for she had left Vitagraph two years earlier. (*My Official Wife* was her last film for that company.)

Trotsky himself wrote: "Of the legends that have sprung up about me, the greater number have to do with my life in New York ... the newspapers had me engaged in any number of occupations, each more fantastic than the one before ...

Clara Kimball Young in My Official Wife, *1914, with the actor mistaken for Leon Trotsky.* (*National Film Archive*)

"I must disappoint my American readers. My only profession in New York was
that of a revolutionary socialist . . . I wrote articles, edited a newspaper and ad-
dressed labour meetings."[189]

But I still nourish a faint hope that Trotsky had forgotten an afternoon spent at
Fort Lee or Flatbush and that a Russian story will surface from obscurity, bearing
the unmistakable close-up of the founding father of the Red Army.

THE COSSACK WHIP   The apotheosis of anti-tsarist films was produced by the Edison Co., written by Paul Sloane, directed by John Collins, and
played by Viola Dana and Franklyn Hanna. One remarkable aspect of this film
was its technique: Collins used fast cutting, and the occasional tracking shot together with elaborate wipes, which suggested a rewarding partnership with cameraman John Arnold.

Also remarkable was its theme of revenge. The other anti-tsarist films showed
the brutality of the regime and the flight of the revolutionaries to the United States.
This was one of the few films in which a victim reaches safety, then returns to
Russia to mete out vengeance to her tormentors. As the original program said,
"The sensation of the spectator is a compelling desire to applaud."[190]

Other films compared the Russian insurrection to the American Revolution.
This one, while equally sympathetic, depicted the rebels' clandestine meetings in
the same way as did the later anti-Bolshevik films. The composition and lighting
were based on paintings; the later films would heighten the sinister lighting and
use the same compositions to disturb the audience, with reminders of how easily
another revolution could happen here.

The story concerned Darya (Dana), daughter of a muzhik. Cossack police take
her relative to prison. The revolutionists decide they must strike; the prison train
is ambushed and the guards attacked. Fedor Turov (Frank Farrington), prefect of
police, orders a raid on the whole district. The sequence is astonishing: it opens
with mounted Cossacks on the skyline breaking into a gallop across the snow, and
these shots of charging horses are intercut with flashes of screaming, panic-stricken
villagers. Some of the flashes are a mere twelve frames; this is a pioneering example
of the rapid cutting which, ironically, the Russians made famous, and is the earliest
I have seen.[191]

Darya conceals herself, but her sister, Katerina, and her sister's lover are
dragged to headquarters. Turov orders the lover taken to the notorious "stone
cell," where he is shackled and flogged. Katerina is forced to submit to Turov to
save her lover, but he is killed anyway, and she is then flogged herself and thrown
out into the snow. Before she dies, she reaches Darya, who vows revenge. The
revolutionist Sergius (Richard Tucker) gets Darya a job with the Imperial Ballet
Company as the best method of hiding her.

She goes to London and Paris, returns to Russia a star, and is introduced to
Turov. When he makes his usual advances, Darya grows quite flirtatious and even
requests the privilege of visiting his famous "stone cell." She allows herself to be
shackled while he playfully demonstrates the technique. "Now you pretend you're
my prisoner," she says, and when he is securely pinioned she produces the Cossack
whip from beneath her dress and attacks Turov with frightening energy. That this

Viola Dana in John Collins's The Cossack Whip, *1916. (George Eastman House)*

scene would appeal to those with sadomasochistic tendencies would not have occurred to the censors of the time; it was not even cut for England.

"That whip was so long and heavy I had one hell of a time pulling it out from
its hiding place," said Viola Dana. "The part should have been played by an older
girl."[192]

Turov's aide bursts in, and Darya thinks it's all over for her. But the officer
gives her the revolutionary password, and, as she leaves the cell, he declares, "I
am going to take a monster from the world," and shoots Turov. The screen is
tactfully blacked out by a wipe, obscuring Turov at the moment of the killing,
then clearing to show him slumped against the wall, held up by his shackled arms.

The film ends as do most of these stories: escape and arrival in the Land of
the Free, with the Statue of Liberty arousing applause from the audience. Although
shot in the winter of 1915–1916, it was delayed in release and did not appear before
the end of 1916.[193] Thus, for some audiences, it would have been unusually topical,
coinciding with the news of the February 1917 revolution.

Wid's described it as "the old Russian story of the oppressor who whipped
men and ruined the women,"[194] but admitted it had one or two good twists. *Variety*
thought it one of the most vivid pictures, pictorially, that Edison had ever turned
out.[195] And everyone praised the work of Viola Dana; she never forgot the personal
appearance she made when the film was shown on the Lower East Side. The crowd
tore off buttons, grabbing at her clothing, "wanting any remembrance of me,
because they identified with the part I'd played."[196]

THE FALL OF THE ROMANOFFS   The strangest film about
the Russian Revolution went into production in 1917, after the revolution of February, to be released before that of October. It was called *The Fall of the Romanoffs*[197]
and accompanying the title, like some magic ingredient: "with Iliodor."

The central character was Rasputin. Everyone knew by this time that he was
the drunken lecher who had become the power behind the throne. Although the
newspapers portrayed him as a brutal, evil man, he was actually a pacifist and a
healer. For all his faults, the royal couple regarded him as a godsend, for Rasputin
was able to relieve the hemophilia of the tsarevich. "Whatever Rasputin's other
talents might have been," wrote Alex de Jonge, "perhaps the greatest talent of all
was his ability to calm and comfort troubled souls."[198]

The Fall of the Romanoffs, *1917, Alfred Hickman as the tsar, Nance O'Neil as the
tsarina. (Wisconsin Center for Film and Theater Research)*

Because of her dependence upon Rasputin, it was assumed that the tsarina and he were lovers. During the war, rumors that the German tsarina and Rasputin were trying to make a separate peace led a group of aristocrats to kill him. "To preserve the old regime," wrote the sister of one of the assassins, "they struck it, in reality, its fatal blow."[199]

The Fall of the Romanoffs should have been called *The Fall of Rasputin.* The royal family were merely supporting players in the duel between "The Holy Devil" and "The Sinful Angel," Iliodor. But who, or what, was Iliodor? In the many books I had read about Russia and the Revolution, never once in over twenty years had I encountered his name. I began to suspect that he was just another charlatan, a Russian immigrant who had sold a movie company a story they couldn't refuse. Seventy years after the events, he has not so much as a footnote in most of the definitive works. But, in 1985, I was led to a book by Alex de Jonge, *The Life and Times of Grigorii Rasputin,* a work of exceptional scholarship, which gives a full account of the career of Iliodor. He was of far more consequence to Russian history than I suspected, and he thus makes the film of more consequence, too.[200]

Iliodor, whose real name was Sergei Mikhailovich Trufanov, was initially better known to the Russian people than Rasputin; tens of thousands followed him. Born a peasant, he grew up believing the tsar was a god on earth whose enemies were revolutionists and Jews. At twenty-three, he became a priest and adopted the name Iliodor. His first experience of urban poverty caused inner turmoil; it led him to preserve his idolatry for the tsar as he poured scorn on those who surrounded him. He thus aroused the anger of the authorities *and* the revolutionaries. His disciples built him a fortresslike monastery at Tsaritsyn,[201] from where he preached his doctrine of resistance to authority to defeat revolution. The tsar ordered his eviction, but Iliodor appealed to Rasputin, who received him warmly and persuaded the tsar to rescind the order. When Rasputin returned the visit, he was received by Iliodor's followers with a display of mass hysteria that greatly impressed him.

Rasputin and Iliodor took a river journey together. Rasputin spent the time talking indiscreetly about himself, and Iliodor memorized everything (and used it in his eventual exposé). "The tsar thinks I'm Christ incarnate," he revealed, showing Iliodor letters written him by the royal family. Iliodor begged him to give him some; Rasputin told him to take his pick.

Iliodor was shocked by Rasputin's behavior toward women, but nonetheless became a disciple. Rasputin protected him, even when the local governor laid siege to his fortress.

Iliodor's gratitude took a strange form. He turned against Rasputin, and, with Bishop Hermogenes, lured him to a sort of ecclesiastical kangaroo court, where they confronted him with his sins and struck him repeatedly with a cross, while a halfwit called Mitia the Blissful tried to castrate him.

Rasputin managed to escape. Hermogenes was imprisoned and so was Iliodor, who chose this moment to release the letters he had acquired from Rasputin. One, from the tsarina, began: "My much loved never to be forgotten teacher, saviour and instructor, I am so wretched without you."[202] The letters caused precisely the damage Iliodor intended. Iliodor renounced the priesthood; the Holy Synod unfrocked him.

Iliodor escaped and set about starting a revolution on October 6, 1913, the tsar's name day, but his aide betrayed him to the police. Once again he got away; disguised as a woman, he fled to Finland and then to Norway, where he worked on his exposé of Rasputin. He reached America in June 1916 and set about trying to make money from his story. The Russians offered him $25,000 to suppress it. He agreed, intending to double-cross them, but they double-crossed him first, and he only got $1,000. The Russians sent over an assassin, but he was too late; the exposé was serialized in 300 newspapers.

Iliodor, a rabid anti-Semite, must have been staggered to discover what the Jews had achieved in America. He met the flamboyant Lewis J. Selznick, born Zelenik in the Ukraine, who had joined forces with Herbert Brenon and placed Iliodor under contract for a moving picture. (Iliodor had been signing contracts for his exclusive services elsewhere, causing massive legal wrangles and general annoyance.) Selznick is famous for sending a telegram to the former tsar:

NICHOLAS ROMANOFF

PETROGRAD RUSSIA

WHEN I WAS A BOY IN KIEV SOME OF YOUR POLICEMEN WERE NOT KIND TO ME AND MY PEOPLE STOP I CAME TO AMERICA AND PROSPERED STOP NOW HEAR WITH REGRET YOU ARE OUT OF A JOB OVER THERE STOP FEEL NO ILLWILL WHAT YOUR POLICEMEN DID SO IF YOU WILL COME TO NEW YORK CAN GIVE YOU FINE POSITION ACTING IN PICTURES STOP SALARY NO OBJECT STOP REPLY MY EXPENSE REGARDS YOU AND FAMILY

SELZNICK

NEW YORK

The cable may not have actually been sent to Russia, but it was apparently released to the press.[203] Selznick must have felt that if he had the real Iliodor, he might as well have the rest of the cast.

Iliodor was flattered by having a picture corporation named after him. (Half the stock was bought by theatrical promoter Al Woods.) He had one of the top directors in the country, Herbert Brenon. Austin Strong and George Edwardes-Hall wrote a scenario from his book.

The film was a farrago of nonsense, yet the very distortions of historical accuracy throw fascinating light on Iliodor's attempts to alter the facts to enhance his prestige. In the screenplay Rasputin's disciple Anna Vyrubova, the tsarina's best friend, becomes a gypsy who loves the priest and supplants his wife. Prince Felix Yusupoff, Rasputin's assassin, becomes the tsar's messenger, bringing the healer to the Winter Palace. Rasputin, soon a power behind the throne, enlists Iliodor to help quench the fires of revolution. Iliodor speaks; the revolutionary spirit abates; Iliodor becomes famous. Rasputin brings him to court to act as his teacher. He orders a Jewish pogrom; Iliodor protests. He tempts him with an orgy; Iliodor flees in horror. At the climax, the tsarina installs a wireless telegraph in her dressing room to communicate with the kaiser and Rasputin is dispatched by airplane to conclude a separate peace. Prince Felix, realizing that Rasputin is a monster devouring Russia, decides to kill him.

Iliodor at last gets his hands on Rasputin (Edward Connelly) in The Fall of the Romanoffs, directed by Herbert Brenon. (Museum of Modern Art)

No one yet knew how Rasputin had died—Prince Yusupoff lied about the murder, preferring to keep the details for his memoirs. So it was left to the scenario writers' imagination: a horseman crashes through a window to land on a banqueting table, riding down the center to cover Rasputin with a gun. Rasputin is then given a pistol to finish himself off.

The sequence paled against the facts. As Trotsky said of the murder, "It was carried out in the manner of a scenario designed for people of bad taste."[204] In December 1916, Rasputin was lured to Yusupoff's palace and fed with cakes laced with cyanide, which had no effect. Yusupoff tried adding cyanide to the wine, but the man was unkillable. Yusupoff shot him. Rasputin still would not die and tried to strangle Yusupoff. He was eventually thrown into the Neva.

The last part of the drama was all that was known, so the film ended with the body being thrown from a bridge. A woman rushes to the city, crying, "Rasputin is dead and Russia is free," and, with an odd sense of chronology, the revolution breaks out then and there.[205]

The ending of the picture was left open—to be dictated by events. Brenon expected to end it with a scene of the tsar at the railway station, receiving news of his overthrow. But the news changed from day to day, and the conclusion was left deliberately vague.

Iliodor as himself in The Fall of the Romanoffs. *(Museum of Modern Art)*

The Fall of the Romanoffs was accorded the most lavish advertising campaign ever given a picture before release. The premiere, on September 6, 1917, was held at the Hotel Ritz-Carlton in New York. Among the prominent guests was William A. Brady, who had every right to be there—but it so happened that his company, the World Film Corporation, was busily completing a rival version of the Rasputin story, *Rasputin, The Black Monk.* Brady had the temerity to shout across the lobby, as the distinguished audience made its way to its limousines, that he had "beaten Brenon to it." Brenon heard him, harsh words were exchanged, and soon the two Irishmen were punching away. The diminutive Adolph Zukor ran foward to separate them.[206]

William Brady had been right. *The Fall of the Romanoffs* may have opened first and may have done excellent business at the Broadway Theater, but when the rival version opened there was a near riot in Columbus Circle. A huge crowd became so impatient it smashed down the doors of the Park Theatre. Police reserves had to be called out. Brady's film owed all this to Selznick's advertising campaign, which had made Rasputin a household word in New York.

Brenon's publicity claimed the most enthusiastic press reaction in the history of the silent drama—two years after *The Birth of a Nation,* that was going a little far. The picture, and its cast, were highly praised, all except Iliodor. Nobody thought Iliodor was any good as Iliodor. Sensibly, Iliodor did not wait for the reviews. He vanished. *Wid's* reported he was back in Russia—in which case he was just in time for the next revolution, for by now it was October 1917.

Iliodor did return to Russia, to start religious uprisings against the Bolsheviks. But he was soon converted, and became one of the leaders of the "Living Church," an artificial creation set up by the Soviet government to undermine the unity of the Russian Orthodox Church. Iliodor referred to himself as "Pope," a title he dropped in favor of "Patriarch." The Living Church was dissolved in 1922.[207]

Before he left America he had played fast and loose with his contract again, offering his services as actor to the Russian Art Film Corporation.[208] And he had quarreled with Brenon over ownership of the negative of *The Fall of the Romanoffs.* Not that one could guess at conflict from the dedication in his book: "To my good friend, the Admirable Herbert Brenon, Motion Picture Artist and Poet." Was this inscribed by Iliodor before the falling-out, or was it added later by the book's ghost-writer, Van Wyck Brooks?[209]

Iliodor turned up again in New York in 1922 to preach at the Russian Baptist Church, and became a daily visitor at the chambers of the district attorney, attempting to get redress against one Al Gilbert and the Sunrise Picture Company for failing to live up to a contract to star him in *Five Days in Hell.* What happened to him after that is clouded in mystery. I have written repeatedly to historians in the Soviet Union. None have replied. Perhaps Iliodor has been written out of their history books, too.

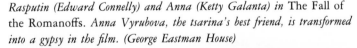

Rasputin (Edward Connelly) and Anna (Ketty Galanta) in The Fall of the Romanoffs. *Anna Vyrubova, the tsarina's best friend, is transformed into a gypsy in the film. (George Eastman House)*

THE RUSSIAN REVOLUTIONS   Although it hastened the end, Rasputin's death was not enough by itself to bring about the fall of the Romanoffs. As no revolution materialized, the revolutionaries became increasingly demoralized. Lenin, exiled in Switzerland, thought the best thing he could do would be to emigrate to America. He doubted that his generation would live to witness the decisive battles of the revolution.[210] Trotsky was about to leave for America himself; Stalin was in Siberian exile.

Thus, none of the future Bolshevik leaders were present when the Revolution at last broke out in Petrograd in February 1917,[211] so swiftly and spontaneously that Russian filmmakers forgot to photograph anything on the vital first three days. They did not sort themselves out until March 1, when they filmed the aftereffects of revolution—the burned-out prisons, the ashes of official records, policemen in civilian disguise caught by the crowds. The material was compiled by the Military-Cinematographic Department of the Skobelev Committee into *The Great Days of the Russian Revolution from February 28 to March 4 1917.*[212]

Now that autocracy had gone, the people wanted peace—peace with victory. But army discipline had been shattered, and soldiers were deserting the front lines in droves. Alexander Kerensky, leader of the Menshevik government, staged a disastrous major offensive against the Germans in June. The people, desperately short of food, rioted in favor of Lenin's Bolsheviks. The provisional government crushed an uprising in June, which it blamed on the Bolsheviks, and films were made to denigrate them—*Lenin & Co.*—and link them to the Germans—*A Stab in the Back.*

It was essential for the government to persuade America that despite the desertions and the disasters, Russia had no intention of withdrawing from the war. John (Ivan) Dored, a Russian who had lived in Los Angeles and worked as a cameraman, traveled to the United States to organize the editing and presentation of Russian battlefield footage. *Russia to the Front* was ready in a couple of months, and in September 1917 was presented at the Rialto, New York. Scenes of action against the Turks were followed by astonishing shots of the funeral procession of the victims of the Revolution, when virtually the entire population of Petrograd turned out to pay their last respects. One prominent family was not present; a subtitle explained that the tsar and tsarina were now "in an ordinary railway coach on their way to Siberia."

How the immigrant audiences must have loved that! Reviewers praised the high photographic standard of the pictures, which had the quality "of conveying more clearly, more impressively than anything else possibly could the immense significance of the Russian Revolution in world civilization." In the September 17, 1919, *Moving Picture World* one reviewer wrote: "One could scarcely view these scenes, in which surging masses of individuals of all classes joined hearts as one in celebrating what was not only the greatest event in the history of their country, but one of the greatest events in the history of the whole world, without being aroused to a high degree of enthusiasm and admiration for the heroes of the hour."

But in Russia, enthusiasm for the war had evaporated, and the failures of the provisional government rallied the masses to Bolshevism, whose slogan—"peace, land and bread"—proved irresistible. On October 26, 1917 (old calendar), as the Red Guards besieged the Winter Palace, a congress at Smolny consigned Kerensky's provisional government "to the rubbish heap of history."*

When news of the February revolution reached America, a young Russian immigrant called Herman Axelbank, office boy at the Goldwyn Company in New York, remarked, "I wish I could take moving pictures over there; we don't have any of our own of 1775."

A few years later, Axelbank met a cameraman traveling to Eastern Europe. He commissioned him to film Lenin and Trotsky, pawning his possessions and borrowing from friends to pay the advance. The cameraman returned, in 1922, with film of the Kronstadt Mutiny and the Trial of the Socialist Revolutionaries. And so began the Axelbank Film Collection of Imperial and Soviet Russia.

Axelbank was never a Communist, nor was he particularly interested in politics. In 1921, however, he helped the Friends of Soviet Russia produce *Russia Through the Shadows* to raise funds for Soviet famine relief. The following year, he assembled *With the Movie Camera Through the Bolshevik Revolution* in three reels from material in his collection. In 1924, he made *The Truth about Russia.* And in 1928, he began work on his epic, *Tsar to Lenin,* for which he had the assistance of Max Eastman, who went to Turkey, to Prinkipo Island, to film Trotsky in exile, then edited the film and spoke some of the narration. The picture was not premiered until 1937, when American Communists who supported Stalin picketed the theatre to protest the portrayal of Trotsky.

Although the Soviet government bought footage from him, Axelbank attributed various fires and thefts to the work of Soviet agents. Nonetheless, the collection survived until Axelbank died in 1979, when it was split up, part going to the Hoover Institution and part to a German collector.

BETWEEN TWO FLAGS   A Russian-born Jew named Jacob Rubin, an unusual combination of prominent banker and convinced Socialist, traveled to Russia in 1919 as a supporter of communism. He landed at Odessa and was thrown into jail by the Whites. Under sentence of death, he endured unspeakable privations until the American Red Cross obtained his release. He could easily have escaped in the evacuation of Odessa, but, realizing he was witness to history and anxious to join the Red cause, he remained. Though shot at and shelled, he survived to welcome the Reds, with whom he got on so well that for a time he controlled the government of Odessa. With his knowledge of American business practices, he transformed the inefficient Russian methods. He was able to prevent a Red Terror, to abolish capital punishment, and to give the Jews of Odessa religious freedom.

---

*The palace was defended mainly by women—the Woman's Battalion of Death—few of whom were hurt. Casualty figures varied from zero to six. It was said there were more injured when Eisenstein stormed it again for *October* (1927).

The frantic population evacuates Odessa before its occupation by Soviet troops in Between Two Flags, *1920.*

Even though elsewhere the Soviets were executing thousands of people daily, they were sensitive about the worldwide publicity given to the Red Terror. Jacob Rubin, still an idealist, regarded these stories as wild exaggerations, like tales of German terror in the war. At a meeting to discuss the problem, a commissar put the question directly to the *Americanitz.*

"The thing to do," Rubin replied, "is to fight the White guards with their own weapon. That is, show the world the White Terror—the atrocities committed by the Denikin regime during its occupation of the Ukraine. The way to do this is by producing a moving picture, showing the pogroms upon the Jews, the raids upon stores and market-places, the cruelty, the injustice, the extortion, the graft, the many executions."[213]

The suggestion was applauded and adopted unanimously. A committee of five, with Rubin as chairman, was appointed to write the scenario. It became the story of his own experiences, his prison life, his death sentence, his release, and the series of White atrocities he had witnessed or learned about. The film was to be called *Between Two Flags,* and it was to be directed by Alexander Arkatov,[214] who had made Jewish films before the Revolution. Rubin was to play himself.

The scenario was so enthusiastically received that 500,000 rubles were appropriated for its production. Rubin was appointed *natchalnik* (chief) of foreign propaganda, given a smart khaki uniform and a regiment of soldiers, and authorized to requisition transport and other supplies for the picture.

Completed in five weeks, the film was first shown to an audience of 500 in the former palace of a sugar king. "There was such a demonstration of enthusiasm as I never witnessed in the United States outside of a political convention."[215]

The liberal regime in Odessa displeased Moscow, and Rubin was deposed and left the city. His fate might have been sealed had it not been for the film, which mitigated the anger of the commissars, who regarded it as "valuable propaganda." It was fortunate that Rubin did not stay in Odessa, for when the Whites recaptured the city they staged a public bonfire of *agitki* (propaganda films), arrested a director, and shot one of the actors.[216]

Disillusioned, Rubin remained in Moscow for some time, but he longed to return to America. When he finally received his visa, a last-minute impulse caused him to try to smuggle out his film—a foolhardy action that caused him agonies of fear on the long train journey to Estonia. Had not a blizzard felled the telephone lines, he would have been escorted back to Moscow under arrest, for his theft had not passed unnoticed. He was so frightened that he handed the film to the secretary of the Estonian Legation, and his book makes no further mention of it. Presumably, though, as the secretary's diplomatic baggage was exempt from search, the film came through safely. Although there is no sign of it, alas, either side of the old Iron Curtain.

A still from Between Two Flags, *1920. From Jacob Rubin's book* I Live to Tell.

The death of a Communist. Reenactment of a scene which occurred at the Odessa Prison, January 18, 1920. As he leaped to his destruction this Communist-patriot cried, "Welcome, Liberty!" (From the motion picture made under Communist auspices, directed by Mr. Rubin.)

Jacob H. Rubin, author of Between Two Flags.

The American picture business had taken little notice of the February revolution, and it studiously ignored the new one. Yet there was an audience passionately concerned with events in Russia. *The Fall of the Romanoffs* and *Rasputin, The Black Monk* had played to packed houses. An "unprecedented box-office rush" led to special midnight performances at New York's Rialto of news films of the February revolution, and a "special" featuring the Man of the Hour, *Kerensky in the Russian Revolution of 1917,* was released with the slogan "Action Pathos Thrills." Even though its subject was on the run, audiences crowded the theatre. Yet when the October Revolution occurred, no feature film was made about it.[217]

Author Gilbert Seldes had his own theory about this: "The October revolution, as opposed to the Kerensky one, was the first revolution in any country since 1776 which was not based on *our* revolutionary principles. Given slight differences, the French revolution, the 1848 movement, the upsetting of kingdoms on the Continent, even the February revolution meant democracy. They were following us. And bang, in October 1917 occurred a revolution which had the audacity, the goddam crust, to say that the American revolution was not the last one . . . as far as anyone was aware at all of what was happening, the awareness brought home to them this fantastic fact; that for the first time in nearly 150 years—we were not the New World. The Russians had started a new system; what right did they have? We invented revolution, and they turned it against us. The reflection of this in our movies was preposterous beyond words."[218]

This reflection, like the sun blazing on glass, blinded people to the truth. The truth, or such fragments of it as we now believe, was frightening enough. The movies poured in generous portions of melodrama to make the incredible merely unacceptable.

LAND OF MYSTERY   Considering the fear aroused by the very name of Bolshevism, it was an act of considerable courage—or bravado—to take a film company into the burning cauldron of Russia—or at least Lithuania. But this is what American director Harold Shaw did in 1920 for a British film called *Land of Mystery.*

To make such an expedition required the support of men in high places. One such man was associated with this project from the beginning, for he wrote the story. Publicity referred to him as "Basil Thompson [sic] of the Secret Service." Such a claim can usually be discounted. An officer in the secret service would hardly remain secret by advertising his job in the newspapers. But Basil Thomson was an exception. He was not only a genuine secret service man, he actually commanded an entire section of British Intelligence.

The son of the Archbishop of York, Thomson was called to the bar after a distinguished career in the Colonial Service. He then became governor of a prison and, in 1913, assistant commissioner of the Metropolitan Police. In 1919, the Special Branch was expanded into a civil intelligence department and Thomson became its director.[219]

"The new Directorate was funded with Secret Service money," wrote Nick Hiley, "and was permitted to operate both in the United Kingdom and abroad to counter the threat of Bolshevism."[220]

Thomson, described by a colleague as having "the 'Red' bee buzzing long and loud in his bonnet," appeared convinced that Britain was "seething with revolution and might well blow up any day."[221] The *Daily Herald* called his organization the "Blood and Shudders Branch."[222] He had been associated with an official film project during the war, and he evidently regarded *Land of Mystery* as a thoroughly worthwhile method of combating the Bolsheviks.

Another curious character behind the venture was Boris Saïd, an associate of the theatrical impresario Gilbert Miller. He was revealed in a court case to be an agent of Imperial Russia,[223] but it seems likely that he was also working for—or with—Thomson's Directorate of Intelligence.

The scenario for *Land of Mystery* was adapted from Thomson's story by Bannister Merwin, a former Edison man. Director Harold Shaw[224] also came from Edison, as did his future wife, the leading actress Edna Flugrath. Although she and her parents were born in America, Flugrath was as fluent in German as in English, which proved an advantage at the first location—Berlin, where from the window of her hotel she saw "machine guns being rushed through the street firing showers of shot indiscriminately into the people."[225]

Only with the utmost difficulty were she and the company able to get out of Germany. They moved to the town of Kovno* in Lithuania, newly independent of Russia and struggling to stay free of the Bolsheviks. Edna Flugrath was appalled by the filthy living conditions and the famine: "So desperately destitute were these poor people that their empty stomachs overrided their moral conceptions and they

*Now Kaunas. Lithuania was part of the Russian empire. Freed in 1917, it was given its sovereignty by Lenin in 1920. It was invaded by Poland that same year and was annexed by the USSR in 1939 under the Hitler-Stalin pact.

Stanley Rodwell, the young British cameraman of Land of Mystery, *1920, with his American Bell and Howell camera. (Ken Rodwell)*

would shoot a person for bread. I used to lay awake at night and count the shots, and on one occasion I counted fourteen—fourteen victims to the uncontrolled hunger of the poor starving people."[226]

So dramatic was this location trip that another player, John East, kept a record of it, describing it as one of the most eventful experiences in a crowded half century of acting. East's grandson wrote it up at length in his book, *'Neath the Mask.*[227]

Kovno, the scene of heavy fighting during the war, was in ruins. It was bitterly cold. The company had grown accustomed to the sight of corpses in Berlin; here, however, bodies by the roadside were the victims not of machine guns but of starvation. The vegetable fields were patrolled by armed guards day and night, and a constant stream of refugees filed through the town.

The filming began with a scene of the Bolshevik flag being torn down to be replaced by a Lithuanian one. "The actor assigned to this task narrowly missed death when troops opened fire on him."[228]

On their return journey to Berlin, members of the company were relieved of "surplus eatables" under the pretext of requisition. The police did not discover the silver candlesticks and the icon which East had himself requisitioned from a ruined church and sewn into the lining of his overcoat.

Was it worth the misery?

The Kine Weekly felt that Harold Shaw and his company deserved congratulations for their enterprise in taking such a hazardous trip, but backgrounds did not make a photoplay. The magazine objected to the creation of a bad precedent—the use of a character well known in world affairs, under a slightly disguised name. "At least one writer in the lay press, deceived by a similarity of names, had stated that this is a true story of a living man, mentioning the man's name."[229]

Even the most outrageous of American propaganda films had not descended to lying about the private domestic life of a living individual, the weekly said, and it would be very bad for the reputation of this country were it to start here.

The film company made no bones about it. It announced at a press lunch that the film was about Lenin. The character was called Lenoff, and he was portrayed by Norman Tharp as the son of prosperous peasants—*kulaks,* no less. (Lenin was actually the son of a college teacher.) Lenoff loves a peasant girl, Masikova (Edna Flugrath). They become engaged, but Masikova encounters Prince Ivan (Fred Morgan), a member of the royal family, who sends her to the Imperial Ballet. She becomes his morganatic wife. This arouses in Lenoff a hatred of the regime and of society in general; he throws himself into the Bolshevik cause. Three years after the outbreak of war, he returns from exile to head the revolution. Upon the downfall of the tsar, Masikova and the prince escape. Lenoff tries a friend by telephone for aiding their escape and condemns him to death. He quarrels with his mother, and she is shot inadvertently as a substitute for this friend, who

The only surviving photograph taken at the Land of Mystery *location, Kovno, Lithuania.* *(Ken Rodwell)*

manages to buy himself off. When he hears what has happened, Lenoff goes mad. The final scene shows Masikova and the prince arriving in England.

The film had many similarities to the 1916 *The Cossack Whip.* The realism of its backgrounds startled English audiences, accustomed to a cruder standard of art direction in their native films. *The Bioscope* praised the enthusiasm with which Shaw had treated his subject: "One of the most dramatic episodes is where a mad fanatic, jumping on to the High Altar, declares that 'there is no God or I should die this minute,' to be taken at his word by a young soldier who, shocked at the blasphemy, shoots him down on the spot."[230]

The re-creation of the Imperial Theatre, showing the vast audience rising at the entrance of the tsar, was regarded as "a masterpiece of staging."[231] A similarly glittering event was held at London's Winter Garden Theatre, Drury Lane, where impresarios George Grossmith and Edward Lurillard gave the film a magnificent premiere, graced by an array of dignitaries quite remarkable for a mere film. Thanks to Sir Basil, the Home Secretary came, together with the French ambassador, the Dutch consul general, and the cream of London society. They were not disappointed. Loud applause was reported for the real "Russian" scenes. Many called *Land of Mystery* a masterpiece to compare with Griffith's finest in its portrayal of the dark despotism of tsarism and the "even greater tyranny under Lenin."[232]

But there was a sour note. "It has been claimed that this film has an historic value," said *The Kine Weekly.* "There is not an historic scene in it. The years 1914 to 1917 are simply dropped out. It has been said that it shows 'the birth of Bolshevism.' The question of Bolshevism is not touched; neither a capitalist nor an industrial worker appears, the characters being exclusively Romanoffs, ballet girls and peasants. But the fact that it is propaganda is indisputable, because the hero is a Romanoff and the villains are peasants."[233]

THE JEWS

A Jewish producer once explained the attraction of the picture business for members of his faith: because the commandment forbidding the making of graven images precluded them from practicing the sculptural or graphic arts, many found an outlet in music; but the theatre, and now films, provided an opportunity to manipulate an art that was not representational within the meaning of Mosaic law.[234]

The motion picture also attracted Jews because it was a new business, with no tradition of prejudice. Like vaudeville, it was a branch of the legitimate theatre, the management of which was predominantly Jewish, David Belasco and Marcus Loew being the most notable examples. Exhibiting pictures required a relatively small investment, and the potential audience was vast. The Lower East Side, in 1908, had forty-two of New York City's 123 movie theatres, for tenement dwellers were fervent picture fans.[235]

While the heads of the industry in the twenties were mostly Jewish, by no means all came from the ghetto. (Jesse L. Lasky was born in San Francisco.) And it should not be thought that Jews were exclusively interested in finance. They could be found in every stratum of the industry: writers (Alfred A. Cohn, Julien Josephson), cameramen (Hal Mohr, David Abel), directors (Ernst Lubitsch, Harry Millarde, John Stahl, Sidney and Chester Franklin—even the de Milles were partly Jewish), and players (Theda Bara, Ricardo Cortez, Carmel Myers, Alma Rubens). The Talmadge girls got the balance right for the early days of pictures—they were half Jewish and half Irish!

A surprising number of Jews on the financial side came from the garment industry; with its emphasis on fashion and public taste, it provided useful training.

It cannot be denied that in the beginning Jews encountered a certain amount of prejudice in Hollywood, where the residents, mostly Presbyterians, objected to the movie invasion and particularly to the Jews. And I found this description of a new executive in a letter of the time: "A little fat, sawed off, undersized, hook-nosed Jew simp by the name of Selznick (you don't pronounce it, you sneeze it)."[236]

But outspoken anti-Semitism faded away in a business dominated by Jews, and despite the quips of Marshall Neilan, whose hatred of money men was notorious—"an empty taxicab drew up and Louis B. Mayer got out"—at least one Jewish filmmaker could assure me that he experienced no racial prejudice whatever in the industry.[237]

Dore Davidson as Isadore Solomon, Virginia Brown Faire as Essie Solomon, and William V. Mong as Clem Beemis in Welcome Stranger, *1924, directed by James Young for Belasco Productions. A Jew arrives in a New England town and the mayor and leading citizens try to get rid of him. A hotel handyman (William V. Mong) persuades the Jew to invest in an electric light plant for the town and when he brings this boon to the populace, they honor him. (National Film Archive)*

———

The Jews were treated more liberally in America than in any European country,[238] but the more immigrants arrived, the more anti-Semitic the United States became. Those who came from Germany in the mid-nineteenth century had been assimilated, and many had reached the middle class. When the influx of Jews from Eastern Europe arrived, those already established were dismayed. They themselves had experienced virtually no anti-Semitism, but they feared that the impoverished newcomers would threaten their hard-won status. They were charitable, but they kept themselves apart.

The ghetto dwellers were surrounded by hostility, for they often had the Irish on one side and the Italians on another. To reach other parts of the city, a Jew had to cross these Catholic enclaves, receiving a beating from time to time in the name of Christianity. These rivalries were immortalized in *The Cohens and the Kellys* films. "There are three races here," said a title. "Irish, Jewish and innocent bystanders."[239] And even within the Jewish quarter, there was prejudice according to national origin.[240]

It was when the Jews began to leave the ghetto that anti-Semitism flourished. Clubs and resorts advertised "No Hebrews," and as Jews moved into prosperous neighborhoods, Gentiles moved out. Denigration of the Jews became part of popular culture in newspapers, songs, vaudeville, and moving pictures. Much of it was the humor of stereotypes, applied indiscriminately to every race and nationality—but some of it was vicious.

Since the beginning of the cinema, Jews had been ridiculed, but the Rosenthal case made their criminal element front-page news, and the movies saw a proliferation of Jewish villains with names like Moe "The Fence" Greenstein or "Moneybags" Solomon.

"Whenever a producer wishes to depict a betrayer of public trust," ran the report of the Anti-Defamation League, "a hard-boiled usurious money-lender, a crooked gambler, a grafter, a depraved fire bug, a white slaver or other villains of one kind or another, the actor was directed to represent himself as a Jew."[241]

In 1908, Police Commissioner Theodore Bingham had claimed that half of New York City's criminals were Jews,[242] thus it would have been as reprehensible to sweep their sins under the carpet as to portray all Italians and Irish as pure in deed. And some of the films dealt with Jewish criminals without racial rancor.

A Female Fagin was made by Kalem in 1913. The most offensive thing about it was its title, without which few people would realize that the old woman is Jewish. Her name is Rosie Rosalsky, a clue only to the most knowing. Given every opportunity to carry on like a burlesque Jew, she is nonetheless restrained, a Fagin in deed only. She lives in a tenement and runs a school for thieves. Her pupils are two charming Jewish girls who work in a department store. It doesn't take long to realize that in this East Side story almost everyone is Jewish.

At the dry goods counter, one of Rosie's girls steals money from a customer's purse and shoots it through the pneumatic tubes to her accomplice at the cashier's booth. The customer raises a fuss, but nothing can be found. The owner's daughter, Grace, decides to investigate. She leaves a pendant as bait; that night she spots

Frame enlargement from A Female Fagin, *1913. The men from the store are led to the school for thieves. (National Film Archive)*

one of the girls wearing it at the nickelodeon. She reports the incident, and the girl is called into the manager's office. She might have got away with the theft, but Grace takes her position for a while, and, thanks to the pneumatic system, becomes the receiver of stolen property from the dry goods counter. The girls, confronted with their crime, break down and plead for mercy. A bargain is struck. They reveal the whereabouts of their teacher, and a group of men from the store, with a policeman, swoop down on Rosie, who is very roughly treated. The picture ends with the girls, looking happier, boarding with Grace and her new husband in their comfortable home. And her husband proves to be the department store manager.

Investigations after the Rosenthal case revealed such a network of Jewish crime that uptown Jews feared a pogrom if they did not act. Their organization, the Kehilla, created a Bureau of Public Morals to deal with the criminals themselves—and they were astonishingly successful.[243]

In 1914, a meeting of the Committee for the Protection of the Good Name of Immigrant People was called to discuss what it called "a notorious evil"—the imputation of the Jews, in certain films, of the crime of arson. Statistics proved the charge without foundation—"the Jews commit no more crimes of such a nature than any other nationality." Several film companies, Edison, Kalem, Lubin, and Universal, sent emissaries, but their advice was only to get in touch with the National Board of Censorship.[244]

Nevertheless, direct references to Jewish criminals began to disappear from the screen, partly because more Jews were taking control of the picture business, partly because Jewish crime was itself fading out as the Italians took over the big cities.

But 1913 had seen perhaps the worst example of American anti-Semitism.

THE LEO FRANK CASE   Leo Frank, a Jew from Brooklyn, was arrested for the murder of a girl at a pencil factory he managed in Atlanta, Georgia. His trial was transformed into an anti-Semitic propaganda campaign—former senator Tom Watson of Georgia, a Populist leader, wrote, "Our little girl—*ours* by the eternal God!—has been pursued to a hideous death and bloody grave by *this filthy perverted Jew of New York.*"[245] Detective William J. Burns, hired by the Frank defense, only just escaped an angry mob for "selling out to the Jews."[246] The trial itself was a tragic farce—the true culprit was the principal prosecution witness—and Frank was sentenced to hang.

William Randolph Hearst expressed concern about the injustice of the Frank case; Senator Watson called him a tool of the Jews and cited the film Hearst had produced as an example. Hal Reid also produced a film, *Leo M. Frank (Showing Life in Jail) and Governor Slaton.* Frank's mother and the governor's wife appeared in it. When it was shown in New York, Reid delivered a glowing tribute to Frank and his mother. He was also impressed with Slaton, who had received more than a thousand messages warning him that if he commuted Frank's death sentence his own would follow. "But with the confidence of his wife, who kissed him when he announced his determination, the Governor did the thing he thought should be done."[247] Reid showed this film together with his anticapital punishment story, *Thou Shalt Not Kill* (1915).

"Incidentally," said *Variety,* "Mr. Reid talks more interestingly of the Frank case off stage than he does upon it, telling inside stuff such as he found out when in Georgia. Mr. Reid mentioned some unpublishable phases of the Frank murder matter that appear to bear out his assertion of Frank's persecution."[248]

Director George K. Rolands, of Russian-Jewish origin, made a five-reel reenactment called *The Frank Case,* which prophesied that Frank would be acquitted. The National Board of Censorship and the New York City license commissioner both banned the film because the case was being appealed to the U.S. Supreme Court, and any film on the subject would be in contempt of court. Although exhibitors protested that it was no more in contempt of court to review the case on film than in print, the picture was banned in Louisville, Kentucky—the first direct interference on the local level since the Jeffries-Johnson fight pictures were barred.[249]

Despite new evidence, the Georgia courts refused Frank a retrial, and he lost his appeal in the Supreme Court. Although two justices strongly dissented, the majority refused to intervene on the grounds that it was not a matter within federal jurisdiction.[250]

Having commuted Frank's sentence, Governor Slaton ordered him secretly transferred from Atlanta to a prison farm. A furious mob was only prevented from hanging the governor and blowing up his home by the arrival of troops; in any case, Slaton had to leave Georgia and abandon his political career.

At the prison farm, a convict slashed Frank's throat. While Frank was recovering, Tom Watson urged direct action: "Once there were *men* in Georgia, men who caught the fire from the heavens to burn a law which outraged Georgia's sense of honor and justice."[251] To Watson's triumph and delight, on the night of August 16, 1915, twenty-five men took Leo Frank from his sickbed and hanged him. "Lynch law is a good sign," Watson had written. "It shows that a sense of justice yet lives among the people."

Before the corpse was cut down, Pathé News managed to get shots of it which were included in its weekly newsreel. Atlanta police did not object to the film itself, but they strongly objected to the way manager Logan of the Georgian Theatre advertised it. He drove through the city in a large truck, with a set of chimes playing and a sign splashed along the sides: "Leo M. Frank lynched. Actual scenes of the lynching at the Georgian today." The theatre had an exceptionally large Jewish patronage, and Logan alienated them all.[252]

Gaumont News, released through Mutual, also showed shots of the lynching ground, the crowds assembled there, and the judge who asked the onlookers to let the body be taken home in peace. Another scene showed Mrs. Lucille Frank, the widow, picking flowers, probably shot days earlier but nonetheless a useful bridge to the funeral.[253]

In Philadelphia, picture and vaudeville theatres were visited by the police and "requested" to refrain from showing any film depicting the Frank hanging or the trial. Managers cooperated to the extent of removing the item from the newsreels.[254]

"During the hysteria surrounding the lynching," wrote Steve Oney, "the Ku Klux Klan . . . held its first cross burning atop Atlanta's Stone Mountain, thus reinvigorating itself for a new life."[255] As for Tom Watson, his anti-Semitism brought him new glory in 1920, when he was reelected to the Senate seat he had held thirty years before. Once he had been a radical. Now, attracting disparate elements from both extremes, he became a bewildering combination of arch-patriot and opponent of Red-baiting, militarism, and the trusts. When he died, two years later, the Ku Klux Klan sent a cross of roses eight feet high.

The State of Georgia did not grant Leo Frank a posthumous pardon until 1986.

HENRY FORD   The automobile manufacturer Henry Ford was also a radical in many ways; he too was opposed to militarism and the trusts. His contempt for Wall Street was well known. A populist, he was convinced that the world war had been fought for the benefit of big business, and since big business was controlled by "International Jewish Finance," in his eyes the war was all the fault of the Jews.

Had this been his privately held opinion, it would have been no concern of history. But Ford took over a small weekly newspaper, the Dearborn *Independent,* and boosted its circulation by making his customers his subscribers. And he used his newspaper to propagate his ideas—it was the *Independent* that offered the notorious forgery *The Protocols of the Elders of Zion* to the world.

Ford's anti-Semitism brought joy to the Corn Belt and did wonders for Klan recruitment. Referring to the Leo Frank case, Ford's paper said it was "not without reason that the Ku Klux Klan had been revived in Georgia."[256]

The *Independent,* which called itself "the chronicler of neglected truth," had already attacked Hollywood by printing the "confessions" of a "producer" who declared he would rather see his daughter dead than on a studio lot.[257] This was in keeping with the theme of *The Protocols,* which urged Jews to stoke the fires of immorality to prepare for the immolation of the Aryan world and the eventual seizure of power by the Jews. Ford called upon the American people to rise up and protest at the "Jewish control" of the people's entertainment.[258]

Moving Picture World splashed its reply across two pages: "If the screen were Jew invented, Jew owned and Jew controlled, it would stand today as the greatest monument to Jewish achievement in all the history of that race because no other thing in modern or ancient life has developed with such amazing speed, with such astonishing progress toward perfection and with such tremendous service to all mankind."

There were Jews, "and some mighty good ones," in the picture business, and it was a cause for pride that no bigotry had barred them. But the business had attracted men of all races and religions. "Down to this very day and hour there never has been a control of any group of religionists or racialists and there is no movement evident toward such an end."[259]

Of course, by 1921 the industry *was* largely controlled by Jews, but they could hardly be accused of forcing Jewish propaganda on American audiences. They did not misuse their power in the way Henry Ford was currently misusing his.

One casualty of this was the *Ford Educational Weekly.* Between 1914 and 1921, Ford released a film a week—factual one-reelers which were often of great educational value—offered free until 1919, when a nominal charge was levied. The fee, together with Ford's anti-Semitic campaign in the *Independent,* finished the series, although there is no evidence whatsoever that the films themselves were anti-Jewish. Circulation dwindled from 7,000 to a mere 1,300 by August 1920, and in December 1921, the series was canceled.[260] Exhibitors told Ford that if he wanted a release, he would have to build his own theatres.[261]

Henry Ford was not dissuaded from his campaign until 1927, by which time immense damage had been done: anti-Semitic articles from the *Independent* had been published in book form and translated into many languages. Among the industrialist's many admirers was Adolf Hitler, who is said to have hung a large picture of Ford in his Munich headquarters and incorporated passages from the articles almost verbatim in *Mein Kampf.* And in one of those paradoxes of which history is full, Hitler's future propaganda minister, Dr. Joseph Goebbels, would express the unbounded admiration for Hollywood which Henry Ford could not. Although he knew, if only from Ford, that Jewish talent and finance lay behind virtually every production, he held regular screenings in the 1930s and 1940s to show his men the standard for which they must aim. His diaries record how impressed he was with *Gone With the Wind,* the brainchild of Lewis Selznick's brilliant son David. He ran *Ben-Hur* (1925, reissued 1931) several times: "Old Jewish hokum. But well made."[262] One of Dr. Goebbels's most cherished beliefs was that the Jews had made no contribution to world culture. To prove this, he was willing to burn their books but not, it turned out, their films.

In 1937, whether he liked it or not, Henry Ford received a decoration from a grateful Hitler.[263] By this time, he had apologized to the Jews, so the award was an embarrassment. But apology or not, the Jews did not forgive him. In at least one recorded case, Jews refused to allow pictures of Ford to appear in a news-reel.[264]

Against such a background, is it any wonder that the Hollywood producers avoided the subject of their own people? Many believed that any treatment might spread anti-Semitism. In any case, they craved acceptance as Americans. Of the films that *were* made, most dealt with poverty, and this brought the inevitable reaction from the Jewish establishment: "Why do you not show the successful ones, with their beautiful homes?"

And yet the subject could not be completely ignored because for some reason several of the biggest hits of the American stage and screen were stories about Jews. *Abie's Irish Rose* ran for 2,532 performances on Broadway.[265] *Ben-Hur* was a phenomenon on the stage years before it was filmed. And *The Jazz Singer,* with Russian-Jewish Al Jolson, introduced the era of talking pictures.

Of course, anti-Semites argued that most Hollywood films were Jewish pro-paganda anyway, with their emphasis on sentiment, mother-love, and the under-dog. But that would suggest that the Irish, whose stories are full of such elements, are one of the Lost Tribes of Israel.

The Jew on the silent screen was not "invisible" as claimed by one historian,[266] although to say he appeared in "a vast number of films," as suggested by an-other,[267] is somewhat overstating the case. But enough films with Jewish themes were made to throw fascinating light on the attitudes and concerns of the time. When the characters were portrayed with sympathy and admiration, the films helped to counter anti-Semitism. But the emphasis on assimilation, however grat-ifying to the federal authorities, dismayed Orthodox Jews, for whom assimilation was a tragedy. "Jews in hiding," they called these new Americans.

As historical records, these films are priceless. They caught the streets of the ghettos when they were full of life, jammed with pushcarts and teeming with people. They recorded ritual and ceremony, and preserved the look of dress and costume. They re-created the pogrom and the process of immigration. They filmed the lives of ordinary people in what must seem to people today extraordinary circumstances. Had all these films been allowed to survive, what a history of the Jewish people would have been displayed!

SIDNEY GOLDIN   If any man could be said to have depicted the suf-ferings of the Jewish people on celluloid, it was a Russian Jew called Sidney Goldin. Born in Odessa in 1880, he moved to America as a child and made his debut in the Yiddish theatre in Baltimore at fifteen. The picture business knew him as a rotund comedian and comedy director, although he made at least two highly prof-itable dramas, *The Adventures of Lt. Petrosino* (1912) and *New York Society Life in the Underworld* (1912). H. Lyman Broening, his cameraman on comedies at the Cham-pion studios, retained a warm but bizarre memory of him: "He was nice, a great big oversize guy. . . . He'd sit down and start directing a scene and right in the middle he'd fall over and snore—sound asleep. He used to call me 'Mr. Leeman,' sounded better to him, I guess. He said, 'Now, Mr. Leeman, when I go to sleep you come and wake me up—don't hesitate. Come and shake me. I can't afford to fall asleep in the middle of these scenes.' So I got to be a bosom friend because I would always wake him up."[268]

After a period with scenario writer Lincoln J. Carter in Chicago, and with Essanay, he joined Universal in 1913 to direct for the Victor Feature Film Company and Imp[269] at Fort Lee. His first film for Imp was a three-reeler, *The Sorrows of Israel* (1913), which dramatized the plight of Russian Jews who could join society by converting to the Russian Orthodox faith, but only by sacrificing family ties. It involved pogroms and rescues by nihilists and ended with the statutory last scene of the couple sailing past the Statue of Liberty.[270] It was ideal fare for the tenement districts and was popular enough to encourage Mark Dintenfass, supervisor of the Champion studios and head of Universal's foreign department, to put more Russian-Jewish films into production. Goldin's *Nihilist Vengeance* (1913), a two-reeler, was the story of the Jewish daughter of a banker and her love for a prince.

Irene Wallace, who had a small part in this film, played the lead in Goldin's *The Heart of a Jewess*—Rebecca, a garment worker who pays for her Russian lover to come to America and go to medical school. Once he succeeds, he drops her for a wealthy girl,[271] and on their way to the wedding the couple's automobile knocks down poor Rebecca. The picture was praised for its atmosphere and for its scenario. "It is a pleasure," said *Moving Picture World*, "to see Jewish people play Hebrew roles of comedy and sympathy, especially after so many sickening caricatures have affronted vaudeville audiences for years."[272]

Actually, Irene Wallace was not of Jewish but of Northern Irish extraction.[273] She played the lead in *Bleeding Hearts or Jewish Freedom under King Casimir of Poland* (1913), a highly colored three-reel melodrama in which wandering Jews, banished from other lands, arrive in Poland in the fourteenth century and plead for sanctuary from King Casimir, who allows them to stay. (The film did not show how Casimir created ghettos to isolate the Jews.) A reviewer complained of the "continuous violence" and declared that reproductions of history's darker pages were gloomy and "should remain in the dust of the past."[274]

A far more valuable film, if only it had survived, would have been *How the Jews Care for Their Poor* (1913), Goldin's last for Imp. It was intended as a one-reeler, dealing with the work of the Jewish philanthropic societies but was expanded to two reels for the annual banquet of the Brooklyn Federation of Jewish Charities on December 21, 1913.[275] Although it had scenes of great documentary importance, showing the work of hospitals, it was not a documentary but a simple story of Jewish immigrants from Russia. A mother dies, and her children are cared for by her brother. When he falls ill, they are taken into the Brooklyn Hebrew Orphan Asylum. The brother, recovered, is so impressed that he leaves the children at the asylum. When the small boy grows up and graduates, he delivers a lecture at the Brooklyn Federation, thanking them for all the help they had given his family over the years.[276]

Nineteen thirteen was a notable year for Goldin. He not only managed to make films for Victor, Imp, and Champion, under the Universal banner, but somehow managed to make a film for Leon J. Rubinstein of the Ruby Feature Film Company, even before his Universal contract had expired. This was called *The Black Hundred or The Black 107*.

The Black Hundred was a virulently anti-Semitic group in Russia, whose slogan was "Beat the Yids and the intelligents; Save Russia."[277] The tsar gave them his approval, and by 1909 they had succeeded in butchering 50,000 Jews.[278]

Goldin's *The Black Hundred* was based on a famous contemporary Russian case in which a Jew named Mendel Beilis had been falsely accused of the ritual murder of a Christian boy. The film featured the celebrated Jewish actor Jacob Adler as Beilis and Jan Smoelski in a leading role. According to the publicity, Smoelski had been a revolutionary agent in St. Petersburg for two years, penetrating the councils of the Black Hundred, but he was discovered and had to seek the aid of the nihilists in order to flee the country.[279]

Sadly, *The Black Hundred* was not considered a good picture and was not taken seriously even by the commercial reviewers. But *Variety*'s critic conveyed the hunger of the ghetto audiences for such films:

"I caught the Ruby home-made Beilis in the thick of the movie-mad section of Rivington Street Sunday. Go to Rivington Street, just east of the Bowery, any Sunday after luncheon when there's a racial film on the circuit if you want to know what a human gorge is. Surprisingly, the fee at the Waco theatre there for the Beilis show was only a nickel. . . . But at that, *The Russian Black 107* [sic] isn't worth more. It's mushroom stuff. About the only sympathetic note its three reels contain is in the personality of the player selected to impersonate the much-advertised Beilis.

"A small body, a gaunt care-lined face, and an expression of unchanging and genuine apprehension, make one follow him through the theatric situations in which he is placed. . . . The manager of the Waco must have realized the playlet's artificial texture, for the operator whipped the reels along at a sixty-mile clip, the persons zig-zagging on and off the screen like dance puppets. Although poor Mendel has a hard time of it on the screen, nary a bit of applause comes from the packed audience when the mimic jury acquits him.[280] In some sections, the film may create a religious outbreak, for Mendel's chief oppressor is shown to be a Russian priest who makes the sign of the cross while plotting the Beilis ruin."[281]

When *The Black Hundred* reached England, the London County Council received a note from the Imperial Russian Consulate requesting that the show, at the Oxford Music Hall, be stopped. The council complied, for precisely one day, and then rescinded the ban. The Russian consul general was startled when he learned of this. "They will never dare to show that film," he said. "They must not. . . . The pictures are a grave slander on the Russian police and the Russian people."[282]

Sidney Goldin subsequently made a five-reel feature called *Escape from Siberia* (1914), which again emphasized the regime's brutality. A Russian count is stripped of his military rank by his own father when he announces his engagement to a Jewish girl. The nihilists are the heroes, and the final sequence shows the lovers' safe arrival in the Land of Liberty.[283] Goldin also made an ambitious version of

East and West, 1923, *directed by Sidney Goldin, with Molly Picon, Sidney Goldin (third from left), and Jacob Kalich (right). (National Center for Jewish Film)*

Karl Gutzkow's 1847 play *Uriel Acosta,* which came out in July 1914, with the Yiddish actor Ben Adler and Rosetta Conn. *Moving Picture World* was disappointed that Goldin had tried to improve on the play and felt that the dramatic moments in the life of this great Jewish philosopher had been spoiled.[284] And *Variety* commented, "In Jewish settlements, colonies, or neighborhoods, this picture will excite interest . . . otherwise it won't create a ripple."[285]

All of this must have been thoroughly discouraging to Goldin. He briefly turned back to comedy for a parody on *Traffic in Souls* called *Traffickers on Soles* (1914) in which the cops were Irish and Jewish, each squad led by an officer of the opposite persuasion. In 1915 he joined forces with the best-known Yiddish actor in America, Boris Thomashefsky, who had opened America's first Yiddish theatre in New York, in 1902. Thomashefsky had become an impresario, and he felt there were enough Jews in the country to support photoplay versions of Yiddish stage successes. The Boris Thomashefsky Film Company produced *The Jewish Crown, The Period of the Jew,* and *Hear Ye, Israel!* Thomashefsky played the lead and Goldin directed all of them, but while the trade press reported that they had been made, there is no record of their release or of the Thomashefsky Film Company's survival.

What happened to Goldin during the war is unclear. Afterward he went to Europe and ran the Eclair studios in Paris for a while. Then he moved to Vienna, where, in 1923, he directed Molly Picon and her husband, Jacob Kalich, in *East and West (Mizrakh un Marev).* According to Molly Picon, the film was popular with all audiences—in America it was called *Mazel Tov*—and in Vienna did better than Chaplin's *The Kid.*[286] Goldin also made *Yisker* with Maurice Schwartz in 1924. He returned to America in 1925, reverting to acting for a living. In 1929 he wrote and directed his last silent, *East Side Sadie,* which contained sound sequences and introduced his daughter, Bertina Goldin, to the screen. She played a part similar to Irene Wallace in *The Heart of a Jewess,* a sweatshop girl who pays to put her boyfriend through college.[287]

Goldin then joined forces with independent producer Joseph Seiden to make Yiddish talkies. He came out of retirement to make *The Cantor's Son,* based on actor and singer Moishe Oysher's life story. Goldin had a heart attack halfway through production and died on September 19, 1937.[288]

HUMORESQUE   The first Jewish classic was financed and produced by William Randolph Hearst, for his Cosmopolitan Productions, and it very nearly failed to appear.

It was directed by twenty-seven-year-old Frank Borzage, a non-Jewish Italian from Salt Lake City who had come to Los Angeles as a Shakespearean actor in a traveling stock company, fallen in love with the climate, and become an extra at Universal. He applied for a job as a character actor at Inceville and was promptly

Cosmopolitan Productions

HUMORESQUE

FEATURING Alma Rubens

Story by Fannie Hurst

Scenario by
Frances Marion

Directed by
Frank Borzage

A Paramount Artcraft Picture

made leading man. The American Film Company at Santa Barbara gave him his first chance to direct. His films were characterized by a strong feeling for people; there was a refreshing realism about his work which marks it as exceptional, even today.

Hearst wanted Borzage to direct a sophisticated story by Robert W. Chambers. Borzage recalls that he replied that he didn't like that type of thing: "Have you got any human interest stories?" He was offered a book by Fannie Hurst: "There are a lot of short stories in it. You might combine three or four to make a feature film out of them. Take it home and read it."

"So I took it home," said Borzage. "The first story was *Humoresque;* it was a short one. I knew that was it. So I called Frances Marion, who was my writer. I said, 'Frances, I've got the story.' I wanted her to read out loud for me—I had a reason for this. So she read it out loud, and she couldn't quite finish it. The chords in her throat welled up and I said, 'That's the test. That's what I want. That's our story, don't you think?' 'Oh, yes,' she said. So that's how *Humoresque* was started."[289]

The combination of Frances Marion and Frank Borzage was a powerful one, for Miss Marion shared Borzage's ability to convey emotion. In an industry devoted to melodrama, it was a rare gift. Miss Marion was much in demand, having written for Maurice Tourneur, Albert Capellani, and Mary Pickford and the screenplays for *The Yellow Passport* (1916) and *Darkest Russia* (1917). She and Fannie Hurst were friends, and it was Hurst who took her to the Yiddish Theatre to watch Vera Gordon.[290]

A veteran of the Yiddish Theatre, Vera Gordon came from Russia. *Humoresque* was her first picture. "We were sixteen weeks making the picture," she said, "but every minute was a delight and it did not seem like acting a part. You see, I know the East Side—the daily life of the people, their love of home and kindred. Like them, I have known the hand of oppression, the longing to rear my family in freedom. Because of this, I could give myself to the part."[291]

Frank Borzage selected Gilbert Warrenton, who would later become the principal exponent of the moving camera and the "German" style in Hollywood, as cameraman. Hearst had no studio, and there was none available in New York, so the company took over an old beer hall, the Harlem River Casino, closed because of Prohibition, on One Hundred Twenty-sixth Street and Second Avenue.

Because sets for another picture occupied the main floor, Borzage and Warrenton had to work in the basement. Fortunately, their sets needed low ceilings anyway, but whenever the crew upstairs boosted the current, all their lights would blow.

For the scene where the mother goes to pray for her children, Joseph Urban built a stylized synagogue on the main floor. Warrenton suggested putting a shaft of light through a little window with the Star of David above the set. To make it more visible, he had two Irish electricians and a couple of prop men breathing smoke from cigars on to the set. Borzage was delighted with the result.

The opening sequence was shot on location on the Lower East Side. Said Warrenton: "To get rid of the crowds, which in that territory were awful, we secreted the camera in vans, and in one case used a pushcart. We also worked out of windows. In the ghetto, the buildings are close together. There are little

Mama Kantor (Vera Gordon) at the synagogue in Humoresque, *1920.*

platforms on the fire escapes . . . we also got up on these to shoot across at the opposite building, or down the street. Of course, we were not observed.

"We shot underneath the elevated, where the lighting was bad. Even when the sun is on the right slant, there is no room for the light to get between the ties that hold the rails. We did our exteriors as best we could under these conditions, and when I had to, I would plug in a booster light. We didn't like to do this because it attracted attention. By doing it pretty fast, we got away with it a couple of times, and that's how we got our exteriors."[292]

Sadly, these glimpses of life on the Lower East Side are all too short.

Humoresque, released in 1920 and long considered lost, was rediscovered in 1986

From Motion Picture Directing *by Peter Milne (New York: Falk Publishing Co., 1922.)*

THE JEWISH TYPES IN FRANK BORZAGE'S "HUMORESQUE" HAVE
BECOME WORLD RENOWNED

by Bob Gitt, of UCLA Film Archives, and Ron Haver, during a search of the Warner Bros. Studios in Burbank. (Warners had acquired the original in order to remake it.) Although it has much to commend it, like all too many once influential films, its attributes are no longer remarkable. Its style of highly wrought sentimentality became identified with Hollywood for four decades and is common to a hundred other pictures. Though well directed and well photographed, it is basically hokum.

The ghetto scenes, however, cannot be overlooked, although real exteriors are often intermingled with studio. In one sequence, a small girl takes a dead kitten from a garbage can, trying to warm it back to life; the boys who crowd around her end up by punching each other to pulp. This vivid ghetto atmosphere gives way to a more theatrical portrayal of life on Fifth Avenue. American films were never so picturesque dealing with the rich as with the poor! Nevertheless, the emotion of *Humoresque* is so near the surface that while you may note a certain disappointment in your reaction, you will also note the lump in your throat.

Fannie Hurst's short story ended as Leon goes to war.[293] The expanded story by Frances Marion begins before the war. Abraham Kantor (Dore Davidson) works in his brass shop, converting factory-made candlesticks from Brooklyn into aged antiques from Russia. His wife (Vera Gordon) cares for a large family which includes a mentally defective child, whose condition she blames on all she suffered in Russia.

The youngest son, Leon (Bobby Connelly), ruins his new suit, given him for his ninth birthday, by fighting for a girl, Minna Ginsberg (Miriam Battista). His father is angry; his mother forgiving. She sends Abraham out with Leon to buy him a birthday present. Leon sees a violin and becomes obsessed with it. Abraham says at four dollars it is too expensive and drags him away, protesting and tearful.

When Mama hears about this, she is profoundly moved. She had long prayed that one of her children should be a musician.

"Always a moosician," grumbles Abraham. "Why not pray for a business-man?"

From the depths of the shop, Mama produces an ancient and dusty violin she has kept for just such a moment as this. And to her intense satisfaction, Leon proves he has talent. Soon, he gets the four-dollar violin and Mama goes to the synagogue to give thanks.

From the boy playing, we dissolve to Leon the young man (Gaston Glass) ending his first concert tour with a recital for the king and queen of Italy. It is ten years later. Leon re-encounters the girl from the ghetto, now Gina Berg (Alma Rubens), pursuing a singing career. They become engaged.

The Kantors are no sooner back in New York when America enters the war and Leon joins the army. Before he goes, he stages a concert for his own people— the people of the ghetto. (And the shots of the audience reveal that Borzage filled the concert hall with authentic Lower East Siders.) He plays the Kol Nidre, the prayer of atonement, and then his people call for him to play *Humoresque,* "that laugh on life with a tear behind it." The concert is a wild success, and Elsass, the great manager, offers a contract at $2,000 a concert. But Leon says he has signed a contract with Uncle Sam. Mama Kantor is overwhelmed with sadness—surely, such a genius could be excused? But Leon refuses to hide behind his talent. "Look at Mannie," he says, "born an imbecile because of autocracy!" Before he goes, he plays *Humoresque* to bring a smile to his mother's lips.

The war ends. The troops return. A car arrives at the Kantors' home, and an officer steps out. But it is not Leon—just a buddy to report that the boy is lying wounded in the hospital. A doctor explains to the anxious Gina that it was a shrapnel wound—a terrific effort would be his only hope, but not in his present state of mind, for Leon has given up, convinced he will never use his arm again.

Gina tends him in his convalescence, with constant assurances that she loves

Humoresque, 1920. Leon Kantor (Gaston Glass) plays a concert for his own people—portrayed by Jews from the Lower East Side.

him. He answers, "Then you must leave me. My career is ended. I will not have you sacrifice yourself to a cripple."

She walks away, heartbroken and falls in a faint. Leon rushes forward and lifts her up. He realizes that he can move his fingers, and, as Gina recovers, he reaches for his violin and tries to play the instrument. Mama Kantor hears Humoresque.

"God always hears a mother's prayers," she says. Replies Abraham, "I suppose a papa's prayers have nothing to do with it?"

When the picture was finished, it was shown to William Randolph Hearst, who loathed it. Not that Hearst was anti-Semitic; in later years, despite being called a fascist, he interceded with Hitler on behalf of the Jews. It was simply that he could not understand why anybody would want to show the seamy side of life and call it entertainment. "The remarks from the releasing company [Paramount] bore out this theory that audiences would reject the picture."[294] The head of Paramount, Adolph Zukor, also detested Humoresque, saying to Frances Marion, "If you want to show Jews, show Rothschilds, banks and beautiful things. It hurts us Jews—we don't all live in poor houses."[295]

Hearst and Zukor decided not to release the film. It would require an elaborate advertising campaign, and they felt there was little point in throwing good money after bad. Frances Marion told me that it was only because the Criterion Theatre had run short of a film that they were obliged to put it on. It was booked in for a prerelease run of several weeks, to follow DeMille's *Why Change Your Wife?*, that glamorous medley of sex and wealth. A press preview on May 4, 1920, suggested that Hearst and Zukor had been right. *Variety* said, "It proved to be something exhibitors should not bank on too heavily. Up to the middle it seemed like a wonderful picture, then it began to slip.... The continuity by Frances Marion was inadequate, and unless Miss Marion soon values her reputation more than her profits she will have to look alive to preserve what's left of the former."[296]

But when the picture opened at the Criterion, it was an immediate sensation. "Never before," said *Picture Play*, "has such a perfect atmosphere of reality been communicated to the screen. Any fine work of art must have the power of drawing the spectator into its very center. This *Humoresque* accomplished. The life of the Jewish family is your life while you sit and watch the screen. You are as much a part of it as your teeth are part of you. I predict that it will live for years, and will be held up as a standard for aspiring artists to aim at."[297]

A vital ingredient for the film's success was its emphasis on mother-love. Curiously, the cinema had not paid a great deal of attention to mothers. There had been stories of maternal sacrifice, there had even been stories about abominable mothers. But a film which bombarded the emotions with scenes of maternal heartbreak—with a Jewish mother at that—could hardly have been more perfectly timed. The postwar generation was rebelling against its parents, and the story exploited their suppressed sense of guilt while it (briefly) restored their parents' confidence.

Fannie Hurst (who was herself Jewish) was as surprised as Cosmopolitan by the success of the film. "The impact of *Humoresque* was quite extraordinary," she said. "It's been done several times since and it still brings in the most wonderful royalties! Yet the original wasn't elaborate. It was a simply made picture. I had no part in the production. I had nothing to do with the filming of any of my books.

"A cousin of mine, who was a writer herself, accompanied me to the special showing at the Ritz-Carlton for an invited audience.

" 'Why, it's a travesty of the story!' she said. 'The liberties they've taken!' I made a sound signifying agreement, but actually I thought they'd done rather well. I enjoyed it.[298]

"The film was directed by Frank Borzage, a rough and ready man whom the cast found somewhat abrasive. But I liked him—he had a real feeling for his work, and the film put him on the map. That's what pleases me most, I think, that my stories have put people on the map."[299]

New York City set its stamp of approval on *Humoresque* by giving it one of the longest runs ever recorded for a feature picture. (It played for twelve weeks and broke box office records.) *Photoplay* awarded the film its first Gold Medal— the 1920 equivalent of an Academy Award. Wrote Frances Marion: "Nobody was more surprised—and hurt a little—than Mr. Hearst, who had just released another Marion Davies million-dollar opus which was playing to half-empty theatres."[300]

The stunning success of *Humoresque* proved that audiences did not want their realism unadulterated, when a little hokum could make even squalor and mental disease acceptable, evoking a tear rather than a grimace. It set the standard for future Hollywood films about the plight of the Jews. Virtually all the silent productions were affected by an overdose of sentimentality, in the hope of repeating Borzage's success.

HUNGRY HEARTS   The long-lost *Hungry Hearts* was recently discovered in England and deposited with the National Film Archive. A remarkably complete account of the production can be put together from the interoffice memos and telegrams preserved by the legal department of Metro-Goldwyn-Mayer. It is thus possible for once to follow a social film from conception to release—and to observe the gulf between what was intended and what was achieved.

Hungry Hearts is a quiet film, with relatively little which could be described as melodramatic or sentimental. It was made so simply it might have passed as a poverty row production were it not for the obvious commitment of those on both sides of the camera.

When it was first proposed by story editor Ralph Block, Sam Goldwyn was enthusiastic, but he wanted an Americanization picture rather than a Jewish propaganda film.[301] This may have been due to the fact that his associates in New York had just turned down Sophie Irene Loeb's book *Jewish Epic* on the grounds that they did not favor Jewish plays.[302]

Goldwyn himself was an immigrant from Russian Poland, and when he approved the synopsis, he wrote, "Important you emphasize value old people in Russia attach to candles and other sacred things they part with to raise money for transportation to America. This is sure fire."[303]

The story was based on a group of short stories by Anzia Yezierska, collected under the title *Hungry Hearts*. Yezierska was also born in Russian Poland, about 1881. When she was nine, her family came to America and lived on the Lower East Side. Her sisters went straight into the sweatshops; Yezierska went to public school and learned English. She started work at about age fourteen or sixteen. At seventeen, determined "to be a person," she left home and began writing. In December 1915, *Forum* magazine printed her first published story, "The Free Vacation House." She won an award for the Best Short Story of 1919 with "The Fat of the Land." She handed the child she bore (during her second brief marriage) to its father and returned to her independent life.[304]

An enthusiastic item by a Hearst columnist aroused the interest of Hollywood in *Hungry Hearts*, her first book: "Here was an East Side Jewess who had struggled and suffered the desperate battle for life amid the swarms of New York. She had lived on next to nothing at times. She had hungered and shivered and endured. Why? Because she wanted to write. And that, ladies and gentlemen, is all there is to genius. An undying flame, an unconquerable hope, an unviolable belief that you are God's stenographer."[305] Actually, she had graduated from Columbia University and worked for a time as a schoolteacher.

Sara (Helen Ferguson) with her admirer, the rent collector—nephew of the landlord (Bryant Washburn) from Hungry Hearts, *1922.*

Yezierska's agent, R. L. Griffen, sold her book to Goldwyn for $10,000, and the company invited her to work on the scenario at a salary of $200 a week. And so, in January 1921, this red-haired girl with a lifelong hatred of the rich set out for Hollywood—a famous writer.

The Goldwyn people were surprised by her disdain for luxuries. She refused any special treatment and would accept only a lower berth on the train.[306] They booked her into an expensive hotel. "I could not stay," she said. "I would have lost myself . . . I did not feel comfortable being waited upon. It smothered me. I told them I must go away and stay in some simpler place."[307] She also abandoned her chauffeur-driven limousine and took the trolley to work—though once was enough and she returned to the limousine.

Few of the studios regarded writers with the same respect as directors, but in 1919 Goldwyn had formed Eminent Authors, Inc., and had invited some of the most distinguished writers to Hollywood. When Yezierska arrived at the studio she was given an office alongside such celebrities as Rupert Hughes, Alice Duer Miller, and Elinor Glyn. She was astonished at being given stacks of fresh paper; her writing had been done on the backs of envelopes and scraps of wrapping paper. She had been assigned an eager secretary but had no idea how to employ her. Her method of composition was not a nine-to-five affair. The aura of luxury made her impotent as a writer.

Yezierska was interviewed by reporters and her story translated into such headlines as "Sweatshop Cinderella," "Immigrant Wins Fortune in Movies," "From Hester Street to Hollywood."

She received a gift of roses from Paul Bern. "Thank you for giving us a book that'll blaze a new trail in pictures," he said. "You're what I call a natural-born sob sister."

"Do you mean that as a compliment?"

"I mean you've dipped your pen in your heart. You've got the stuff that will click with the crowd—the stuff that'll coin money."[308]

She detested Bern on sight; his dark Hester Street face seemed betrayed by his slick, movie star appearance. But it is hard to know how much of Yezierska's recollection to trust. In her memoirs she had Bern assure her the picture would have a million-dollar budget, which was ludicrous, and around three zeroes more than it did cost.[309] And there are many other discrepancies.

Bern, one of a large family, had come to the United States from Germany when he was nine and his parents were over sixty. The family lived in the New York ghetto with packing cases as furniture for a time, but, like Chaplin, whom he resembled in many ways, Paul used his wits to struggle free of poverty. Bern was said to be a nephew of Sigmund Freud,[310] and certainly his analysis of pictures was unusually perceptive. An intellectual, he was described by his friend Sam Marx as "soft-spoken, with a slight Teutonic accent and gentle Continental manners."[311] Known as the best-read and most generous man in Hollywood, he had little in common with the character sketched by Anzia Yezierska.

In Yezierska's account, Paul Bern is quite clearly a director. Certainly he had codirected a couple of pictures, and his experience included acting, writing, and even managing a film laboratory. But at this stage of his career he was both head cutter at Goldwyn and a producer. True, he had his heart set on directing *Hungry Hearts,* but Goldwyn's heart was harder. This was to be a superspecial and he wanted "Hamburg" to direct it. "Therefore cannot consider Bern's feelings in the matter," said his telegram, bluntly.[312]

I had never heard of a director called Hamburg. As I read these telegrams to and from the home office in New York, I came upon other unfamiliar names—a Frenchman called Bordeaux, a man called Glasgow—and I realized that to avoid other studios indulging in industrial espionage, directors' names were in code. "Hamburg" referred to E. Mason Hopper.

Born in Vermont and educated in Maryland, Hopper began acting at the age of fourteen. And that was the least surprising fact of his career. He was also a baseball player with a minor-league team, a cartoonist—he used this talent on the vaudeville stage—a student of chemistry, and he even invented a windproof matchbox.[313] He became an interior decorator and a student of architecture and wrote sketches for vaudeville. He joined Essanay in 1911 as a writer and became a director, known as "Lightning" Hopper for his skill at cartooning, and directed Gloria Swanson and Wallace Beery, whose comic talents he helped develop. According to his own count, he made around 350 silent pictures and wrote 400 produced scenarios. And yet he remains unknown.

"E. Mason Hopper could have been one of the finest directors," said his former assistant William Wellman, "but he was completely crazy. He'd rather cook than make pictures; he was a much better chef than he was a director. He was a little screwy, but he had great talent."[314]

Ethel Kaye, the first choice to play Sara in Hungry Hearts—*later dropped in favor of Helen Ferguson. (National Film Archive)*

Yezierska had taken more kindly to the scriptwriter, Julien Josephson, a sandy-haired young man of endearingly scruffy appearance who had written some of Charles Ray's tales of small-town life. She and Josephson worked on a story outline during her four-week stay in California. "We spent days and days in the search for one slim thread of truth," she said. "Not one false note must be struck. And we did not force it. Not one line. When the sterile days came, we just sat back and waited and then after a while the life of the thing itself carried us forward so that it wrote itself as a story should."[315]

She was equally impressed with the sets, designed by Cedric Gibbons. "We walked out of the office building to the studio lots and saw an East Side tenement, the rusty fire escapes cluttered with bedding and washlines, a row of pushcarts that seemed to come directly from the Hester Street fish market, a whole city humming."

The sight of men working on the thatched roofs of the village houses transported her to her childhood. "The past which I had struggled to suggest in my groping words was recreated here in straw and plaster. . . . I closed my eyes and could almost see Mother spreading the red-checked Sabbath tablecloth. The steaming platter of *gefüllte* fish, the smell of fresh-baked *hallah,* Sabbath white bread. Mother blessing the lighted candles, ushering in the Sabbath. 'This interior is perfect,' I said to Josephson."[316]

Once her four weeks were up, Yezierska returned to New York to fulfill her commitment to a series of lectures. She left behind a massive story outline— "enough for a twenty-reel picture," groaned the front office[317]—and a reputation for being "difficult."[318] With her socialist sympathies, she did not hesitate to take financial advantage of the studio. To keep her happy, the studio promised to submit Josephson's slimmed-down "technical continuity" for whatever comments she might care to make.

A few months later, the studio began casting the picture. Sam Goldwyn, in New York, tested a Russian-Jewish girl called Ethel Kaye[319] and decided that she should play Sara,[320] although a few days later he had second thoughts and suggested that Alma Rubens, another Jewish actress, might be more suitable.[321]

"Organization unanimously and definitely opposed to Rubens for *Hungry Hearts,"* replied Abe Lehr, who ran the studio. Leatrice Joy was also turned down. So was Carmel Myers, the daughter of a rabbi, who had just appeared in *Cheated Love:* "Good actress, but too American."[322] So Ethel Kaye got the part.

The role of the mother was even more crucial. Augusta Burmeister, who had played in George Loane Tucker's wartime comedy-drama *Joan of Plattsburg* (1918), impressed Goldwyn, but when he brought Yezierska in for her opinion, she thought Burmeister looked more Irish than Jewish.[323] Jacob Adler's wife was interviewed. An actress called Cottrelly was considered. Yezierska said she was not the type. Goldwyn suggested having Mary Alden, a celebrated Hollywood character actress who had been in *The Birth of a Nation,* study Jewish mannerisms.[324] Lehr replied: "Unanimously thought here Mary Alden could not possibly acquire Jewish mannerisms in short time between now and starting of the picture."[325] Lehr made an appointment to see Madame Thomashefsky, but she failed to turn up. None of this came to anything.[326] With the start of production looming. Goldwyn took Yezierska's advice and settled upon the Russian stage actress Sonia Marcel, who left at once for California.[327] Lehr informed Goldwyn that Bryant Washburn had been selected for the juvenile lead, a surprising choice, for he was a very American actor, popular in light comedy. But Lehr justified the decision by calling Washburn "the only juvenile leading man we know of who acceptably photographs Jewish."[328] Perhaps equally important, he had been six years at Essanay and was a friend of Hopper's.

Goldwyn asked Lehr if he wanted Yezierska to come out again. Lehr answered: "Don't want Yezierska as aside from her being a hindrance to Hamburg she will make impossible a sane shooting schedule."[329] Last time, he explained, they either had to get her out of California or face devoting years to the development of her continuity.[330] "I suppose she is just as much of a nuisance in the home office as she was here."[331]

From New York, Yezierska had complained bitterly that the scenario was being reedited without her approval. Cleverly, she argued that unless she were consulted at every stage, Goldwyn's policy, which had given authors complete faith in him, could not be carried out, endangering both artistic integrity and money-making potential.[332] Lehr assured her that nobody was contemplating murdering her brainchild.

And it was true. The creative people associated with the film were devoted to it. They were convinced they had a great picture, and they worked on it with enormous enthusiasm.

Shooting began in late September 1921, and Lehr happily cabled Goldwyn: "Have never screened in any single day a finer or more satisfactory collection of rushes than what we saw today. Opening episode is full of beauty and convincing realism."[333]

But the euphoria was short-lived. In the eight months between the making of her test and her appearance in the picture, Ethel Kaye, in the eyes of everyone at the studio, had changed. "She has lost something that makes her acceptable," wired Lehr enigmatically, "and consequently took her out of part this morning after exhaustive consideration. As emergency measure we put Helen Ferguson in part."[334]

Helen Ferguson was another veteran of "Lightning" Hopper's playground, one of the hopefuls who turned up and sat on the extra's benches, hoping for a job. She was thrown out again and again by the casting director, E. J. Babille, who told her bluntly that she simply wasn't the type for pictures. She refused to believe him. When she signed a contract for the lead in *Hungry Hearts,* it was poetic justice that the assistant director should have been the same E. J. Babille.[335]

Ferguson was delighted with the part, which proved the only major role she was ever to play. "I'm not a Jewess," she said, "and have always hated the little hump on my nose. I now love it because it brought me the part I love so."[336]

In a letter, she assured Yezierska that she would not simply act the part, she would *be* the part. To this end she went to Temple Street, the Jewish district of Los Angeles, and took a job in a delicatessen. The owner, Abe Budin, was a Russian-Jewish immigrant who lived with his family behind the store. "Warm-heartedly, they asked me to live with them for a while. So I lived with these people and it got so it didn't smell right any place unless it smelt of *gefüllte* fish."[337]

Abe Budin was given the role of Sopkin the butcher and played it most proficiently.[338]

If one member of the cast is replaced, the others fear for their jobs. This is the time to make changes; soon it will be too late. And the ax duly fell on Sonia Marcel. Lehr wrote to Goldwyn: "We have gone along from day to day with hope that . . . Sonia Marcel would give us an improved performance but in spite of everything that Hopper can do and talk that I have had with her we feel she will kill our picture if we go on. . . . She is photographically almost impossible for this part because of hard straight mouth and hawk nose that even in slightest profile gets over hardness which makes her repellent in her sympathetic scenes. . . . Her personality is negative and instead of giving us simplicity of peasant Jewess she is giving us intensity of an intellectual woman dressed in peasant's clothes . . . With Ferguson only moderately acceptable we are apparently doomed with definite failure if we go on."[339]

Lehr suggested recasting with Cottrelly as the mother and Celia Adler as the

Helen Ferguson as Sara, the immigrant in Hungry Hearts.
(National Film Archive)

daughter. To suspend production and make the necessary retakes would cost $10,000. "We must face this unless we are willing to accept mediocre production . . . we are faced with expense through extra production time it takes Hopper each day to get over Marcel's scenes even passably."[340]

Production was suspended. Goldwyn wired that to replace Marcel he and Yezierska had chosen Russian-Jewish actress Rosa Rosanova,[341] a veteran of twenty-two years on the Russian and American (Yiddish) stage. He saw no hope of finding another Sara, so it was decided to retain Ferguson.

When production resumed, Goldwyn complained that Hopper was inclined to be "too realistic" in his direction of the East Side characters—in other words, they were too Jewish—and he asked Lehr to keep a close watch on him.[342]

Hopper transferred Yezierska's story and Josephson's continuity with care and dedication. And he created one of the best, albeit one of the simplest, Jewish pictures of the entire silent period.

Hungry Hearts opens in that same thatched hut Anzia Yezierska had seen on the back lot, where Abraham Levin is forced by the tsar's harsh law to hold services in secret. "Abraham, gentle, pious, impractical, who, in 1910, solved all problems according to a book written in 1200."

A Cossack policeman (German actor Bert Sprotte) bursts into the hut, threatening Abraham with ten years in prison if he catches him again. The Cossack stamps on the Sabbath bread and slashes at Abraham's wife, Hanneh (Rosanova), with his whip.

"*Oi weh!*" cries Hanneh. "Is there no end to our troubles?"

A letter from America is read by Abraham to a gathering of villagers: "In America, they ask everybody who shall be President and I, Gedalyah Mindel, have as much to say as Mr. Rockefeller, the greatest millionaire."

Sara, Abraham's daughter, longs to go to America, as does Hanneh, but Abraham asks where he is to get the money.

"Let us anyhow sell our fur coats," urges Sara. "It must be always sunshine in America."

They sell all their possessions, beg, borrow, and at last reach New York. They are dismayed by the ghetto (we see brief shots of the real Lower East Side) and even more dismayed by the tenement Gedalyah Mindel (Otto Lederer) has found for them.

"*Gottiniu,*" gasps Hanneh. "Like in a grave so dark."

"It ain't so dark," says Gedalyah, "it's only a little shady."

And for this they must pay ten dollars a month.

Abraham tends a pushcart in the crowded street, but keeps his nose in his beloved Talmud. "He who studies," it tells him, "will not follow a commercial life, neither can the merchant devote his time to study."

Abraham's landlord, Benjamin Rosenblatt (George Siegmann), a burly, brutal-looking man, has a good-looking young nephew, David Kaplan (Washburn). David calls on his uncle to tell him that the Supreme Court has made him a lawyer.

"*I* made you a lawyer," shouts Rosenblatt, showing him his financial outlay down to the smallest car fare. He orders him to start collecting rents, as a return.

Abraham loses his pushcart to a thief and asks Sopkin the butcher to buy his watch. Sopkin doesn't want it, but he is a kindly soul and takes it anyway. Abraham uses some of the money to purchase a hat for Hanneh. She is touched, until she learns the source.

Day after day, Sara scrubs steps and cleans rooms for Rosenblatt. For this he gives the family their flat rent-free. To her mother, Sara mourns the lack of a social life. "I'm not jealous, but why should they live and enjoy life and why must I only look on how they are happy?" When Mindel offers her a job in a shirt factory, she accepts. This means the Levins start paying rent—and David Kaplan becomes a frequent visitor.

He stays to supper one day and is clearly attracted to Sara, but Abraham monopolizes the conversation. "I am an ignorant woman," Hanneh whispers to him. "But if there is anything in the Talmud about getting a daughter married by her father doing all the talking, *show* it to me!"

Hanneh is deeply impressed by the gleaming white kitchen in the home of

Helen Ferguson works with Abe Budin in his delicatessen store. Budin played Sopkin in Hungry Hearts. *(National Film Archive)*

Hungry Hearts: E. A. Warren (Abraham Levin), Helen Ferguson (Sara), and director E. Mason Hopper. (National Film Archive)

Benjamin Rosenblatt (George Siegmann) yells at his nephew (Bryant Washburn): "I made you a lawyer!" and shows how much it cost him, in Hungry Hearts.

wealthy Mrs. Preston (Frankie Raymond), whose washing she delivers. "If only my children could live to have such beautifulness." And why not? Hanneh spends her hard-earned money on white paint and begins to transform her kitchen.

She invites her neighbors to admire the new grandeur. "To such a tenant," says Sopkin, "the landlord ought to give a medal."

The landlord cannot understand why his rent collector should spend two hours every time he goes to the Levins, and walks over to find out. He smiles as he sees the white paint but the smile vanishes when he sees David holding hands with Sara. He calls the Levins "starving nobodies."

"They are not nobodies," replies David, indignantly. "They're fine people from Russia."

"*Fine* people! Low-down greenhorns—schnorrers!"

David tries to reason with his uncle but he is crushed, and Sara sees their future crumble. As a parting shot, Rosenblatt says, "Because you've got such a fine painted-up kitchen—your rent will be doubled."

Hanneh is mortified. She rushes downstairs to plead with Rosenblatt, who responds, "If you don't pay more another tenant will." A policeman confirms his rights.

"Is there no justice in America?" she asks.

She returns to her flat, shuts the door, and leans her head against the wall, smoothing the paintwork with her hand and weeping. "No, the landlord ain't going to get the best from me." She grabs a meat cleaver and hacks at the wall with ferocious energy. The plaster crumbles. She attacks the cupboards, shelves, and crockery. The janitor rushes in, and she chases him out with her incongruous weapon. Smash—smash—Abraham and Sara rush in and try to hold her, but she breaks free. She has gone berserk, and there is nothing they can do to restrain her. Rosenblatt arrives and is apologetic. Not until two policemen over-power her does the destruction stop. "The Cossack!" she cries, as they drag her out.

Hanneh's case comes up the next morning. The judge asks if she has an at-torney, and David steps forward, to Rosen-blatt's fury. Hanneh tells her story clearly and movingly, and even the judge is touched.

"How could you raise this poor wo-man's rent?" he asks Rosenblatt. "You who were once a poor immigrant yourself?" He dismisses the case, and Rosenblatt's an-ger is so violent he is fined for contempt of court.

"Their second summer in a new land." The Levins now have a smart home in the suburbs. Before this sequence goes much further, the surviving version abruptly ends.

In Hungry Hearts, *Abraham (E. A. Warren) and Sara (Helen Ferguson) restrain Hanneh (Rosa Rosanova) without success; she smashes up their kitchen. (National Film Archive)*

All Yezierska's stories were in some degree autobiographical. Her father, like Abraham, was a Talmudic scholar, although he was a tyrant—more like Rosenblatt than the quiet old man of the film. Anzia herself had a burning eagerness to become an American, to acquire American clothes, like Sara in the picture.[343] But the film smoothed away the underlying anger and all hints of Yezierska's socialism. Gone is the wretchedness of the girl in the ghetto, her agitation for higher pay in the shirt factory, the passiveness of the other workers, and her subsequent despair: "At least in Russia she had the hope of America!"[344]

The original story, "The Lost Beautifulness," dealt only with the episode of the painted kitchen. Hanneh, the mother, converts it because her soldier son is returning from France. There is much more emphasis on relentlessly rising prices. Mrs. Preston, the wealthy woman, treats her as a friend and talks to her of de-mocracy. The courtroom scene is also very different. In the story, the judge agrees with the landlord. Hanneh is evicted. The soldier returns to find his mother sur-rounded by a heap of household things on the sidewalk, dumped there in the rain.

The picture was completed at the end of November 1921 and was edited by Robert Kern as a nine-reeler, under Paul Bern's supervision. It was shipped to New York with the strict understanding that Anzia Yezierska would not be permitted to dominate the final ending.[345] Some people at the home office in New York felt the climax was not strong enough emotionally: it was all very well seeing Hanneh tear up the apartment with a cleaver, but unless one saw her trying to collect the money to paint it, the impact was diminished. Extra scenes were shot of Hanneh working her fingers to the bone, scrubbing offices until the early hours, and returning through the deserted ghetto streets. (None of this is in the surviving version.)

E. Mason Hopper directs "East Side crowd" for Hungry Hearts. *The man on the left, with boots, is a member of the crew. (National Film Archive)*

A studio preview was attended by Elinor Glyn and Montague Glass, author of *Potash and Perlmutter* (1923). Both were extravagant in their praise, but Glass was particularly struck. He said it was "a perfect human document" and "the finest picture he ever saw." He could not suggest a single improvement. He also commented about the fine judgment shown in the spoken titles.[346]

By this time Sam Goldwyn had been replaced as president of the Goldwyn Company by Frank J. Godsol, who set about signing Glass to rewrite the titles. He also requested that all positive offcuts be sent to New York. Bern, Kern, and Hopper were dismayed at this clear indication that Godsol was about to tamper with their film. When Lehr protested on their behalf, Godsol said Glass hadn't changed his opinion; he just saw a few splendid opportunities for humorous titles. "The ending is not good and can never be made good, but Glass has figured out a way to make it more logical."[347] (Glass would also insert quotations from the Talmud, to make clear the identity of the book the old man consulted.)

Maybe Glass could work with Bern? But Bern was so violently opposed to the reediting that he refused to cooperate. "I appreciate his feelings," said Godsol, patronizingly, "but we are closer to exhibitors than he is."[348]

When Glass finished his work, the studio people were horrified at the increase in the number of titles. So they made up two versions, the home office version with all Glass's titles intact and a studio version containing many of them but recut by Kern and Bern. It was not the film they started with—Godsol had lopped more than two reels out of it because he felt it was "draggy and boresome"[349]—but it was a reasonable compromise. Both versions were sent to New York, and the studio people waited in suspense for Godsol's reaction. To their intense relief, he accepted their version.

When Anzia Yezierska finally saw what had been made of her stories, she was horrified. She realized she could do nothing to prevent the desecration of her idea and felt as if she had been raped. "But I lived through it. And here is my message of faith; for all this desecration, for all the violation of an integral thought, I feel that the idea still lives and goes on. And it is, after all, a great and good thing to have even the fraction of one's idea live."[350]

Before the film was shown to the press, it was shown privately to Lillian D. Wald, the noted settlement worker, and to magazine editors. *The American Hebrew* wrote an enthusiastic report of this "epic of the immigrant." Variety acknowledged that there were many touching passages, "but it is entirely devoid of dramatic action and one is constrained to fear that its appeal will be limited . . . Here's a big subject—the theme of the Americanization of an alien family delivered raw in New York from the oppression of Russia. But out of this rich material it does seem the incidents that have been picked are petty. Certainly they are inadequate for a feature length picture."[351]

One can sympathize with this attitude, for *Hungry Hearts* might have been the kind of intimate epic achieved, decades later, by Elia Kazan with *America, America.* But now its very quietness seems an asset. The lack of manufactured drama is refreshing. The titles are full of wisecracks. Yet the degree of stereotyped Jewish behavior is minimal compared to what might have been.

The picture is no documentary; suffering and poverty are talked about rather than experienced. It is in no way a political film. The ghetto is a fact of life, and no one is blamed for it. In common with most films of the 1920s which touch upon poverty, the rich are glimpsed as kindly, charitable people. When Hanneh admires the lady's kitchen, she is rewarded with a gift of a geranium. "It chokes me how good you are," says Hanneh. "I can't get it out in words."

Hungry Hearts may be more of an entertainment than a social film, but its slice-of-life approach gives it unusual value. The picture of downtrodden Jews may border on the sentimental, but the feeling is right. The central theme is money. Knowing that many in the audience suffered from prejudice, Josephson made the father a man with no interest in money at all. In European communities, Jews who had money supported those who did not. The film makes it clear that in America the system is harsher—"Nobody's a somebody before he can earn money in America," says Mindel to the new arrivals. And the fact that the grasping landlord is portrayed as a Jew, too, was a unique touch in a film of this sort. ("Perhaps overdrawn," said *The American Hebrew*.)[352]

The film's main drawback, from the cinematic point of view, is its dependence on titles. The first half is a perfect example of a silent talkie. It is soberly and competently directed, albeit without flashes of imagination. The art direction was highly praised: "No one who knows the Lower East Side could find fault with a single scene," said *The American Hebrew*.[353] Yet there is an empty look to interiors which Gibbons did not overcome, and I suspect this was due more to the poverty of the budget than to that of the story. The happy ending was attacked by almost every critic—"an oozily sentimental finish," said Frederick James Smith[354]—and the sight of Abraham in his battered old clothes against the gleaming white of the suburban home is ludicrous. Mercifully, very little of this survives.

The print, which was discovered in 1978 by John Cannon,[355] is missing several important scenes—such as those aboard ship. (One review refers to the "touching moment" as the family sights the Statue of Liberty.) And the pace of the picture is fractured by the chunks torn from the heavily run positive. About fifteen minutes appear to be missing. Between that, and the cuts and changes made between completion and release, the impact of the original is much reduced.

Although the film was selected as one of *Photoplay*'s Eight Best of the Year and received an honorable mention in Robert Sherwood's *Best Moving Pictures of 1922–1923*, it was not a major moneymaker for Goldwyn. It led to very little for its star; she hardly worked at all for the following eight months. And it was three years before Hollywood tackled the subject of Jewish immigration again.

SALOME OF THE TENEMENTS   Anzia Yezierska made one more contribution to the silent cinema: *Salome of the Tenements* (1925), which was directed by the Canadian-born Irishman Sidney Olcott for Famous Players–Lasky. Her agent sold it for 50 percent more than she had been paid for *Hungry Hearts*. But Yezierska had little to do with the making of the film.[356] It was scripted by her old friend Sonya Levien, who had once been fiction editor of *Metropolitan Magazine* and had virtually started Yezierska's career when she had bought some of her stories. The lead was given to the Jewish actress Jetta Goudal, and there was a strong representation of Jewish players, including José Ruben, Lazar Freed, Irma Lerner (a friend of Yezierska's), Sonia Nodell, and Elihu Tenenholtz.[357] (According to *Picture Show,* Tenenholtz gave "one of the most masterly portrayals of Jewish life ever seen on the screen.")[358]

The story was a more cynical view of ghetto life than *Hungry Hearts;* it was about the next generation, the children of the immigrants. Sonya Mendel grows up with good looks and a sharp wit and works as a reporter on the *Jewish Daily News.* She pursues millionaire John Manning (Godfrey Tearle), who has endowed a settlement house on the East Side and wages war against local grafters. Sonya, known as Salome because of the string of scalps at her belt, borrows money from a loan shark so that she can improve her apartment in order to impress Manning. She is determined to marry the philanthropist and succeeds, but does not reckon with the grafters. They use her debt to blackmail Manning, forcing him to relax his campaign against them. Sonya proves her love, showing herself willing to go to prison rather than allow her husband to give up his work for the people in the ghetto.[359]

Salome of the Tenements, *1925, with Jetta Goudal, center, directed by*
Sidney Olcott. (George Eastman House)

Sonya was partly based on Rose Pastor Stokes, a Russian-Jewish social worker
who became assistant editor of the *Jewish Daily News* and married a philanthropist,
millionaire Graham Stokes. It was also a portrait of Anzia herself, who became
romantically involved with the philosopher and educationist John Dewey. She
remained particularly fond of the character.[360]

Reviewers praised the "rare types" who enlivened the atmosphere, but considered it "a mighty wishy-washy tale at best" which would get money only in towns
with large ghetto populations.[361] A fan from Medford, Massachusetts, thought the
producers should be locked up. "This is without doubt the worst picture I have
ever seen. If I saw one more like it I think I should give up being a fan for
evermore. Please refrain from any more 'anti' or 'pro' propaganda pictures of the
kind of *Salome of the Tenements.*"[362]

EDWARD SLOMAN   Was Edward Sloman the most socially conscious director of his time? Just look at his achievements: in 1915 he made *The Inner Struggle,* a tragedy of life in a leper colony. The same year he directed *The Convict King,* about the convict labor system. In 1916, he released *The Law's Injustice,* about legal and political corruption, and *Dust,* about conditions in factories and the hypocrisy of rich people who spent lavishly at Belgian relief galas, where their generosity was visible, but who allowed their workers to starve. In 1921, he made *The Ten-Dollar Raise,* dedicated to the underdogs of the world. And this does not take into account his Jewish pictures.

Yet if anyone personified the kind of filmmaker who made social films without being aware of the fact, it was Edward Sloman. He was the last man to be described as a crusading reformer. He had made so many pictures, he said, he had trouble recalling them. He thought he had made only three films with Jewish backgrounds; I can account for at least seven. Behind many of his early social films was the young radical Julian Lamothe, scenarist; one should beware of ascribing to the director the idea and story of films which were so often assigned to him.

Sloman came from a poor background, but apart from his Zionist sympathies he was never involved in politics. His style of filmmaking was what would now be called traditional, except that rather than following tradition, he was one of those pioneers who helped create it. His attitude was encapsulated in a letter he wrote to me in 1967: "Saw an old picture the other night on television, *How Green Was My Valley,* the story of a coal-mining town in Wales—and it was perfectly beautiful. It was so far ahead of most pictures made today—and especially the so-called *art* pictures from the Continent—there was no comparison. Here was sheer entertainment (not pictures that are supposed to tell us how to live). It was 'hocum' [sic] but nice 'hocum,' the 'hocum' that the ordinary person who goes to see pictures doesn't recognize as such; he enjoys every minute of it and loves it!"

How Green Was My Valley, made by John Ford in 1941, was indeed a beautiful production, but it was an idealized and romanticized view of life in a mining village. It no more dealt with the realities of coal-mining than *The Sound of Music,* another Sloman favorite, dealt with the realities of refugees.

So Edward Sloman is included in this volume as an outstanding contributor to the films of social importance more by accident than design. Yet some of his films have a significance quite apart from their value as entertainment.

Sloman was born in London in 1883. He emigrated to Montreal around 1901. His skills as a photo-engraver were much in demand, and he moved to a more profitable job in Minneapolis. Fascinated by acting, he paid for lessons from Fred Carr, a former leading man for Otis Skinner. Carr was so impressed by his pupil's ability, he said he wouldn't charge Sloman for lessons if he would help Carr teach. Sloman became a professional actor and director and appeared in a staging of Clyde Fitch's *The City* (1909), a story of drug addiction.

Edward Sloman with inhabitants of the Jewish quarter of Los Angeles who were hired as extras for the shtetl *scenes of* Surrender, *1927.*

He married Hylda Hollis, and together they toured with Eva Tanguay in vaudeville. When Tanguay was blackballed by the booking agencies because she preferred to book her artists herself, the Slomans were blackballed along with her, so they went to California to act in motion pictures. Sloman's stage experience caused him to be promoted abruptly to director, at Lubin's West Coast studios. For three years he worked at the Flying A studios in Santa Barbara, until they closed. For Benjamin Hampton he made the highly successful *The Westerners* (1919) before joining Metro. And in 1922 he made a Jewish story for J. L. Frothingham: *The Woman He Loved.*

"Direction came very easily to me," he said. "It was hard work but I knew what I was doing. You see, when I was acting in pictures, I never knew what I was doing. An actor never saw a script. That's what started me writing, you see. If I hadn't written some of the things I worked in, I wouldn't have known what the hell I was doing. I always worked at night on my script for the following day—I always visualized everything."[363]

Sloman never encountered anti-Semitism in Hollywood, but those who imagine Hollywood to have been a tightly knit Jewish enclave might be surprised to know that he had a rough passage in the 1920s and '30s, despite the success of so many of his films. For instance: J. L. Frothingham was backed by financier E. F. Hutton. When Hutton withdrew, Frothingham turned his assets over to Mike Levee, owner

Surrender, 1927. Lea Lyon (Mary Philbin), the Rabbi (Nigel de Brulier), and Constantin (Ivan Mosjoukine), in Edward Sloman's version of the play Lea Lyon, *about a Cossack prince's threat to burn a Jewish village unless a village girl surrenders to him; Jewish customs were carefully reproduced.*

of the studio. The assets included the negative and print of a picture Sloman had written but had not been paid for.

Sloman recalled, "When I presented my bill to foxy Mike Levee, he not only hired my lawyer away from me, but threatened me with a blackball if I ever dared to collect that money for the story. So I collected and he blackballed me—with the result that I didn't direct for almost two years."[364]

Two years seems to be an exaggeration, but certainly Sloman was driven to putting his own money up for his next production, *Blind Justice,* released as *The Last Hour,* with Milton Sills. He was talked into selling it to Mastodon Pictures, a States Rights outfit run by the notorious C. C. Burr, who succeeded in cheating him once more.

Sloman's agent, Edward Small, was a friend of the studio manager at Universal, Julius Bernheim. He persuaded Bernheim to offer Sloman a job. "Bernheim did so, at the lowest salary ever offered to a director, hoping I would turn it down. But I accepted."

His association with Universal brought Sloman his biggest hit and the most popular of all the Jewish pictures of the silent era: *His People.*

Among the first three-reel films to be directed by Sloman was *Vengeance of the Oppressed* (Lubin, 1916), in which he also played the lead. Yet on the list of films he compiled for me, he could not even recall the title and referred to it alternately as "Russian picture" and "Jewish picture." The script was credited to Wilbert Melville, the manager of the studio, and Julian Louis Lamothe. The only drawback to the picture, according to *Moving Picture World,* was that the opening was so powerful that the authors could not increase that impact as the story neared its climax. The opening dealt with the cruelties exacted on the Jews by the Cossacks.

"A more striking and realistic picturization has seldom been produced," said one critic, "even the crucifixion of the mother lacks any tendency towards artificiality." Sloman's playing of the part of Aaron was highly praised: "It is most realistic, being unspoiled by any tendency to overact."[365]

The story was about a Jewish student, Aaron, whose uncle in America sends money to enable his family to emigrate. A pogrom shatters the plans and only Aaron and his daughter reach the United States. Years later Aaron becomes financially successful and is asked to assist in the negotiation of a loan to Russia. One of the negotiators proves to be Sergius Kosloff, the man who killed Aaron's mother and wife. Aaron plans his vengeance, "and in his dying moments he had the pleasure of seeing his enemy killed, decoyed by a woman."[366]

"In doing the thing as a Jew," said Sloman, "I was tied up to a gate and lashed with a cat o' nine tails. We were using the 1st Cavalry for the Cossacks, and I said to the guy who was going to lash me, 'You're going to hear an awful lot of yelling. But don't take any notice. You keep doing it.' The lash was made of felt instead of leather—didn't make any difference. I was yelling at him to stop, and he didn't stop. He tore all the skin off my back. I carried those scars on my back for many, many years."[367]

HIS PEOPLE   Sloman's grand contribution to the films about Jews was *His People* (1925). "This is my favorite film, not because it was the best thing I'd done, but because it was such a sure-fire picture. I knew when I started that it was going to be a great hit."[368]

His confidence was based on Isadore Bernstein's story, "The Jew," and Rudolph Schildkraut's performance. The title *The Jew* was quickly changed to *His People,* and advance publicity explained that the story had been written around Alexander Carr's ability to portray a lovable character and fill it overflowing with humor and pathos.[369] "Mr. Laemmle offers a surprise in this one!" The surprise was that Alexander Carr was not in it.

Carr was a Jewish stage actor who had worked for Goldwyn in *Potash and Perlmutter.* He was notoriously temperamental, a fact which would have been well known to Universal. *His People* had a fairly large cast, but essentially it was a one-part movie; the entire picture hinged around the father, David Cominsky. This part could have been played by either man, but Universal settled for Schildkraut.

The character of Sammy, the devoted son who becomes a boxer with an Irish name, was based on the prize fighter Benny Leonard (who also inspired the 1927 Alfred Santell film *The Patent Leather Kid).* Some of the scenes bore a similarity to the stories Leonard told of his parents when he first became a boxer.[370] Edward Sloman picked George Lewis from the ranks of the extras to play this part.

Bernstein wrote his story in 1921. Born in New York, he had spent fourteen

His People, 1925, directed by Edward Sloman. Rosa Rosanova as Mamma Cominsky and Rudolph Schildkraut as David Cominsky. (National Film Archives)

years working on the *Christian Herald* and had been superintendent of Boys' Institute and athletic instructor at the Five Points Mission, New York. He entered the picture business in 1909, taking over Western Universal in 1913. Bernstein had written the script for a 1915 Jewish film called *Faith of Her Fathers.* That same year he resigned, but his problems with Carl Laemmle, the German-Jewish president of Universal Pictures, were never so serious that he could not return, and he became a supervisor and executive as well as a writer. He knew the Lower East Side, and several of the incidents in *His People* were autobiographical.

Every producer to whom he showed his story turned it down. Even Universal felt it had no hope of success. Finally, Bernstein got Carl Laemmle himself to read it, and Laemmle decreed that it was to be produced.[371] With the amazing success of *Abie's Irish Rose,* it was a foregone conclusion that Hollywood would eventually make a Jewish-Irish story.

Universal's new studio manager, Raymond Schrock, called Sloman into his office and handed him the three typewritten pages of *The Jew.* "There was only a germ of an idea in this story," said Sloman, "but it was a good one. So, with the help of Al Cohn,[372] who had written a similar story for Warner Bros., Charlie Whittaker and myself, we took a couple of sequences between us and started to write a script.

"Our combined efforts evidently jelled perfectly, because before the picture was actually finished everybody in the studio seemed to know that we had a great big hit on our hands."[373]

Before Sloman had finished editing the picture, Carl Laemmle ordered it sent to New York. Sloman had to follow, completing the editing on the East Coast. The picture's name caused problems: Universal pictures always opened with the title "Carl Laemmle Presents" and in the light of all the jokes about Laemmle's kindness to his relatives it was asking for trouble to open with "Carl Laemmle Presents His People." So it was changed to *Proud Heart*, perhaps recalling *Hungry Hearts*. This, however, was attacked in the press as "meaningless, trite." Universal appealed for a better title. Meyer Schine, of Schine Theatrical Enterprises, a large New York circuit, came up with *Common People*, pointing out that it suggested the significance of the picture and was maximum box-office value. Universal agreed and the title was announced while the film was still playing at the Astor, but as no one else liked it, the name reverted to *His People.*

The picture had been booked into the Astor while *The Phantom of the Opera* was still doing $10,000-a-week business there, so certain were Universal's executives of creating a new hit. And a hit it was.

The premiere was attended by many prominent Jews, including Henry Morgenthau, former U.S. ambassador to Turkey; Bernard Baruch; Judge Otto A. Rosalsky; and lawyer Nathan Burkan. Rudolph Schildkraut did not attend, as he was acting in a play, but his son Joseph was there. The picture got a tremendous reception, and when it was known that Sloman was present, he received great applause. The critics were unanimously enthusiastic . . . almost. One critic said he hoped a film would one day exploit Schildkraut's magnificent and powerful pantomime, "which, I am sad to say, are but faintly called upon in *Proud Heart.* The photoplay is sentimental-comedy-melodrama of the Ghetto—a few dabs from *Humoresque,* a pinch of *Abie's Irish Rose* . . . it could scarcely fail of sound financial success." But he admitted that in the development "there was a modicum of honest sentiment, feeling, simplicity and sincerity."[374] The other critics admitted the picture was hokum, but said it was nonetheless human, true, and magnificent. Schildkraut was compared to Emil Jannings in *The Last Laugh. His People* was a sensation in London; Sloman must have been gratified by the *Kine Weekly* review which said the picture had "a sprinkling of Dickens and Zangwill."[375] It broke records in London and at theatres across the United States. One exhibitor said his conscience was troubled when he thought of the low price he had paid for the picture, and he sent an extra 20 percent to Universal.[376]

Out-of-town reviewers thought the re-creation of New York flawless. Critics from the ghetto, however, felt the sets were "rather artificial and poorly lighted" and complained that some of the titles were inane. (Nonetheless, they loved the picture.)[377]

The Jewish reaction was unreservedly enthusiastic:

"A street in the ghetto. A cross-section of swarming, teeming humanity. A page from Life with its stark, staring realism," wrote Sam B. Jacobson in a Jewish Los Angeles paper. "One can almost smell the smells of this city within a city that is shown so realistically on the screen.

"This is the first time that a film has so vividly portrayed the lives and environment of the Jewry of a metropolis."[378]

After a lengthy paragraph praising Schildkraut, Jacobson added: "Can't you see the little Cominsky family as the old father pronounces 'kiddush' with his 'brosha' over the wine and the final 'moitze' over the bread? Not once does he omit to kiss the 'mezuzah' as he leaves or enters his home. And true to his traditions, he blesses his first born when he believes that he is on his dying bed.

"Rosa Rosanova is perfect as the subjective, yet doting mother. The sweet smile of faith as she finishes her 'benching' of the Shabbas candles is the same smile that thousands of Jewish mothers have worn down the ages. Her quick sympathy for the misunderstood younger son is the sympathy of an intuitive mother heart."[379]

He reserved his highest praise for the director.

"Edward Sloman is responsible for one of the finest pictures ever made. He has done, with *His People,* more to eradicate with one blow prejudice and racial hatred than any other agency has accomplished.

"It is a picture that only a Jew could have made. Carl Laemmle, a Jew, who produced it, Isadore Bernstein, a Jew, who wrote the original story, and Edward Sloman, a Jew, who directed it; all have earned the thanks of the Jews the world over for their participation in the greatest piece of propaganda that has ever been presented to the public."[380]

Because *His People* was made by Universal pictures, it was aimed, as were virtually all their films, at the audience of small-town America, and the Jews were as sentimentalized and caricatured as the Irish. But because it was obviously written from experience, the film carries an impact. Time has made even the obviousness touching. Fortunately, the leading roles were given to Rudolph Schildkraut and Rosa Rosanova, both of whom look perfect; Schildkraut, particularly, gives a marvelous performance. Arthur Lubin is convincing as the erring son, but George Lewis is too bland and two-dimensional to be effective as Sammy. The Irish family, represented by Kate Price and Blanche Mehaffey, is overdrawn.

The prologue—supposedly 1914, but no concessions are made to period—establishes Sammy as a tough little newspaper boy, defending his studious brother against the aggressive Izzy Rosenblatt. Ten years later, the boys have grown up and Sammy, caring little for religion, is enamored of the Irish girl across the way. His strict father is dismayed by Sammy's inattention during Shabbas. He manages to break away by telling his father he is going to night school—"What are you studying, box fighting?" "I'm studying to be an expert finisher." When a mischievous neighbor shows the father a flyer announcing "Battling Rooney" fighting in a nearby tournament, the father recognizes his son. He throws him out of the house. The same day, the family favorite, Morris, packs and leaves—he has taken a flat uptown to help his career. The family is broken up; the mother bursts into tears.

Morris's uptown commitment is female, the daughter of a former judge named Stein.[381] To give himself greater leverage when he asks for his sweetheart's hand, Morris convinces the wealthy judge that he is an orphan and that he has made his way unaided and alone. This also avoids the embarrassment of bringing his ghetto parents face-to-face with his prospective father-in-law.

Needing money to fuel his courtship, Morris turns up at home, saying that his entire career depends on his having a dress suit. The old father has an idea, and on an icy December night, with snow driving fiercely in a gale, he sets out.

"But, Papa, you said you wouldn't go out on a night like this for a thousand dollars," says Mother.

"Well, if they give me a little less, maybe I take it."

He staggers through the blizzard to a pawnbroker and there removes his magnificent coat which he has brought all the way from Russia and which he would not part with for anything. The pawnbroker affects derision for it, but they settle for twenty dollars. "Twenty dollars won't buy me a dress suit," says Papa.

"Why didn't you say?" The pawnbroker has dress suits fit for a king.

While Morris is protesting to his mother that he can't wait much longer, the old man, deprived of his overcoat (ref Gogol!), soaked and buffeted, staggers home. He is bowled over by a passing vehicle, and Sammy, out for a training run, helps him up without guessing his identity. When the old man reaches home, Morris is sickened by the sight of the dress suit. "But where's the *money?*" However, he takes the suit to humor his parents. No sooner is he outside than he tosses it into a trash can.

The father catches pneumonia and cries out for Morris, to give him his last blessing. A telegram greets the boy at his uptown flat, but his girlfriend is more demanding—"You needn't come if there is anything more important than me." Of course there isn't; how can he tell her of his father's illness—he, an orphan?

So the son receiving the blessing is Sammy; the father is too ill to notice the difference. While the family, and the Irish family, too, stand around and weep, the doctor smiles—he is over the crisis and will pull through.

"It was my Morris—he gave me strength," says the old man.

But instructions from the doctor are grim; unless the old man goes to live in a better climate, he will die. Sammy therefore forces himself into a tournament; the prize money is $1,000. Meanwhile, the mischievous neighbor cannot wait to show the father the column in the Jewish paper about the smart marriage uptown—Morris Cominsky, an orphan, who rose to an important position in Judge Stein's legal firm entirely on his own! "This cannot be my Morris." "But it wasn't your Morris who came when you were ill—he was too busy. It was Sammy. And Sammy is fighting for you now."

Intercut skillfully with the boxing match, in which Sammy is being beaten to a pulp, the old man sets out for the wedding reception. Meanwhile, Mrs. Cominsky, under the guise of being taken to a movie show by Sammy's Irish sweetheart, finds herself a spectator at the boxing match. Horrified by the injuries her son is sustaining, she nonetheless hurls herself to the front and yells at him that he must win—for his father.

The father gains admittance to the great house and upon being told that the bridegroom has no father—there must be some mistake—confronts his son, to Morris's intense embarrassment. It is an absorbing and impressive scene, albeit highly theatrical. The old man, hearing from Morris that he has never set eyes on him before, apologizes. His own eyesight is weak. With dignity he departs.[382]

A coincidence of Dickensian proportions: at the subway station Sammy, the Irish girl, and the mother sit down exalting in their win and the thousand-dollar check. Suddenly they see the old father being helped down the steps by the neighbor. When Sammy hears what has affected the old man so badly, he takes a taxi

Edward Sloman (left) with Rudolph Schildkraut, who had just arrived at Universal City for what the press agent termed "his debut in motion pictures." He had already made films in Europe.

to the same address and forces his way past the butler. "You denied your father. I wait to hear you deny me, your brother." Sammy frog-marches Morris away from the reception and throws him in front of his father. "I—I've been a selfish cur." But the father is so anxious to forgive his favorite son, the first-born, that he even has a reconciliation with Sammy. He admits he has been stupid. "I looked for success for my children in the only thing I knew—learning. But success in this country can even mean a box fighter."

Rudolph Schildkraut, the father, could hardly have been better. A star of the German theatre, an actor with Max Reinhardt, and a veteran of the cinema, Schildkraut came from Rumania. As a young man, he misguidedly accepted the role of Jesus in a Passion Play one Easter; the crowd quickly realized that he was a Jew and attacked the stage.[383]

Schildkraut had been to the United States before: he had made his debut at the Peoples' Theatre in 1911, left in 1913, and returned in 1920. His family accompanied him, and Joseph, his son, was the first to become a film star, thanks to D. W. Griffith's *Orphans of the Storm* (1921).

Schildkraut was a revelation to Edward Sloman. "He was such a consummate actor," he said. "In the silent days, a good director was a good actor at the same time. While the camera was going he could tell the actor what to do. But with the old man, his technique was so perfect, I'd just have to say to him, while the camera was going, 'Tighter, poppa, tighter,' and he would ease the action into perfect balance."[384]

For the scene in which old Cominsky confronts his son at Judge Stein's party, thirty extras were seated around a table. Hollywood extras were well known to be the most hard-boiled and least impressionable people in the business. Toward the end of the afternoon, with everyone wilting under the hot lights, Schildkraut made his appearance at the end of the table. The extras watched cynically as Schildkraut worked his theatrical magic. Slowly he worked to the climax, and when he heard his son deny him he scarcely stirred. He apologized brokenly to the guests. His eyes overflowed with tears as he turned and blindly left the room. When Sloman called "Cut" the extras were weeping openly.[385]

WE AMERICANS   Edward Sloman made one more important film for Universal, *We Americans* (working title *Heart of a Nation*), based on a 1926 play by William Herbert Gropper and Max Siegel which starred an actor from the Yiddish theatre called Muni Wisenfrend (Weisenfreund), who became better known as Paul Muni. Said Sloman: "He was very anxious to do the picture, but all we saw was a young man in the stage make-up of a middle-aged man, and we were afraid he wouldn't be convincing on the big screen. So we took George Sidney. Only a few years later, Muni became the biggest star on the Warner lot, celebrated for his make-ups."[386]

The script was by Alfred A. Cohn, who doubled as the Los Angeles harbor commissioner with the Immigration Naturalization Service. He expanded the play, which was a drama of three immigrants. A Russian Jew (Levine: George Sidney), a German (Schmidt: Albert Gran), and an Italian (Albertini: Michael Visaroff) come to America ten years before the war. Their children grow up, and the sons enlist. Levine's daughter leaves home, sets up a smart interior decorating studio,

We Americans, *1928. Mr. Albertini (Michael Visaroff), Mr. Levine (George Sidney), and Mr. Schmidt (Albert Gran). (Museum of Modern Art)*

The immigrants learn to become citizens: We Americans, *1928. The teacher is John Bleifer, who was also technical adviser on* Surrender. *(Museum of Modern Art)*

and falls for a wealthy young society man. The immigrants are now alone. Since they cannot read or write, they are persuaded to go to night school, where they learn the principles of Americanism. This has a magical effect and they *become* Americans.

The picture was a tear-jerker; the moment that not even hard-boiled reviewers could resist was one in which Mrs. Levine, learning the Gettysburg Address, reaches the line "and they had not died in vain" when she is handed a telegram informing her of the death of her son at the front.

It is a tragedy that Universal allowed their silent films to rot or burn. *We Americans* would today be of immense historical importance, for it included sequences showing the process of immigration. In response to a request from Will Hays for pictures that would speed up the Americanization of immigrants, Universal asked him to help shape the story by enlisting welfare professionals who worked with the newcomers. Under the chairmanship of former governor Carl Milliken, standing in for Hays, the MPPDA organized a luncheon at the Waldorf-Astoria to which were invited a number of these people, including Commissioner of Immigration Benjamin A. Day and Dr. John Finley of the Council for Adult Education of the Foreign Born.[387]

"One after another these men and women, every one of whom had countless personal experiences from which to draw, talked; and while they talked, the pencil of the director moved as he made his notes."[388]

Sloman decided to begin his picture before the immigrants reached land, so the first scene was photographed aboard the S.S. *George Washington* at quarantine, then at the Statue of Liberty, and finally at Ellis Island.

Commissioner Day put the facilities of Ellis Island at Sloman's disposal. Since the scene was supposed to have taken place in 1907 or 1908, Sloman called in Inspector Baker, who had been attached to the facility since its opening. Baker showed Sloman the parts of the area that were original; fortunately, the piers and the main building, with its glass-covered archway, had not been altered. It was ideal for filming because it had been designed to admit as much light and air as possible for the benefit not only of the immigrants but also of the authorities.

Twenty scenes were shot at Ellis Island, and still pictures were made of the building so that sets could be put up at Universal studios and the rest of the scenes shot there.

Inspector Baker took the film people on a tour, showing exactly what happened to the immigrant from the moment he stepped on the dock—all of which would eventually appear in the film.[389] He was asked if the costumes had changed in the twenty years.

"Not a chance," he replied. 'They haven't changed in two hundred years. I see the same kinds of clothes coming in here from Italy, Scandinavia, Ireland, France, Germany and Spain as I saw coming in from these same countries twenty years ago, and I'll venture that in the next twenty years they will be the same. Mr. Sloman need have no fear of getting plenty of character in the costumes of the immigrants, but I would suggest that he wait for one of the immigrant ships from Italy before taking some scenes. They are the most colorful of all the immigrants."[390]

Commissioner Day explained to Sloman that not nearly as many newcomers arrived at Ellis Island as before the war, thanks to the government's new practice of having prospective immigrants examined by U.S. officials in the country of origin. "This prevents a great deal of useless travel, of disappointment on arrival here."[391]

Motion Picture Magazine called *We Americans* the first film to glorify the pants-pressers. "If you have tears, prepare to shed them now. For *We Americans* is especially constructed for the stimulation of the lachrymose glands. It is a rather skillful mixture of the Jewish-Gentile theme, the war and the waving of the flag. But, Lord, how they'll love it!"[392]

THE JAZZ SINGER   Anne Nichols's play *Abie's Irish Rose* had a lot to answer for. Its phenomenal success led to a proliferation of Hollywood comedies— *The Cohens and the Kellys, Clancy's Kosher Wedding, Frisco Sally Levy, Kosher Kitty Kelly, Private Izzy Murphy, Sailor Izzy Murphy,* and endless subplots about the conflicts between Catholic and Jew.

The Jazz Singer, as a play, was written as a reaction to *Abie's Irish Rose;* it was an attempt to deal seriously with the problem of assimilation. Its author, Samson Raphaelson, had been electrified by Al Jolson in a musical called *Robinson Crusoe Jr.* in 1916. Jolson's absolute absorption in his song, the way he flung out his white-gloved hands as he knelt on the runway projecting into the heart of the audience reminded Raphaelson of a cantor embracing the audience with a prayer. Raphaelson wrote a story called "The Day of Atonement," published in 1922, about a young Jew from the Lower East Side who was trained to be a cantor, like his father, but who forsook the synagogue for show business, changing his name from Jacob Rabinowitz to Jack Robin and falling for a shiksa—a Gentile girl.

This is precisely what had happened to Asa Yoelson, who had changed his name to Al Jolson and who was struck by the similarities between the story and his own life. He tried to interest several film producers in the idea, but no one wanted Jewish stories. Raphaelson and Jolson met around this time and discussed the story, but Jolson wanted it reworked into a musical revue, with all the hokum that would imply. So Raphaelson rewrote it as a play, which opened in September 1925 at the Fulton Theatre, where *Abie's Irish Rose* had had its premiere. It starred George Jessel, a vaudeville comic. Reviews were mixed; the New York *Post* commented that the play was literate and interesting, its bunkum obscured by careful construction and sympathetic treatment.[393] Audiences were average to begin with, but then, after the Jewish holidays, they picked up remarkably. Warner Bros., which had placed Jessel under contract, now began negotiations to purchase the play for its leading director, Ernst Lubitsch.[394]

Warners was prevented from releasing its film until May 1, 1927, to protect the play's national tour. Meanwhile, Jessel had made *Private Izzy Murphy* for the studio in Hollywood before returning to take the play on the road. Lubitsch then left to make a film for MGM. Warners launched the Vitaphone system with *Don Juan* and followed it with another sound program in which Jolson and Jessel were represented in separate shorts. When Jessel returned to Hollywood he found prep-

Al Jolson in The Jazz Singer, *1927. (Museum of Modern Art)*

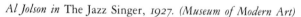

Cantor Josef Rosenblatt played himself in The Jazz Singer, *1927. (Museum of Modern Art)*

arations complete not for the silent film he anticipated, but for a film with sound sequences. This, he thought, was out of line. According to *Moving Picture World*, he demanded $100,000, on top of the $100,000 he was getting for the role, for Vitaphoning.[395] Warners got Jolson, the most successful figure in vaudeville, for $75,000, with a contingency should the picture go over schedule.[396]

The scenario was written by Alfred Cohn, who might have tailored it for Jolson, so strongly did he emphasize the sentiment and melodrama of the original play.[397]

The cameraman, Hal Mohr, went with director Alan Crosland to New York to shoot the opening of the film on the Lower East Side, tracking shots that are among the best surviving records of the ghetto. The choice of Crosland was made on practical rather than aesthetic grounds. He had directed *Don Juan;* even though he had made it as a silent film, adding the music afterward. He had directed *When a Man Loves,* which also used Vitaphone for its orchestral accompaniment, and had more experience with the new process than any other director. His brother was prominent in Western Electric, manufacturers of the Vitaphone equipment. But if only Lubitsch had stayed at Warners to make this film! For Crosland made it so melodramatic the picture looks as though it were made at the dawn of the silent picture rather than at its twilight.

Among the small part players was a Jewish actor from Russian Poland called Joseph Green. Rudolph Schildkraut, his friend and mentor, helped him get a bit part in the synagogue scene. Green remembered, "When we made the scenes in the synagogue, the Warner brothers, they put their father in charge—he was an elderly gentleman—and Josef Rosenblatt, the cantor, who played himself.[398] So for that day, they all refused to use English and all spoke Yiddish on the set. Even the director spoke Yiddish.

"The fact is that I never left this studio until the last minute. I followed from morning until night every day what went on. I was enchanted with this new phenomenon, talking pictures. And when this picture was over, I felt that this was what I was going to do in the future. I had already a background of theatre, naturally. But it was too early. Only a few theatres had the equipment for talking pictures. So I went back to New York."[399]

Green eventually became the leading producer-director of Yiddish pictures in the 1930s, with such productions as *Mamele* and *Yidl Mitn Fidl (Yiddle with His Fiddle)*.

The Jazz Singer, according to Green, was acceptable to the public because it was not totally concerned with the Jews, as were his pictures, but, like *Abie's Irish Rose,* was about Jews and Gentiles. Warners called it "a Supreme Triumph," which was true, if only financially. Reviews for the film were as mixed as for the play, but the public jammed the theatres to see and hear Jolson.

Samson Raphaelson was dismayed. "A dreadful picture," he said. "I've seen very few worse." He objected to the cantor (Warner Oland), his whiskers so beautifully combed he looked as if he had been to a beauty parlor. "And the mother (Eugenie Besserer) was made just too spotlessly clean, as though she were demonstrating stoves or refrigerators . . . I had a simple, corny, well-felt little melodrama, and they made an ill-felt, silly, maudlin, badly timed thing of it. There was absolutely no talent in the production at all except for the cameraman.

"The big moment was ridiculous—when Jolson's rehearsing his big show, and he hears his father is dying, and his mother comes to beg him to replace his father on the eve of the Day of Atonement, and it's dress rehearsal afternoon and as his mother is begging him, he's suddenly told, 'Go on for your number,' and he has to leave his mother behind as he goes on for his number.

"Now that situation was basically from my play, but in my play the song I had him sing was—Lord Almighty, the one thing I wouldn't have him sing was a song about *mother.* There's a limit . . ."[400]

The Jazz Singer has passed into legend as the first talkie, even though dialogue films had been made years earlier. It was essentially a silent film interrupted by songs, and it contained one lengthy monologue from Jolson. Whereas *Don Juan* had been given a recorded score to demonstrate how Vitaphone could enrich the silent films, *The Jazz Singer* altered the direction of sound and ensured that dialogue would triumph.

THE YOUNGER GENERATION   Frank Capra's *The Younger Generation* (1929) was adapted by Sonya Levien from Fannie Hurst's play *It Is to Laugh.* The Jewish star Ricardo Cortez (whose real name was Jacob Krantz, or Kranze) played an unsympathetic role as an East Side boy who grows up to be a wealthy antique dealer, taking his family with him to an uptown palace. They hate the place. The old father (Jean Hersholt) pines for his daughter Birdie (Lina Basquette), who has married a boy jailed on a frame-up and who is barred from the mansion. Even her letters are destroyed. Worried at the lack of news, the old man defies his son and returns to his old neighborhood. And there he discovers that he is a grandfather. With an armful of presents, he returns to the palace, to be ordered up the service stairs by the doorman. The son emerges at that moment, with some distinguished guests, and Papa appeals to him.

Rosa Rosanova and Jean Hersholt in Frank Capra's The
Younger Generation, *1929.*

"How many times do you have to be told that servants must not use the front
entrance?" the son snaps.

The old man, deeply shocked, staggers out with Mama to a park bench, where
he collapses and has to be carried home by the police. With the old man near
death, the son allows Birdie to visit him, and the family is briefly united when
Papa dies. Birdie takes Mama back to Delancey Street, leaving the son to a lonely
celebration of his wealth. His butler draws the Venetian blinds, and shadows like
bars fall upon his face.

The story owed much to *Humoresque* and *His People,* and it was provided with
talking sequences, like *The Jazz Singer.* Sound is cleverly introduced. The old man
has a letter, which he cannot read, from Birdie—he takes it to a friend, whose
young son reads it aloud. The musical score gives way to the boy's voice, which
is natural and amusing. The rest of the dialogue is delivered at the slow pace of
the period, but Capra manages to keep the talking sequences homogeneous.

The picture was produced by Jack Cohn, and he and his brother Harry must
have laughed up their sleeves at the name of the family in their Jewish picture—
Goldfish, the original name of their rival Sam Goldwyn.[401] The son changes it to
Fish, as in Hamilton Fish, one of the New York 400, although this was considered
too risible for the foreign release and the name became Gold.

ABIE'S IRISH ROSE   *The Jazz Singer* may be a landmark of film history, but as a piece of cinema it is second-rate. So it is with *Abie's Irish Rose.* The
play, by a poverty-stricken girl in her early twenties called Anne Nichols, who was
not Jewish, received the usual round of rejections before it was staged. And it then
received a roasting bordering on personal insult from the critics. It would not,

they said, last a week. Anne Nichols's revenge was sweet: the play ran for years, breaking theatrical records and earning her a reputed $8 to $10 million.[402]

The strange thing about this burlesque comedy was that it was based on a true story. Anne Nichols, despite her youth, had written plays for Fiske O'Hara. As she told it: "One evening [O'Hara] told an interesting story of a young friend of his, a Jew who had fallen in love with an Irish girl. The couple had married secretly, and were trying to win the affection of the boy's father by having the girl pose as a Jewess. One evening the father had unexpectedly entered the girl's room, where she was lying down, and, to his horror, he saw a crucifix hanging over the bed. He had rushed from the house, furious with the young couple.

"The story amused us all, but it left a deep impression on me. Almost immediately after my guests had gone I went into the library and sat down to write a play based on the story. I wrote continuously, often working all night, and when I read the final manuscript I was convinced I had a good play. A play that had enormous commercial value, because it was a story of true life, its psychology being obvious to all who would see it, and back of it lay the religious prejudices of generations. I told my mother that I had a 'million dollar play' and that *Abie's Irish Rose* would make me a rich woman."[403]

When this play, in which stereotyped Jews conversed in funny accents with equally stereotyped Irishmen, was transferred to the screen, it was not made as a talkie—although this was 1928—but as a silent film.

First-rate people were assigned to it. The scenario was written by Jules Furthman *(The City Gone Wild, Barbed Wire, The Docks of New York),* with titles by Julian Johnson, former editor of *Photoplay,* and Herman J. Mankiewicz, who would write *Citizen Kane* with Orson Welles. It was directed by Victor Fleming, who was capable of very good work and would one day make *Gone With the Wind.* But stuck with a silly play which was so popular they dare not change it, they merely put it on film. The picture has a superb opening, which is pure cinema and the only real contribution of these distinguished talents. Beautifully shot by Hal Rosson, it shows the arrival of the immigrants and the birth of their son in the ghetto. The children go to school, pledge allegiance to the flag—we see close-ups of the various races, and for once Orientals and blacks are included. From the feet of the children marching into the schoolhouse we mix to the marching feet of soldiers. "So they went to that baptism of fire and thunder—Catholics, Hebrews, and Protestants alike—newsboys and college boys—aristocrats and immigrants—all classes, all creeds, all Americans." An injured soldier asks for a priest; instead, a bearded and steel-helmeted rabbi approaches him: "Have no fear, my son, we travel many roads—but we all come at last to the father."[404]

Once the play proper begins, the temperature drops. The two young people, Abie (the Irish Charles Buddy Rogers) and Rosemary Murphy (the Irish Nancy Carroll), meet in France and return home, get married secretly,[405] and face the wrath of their parents. Abie introduces his bride as Rosie Murpheski. To placate one set of parents they are remarried by a rabbi and to placate the other by a Catholic priest. But they please them both by producing twins and naming one Patrick Joseph and the other Rebecca.

The curious thing was that the film was released as a twelve-reel silent, com-

Charles "Buddy" Rogers and Nancy Carroll in Abie's Irish Rose, *1929.*

plete with carefully depicted religious scenes, on which, Paramount proudly announced, a rabbi and a priest had acted as technical advisers. And it was highly praised: "From one of the worst plays ever written has come one of the best films ever made," said *The Film Spectator*.[406] It was then recalled, cut down to seven reels, and given sound—Jean Hersholt singing the Kaddish and Nancy Carroll singing and dancing were highlights.

"Use of added sound makes *Abie* a different matter," said *Variety*. "Most of the serious religious material has been eliminated and the story treatment has been greatly tightened. . . . Generally speaking, sound has heightened the effect of the picture. Also the footage has been cut 40 minutes and the story moves much faster. On both counts the picture is greatly improved. Indeed, to the point where it looks like a run prospect at the Rialto instead of an utter flop for $2."[407]

Variety was wrong. The film was not an outstanding financial success. "I can't understand why it didn't do phenomenal business," wrote Jesse Lasky, "since the picture was every bit as bad as the play."[408]

Apart from the opening reel, and the fact that a phenomenon of American popular culture has been preserved, one of the few points of interest is the presence in the cast of Ida Kramer and Bernard Gorcey. Both played the same parts as in the stage version—Mr. and Mrs. Isaac Cohen. Gorcey was the father of Leo Gorcey, who appeared in *Dead End;* Ida Kramer was a veteran of the Yiddish theatre.

The film upset Orthodox Jews so much that the Motion Picture Project—now known as the Jewish Film Advisory Council—was formed to combat films like this and *The Cohens and the Kellys*.[409] It was a dismal end to a remarkable epoch of Jewish pictures.

ROOSEVELT, TAFT or WILSON?

WHO WILL BE THE WINNER NEXT NOVEMBER?

WE DO KNOW THAT YOU, MR. STATE RIGHT BUYER, WILL BE
IF YOU PURCHASE THIS LIVE FEATURE JUST RELEASED

THE WAGE EARNERS

A Story of

LABOR vs. CAPITAL

3000 FEET   **100 SCENES**   **3 REELS**

Everybody will want to see *The Wage Earners.* They will all want to see this great picture of Labor and Capital. Many thrilling and exciting scenes, such as the big train wreck, auto wreck, the wild ride on the handcar, the flying leap onto a moving train, the big walk-out, the mob scene and many others. This feature will be a fast seller, so better get in touch with us at once regarding territory wanted, as waiting has cost many a state right buyer very dearly.

**Elegant line of Paper, Banners, Heralds, etc.
Always watch for our next release. Out soon,**

SECRET SERVICE STEVE

STORY OF THE SMUGGLING ALONG THE CANADIAN BORDER

COMING OUT SOON—Midnight Ride of Paul Revere

**WATCH FOR THIS ONE
WITH YOU SOON** QUO VADIS

ATLAS MFG. CO., 411 Century Bldg., St. Louis, Mo.

Chapter Eleven

INDUSTRY

From Moving Picture World,
*October 19, 1912. (Academy of Motion
Picture Arts and Sciences)*

CHILD LABOR

"Probably no other evil of modern industrialism has had a more devastating effect upon the home and family than child labor," said Judge Ben Lindsey.[1] But his attempt to impose Colorado's child-labor restrictions on a local cotton mill led to the closing of the factory.[2] The families who depended on their children's earnings and were now reduced to the bread line did not thank the judge for his moral rectitude. It is significant that his attempt to make a film on the subject did not succeed. Relatively few films on this most provocative of topics were produced, perhaps because of this very paradox: the children working down the mines or in the factories were usually there with the knowledge and complicity of their parents.

By 1900, with more than 1,790,000 child laborers in America, most industrial states had enacted some form of protective regulation, but few of them had enough power to be effective.[3] The problem was at its worst in the South.

Carl Laemmle, president of the Universal Film Manufacturing Company, took frequent tours among small-town exhibitors, and it was while visiting the Mississippi Valley that he became aware of the widespread use of child labor. The result was a two-reeler called *The Blood of the Children* (1915), written by Bess Meredyth and directed by Henry MacRae.

Shot partly in a cotton gin, the film was an exposé of conditions in cotton factories, both in the South and in New England, where lint was a constant hazard to health. William Clifford played a senator ready to vote for a child labor bill, whom two mill-owners (Sherman Bainbridge and Rex de Rosselli) attempt to buy off. Overcoming his anger, the senator tells them, in a series of flashbacks, of his days as a factory employee and later owner and of the number of men, women, and children who were injured each year or who died from disease. The mill-owners are won over to his side, and they put the bribe money into a fund to support the passage of the act.[4] Prints of the film were sent to Atlanta and New Orleans for exhibition to cotton men, many of whom admitted that the conditions shown in the film were all too true.

The fight against child labor had been initiated largely by settlement workers. In 1903, Lillian Wald put forward a proposal for a children's bureau. President Theodore Roosevelt invited her to Washington, but nothing much happened until 1909, when Roosevelt called a White House Conference on the Care of Dependent Children. Miss Wald testified before a Senate committee, comparing the treatment of children to that of pigs. A bill drafted by Wald and Florence Kelley of Hull-House eventually received President William Howard Taft's signature in April 1912, but it achieved little. The problem persisted, and in 1920 one of the most famous settlement workers made a film on the subject.

Sophie Irene Loeb, who had been brought to the United States from Russia at

Children forced to work at making artificial flowers: Child Labor, *1913. From* Moving Picture World, *January 18, 1913.*

the age of six, was a reformer and sociologist who, like Jane Addams, succeeded in bettering the society in which she lived.[5] She is remembered in particular for her work in connection with child welfare. Besides books, she also wrote a film called *The Woman God Sent* (1920) dealing with the efforts of a young woman (Zena Keefe) and a senator to enact a law forbidding child labor in factories. It was directed by Larry Trimble.

"The hammer of propaganda is skillfully wielded," said *Photoplay*, "for the picture is well told and holds your interest."[6]

The fact that child labor should still be an issue at the end of the Reform Era is an indication of the strength of the opposition. The industrialists had found an all-purpose answer to their critics; they described the issue as "a Trojan horse concealing Bolshevists, Communists, Socialists and all that traitorous and destructive brood."[7]

Back in the 1890s reformers thought that photographs showing children at work would arouse so much sentiment that none but the most rabid capitalist would stand in the way of a Constitutional amendment. They were fortunate to acquire the services of a great photographer, Lewis Hine. As staff photographer for the National Child Labor Committee (NCLC), he smuggled his camera into factories, risking violence from foremen and mill-owners, and produced a series of brilliant still pictures.

"Winning the confidence of the children," wrote Robert Doty, "he would interview them while scribbling notes on a pad inside his pocket. These would be rewritten later, in a legible form. . . . These photographs and information formed the backbone of the publicity efforts of the National Child Labor Committee. They were used to illustrate booklets, posters, magazines and even as source material for several films."[8]

CHILDREN WHO LABOR   One of these films was *Children Who Labor* (1912); written and directed by Ashley Miller, made by the Edison Company in cooperation with the National Child Labor Committee and highly praised for its artistry. It featured the Flugrath sisters, later known as Viola Dana and Shirley Mason, and it was filmed in Paterson, New Jersey, and at the Bronx studio.[9] A print survives at the Museum of Modern Art, New York, confirming that a great deal of care and skill went into it. But it cannot compare with the work of Lewis Hine.

It is an unlikely but nonetheless compelling little melodrama, with good lighting and inventive art direction. The playing is unrestrained, although Viola Dana is both natural and beautiful. The film opens with a title, "The appeal of the child laborers," and an allegorical double exposure shows the figure of Uncle Sam looming over lines of children filing into a factory beneath a lowering sky. They raise

John Sturgeon (left), Robert Conness (right), and Viola Dana (center). From Edison Kinetogram, *London Edition, May 1, 1912. (David Robinson)*

Thomas A. Edison

SCENE FROM
CHILDREN WHO LABOUR
FILM No. 6981
Released May 29th, 1912

their hands beseechingly; Uncle Sam takes no notice. Over the factory appears the word "GREED."[10]

Outside the gates, an Italian (John Sturgeon) vainly tries to get work. No men are wanted; the foreman is far more interested in his daughter. Members of the NCLC endeavor to persuade Hanscomb, the factory owner (Robert Conness), to abolish the evil, but he refuses. Nor will he listen to the Italian who pleads with him when he drives up to the factory. The daughter is put to work.

Hanscomb's wife (Miriam Nesbitt) takes a train journey with her daughter Mabel (Mason). Playing on the observation platform, the girl drops her handkerchief and steps off the train to retrieve it. The train pulls out without her. She is stranded in the town where the Italian lives, and he and his wife give her shelter. Her mother is frantic, but not even a detective can locate the child. The needy Italian reluctantly sends Mabel to the factory along with his own child (Dana). Hanscomb becomes an even more ruthless employer and expands his empire— buying another factory, the very one in which his daughter is employed. During a visit to the factory by the Hanscombs, Mabel collapses and is rushed home on a stretcher. Kindhearted Mrs. Hanscomb calls on the Italian with sustenance and discovers her daughter. The child refuses to greet her father until she has berated him for employing children. Hanscomb is converted and we see grown men taking over the work, but the film ends with a reprise of the opening scene, Uncle Sam now looking with concern at the upraised arms.

"Sincerity glows in every one of its scenes," said *Moving Picture World*. "This reviewer has heard audiences receive good pictures before, but he has never heard the applause that this picture got."[11]

THE CRY OF THE CHILDREN In 1912, a presidential election year, the Thanhouser studio released a film which was described as "the boldest, most timely and most effective appeal for stamping out the cruelest of all social abuses."[12] Woodrow Wilson, the Democratic candidate, cited it as an instance of the outrages permitted by the Taft administration, even though Taft's signature on the Child Labor Bill was hardly dry.[13]

Thanhouser used the words of Theodore Roosevelt, who had formed the breakaway Progressive party, in the advertising, suggesting he had endorsed the film: "When I plead the cause of the overworked girl in a factory, of the stunted child toiling at inhuman labor . . . when I protest against the unfair profit of unscrupulous and conscienceless men . . . I am not only fighting for the weak, I am fighting also for the strong."[14]

The Cry of the Children, seen today, is a primitive film. Conceived in the direct-to-camera style of 1912, it nonetheless achieves a kind of elegiac quality through its use of the poem by Elizabeth Barrett Browning[15] from which it takes its title and the solemnity with which its players conduct themselves. The poem does not dictate the story, but a prologue illustrates the lines:

> *The young lambs are bleating in the meadows,*
> *The young birds are chirping in the nest . . .*

But the young, young children . . .
They are weeping . . .
In the country of the free!

The day starts before dawn at the millworkers' home. Father wakes first, and we see him tying his boots by candlelight. The wife and two of the children are careful not to wake little Alice, who is to be kept from "the shadow of the factory." After a meager breakfast, they go to work and are checked by the supervisor at the gate. The mill-owner and his wife leave their palatial home in a luxurious car for a tour of the factory. One glimpse is enough for the wife; she retreats, deafened by the roar of the machines.

At the end of the day, Alice takes her bucket to the stream. The owner's wife sees her from her car and chats to her. Enchanted by her radiant good nature, she offers to adopt her, but Alice loyally refuses to leave her family.

The millworkers strike for a living wage, but the owner stands firm and, after months of privation, the workers are defeated. The owner gathers his supporters for a celebratory supper and reads them the news: STARVATION WILL SOON FORCE MILLWORKERS TO ABANDON STRIKE—Large Families Endure Heavy Hardships—Children Cry for Bread.

The owner is congratulated.

Weakened by hunger, the mother collapses and little Alice is obliged to go to work in her place. "All day she drives the wheels of iron." The mother's illness worsens, and to help her family Alice offers herself for adoption. But now the owner's wife is repelled by the child's haggard appearance.

"It is good when it happens," say the children,
"That we die before our time."

Exhausted by overwork, Alice collapses at her machine. The supervisor lays her on a chair in the owner's office. Her father is summoned to remove her.

From the sleep wherein she lieth none will wake her
Crying, "Get up, little Alice! it is day."

After the funeral, the family encounters the owner and his wife in their car. The wife is full of tearful self-reproach. In an astonishing series of dissolves, unique for their time, the mill-owner and his wife are linked in responsibility to the factory and the wage-slaves who work in it yet are shown to be as touched by grief as the bereaved family itself: the husband takes the wife's hand, mix to a long shot of a factory complex, to the supervisor pushing Alice back to work, and her collapse, to the father and mother at the graveside, and back to the owner holding his wife's hand. She breaks free and, choking with sobs, sinks to a chair. And then we mix back to the long shot of the factories.

Intended to form part of a series called *Can Such Things Be?*—which was not completed—*The Cry of the Children* is an unusually restrained and moving film for

1912. The performers are comparatively natural except for Marie Eline, "the Thanhouser kidlet," as little Alice.[16] She hops, skips, and jumps until her demise at the factory comes as a welcome relief.

The Cry of the Children would be called naïve today, and with justice. Its treatment is sentimental, its story only a variation of the hoary melodrama of the mill girl who resists the owner's advances until she must yield in order to buy medicine to save her mother's life. Yet it carries evidence of a more creative mind than one normally encounters in a picture of 1912. The director (who is unknown, alas)[17] used a real mill for the interiors (which tend to be underexposed as a result). One or two shots carry the influence of Lewis Hine, though they lack his pictorial flair. And while the cutting between poverty and luxury is as obvious as in Edwin S. Porter's 1905 *The Kleptomaniac,* the editing is handled with a trifle more skill than in most productions of the time.

W. Stephen Bush considered the film so important he devoted a lengthy essay to it in *Moving Picture World:*

"More than two generations have passed away since Elizabeth Barrett Browning told of 'the children weeping ere the sorrow comes with years.' Since that time, great efforts have been made by many good men and women to stop this evil. The best that had been accomplished was a law establishing a Federal Bureau, which could do nothing but investigate conditions. However, it could arouse public sentiment through the publication of reports. We are glad to say that the Thanhouser picture will accomplish the same results . . . the arousing of public indignation. The pictures are admirably conceived, do not at any time go beyond the line of probability and bring home their lesson in a forceful but perfectly natural and convincing way. . . . While the picture skillfully paints the extremes of our modern social life, it has steered clear of the fatal error

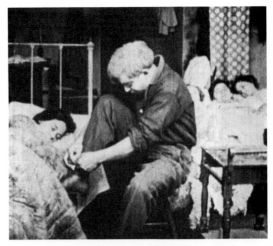

Frame enlargements from The Cry of the Children, *1913. Before dawn, father (James Cruze) rises.*

Marie Eline as Alice at work in the mill. Frame enlargement from The Cry of the Children, *1913.*

Alice (Marie Eline) collapses at the mill. (Gerald McKee)

of the old time melodrama in which, instead of human beings, the spectator was compelled to see a set of angels and a set of devils. *The Cry of the Children* makes it plain that the mill-owner is as much a creature of circumstances and surroundings and economic conditions as the laborer.

"The report of the Federal Bureau will be read by hundreds, at best, while the picture will be seen by millions . . . we will confess ourselves much mistaken if *The Cry of the Children* will not serve as a valuable campaign argument long before the votes are counted in November."[18]

SOCIALISM AND POPULISM

Five times the Socialist candidate for president, Eugene Debs seemed within reach of the White House in 1912. A few years later he was in jail. While the fire of socialism swept over Europe, its flames found damper fuel in America. The working class was divided. American workers (many of them foreign-born), alarmed by the increasing influx of immigrant labor, formed trade unions to protect their own positions, unions which were not allied to a political party, as in England. Samuel Gompers, British-born head of the American Federation of Labor, rejected socialism and depended on the self-interest of the workers to improve conditions.

Socialism and anarchism were confused, intentionally by the press, unintentionally by the public. And whenever the workers resorted to violence, they made it easier for the authorities to act against socialists, anarchists, and unionists alike.[19]

In April 1911, John J. McNamara, secretary of the International Association of Bridge and Structural Iron Workers, and his brother, James B., were charged with dynamiting the Los Angeles *Times* Building on October 1, 1910. Twenty-one people were killed.

The American Federation of Labor produced *A Martyr to His Cause* in 1911 to defend the McNamaras; it depicted John as the innocent victim of open shop militants and had him pleading to the public "to suspend judgments . . . until opportunity for a fair and full defense had been afforded."[20] The film attracted large audiences until the McNamaras pleaded guilty. After the trial Clarence Darrow, their attorney, was himself tried—and, after two trials, acquitted—for attempting to bribe a juror.

The McNamara trial was worked into a film called *From Dusk to Dawn* (1913) in which Darrow played himself. It was written and directed by Frank E. Wolfe, whose ambition was to "take Socialism before the people of the world on the rising tide of movie popularity."[21] Produced by the Occidental Motion Picture Company of California, the four-reeler was advertised with a significant slogan: "85 Per Cent of your Theatre-Goers—the Numberless Working Class—Will Want to See This Picture."[22]

The main part of the film dealt with Daniel Grayson, a union man forced to leave an ironworks, who is involved in strike, riot, and explosion. Eventually, he is nominated for governor on the working-class ticket. All parties unite to defeat him. Then comes the "conspiracy" trial. With Darrow found not guilty, a wave of enthusiasm carries Dan to victory.[23] There was irony in this, for Job Harriman, running for mayor of Los Angeles on a Socialist ticket, was soundly defeated as a result of the McNamara case. Also defeated was Frank Wolfe, running on the same ticket for city councilman.

The nickelodeon was not a forum for politics, and films on working-class themes were rare. Tom Brandon has established the fact that of 4,249 films reviewed in the trade press in 1914, a mere nineteen were directly political. Seven were prolabor (one being *Germinal* from France), six antilabor, and six "populist."[24]

The populist films have been mistaken for socialist tracts because populism embraced certain socialist ideas. Formed in 1892, the People's party was a coalition of those united by fear of big business, disgust with corruption, and sympathy for labor. America was divided into "producers"—those who worked with their hands—and "nonproducers." But populists did not want the means of production owned by the state; they cherished the system of free enterprise and opportunity for the individual. And they prided themselves on being "home-grown"—not like that imported doctrine of socialism—and were distinctly unfriendly to immigrants.[25] Populist films about poverty or capital versus labor refused to condemn the system but blamed the grafting politician or the selfish millowner. Once the villain was removed, the sun came out and the workers marched happily back to their machines.

Films which adopted a socialist view were few and far between. The miracle was that any were made at all.

The Eclair production *Why?* (1913) asked unpalatable questions: "Why do we have children at hard labor?" "Why do we have men who gamble at the race track?" "Why are trains run so fast that fatal accidents occur?" (It had been revealed, in 1912, that railroad travelers had sustained more than 180,000 injuries—10,000 of them fatal—in a single year.)[26]

H. C. Judson wrote that it was not within the province of a reviewer to discuss politics, yet the exhibitor had to take careful account of them, for what might appeal in one neighborhood might infuriate another. He dare not wholly commend this film.[27]

"The motive of the story," wrote another critic, "is to show the manner in which capital and labor clash. Much of it is socialistic doctrine, strongly presented . . . perhaps too strongly for many audiences."[28]

The picture employed photographic trickery in the French style. In a dream, the wealthy hero travels the word and is struck by the hardship of labor. He sees children working on a factory treadmill, women working at half pay and using blood to make red thread, horses being killed because their owners would not insure them. To demonstrate that it is impossible to kill capital, he shoots the child-labor employer who is transformed into a bag of gold. The hero is invited to a feast; working men break in, demanding a seat at the table. Frightened capitalists rally round the generals as they shoot the people, who fall beside the food-laden table.

"Following this comes the most sensational picture we have ever seen; it is nothing less than the burning of the Woolworth Building and all the other build-

The Socialist allegory, Why?, *1913. Child laborers on the treadmill of the Almighty Dollar.* (Robert S. Birchard Collection)

ings in the lower part of Manhattan Island. They are shown all going up in red fire and it is indeed a tremendous spectacle."[29]

H. C. Judson did not think the picture taught anarchy. It was only a dream, after all: "Things are bad enough, but they are not as this picture shows them."[30]

In 1914, a multireel spectacular appeared from an independent company called the United Keanograph Film Company of Fairfax, California. Entitled *Money,* it was said to have 2,000 extras. James Keane, president of the company, wrote the scenario and directed the picture. George Scott was the cameraman;[31] the picture was shot largely on location.

In a scene filmed at the Union Iron Works in San Francisco, Baroness von Saxe, a member of an aristocratic German family, appeared with her daughter, Leonora. Her unlikely interest in the cinema arose because her father, a general, was the first nobleman in Germany to install a projection machine in his *Schloss.* The baroness explained to the press that some of her happiest moments were spent in the theatre watching American films, so she was only too pleased to distinguish another with her presence. Had she been aware of the content, she might have hesitated. Announced as a six-reeler, advertised as a seven-reeler, but reviewed as a five-reeler, *Money* was described as "the frankest kind of socialism."[32] It was, perhaps, inspired by *Why?,* for one of its big scenes had the starving workers storming a banquet.

The melodramatic coating to the political pill dealt with the pursuit of a stenographer by the youthful partner in a steel works, a pursuit which involved mistaken identity and a chase by car and boat. But because it was a political film, there were three villains: the capitalist who reduces wages, gives banquets, and oppresses the poor; his young partner; and an anarchist who aids and abets him. The hero was a poor worker, who took the daughter of the capitalist to see poverty in all its squalor and misery.

"When Keane hired 2,000 'roughnecks' to storm the palace of Croesus, at which was being held the Million Dollar Dinner," said *Moving Picture World,* "he wanted the consequent battle between them and the police to look like a battle. . . . One of Keane's jokeful friends 'tipped off' the police that an attack in all sincerity was being made. The effect of a hundred coppers wielding clubs on 2,000 underworldlings . . . can be imagined."[33] A typical piece of publicity nonsense of the time, which undermined the talent Keane must have had as a director, for the action had "snap and fire."[34]

Money was first shown at Grauman's Savoy Theatre in San Francisco on September 2, 1914. Among the audience of 1,500 was a Judge Lawlor, who declared: "The most powerfully written, intensely acted and photographically perfect picture I have ever witnessed."

Other local personalities included Andrew J. Gallagher, president of the San Francisco Labor Council, who called it "the greatest labor picture ever thrown on the screen. Every union man SHOULD and I know WILL see it."[35]

UPTON SINCLAIR   What did socialists think of the American motion picture? Upton Sinclair left his thoughts on the subject in a letter to Nicolai Lebedev of Proletkino, Moscow: "The moving pictures furnish the principal intellectual food of the workers at the present time, and the supplying of this food is entirely in the hands of the capitalist class, and the food supplied is poisoned. I cannot speak concerning the moving pictures of Europe, but I can tell you that so far as the American workers are concerned the moving pictures are vile beyond the possibility of words to describe, and the whole industry is so completely controlled by big business that there is practically no chance of breaking in with a true idea."[36]

Sinclair's own experience with the picture business had been brief and unhappy (and worse was to come in the 1930s, when he financed Sergei Eisenstein's *Que Viva Mexico!*). He was so disgusted that he had given up all idea of using the new medium to express his ideas:

"Again and again some smooth-spoken gentleman, wearing silk stockings and the latest tailored clothing, and perhaps a diamond ring on his finger, comes to me to propose to put my ideas into a moving picture. With time I discover that what he really means to do is to use my name as a means of selling stock, sometimes to a few friends of mine who happen to have money, and other times to the gullible public.

"Time and again I have had propositions to make one of my novels into a picture but always upon condition that I would 'leave out the Socialism.' And of course I have turned such propositions down."[37]

One of these smooth-spoken gentlemen was Herbert Blaché, educated in England and France and the husband of Alice Guy Blaché. Like others of his kind, Blaché wanted to exploit the name of the author but little of his work. Sinclair needed the money and tried to disassociate himself from the film. Blaché sent him a telegram offering $500 cash: "Cannot very well agree to purchase story without your name and you must yourself realise the necessity to alter the story as it is impossible to produce a good picture with the story in present form and you would not want a bad picture."[38]

Sinclair relented and the picture was released in 1917 as *The Adventurer*, "based on the famous novel by Upton Sinclair." But Sinclair never wrote a novel of that name. The scenario, which had elements of a play within a play called *The Pot-Boiler*, was written by Harry Chandlee, who would, during the Red Scare, write a profoundly anti-socialist picture, and Lawrence McCloskey. The featured players were Marian Swayne and Pell Trenton. At least the film retained something of Sinclair in its exposure of graft and dishonesty in organized charities, but basically it was a melodramatic thriller.

Sinclair does not appear in Benjamin Hampton's book of film history, nor does Hampton appear in Sinclair's autobiography. With good reason, as Sinclair related: "A friend of mine undertook to make a moving picture version of my novel *The Moneychangers* [sic] and I helped in the making of a scenario, which faithfully followed the story. But after the scenario had been read, the producer [Hampton] told me that it was not suitable for a moving picture; it was, he said, 'a grand opera.' I was very much impressed by this pronouncement even though I did not understand it. The producer said that he would have to make another scenario for the picture, and he made one. And then I discovered the difference between a motion picture and a grand opera. In a grand opera the heroine dies in the last act. While in a moving picture she marries the hero amid a shower of spring blossoms, and lives happily ever after in the imagination of the feeble-minded audience.

"So it happens that there is a picture entitled *The Moneychangers* by Upton Sinclair going the round of the United States, presumably a great many members of the working class go to see it, expecting to see something of mine, but as a matter of fact it has literally nothing to do with anything I ever wrote. My novel tells how Pierpont Morgan the elder caused the Wall Street run of 1907. The thing which is called *The Moneychangers* in the moving picture version is a blood-and-thunder melodrama of the drug traffic in Chinatown. And lest people should think that I am growing wealthy out of thus exploiting the incredulity of the workers, let me say that I was unable to stop the picture and as usual the financial organizations which are distributing the picture have made off with all the profits."[39]

It should be pointed out that the "feeble-minded" viewers for which *The Money Changers* was altered was precisely that working-class audience Sinclair refers to in another context. It was not merely for the middle class that happy endings were invented. The film was a commercial success, in any case, grossing $100,000 by March 1921.[40]

In 1918, Sinclair was approached by two delegates of the Brotherhood of Railway Trainmen, who proposed a propaganda film to advocate continuing govern-

Filming Upton Sinclair's The Money Changers, *1920. Jack Conway in the director's chair, Harry Vallejo at the camera. Players relax while opium scene is shot.*

ment control of the railroad system. Sinclair agreed to write a scenario and accepted the post of editor of the Motive Motion Picture Company (MMPC). The director-general of the company was David Horsley, who, with his brother William, had founded the first studio in Hollywood in 1911.[41]

Sinclair was paid an advance of $300 for his work, and he duly presented an outline for the scenario. Brave announcements were made, Samuel Gompers was conferred with and was "vitally interested." But nothing was filmed.

"I realize now," said Sinclair, "that I put myself in an unfortunate position by permitting them to sell stock upon the basis of my work, and I will never make that mistake again."[42]

But Sinclair did not give up. In 1917, he tried to interest D. W. Griffith in *The Daughter of the Confederacy,* and in 1918, he wrote a synopsis for a comedy called *The Hypnotist* for Charlie Chaplin.[43] Neither was made.

A CORNER IN WHEAT   The socialists were only too anxious to use motion pictures to further their cause. Jack London's *The Valley of the Moon* was filmed by the Bosworth Company in 1914; its story of a young couple freeing themselves from the suffocating grasp of a big city and escaping to the wilds of California carried a socialist message.

The Valley of the Moon, 1914, *from Jack London's novel. The battle in Oakland between strike-breakers and teamsters. The picture was used as Socialist propaganda. (Robert S. Birchard Collection)*

"The strike scenes where a huge mob battled with the police, where the patrol wagons seemed to trample the rebellious workers, where men lay with broken heads and bleeding freely in the open, were, like the scenes which started the picture, true to the spirit in which Mr. London painted them—brutal, revolting and truthful,"[44] reported the New York *Dramatic Mirror.*

But such presentations frequently encountered the opposition of the police. In Pittsburgh, they put an outright ban on the showing of socialist pictures on Sunday. "So they won't allow you to show moving pictures, eh?" asked a socialist member of the Allentown (Pennsylvania) City Council of his packed audience. "If it were a booze joint, it probably would be given police protection."[45]

Nothing encouraged socialism so much as the behavior of the robber barons, whose companies wielded the power of the multinational conglomerates of today. D. W. Griffith's pioneering *A Corner in Wheat* (1909), taken not from Frank Norris, but, as Russell Merritt has discovered, from Channing Pollock's 1904 play, *The Pit,** was full of striking imagery and the kind of intercutting that would serve the cinema for decades. A scene inspired by Jean Millet's painting *The Sower* opened the film, which dealt with a great wheat speculator whose intrigues would wreck the lives of these simple farm laborers. "No subject has been produced

---

*Based on Norris—and Norris used similar intercutting in *The Octopus.*

Contrasts from D. W. Griffith's A Corner in Wheat, *1909. The Wheat King lauded for his acumen . . .*

. . . the poor confronted by crippling prices. (Museum of Modern Art)

more timely than this powerful story of the wheat gambler, coming as it does when agitation is rife against that terrible practice of cornering commodities that are the necessities of life," said *The Biograph Bulletin.*[46]

Griffith shows the excitement in the wheat pit at the stock exchange, "where we see them struggling like ravenous wolves to control the wealth they did nothing to create."[47] "The Gold of the Wheat" is represented by a lavish banquet where the Wheat King is lauded for his acumen, "The Chaff" by a bakery where the poor are confronted by crippling prices. A mother is forced to go without. The bread fund for the poor is reduced, and the police club the unlucky ones away from the bread line. At the moment of his triumph, when the Wheat King is told he has cornered the world supply, he trips and falls into one of his own bins of wheat, to be smothered, symbolically and literally, by his source of wealth. The film ends with a haunting shot of a figure broadcasting the seeds for next year's crop—alone in a vast landscape.

One feels the film is not so much silent as gagged—having to convey points by waving arms, notices, and letters. The silence has yet to become eloquent. Nevertheless, a modern critic, Richard Schickel, calls it "a model of compression" and says, "Even now, one can scarcely speak too highly of the film."[48]

The film was made again in 1914, when the cinema was growing more sophisticated and the story could fill five reels. The director was Maurice Tourneur, newly arrived from France, who, for a few prolific years, looked set to steal the crown from Griffith's head. *The Pit* set a new mark for artistry and realism, with an almost full-size replica of the Chicago Board of Trade built by Ben Carré and filled with 500 extras.[49]

C. Gardner Sullivan, who so often wrote new versions of Griffith films, reworked *A Corner in Wheat* with *The Corner* (1915), about millionaire David Waltham's attempt to corner the country's food supply. We see the effect of his scheme on the family of a prosperous workingman who loses his position and then his savings when there is a run on the bank. His children are starving. He breaks a bakeshop window and steals four loaves, for which he is sent to the workhouse for thirty days. His wife, left destitute, is forced to sell her body to obtain food for her children.

Unusually for a film of this period, the husband is shocked, but does not blame her. He sets out to capture Waltham, ties him up in a warehouse surrounded by the food he has been stockpiling, and leaves him to starve to death. The picture ends with cases of food toppling over and smothering the millionaire.[50]

The New York *Dramatic Mirror* thought the film "startlingly well acted" by George Fawcett and Willard Mack, and *Variety* considered it among the best Ince productions. It was directed by Walter Edwards. Memories were short, and no reviewer connected it with the 1909 Biograph.

A remarkable socialist drama called *Dust* was made in 1916 for Flying A by writer Julian Lamothe and director Edward Sloman. A symbolic opening showed the laboring class coining their lives into money for their employer, a vision of the idealistic hero of the film, the young sociologist Frank Kenyon (Franklyn Ritchie).

The Corner, *1916. The impoverished wife (Clara Williams) "sells her body" to the rent collector (Charles Miller) in order to survive. Directed by Walter Edwards, written by C. Gardner Sullivan for Thomas H. Ince. (George Eastman House)*

Dust was a clever title, referring not merely to the poor—"dust beneath the feet of the rich"—but to the deadly dust of the woolen mills which, so far as the workers were concerned, was as destructive as war itself.

During the war, the concern and compassion of so many films of the Reform Era were replaced by hatred of the Hun. With the armistice, the Hun was transmuted into the Bolshevik.

In November 1918, the following letter was circulated to the heads of the film industry by David Niles, chief of the motion picture section of the U.S. Department of Labor:

"Gentlemen:

"The Motion Picture undoubtedly shortened the war by at least two months. This is the opinion of officers in the army who are in a position to know. The Motion Picture can do more to stabilize labor and help bring about normal conditions than any other agency. An injudicious use of Motion Pictures, on the other hand, can do our country incalculable harm.

"Constructive education will do infinitely more good than destructive propaganda. To portray the villain of a photo-play as a member of the I.W.W. or the

Bolsheviki is positively harmful; while portraying the hero as a strong, virile American, a believer of American institutions and ideals, will do much good."[51]

Directors and producers had to consult Niles before embarking on films about socialism or labor unrest, and he warned those who failed to cooperate of Federal censorship.[52]

Socialist projects, like Upton Sinclair's for the railroad men and Frederick Collins's for *McClure's Magazine* on the achievements of American labor, collapsed. Antisocialist films proliferated in the postwar atmosphere of reaction. And whether Niles's department approved or not, Bolsheviks were the all-purpose villains.

"There is much freedom of thought that should be imprisoned," wrote the editor of *Photo-Play Journal,* "especially at this critical time in our national history. We should not lose sight of the fact that there are some writers with wildly socialistic ideas which should not be permitted the privilege of visualization."[53]

That was written in 1919, the year of the Red Scare.

THE RED SCARE

Charlie Chaplin entertained two prominent people at his studio in 1918. One was General Leonard Wood, former U.S. Army chief of staff, who had organized the Rough Riders with Theodore Roosevelt in the Spanish-American War. The other was Max Eastman, an American aristocrat who had become the country's leading socialist writer. He had edited *The Masses* until its suppression; he supported Lenin and Trotsky and said so in his new paper, *The Liberator.*

In 1919, Chaplin was accused of financing Eastman's paper and of being a parlor socialist. Chaplin agreed he was a friend of Eastman's but denied backing his magazine: "I am absolutely cold on the Bolshevism theme; neither am I interested in Socialism. You know my war record. If *The Liberator* is seditious, it certainly should be suppressed."[54]

At the same time, General Wood noted with approval a clergyman's call for the deportation of Bolsheviks "in ships of stone with sails of lead, with the wrath of God for a breeze and with hell for their first port."[55]

Such was the atmosphere during the year of the Red Scare, of which William E. Leuchtenburg has written, "Perhaps at no time in our history has there been such a wholesale violation of civil liberties."[56] Anarchists, aliens, Jews, socialists, pacifists, labor leaders, unionists, and even "hysterical women" were wrapped up together and popped into the same compartment of the popular mind: "Reds."

Attorney General A. Mitchell Palmer launched the Palmer Raids on November 7, 1919. In a number of cities, members of the Union of Russian Workers were arrested and treated brutally by the police. President Woodrow Wilson was ill and may not have known. The following month 249 aliens, virtually none of whom had committed an offense, were deported to Russia on the army transport *Buford* (the same ship Buster Keaton would use in *The Navigator* in 1924). Most of these people were anarchists, not Bolsheviks, and while some professed violence, like Emma Goldman and Alexander Berkman, others were passionately nonviolent.[57] The Commissioner of Ellis Island, Frederic C. Howe, resigned over the deportation issue.

The turn of the Bolsheviks came in January 1920 when, in a single night, more than 4,000 alleged Communists were arrested in thirty-three cities. In one town, prisoners were handcuffed, chained together, and marched through the streets. But by the end of 1920, as the threat of a Communist takeover of Europe receded, the Red Scare faded and the Wilson administration was replaced by the government of Warren G. Harding and a desire for "normalcy."

As the Palmer Raids climaxed a long campaign against the left, so the Red Scare films were antisocialist tracts given new relevance by the word "Bolshevism."

BOLSHEVISM ON TRIAL   *Bolshevism on Trial* was adapted from the novel *Comrades* by the Reverend Thomas Dixon, a Southern populist who also wrote *The Clansman,* on which *The Birth of a Nation* was based. Published in 1909 as "A Story of Social Adventure in California," *Comrades* was a satire on Upton Sinclair's socialist experiment at Helicon Hall (sometimes referred to by those writing of the experiment as Halcyon Hall!) at Englewood, New Jersey, in 1906–1907. This colony had been a success, most obviously with children, but the press ridiculed it, deciding Sinclair had started it in order to provide himself with plenty of mistresses.[58]

The picture was originally entitled *Shattered Dreams.*[59] The new title was adopted to boost it at the box office with the lure of the latest headlines. The film was an attack on socialism, intended to make it seem ludicrous in theory and impossible in practice.

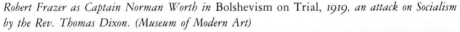

Robert Frazer as Captain Norman Worth in Bolshevism on Trial, *1919, an attack on Socialism by the Rev. Thomas Dixon. (Museum of Modern Art)*

The plot is a hotchpotch about a true-blue capitalist, Colonel Bradshaw (How-ard Truesdell), whose inventions have "created work for thousands." He is furious to discover that his son Norman (Robert Frazer) has fallen for a Red, a college girl named Barbara Alden (Pinna Nesbit). She takes Norman to the slums, where he is horrified by the squalor and begs her to leave such wretchedness to the charity workers.

"If you love me," she says, "you should help me."

Herman Wolff (Leslie Stowe) is a professional agitator; beetle-browed and villainous in every way, he sits at his desk surrounded by socialist pamphlets and a volume by Karl Marx.[60]

Posters on the exterior of a meeting hall make it evident that the scene was filmed in December 1918 and that the next event at the hall was to be a ball in aid of the Galician town of Przemysl, besieged by both Russian and German forces. Even more fascinating, the posters reveal that the heroine's name was to have been Barbara Bozenta. One can only assume that by 1919 the foreign name would have lost her a degree of audience appeal.

Wolff uses the meeting to raise funds to purchase "the one spot on earth where they can all be free"—Paradise Island in Florida, with its vast hotel.[61] Norman, carried away by the rhetoric, offers to buy the island. But the first few days in paradise prove purgatorial. No one volunteers for menial labor, and when the jobs are imposed the response is: "Unwilling labor is slavery!" A festive ball revives spirits and everyone is delightfully equal except the electricians in the basement. "Pretty soft for dem—dancin' while we sweat for nothing a week," says one. "Let's give 'em a dose of darkness." He pulls a switch and causes alarm on the dance floor. The lights are not restored by the electricians until Norman pays them out of his own pocket.

But then strikes spread like wildfire, Wolff deposes Norman and seizes power, and makes a speech not even the maddest socialist would dream of making: "Com-rades, we can spread the Red Brotherhood over the world and come to power and riches." Religion will be abolished, marriage laws banished—no wonder the white-garbed forces of righteousness race to the rescue. It can't be the Ku Klux Klan this time, so it's the U.S. Navy.

At this point appears the one memorable image of the film—a reversal of the scene in so many later Russian films when sailors tear down the Imperial banner and replace it with the red flag. An officer orders the red flag removed, and Colonel Bradshaw runs up the Stars and Stripes. The sailors cheer. It was an axiom of the industry that the one sure way of ensuring applause was to end on the United States flag, and this picture fades to its end title with the somewhat superfluous words "AMERICAN MOTION PICTURE."

Just before the picture's release, the trade press grew so excited it inadvertently caused a crisis. *Moving Picture World* felt the antisocialist propaganda was so strong it ought to have government support. It advocated exhibitors sending letters at-tacking socialism to the press—"then the battle is on." It told its readers to exploit the fears of factory owners by linking socialism to Bolshevism—they would buy blocks of seats for their employees.

The U.S. Navy storms the Red enclave in Bolshevism on Trial, *1919. (Adam Reilly)*

"Put up red flags and hire soldiers to tear them down . . . come out with a flaming handbill that the play is not an argument for anarchy. . . . Work out the limit on this and you'll not only clean up, but profit by future business."[62]

The protests flooded in, and *Moving Picture World* was forced to print a retraction. The producer, Isaac Wolper of the Mayflower Pictures corporation, and the distributor, Lewis J. Selznick of Select, were driven to deny that the film was propaganda and disowned their advertisements.

A year after this picture came out, its director, Harley Knoles, set up an independent production company in Los Angeles. He thought it would be equitable if he, his cameraman, the leading players, and the scenario writer all drew the same salary. He must have been staggered by the headline in *Variety:* "Communist Scheme Tried in Pictures." The reporter described the idea as "Bolshevistic."[63]

Not long afterward, hounded by creditors, Harley Knoles moved to England.

DANGEROUS HOURS   Although prevailing opinion did not distinguish socialism from Bolshevism, it became a matter of box-office expediency to do so. When Thomas H. Ince announced a project called *Americanism (versus Bolshevism)* he quoted Samuel Gompers: "If I thought that Bolshevism was the right road to go, that it meant freedom, justice and the principles of humane society and living conditions, I would join the Bolsheviki. It is because I know that the whole scheme leads to nowhere, that it is destructive in its efforts and in its every activity, that it compels reaction and brings about a situation worse than the one it has undertaken to displace that I oppose and fight it."[64]

Americanism was released in 1920 as *Dangerous Hours.* I wrote about this Fred Niblo film in *The Parade's Gone By . . . ,* but looking at it after a gap of twenty years, I was amazed by it once again. I knew it was an attack on socialism, but I never realized how vitriolic it was, nor did I remember artist Irvin Martin's painted title backgrounds, which contained lurid symbols of death and destruction.

The film depends on the titles. The images are cut very fast, as if the editor[65] could not wait to get to the meat of the scene—the text. It is another silent talkie. The performances are either wooden—Lloyd Hughes in particular—or absurd, and although the exterior sets of factory, shipyard, or Russian town are elaborate, they remain sets, and Niblo's direction is too pedestrian to bring them all alive. The film is not badly made; it is simply prosaic. Had its visuals had the passion and hatred of its titles, *Dangerous Hours* might have been dangerous indeed.

The cinema was a populist medium. It favored the ordinary man, and it was surprisingly hard to make a right-wing film which denigrated him. Audiences responded with distaste to scenes of workers being beaten. Thus, the crowd had to be portrayed as a mob, snarling, waving cudgels, or tearing a town apart. There are just four policemen coping with the strikers in the opening scene of *Dangerous Hours;* in the attack on the shipyard town there are none at all.

But there was a strenuous effort to distinguish between the honest union man and the Bolshevik agitator. The strikers have "an honest grievance," but we see another group, obviously based on the International Workers of the World, who are described as "the dangerous element, following in the wake of labor as the riff-raff and ghouls follow an army." Among them is John King (Hughes)—"graduate of an American University—but . . . owing to his ardent sincerity, rich soil for the poisonous sophistry of fanatics, drones and dreamers"—and foreign-born Sophia Guerni (Claire Du Brey), the movement's vamp, who feigns passion for him. He is attracted by her, "translating the feverishness of her shallow, thrill-craving soul as the Sacred Fires of the New Womanhood."

The meeting of the revolutionaries in Sophie's Greenwich Village studio is strikingly lit by George Barnes and given a smoky, conspiratorial atmosphere. The faces are carefully selected to send a shudder through the audience. There are even a couple of lesbians—"intellectuals abandoning their 'mighty interests' for the cause."

Other major characters include Mary Weston (Barbara Castleton), "a sweet type of American womanhood," who loves John and who just happens to have inherited her father's shipyard, and Russian agent Boris Blotchi (Jack Richardson), "one of the bloodiest butchers of the Revolution." (A blood-spattered cleaver decorates his titles).

At Mary's shipyards, strikers refuse to have anything to do with the "four-flushing Bolsheviks," and thus the film assuages the A.F.L. But the Bolsheviks try to seize control and at last King realizes their true purpose. "You are not interested in humanity—but murder! . . . We in America do not fight that way and what you say shall not be. This is America!"

Bolshevik conspirators from Dangerous Hours, *1920. (Museum of Modern Art)*

The titles blossom in stars and stripes, but King is beaten up and abandoned, while the Bolsheviks carry "the Freedom of the World" to town. This played on the same fears as the German invasion pictures: a church is set on fire, a lavish home destroyed. King staggers into town, takes on Blotchi single-handed, and blows up the Bolsheviks with their own fiendish bombs. The picture ends happily with glimpses of contented workers in the shipyard and agitators, tarred and feathered, being carried out of town on a rail.

C. Gardner Sullivan brought to this Donn Byrne story the black and white politics of a Western.[66] "Draw a strong line between laborers and agitators," advised *Moving Picture World,* whose exploitation advice was considerably muted after its embarrassment over *Bolshevism on Trial.*[67]

The president of the Saginaw, Michigan, Manufacturers' Association announced that he would buy 5,000 tickets for his employees to see *Dangerous Hours:* "I consider this production a most powerfully appealing picture for fairness, squareness and truthfulness and the very best method with which to combat the most dangerous evil that has confronted America since the subjugation of the diabolical Hun."[68]

More than any other event of the Russian Revolution, the nationalization of women caught the imagination—or lack of it—of scenarists. Instead of what it was—a mobilization order to bring women into the labor force—American films passed it through the filter of melodrama and portrayed it as a license to rape. It lay behind one of the most lurid moments in *Dangerous Hours:* we see a soldier walking out of a cell, leaving a half-naked woman lying unconscious, and then a representation of Lenin addressing the Supreme Soviet, followed by columns of soldiers tramping past the body of a dead woman and her baby. Boots stamp on her outstretched arm.

"The nationalization of women was not invented by a motion picture producer," said Gilbert Seldes. "It was published as a fact in all of our newspapers. The assassination of Lenin occurred seven times, until the poor man died of natural causes. For something like ten years, the most respectable and even then I suspect in many ways the best newspaper in this country—I'm speaking of the *New York Times*—did not have a true word out of Russia."[69]

THE NEW MOON   Soon after the Bolsheviks seized control of Russia, the American papers announced the abolition of the marriage law. The Soviet province of Saratov had decreed that it would be unlawful for a man to possess his wife alone but that she would become public property. This would ensure the propagation of a declining race.

"Such a story . . . had never been equaled in history," wrote H. H. Van Loan, a former newspaperman who had become a successful scenarist. "It was a tremendous piece of news, and the most barbarous document ever conceived by the most brutal forces of man."[70] He claimed to have seen the original decree (actually a forgery).[71] "It was horrifying. After reading its sixteen articles I wondered if I

Russian frightfulness—and Orel Kosloff (Stuart Holmes) isn't even a Bolshevik, although he is "in the pay of a foreign government." New Moon, *1919, directed by Chet Withey, from an H. H. Van Loan story, with Norma Talmadge.*

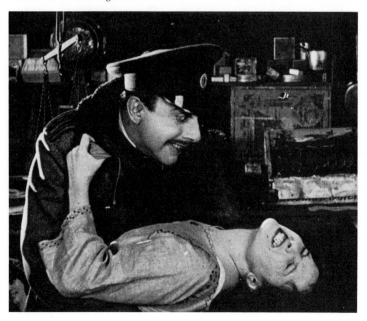

couldn't, in at least a small way, prevent that decree from becoming active in the other provinces of Russia. At least, I could reveal to America and the rest of the civilized world the illiterate souls of a degenerate group of leaders."[72]

Van Loan wrote a story called "The New Moon" and sold it to Joseph Schenck for Norma Talmadge. It was directed by Chet Withey in 1919 in so exaggerated a fashion that even *Variety* was driven to call it "cheaply melodramatic."[73] Although it merely recalled the old anti-Russian pictures, with aristocrats escaping from revolutionaries instead of the other way around, it was taken more seriously than it deserved. "The newspapers have prepared people to expect any sort of outrages . . . so that nothing can well be presented, however brutal it may be, that is likely to be dismissed as an exaggeration," wrote Wid Gunning.[74]

Julian Johnson of *Photoplay* was not hoodwinked, however. "Good morning," he wrote. "Have you written your Bolshevist story yet? H. H. Van Loan has written his, and here it is. It is the sort of story you always find the literarily ambitious Dubuque young lady writing about New York; that is to say, she doesn't know a blamed thing about New York except what she has read in the papers. And while I am wholly ignorant of Mr. Van Loan's real and first-hand knowledge of Russia, his atmosphere and phraseology sound like studious cramming out of the *Saturday Evening Post,* the *Literary Digest* and the morning front pages, rather than resembling a personal reflection."[75]

Van Loan was hurt to the quick by this review. He retorted that he had represented a chain of American newspapers abroad, had traveled the length and breadth of Russia, and would vouch for the accuracy of the detail in his story.[76]

The nationalization of women soon became a staple ingredient of movie hokum. *Common Property* came out at the end of 1919; Universal, having digested their H. H. Van Loan, set their story in that same "Saratov."

"This decree may not be authentic," admitted *Picture Play,* "but it carries a forceful idea for dramatic exposition."[77] The picture made inventive use of the American Expeditionary Force to Russia; troops arrive in the nick of time to rescue the women from a fate worse than death. "One can overlook their presence under the circumstances," said *Picture Play,* "for it is easy to violate truth where the madmen of Russia are concerned."[78]

THE BURNING QUESTION   In October 1919, 17,000 Roman Catholic churches began showing films in their parish halls on a nonprofit basis.[79] Films were produced especially for this network, to the distress of the exhibitors, whose trade suffered as a result.[80] *The Burning Question,* one of the first releases, attacked foreign-born (i.e., Jewish) agitators.[81] In case anyone was in any doubt, one title linked the three New Evils: "Socialism . . . Bolshevism . . . Anarchism . . ." After a skittish opening—an employee caught smoking his boss's cigar—the humor evaporates and the film becomes Very Serious. The contractor is waging war on Reds. "Unless Bolshevism is checked," he says, "its evil influence will crush the whole world." Conviction is undermined by a subsequent title, "The Day the United States Declared War." But this date was April 7, 1917, a full six months before the October Revolution; when the word "Bolshevik" was still virtually

The Burning Question, *an anti-Bolshevik melodrama made in 1919 by the Catholic Art Association. (John E. Allen)*

unknown in America. Russia was ruled by the Social Democrat Alexander Keren-sky with the financial support of the United States.

Having lost its sense of direction as well as its sense of humor, *The Burning Question* now loses its point in a lengthy subplot on the battlefields of France to show "the great work done by the Knights of Columbus."[82] "By the time the war is over, the Bolsheviks have to indulge in sabotage and rape to help us remember how they were trying to wreck the United States. By which time, we are too bored to care.

It was not long before the forces of anti-Semitism joined with those of anti-communism, although the first example came from an unexpected source, the playwright Augustus Thomas. He had been responsible for the film of Upton Sinclair's *The Jungle* (see pages 472–78), which was regarded as powerfully social-ist. His *The Volcano* (1919), a distinctly antisocialist film, was made by the same team, directed by George Irving under Thomas's supervision for producer Harry Raver. The original version was strongly anti-Semitic[83] (the audience cheered it in some theatres),[84] and it was only as a result of a campaign by a Yiddish newspaper that Raver was forced to make alterations.

The portrayal of Jews as Bolsheviks was a reflection of the popular belief. Allen Holubar made a picture for Universal called *The Right to Happiness* (1919), which opened, like the earlier anti-Russian pictures, with a pogrom that separates the two daughters of an American who happens to be living on the outskirts of the Jewish quarter of St. Petersburg. He retrieves one, but mourns the loss of the other, who is given a home by an outcast Jewish family and grows up a Red revolutionary. "Lenine and Trotzki send her to America to stir up trouble, and, of course, she stirs it up in her father's factory without knowing who he is. In the end she is shot trying to protect her sister from the mob that has journeyed down to Long Island to attack her father's house. The story ends in a haze of inconsistencies, with everyone weeping, and repenting and shouting nonsense about love."[85]

Universal publicized it as "The Greatest Love Story Ever Told"[86] and the public liked it. One theatre owner was so rapturous that his letter was used in the ads: "We had throngs of eager patrons lined in front of our box offices . . . exceeding our greatest expectations."[87]

Arthur Guy Empey, the famous soldier who turned his book *Over the Top* into a film in 1918, came up with a sequel called *The Undercurrent* (1919) in which he played an American soldier returned from France and working in a steel mill. He falls prey to Red agents. Empey favored the deportation of radicals—"My motto for the Reds is SOS—Ship or shot"—and his picture was a diatribe. Julian Johnson thought it showed little knowledge of the subject beyond "a perusal of newspaper headlines."[88]

The film was directed by Wilfred North, who had made *The Battle Cry of Peace* in 1915. *Variety* considered that Empey's popularity had run its course (this proved

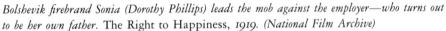

Bolshevik firebrand Sonia (Dorothy Phillips) leads the mob against the employer—who turns out to be her own father. The Right to Happiness, *1919. (National Film Archive)*

accurate) and that the film, like his acting, was ragged and crude. But it admired the fact that it exploited "the evils of Bolshevism" and approved particularly of one episode in which a woman Red, "seeing that the law is about to checkmate her career, draws a revolver, kills her cringing associates, and fires the lead into herself. This bit is worthy of no less a Russian than Turgenev."[89]

But the audience at the Capitol Theatre, New York, far from being alarmed by it, laughed at this superpatriotic drama.

LAND OF OPPORTUNITY   In the same year, 1919, a nationwide "Americanization" process began. Progressives hoped this would mean aid for immigrants. But in postwar America it meant a tough "Love us or leave us" policy. The melting pot had been replaced by the branding iron.

In December 1919, Franklin Lane, Secretary of the Interior, met with a group of producers and distributors to discuss the making of "Americanization" films "for the purpose of counteracting Bolshevism, radicalism and discontent against the U.S."[90] A committee was formed, which included Adolph Zukor, Lewis J. Selznick, and Lane as chairman. To prove how unlike the Bolsheviks they were, the producers took advantage of the situation to raise the price of the films. Exhibitors protested,[91] but they were not supposed to make a profit any more than the producers were. The idea was *circulation.*

Lane said that he knew of no better weapon to stop the grave menace to civilization than the motion picture.[92] He suggested that the industry organize immediately to spread the story of America as exemplified in the life of Abraham Lincoln. A round robin was sent to authors asking them to contribute screenplays for one- or two-reelers "not praising the government to the skies as perfect or Utopian"[93] but pointing out in simple lessons the advantage of the republican system and the need for united and patriotic sentiment.

Selznick produced a two-reeler called *Land of Opportunity* especially for the committee. Ralph Ince, who directed the film, was featured as Lincoln and also played Merton Walpole, "an idler with an inherited fortune—busy with 'pink' theories for lack of a real share in the world's work." The story is set in a club, where this unlikely member assails his rich friends for buying their way into the courts and government and blinding the eyes of the poor by gifts to flashy charities. The others, who have no answer to this, accuse him of being a "Bolshevist," and of belonging to the herd of uplifters who never lift anything but their voices. They walk out, leaving him with an elderly butler. "They don't understand," says Walpole, gazing at the pages of his book, *Classes versus Masses* by Yakem Zubko.

"Pardon me, sir," says the butler, "but it is you who do not understand." And he tells, in flashback, a story of how Abraham Lincoln, campaigning in a rural district and hearing of a boy on trial for murder in a nearby town, walked twenty miles to take charge of the defense and win the boy's freedom.

"You tell the story as though you had been there," says Walpole.

"I was the boy," says the butler. "And the same America that gave Lincoln the opportunity to rise from a rail-splitter gave me justice in the courts—freedom —work—the opportunity to save—the field to serve."

Left alone with his thoughts, Walpole tears out the pages of his subversive book and throws it on the fire. The film ends with the title "AMERICAN MOTION PICTURE."

This curious anecdote, well produced though it was, hardly brought the socialist case crashing in ruins—it merely suggested the haphazard nature of American justice. The producers intended to release *Land of Opportunity* on Lincoln's Birthday and to follow it with fifty-two more such films at weekly intervals.[94] But the Red Scare was running out of steam, and in the end only a few more anti-Bolshevik films appeared.

STARVATION   Hard as it is to believe, one film used the hungry masses of Europe to preach an anti-Bolshevik sermon. Behind it, thinly concealed, was Herbert Hoover, whose American Relief Administration was feeding the starving millions. And behind him was George Barr Baker, a lieutenant commander in the navy, who was based in Paris, where he worked as a publicist for the A.R.A. Historian Bert Patenaude, who has examined Baker's papers in the Hoover Archives at Stanford University and who found documents quoted here, describes him as "a cultivated man, very sharp politically and with a good sense of humor."[95] Baker, like Hoover, was dedicated to the overthrow of Bolshevism, and he devoted months of his life, and thousands of dollars of his own money, to the documentary *Starvation* (1920).

The A.R.A. cause was aided by a number of newsreel cameramen, including George Zimmer, a navy photographer who shot most of *Starvation*, edited it, and received credit as director. Another was Donald Thompson,[96] a maverick from Canada, who was paid by *Leslie's Weekly* in New York. His footage and still pictures of child welfare work was "the best the A.R.A. has ever had."[97]

Baker went into partnership with a shady distributor called Fred Warren. When he sent out invitations for the premiere, he was careful to distance himself from Warren: "We have not been able to control the announcements because the matter is now in the hands of the professional moving picture people and they use the methods of Barnum wherever possible. They have used Mr. Hoover's name too freely in spite of all my efforts, nevertheless, every incident in this picture is absolutely authentic. . . . I do not believe that any woman in the working class who sees it will sit down at home with her children and calmly permit talk of direct action and other forms of radicalism."[98]

Of course it was not the working class Baker had invited to the premiere, on January 9, 1920, at the Manhattan Opera House. He had invited the very rich—Otto Kahn—the very powerful—William Randolph Hearst—and the very influential—the editors of all the big newspapers.

The critical reaction was just what Baker needed. "Pictures of the worst cases of children—with protruding bones, swollen abdomens, and tight eyelids—brought sympathy and tears and relief at the thought that America was doing something to alleviate their sufferings."[99]

"No fair minded person," said *Variety*, "no matter what their leanings politically, could view this picture, particularly the scenes showing the frightful con-

FIRST SHOWING IN ANY LAND

FREDERICK B. WARREN
presents

The Tremendous Picturization of

HERBERT HOOVER

and the American Relief Administration Work in

STARVATION

Made under the Complete Supervision
and Direction of

GEORGE F. ZIMMER

Covering These Countries:

RUSSIA	POLAND	AUSTRIA
COURLAND	LETVIA	ESTHONIA
UKRAINIA	HUNGARY	EAST GALICIA
TURKEY	ARMENIA	RUMANIA
GERMANY	HOLLAND	BELGIUM
FRANCE	SWEDEN	DENMARK

ITALY, with glimpses in other lands

Photographed by eight daring camera-men frequently facing death. It is the only record the world will ever have of the hunger and salvation of a Continent; of the greatest disaster in the history of Civilization.

In the prints for the other large cities and the various sections of the United States there have been prepared sections of this picture dealing with men and women local to those particular regions, so that, as seen nationally, each section of the nation will see its own people, photographed in Europe, engaged in their splendid work of humanity as the representatives of the American people and the generous American pocketbook.

(Herbert Hoover Archives, Stanford University)

ditions in Russia, where the red banner of the Bolsheviki flies, and still have the slightest doubt as to whether or not a condition of government such as they have now is the best for the people."[100]

Included in *Starvation* was footage of Bolsheviks being hanged and executed by firing squad. This all had a most unfortunate effect on audiences; Whites shot by Reds might have been more salutary. But here sympathy went to the victims. The scenes "left one cold with an unameliorated terror," said the *New York Times*.[101]

Moving Picture World found a way of dealing with it, however: "At every point we have before us the contrast between the American way of dealing with a festering situation, and the unmerciful and less efficient way of the Central Powers. America erected a bulwark of food to stem the tide of the Bolsheviki, while the brutal methods of hanging and shooting . . . were resorted to as the only remedy by those of a lesser understanding."[102]

"It is the first really powerful anti-Bolshevist and anti-Radical lesson offered in the United States," Baker wrote to Alexander J. Hemphill of the Guaranty

Trust Company, "which carries with it by indirection, instead of having all the earmarks of propaganda, the story of what happens to countries which abolish law and God and refuse to understand that without work there is no bread."[103] He gave the film its slogan: "The United States of America fights nations and men—but never women and children."

It was not the ideal time for such a film. The price of food had soared in the United States thanks to the war, and by 1919 the cost of living was 79 percent higher than it had been in 1914.[104] Food riots had scarred American cities only a couple of years earlier. Attendance at performances of *Starvation* was patchy, and the film was forced out of the Manhattan Opera House two weeks into its run.[105]

The film was hastily reedited. "The material very much shortened, and the shock very much reduced," Baker wrote to Hoover. Having put $18,000 into the venture, he declared his confidence undiminished; he wanted to go ahead with it, "doing away with the professional crowd and reconstructing according to our ideas as generally carried out in the A.R.A. This plan does not involve you in any way."

He had said he would not get Hoover into trouble, and "I have not done so. The enclosed clippings indicate that the public is not led to believe that you have any interest in the film."[106] *Variety* must have been among these clippings: "It was said to be propaganda for Hoover in his attempt to secure the presidential nomination, but there was so little of Hoover, it was propaganda of the subtlest kind."[107]

Baker had a long talk over lunch with independent film distributor Fred Warren, then watched the film again. He drew up a list of cuts and alterations—a shot of Zimmer went from the opening—and suggested a new approach: "I would start off . . . by showing that even after the war much that was beautiful remained in the various countries of Central Europe; fine buildings and bridges undisturbed; that life was still worth living. Gradually I would drift into the question of Bolshevism as an after the war terror, and while doing this would show the blown bridges, White armies, and general scenes of the desolation which comes from revolution and unemployment. After all of this misery, which apparently began to spread widely with the initiation of Bolshevism, I would show the result; the bread lines and the starving children . . . As a climax to this, I would show the little naked girl, the little girls who are being stripped and weighed by the doctors and nurses, and who, if they are proved to be normal weight, will not be fed again until they begin to show fresh signs of the effects of starvation."[108]

The film went round the country but never recovered from its initial failure, and Baker lost nearly $11,000.[109] Hoover was not elected president until 1928, but Baker worked under Calvin Coolidge and was closely associated with Hoover during his presidency.

In 1923, Baker wrote to the Income Tax Bureau: "The film had various degrees of misadventure over a considerable period. It was always just about to be made to pay. However it never did reach that point and I paid the losses out of my own pocket, as indicated by my tax return. My advice to a young man about to risk money in motion pictures is—'No.' "[110]

———

WILSON PALE AFTER VIEWING FILMS OF AN EXECUTION OF EIGHTEEN BOLSHEVISTS

Motion Pictures of Killing of Prisoners Condemned by 'White Terror' at Mitau Shown at Peace Conference; Why Von der Goltz Was Ordered from Russia

By Lieutenant Frank O. Johnson, U. S. A.

Especially assigned to make a cinema record of American relief in Russia.

(Copyright, 1919.)

THIS is the story of a unique record in the archives of the Peace Conference, not a record of parchment, but of celluloid. It is the story of how a motion picture film became a deciding factor in the deliberations of the greatest legislative body of modern times. Now that the Peace Conference has been officially closed, the facts in this connection and the circumstances surrounding this remarkable celluloid document can be set forth without betraying any governmental confidence.

While the statesmen at the Peace Conference were debating the conflicting reports of Germany's activities on the eastern front, when she was officially suing for terms on the western front, there arrived in the closing days of the deliberations, by special messenger from the far-off Russian frontier, the first visualized proof of the real conditions.

It was not in the form of written documents, but in the deadly proof of the unfailing camera, made in a corner of Europe where a camera had never penetrated before, and the story told by the films was probably the most amazing ever developed in a laboratory.

For the first time in the lives of men a motion picture camera had been trained on a wholesale execution from the moment of its start to the hasty covering of the grave on its completion—an execution so callously cold-blooded that no other proof could stand as a convincing evidence of its atrocious details.

Eighteen Men Executed at Mitau.

On the evening of May 26, 1919, eighteen men were slaughtered at Mitau, Russia, by a firing squad, part of the German army of occupation, which, under pretence of quelling the advances of the Bolshevists, had been conducting a campaign of frank conquest for weeks.

Every incident of the execution was caught by the camera, from the reading of the death sentence to the toppl... —into their common grave. Certainly no... been introduced into the proceedings of a... and the response to it was immediate an... As a result the Allied Government... shown by the motion picture films, at o...

front, in the name of so-called repulsion of Bolshevism.

And still that tension of waiting, waiting! The four of us Americans were feeling it creeping more and more surely through our veins. Those in charge of the execution were laughing and jesting, for Bolshevist executions, we had found, were a matter of almost daily occurrence at Mitau.

We had almost exhausted our cigarettes, for we had given one package to the authorities as the price of our admittance with our camera to the scene. A package of cigarettes to witness the execution of eighteen men for a motion picture film! And now they were beginning to worry for fear darkness would come before the pictures could be made. They had sent a messenger uptown to hurry up the death warrant, but it was necessary finally to send our own machine after him.

Across the gray, sluggish river the sun was setting in a great red ball—a fitting symbol to the tragedy about to be enacted before it should sink for the night. But would the waiting never end?

And then, slowly, creakingly, the heavy iron door swung inward. A squad of guards, wearing the Iron Division insignia of the German army, stepped out and stood on either side, a double, stolid line with fixed bayonets. Down the pathway of bayonets, cowering, fearful men in ragged clothes and with sunken eyes, began to come like frightened sheep. They did not know yet whether it was to be another reprieve of life for them or immediate death.

Every furtive glance sought mutely for some evidence of hope, some sign of what was coming. Several of them were but mere boys. And so these were Bolshevists—the Bolshevists we had come to Russia to study! It was our first close-range view of what we had been told was the heart of Baltic Bolshevism, and we stared almost rigidly at attention as the doomed men passed before us.

DOOMED MEN FACE CAMERA.

An army officer gave a curt command and motioned to us. He was performing the first part of his agreement to us for the package of cigarettes we had brought. Four abreast the huddled men were ordered to step forward and face the camera. None of them ever had seen a motion picture camera before, and they stared at us, uncertain and

fields, ...
new gr...
sun was...
there w...
spare f...

The s...
into an...
tumbled...
a long, ...
the rec...
pants, ...
died me...
sharp ...
comman...
their sh...
Russia, ...
peasants ...

Into ...
cast the...
looking...
now—bu...
shriekin...
The ca...
It had ...
even de...
the pris...
on the ...

DEATH ...
Over ...
ed at th...
ventiona...
to witne...
ribe the ...
to eterni...

Three ...
dered to...
trench v...
on the g...
no hesit...
parently ...
Nothin...
less stol...
men alm...
it came ...
caught h...
ishly. T...
its work...
used to ...
as to cate...
stood, fo...
tim's he...
were stil...
they cru...
camera ...
ing up t...
owners f...

After t...
of three ...
seemed ...
others. ...
at the te...
brink an...
a guard. ...
In this ...
their dea...
join the ...
At last ...
execution ...

Perhaps the most effective anti-Bolshevik film did not deal with Bolshevism at all. It was D. W. Griffith's epic of the French Revolution, *Orphans of the Storm* (1921). Griffith succeeded brilliantly in recreating the Terror at his new studio at Mamaroneck, on Long Island Sound, not far from the homes of some of the wealthiest people in the country.

Before portraying the bloodthirsty behavior of the mob, Griffith declares in a memorable title: "The French Revolution RIGHTLY overthrew a BAD government. But we in America should be careful lest we with a GOOD government mistake fanatics for leaders and exchange our decent law and order for anarchy and Bolshevism."[111]

THE ETERNAL CITY   The first version (1915) of Hall Caine's *The Eternal City* was a film of socialist idealism. Caine lived in Rome when he wrote the novel, which was published in 1900, and told of the establishment of a socialist state and the appointment of a prime minister who put into effect the Christian socialism of Giuseppe Mazzini. The film was made on location in Rome, with the cooperation of the Italian government and the Vatican, and was exhibited throughout the world, "apparently without offence," said Caine, "except perhaps in certain states of America."[112]

Famous Players made the first version, and Sam Goldwyn decided to remake it in 1923. Caine assumed that he would film the story as he had written it, but he reckoned without Benito Mussolini. He was informed that the representatives of the Italian government in Washington objected to the subject and Mussolini himself had denied them all facilities in Rome for a film that would be based on the socialistic *Eternal City.*

Caine tried to withdraw from his contract, but the Goldwyn people told him they considered location scenes in Rome essential and that they had already spent a great deal of money preparing for them. They had been promised full civilian and military cooperation for a film which supported Fascist policy and argued that a free adaptation of the story was the only way out of the impasse.

"To this I objected," wrote Caine, "that it would be false to the theory of my story to put Mussolini and Fascism into the places of Christian Socialism and the disciple of Mazzini; but the ultimate result of prolonged and sometimes painful legal negotiations was that I consented that an independent scenario should be written by another author, under her own name, and coupled with the name of my book. This has now been done, and the film shortly to be released will present a picture (no doubt vivid and faithful) not of the triumph of Socialism as dreamt of and desired by me, but of the triumph of Fascism as foreseen and desired and brought to pass by Signor Mussolini."[113]

Like so many adults, Caine was bewildered by the whole experience. Why on earth would a film company buy a novel which had sold a million copies and render it unrecognizable to its devoted public? He could not understand, either, why Christian socialism, a worldwide movement, should be replaced by fascism, which was confined to Italy and of no appeal to any other country.

The official publicity was as mendacious as ever:

"It isn't often that an author, and one of the most noted in the world at that,

Free extras for The Eternal City, *1923.* Fascisti *at the Coliseum, Rome. (Museum of Modern Art)*

will agree to allow his story to be altered for the screen. . . . But such was the case with Sir Hall Caine's immortal story of love and adventure. . . . Many producers had sought to purchase the film rights to the story before George Fitzmaurice made the successful offer. Not only was he able to induce the titled English novelist to agree to the changes, but the latter even assisted in working out the continuity, in conjunction with Ouida Bergere, Fitzmaurice's wife.

"The story was written years before the Fascisti of Italy had been thought of; but due to the modernization of the tale, and the persuasive tongue of Producer Fitzmaurice, Premier Mussolini, the chief of the Fascisti, appears in the picture."[114]

Actually, Hall Caine had tried not merely to withdraw, but to stop the production while the company was on location in Rome, as he saw the film developing into Fascist propaganda.[115]

Goldwyn proceeded with the film, which turned into a very curious production indeed. David Rossi, an Italian orphan, has been cared for by a tramp (Richard Bennett) and is adopted by Dr. Rosselli, a pacifist, who rears him together with his daughter, Roma. They grow up (and become Bert Lytell and Barbara La Marr). David joins the army at the outbreak of war and Roma becomes a sculptor with the financial assistance of Baron Bonelli (Lionel Barrymore), the covert leader of the Communist party. David is reported killed.[116]

This is how the *Daily Worker* recounted the rest of the plot: "Despite the fact that this wealthy, world-wise Baron buys up her 'masterpieces' and pays her board bill, she returns pure and undefiled to her young lover who wasn't killed after all. . . . The rich art patron, Baron Bonelli, is made into a war profiteering capitalist, who seeks to become Dictator of Italy by the road of the proletarian revolution. The wickedness of 'red strikers' is pictured by putting axes into the hands of a crowd of roughly dressed 'extras' and setting them to making kindling out of a railroad coach. . . . The brave youths return from the war, and find that their medals and banners are not properly respected. So they organize into mobs, and fling stilettos bearing anti-strike warnings at darkened doorways. When the reds organize to counter-attack, they are dispersed by the police, but the title-writer explains that Italy was fortunate in having a King with enough sense to turn the government over to Mussolini, the 'man of the people.' Mussolini and the King appear in person, of course."[117]

The film's cameraman, Arthur Miller, has recorded in his memoirs how scenarist Ouida Bergere had altered the story to include Mussolini and the Fascisti: "Mussolini was so impressed with the idea that his office was open to us at any time." Blackshirts were provided to help with crowd control: "They did anything we asked of them. One Sunday we shot in five different locations in Rome, walking two thousand extras from one location to another and ending at the Coliseum."[118]

As the advertisements said, "3,000 years ago they began building sets for *The Eternal City.*"[119]

Unhappily, Mussolini saw *The Man From Home* (1922), which Fitzmaurice had also made in Rome, and was apparently infuriated by its portrayal of Italian nobility. He demanded to see Fitzmaurice, who left for New York, and Miller sneaked out of Italy via Venice, with the last of the negative. "If the blackshirt boys had gotten their hands on the film that would have been the end of it."[120]

THE VOLGA BOATMAN In 1926, the International Motion Picture Congress, held under the auspices of the League of Nations International Commission on Intellectual Co-operation, declared that while Russia should henceforth be treated in Western films in such a way that its "ancient culture" would be respected, the present government and conditions within the Soviet Union were to be ignored.[121]

But it is hard to ignore a regime with whom you are anxious to trade. The anti-Bolshevik films had died out by the early twenties, although some were still in circulation in Europe, representing the tip of an iceberg of propaganda freezing the waters between Russia and the United States. Lenin's adoption of the New Economic Policy in 1921 suggested that capitalism was returning, albeit to a limited degree. And it altered America's attitude. Russia had begun to look outward, and American tourists had begun visiting Moscow, prompting the Russian comedy *Mr. West in the Land of the Bolsheviks,* which used serial techniques to parody the American image of Soviet Russia.

The one gesture of goodwill, the one picture which portrayed the Bolsheviks in a relatively favorable light, was made by perhaps the most conservative figure in Hollywood, Cecil B. DeMille. That film was *The Volga Boatman* (1926).

DeMille had been considering a film on the Russian Revolution, and to this end he had brought in books by Upton Sinclair and John Reed, and even *The Outline of the British Labour Movement*. According to a DeMille biographer, John Kobal, he had, for a while, "an idealistic sympathy with the Russian Revolution." DeMille admitted in his autobiography that had he made *The Volga Boatman* in the 1950s, he would have been ordered before the House Un-American Activities Committee. "In 1925 most of us were more naive politically. Prohibition seemed a more burning issue than Communism. Not that *Volga Boatman* was communistic in either its inspiration or its effect; but we were still close enough in history to the tyranny of the Czars to look upon their overthrow with at least guarded optimism. And to the average American at that time Russian Communism had not yet been revealed as a tyranny far worse than that which it replaced."[122]

The left-wing writer Konrad Bercovici had written an outline for the story, which DeMille handed to Lenore Coffee, and she came up with a scene which caught DeMille's interest at once, a scene which would show that the Bolsheviks and the aristocrats could behave equally badly once in the saddle.

"When the Bolsheviks are victorious," said Coffee, "in capturing a palace filled with women in beautiful evening gowns, wearing superb jewels, and men in Court dress with decorations, the Volga Boatmen harness these proud people into the ropes which pull the barge, while they watch in triumph from the boat."[123]

The aristocrats were played by real White Russian emigrés. William Boyd (later Hopalong Cassidy), played the hero, wearing an armband with the Cyrillic letters KOM POL., indicating his status as a political commissar. The film is every bit as preposterous as the most lurid of the anti-Bolshevik films, but with DeMille's characteristic good luck, he got away with it—at least as far as the public was concerned.

"A beautiful picture," wrote a fan. "Mr. DeMille idolized the Bolshevists, with their demoralization of social life, but the horrible realities of the Russian Revolution are forgotten for a time, while we sit entranced with this stirring romance."[124]

Critics thought it artificial. Said *Picture Play:* "All we learned about the revolution from this film is that the Red gentlemen invariably craved the aristocratic gals, and that the boys with the 'clean white hands' constantly yearned to carry on with the lady peasants. That, in fact, is the whole story of the film."[125]

What makes it all the more surprising that this film was made is that it was financed by Jeremiah Milbank, DeMille's backer, who had a horror of his films being used as Communist propaganda. When John Hampton, owner of the Silent Movie Theater in Los Angeles, tried to acquire the film years later, he found it exceptionally difficult—probably because of its political associations.

DeMille made much of his team of researchers and historical advisers, but he conveyed no feeling for authenticity at all. The technical adviser, a former Russian general, said: "They wanted to put it into the present day and make it a Bolshevist film, but I told them that Volga boatmen haven't existed for over fifty years. They got all the details and the costumes wrong. Oh, absolutely. And because I really tried to get things right and tried to insist, they paid me my money and turned me out. I tell you that the job of the technical expert is to say, 'Yes, that's all right; yes, that's all right'—whatever they do."[126]

The film did surprisingly well in America (it cost $497,356 and grossed

Prince Dmitri (Victor Varconi) faces the stern gaze of Bolshevik commissar Feodor (William Boyd) in The Volga Boatman, *1926, directed by Cecil B. DeMille—the only American film to present the revolutionaries in a relatively sympathetic light. (Museum of Modern Art)*

$1,275,374, according to figures from the DeMille Estate), and it was even shown in Russia. One film showing Bolsheviks in a dimly favorable light, however, could hardly cast into the shadows a dozen showing them as they knew the Americans really thought of them.

"The tendency has been to brutalize the acts of Socialistic revolutions," said *Motion Picture Magazine,* when the United States finally recognized the U.S.S.R. in 1933. "No attempt has been made to qualify the brutalities as natural impulses, under the eye-for-an-eye creed, in retaliation for centuries of oppression and serfdom. The first sympathetic presentation was probably DeMille's *Volga Boatmen.* Yet no charge can be made that this picture contained dangerous propaganda."[127]

Or, as *Picture Play* put it, "DeMille had made the Russian Revolution safe for American audiences by making it merely a movie."[128]

Two supposedly lost films of this period—both of which I have seen in a private collection in England—display a fascinating contrast in their handling of radicals. *The One Woman* (1918) is a diatribe against socialism written by the Reverend Thomas Dixon and made by his company. *The Lion's Den* (1919), written and directed by George D. Baker, is a far more typically American film—moderate, sensible, and humorous. But in each film, a clergyman takes political action, alienates his congregation, and arouses the anger of powerful men.

Despite the fact that *The One Woman* was directed by the brilliant Reginald Barker *(The Coward, The Italian),* it is essentially a silent talkie. A fire-eating pastor (Lawson Butt), whose vitriolic sermons are the sensations of the day, is warned by his deacon: "You are driving the best people out of your church with your socialist rubbish." A female admirer (Clara Williams) encourages him to regard himself as a leader of men, but when he tries to raise money for a temple, a friendly banker warns him that socialism strikes at "the heart of human society—the Home." He uses chickens as an example: "Full brothers, yet ready to fight at the drop of a hat, why? Both want the same pullet! Man, too, is a fighting animal, and when Socialism comes to pass, the EAGLE will light in the barnyard—and then—good night, roosters!"

This somewhat bizarre lesson gives way to a red-hot affair between the pastor and his female acolyte. The pastor's wife remains steadfast, refusing the advances of a politician, even when the man becomes governor. The pastor is engulfed "in a whirlpool of violent radicalism," and when he finds his banker friend taking advantage of his mistress, he kills him during a fight. He is brought to trial and sentenced to death. His wife, still loyal, appeals to the governor, who admits he sanctioned the death penalty to clear the field for himself. "Your love for this man is a thing divine," he says. "You have nailed me to the cross. Marriage *is* a divine sacrament. I bow to the will of God and grant him a new trial." And the pastor, pardoned, returns to the bosom of his family, rejecting what Thomas Dixon clearly considered to be the politics of the farmyard.

The Reverend Sam Webster (Bert Lytell), in *The Lion's Den,* is no socialist. Instead of trying to destroy capitalism, he joins it. But he, too, rails against injustice, virtually emptying his church by attacking his congregation for its complacency. How can the members allow their boys to hang around the pool hall, smoking, swearing, and listening to salacious stories? There should be a boys' club in town! He tries to raise funds, but is made to feel like a beggar. Webster reminds the richest man in the area, grocer Stedman, that he has won his wealth from the town and asks him to put up the first $500. Stedman writes a check—for a mere twenty-five dollars. Infuriated, Webster tears the check up in front of him and goes into business in opposition. At first Stedman uses underhanded methods to force his new rival to the wall, but Webster gathers all the boys at a movie show and puts a proposal to them: each one to become a partner and every penny he makes will go toward the club. The boys enter the scheme with enthusiasm, and soon Stedman is defeated. In a melodramatic ending, Stedman's clerk sets fire to his store and the boys have to rescue him. He then agrees to build their clubhouse.

Such an ending was unnecessary for so exuberant and realistic a portrait of small-town life. (The small town was Hollywood.) The shots inside the pool hall and barbershop are fascinating and give the film a value not apparent when it first appeared, when it was dismissed as mere program fare. The movie theatre sequences show the boys roaring with laughter at a Chaplin comedy (Metro made its own with a Chaplin imitator). *The Lion's Den,* which was adapted from a *Saturday Evening Post* story by Frederick Orin Bartlett, acknowledged the tyranny of some capitalists, but showed that society didn't need a Bolshevik revolution to get rid of them.

CAPITAL VERSUS LABOR

The long struggle between capital and labor reached a peak of violence when the motion picture was present to reflect it and sometimes to record it.

A strike was usually regarded by an employer less as a legitimate expression of a grievance than as a declaration of civil war. He did not seek negotiation—he sought strikebreakers. He did not offer arbitration—he stockpiled guns and gas grenades. To give the strikers a "rifle diet," he hired an army of "guards"—often gangsters. The strikers were sometimes driven to do the same. Politicians automatically sided with the employer and used the National Guard as a private army. The railroad baron Jay Gould put it succinctly: "I can hire one half of the working class to kill the other half."[129]

The more civilized employers felt a paternalistic responsibility toward their employees. A railroad president wrote: "The rights and interests of the laboring man will be protected and cared for—not by the labor agitators, but by the Christian gentlemen to whom God has given control of the property rights of the country."[130]

When model towns and model factories were built, notably by the sleeping-car tycoon George M. Pullman, rents were high and the company kept the workers in a state of feudal serfdom. Wage cuts led to rent arrears. A series of smaller strikes over this issue culminated in 1894 in a massive one, led by Eugene Debs, which was put down by troops with considerable ferocity.

But not all strikers were browbeaten and defenseless. In a country where the right of the citizen to bear arms is (tragically) written into the Constitution, guns were all too easily available. And it took the merest flick of a trigger finger to transform solidarity into slaughter.

Armed conflict was never part of socialist policy. During the 1877 railroad riots, *The American Socialist* declared that laborers "have no legal or moral right to insist that certain men who have been employing them shall pay them whatever wages they demand. They have a right to quit work and seek better pay elsewhere, but have no right to make war or destroy property or prevent others from taking their places at the reduced wages."[131]

Employers' associations financed an anti-union open-shop campaign at the turn of the century. (Los Angeles was well known as a nonunion town—one reason the film industry settled there.) Most workers distrusted the unions, which were infiltrated by the employers' spies. But without solidarity, no strike could succeed. The I.W.W. was formed in 1905 as a militant organization dedicated to the idea of "One Big Union" and determined to challenge the conservative policies of the A.F.L. Notoriety came quickly: the former governor of Idaho, Frank Steunenberg, who had beaten striking miners at Coeur d'Alene, was killed by a bomb, and Big Bill Haywood, one of the founders of the I.W.W., was among those arrested. Sentenced to twenty years in jail, he fled to Soviet Russia—an act which incensed even his supporters—and never returned. He died in Moscow in 1928.

The I.W.W. were known as "Wobblies," and the initials were translated as

An I.W.W. (Industrial Workers of the World) parade in Los Angeles on May Day, 1913.

"I Won't Work." The movies had endless fun with them in comedies, but never took them seriously. Or perhaps they took them too seriously, for no film was made which dealt with them directly. They were invariably referred to, mysteriously, as "outside agitators." But the I.W.W. achieved the solidarity other unions never attained. It offered to organize anyone, even the despised Chinese and Japanese,[132] and won many strikes, for, unlike most socialists, its members believed in violence. They did not, however, believe in the power of film.

The film industry had an early encounter with the I.W.W. in 1914, when a crowd scene involving 600 extras was disrupted by demands for higher pay. Otis Turner was filming *Damon and Pythias* at Universal, and the strikers, playing Greek soldiers returning from a victorious campaign, were armed with swords and spears. Universal, fearing a riot, solved the problem by firing the lot of them and hiring another 600 extras to complete the scene a few days later.[133]

The majority of the capital-versus-labor films used the subject as the focal point for melodrama, the villain being a mill-owner or superintendent. Vitagraph's *The Mill Girl—A Story of Factory Life* (1907) was the classic tale of the boss who desires a working girl. Her worker fiancé defends her honor. The boss hires thugs to ambush him, but he proves too strong. Fire breaks out at the factory, and the boss seizes his chance to ravish the girl. The hero climbs a drainpipe to rescue his sweetheart.

Sophisticated in technique, if not in story, *The Mill Girl* contained an interior of a genuine cotton mill. But its makers had not the slightest interest in social conditions. Nor had Selig, which made *The Power of Labor* in 1908. This one-reeler portrayed a mill superintendent acting with such brutality that no one would believe it had similar cases not been reported. An absentee owner leaves his steel mill in the charge of John Flack, a man with a criminal past. Flack plays the stock market and, when he needs extra cash, orders a cut in wages. A worker emerges as a champion of labor, and Flack has him kidnapped and thrown into a blast furnace. Unexpectedly, the owner returns to the mill and Flack is confronted by the worker he thought he had killed—who proves to be the owner's son. After a fight, Flack meets the fate he had reserved for his antagonist.[134]

Variety thought it "a dramatic triumph,"[135] and *Moving Picture World* described it as "a powerful argument for fair play between employer and employee."[136]

Industrial unrest was feared as much by the bosses of film companies as those of regular factories, so the majority took care to avoid controversy in their films. But some were openly anti-labor, like Kalem's *The Molly Maguires, or the Labor Wars in the Coal Mines* (1908). The events had long since passed into history, but by reviving memories Kalem drew parallels with the I.W.W.

In the Pennsylvania coal fields in the 1870s, the Molly Maguires were said to be terrorists, killing bosses who were hated by the workers, provoking strikes, and murdering alien miners—but no one has proved that the band ever existed. The detective Allan Pinkerton and his spy James McParlan were the source of most of the stories, but labor historians have accused them and the coal ring of inventing the Molly Maguires.[137]

Pinkerton planted spies among the miners. During the strike, the coal ring's private army, the Coal and Iron Police, was reinforced and its attacks on the workers passed off as Molly Maguire operations. After five months, the starving miners gave up; those not blacklisted returned to work with a 20 percent wage cut. Some radicals were found dead in disused mine shafts. Others were branded as Molly Maguires, which was enough to hang a man. McParlan produced his "evidence," and in 1876 the first trials of the Molly Maguires began. July 21, 1877, became known as "Pennsylvania's Day with the Rope"; ten were hanged that day, nine more later.[138]

The Kalem film was a re-enactment in one reel and eight scenes. Even by the standard of 1908, *The Molly Maguires* was not rated highly. "Created no strong impression," said *Moving Picture World.*[139]

The attempt of some film companies to quench the flames of industrial conflict was occasionally a little too obvious, as in *The Right to Labor* (1909). Said *Moving Picture World:* "The closing scene, where Capital and Labor grasp hands and the angel of prosperity waves the olive branch above them, is well worth preservation as an inspiration to conservative action when any dispute of this character arises."[140]

Most people felt that the bridge between capital and labor had long since been burned. But Vitagraph's *Capital vs. Labor* (1910) was optimistic. An industrialist's daughter, courted by both an officer of the militia and a clergyman, cannot decide which to marry. When a strike at her father's factory develops into a riot, the officer runs off to alert his troops. The mob attacks her house, breaking the doors and windows and threatening her father. "While the fury of the mob is at its height, the young minister rushes into the room, checks and silences the strikers, and gains from their employer all their claims and privileges. Naturally, the young clergyman has won the respect of the capitalist, the cause of labor and the heart of the young girl."[141]

Directed by Van Dyke Brooke, the picture featured Maurice Costello, Harry T. Morey, and Earle Williams. As Lewis Jacobs wrote, "The message of the film, that capital would accede to labor problems if approached properly by the right people," prompted *Moving Picture World* to call the film 'one of the most extraordinary motion picture dramas of the year . . . powerful in its purpose.' "[142]

The paper added that it was much too realistic to be comfortable. "Perhaps the picture will have a salutary influence during the season when strikes pervade the air.' "[143]

A surprising number of films used the device of an owner's son who works incognito at the factory to experience conditions firsthand. Sometimes he organizes the strike, sometimes he stops it. In Thanhouser's *The Girl Strike Leader* (1910), he falls for a radical. Her strike is crushed, but she accepts his hand in marriage, whereupon he reveals his identity and gets his father to restore a wage cut. These were films designed to offend no one and, apart from the odd documentary scene, were of no great significance.

Vitagraph's *Tim Mahoney, the Scab* (1911), however, was one of the most talked-of films. Its neutrality was deceptive; for once, the filmmakers put the case for the ordinary human caught up in conditions beyond his control. Wrote *Moving Picture World:*

"Tim is a union man . . . and he also believes in the righteousness of this particular strike. But the strike finds Tim, in spite of union help, if there is any, unprepared. His children are hungry when the story opens, and are going to be hungry three times a day right along. Tim's case is special. We are not shown just what elements make it harder for him than for all the others, but we see at first he is loyal to the union.

"It's a weakness of the photoplay that it cannot tell us plainly all the reasons that there were for such a step, but on the other hand, it's the photoplay's strength that it can picture so vividly the state of mind in which Tim makes his decision."[144]

Tim is judged harshly, and the other youngsters stone his children.

"When the works open again and Tim stands at the door while his former friends pass by, five or six pass him, some with contempt, and one looks upon him, Tim Mahoney, his old friend who is now a scab, with such wonder that the fact seems not believable. It is a shaft that goes home to Tim's heart. . . . That scene has not been beaten in any picture, so far as we know."[145]

Alice Guy Blaché, as a director of Solax, was a factory owner herself, and her films on labor problems were thus unlikely to contain much of a radical flavor. Gerald Peary, who has seen some of them, says they were "reactionary . . . stringently anti-strike, pro-management and deal typically with a worker protagonist forced to strike against his will who discovers proof of the 'goodness' of the boss and leads the men back to work, and away from their 'unreasonable' demands."[146]

This is certainly true of *The Strike* (1912). It is impossible to know whether

Madame Blaché directed it, but she would have supervised it even if one of her employees did the actual directing. At a meeting in a union hall we are introduced to the Agitator (who looks Italian) and the Hero, Jack Smith (who looks Anglo-Saxon). Jack is appointed to speak to the boss, but the latter refuses the workers' demands. They pour out of the factory and, ignoring their employer's pleas, express their anger by smashing windows. The union committee decides to wreck the factory at midnight. Once again, our man Jack gets the short straw. After hiding the bomb, Jack goes to a mass meeting which is hardly under way when he is called to the phone. A split-screen effect conveys that his home has caught fire. Jack runs out and flags down a car. It contains the boss. Together they speed to the burning house and rescue Jack's wife and child. And Jack disposes of the bomb. Next morning, the workers deliver a letter via Jack's little girl: "We've had enough strike, boss, and are all ready for work. We all think you're a fine fellow after last night, so let the whistle blow." At the factory, the boss stands beside the little girl and shakes the hand of each worker as he reports for duty.

The film is melodrama rather than propaganda, but the message is strong, nonetheless: survival means cooperation. It is perhaps significant that the "hero" seems committed to placing a bomb in the factory, as though, after the McNamara case, Madame Blaché imagined all discontented American workers were potential dynamiters.

How different is Solax's *The High Cost of Living,* a courtroom drama also made in 1912. Joel Smith, an old ironworker, tells his story to the judge. He has given half a century to his employer. While the cost of living has soared, he and the other workers have had no raise in pay. They strike, but the boss stands firm. Faced with starvation, Joel tries to beg, but cannot bring himself to do so. His only alternative is to go back to the forge. A young worker calls him a coward; they fight with sledgehammers, and Joel kills the youth. In jail, he hears of the death of his youngest child. Joel pleads with the judge to put an end to his sufferings.

The old man is played by a young actor, in unconvincing make-up. Equally artificial are the sets. But what a fascinating glimpse into the conditions of the time this film represents!

Mindful of their audience, manufacturers usually avoided showing workers at each other's throats. But the Selig film *The Girl at the Cupola* (1912), directed by Oscar Eagle, dealt with the painful subject of industrial inefficiency. Jessie Wilson (Kathlyn Williams) is engaged to Jack Berry (Charles Clary), who is known as "the Business Doctor" for his success in reviving ailing companies. Jessie's father runs just such a company, the Wilson Iron Foundry. Jack Berry takes the reins and fires the elderly workers, explaining that more expert men are required.

Jessie, furious with Jack, supports the employees who go out on strike. She tips them off when Jack brings in a trainload of strikebreakers. The strikers fortify themselves at the saloon, then pounce on the new men. Jessie retreats to the factory to protect Jack, but the fighting men burst in. They find him at the cupola door, trying to keep the fire burning. They almost kill him before Jessie, heating an iron in the furnace, repels them.

A week later a letter is circulated by Wilson: "My daughter has pleaded your case and won. Men over 60 years of age will be pensioned; all others may go back to work."

The print ends here, so we don't see how the Business Doctor copes without his expert foundrymen. What is fascinating, apart from some fine exteriors and shots of the foundry in action, is to see a film, albeit only mildly pro-labor, which condones violence.

Thanhouser's *The Strike* (1914), directed by Henry Harrison Lewis and Carl Louis Gregory, who was also the cameraman, deplored violence. Although its aim was to show the need for arbitration, reviewers found it far too partisan toward the employers: "The one error seems to be the placing of labor unions in a too unfavorable light, even granting the dangerous character of professional agitators such as Black, the troublemaker in this story. We are shown the worst elements of organized labor and none of the better; whereas capital is the virtuous, innocent party, save for a persistent obstinacy in refusing to compromise."[147]

The film does not say so, but the implication is that Black is an I.W.W. man. He enters the contented village of Peacedale and unionizes the employees of the Trask factory. When a worker is fired for incompetence, Black triggers a strike, which brings misery and poverty to the community. A worker who protests is beaten up. Finally, Black dynamites the factory. Trask declares that rather than rebuild it and have to deal with such an impossible man, he will quit the business. And so he does, leaving the community shattered and without prospect of employment.[148]

AN AMERICAN IN THE MAKING   Thanhouser had made *The Cry of the Children,* and its policy was not wholeheartedly anti-labor. But it was perhaps significant that the company made films "sponsored" by the big corporations. A good example is *An American in the Making* (1913), which Thanhouser identified as a safety-first film produced by the National Social Betterment Association.[149] Actually, it was produced under the direction of the United States Steel Corporation, and its Committee of Safety, for the Bureau of Mines.[150]

A Hungarian peasant receives passage money from his brother in America. He kisses his parents with joy and starts packing. We see him arrive in America, disembarking from the Ellis Island ferry at the Battery.[151] A label on his coat is clearly visible; Bela Tokaji, Gary, Indiana. Unusually for an immigrant film, an American comes to his aid and helps him load his heavy trunk on his shoulder.

His brother greets him at Gary and shows him the workingman's model city. Bela works hard, attends night school, becomes a skilled laborer, and marries a schoolteacher. "His happiness as the head of a family is shown, and also the interest which the great Corporation takes of its employees, and their willingness to advance those who are ambitious and competent."[152]

Up to this point, the film might be a thinly disguised recruiting film for cheap foreign labor. Only at the end comes the sequence which justifies its description as a safety-first film: shots of the protection installed on machines, guards over belts and pulleys, and the fans used to cool the fierce heat of the steelworks. (Such evidence was also good for recruiting.) There are some impressive shots of Bes-

The Workman's Lesson

Produced in co-operation with the U.S. National Association of Manufacturers

The National Association of Manufacturers showed this at their convention at the Waldorf-Astoria Hotel, New York. An Italian is put to work on a lathe; he leaves the safety device open and mangles his arm. Bigelow Cooper (left) and George Lessey. (David Robinson)

semer converters, showering the screen with sparks. The picture ends with the immigrant's son going to school—another American in the making. (Gary's schools were the country's leading exemplars of progressive education.)

The attitude of the employer was revealed in a U.S. Steel publication which referred to the film as the story of an "ignorant Hungarian peasant . . . stupid and uneducated," who prospers thanks to the company's safety and welfare programs.[153]

The yellow press, which found no space to discuss documentaries in the normal course of events, leaped on this one. "Samuel W. Gleason, superintendent of the Gary steel mills, is wondering what his daughter, Mary Louise, will say when she gets back from California and finds a majority of the workmen believe she is the heroine of the courtship. The mill scenes, the office scenes displayed in the movie being real, it is puzzling the superintendent how to suppress the belief among the workmen that the remainder of the scenes are real."[154]

C. J. Hite, president of Thanhouser, angrily replied that the Gleasons had not insisted on changes; the film did not tell the story of the superintendent, nor did it portray the courtship of his daughter: "The film merely tells the story of an immigrant who gets a job in the steel works and is enabled in time to buy a little house and marry a young school teacher. The whole article is an injustice to Mr. Gleason and his daughter, who were not mentioned even remotely in the film."[155]

Employers did not often sponsor entertainment films. Their use of the moving picture reflected their self-interest. During strikes, some employed cameramen to film disturbances so that troublemakers could be recognized and charged.[156]

So few pictures supported labor that union men protested. In 1910, delegates to the American Federation of Labor convention had called for a boycott of movie theatres which showed antilabor films. The "boycott" was too mild to have any effect. In 1915, union men were still protesting—still far too mildly. One wrote to a Washington paper that he resented "these flagrantly unfair and prejudiced attacks upon the workers of the country, and on more than one occasion have expressed my opinion to the managers of the theaters, who have usually replied that this is the sort of play the film companies furnish, and that they are obliged to take what they can get. If this is the case and if it is the result of a definite policy of the film manufacturers to discredit working men, who are the chief patrons of the 5 and 10 cent houses, I should think this would be a subject which union labor might do well to look into."[157]

But at least one film presented a strike with approval. George Melford's *The Struggle* (1913), from a story by Henry Albert Phillips, was praised for its unusual

Steel workers played alongside the actors in this drama, directed by George Melford. The Struggle, *1913, was one of the few films to sympathize with strikers. Paul Hurst plays the brutal foreman (left). From* Moving Picture World, *June 7, 1913. (Academy of Motion Picture Arts and Sciences)*

theme: the scandalous absentee owners of industrial property, who take the profits but care nothing for the welfare of their employees. Melford staged scenes in a rolling mill, and steelworkers played alongside the actors. The foreman whose brutal behavior causes the strike was played by Paul C. Hurst, who specialized in villains (and later became a director).

Melford returned to this theme in 1915 with *Out of Darkness*, a Lasky feature from a Hector Turnbull scenario. An accident causes Helen Scott (Charlotte Walker) to lose her memory, and she is obliged to earn her living (thirty cents a day) in a Florida canning factory where hundreds of children are employed. The workers strike, and the factory is set on fire. A mob tries to kill the manager. The excitement restores her memory—she recalls that she is the owner of the factory. "She sets to work to rebuild it to conform with the laws of sanitation and humanity."[158]

The Strike at Coaldale (1914) presented a more ambivalent situation. This Eclair drama featured Stanley Walpole as Joe Gregory, a power in the union and an engineer on the Coaldale Railroad. Conditions are bad; a strike is threatened. Edith Harland (Mildred Bright), daughter of the president of the line, pleads with Joe to avert the strike. The president, a proud and autocratic man, rejects the workers' demands. The strike begins.

The president hires strikebreakers; violence erupts. Edith suffers a concussion and must be rushed to the hospital, but no trains are running. The president pleads with the strikers, who refuse to cooperate. Joe Gregory intercedes: a human life is at stake, says he. Do the men want to be branded as murderers? But they are adamant, so Gregory takes a train out himself. The strikers set fire to a trestle bridge in the path of the locomotive, and Gregory, risking death, drives through the flames.

He gets Edith to the hospital in time, but Gregory is repudiated by his union. The strikers capture the president and threaten to kill him. Gregory appeals to them, successfully this time, and regains his former position. Then he turns on the president and, with Edith, pleads the strikers' cause. At last, the men's demands are met. And Gregory is promoted to superintendent of the Coaldale Railroad.[159]

All this in one reel! *Moving Picture World* thought it achieved "perfect direction and the strike is most realistic." A railroad trestle was actually burned for the making of this picture, costing the Eclair Company hundreds of dollars.[160] Pennsylvania and Ohio censors banned the film because, despite the desperate acts committed by the strikers, it was still regarded as being prolabor,[161] too inflammatory to be let loose on the people without being slashed to ribbons.

A film about a labor leader was an unlikely subject for a feature, yet Favorite (not Famous) Players produced a six-reeler called *The High Hand* in 1915.[162] Directed by William Desmond Taylor, it showed "Honest" Jim Warren (Carlyle Blackwell), a former foundryman, waging war against entrenched graft and rising to governor. Oddly enough, the film's history worked against it in the opinion of reviewers: "That he himself, feeling unable to cope with political conditions by open-handed methods, stoops to do the same kind of dirty work that his opponents do, even with the clean purpose of doing away with bad conditions, is the story's most hampering burden," said *Moving Picture World*, admitting that in real life the man might have done just that, but in the story the audience's interest in him drops as a result.[163]

Considering that most films—populist, socialist, or simply the many apolitical melodramas—showed factory owners as villains, it is surprising that the industrialists permitted film people anywhere near their property. (Perhaps they never went to the movies.) Homestead Mills, Pennsylvania, was used as location for *The Cave Man* (1915); Galloway Oil Fields, near Franklin, Pennsylvania, for *Those Who Toil* (1916); and cotton mills at Anniston, Alabama, for *The Quality of Faith* (1916).

The whole town of Las Vegas, New Mexico, turned out to help Romaine Fielding stage *The Golden God* (1914), a capital-versus-labor epic set in 1950, when "giant labor will strike its tyrant Gold."[164] Fielding imagined that by that time, labor unrest would be on the scale of a small war, and with the example of Ludlow (see pages 481–83), no one could blame him.

Fielding himself led a cavalry charge in a car fitted with a machine gun, while a fleet of airplanes flew overhead. The National Guard, surprisingly (considering its record in the suppression of strikes), cooperated in all this.

When a film was intended to condemn the very manufacturers whose cooperation it sought, the filmmakers were forced to disguise their intentions. So it was with the most notorious of all anticapitalist films of this period, *The Jungle*.

THE JUNGLE   An ironic paragraph appeared in the trade press in April 1914, in a review of a Victor film called *U.S. Government Inspection of Meat:* "It was seven years ago that the present law came into effect, requiring veterinary inspectors authorized by the U.S. Government to be stationed in every slaughtering and packing establishment of importance in the country. These experts safeguard the public health by detecting tuberculosis and other diseases in animals and carcasses. But the average person knows little about how this work is carried on. The film goes into practically every detail of the inspection work. . . . The various scenes have been taken in one of the biggest slaughtering and packing establishments in the country."[165]

The reviewer stopped short of saying where the scenes had been shot, for the very name "Chicago" summoned up horrific images from Upton Sinclair's novel *The Jungle*, a film version of which would be reviewed in this same column within a couple of months. *The Jungle* was the most scathing indictment of an industry ever written. Published in 1906, it was described by Jack London as "the *Uncle Tom's Cabin* of wage slavery."[166] The meat packers did all they could to suppress it. But a congressional committee vindicated Sinclair and the public outcry brought about the Meat Inspection Act of 1906. An American industry, responsible for poisoning its own country's troops in the Spanish-American War, was reformed by a book.

By the time the film version of *The Jungle* appeared, the passage of the Pure Food and Drug Act had improved the situation. But it was still far from satisfactory, and films like *Poison* (Kalem, 1915) charged the food industry with continued negligence.[167]

The Jungle, turned down by five publishers, had been translated into seventeen languages. "I aimed at the public's heart," wrote Sinclair, "and by accident I hit it in the stomach."[168] The book is so graphic and uncompromising that certain passages are still hard to read without a sense of nausea. As an indictment of the meat-packing industry, it is shattering. Yet it was not meant to be so restricted: Sinclair intended it as a study of the worst effects of capitalism, followed by a lecture on socialism.

The story centers on a Lithuanian immigrant named Jurgis and his family, who arrive in Chicago (Packingtown in the film) and go to work in the stockyards. Jurgis is laid off when he sprains his ankle, and soon his family faces starvation. He beats his son to force the lad through the snow to work.

A member of the family dies from eating poisoned food—much of what the packing plant ships to the public is poisoned in one way or another. (Occasionally, a worker will slip and fall into one of the vats. There is no way the others can get the body out, so he goes on to be processed as pure leaf lard.) Jurgis eventually gets a new job in the fertilizer plant, where all workers are doomed, so appalling are the conditions. He takes to drink, discovers his wife is earning extra money as a part-time prostitute, smashes the head of the man who led her to this fate, and is sent to jail for thirty days. When he is released he finds that his family has been evicted. His wife dies in childbirth; Jurgis becomes a hobo. He returns to the Chicago packers as a strikebreaker and is promoted to foreman. But it doesn't last, and soon he is back on the streets again, facing a slow death by starvation in the icy winter. Dropping in at a political meeting to keep warm, he is introduced to socialist doctrine and becomes a new man. He takes part in a wildly successful socialist campaign, and the story ends on a note of optimism: "We shall bear down the opposition, we shall sweep it before us—and Chicago will be ours! CHICAGO WILL BE OURS!"[169]

Margaret Mayo, wife of dramatist Edgar Selwyn, adapted the book as a play, but Sinclair considered it poor. It came to New York and lost money—much of it Sinclair's. So the scenario for the film was taken from the novel, following it closely, although a layer of melodrama was inevitable. "But all the scenes of the packing house and the doping of the meat are shown, and likewise all the sufferings of a working-class family."[170]

The film was produced by the All-Star Feature Corporation, whose president was Harry Raver, a former publicity man with a circus. The vice president was Archibald Selwyn, the theatrical producer, and its director-general Augustus Thomas, the distinguished playwright.[171] All-Star publicity stressed that every film would be made under the personal direction of Thomas.

This was the 1914 equivalent of Arthur Miller directing films of his own plays. A former newspaper reporter, illustrator, and law student, Thomas had written his first successful play, *Alabama,* in 1891. He was probably best known for *The Witching Hour* (1907). More significantly, he had been a labor leader for six years while working as a railroad brakeman.[172]

To help Thomas with the technical side, two other directors, George Irving and John H. Pratt (who also acted in the film), were brought in. Virtually all the players were active on the Broadway stage and had to be rushed back to the theatres every evening. Picture people wondered how All-Star got the footage of the stockyards without the owners realizing the true nature of the film. In fact, the yards were filmed in New Jersey rather than Chicago,[173] and, according to William S. Hart, All-Star represented its film to the meat packers as something other than *The Jungle*. The meat packers granted permission for exteriors to be filmed at their yards, and the company matched these exteriors with studio interiors "showing all sorts of frightful stockyard stuff that was as revolting as it was untrue."[174] (Why Hart took the meat packers' side is unknown.)

The picture cost $17,000.[175] Sinclair himself considered it "a great success" and "an honest attempt to represent my ideas."[176] *Moving Picture World* called it "somewhat daring and powerful. Many gripping scenes obtain, especially where Jurgis, after a desperate struggle, flings the foreman into the cattle run of the stockyard. The mob scenes during the strike against a reduction of 20 per cent in wages, ordered by the packing house magnate, on account of the extravagance of his family, are cleverly directed and extremely realistic."[177]

The cast included George Nash, Gail Kane, Robert Cummings, Clarence Handyside, Julia Hurley, and Ernest Evers. Upton Sinclair was seen at the start at his typewriter, and he acted in the closing scenes, playing the socialist orator. He appeared onstage when the film was shown at the Broadway Theatre in New York.[178]

Clement Wood, writing in the socialist paper *Appeal to Reason* (which had first published the novel), described the film with enthusiasm: "And all this being shown in pictures that stir the brain and tear the feelings, that bring tears to the eyes of women and men, that shock and arouse and awake . . . all combine to drive the lesson of Socialism home with a point and a snap that it has never before possessed."[179]

Variety's critic Sime (Sime Silverman, the paper's founder) was one of the few dissenters on June 6: "More misery! And the gloom in *The Jungle* was laid on with a shovel. This is not a feature picture of wild animals, just about wild socialists, that's all—and the Lord knows that's enough."

The picture opened on June 1, 1914, at the 2,000-seat De Kalb Theatre in Brooklyn, and later at the Broadway Theatre in New York City. It had a two-week run at Woodley's Theatre in Los Angeles before moving to Clune's, where *The Birth of a Nation* would open. Here it was accompanied by a twenty-piece orchestra and, according to Sinclair, was highly profitable.[180] "The board of censorship barred it from Chicago," he wrote, "and you will understand that this is a compliment to its truth."[181]

By the end of 1915, Sinclair began receiving disturbing reports. One correspondent told him that some of the best scenes were missing or incomplete and the film kept breaking. Sabotage was suspected, but actually the prints had been run to death. New copies were made and fan mail from socialists across the country flooded in, calling *The Jungle* the best socialist film in existence.[182] Sinclair felt that Augustus Thomas had more honesty and fair-mindedness than the average. But those who handled the picture, Harry Raver and Co., "milked the company of the profits, and then threw it into bankruptcy and I got practically nothing from this play."[183] What he did get, however, was the negative, which his wife

(Pacific Film Archive)

purchased for $250 during the bankruptcy proceedings. He made many attempts to have the film shown and in 1920 began negotiations with Joseph D. Cannon, founder of the Labor Film Service, to reissue it.

Cannon was a Seattle-born Socialist candidate for governor of New York who had been an organizer with the International Union of Mine, Mill, and Smelter Workers of the Mining Department of the A.F.L. He was a great admirer of Sinclair's work and thought parts of the picture "splendid," but that overall it did not measure up to the novel. *"The Jungle* is entitled to something bigger and better than that."[184] He suggested cutting certain scenes and filming additional material.

Sinclair was happy about these changes,[185] and Cannon agreed to distribute the film, perhaps through Pathé—although they soon dropped the idea. For a while nothing happened, and Sinclair, with his very low opinion of moving picture people, suspected he had been double-crossed yet again. But Cannon was fighting to survive in an atmosphere poisoned by the Red Scare. Once he had found the money, he embarked on all the changes he had promised, spending the sum of $2,498.13. In August 1921, he submitted the film to the National Board of Review (together with *The Contrast,* about a coal strike).

"One heavy-set man of about fifty became almost choleric," he wrote to Sinclair. "He branded *The Jungle* as the most un-American picture that was ever shown. The very idea that we invited foreigners to come over here and then even to intimate that they received any such treatment as shown in *The Jungle* was an outrage."[186]

The subcommittee turned the picture down, and Cannon appealed for a showing before the full board: "Two members of the Board were friendly, not friendly perhaps to *The Jungle,* but friendly to common sense. They felt that in the end an adverse report on the picture would hurt the board more than it would hurt the picture, although it would have been extremely embarrassing to Labor Film for the time being." At the end of an exhausting, four-hour session, Cannon reported that both *The Jungle* and *The Contrast* had been passed. But he warned Sinclair, "There is going to be a terrific fight to keep *The Jungle* off the screen."[187]

The Jungle was passed . . . with cuts. "You remember when they held their noses while passing the yards. We had put a title in there 'Not just the "sweet" land of liberty.' Some members of the Board objected that that might be interpreted as unpatriotic."[188]

Cannon reported that Armour and Company had asked *Exhibitors Trade Review* for details of the personnel of the Labor Film Service.[189] And Augustus Thomas, presumably regretting his association with the film, wrote to the Labor Film Service denying any connection with *The Jungle.* (By this time, Thomas had made the antisocialist film *The Volcano,* and he undoubtedly knew that he would be selected as executive chairman of the governing body of theatrical producers, the Producing Managers Association, to which he would be appointed in 1922.) Sinclair was baffled and, somewhat naively, wrote to him: "I am not sure whether this is a lapse of memory on your part, or some misunderstanding on my part as to the meaning of the word 'direct.' "[190] He recounted how he had watched Thomas, apparently in full charge of the making of the film, giving instructions to the actors and how his name had been used in the film's advertisements. Thomas's reply is missing, but somehow Sinclair became convinced that *another* man with a similar name had done the work, for in his autobiography he wrote: "An odd confusion there—the show was being directed by A. E. Thomas; I took this to be Augustus Thomas and named him so as the director, greatly to his surprise."[191]

A. E. Thomas was also a playwright who specialized in light comedies. He was never credited as being part of All-Star, whereas the name of Augustus Thomas was boasted in almost every advertisement. But even if there was confusion, and A. E. Thomas had been mysteriously introduced into All-Star, posing as his namesake, there is one other fact to be taken into consideration. The star of *The Jungle* was George Nash. And George Nash was Augustus Thomas's favorite actor.

In November 1921, the Assistant Secretary of the Department of Agriculture, C. W. Pugsley, wrote to the Labor Film Service that *The Jungle* gave an erroneous impression of the conditions existing at packing houses under the supervision of the federal meat inspection force.[192] He objected to the display of filthy conditions in the manufacturing of sausage: the scene showing that the contents of a tank in which an employee had been scalded to death is manufactured into edible lard, the scene showing a spoiled ham. And the department had worked out a way to play upon the feelings of the Labor Film Service: "You are doubtless familiar with the condition of agriculture at the present time. The prices of grain, forage and other farm products are ruinously low. The film will certainly interfere with the consumption of meat and such interference will be to the great disadvantage of farmers and consumers directly and labor indirectly."[193] Furthermore, the department did not consider adequate the insertion of statements, suggested by Cannon, that there was now a federal inspection of meat and that the packing houses were sanitary.

Cannon sent this letter to Sinclair, who replied, "I will carefully cherish their letter."[194] And when the picture was presented at Tucson, Arizona, on Labor Day 1921, Sinclair declared: "The condition of the stockyard workers is exactly the same today as in 1906."

In 1922, Cannon spent a great deal of money on publicity for the new version of *The Jungle.* He had a new print struck, but he was horrified by the result, for the laboratory had done a wretched job. "The thing has done us irreparable harm," he said. Worse news followed for the perennially hard-up Sinclair: The Labor Film Service could send him no money.

The laboratory's excuse was the one used to this day: it's an old film, what do you expect?[195] There was a further setback when it opened in May at the Fifth Avenue Theatre, for the picture drew a response very different from its first appearance in 1914. The left-wing New York *Call* attacked it so vehemently, accusing it of overemphasis and melodrama, that Cannon was driven to defend the film in print.[196]

In June, the picture was booked into the Winter Garden Theatre on Houston Street and Second Avenue.[197] The month's run proved a disaster. That, and the faulty film, came close to putting Labor Film Service out of business.[198] Sinclair came east to help with the publicity, but exhibitors would have nothing to do with Labor Film Service. "The financial interests which control the trade were too strong to overcome," wrote Sinclair.[199]

The following year came enquiries from Russia. The president of Politkino, Joseph Malkin,* asked Sinclair to send *The Jungle* to the Soviet Union. Sinclair explained that he had examined the negative and found it absolutely ruined: "When it was unwound this time great strips of the material came off entirely, so there is nothing left." Sinclair was probably mistaking the simple breaking of joins with disintegration of celluloid, but in any case he decided the only course was to make a duplicate negative from his print. "I take it you would rather have a picture which is poor from the technique point of view, but which speaks to the working class in its own language, rather than have the most perfect and costly reproduction of the trash and corruption which fills our moving picture theatres at the present time."[200]

The Russians decided they could not afford a negative, even at cost, but after fresh negotiations they imported the picture. So did the Scandinavians. In 1927, Sinclair attempted to distribute the film himself, but encountered even stiffer resistance. The New York censors reported, "Too many immoral scenes and subtitles. At the conclusion of the picture and throughout there is an attempt to force Socialistic propaganda on the minds of the audience, with a general denunciation of factory workers as the slaves of greed. The picture is immoral throughout, both in theme and subtitle, and is unsuitable for public presentation."[201]

The only way the censors would permit it to be shown was in fragments. They demanded the removal of the following titles: "This ham is rotten," "We sell every

---

*One of the emissaries sent by Lenin to D. W. Griffith asking him to take charge of the Russian film industry (William Drew).

part of the pig except the squeal," "The workmen refuse to accept the wage cut—
they are underpaid as it is," "They grind up the workers as well as the animals
in their great machines. They turn sweat and blood into gold. They care nothing
for the workers save the money they can make out of them. The workers are slaves
of greed."[202]

And besides the titles, many scenes had to be sacrificed.

By the time he wrote his autobiography, Sinclair had changed his mind about
the quality of the film: "It was a poor picture; the concern went into bankruptcy,
and so ended another dream. All I got was the film, and I loaned it to some
organization and never got it back. Whoever has it, please return it!"[203]

THE TRIANGLE FIRE   Safety precautions in factories and sweatshops were rudimentary at best; 15,000 people were killed in industry every year,
and half a million were crippled.[204] The greatest danger was fire. On March 25,
1911, a blaze at the Triangle Shirtwaist Company in New York killed 146 girls, some
in the flames and others who jumped out the windows. Overcrowded, poorly
ventilated, the floor littered with combustible material, the place was a tinderbox,
and when the owner bolted the steel door leading to the stairway to prevent
"interruption of work" by employees using the toilet,[205] he condemned most of
them to death.

Selig's The Still Alarm, *1911, came out two months after the Triangle Fire and was thus highly
topical, even if it was based on an old play. Selig remade it in 1918. (Robert S. Birchard
Collection)*

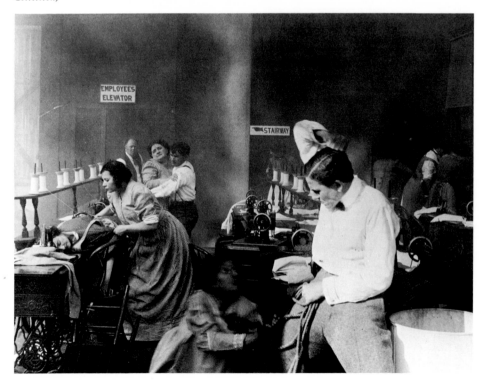

The Crime of Carelessness (1912), written by James Oppenheim, a former settlement worker who had scripted *Hope,* was produced by Edison for the National Association of Manufacturers, so it could hardly lay the blame entirely on employers. But while it shows a worker causing a fire, it has the employer admitting his own responsibility, too.

A worker called Tom (Barry O'Moore) becomes engaged to Hilda (Mabel Trunnelle), who works in the same mill. They plan their future home. Although reprimanded for smoking, Tom lights up in the cellars, discarding a match which ignites a pile of rubbish. As the flames spread, the workers panic. Hilda rushes to the nearest fire door to find it locked; she faints in the heat. Tom races back into the inferno and rescues her. When he admits his responsibility for the fire, he is discharged. All the workers are laid off; the feeling against Tom is so strong he cannot get work. He becomes poorer and poorer, and he lives with the agony of having crippled Hilda. He considers suicide.

Visiting the mill-owner (Bigelow Cooper), Hilda accuses him. "It's your fault I have crutches," she shouts, referring to the locked fire door. He is stunned and sits for a moment in shock. At length, he writes a letter to Tom, admitting they are both to blame and offering him a job in the new factory.

A couple of interiors were filmed in a real mill, but the acting is exaggerated, and the burning factory is a palpable miniature. The one-reeler is primitive in every way, but it undoubtedly caused people to think—a considerable achievement in itself.

As Steven Ross points out, however, the fact that mill and garment factory owners had persistently ignored union demands for improved safety conditions was overlooked.[206]

Based on the Triangle fire, and widely admired at the time, although forgotten since, was a three-reeler called *The Locked Door* (1914). Produced in collaboration with the Fire and Police Departments of New York City, it was written by W. B. Northrup, and directed by Tefft Johnson, who played a leading role.

"Among photoplays with a deeper purpose than that of fleeting entertainment," wrote the New York *Dramatic Mirror,* "*The Locked Door* must be given a prominent place. With the horror of the Triangle fire fading into the shadow of years, it is quite worthwhile to produce a picture illustrating the way to invite and the way to avert another such catastrophe."[207]

The film contrasted the attitude to safety of two companies. In the Atlas Syndicate loft, run by Jacob Emanuel (Edward Elkas), young women work at sewing machines with scarcely any elbow room between them. The narrow aisles are littered with discarded material; the foreman is a chain smoker. The door to the hallway is locked, and fire extinguishers are regarded as a needless expense.

In the same building, one flight up, Arnold Forsythe (Tefft Johnson) and his son (William Dunn) run a much safer establishment, fitted with fire extinguishers, sprinkler pipes, and containers for waste material. Stella Rubinow (Eulalie Jensen) is discharged for repeatedly breaking the safety rules and gets her revenge—and another job—by telling Emanuel of a door in Forsythe's factory that violates fire ordinances by opening in, not out. Emanuel, who has often been threatened by Forsythe, calls in the Fire Department. Forsythe demonstrates his safety devices

Viola Dana and director John Collins (perched at the foot of the bed) on the set of The Children of Eve, *1915. Ned Van Buren at camera, with Robert Walker, the leading man, and assistant Albert Kelley. Filmed at Edison Studios, Bronx, New York. (George J. Mitchell)*

and promises to fix the door—then suggests an examination of Emanuel's factory. The old man is shocked when he sees the inspector and complains that he cannot afford proper fire prevention devices. "You'll have to afford it," says the inspector, threatening to close him up in a week. When he has gone, Emanuel creeps upstairs and sets the Forsythe factory alight. The safety devices save Forsythe's, but the Emanuel floor is soon consumed in flame.[208]

The Children of Eve (1915), a Lower East Side drama, directed by John Collins and starring Viola Dana, climaxed with a horrific fire sequence (with the inevitable locked door) shot at Fort Schuyler. An empty four-story brick factory, filled with waste film and gasoline, was set alight. It burned too well, and Ned van Buren, the cameraman, was marooned on a camera platform sixty feet above the ground, in considerable danger, until the front of the building collapsed and the heat was reduced.[209]

The same year, John Noble made *The High Road,* a Metro five-reeler adapted from an Edward Sheldon play. It was a pre-Hays picture in every sense, with the leading character, Mary Page (Valli Valli) becoming the mistress of a man in the city. After three years, she "suddenly awakens to the enormity of her offense" and leaves for a job in a factory. She leads a strike which is unsuccessful. The girls are forced to work overtime to make up for lost orders. To prevent anyone leaving early, the manager locks the door. The building catches fire; panic and terror lead to many casualties.

In the last sequences, Mary Page prevents the factory owner from avoiding the blame.[210] (The owners of the building destroyed in the Triangle fire brought in a devious lawyer who won their acquittal, proving that the deaths of the garment workers were all their own fault.)[211]

THE LUDLOW MASSACRE   The Ludlow Massacre of Easter 1914 was triggered by a strike at the Colorado Fuel and Iron Company, owned by John D. Rockefeller, Jr. The company was run as a dictatorship—it even censored the movies its employees saw.[212] The workers were housed in deplorable conditions.[213] When the United Mine Workers attempted to negotiate such improvements as an eight-hour day, the company refused even to enter discussions and forced striking employees to move from these company-owned houses to union-built camps which were even worse—pits covered with tents.

After a savage battle at Trinidad, Colorado, the National Guard arrived to be welcomed by the strikers as peacemakers. The Guard imposed a truce, but when Governor Ammons decided it should be used to protect strikebreakers, the truce was shattered.

The strikers at Ludlow took on the militia, who blazed away at them with rifles and machine gun for hours. The Guardsmen charged part of the camp, where women and children were sheltered, and doused the tents with kerosene. "There rose up," recalled a lieutenant, "the most awful wail I ever heard in my life."[214] The flames roared through the camp; soldiers and guards fired at anyone trying to escape. When the fire died down six adults were found shot in their tracks; eleven children and two pregnant women were found burned to death.

The strikers' grief and fury caused the warfare to spread as the fire had done. Governor Ammons appealed to President Wilson, and Federal troops put an end to Colorado's civil war, in which more than forty people had died.

Congressional investigations laid the blame on John D. Rockefeller, Jr., who had become a figure of odium in both working-class circles and on the screen.

By a remarkable coincidence, two future Hollywood cameramen, Harry Perry and Victor Milner, were on opposite sides of the Colorado coal mine war. Perry had joined the National Guard for fun, but in 1914 he was called out on strike duty near Trinidad, and, as he put it, "The fun was running out. I will always regret having had any part in those infamous days of 1914.

"The National Guard had been called to duty to restore order. Our troops were posted over an extended area, on the fringe of engagements between rightfully bitter, striking coal miners and some very tough, company-hired strike breakers.

"Many of us who had to serve felt that we were being 'used,' to help the mine owners more than the miners—who had really been getting a raw deal for too long a time. They worked extremely long hours underground for terribly inadequate pay."[215]

One afternoon Perry was drowsing in his saddle when explosions of dust erupted on the ground.

"Looking up, I saw the flash of rifle fire repeated in the hills. Somebody was trying to kill me. Crouching low over my mount's shoulder, I wheeled him about and gave him the spur for both our lives. Thank the Lord, whoever was shooting was a lousy marksman!"[216]

Milner, at that time known as Miller, was a newsreel cameraman covering the strike for Pathé News. He, too, came under fire—although from the other side.

"The most hostile reception that I ever received," he wrote, "was in the city of Trinidad, Colorado. The editor of the Denver Post informed me that there was a real mean strike going on. The miners there were justifiably striking for better wages, treatment and living conditions. The owners of the mines who for all purposes owned Trinidad were militantly determined to break the strike. Up to the time I got there, they had been able to prevent any news not to their liking getting out of the area. When I checked into the hotel, I was met by the local sheriff and told that I had better not take my camera out of the hotel, if I knew what was good for me and wanted to remain healthy. He also told me to leave town the following day. He did let me wander out of the hotel that evening and I dropped into a local bar where I met a few miners. When they learned my business, they arranged to get my camera, film and suitcase smuggled out of the hotel. Early the next morning they took me to the scene of the strike. It was really a battlefield, trains had been sandbagged and everyone was armed to the teeth."[217]

Denver *Post* reporters filled in the next chapter of the event, which Milner was too modest to describe. Their account is undoubtedly exaggerated, but the conflict at Ludlow was murderous enough to justify some of it. The reporters were amazed at Milner's courage and gave him considerable space in the coverage of the fight:

"The bullets came so fast and thick about the newspapermen at the depot that the telephone and telegraph wires overhead were repeatedly struck, as if from hailstones. The zip-zip of the dying lead continued unabated all about the station for twenty minutes, but not a person was scratched.

"But what was even more remarkable and what will explain at least in a large measure just why it is that so many shots are wasted in a gun fight of this character, was the escape from injury of Victor Miller, cameraman for Pathé's Weekly. He stood out in the open, grinding away at his camera as calmly as though he was taking moving pictures of one of those 'actor' battles.

"All about him, kneeling, lying flat, or crawling across the ground almost beneath his feet, the strikers were emptying their rifles at the approaching guards. Over on a hillock came the rat-tat-tat of a machine gun that was belching 250 steel-jacketed bullets a minute in the direction of the miners.

"Those bullets sang a song of promised death as they whirred just over Miller's head. Watching him closely, and noting from the freight cars on adjacent side-tracks to his rear the course of the bullets, it was seen that he was directly in the path of the big gun's hail of lead. It seemed that he must be struck. But still he continued to grind away, and even after the guards had retreated to their train and it had pulled out around the distant curve, Miller remained on the job, taking 'movies' of the returning miners, who had started in the futile pursuit of the guards.

" 'I didn't have time to get scared,' said Miller, packing up his camera. 'It was too rare a chance for a real battle picture for me to think of anything else but the work ahead of me. . . . After it was all over I began to think of the many narrow escapes I must have had, but it was all over then, so why worry?' ''[218]

In a letter to me, Milner added the climax to the incident: "I got a car to drive me out of town. Somehow the locals learned about it and chased me for a long way. I am sure to this day that if my Model T hadn't been a bit faster than theirs I would have been buried in Trinidad. I don't think I was ever more scared in my life, but the pictures I took were of considerable value in getting public opinion and the law on the side of the miners. This was probably my most humanitarian achievement."[219]

When the newsreel was released in Colorado, it was confiscated by the state's attorney general and used as evidence in the prosecution of the striking miners.[220]

Selig joined in the labor wars with *The Lily of the Valley,* a 1914 Colin Campbell production which reminded a reviewer of "the very tragic conditions in Colorado recently."[221] The picture opened with a pitched battle. A militia lieutenant (Joe King) is half crazed by the killing of his sister, a mission worker, by strikers. He infiltrates the workforce and meets a girl (Bessie Eyton) as driven by revenge as he. She swears to kill the man who fired the machine gun which killed her father and brothers. That man happens to be the lieutenant; they fall in love and are on the verge of marriage when another strike breaks out and she discovers the truth. "Fortunately, he is killed by a bullet from the guns of the strikers," said the New York *Dramatic Mirror* unequivocally, "and the offering closes, as it opened, sadly."[222] The reviewer thought there was too much slaughter; otherwise he admired the film. "The mob in the attack on the factory shows its disorganized and alarming poverty as contrasted with the clean-cut and efficient militia and the smug satisfaction of the plutocrats."[223]

The synopsis of "Old King Coal," an episode of the 1915 Universal serial *Graft,* described "the usual misery attending the coal strikes; the brutality of the militia, and the savagery of the strikers towards strike breakers." At the end, "The militia quell the riot with the usual loss of life."[224]

The Blacklist (1916), a drama based on the system by which the big mining companies exchanged information about suspect employees, was written by Marion Fairfax and William de Mille, who also directed it. Fairfax obtained much of the material from firsthand interviews.[225]

According to *Variety,* "Superintendents of the mines are the real oppressors in most instances, the owners being uninformed of the local conditions. At one of the mines the state of affairs reaches fever heat over the killing of a miner by an armed guard. It causes unrest in the camp and the school mistress for the company (whose father is a miner) writes to the president complaining of conditions. He immediately leaves for the mine. Things become acute with his appearance and at first unwilling to give in to the demands of the men he is confronted with a strike. A number of the strikers are killed by the guards who use a rapid firing gun

William de Mille's drama based on the Ludlow miner's strike, The Blacklist, *1916, with Blanche Sweet (center). (DeMille Collection)*

against the orders of the president. The strikers have a meeting in which the one drawing a black pea from a bag is to kill the president. The school mistress is the unfortunate person."

She goes to the office but cannot bring herself to do it. Her dying father renews her courage, and she loads her gun with two bullets, one for the president and one for herself. "He in the meantime has fallen in love with her, the feeling being mutual between them. She has to fulfill her vow and fires at the man, only wounding him. In the ensuing struggle the other shot explodes with no material damage. His wound is slight. When recovering he grants the demands of the men and he and the school mistress intend to run the mine in co-partnership from then on."[226]

Variety omitted to mention that the schoolteacher (played by Blanche Sweet) was named Vera Maroff and was the daughter of a Russian anarchist, head of a group planning the overthrow of the corporation. The New York *Dramatic Mirror* called it "a socialistic drama." It thought Cecil B. DeMille had made the film and congratulated him on his realistic battle scene: "A spectacular climax was reached in the burning of the tent camp of the striking miners."[227]

Upton Sinclair was infuriated by the film, particularly since William de Mille was a friend of his: "He wrote me that he had made a drama of the struggle between capital and labor; he had really told the truth, he said, and I would be interested. So I went. Here were scenes in which the tent colony of the strikers was burned down by the mine guards—quite an unusual lot of industrial truth. But in the very beginning, I noticed that the movie star had had her hair dressed by a hairdresser ... If I had not been told on the screen that this was a miner's cabin and a miner's daughter, I would not have recognized it ... The strike was fought through and the problem of capital and labor solved. And how was it solved? Why, of course, there is only one way to solve the problem of capital and labor in the movies. It was solved by the daughter of the miner marrying the handsome young son of the owner of the mine." Sinclair admitted he could not recall the exact details—he was writing for *Screenland* in June 1930—but he intimated that he did not hurt William de Mille's feelings by telling him his opinion.

A more important truth the movies could not tell, and that was why the owner of the coal mine did not pay a living wage. "If he made terms with the union which didn't please the coal mine owners' association, he would be blacklisted and have his credit cut off; then he would find he couldn't get coal cars and before he knew it he would be out of business."[228]

Sinclair may have found the interior of the miner's cabin unconvincing, but the exteriors were authentic enough. De Mille took his company to a small mining town in Nevada for locations, where he found conditions more relaxed than in Colorado. The superintendent gave the miners a day off to play in mob scenes— the company being handsomely rewarded by the Lasky Feature Play Company.[229]

Schoolmistress Vera Maroff (Blanche Sweet) pleads on behalf of the children in
The Blacklist, *1916, William de Mille's drama of the Colorado mining camps.*
(DeMille Collection)

The San Francisco *Call and Post* considered *The Blacklist* a masterpiece, "with compelling situations, great story, flawless acting and wonderful photography."[230] After the film's first engagement at the Strand in New York, the Labor Forum endorsed it and sponsored an additional showing at Washington Irving High School to support their cause. William de Mille was rewarded by being placed on a blacklist himself. The Bureau of Investigation listed him as one of Hollywood's leading radicals.[231]

D. W. Griffith made John D. Rockefeller, Jr., responsible for the massacre of strikers in his *The Mother and the Law* (1914), which became "The Modern Story" in his massive *Intolerance* (1916). Using information from the report of the U.S. Commission on Industrial Relations, the film showed strikers being attacked by National Guardsmen with rifles and machine guns. Griffith shot the sequence in the streets of Los Angeles, staging part of it against a huge advertising sign: "The same today as yesterday."

We see Rockefeller (Sam de Grasse)—called Jenkins in the film—disbursing charity at the expense of his employees.[232] We see him supervising the morals of his workers by visiting a dance. (In reality, after the strike, Rockefeller had danced with miners' wives.) From the sidewalk he picks up a dime. The 1916 audience would know that Rockefeller's father liked to hand out shiny new dimes to small children.

But Griffith dared not sail too closely to the wind. His workers are not miners. They are not shown to be immigrants. Only one or two are armed. And while there is no atrocity like the burning of tents at Ludlow, even the use of machine guns by National Guardsmen is thought to be embarrassingly far-fetched by modern viewers unfamiliar with the labor wars.

Griffith could not have perpetrated so radical a scene in the year of the Red Scare, when he reissued *The Mother and the Law*. He was obliged to put this title into the strike sequence: "The militiamen having used blank cartridges, the workmen now fear only the company guards."[233]

Rockefeller came under more direct fire in a one-reel Lubin film, *Two News Items* (1916), written by the prolific Julian Lamothe and directed by Edward Sloman. A reporter is reprimanded by his editor for his poor sense of news value. The body of a woman, identified as Katie Eagen, is found in the East River, but this is deemed to be of little interest, whereas news of a prominent person gets front-page headlines. The film delves into the dead woman's background. Katie (Adda Gleason) is a typical product of the tenements. Her husband Dan (Jay Morley) works in the great factory of millionaire "John Rockland" (L. C. Shumway), who also owns the tenement in which they live. Drink causes Dan to maltreat Katie, but when she tells him she is pregnant, he helps her to save money—for the baby's sake.

Then Rockland cuts wages by 25 percent and a strike breaks out. Katie clings to the baby's savings, but the rent collector is both punctual and insistent. Dan goes to Rockland's magnificent home to appeal to him, but is thrown out. With all their money spent, they are faced with eviction. Dan secures a job as a janitor

The militia opens fire on the strikers, as at Ludlow. A scene from the modern story of Intolerance, *1916.*

at the Children's Outing Association, but Rockland, on one of his charitable tours, spots him and has him discharged. Dan decides to break into Rockland's mansion and steal the money that is rightly his. Rockland has him arrested. The men arrive to dispossess Katie, who is already wild with grief. As the *Lubin Bulletin* put it: "She told them to take everything, and holding the baby's things tightly to her, she made her way blindly to the river, a victim of John Rockland.

"The same paper also contained the reporter's other bit of real news, in front-page headlines: 'JOHN ROCKLAND AGAIN CONTRIBUTES TO CHILDREN'S OUT-ING ASSOCIATION/NOTED PHILANTHROPIST GIVES CHECK FOR $50,000/TEN THOUSAND CHILDREN TO BE MADE HAPPY BY WEEK IN COUNTRY.' "[234]

WHO PAYS?   While serial manufacturers were vying with each other to make the most lurid and implausible tale of the week, Pathé released a series of thought-provoking social dramas, complete within themselves, entitled *Who Pays?* (1915). Featuring Ruth Roland and Henry King in twelve episodes of three reels each, *Who Pays?* used the same basic cast in each story, though they played different characters.

"The series had a sociological twist, as it put up to the spectators the question as to who was morally responsible for the various and sundry misfortunes suffered by the principal characters," wrote Alfred A. Cohn in *Photoplay.*[235]

The entire series was discovered by UCLA Film Archives a few years ago, at

Henry King and Ruth Roland in Toil and Tyranny, *the final episode of*
Who Pays? *1915, in which a worker is robbed of his livelihood through a
momentary flash of temper. (Robert S. Birchard Collection)*

Ruth Roland's former home. I have viewed the final episode, "Toil and Tyranny."
Although the performances tend to be of the shaking-fist variety, the film is a solid
piece of work, well photographed on authentic locations and marred only by an
unusual lapse of editing in the final sequence. (Shots are fired at a car, and there
is a cut to the window several long seconds before the holes appear in the glass.)

Whatever its failings, "Toil and Tyranny" is a powerful piece of socialist
propaganda,[236] showing how a man can be robbed of his livelihood through a
momentary loss of temper. The intercutting of scenes of poverty with the indolent
life of the boss's daughter would have delighted Soviet directors of a decade later.
Once again, however, the capitalist system is not blamed so much as the tough
old curmudgeon of a boss.

Karl Hurd (King) works for lumber tycoon David Powers (Daniel Gilfether),
who condemns him to long hours for low wages. When he rests to recover from
a fit of exhaustion, the foreman treats him so badly that Hurd slugs him in a
sudden fury and runs away. Powers and his cold-blooded legal adviser, Travis
(Edwin J. Brady), watch as the foreman corners Karl and batters him with a plank.
"If you handled these fellows any other way, they wouldn't understand it," remarks
Travis.

As Karl is brought home to an overworked wife who already suffers from
consumption, Powers officiates at a splendid luncheon for his daughter Laura
(Roland), whom he idolizes. Despite a fractured skull, Karl is obliged to return to
work long before he has recovered, so low are the family's resources. But no sooner
does he set foot inside the mill than Powers fires him.

When hours are extended with no extra pay, the workers strike. Powers brings in police and strikebreakers. Travis convinces him to evict the strikers from their company houses. Laura, shocked by all she has seen and heard, can stand no more and pleads with her father to treat his men decently. She is particularly concerned with the plight of Karl Hurd; his wife has just died, he has to care for his daughter, and he is being thrown out of his home. Powers is unmoved.

The strikers determine to confront the boss in his limousine and give him a beating. Hurd, who blames all his agony on Powers, steals a revolver and opens fire on the car himself. How could he know that Laura had borrowed it and was using it to aid the strikers' families? And it is she who is killed. As a final title puts it: "Who pays for this tragedy of toil and tyranny?"

Who Pays? was made at the Balboa Studios, in Long Beach, California. It was an experiment, but it did good business and was regarded as a success.[237] The same studio, however, turned out a series called *The Grip of Evil* as an antidote to *Who Pays?* An episode entitled *The Dollar Kings* was a capital-versus-labor story showing that the same evil existed among the workers as in the upper class. A young man creates a capitalist Utopia—a factory in the country, good wages, sunshine, and fresh air. His ideal is wrecked from within by agitators. Humanity was shown to be in the "grip of evil."[238]

FIRES OF YOUTH   As one of the few surviving capital-versus-labor films, *Fires of Youth* (1917) should by rights be a brilliant example, with a panoply of documentary sequences, a sophisticated and radical story line, and a stunning climax. In fact, it is primitive, looking many years earlier than its date. Its direction is incorrectly credited to Rupert Julian. Written by Agnes Christine Johnston, it is actually one of the very few extant works of Emile Chautard, a Frenchman whom Josef von Sternberg acknowledged as "a studious and cultured man with exceptionally high standards . . . not only well qualified to direct but a gracious teacher."[239]

A Dickensian fable about a small boy's friendship with a lonely old mill owner (Frederick Warde) and a fantasy of a ruthless boss who becomes an ordinary worker, the film was an attempt to counter socialist propaganda by preaching tolerance. The error of the "bad" boss is ignorance, not cruelty. The picture is quite well put together for all its obviousness, but there are some outrageously theatrical performances, particularly from Warde, a celebrated stage actor.[240]

The most fascinating aspect of the film is that it features the legendary Jeanne Eagels. She had recently been George Arliss's leading lady[241] and had played a streetwalker in Thanhouser's *The World and the Woman* (1916), her first film.

Filmed by Thanhouser in and around New Rochelle, New York, *Fires of Youth* included footage shot at a factory, which was vivid, though tantalizingly brief (in the surviving version of three reels cut from five). Dilapidated houses and industrial areas were well photographed by Chautard's French cameraman, M. Bizeul, although the surviving print is a miserable dupe.

The picture was not much of a success, judging by an exhibitor's report from the Dreamland Theater in South Carolina: "Hardly an ordinary business—no business."[242]

"Considered as a whole," said *Wid's,* "the story was very old stuff." Wid thought that Jeanne Eagels was very effective but that some of the extras were bad: "The scene outside the mill owner's home where a group of extras was going to do violence was awful. They shoved one another around in the usual manner, with much arm waving, and of course there was one gink that wanted to fight his way through, and somebody wished on us the title 'Let me get at him!' Oh boy, why will they do those things!"[243]

While the war gave an unpatriotic tone to capital-versus-labor stories, it provided an ideal villain in the person of Count Bernstorff, the German ambassador to the United States. In *The Key to Power* (1918) he was shown organizing coal shortages to wreck industry and freeze the population.[244] Produced by the Educational Film Corporation, *The Key to Power* was not a documentary so much as an industrial melodrama. Directed by William Parke, from a scenario by Caroline Gentray and E. Lloyd Sheldon, it was shot in the coalfields of West Virginia.

Another made-to-order villain was the war profiteer—a man who cheated the government on vital contracts. Arrow's *The Profiteer* (1919), directed by J. K. Holbrook, leveled the spotlight on a vicious character who might have appeared in many more films were it not for the fact that war profiteers were at that very moment buying stock in picture companies and (as in the case of Frank Godsol and Goldwyn) were soon to take over the company itself.

The industrial disturbances of 1919 caused the subject to disappear from the screen except in the anti-Bolshevik pictures. And the Republicans planned to bring federal censorship to bear in the hope of calming the situation: "UNCLE SAM TO EMPLOY SCREEN ON BIG SCALE TO STILL UNREST," said *Variety.*[245] Herbert Hoover was the choice for the first national censor.

"A major industrial idea is back of this movie," said *Variety.* "It is to be an important part of the 'back to the farm' movement and the attempt to keep labor stationary and happy and prevent expensive turnovers. . . . Wealthy commanders of industry since the war have realized the prime importance of amusement to replace the influence of liquor."[246]

THE CONTRAST   "We are going to make the projecting lens a weapon for labor," declared one of the men involved in producing prounion films. After the war, while it was still possible to make films relatively cheaply ($500 to $2,500 for a one- or two-reeler), nearly a dozen radical groups produced and distributed their own pictures—the Federation Film Corporation and the Labor Film Service among them.[247]

Joseph Cannon, the field director of the Labor Film Service,[248] was angered by the way the motion picture was being used to distort socialist ideals and the activities of labor. The Labor Film Service, incorporated in April 1920, planned to combat the Red Scare pictures with films which would not be mere propaganda

Anita Loos and husband John Emerson and the headline: GOVERNMENT ASKS FOR INJUNCTION
TO HALT GREAT SOFT COAL STRIKE. *In 1921, virtual civil war reigned in West Virginia as
mine owners hired private armies to protect their property.*

but which would be based firmly on fact. The company intended to produce
Animated Labor Review (newsreels), Lecture Lyceum (films and slides), and films
on labor and construction as well as "dramas based on the writings of the icono-
clasts" such as Dickens, Jack London, and Tolstoy.

In August 1920 the Labor Film Service began showing weekly news reviews,
the first of which, besides an item on a Socialist party picnic at Manhattan Casino,
contained shots of Eugene Debs in prison garb. This aroused "a storm of applause."[249]

That same month, Cannon wrote to Upton Sinclair to tell him about the weekly
news reviews and to say that his company was negotiating with the Interchurch
World Movement ("this is strictly confidential") for the privilege of visualizing
the report of that organization on the recent steel strike. While admitting that he
lacked the capital to produce a feature picture, Cannon was convinced that this
film would prove such an effective method of publicity that "the Garyites will find
it difficult to get any sympathy from the public."[250]

Cannon sent details of the second Animated Labor Review, which featured a
strike (some would term it a mutiny) by Italian sailors aboard the S.S. *Calabria,*
which was carrying munitions and Polish reservists to reinforce the White Russian
army. Such explosive subjects were not often seen by the general public; the New
York Police Department made sure of that. When Cannon tried to launch a labor
film magazine, the department refused him a license.

The Kansas Board of Censors rejected *The Contrast* (1921), produced by the
Labor Film Service and dealing with the coal strike, precisely because it depicted

a coal strike—in which the miners appeal to the railroad men to join them. The film had been financed by contributions from miners in West Virginia, Ohio, and Pennsylvania and showed scenes of cave-ins caused by the owners' negligence.[251]

The board received a shock when Cannon took it to court. Judge F. D. Hutchings said, "I don't believe the board of censors has the authority under the law to pass upon a social question so long as the picture in question does not depict immoral, obscene or inflammatory scenes."[252]

The Kansas attorney general claimed that the picture was a violation of the state's Industrial Court Law, which made it a crime for men engaged in essential industry to strike.[253] Attorneys for the distributors responded that *The Contrast* was basically a love story woven around the industrial situation, and they invited the court to see it. Kansas was given twenty days in which to file its rejoinder, but the state's machinery ground exceeding slow. Seventeen months later, with the strike already history, the film was passed—with the elimination of several scenes of violence, the funeral of a striker and a scene showing "a minister denouncing labor at a meeting of capitalists."[254]

Yet it proved the biggest success of all the Labor Film Service films. *The Contrast* was written by John W. Slayton and directed by Guy Hedlund; it was shown across the nation, often in secret. "Its aim was to dramatize the contrast of the life of the poor and the rich in the United States; for example, a starving girl steals off with garbage that a pampered dog passes up."[255]

So violent a change had the American cinema undergone that the kind of film which would have been seen on the screen of any nickelodeon now had to be shown in secret, its makers condemned by labor leaders as "radical." The stage for the House Un-American Activities Committee was now set. The wonder is that it took another thirty years for it to materialize.

THE F.F.C.   The Federation Film Corporation was a Seattle-based company founded in 1919 by radicals and militant trade unionists. Their first important film was *The New Disciple* (1921), set in the small town of Harmony, where industrial relations are calm until the advent of the war. Then the class struggle begins. The town's leading capitalist becomes a profiteer. "There are stool pigeons and raids and an attempt at installing the 'American plan' in the shops." The hero, John, returns from the war and leads the workers in reestablishing Harmony by allowing the workers to take over the mills with capital secured from the farmers in the area. "As the workers are the greatest consumers of farm products, it is to the advantage of the farmers to stand by them and break the strike. The big climax comes when the farmers outbid the capitalists in the foreclosure of the mills."[256]

The film was written by William Pigott from a story by F.F.C. director John Arthur Nelson and was directed by Ollie Sellers.[257] Inspired by Woodrow Wilson's *The New Freedom* (1913), it used passages from the book in the titles. *Photoplay* thought the story could have been made into a stirring and intensely significant picture, "but it falls rather flat through lack of subtlety, mediocre direction and an indifferent cast." It did, however, consider the film suitable for the family— after a tiring day. "And that's commendation—if you think it over."[258]

Variety was more scathing: "There was only a sprinkling of people in the orchestra [seats] at the opening, and the film shows nothing calculated to bring them in. It has little entertainment value and even less value as propaganda."[259]

Even the *Daily Worker* agreed: "Its ideology would certainly not stand the test of Communist principle; from Main Title to 'The End' it reeks with the 'Social Compact' reformist viewpoint of those who call their unionism 'pure and simple.' The picture is just this—pure enough for the babies and simple, too—too simple. It even has the praise of Sam Gompers."[260] Steven Ross asserts that Gompers refused to help either the Labor Film Service or the F.F.C., fearing them "too radical" and "tainted with communism." In 1920, the youthful J. Edgar Hoover put agents on to the Labor Film Service, and they supplied him with extensive reports.[261]

The largest American Federation of Labor campaign involving film was its "union label" drive of 1925, for which the film *Labor's Reward* was made. The Union Label Trades Department of the A.F.L. checked the script, which was produced by the Rothacker Film Manufacturing Company.

"After depicting scenes in the slavery days of antiquity and the slave markets where white men and women were sold on the auction block, the story comes down to the latter part of the nineteenth century. . . . The ten-hour day put in by Mary taxed her every energy. One day . . . she fainted and was sent home.

"Tom was a union man. . . . He took advantage of every occasion to impress upon his fellow workers that they should buy nothing that did not bear a union label. He assured them that the union label represented that the articles . . . had been made in sanitary workshops . . . that safety appliances protected the workers and in purchasing union-labeled articles they were adding to the wages and bettering the working conditions of those who produced them."[262]

One of the girls expresses sympathy for Mary; the forewoman discharges her, and the girls go on strike. Mary, recovered, joins the picket lines and helps form a union. The strike is won, and the sweatshop becomes a union shop with an eight-hour day.

"Scenes in and about the homes of union and non-union men are shown and the difference is so great that it will be an impressive lesson to those who see the picture. . . . In the non-union shops, the workers are sullen and look suspiciously around as if afraid of being reprimanded or discharged. . . . In the union shops, the men and women hold their heads high, bear a contented look and sing or whistle while running the machines."

A short history of labor was provided via the subtitles to demonstrate the benefits of membership in a trade union.[263]

The drive, which opened on October 10, 1925, covered thirty states; the film was seen by an estimated 479,000 people. But the A.F.L.'s continued refusal to support the makers of the more radical labor films meant that even independent distributors and exhibitors regarded them as too much of a risk, while the main theatres, controlled by the big chains with their Wall Street finance, would hardly consider them appropriate family entertainment.[264]

MEN OF STEEL   Director King Vidor's desire to make films on epic themes—steel, wheat, and war—was only partly realized in the silent era. He made his great war film, *The Big Parade* in 1925, but wheat and steel had to wait for sound.

An epic of steel was, however, undertaken at this period at First National. The story and scenario for *Men of Steel* were written (with John Goodrich) by Milton Sills, who played the leading role. It was suggested by Ralph G. Kirk's *Saturday Evening Post* story "United States Flavor," published in 1924.[265]

Sills, who had starred in *The Honor System* in 1917, was one of the few highbrows in pictures. A former fellow in philosophy at the University of Chicago graduate school,[266] he had also had a thorough stage training. His ambition was to become a director. An outspoken critic of the average film, he wrote: "The motion picture, although quite an art in its present state, is still in its mediocrity . . . Producers have been made to believe that the 20,000,000 people who make up the daily motion picture audience average are but twelve years of age in intelligence. Fearing that an adult type of photoplay might be 'over the heads' of the average audience too many producers have made pictures so silly, so puerile that a good percentage of the public is cynical in its attitude toward the screen."[267]

The Honor System had convinced Sills that artistic things could be done in pictures, but he was too often cast as a tough he-man in unchallenging melodramas. Although one might have thought he would be more uncompromising, his script for *Men of Steel* proved a combination of social drama and hokum—the same kind of hokum that made him so impatient. He admitted it had a lot of old stuff in it, "but it's the background and the manner in which the story is handled that is turning it into a big and unusual picture. Steel pictures have been done before, it's true, but never on so large a scale or with such a painstaking effort to achieve realism."[268]

Sills was profoundly impressed by *The Big Parade.* "But we can't have many movies that truly picture life," he said. "We can't really present sex problems, nor social problems, nor marriage problems, nor any other kind of problem, because the censors won't let us!"[269]

In *Men of Steel* (1926), an immigrant mine laborer called Jan Bokak (Sills) is wrongly accused of murder, escapes, and becomes a labor leader at the steel mills owned by "Cinder" Pitt (Frank Currier). Agitators try to wreck the mill, and Jan is seriously injured saving the life of Pitt's daughter, Clare (May Allison). He becomes engaged to her, but he has left a fiancée called Mary (Doris Kenyon) in the mining town. Mary's mother confesses on her deathbed to being the estranged wife of Pitt, the millowner. Mary finds her way to the Pitt home, sees Jan with Clare, and accuses him of murdering her (Mary's) brother, Anton. But Jan forces a confession from the real murderer, Massarick (Victor McLaglen). On the day of Jan and Clare's wedding, Mary is hurt in a car smash and Jan decides to marry her instead, incurring the wrath of the workers. Pitt learns of Mary's parentage and quells the mob, assuring them that Jan will get half interest in the mill.[270]

The director was the French-born George Archainbaud, whose most outstanding film this proved. The foster son of Emile Chautard, he turned out many conventional films from 1915.

The picture was made on location at the huge Ensley Mills of the United States Steel Corporation in Birmingham, Alabama. Judge Elbert Gary, chairman of the corporation, traveled to Birmingham to organize the facilities required by the picture company. No professional extras were required for the mill scenes—the steelworkers played themselves.[271]

"It was very difficult," said Sills, "and we had to work under very trying conditions—the heat from the furnaces, the gas fumes and the constant noise were not conducive to inspired acting—but I believe that we have managed to get into the film the real spirit of the steel industry."[272]

The publicity declared it took two years to produce *Men of Steel,* a claim not borne out by Milton Sills's crowded acting schedule. *Variety* thought it qualified as a corker: "A big picture with some faults, but so many thrilling virtues it should stand up beautifully as a de luxe program feature."[273] Its demerits were its length—ten reels—and its comedy, "both deplorable."[274] But it was handsomely produced. "Included among the thrills are the many industrial scenes; molten steel in its red, flaming color, also in the white heat state; the crash of a water tower into the molten steel with the subsequent spattering of the vicious liquid over many people (badly done in miniature but effective); and most impressive of all, the burial of a man who fell into a pot of molten metal."[275]

Photoplay thought it a box-office picture if ever there was one and felt Milton Sills gave his best performance since *The Sea Hawk:* "It is an unusual characterization, reaching its high point in a remarkable scene in which the starving Jan Bokak steals a dinner from a dog."[276]

Motion Picture Magazine called it "a moving, rugged story." As the raw ore enters the crucible to emerge as steel, so the raw, stolid workman becomes through a refining process a power in the community. "That's the idea behind this picture, regardless of any plot ramifications. Some may scoff at its obvious treatment, and its melodramatic fireworks (they do become a trifle far-fetched) . . . but these scoffers will have missed the simplicity of its theme, the ruggedness of its action, and the lusty vigor of its characterization. . . . The impression gathered is one of a surging realism which swallows up its hokum. The energy of America is being released . . . it presents a kaleidoscopic sweep of events—moving graphically and directly to a climax."[277]

V. Hagedorn of Minnesota wrote to *Picture Play* to say he found the picture engrossing. "But I really was amazed at the presentation of the Mesaba range. I just wish the director had taken a little trip up here and looked around for himself. Mesaba is large. None of our mines is as small as the one pictured in the film. Here in Nibbing we have the largest open-pit mine in the world, and believe me, it is some hole! It seemed rather ridiculous the way Doris Kenyon dressed as a range girl. You could never at any time in the past have found an American girl dressed in that way here. . . . I feel highly indignant at the way we were represented and I speak not only for myself but for my many friends who have dwelt here and have watched the range grow from timber country to ore mines."[278]

The ads claimed "Two Years in the Making—Will Live for Decades." But the picture was destroyed along with so many other "obsolete" productions, depriving us of the most graphic documentation of a 1920s steel mill ever put on film.

Above: Filming Men of Steel, *1926, in the Open Hearth Section of the Ensley Mills of the Tennessee Coal and Iron Company, Birmingham, Alabama. (Museum of Modern Art). Left: Hooker Grimes (George Fawcett) buried alive in tons of iron ore in the hold of a Great Lakes ship of which he is captain, in* Men of Steel. *(National Film Archive)*

Above: According to custom, a man who falls to his death in a vat of molten metal is buried in that vat, amid impressive ceremonies. The steel mill officials attend, with workers, and even supply a choir. (Museum of Modern Art). Below: The Men of Steel *company acts as host for Major Dodge of the United States Steel Corporation and officials of the Ensley Mills; director George Archainbaud is master of ceremonies at a Thanksgiving dinner. (Museum of Modern Art)*

THE PASSAIC TEXTILE STRIKE   The tumultuous labor confrontations bequeathed precisely one feature film to record a strike as it happened. I put off writing this book until I saw that film. I had long accepted it as "lost," but I could not see how this history could be written without a glimpse of at least part of it. Not that I expected a masterpiece. Highly paid film technicians would hardly want to be involved in a film supporting a strike. And amateurs, however skilled, seldom produce brilliant films.

What I hoped for was another view, a contrast to the stereotyped melodrama about factory life in which foul conditions were attributable only to foul characters. I wanted an unadulterated view of reality.

It was during a visit to the Museum of Modern Art in 1983 that the subject came up. Film curator Eileen Bowser was showing me around the museum's new premises when she told me her department had acquired the collection of the late Thomas Brandon. Knowing him to have been a distributor of labor films, I mentioned the subject of my new book.

"Oh," said Bowser, "then we have something for you. We have found *The Passaic Textile Strike.*"

Before I had time to recover, the museum staff had organized a viewing. As a work of cinema, the film proved to have only one sequence of merit; the prologue. Significantly, this is fiction, acted by Polish immigrant workers and showing the sort of events that set the scene for the strike. It lasts a mere few minutes; it shows the living conditions and portrays the bosses—in this case a Mr. Mulius—in a villainous light.

After that stereotyped but promising beginning, the film develops into an extended newsreel. Union meetings and propaganda were dependent on words, and so is this film. Lengthy subtitles, written by Margaret Larkin,[279] accompany virtually every shot. Some scenes are clearly reconstructed, others covered as they happened. Silent newsreels tend to show history as the movement of crowds, and this film follows that tradition: the endless picket line, the ecumenical demonstration by the local churches in support of the strike, the arrival of relief trucks, hailed by the beleaguered workers. It is a "mass film" in true Communist style, the first such film ever to be made in America.

When individuals are picked out, they are likely to be hectoring orators or demonstrators displaying their wounds to the camera. The effectiveness of the faces of ordinary workers, which so enlivened the documentaries of the thirties, had not been thought about. (Eisenstein's *Potemkin* had yet to be seen in the United States.) When faces are shown they are included in groups—batches would be a better word—posed as if for the standard group photographs of the time. Even so, the faces are extraordinary. They belong to another world, another age—ancient, gnarled, peasant faces. The presence of these almost-old people from Central Europe, some still wearing traditional peasant clothes, gives the film a poignant sense of reality no reconstruction could achieve. The sight of the young, jackbooted cops, swinging their clubs, inevitably reminds one of the fate lying ahead for the Poles and Slavs who stayed at home. The people on screen will be clubbed and gassed,

Striker Martin Winkler under arrest in The Passaic Textile Strike, *1926. Civilian vigilante in background. (Martha Stone Asher)*

too, but the support of their comrades will be so solid that the forces of law and order will be brought if not to law, at least to some semblance of order.

Since 1926 is still within living memory, I set out to trace some of the survivors of that strike. Eileen Bowser gave me the address of Albin E. Zwiazek, who was only a schoolboy at the time, although he had vivid recollections. His family was employed in the textile industry in various plants throughout the area. His mother had had to give up her job in 1925 because of tuberculosis, which was especially prevalent around Passaic. His father, from Poland, was a striker, and so were other members of his family. He attended many strike meetings with his father. "The meetings were raided by the police many times. The freedom to assemble is granted to Americans by our constitution, but the police and National Guardsmen ignored this. I have seen strikers beaten by police as well as scabs beaten by strikers."[280]

He saw a woman worker, returning from the Forstmann plant, knocked over in the street. Two men jumped from their car and kicked her. A neighbor's house was bombed during the night.

"Many people with cameras were running around making photographs and films. We used to leave early for school so the strikers would recruit us to picket with them. We did it to get our pictures in the newspapers. Of course, we also wanted the strikers to win out."[281]

Mr. Zwiazek did not see the film during the strike, but finally saw it at the

Gus Deak (left) in The Passaic Textile Strike, 1926. *(Museum of Modern Art)*

Museum of Modern Art's tribute to Thomas Brandon on February 22, 1983. He advised me to contact Gustav Deak, the retired city manager of nearby Garfield, New Jersey. Since Mr. Deak appeared in the film and was a leader of the strike I was only too eager to make contact. It was some months before I had a reply, for he had suffered a minor stroke. By that time, I was in New York, able to take a bus to Garfield and meet him. In his late seventies, he was a handsome, stockily built man who, despite his stroke, had an excellent memory. But he could not recall one vital fact—the identity of the director.

"I was in the film, but I had no knowledge of who the contractor was or how they hired this man. It was an independent group, and it was all handled by the Relief Committee. Alfred Wagenknecht, who was head of the Relief Committee, wanted me to work with the director of the film. I don't remember his name. He was not involved with the party. He was working for pay. He was not a sympathizer with the strike at all. He was a director, hired from an independent company. And he had all the equipment. He knew his business.

"I had to assemble the cast for him, so he said, 'Okay, you're going to play this part.' That's how it all started. Most of the people in the cast I knew, and I put the cast together, naturally with his okay. He directed the picture, and the script was his."[282]

This director (there may have been two) was eventually fired, and the Relief Committee asked Sam Russak to take over. He was a professional still photographer with some experience of motion pictures. He was also a labor activist and an ardent supporter of the strike. According to Sam Brody, "there would have been no film without him. He did the whole thing practically on his own."

Brody was later celebrated as the cofounder, with Lester Balog, of the Film and Photo League. Balog and Brody served as cameramen, along with Bill Schwartfeller. "I used a hand-held 35mm DeVry," recalled Brody, "and a borrowed Bell and Howell Eyemo. I went to Passaic on four or five occasions and covered certain peripheral phases of strike activity, mainly strike relief. I don't remember being attacked by the police, but I was there when many heads were bashed in."[283]

To Martha Asher, at the time a member of the Young Communist League who came from New York to work with strikers' children, the police violence was a response to open rebellion. The fact that the strike had been initiated not by trade unions but by a political party—and the Communist party at that—undoubtedly scared them. "The attacks of the authorities were so great they fired up the whole East Coast. In the town itself, the entire community came to support that strike. Doctors would give free service—'pay me when you get back to work.' Storekeepers would give you credit as long as they could hold out. The small landlord suffered rather than evict. Food was donated from all over the country. Strikers would come in with their card to one of the relief stations, and they would get a certain amount of food, according to how many were in the family. The film was used to raise money for this relief."[284]

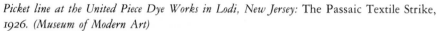

Picket line at the United Piece Dye Works in Lodi, New Jersey: The Passaic Textile Strike, *1926. (Museum of Modern Art)*

The film was only part of the enormous publicity given to the strike. Passaic was close enough to New York for newspapers and newsreel companies to rush cameramen down at short notice. It has been suggested that the film used scenes from newsreels. Some of the scenes suggest the skill of a professional behind the camera, but I cannot imagine the major newsreel companies supplying material to the strikers. For one thing, they would want too much money. For another, this was the first important strike in American history to be instigated and led by the Communists.

For the Communists behind the film, it was a tremendous risk to spend thousands of dollars on a movie rather than on food for strikers' families. People remembered the Paterson Pageant* at Madison Square Garden, and the "disappearance" of the profits—in many people's minds, into the pockets of the organizers. But presumably Alfred Wagenknecht and his committee remembered Lenin's words: "For us, the cinema is the most important of all the arts." And what better weapon to help in the fight toward "One Big Union"?

At the turn of the century, the McKinley Tariff Act of 1890 and the 1897 Dingley Tariff Act made it profitable for foreign manufacturers to operate in the United States. Most of the mill-owners in the Passaic area were German. The little town exploded into a full-scale industrial center, the country's chief producer of fine woolens and worsteds.[285] The surrounding towns—Clifton, Garfield, Lodi, and Wallington—became part of the complex. To the north was Paterson, the silk center.

The German mill-owners filled the towns with Poles, Russians, Ukrainians, Slovaks, Hungarians, and Germans. They were said to have men stationed at Ellis Island to carry out their plan; by hiring so many different nationalities—and tongues—they avoided worker solidarity.[286] Certainly the workers remained hopelessly disorganized.

During the war, the German bosses were temporarily unseated or replaced. Workers went overseas and learned English in the army. They came back, their heads full of idealistic slogans, only to be disillusioned. The Germans returned, hours were increased, discipline heightened, speed-ups imposed. The introduction of new machinery transformed skilled men into unskilled and threw many out of work. For those who remained, sanitation and other conditions in the factories and the disease-ridden slums were appalling.

In October 1925, due to depression in the industry, a 10 percent wage cut was imposed. Three hundred and eighty workers promptly went on strike at the Passaic Worsted Spinning Company. Albert Weisbord, a graduate of Harvard Law School, had been elected leader and spokesman for the United Front Committee of Textile Workers of Passaic and Vicinity. Weisbord, who was only twenty-five, was a Communist, and the participation of Communists strengthened the opposition.

---

*The I.W.W. organized a silk strike, led by Bill Haywood and Elizabeth Gurley Flynn, at Paterson, N.J., in 1913. John Reed staged a Pageant of the Strike in Madison Square Garden with a cast of millworkers. The managers announced a profit of $10,000; later it proved to have sustained a loss of $1,000, triggering a financial scandal. People complained that the money should have been used for relief. (Graham Adams, Jr. *The Age of Industrial Violence 1910–1915*. New York: Columbia University Press, 1966, p. 97.)

Picket line going to afternoon strike meeting near Belmont Park, New Jersey: The Passaic Textile Strike, *1926. Steel helmets are worn as protection from police attacks. (Martha Stone Asher)*

"Weisbord was a brilliant man and a good speaker," said Gus Deak. "He asked me, working at the Botany Mill, if I knew some young men to get organized. I called them together and we had about twenty-five. Then we moved inside the mill and organized there. I was in the Finishing Department and in two or three months we organized membership of about one thousand, right in my department. But it was hard to get a meeting place; we had to meet secretly."[287]

To maintain secrecy, when hundreds of workers were flooding on to the streets after late-night meetings, was equally hard. Weisbord ordered a strike before the opportunity was lost.

On January 21, 1926, a worker was fired from the Botany Mill for being a union member. The next day, Vice President Colonel Charles F. H. Johnson told a committee from the United Front that all union men would be fired. Johnson had a fear of communism, which he had seen in action when he visited Russia.

On January 25, Gus Deak and forty-five other delegates stopped their machines and confronted Johnson as a committee. "We demanded the restoration of the 10 percent wage cut," said Deak. "This was rejected by Colonel Johnson, who asked the committee to stay in his office to discuss the matter. We found out that one of his clerks had called the police, so we rushed back to our departments and called the strike. On our call, one thousand employees walked out. We immediately formed a picket line around the gates of the mill. The next day we pulled out the entire plant [of four thousand]."[288]

"Children were trampled down and men and women were injured in a mad flight before enraged police charging the strikers' picket line at the Gera Mills in Passaic." The Passaic Textile Strike, *1926. (Martha Stone Asher)*

In the second week, workers from other mills walked out. The police were short-tempered and charged the crowd frequently. "The first month was not too bad," said Gus Deak, "but when they found they had these massed picket lines, they decided to break them up. They hired extra cops and probably fed them a lot of whiskey. And when they were half drunk they were fearless. So they were really tough with the people—they beat them up and clubbed them, and that was how they broke the picket lines."[289]

Deak was himself clubbed and restricted to the office thereafter by Weisbord. The police, finding tear gas ineffective, turned powerful fire hoses on the strikers, in bitterly cold weather. The next day's newspapers carried vivid pictures, and the police turned their anger on cameramen—press and newsreel.

Karl W. Fasold of Pathé News was beaten up by a posse of policemen, while John Painter of Fox News had his tripod wrenched off and used as a weapon with which to batter his $2,000 Akeley camera to "a mass of junk."[290] The police did not realize that three cameramen were operating from roofs and fire escapes.

The following day, the newsreel men took to an airplane, while thousands of strikers paraded past the mills, many with steel helmets and gas masks they had worn in the army. An armored car, of the kind used by banks, rumbled through the streets packed with cameramen, together with a sedan with bulletproof glass marked "News photographers getting pictures at the Passaic front."[291]

The idea of using motion pictures to raise money had occurred to the Relief Committee early in the strike,* but Alfred Wagenknecht was unquestionably the driving force behind the making of the film.[292] According to him, the Relief Committee had invited two professionals from Boston to undertake the film. Wagenknecht said: "They knew what we wanted but they hung around in their studio, planning fake scenes and talking of putting pretty girl strikers into the foreground of the film with lots of romance for the American movie public. We protested and told them to go to the picket lines and relief kitchens. But they did not like the idea of having their heads battered by police clubs for taking pictures of the lawless cossacks doing their stuff, so we had to get rid of them.

"We then bought a movie camera and a projector, got together a staff from the strikers and photographed the real happenings. It was dangerous but it was genuine adventure, not the warmed-over thrills carefully dolled up by Hollywood methods."[293]

The United Front Committee began showing its footage even before the film was complete, probably thinking the strike would be over before the film was ready. The fact that the strike dragged on for so long gave the film exceptional value, both as a historical document and as a fund raiser. One of its "scoops" was the arrest of Albert Weisbord, on a trumped-up breach of promise charge, even though part of that scene was staged.

Ten thousand people had joined the United Textile Workers as a result of the

After the police attack on cameramen, these men from the newsreels returned properly prepared. (Albin Zwiazek)

*On February 24 the committee had presented *Labor's Reward* and, to celebrate May Day, the Soviet feature *Polikushka*. They also staged plays about the strike.

strike, and Weisbord wanted them to affiliate with the American Federation of Labor, despite that organization's opposition to the Communists. The A.F.L. insisted that he step down, and he agreed to do so in September 1926. In gratitude, the strikers gave him gifts including a gold watch and a silver loving cup. Gus Deak was elected to succeed him.

Only strikers were permitted to attend the first showings of the film in September 1926. Robert Wolf, writing in the *Daily Worker,* said he had seen more interesting movies—one or two—but he had never seen a more interesting audience:

"They were packed into Belmont Park . . . and as far as I could see the only reason there weren't sixteen thousand instead of ten was that there wasn't room. Gustav Deak, the young chairman of the strikers' local, came out on the screen. 'There's Deak,' yelled the crowd, hugely delighted . . .

"The movie itself was a first-class professional production, even to the usual amount of hokum. Before the strike drama there was a prologue which, as far as hokum was concerned, was just a little bit bigger and better hokum than anything I have ever seen on the screen before . . .

"If I did not know that *Potemkin* was not shown here till after the Passaic movie had been produced, I should suspect its continuity writer of having been influenced by *Potemkin.* The scenes came one, two, three, bang-bang-bang-bang—with that dynamic quality that we have learned to associate with all good movies. Scenes were torn out of their chronological order and slight violence [was done] to technical historical details, but [there was] much greater accuracy in the spirit of the strike—in other words, instead of a newsreel, we have a movie."[294]

Kanter's Auditorium at Passaic was jammed for the first public showings, in October. The profits went for the relief of the strikers' children. Said the *Daily Worker:* "The Passaic police have tried unsuccessfully to prevent this celluloid record of their atrocious brutality against the girl pickets and even the children of strikers. The woolen-mill owners likewise take no pleasure in these motion picture photographs of their misconduct.

"But the 16,000 strikers, sustaining a heroic battlefield for three-quarters of a year against police violence, employer greed, detective frame-ups and starvation, are rejoicing in this movie history of their tremendous fight."[295]

The film was taken on tour by Bertha Kuppersmith of the Relief Committee, and in each city labor groups showed their support, not only by buying tickets—and sometimes reselling them and giving the money to the Relief Committee—but by carrying out, without charge, such vital tasks as bill posting.[296] The film was brought back again and again. Distribution was in the hands of the International Workers' Aid, who released Soviet films in the United States.

Ella Reeve Bloor—"Mother" Bloor, the Communist activist—accompanied the film and gave a talk on the strike, telling her audience that for the strike to be sustained, union people throughout the country must furnish the funds. The response was invariably generous, for few strikes had aroused such widespread sympathy.

The Federated Press Labor Letter reported the reaction in Seattle: "A showing

. . . so aroused the members of the Seattle Milk Wagon Drivers that they voted an assessment of 50 cents a member for the benefit of the strikers and their children. The secretary was instructed to send on a check for $200 at once."[297]

Only occasionally did the film encounter opposition; in Erie, Pennsylvania, for instance, the Chamber of Commerce managed to intimidate the manager of a theatre into canceling the booking.[298]

The picture reached New York in November 1926, where it was shown at the New Waldorf Theater, accompanied by a Russian balalaika orchestra. Here it was seen by 3,000 people, grossing about $2,000.[299]

The strike continued with renewed violence, further arrests, and a great deal of prevarication by the A.F.L. It was finally brought to an end in February 1927, after thirteen months, in bitter defeat for the strikers. The wage cut was not rescinded. The workers won merely the right to affiliate with the A.F.L. and a promise that no discrimination would be shown in reemploying them.

Many strikers could not be rehired, however, because the economic problems of the mills had been exacerbated by the strike. Relief funds were still desperately needed. Said a full-page advertisement in the *Daily Worker:* "Passaic Textile Workers Still Need You! Hundreds of families need relief. A year's strike has caused such destitution. Thousands are unemployed. If we are to build a union we must aid until they secure employment. Also—hundreds of strikers are to be placed on trial. Many have been in jail for months. Defense must be provided. Their families must be supported. This aid given now will assist in organizing thousands into a union. You will help in this organization campaign by seeing the motion picture of the Big Passaic Textile Strike . . ."[300]

The film was now the principal source of relief funds for the Passaic workers.[301] But as the memory of the strike faded, so did bookings.

Alfred Wagenknecht moved from one massive strike to another. The *Daily Worker* reported in 1928 that he was supervising the production of a six-reel film called *The Miners' Strike,* covering the sixteen-month struggle in the Pennsylvania coal fields.[302]

Albert Weisbord failed in his efforts to organize the textile workers into one big union. The strike was a disaster for the area. Weisbord was expelled from the Central Committee of the Communist party in 1929. Gustav Deak left the labor movement and became a supporter of Roosevelt and the Democratic party and eventually became city manager of Garfield. "So after being clubbed by the cops, I became boss of the entire police department."[303]

In the early 1950s, a worker approached a Passaic resident called Emil Asher and gave him a copy of the film, on 35mm nitrate, in seven reels (two of which later disappeared). "We showed it around 1955 in Passaic, and about two hundred people turned up," said Asher. "There were quite a few participants from the strike. It was a successful event, although the cops arrived just after the movie was shown."

"After that," said Martha Asher, "it remained in the offices the Communist Party used in Newark, New Jersey. I had resigned from the National Committee, and this was my last day at work. I looked at the metal cans and I said to myself, well, rightfully, I ought to take this. There weren't many people around any more who were participants in the strike. But I decided no, it wasn't mine and I would leave it . . . I remember in the missing reels there were more scenes of trucks loaded with relief, more scenes of terror—probably repetitious, and somebody may have cut them. And there was something included at the end having to do with the settlement of the strike. I must admit when I first saw the film, I didn't view it as a patched-up thing. The whole film was quite precious. Now we take it around and lecture with it. At Paterson Community College recently, we showed it to black kids of fifteen and sixteen from Passaic. About thirty-five of them. Nobody budged, nobody was bored. They took notes and sat all the way through it. They couldn't believe that this is what happened in their town."[304]

Epilogue

Most of the social films managed a happy ending. So should this book. The last thought, however, is not one of mine. Film historian Russell Merritt came up with it as a reaction to this book, and I shall give him the last word.

"Let me try out an idea that may infuriate you. The move away from the social consciousness of the teens to the twenties merry-go-round of comedy, crime, glamour, and sex may not have been altogether a bad thing. The shift of public attention from the antics of Lusk and Palmer to those of Valentino and Swanson may have done more to abate the madness of the Bolshevik witch hunts and Ku Klux Klan revivals than any reasoned arguments for freedom of speech. One of the contributions of twenties movies is that, like baseball, jazz, and national magazines, they brought Americans back together again after years of severe—and, by 1919, hysterical—divisiveness. Your text concentrates on the negative aspect of this—the avoidance of issues that badly required reform and investigation—but it is possible to see another side. Better the trivial than the hysterical. Movies helped deflate the hot-air rhetoric of people like Tom Dixon and Billy Sunday; movies—particularly the great comedies—showed that disillusionment need not be melancholy and that denunciation may be less effective socially and politically than satire and parody.

"The industry was drifting away from social controversy at least two years before the Hays Office was invented, and it is symptomatic that the last great social crusade was Bolshevism; mainstream directors and studios needed no encouragement to look for noncontroversial characters and stories. The challenge became to find topics that would bring audiences together."

Twenty-five years ago I wrote a book in praise of the entertainment film of the 1920s. It was the first volume in this trilogy—*The Parade's Gone By. . . .* I am delighted to find we have come full circle.

Notes

INTRODUCTION

1. *Moving Picture World,* June 21, 1913, p. 1233.

2. *Moving Picture World,* June 19, 1920, p. 1604.

3. Mary Grey Peck of the Motion Picture Committee of the General Federation of Women's Clubs, quoted in *Photoplay,* February 1917, p. 57.

4. *Motion Picture Magazine,* March 1929, p. 114.

5. Robert Sklar, *Movie Made America* (New York: Random House, 1975), p. 123.

6. Russell Merritt, "Nickelodeon Theatres 1905–14," in *American Film Industry,* ed. Tino Balio (Madison: University of Wisconsin, 1976), p. 63. No motion picture theater was allowed within 200 feet of a church, *Motion Picture World,* March 1, 1913, p. 864.

7. *The World Today,* October 1908, quoted in Balio, p. 51.

8. William O'Neill, *Everyone Was Brave* (Chicago: Quadrangle Books, 1969), p. 261.

9. William Drew, *D. W. Griffith's Intolerance: Its Genesis and Its Vision* (Jefferson, North Carolina: McFarland & Co., 1986), p. 10.

10. *Social Hygiene* 5 (1919), p. 27. Quoted in Martin S. Pernick, "Edison's Tuberculosis Films," *Hastings Center Report* 8 (June 1978), p. 27.

11. *The Reformers* (which was written by Frank Woods) was filmed on location in the little town of Hollywood.

12. Lewis Jacobs, *The Rise of the American Film* (New York: Teachers College Press, Columbia, 1968), p. 271. When C. B. DeMille held a contest for film ideas in 1929, he complained that "prosperity has cut down the number of suggestions dealing with social problems," *Screen Book,* August 1929, p. 61.

13. *New York Dramatic Mirror,* December 4, 1915.

14. At this period the term "feature" referred to dramatic films of any length. Eventually, it came to mean films of four or more reels.

15. Sam Ornitz, author of *Haunch, Paunch and Jowl,* a novel of Jewish life, later appeared before the House Un-American Activities Committee as one of the Hollywood Ten.

16. Jan and Cora Gordon, *Stardust in Hollywood* (London: George C. Harrap, 1939), pp. 121–22.

17. Gordon and Gordon, pp. 121–22.

18. *Moving Picture World,* January 13, 1912, p. 112.

19. Q. David Bowers, in his forthcoming study of the Thanhouser Film Company, points out that *Moving Picture World*'s reviews—apart from their simple synopses—were as positive as possible, and the forthcoming announcements were transcripts of studio handouts. The magazine was a promoter of the moving picture. Good or bad, however, the attitudes included in the review is what makes them valuable in the context of this book. Bowers selects the *New York Dramatic Mirror* as the only trade journal which printed reviews worthy of the name. I am indebted to William Drew for searching through microfilms of this magazine and sending me the reviews of social films.

20. *Motion Picture News,* July 12, 1913, p. 19.

21. Carolyn Lowrey, *The First One Hundred Noted Men and Women of the Screen* (New York: Moffat, Yard & Co., 1920), p. 190.

22. *Moving Picture World,* August 9, 1913, p. 640.

23. *Photoplay,* June 1915, p. 42.

24. Phillips Smalley acknowledged the influence of director Edwin S. Porter, with whom the Smalleys worked at Rex, and he may even have worked on this film with them, *Moving Picture World,* January 24, 1914, p. 399. *Suspense* included split screen, unusual angles, and a startling use of close-ups.

25. *Moving Picture World,* August 9, 1913, p. 638.

26. *Motion Picture News,* May 1, 1915, p. 54. Part of the film survives in the Library of Congress.

27. *Variety,* February 4, 1916, p. 29.

28. *Motion Picture Magazine,* May 1918, p. 6.

29. *Wid's* (A Magazine by Wid Gunning), June 15, 1916, p. 647. The story was written by Stella Wynne Herron. Universal turned it into a comedy short in 1932 with the kind of commentary made popular by Pete Smith—"she needed new bootsies for her tootsies"—and in this form it survives in the Library of Congress as *The Unshod Maiden* (one reel).

30. *Variety,* April 6, 1917, p. 22.

31. *Variety,* May 18, 1917, p. 26.

32. *Photoplay,* May 1930, p. 126.

33. Mrs. Wallace Reid to Sue Mc-Conachy, "Hollywood" TV series, 1976 (research interview).

34. Colleen Moore to author, "Hollywood," a thirteen-part series on the silent era, written, produced, and directed by Kevin Brownlow and David Gill (1980).

35. *Photoplay,* October 1928, p. 122.

36. Lester Friedman, *Hollywood's Image of the Jew* (New York: Frederick Ungar, 1982), p. 46.

CHAPTER ONE: CENSORSHIP

1. Edward de Grazia and Roger K. Newman, *Banned Films* (New York: R. R. Bowker, 1982), p. 21.

2. R. A. Liston, *The Right to Know: Censorship in America* (New York: Franklin Watts, 1973), p. 23.

3. Terry Ramsaye, *A Million and One Nights,* 1926. (Reprinted, London: Frank Cass & Co., 1964), p. 473. Jane Addams introduced a resolution which prevented the nickelodeons from being closed, and had them subject to supervision, *Moving Picture World,* May 11, 1907, pp. 147–8.

4. *Moving Picture World,* May 25, 1907, p. 180.

5. *Moving Picture World,* May 25, 1907, p. 180.

6. Robert Fisher, "Film Censorship and Progressive Reform," *Journal of the Popular Film* 4 (1975), p. 144.

7. De Grazia and Newman, p. 14. A judge who proved particularly friendly was William Gaynor, later mayor of New York himself and a supporter of the freedom of the screen. Gaynor grew tougher in 1912 and brought in stricter and more extensive licensing laws.

8. De Grazia and Newman, p. 14.

9. Professor Charles Sprague Smith was an educator, lecturer, and writer. *Who Was Who in America* does not mention his film connection. Besides his work for the board, he directed scenes for a history film for the New York Board of Education.

10. The Charity Organization Society, The Children's Aid Society, City Vigilance League, League for Political Education, Neighborhood Workers Association, Public Education Association, Society for the Prevention of Crime, Women's Municipal League. The Children's Aid Society and the Women's Municipal League withdrew their support after 1910, demanding tougher measures. Robert Fisher, "Film Censorship and Progressive Reform: The National Board of Censorship and Motion Pictures, 1909–1922," *Journal of Popular Film* 4 (1975), pp. 145–46.

11. Lary May, *Screening Out the Past* (New York: Oxford University Press, 1980), p. 204.

12. *Moving Picture World,* March 26, 1927, p. 349. The board's findings were published in its bulletin and circulated to exhibitors as well as to boards of education and police departments.

13. *Moving Picture World,* July 13, 1915, p. 324.

14. *Moving Picture World,* March 8, 1913, p. 973.

15. *Moving Picture World,* February 8, 1913, p. 549.

16. *Moving Picture World,* February 8, 1913, p. 549. The title "Passed by the National Board of Review" was not a mark of approval, it merely indicated that the film would not corrupt anyone's morals. (Some exhibitors spliced it on to films which had not been passed.) The board had no legal powers and claimed it wanted none. In theory at least, local authorities had power enough to punish exhibitors who showed films condemned by the board by revoking their licenses.

17. William H. Short, *A Generation of Moving Pictures* (New York: The National Committee for Study of Social Values in Motion Pictures, 1928, reprinted New York: Garland Publishing, 1978), p. 291.

18. *Moving Picture World,* July 4, 1914, p. 43.

19. Fisher, p. 149.

20. Ibid.

21. Charles Feldman, *National Board of Censorship (Review) of Motion Pictures* (New York: Arno, 1977), p. 112.

22. Despite its opposition to censorship, the footage eliminated by the board in 1916 alone amounted to 46,990 feet and the sales value of the film kept off the market was $156,465, *Motion Picture Magazine,* September 1917, p. 41.

23. Drew, p. 48.

24. Fisher, p. 151.

25. Ruth A. Inglis, *Freedom of the Movies* (Chicago: University of Chicago Press, 1947), p. 78.

26. Short, p. 327.

27. Short, p. 311.

28. Southern Convention of Baptists, Washington, D.C., 1920, quoted in *Variety,* May 14, 1920, p. 35.

29. Inglis, p. 82.

30. Inglis, p. 89.

31. Short, p. 317. Wilton Barrett succeeded John Collier.

32. *Motion Picture Weekly,* November 1915, p. 118. Quoted in D. C. Wenden, *Birth of the Movies,* p. 118. Carl Laemmle's pronouncements were usually written for him by Robert Cochrane.

33. *Moving Picture World,* March 26, 1927, p. 423.

34. *Photoplay,* March 1916, p. 69.

35. *Photoplay,* May 1917, p. 99.

36. *Photoplay,* March 1916, p. 63.

37. *Photoplay,* October 1922, p. 39.

38. *Mutual Film Corporation* v. *Industrial Commission of Ohio* 236 U.S. 230 (1915), quoted in "National Board of Censorship (Review)," notes.

39. William de Mille, *Hollywood Saga* (New York: E. P. Dutton, 1939), pp. 253–54.

40. Robert E. Sherwood, *Best Moving Pictures of 1922–23* (Boston: Small Maynard & Co., 1923), p. 136.

41. De Grazia and Newman, p. 28.

42. De Mille, p. 252.

43. *Variety,* March 7, 1928, quoted in Short, p. 340. Garth Jowett, *Film: The Democratic Art* (Boston: Little, Brown, 1976), p. 114, quotes a survey putting the number of cities at less than 100.

44. Inglis, p. 87.

45. John Collier, p. 426, quoted in Thomas Brandon manuscript, Museum of Modern Art, New York.

46. *Variety,* May 31, 1918, p. 37.

47. *Moving Picture World,* May 3, 1914, p. 473.

48. *Moving Picture World,* September 15, 1917, p. 166.

49. De Grazia and Newman, p. 37.

50. The Portland (Oregon) Chamber of Commerce decided life in the studios of Los Angeles was immoral and sent William G. Harrington to investigate, with police powers and a corps of investigators, *Motion Picture Magazine,* October 1917, p. 67; *Motion Picture Magazine,* November 1917, p. 71.

51. Inglis, p. 66.

52. Quoted by Donald R. Young, *Motion Pictures: A Study in Social Legislation* (Philadelphia: University of Pennsylvania Press, 1922), p. 22 in Inglis, p. 63.

53. Inglis, p. 95.

54. Inglis, p. 87.

55. Ibid.

56. Short, p. 341.

57. The Supreme Court of Nevada sustained the divorce in May 1922; by that time she and Douglas Fairbanks had been married two years. Their popularity survived the storm.

58. Rumors abounded that Olive Thomas killed herself because she discovered she had been infected with syphilis—this rumor led Michael Arlen to adapt the situation for *The Green Hat.*

59. *Variety,* August 26, 1921, p. 37; *Variety,* September 9, 1921, p. 43.

60. *Variety,* February 18, 1921, p. 46. These Fourteen Points banned nakedness, manhandling during love scenes, stories concerned with vice and crime, gamblers, drunkards, and the "morally feeble." Villains should not be identified as holders of any particular religious belief.

61. *Moving Picture World,* May 18, 1917, p. 1099.

62. In 1928 it was revealed that Will Hays had accepted a $75,000 gift and $185,000 loan, representing illegal contributions to Republican party funds, from oil man Harry Sinclair, one of the perpetrators of the Teapot Dome scandal, in gratitude for putting Harding in the White House. Hays was not prosecuted, Sklar, *Movie Made America,* p. 83.

63. Short, p. 332.

64. Raymond Moley, *The Hays Office* (New York: Bobbs-Merrill, 1945), p. 54. For a full account of this campaign, see Jowett, p. 167.

65. Will Hays, *Memoirs* (New York: Doubleday, 1955), p. 333.

66. Hays, p. 344.

67. David A. Yallop, *The Day the Laughter Stopped* (London: Hodder & Stoughton, 1975), p. 259.

68. *Photoplay,* March 1923, p. 27.

69. Short, p. 50. Paul Kelly, an actor jailed for homicide, was allowed to return to the screen.

70. Hays, p. 361.

71. Agreement, December 11, 1928, between Metro-Goldwyn-Mayer and John Gilbert. Courtesy Leatrice Gilbert Fountain. See also *Motion Picture Magazine,* December 1927, p. 81. Film companies proclaimed their virtue in their very names: "The Wholesome Film Corporation," "The John Golden Unit of Clean American Pictures, Inc." (set up by Fox).

72. Hays, p. 436.

73. *Variety,* July 9, 1924, p. 17.

74. *Variety,* July 30, 1924, p. 25. A form of cheating he would indulge in was his agreement with the Authors' League. (See note 91, below, for more detail.)

75. Short, p, 94.

76. De Grazia and Newman, p. 27.

77. Hays, p. 430.

78. Released as *Lily of the Dust.*

79. Mrs. Robbins Gilman, Chairman, Motion Picture Committee, National Council of Women, USA, *Report,* International Council of Women, Geneva, 1927, quoted in Short, p. 356.

80. Short, p. 339.

81. Hays, p. 436.

82. Gloria Swanson, *Swanson on Swanson* (New York: Random House, 1980), p. 298.

83. Hays, p. 436. The Production Code was introduced on February 17, 1930, and it specifically banned films about white slavery, drug trafficking, and venereal diseases. Not until the Legion of Decency stepped in, however, in 1934, was it backed up with any degree of power.

84. Ramsaye, p. 484. The film was *Lady of the Night* (1925). The producers couldn't get away with it scot-free. As Gwen Lee dusts powder on to her feet, Norma Shearer is given a title: "Stop walking back from auto rides."

85. Philip French, *The Movie Moguls* (London: Penguin, 1969), p. 98.

86. Hays had Mary Van Kleeck of the Russell Sage Foundation conduct a survey, and this was one of her recommendations. Film extras who found there was no money stormed one of these employment agencies and several were shot by the guard, *Variety,* March 22, 1923, p. 23.

87. Hays, p. 431.

88. Swanson, p. 298.

89. Swanson, p. 322.

90. *Film Spectator,* December 10, 1927.

91. In 1927 Hays came to an agreement with the Authors' League that books unacceptable in their original form could be accepted if rewritten and made unobjectionable. *The Green Hat* was notorious as a novel, as it dealt with such things as syphilis. The film altered this, changed the story, even the names of the characters, and finally the title; *The Green Hat* became *A Woman of Affairs.*

92. *Life,* August 18, 1927.

CHAPTER TWO: MATTERS OF SEX

1. Margaret Sanger, *An Autobiography* (New York: W. W. Norton, 1938, reprinted Dover, 1971), p. 28.

2. "What Films Are Doing to Young America," address before the National Motion Picture Conference, February 11, 1926, quoted in Short, *A Generation,* p. 214.

3. "What Films Are Doing," Short, p. 215.

4. Short, pp. 313–14.

5. Morris Ernst and Pare Lorentz, *Censored—The Private Life of the Movie* (New York: Harrison Smith, 1930), pp. 7–8.

6. Ernst and Lorentz, pp. 7–8.

7. *Variety,* August 25, 1926.

8. A collection of these, now in the National Film Archive, London, was discovered in an old air raid shelter along with a hand grenade!

9. *Variety,* August 8, 1919, p. 52.

10. *Variety,* January 6, 1922, p. 45.

11. *Moving Picture World,* June 21, 1919, p. 1768.

12. *Motion Picture Magazine,* August 1921, p. 68. *His Naughty Night, Don't Blame the Stork,* and *Up In Betty's Bedroom* do not appear in the AFI catalogues and may be short subjects.

13. *Motion Picture Magazine,* August 1921, p. 68.

14. Clifford G. Twombley, in *Christian Century,* April 13, 1932, p. 480, quoted in Jowett, p. 190.

15. Short, p. 152.

16. *Variety,* March 22, 1918, p. 57. For an excellent study of the vamp cycle, see Alexander Walker, *The Celluloid Sacrifice* (London: Michael Joseph, 1966).

17. Mary MacLane, *The Story of Mary MacLane by Herself* (Chicago: Herbert Stone and Co., 1902, reprinted Jonathan Cape).

18. *Montana Magazine,* July 1977, p. 26. Harold Lloyd parodied MacLane, in *Girl Shy* (1924), playing a young man, terrified of girls, who writes a steamy guide to love—"by the author who knows and knows and knows."

19. Quoted in MacLane synopsis by Michael Yocum, p. 1.

20. Published by Frederick A. Stokes, New York, 1917.

21. *Book News* 35 (May 1917), p. 335, quoted in Yocum, p. 1.

22. MacLane, p. 5.

23. *Moving Picture World,* January 5, 1918, p. 107.

24. November 11, 1917, quoted in *Montana Magazine,* July 1977, p. 32.

25. *Wid's,* January 17, 1918.

26. Ibid.

27. The picture reminded Wid Gunning of a C. Gardner Sullivan story for Thomas Ince, *The Hater of Men,* with Bessie Barriscale: "That had the same general delicacy that handicaps this," *Wid's,* January 17, 1918.

28. *Variety,* February 7, 1918, p. 45.

29. *Montana Magazine,* July 1977, p. 32.

30. *Moving Picture World,* January 26, 1918, p. 525.

31. *Montana Magazine,* July 1977, p. 33. The reference to "kimono"and the opulent surroundings would have been understood by readers of the yellow press as hints that Mary MacLane had turned to prostitution.

32. Quoted in Yocum, p. 3.

33. *New York Dramatic Mirror,* March 17, 1917.

34. Upton Sinclair, *Autobiography of Upton Sinclair* (London: W. H. Allen, 1963), p. 186.

35. Robert S. and Helen Merrell Lynd, *Middletown* (New York: Harcourt, Brace, 1929), p. 114.

36. Lynd and Lynd, p. 121.

37. Judge Ben Lindsey and Rube Borough, *The Dangerous Life* (London: Bodley Head, 1931), p. 216.

38. Lindsey and Borough, p. 259.

39. *Variety,* June 7, 1918.

40. Jim Sleeper, *Great Films Shot in Orange County* (Trabuco Canyon, Cal.: California Classics, 1980), p. 151.

41. *Variety,* November 17, 1916, p. 23.

42. *Photoplay,* February 1917, p. 77.

43. Anthony Slide, *The Kindergarten of the Movies* (Metuchen, N.J.: Scarecrow Press, 1980), p. 88.

44. *New York Dramatic Mirror,* December 1, 1917.

45. *Variety,* November 30, 1917.

46. *Motion Picture News,* April 20, 1918, p. 2388.

47. *New York Dramatic Mirror,* April 20, 1918, p. 560.

48. *Motion Picture News,* April 20, 1918, p. 2388.

49. *Motion Picture News,* April 27, 1918, p. 2564.

50. *Photoplay,* July 1918, p. 96.

51. *Motion Picture News,* April 27, 1918, p. 2536.

52. Kenneth W. Munden, editor. American Film Institute Catalogue of Motion Pictures Produced in the United States. Feature Films 1921–1930 (New York: R. R. Bowker Co. 1971). Credit and Subject Indexes, pp. 1515–1516.

53. *Variety,* January 6, 1922, p. 43.

54. Ibid.

55. Ibid.

56. The film is not known to exist.

57. *Variety,* January 6, 1922, p. 44.

58. *Variety,* January 27, 1922, p. 3.

59. Adapted by Olga Printzlau and Sada Cowan. William spelled his name with a small "d," as did Cecil, nonprofessionally. The film was to have been directed by William, featuring Elliott Dexter.

60. Frank Case, *Do Not Disturb* (New York: Garden City Publishing Company, 1943), p. 311.

61. The film cost $129,349.31 and grossed $1,016,245.87. (Schedule of costs and gross receipts, January 31, 1931, DeMille Estate.)

62. Charles Higham, *Cecil B. DeMille* (New York: Charles Scribner's Sons, 1973), p. 67.

63. *Picture Play,* June 1920, p. 76.

64. *Motion Picture Classic,* April-May 1920, p. 50.

65. *Photoplay,* May 1920, p. 64.

66. *Picture Play,* September 1925, p. 58.

67. Program notes of the Theodore Huff Memorial Film Society, November 24, 1964.

68. By Judge Lindsey and Wainwright Evans.

69. Lindsey and Borough, pp. 255, 263, 273.

70. Lindsey and Borough, p. 246.

71. Olive Carey to author, Carpinteria, California, June 1980. Her father, Joseph Fuller Golden, wrote the song.

72. *AFI Catalogue,* 1921–1930, p. 142.

73. *Photoplay,* October 1928, p. 126.

74. *AFI Catalogue,* 1921–1930, p. 493.

75. Patsy Ruth Miller to author, Connecticut 1964, 1988, and letter to author, January 19, 1988.

76. *Picture Play,* February 1929, p. 100.

77. Unidentified New York paper in Patsy Ruth Miller scrapbook.

78. Sanger, p. 28.

79. Ibid.

80. Sanger, p. 194.

81. Sanger, p. 89.

82. Sanger, p. 92.

83. Sanger, p. 252.

84. *Variety,* March 30, 1917, pp. 27–28. The Message Feature Film Corporation was a unit of the B. S. Moss Motion Picture Corporation.

85. *Variety,* March 30, 1917.

86. *Variety,* April 13, 1917, p. 25.

87. Ibid.

88. *Moving Picture World,* April 21, 1917, p. 51; De Grazia and Newman, *Banned Films,* p. 188.

89. *Variety,* April 6, 1917, p. 21.

90. *Variety,* May 11, 1917, p. 32.

91. Sanger, p. 252.

92. De Grazia and Newman, p. 187.

93. *Moving Picture World,* May 19, 1917, p. 1098.

94. De Grazia and Newman, p. 188.

95. Sanger, p. 252.

96. De Grazia and Newman, p. 17. When, around 1916, Alice Guy Blaché proposed a birth control film to Lewis Selznick, he laughed in her face, Roberta and Simone Blaché, trans., *The Memoirs of Alice Guy Blaché,* ed. Anthony Slide (Metuchen, N.J.: Scarecrow Press, 1986), p. 88. Silent films opposed to birth control included *Valley of Decision* (1916) with Richard Bennett. Clifford Howard, who had written the nudist drama *Purity,* wrote the story, and it was directed by Rea Berger and produced by American Film Co. All three Bennett daughters appeared in it, together with Bennett's sister Blanche Hanson. (Joan Bennett and Lois Kibbee, *The Bennett Playbill* [New York: Holt, Rinehart and Winston, 1970], p. 52.) The curious thing was that Richard Bennett approved of birth control, despite his large family. When Charles G. Norris's *Seed* was filmed in 1931, with Lois Wilson, the birth control aspect was left out.

97. Story by Lucy Payton and Franklyn Hall, scenario by Lois Weber and Phillips Smalley.

98. From the print in the Library of Congress, Washington, D.C. See also Katherine Karr, "The Long Square-Up: Exploitation Trends in the Silent Film," *Journal of the Popular Film,* Vol. III, No. 2, Spring 1974, pp. 107–28. The original title of the film was *The Illborn, AFI Catalogue,* 1911–1920, p. 1021.

99. *Wid's,* April 20, 1916, p. 524.

100. It followed into the Globe *The Dumb Girl of Portici* (1916), the Smalleys' lavish film with Anna Pavlova.

101. *Variety,* April 21, 1916, p. 25.

102. *Moving Picture World,* May 20, 1916, p. 1321.

103. *Moving Picture World,* April 29, 1916, p. 818.

104. *Moving Picture World,* April 29, 1916, p. 818.

105. *Motion Picture News,* October 7, 1916, quoted in Karr, p. 126.

106. *Variety,* July 7, 1916, p. 22.

107. *Variety,* September 22, 1916, p. 32.

108. *Variety,* July 7, 1916, p. 22.

109. This European version was distributed in neutral Holland, the country which had pioneered birth control and where the print was found. A new sequence had been added to the beginning— mothers bring their children to a health clinic, where the authorities ensure they are well cared for.

110. *Pall Mall Gazette,* November 8, 1916, quoted in *The Bioscope,* January 17, 1918, p. 75.

111. *The Bioscope,* November 16, 1916, p. 631.

112. *The Bioscope,* January 17, 1918, p. 75.

113. *The Bioscope,* November 8, 1917, p. 122. A picture called *The Unborn* (1916) was adjusted to cash in on the success of the Smalleys' film. It started as conventional melodrama and suddenly turned into a preachment against abortion. The abortionist's name was Dr. Ahlbad! *Variety,* June 23, 1916. See also *American Film Institute Catalogue* 1911–1920, p. 963, for an account of the legal test case.

114. *Wid's* May 31, 1917, p. 349. The film's original title was *Is a Woman a Person?* Richard Koszarski letter to author, December 8, 1983. The script, which is reprinted in *Film History,* Vol. I, No. 4, pp. 343–66, has a different opening than the released version.

115. *New York Dramatic Mirror,* May 26, 1917.

116. *Wid's,* May 31, 1917, pp. 349–50.

117. De Grazia and Newman, p. 190.

118. *Variety,* May 18, 1917.

119. Lloyd Morris, *Postscript to Yesterday* (New York: Random House, 1947), p. 274.

120. Lynd and Lynd, p. 145.

121. *Moving Picture World,* December 30, 1911, p. 1052.

122. *Motion Picture Magazine,* April 1916, p. 181. The film is preserved in the Library of Congress.

123. Issue of October 1915.

124. Vachel Lindsay, *The Art of the Moving Picture* (New York: MacMillan Co., 1915, reprinted by Liveright, 1970), p. 184. The picture was a box-office failure and another Ibsen film, *Pillars of Society,* directed by Raoul Walsh with a similar cast, was held back for more than a year.

125. Bennett and Kibbee, pp. 44–45.

126. Bennett and Kibbee, pp. 47–48. A student named Walter Wanger approached Bennett for permission to produce the play at Dartmouth, p. 48.

127. *Moving Picture World,* October 2, 1915, p. 90. A novel was also adapted from the play by Upton Sinclair.

128. Ramsaye, p. 619. Thomas Ricketts was a former opera director. Harry Pollard made *Motherhood,* a one-reel birth control picture, in 1914.

129. Bennett and Kibbee, p. 51.

130. *Variety,* October 1, 1915, p. 18.

131. Mrs. Richard Bennett and the mother of the future stars Constance, Barbara, and Joan.

132. This ending was apparently removed before release; reviewers referred to the way he meets his end as "a mystery."

133. Bennett and Kibbee, p. 57.

134. *The Times,* quoted in Harold Dunham, "Research on the Career of G. B. Samuelson," unpublished ms.

135. *The Bioscope,* December 25, 1919, p. 61.

136. *The Kinematograph Weekly,* December 25, 1919, p. 367.

137. The film was reissued in March 1923.

138. *Variety,* March 26, 1920, p. 56.

139. National Vigilance Association Collection, Fawcett Library, courtesy Annette Kuhn, ref. S1 (3).

140. *Moving Picture World,* August 12, 1919, p. 164. These titles do not appear in the incomplete version at the Historical Health Film Collection, University of Michigan. Courtesy of Martin Pernick.

141. And in several other V.D. films. Neither Raymond McKee nor Edward H. Griffith would agree to be interviewed by me, despite my repeated attempts.

142. *Wid's,* April 13, 1919, p. 5.

143. Ibid.

144. *Variety,* April 11, 1919, p. 62.

145. *Variety,* May 9, 1919, p. 57.

146. *Variety,* July 4, 1919, p. 48.

147. *Wid's,* July 11, 1919, p. 1. Lieutenant Colonel William F. Snow was associated with Silverman, and the *AFI Catalogue,* 1911–1920, p. 287, credits him with planning the whole series. Patricia King Hanson, editor. *American Film Institute Catalogue of Motion Pictures Produced in the United States. Feature Films 1911–1920* (Berkeley: University of California Press, 1988).

148. *Variety,* July 4, 1919.

149. Karl S. Lashley, Ph.D. and John B. Watson, Ph.D., "A Psychological Study of Motion Pictures in Relation to Venereal Disease Campaigns," in *Social Hygiene* VII, no. 2 (April 1921), pp. 181–219. Courtesy Martin Pernick.

150. Lashley and Watson, p. 199.

151. "Notes by Joseph Best," January 14, 1949, courtesy Rachel Low and partly printed in her *History of the British Film, 1914–1918* (London: Allen & Unwin, 1950), p. 149.

152. *The Cinema, Report of the Cinema Commission of Inquiry* (London: Williams and Norgate, 1917), p. 84.

153. *Wid's,* February 29, 1918, p. 14.

154. *Variety,* July 4, 1919, p. 42. Ben Lyon played in this film.

155. *Variety,* July 4, 1919.

156. Ibid.

157. Davis was Director of the Section on Women's Work of the Social Hygiene Division of the War Department Commission on Training Camp Activities (of which Raymond B. Fosdick was the head).

158. Helen Ferguson to author, Palm Springs, California, 1970.

159. Ibid.

160. National Vigilance Collection, Fawcett Library, ref. S1.

161. *Wid's,* October 13, 1919. The film was owned by the American Social Hygiene Association of New York and was part of the Public Health Service Campaign, *Wid's,* April 13, 1919, p. 5. It was distributed by Public Health Films, New York, headed by Isaac Silverman and Lieutenant Colonel William F. Snow.

162. *Moving Picture World,* January 4, 1919, p. 100.

163. *Variety,* February 21, 1919, p. 71.

164. *Variety,* July 18, 1919, p. 46.

165. Vivian Van Damm, *Tonight and Every Night* (London: Stanley Paul & Co., 1952), p. 48. Courtesy of Nick Hiley.

166. Dr. Bagley to Parliamentary enquiry "Report of the Joint Select Committee on the Criminal Law Amendment Bill, P.P.," VI, 1920, ques. 2,325, 2,333 quoted in Edward J. Bristow, *Vice and Vigilance* (Dublin: Gill & Macmillan, 1977), p. 151. Another sex education film which perpetuated fear was *The Solitary Sin* (1919), directed by Fred Sullivan and featuring Jack Mulhall, Helene Chadwick, and Pauline Curley. It was banned by New York and in several states, and few periodicals could bring themselves to review it. Yet *Variety* said, "It is so delicately produced that no one could possibly object to any scene in it." *Variety.* May 30, 1919, p. 79. One of the characters goes insane.

167. *Pearson's,* December 1921, p. 244.

168. Ibid.

169. Jane Addams, *A New Conscience and an Ancient Evil* (New York: Macmillan, 1912), p. 3.

170. The use of the word "traffic" in the title of *Traffic in Souls* so upset actress Jane Gail that she pleaded for it to be changed, *Moving Picture World*, December 20, 1913, p. 1420. Jane Gail played a drug addict in the stage play *Dope*, Karr, p. 113.

171. Justin Kaplan, *Lincoln Steffens* (New York: Simon and Schuster, 1974), p. 68. One of Parkhurst's investigators was Frederic Howe, future head of the National Board of Review. And Parkhurst himself later joined the board, May, p. 47.

172. Kaplan, p. 206. Nominal head of the Lexow Committee was Clarence Lexow, state senator from Yonkers. One of its members was William Travers Jerome, Andy Logan, *Against the Evidence* (London: Weidenfeld and Nicolson, 1970), p. 85.

173. Lincoln Steffens, *Shame of the Cities* (New York: McClure, Phillips, 1904, reprinted by Hill and Wang, 1957), p. 203.

174. An episode of *The Downward Path*, the first five-scene film to be copyrighted. Made by the American Mutoscope and Biograph Company, it was intended primarily for peep-show Mutoscope machines and was typical of the risqué films supplied to arcades, or "electric vaudeville." A print is in the Library of Congress.

175. Joseph Mayer, *The Regulation of Commercialized Vice* (New York: Columbia University Press, 1922), p. 43.

176. *Variety*, August 29, 1913, p. 10. *The Lure* was filmed in 1914 by Alice Guy Blaché, *The Memoirs*, p. 85. *The Fight* was filmed (by George Lederer) in 1915, *The Battle*, as *The Money Master*, also in 1915. *The House of Bondage* had been filmed in 1914.

177. Jane Addams, *The Second Twenty Years at Hull-House* (New York: Macmillan, 1930), p. 324.

178. Ramsaye, p. 613.

179. Ramsaye, p. 615.

180. One reason that he left, Tucker said, was that he had produced a picture he did not like—*Traffic*: "I soon would open up the way to an avalanche of this type of picture." He felt he had to flee the temptation of easy money through more such films, *Motion Picture News*, January 13, 1917, p. 228.

181. Ramsaye, p. 616.

182. I. G. Edmonds, *The Big U* (South Brunswick, N.J., and New York: A. S. Barnes, 1977), p. 35. The minutes of the board of directors' meetings at Universal in December 1913 make it clear that the Shuberts had a 33⅓ percent interest, al-though it is not apparent whether it was obtained before or after production, Koszarski letter, December 8, 1983.

183. Edmonds, p. 35.

184. Mark Langer letter to author, September 28, 1984. They did become more involved through various Shubert offshoots and World Film.

185. Jack Lodge, "The Miracle Men," *Griffithiana* 37, December 1989, p. 41.

186. Thomas Monroe Pitkin, *Keepers of the Gate* (New York: New York University Press, 1975), p. 104.

187. Jenks's report was later published, in that significant year of 1913, as *The Immigrant Problem*.

188. Not until 1917 was the first immigration bill requiring a literacy test passed.

189. *Moving Picture World*, February 26, 1916, p. 1275. MacNamara was later responsible for writing and directing a nationalist film, *Ireland a Nation*, which caused riots in New York. See *Moving Picture World*, August 29, 1914, p. 1245.

190. A two-reeler with King Baggot and Jane Gail and almost certainly directed by George Loane Tucker, Lodge, p. 40.

191. The Edison Business Phonograph dated from 1907, and the Dictophone Company was organized in 1908.

192. In April 1912 the Selig Polyscope Company released *Exposed by the Dictograph*, and in 1913 detective William J. Burns was shown setting a trap with a Dictograph in *Exposure of the Land Swindlers* (Kalem, 3 reels). *The Big Boss* (May 1913) also captured a Dictograph trap. Big Tim Sullivan spoke in whispers at the end of his life, believing there were dictagraphs in the walls, Logan, p. 232.

193. The duty list in the police precinct set contains the names of Tucker, MacNamara and even Stern (for Julius Stern, absent studio manager). Cohn has been Anglicized to Cowan.

194. Minutes of Universal Board of Directors, October 28, 1913, courtesy Richard Koszarski.

195. Quoted in Ramsaye, p. 617.

196. Mrs. O. H. P. Belmont and Harriot Stanton Blatch later commended it. Kay Sloan, *The Loud Silents: Origins of the Social Problem Film* (Urbana: University of Illinois, 1988), p. 83.

197. Edmonds, p. 36.

198. *Variety*, December 19, 1913, p. 12.

199. A subplot of the entrapment of a country girl shows signs of the censoring—her beating is removed *in toto*.

200. Charles Feldman, *National Board of Censorship (Review) of Motion Pictures* (New York: Arno Press, 1977), p. 65.

201. *Moving Picture World,* August 29, 1914, p. 14.

202. *New York Times,* December 9, 1913, 8:3.

203. *Variety,* November 28, 1913, p. 12.

204. *Motion Picture News,* January 31, 1914, p. 27. Belasco's attorney must have thought this up; no one seriously considered the motion picture to be on a level with the stage in 1913.

205. *Moving Picture World,* March 21, 1914, p. 1593; Ramsaye, p. 619.

206. Robert C. Allen, *Sight and Sound* (Winter 74/75), p. 50.

207. *Motion Picture Story Magazine,* December 1914, p. 89. Lars Lindstrom found a reference in a Scandinavian newspaper of 1910 to a Dane arrested in Chicago as he was about to deliver two eighteen-year-old Swedish girls to a brothel on South Clark Street. He had met the girls in Copenhagen, provided them with good positions with a Chicago family, and taken them across the Atlantic in a German steamer, letter to author, March 12, 1985.

208. The final raid was not filmed in New York City. The thought of a mass police raid and shootout in the middle of somewhere like Hell's Kitchen evidently deterred the company. Judging by the unpaved streets, it was probably filmed near the studios at Fort Lee, with a larger New Jersey town providing the roofscape.

209. *Picture Play,* September 1916, p. 43.

210. "Ball, Eustace Hale, Traffic in Souls; a novel of crime and its cure; based in part upon the scenario of the photodrama of the same name written by Walter MacNamara, with illustrations from the scenes in the photoplay. C. Dillingham Co (1914) 289p. illus." But MacNamara earned nothing from the picture's success, apart from his salary and "a trifling Christmas present." (*Variety,* January 23, 1914, p. 14.)

211. *Moving Picture World,* November 1, 1913, p. 500, November 9, 1913, p. 613.

212. Original title *Human Cargoes.*

213. *Motion Picture Story Magazine,* December 1914, p. 93. I suspect they showed only parts of *Traffic in Souls.*

214. *Variety,* December 12, 1913, p. 12.

215. *Motion Picture News,* December 20, 1913, p. 31.

216. Ibid.

217. Ibid.

218. Leo Katcher, *The Big Bankroll* (New York: Cardinal, 1961), p. 21. It was also known as "Jewish faro."

219. Night courts had been established in 1907 by magistrate Charles Whitman (later D.A. in New York) to deal with prostitution and were also known as the morals court, Logan, p. 143. *On Record* (1917) showed that girls could be placed "on record" in the night court through no fault of their own, *New York Dramatic Mirror,* May 3, 1917, p. 17.

220. *Variety,* December 12, 1913, p. 12.

221. Herbert Asbury, *The French Quarter* (New York: Knopf, 1936), p. 446.

222. *Variety,* December 12, 1913, p. 12.

223. *Variety,* December 26, 1913, p. 13.

224. *Variety,* January 2, 1914, p. 14.

225. This was probably a 1910 Danish film, *The White Slave Trade,* itself a remake of an earlier Danish film on prostitution.

226. *Moving Picture World,* January 31, 1914, p. 530.

227. *Moving Picture World,* January 3, 1914, p. 53.

228. *Moving Picture World,* January 10, 1914, p. 155.

229. *Variety,* January 2, 1914, p. 15.

230. *Moving Picture World,* January 10, 1914, p. 156.

231. *Variety,* January 16, 1914, p. 15.

232. *Variety,* March 13, 1914, p. 23. This was not the end of London's association with motion pictures. In 1918 he wrote *Her Moment* (also copyrighted as *Why Blame Me?*). It was the story of how one typical victim 'struggled to find her way to the light.' London once more based the story on incidents from his days as investigator. Anna Luther played the immigrant victim, *Motion Picture News,* June 19, 1918, p. 3903.

233. Quoted in Karr, p. 116.

234. *Moving Picture World,* January 17, 1914, p. 276.

235. *New York Dramatic Mirror,* January 14, 1914.

236. *Moving Picture World,* January 17, 1914, p. 276.

237. Ibid.

238. *Variety,* February 27, 1914, p. 21.

239. *Moving Picture World,* February 7, 1914, p. 653.

240. Hampton, p. 42.

241. Herbert Asbury, *The Barbary Coast* (New York: Knopf, 1933), p. 287.

242. Geoffrey Bell letter to author, September 28, 1985.

243. Sid Grauman and Ephie Asher were also involved.

244. Asbury, *The Barbary Coast,* p. 289.

245. Hal Mohr to author, Hollywood, 1969. See also Bernard Rosenberg and Harry

Silverstein, *The Real Tinsel* (New York: Mac-Millan, 1970), and Leonard Maltin, *The Art of the Cinematographer* (New York: Dover Publications, 1978), chapters on Hal Mohr.

246. *Moving Picture World,* November 1, 1913, p. 546.

247. *Moving Picture World,* November 1, 1913, p. 474.

248. Geoffrey Bell, *The Golden Gate and the Silver Screen* (Cranbury, N.J.: Associated University Presses, 1984), p. 107.

249. *Motion Picture News,* June 22, 1918.

250. *Variety,* November 22, 1923, p. 22.

251. *Photoplay,* July 1917, p. 113.

252. *Journal of the Popular Film,* 1973; Karr, *Journal of the Popular Film,* Vol. III, No. 2, Spring 1974, pp. 107–28..

253. Richard Koszarski, letter to author, May 1985. Koszarski, who has a copy of the script, says the film cuts back every few shots to a minister in a pulpit delivering a sermon on the white slave evil.

254. *Variety,* September 1, 1916, p. 20.

255. *Wid's,* September 21, 1916, p. 982.

256. *Moving Picture World,* June 30, 1917, p. 2116.

257. Ibid.

258. Ibid.

259. *New York Dramatic Mirror,* June 23, 1917. Evelyn Brent played Betty Hamlin.

260. *The Penalty* (1920).

261. *The Toll Gate* (1920).

262. In 1920 a bill adding "lewd and lascivious" motion pictures to the list of articles prohibited from interstate commerce was passed by the House of Representatives without debate, *Moving Picture World,* February 7, 1920, p. 878.

263. *Motion Picture Magazine,* May 1925, p. 129.

264. *Photoplay,* June 1925, p. 110.

265. *Classic Film Collector,* 38, p. 17.

266. Mrs. Wallace Reid to Sue Mc-Conachy, Hollywood TV series, 1976.

267. Asbury, *The French Quarter,* p. 430.

268. Asbury, *The French Quarter,* p. 452. Storyville was closed when the secretary of war issued an order forbidding open prostitution within five miles of an army cantonment, and a similar ruling was made for naval establishments. It was the navy who insisted in this case.

269. Priscilla Bonner played the blind girl in *The Strong Man* (1926) with Harry Langdon.

270. Priscilla Bonner letter to author, October 19, 1980.

271. *Picture Play,* February 1926, p. 66. Mrs. Reid said she never regarded herself as a good actress, so while she codirected, she only appeared in the prologue.

272. Carl Miller played in Chaplin's *A Woman of Paris* (1923).

273. This sequence was placed earlier in the picture.

274. A reference to *The Scarlet Letter* by Nathaniel Hawthorne; the A is for Adulteress.

275. *Magill's Survey of Cinema,* Vol. 3, ed. Frank N. Magill (Englewood Cliffs, N.J.: Salem Press, 1982), p. 906.

276. Short, p. 67.

277. *Variety,* February 3, 1926.

278. *New York Times,* February 3, 1926.

279. Bonner letter to author, October 19, 1980. See also Anthony Slide, *Idols of Silence* (Metuchen, N.J.: Scarecrow Press, 1976), p. 72.

CHAPTER THREE: DRUGS

1. *Dope,* scenario by C. Gardner Sullivan, author's collection.

2. Troy Duster, *The Legislation of Morality* (New York: The Free Press, 1970), p. 3.

3. Duster, p. 7.

4. Harry J. Anslinger, U.S. Commissioner of Narcotics, quoted in Katcher, p. 291.

5. Duster, p. 8.

6. William Dufty, *Sugar Blues* (New York: Warner Books, 1975), p. 165.

7. *The Dope Chronicles,* ed. Gary Silver (New York: Harper & Row, 1979), p. 53.

8. *The Biograph Bulletins* 1908–12, ed. Eileen Bowser (New York: Octagon, 1973). These bulletins were the work of Lee Dougherty.

9. *Variety,* October 24, 1913.

10. *Variety,* February 27, 1914, p. 23.

11. The Lubin Film Company scrapbooks, courtesy Linda Kowall.

12. Ibid.

13. *Variety,* February 27, 1914, p. 23.

14. *Variety,* June 5, 1914, p. 17.

15. *Variety.* The film broke attendance records elsewhere, according to Lubin historian Linda Kowall. It was shown at the Tombs, New York, and many other prisons. Special screenings were arranged for Jane Addams at Hull-House and for physicians at Johns Hopkins.

16. *Moving Picture World,* April 4, 1914, pp. 113–14.

17. *New York Dramatic Mirror,* Novem-

ber 13, 1915, p. 32. Frank Reicher made a film with a similar story in 1921, *Idle Hands*.

18. *New York Dramatic Mirror*, December 18, 1915.

19. *New York Dramatic Mirror*, January 1, 1916, p. 30.

20. *Variety*, June 18, 1915, p. 19.

21. *Variety*, December 8, 1916, p. 29. The film was held up for a year—usually the sign that distributors have no faith in it. The attempted suicide was based on the case of the wife of actor Edward Morgan, who was addicted to morphine and tried to kill herself in this manner. Courtesy of John Delph.

22. *Wid's*, December 14, 1916, p. 1174. *Motion Picture News* liked it.

23. *Variety*, July 28, 1916, p. 24.

24. *Wid's*, July 20, 1916, p. 733, and synopsis in the Library of Congress of 1923 reissue.

25. *Variety*, July 28, 1916.

26. Katharine Karr, "The Long Square-Up," p. 119.

27. Bessie Love's diary.

28. Arthur Lennig, *The Silent Voice*, Faculty-Student Association of the State University of New York at Albany, Inc. 1966, p. 45.

29. *Variety*, June 8, 1916, p. 627.

30. Ibid.

31. *New York Dramatic Mirror*, June 10, 1916, p. 31.

32. *Wid's*, April 12, 1917, p. 236. Miss Fischer removed the Teutonic "c" from her name during World War I. Only a short version of this film survives.

33. Paul Armstrong, who had died in 1915, had been the husband of the star of the film, Catherine Calvert.

34. *Mutual Defense League Magazine*, quoted in *Motion Picture News*, May 4, 1918, p. 2700. A remake of *A Romance of the Underworld* by Irving Cummings in 1929 dispensed entirely with the drug aspect.

35. Duster, p. 15.

36. Duster, p. 19.

37. Silver, p. 81.

38. Dr. Ellis Paxson Oberholtzer, *The Morals of the Movie*, quoted in Gerald Mast, ed., *The Movies in Our Midst* (Chicago: University of Chicago Press, 1982), p. 198.

39. Oberholtzer, in Mast, p. 81.

40. *Picture Play*, February 1921, p. 97.

41. *Photoplay*, January 1923, p. 84.

42. *Photoplay*, March 1923, p. 36.

43. *Photoplay*, May 1923, p. 26.

44. Charles "Buddy" Post, *Motion Picture Magazine*, January 1924, p. 21.

45. *Los Angeles Herald*, March 25, 1919. Courtesy Bruce Long.

46. Alice Terry to author, Hollywood, 1971. In the film, Wallace Reid plays a man who builds a railroad.

47. *Los Angeles Herald*, December 19, 1922.

48. Karl Brown to author, "Hollywood," a thirteen-part series on the silent era, written, produced, and directed by Kevin Brownlow and David Gill (1980).

49. Brown to author, 1976.

50. *Variety*, September 9, 1921. *Forever* was premiered in October 1921. While this may not refer to Reid, all the indications are that it does. The reference to peddlers, however, suggests the studio doctor was not his sole supplier, as Mrs. Reid maintained later.

51. Douglas Whitton, "Murder of a Movie Director," unpublished ms. (p. 221).

52. *Picture Play*, January 1923, p. 8.

53. *Films in Review*, April 1966, p. 217.

54. *Photoplay*, January 1923, p. 84.

55. *Los Angeles Herald*, December 19, 1922.

56. *Variety*, January 25, 1923, p. 10. *The Devil's Needle* was reissued in 1923 to cash in on Reid's death.

57. *Photoplay*, April 1923, p. 76.

58. Bessie Love to author, London, 1978.

59. *Variety*, May 17, 1923.

60. *Films in Review*, April 1966, p. 216.

61. *Human Wreckage* pressbook, courtesy Dr. Güttinger.

62. The film also featured Martha Nelson McCan, Los Angeles Park Commissioner; Mrs. Chester Ashley; John P. Carter, former U.S. Internal Revenue Collector; Charles F. Gray, of the Parent-Teachers Association; Dr. L. M. Powers, Health Commissioner, City of Los Angeles; Brigadier C. R. Boyd, Salvation Army, *AFI Catalogue*, 1921–1930, p. 368.

63. *Photoplay*, August 1923, pp. 85–86.

64. Claire McDowell and Mrs. Reid (née Dorothy Davenport) were cousins.

65. Mothers at this period calmed their babies with syrups spiked with opium, which could be bought at any pharmacy, Whitton, p. 222.

66. *Variety*, July 4, 1923. *Variety* also pointed out an error—morphine was used by MacFarland as a stimulant, but the review declared it deadened rather than exhilarated. They were only partly right. "Despite the fact that it is primarily a depressant it has some ability to act simultaneously as a stimulant," Duster, p. 32.

67. *Motion Picture Classic*, October 1923, p. 11.

68. Ibid.

69. Quoted in *Variety*, June 28, 1923, p. 23.

70. Home Office file 45/1159, Public Records Office, London. Courtesy Annette Kuhn.

71. *Motion Picture Magazine*, October 1923, p. 114. In her old age, Mrs. Reid remained an intelligent and lively woman, but so strong were the defenses she had built up against the wounds of memory that she was unable to recall anything more than headlines about the events. "I don't know whether keeping everything sharp and alive is kind," she said. When asked directly about the Wallace Reid affair, she paused for thought and then said, "Isn't it dreadful? Greatest tragedy of my life, of course. I think it's one of those things that's so bitter for you, you just keep the lovely things. I can't offer you a legitimate excuse for not having more detail except loss of memory. But not," she added, "a loss of love," Mrs. Wallace Reid to Sue McConachy, "Hollywood" TV series, 1976.

72. Al Rogell to author, November 1986.

73. Rogell to author, 1986.

74. *AFI Catalogue*, 1921–1930, p. 315.

75. Al Rogell to Bob Birchard, interviews for Directors Guild of America, 1977, and for Kevin Brownlow, 1986.

76. Rogell to author, 1986. The film was made at the old Fine Arts Studio, where *Intolerance* had been shot.

77. William O. Walker III, *Drug Control in the Americas* (Albuquerque: University of New Mexico Press, 1981), pp. 67, 70.

78. Michael Starks, *Cocaine Fiends and Reefer Madness* (East Brunswick, N.J.: Cornwall Books, 1982), p. 45.

79. *Photoplay*, February 1929, p.76.

CHAPTER FOUR: PROHIBITION

1. *Wichita Daily Eagle*, December 28, 1900. The defense held that she was not responsible for her actions, and the charge was dismissed. Shortly afterward, she wrecked two more saloons, *Wichita Daily Eagle*, January 22, 1901. Courtesy J. B. Kaufman.

2. A calendar in one scene says Thursday, November 23 which occurred in 1905 and 1911, letter from Library of Congress to author, October 13, 1977.

3. Sinclair, *Upton Sinclair Presents William Fox*, published by the author, Los Angeles, 1933, pp. 2–3.

4. *Edison Catalogue*, quoted in Lewis Jacobs, *The Rise of the American Film*, p. 19.

5. Jack S. Blocker, Jr., *Retreat from Reform* (Westport, Conn.: Greenwood Press, 1976), p. 15.

6. May, *Screening Out the Past*, p. 14.

7. *Moving Picture World*, June 29, 1912, p. 1217.

8. Addams, *The Second Twenty Years at Hull-House*, p. 222.

9. Blocker, Jr., p. 199.

10. Lindsay, *The Art of the Moving Picture*, p. 235.

11. Martin Short, *Crime Inc.* (London: Thames Methuen, 1984), p. 60.

12. Thomas Dixon, *Southern Horizons* (Alexandria, Va.: IWV Publishing, 1984), copyright Raymond Rohauer, p. 234.

13. *Photoplay*, May 1916, p. 27.

14. *Moving Picture World*, January 24, 1920, p. 553.

15. Hampton, *The History of the American Film Industry*, p. 424. Garth Jowett in *Film: The Democratic Art* (p. 90) thinks it doubtful that many people permanently deserted the public bar for the picture theatre.

16. *New York Dramatic Mirror*, November 6, 1915.

17. *New York Dramatic Mirror*, March 10, 1917, p. 27. The Southern scenes were shot on the Gulf Coast near New Orleans, *AFI Catalogue*, 1911–1920, p. 113.

18. *New York Dramatic Mirror*, March 10, 1917, p. 27.

19. *New York Dramatic Mirror*, June 9, 1917, p. 28.

20. Ibid.

21. *Moving Picture World*, August 23, 1913, p. 848. The secretary and third partner of the Bosworth Company was H. T. Rudisill. Garbutt was also a celebrated sportsman.

22. Kalton Lahue, *Motion Picture Pioneer* (South Brunswick, N.J., and New York: A. S. Barnes, 1973), pp. 14, 77.

23. Mrs. Bosworth was recently persuaded by Paul Spehr to donate such prints as she possessed to the Library of Congress.

24. *Moving Picture World*, January 10, 1914, p. 156.

25. *Moving Picture World*, July 18, 1914, p. 406.

26. Ibid.

27. Sinclair, *Autobiography of Upton Sinclair*, p. 50.

28. *AFI Catalogue*, 1911–1930, p. 475.

29. *Moving Picture World*, August 1, 1914, p. 707.

30. Ibid.

31. Harry Reichenbach, *Phantom Fame* (New York: Simon and Schuster, 1931), p. 225.

32. *Variety*, April 23, 1915, p. 18.

33. Ibid.

34. Ibid.

35. *Motion Picture News*, April 17, 1915, p. 68.

36. Ibid.

37. *Motion Picture News*, May 15, 1915, p. 56.

38. Ibid.

39. *San Jose Mercury-Herald*, October 19, 1916, quoted in Drew, *D. W. Griffith's Intolerance*, p. 131.

40. *Variety*, June 17, 1919, p. 1.

41. *1919 Wid's Year Book*, p. 104.

42. *The Dry Decade*, p. 51.

43. *1919 Wid's Year Book*, p. 104.

44. *1919 Wid's Year Book*, p. 110.

45. *1920 Wid's Year Book*, p. 233.

46. *1920 Wid's Year Book*, p. 235.

47. Ibid.

48. *Variety*, October 24, 1919, p. 61.

49. *New York Times*, June 2, 1920, p. 1, col. 3; June 3, 1920, p.9, col. 1; June 4, 1920, p. 10, col. 1; June 14, 1920, p. 10, col. 1. Courtesy J. B. Kaufman.

50. The term originated in the Southern states when a moonshiner avoided paying tax on manufactured distilled spirits by delivering bottles concealed in the leg of his boots, George E. Mowry, *The Twenties* (Englewood Cliffs, N.J.: Prentice-Hall, 1963), p. 94.

51. Donald Ogden Stewart, *By a Stroke of Luck* (London: Paddington Press, 1975), p. 149.

52. Short, *Crime Inc.*, p. 145.

53. *Variety*, May 20, 1921, p. 46.

54. *Variety*, November 4, 1921, p. 46. She was also arrested for abducting a fourteen-year-old boy who had left home to follow her, *Cinemagazine*, January 5, 1923, p. 23.

55. Morris, *Postscript to Yesterday*, p. 73.

56. *Picture Play*, October 1925, p. 55. Texas was also portrayed, thinly disguised, in films like Lois Weber's *Angel of Broadway* (1927).

57. *Picture Play*, January 1929, p. 55.

58. Allen F. Davis, *Spearheads for Reform* (New York: Oxford University Press, 1967), p. 237.

59. *Motion Picture Magazine*, September 1929, p. 53.

60. Frank Thompson, *William Wellman* (Metuchen, N.J.: Scarecrow Press, 1983), p. 50. The sequence appears in Robert Youngson's *MGM's Big Parade of Comedy*. (1964).

61. *Variety*, August 19, 1925, p. 27.

62. It is almost certain to have been acquired by Warner Bros. when they remade it in 1930.

63. *Photoplay*, August 1924, p. 48.

64. Ince Corporation agreements, August 25, 1923. Courtesy Steven Higgins. George Kibbe Turner was eventually credited with the story, Hillyer and Arthur Statter with the adaptation.

65. Ince Silversheet, no date.

66. Ince Silversheet.

67. *Variety*, July 2, 1924.

68. Letter from Wilbur D. Finch to the Ince Corporation, July 29, 1924. Courtesy Steven Higgins.

69. Laurence Reid, *Motion Picture Classic*, September 1924, p. 94.

70. *Picture Play*, September 1924, p. 56.

71. *Motion Picture Magazine*, September 1924, p. 85.

72. Letter Ingle Carpenter to Ben M. Goldman, July 29, 1925. Courtesy Steven Higgins and J. B. Kaufman.

73. *Santa Ana Daily Evening Register*, August 7, 1924, quoted in Sleeper, *Great Films Shot in Orange County*, p. 106.

74. *Santa Ana Daily Evening Register*, September 4, 1924.

75. A Chicago playwright and later MGM producer (*The Great Ziegfeld*). Reviewers noted the influence of *What Price Glory?* on this film, about two tough men and their misuse of women.

76. Charles Merz, *The Dry Decade* (New York: Doubleday, 1930, reprinted by the University of Washington Press, 1969), p. 114.

77. *Life*, August 18, 1927, quoted in original uncut ms. of *Dark Star* by Leatrice Gilbert Fountain.

78. *Photoplay*, August 1927, p. 92.

79. MGM press book Theatre Arts Collection, Lincoln Center, Courtesy of George Geltzer.

80. *Los Angeles Times*, July 14, 1927, quoted in *Dark Star* original uncut ms.

81. *Film Spectator*, September 3, 1927, p. 12.

82. *Photoplay*, September 1927, p. 55.

83. *New York Times*, July 26, 1927, p. 17, quoted in Leatrice Gilbert Fountain, *Dark Star* (New York: St. Martin's Press, 1985), p. 139.

84. *Photoplay*, December 1927, p. 27.

85. *The People's Chronology*, James Trager, ed. (New York: Holt, Rinehart and Winston, 1979), p. 846.

86. *People's Chronology*, p. 854.

87. William E. Leuchtenburg, *Perils of Prosperity* (Chicago: University of Chicago Press, 1958), p. 215.

CHAPTER FIVE: CRIME

1. A similarity was noted between this and Augustus Thomas's *The Witching Hour* (1907), also filmed in 1916.

2. *Photoplay*, November 1916, p. 57.

3. *Photoplay*, November 1916, p. 86.

4. *New York Dramatic Mirror*, August 26, 1916.

5. J. B. Kaufman letter to author, February 27, 1985.

6. Evelyn Nesbit, *The Story of My Life* (London: J. Long, 1914), p. 50.

7. Evelyn Nesbit, *The Untold Story* (London: J. Long, 1934), p. 51.

8. Jay Robert Nash, *Murder, America* (London: Harrap, 1981), p. 384. A film called *Evidence* (1918, Triangle) had a man kill his unfaithful wife. "But so blameless is his past reputation and so powerful the influence of his friends, that he is declared insane and sentenced to an asylum for a brief period," *New York Dramatic Mirror*, January 19, 1918.

9. *The Unwritten Law* is in the National Film Archive, London; a short reenactment called *The Thaw-White Tragedy* (1906) is in the Library of Congress. It was photographed by Billy Bitzer two days after the event primarily for the amusement arcades and was banned in some cities.

10. Jay Robert Nash, *Bloodletters and Badmen* (New York: Warner Paperback, 1973), p. 373. Ziegfeld put Nesbit lookalike Lilian Lorraine on a swing, flying out over the Follies audience, to recall this incident, Frank Platt, *Great Stars of Hollywood's Golden Age* (New York: New American Library, 1966), p. 123.

11. Nash, *Bloodletters and Badmen*, p. 374.

12. Nesbit, *The Untold Story*, p. 247.

13. *Moving Picture World*, May 23, 1907, p. 180.

14. *Moving Picture World*, July 13, 1907, p. 295.

15. Nash, *Bloodletters and Badmen*, p. 377.

16. Memorandum from Sidney E. Werner, attorney for Harry Thaw, June 17, 1947. Courtesy Lawrence Copley Thaw.

17. *Variety*, August 15, 1913, p. 4. Thanks to her, Hammerstein's made a $100,000 profit during the summer months, "when anything excepting a loss is a Heavenly gift in vaudeville." *Variety*, September 5, 1913, p. 4.

18. This may have been the film with Ethel Grandin in the Nesbit role, filmed at Madison Square Garden, using the very table where Thaw had shot White. *Motion Picture Country Home Lodge Commentary*, July 1971, p. 2.

19. *Variety*, September 19, 1913, p. 2.

20. *Variety*, September 26, 1913.

21. Jacobs, *The Rise of the American Film*, p. 155. Thaw was almost certainly unbalanced, and he was involved in many other newsworthy incidents—mostly brawls of one kind or another.

22. *Variety*, May 8, 1914, and May 15, 1914.

23. Nesbit, *The Untold Story*, p. 249.

24. Nesbit, *The Untold Story*, p. 257.

25. *Variety*, May 4, 1917, p. 28.

26. *Wid's*, June 21, 1917.

27. *Variety*, May 25, 1917, p. 18.

28. *Motion Picture Magazine*, August 1917, p. 12.

29. *The Bioscope*, February 28, 1918, p. 38.

30. *Moving Picture World*, September 21, 1918, p. 1747. Portraits of Nesbit by Dana and Harrington Mann were shown in the film (*AFI Catalogue*, 1911–1920, p. 1062).

31. *Wid's*, December 29, 1918, p. 9.

32. *Photoplay*, May 1919, p. 95.

33. *Variety*, January 31, 1919, p. 52. *AFI Catalogue*, 1911–1920, says she marries the millionaire, p. 1062.

34. *Wid's*, June 15, 1919, p. 39.

35. Allan Dwan to author, "Hollywood" TV series, 1977.

36. Ibid.

37. Ibid.

38. *Variety*, January 6, 1926, p. 1.

39. Samson de Brier letter to author, November 28, 1983.

40. *Motion Picture News*, September 16, 1911, p. 11.

41. *Motion Picture News*, September 16, 1911, p. 14.

42. Ibid.

43. *Motion Picture News*, September 30, 1911, p. 18.

44. *Motion Picture News*, September 30, 1911, p. 22.

45. *New York Times*, November 25, 1911, 3:1.

46. Miriam Cooper, *Dark Lady of the Silents* (New York: Bobbs-Merrill, 1973), p. 146.

47. Cooper, p. 146.

48. *Variety*, March 15, 1918, p. 43.

49. Rumor had it that Rudolph Valentino was poisoned in 1926 by friends of Jack De Saulles, Alexander Walker, *Valentino* (London: Elm Tree Books, 1976), p. 113.

50. *Photoplay*, November 1921, p. 64.

51. John Ince was a director and a brother of Thomas H.

52. *AFI Catalogue*, 1921–1930, p. 233.

53. *Variety*, June 24, 1921, p. 38.

54. *Variety*, July 8, 1921, p. 29.

55. *Variety*, August 26, 1921, p. 39: 1921 Studio Directory.

56. *Variety*, July 1, 1925, p. 22, reported Clara Hamon divorced Gorman on grounds of mental cruelty.

57. *Variety*, September 2, 1921, p. 41.

58. *Variety*, September 28, 1921, p. 46.

59. Ibid.

60. *Photoplay*, November 1921, p. 64.

61. *Photoplay*, February 1922, p. 39.

62. Veronica and Paul King, *Problems of Modern American Crime* (London: Heath Cranton, 1926), p. 33.

63. *Variety*, February 24, 1922, p. 39.

64. *Moving Picture World*, March 9, 1907, p. 24.

65. When the New York Police Department changed its uniforms, Sennett's New York office had sackloads sent to California for the Keystone Cops, Minta Durfee interview, 1963.

66. *Variety*, May 17, 1918; *Variety*, July 5, 1918, p. 34.

67. *Motion Picture News*, July 27, 1912, p. 2.

68. *Variety*, April 17, 1914, final page. "Lineup" meant watch bill or roster, listing men on and off duty; it also refers to identity parades.

69. *Variety*, May 15, 1914, p. 19.

70. *Variety*, April 17, 1914, final page.

71. *Moving Picture World*, November 7, 1914, p. 774.

72. *Moving Picture World*, October 1, 1920, p. 39.

73. Short, *Crime Inc.*, p. 65.

74. *Moving Picture World*, April 11, 1914, p. 226. There was a Universal City before the grand opening of the ranch in 1915.

75. *Variety*. June 11, 1915, p. 19.

76. Ibid.

77. *Film Index*, p. 539; *Moving Picture World*, September 2, 1911, p. 633.

78. *Moving Picture World*, March 11, 1916, p. 1669.

79. Hal Roach to David Gill, Bel Air, 1988.

80. *Moving Picture World*, January 14, 1913, p. 1116.

81. *Moving Picture World*, January 5, 1914, p. 30.

82. Reichenbach, *Phantom Fame*, p. 176.

83. Graham Adams, Jr., *The Age of Industrial Violence, 1910–1915* (New York: Columbia University Press, 1966), p. 197.

84. *Moving Picture World*, February 10, 1912, p. 486; *Moving Picture World*, March 29, 1913, p. 1351.

85. *Moving Picture World*, February 10, 1912, p. 486; *Moving Picture World*, March 29, 1913, p. 1351.

86. *People's Chronology*, 1979, p. 607.

87. *Moving Picture World*, February 22, 1913, p. 759.

88. Ibid. See also rewritten story line in *Motion Picture Story Magazine*, April 1913, p. 85, with illustrations. A letter to the magazine assured readers that this was the only film in which William J. Burns appeared and the only one authorized by him. This statement was necessary because so many other filmmakers had made free with his name.

89. *Moving Picture World*, February 22, 1913, p. 759.

90. *Moving Picture World*, August 8, 1914, p. 843.

91. *Variety*, August 14, 1914, p. 21.

92. *Moving Picture World*, August 22, 1914, p. 1083.

93. *Moving Picture World*, August 22, 1914, p. 1083.

94. *Moving Picture World*, April 19, 1913, p. 289. The film was not released until 1914—it was probably delayed for legal reasons. The picture reminded *Variety* (August 14, 1914, p. 21) of Lasky's *The Little Gray Lady* (1914), another story of counterfeiting. But far from pleasing the Secret Service, this outraged them. Major Metellus Funkhouser showed *The Little Gray Lady* to the head of the Service in Chicago, Captain Thomas I. Porter, who confiscated it. Among the scenes he objected to were shots of a government clerk tearing small portions from bills and then putting them together to form a hundred-dollar bill. But far worse was the scene of the clerk being arrested by a Secret Service man. A friend of the clerk bribes the officer, enabling the crooks to flee the country.

"This is the most objectionable picture I ever saw," said Captain Porter. "It shows bribery of government officials, and also criminality, because of the fact that the alleged hero is shown making the money."

Porter's action was received with protests, since the story was based on Channing Pollock's play, performed many times without complaint, *Moving Picture World*, August 8, 1914, p. 820.

95. Robert Grau, *Theatre of Science* (New York: Broadway Publishing, 1914), p. 88.

96. *Motion Picture Magazine*, June 1931, p. 103.

97. See also Kevin Brownlow, *The War, the West and the Wilderness* (New York: Knopf, 1978), p. 139.

98. Katcher, *The Big Bankroll*, pp. 53, 55. Mizner was coauthor with Paul Armstrong of the play *Alias Jimmy Valentine* and *The Greyhound*, underworld stories which became films. He appeared in Raoul Walsh's *Me, Gangster* (1928).

99. *Photoplay*, May 1920, p. 110. The most famous name among all American detectives, that of Pinkerton, cropped up in a Selznick picture, *A Man's Home*. Far from being flattered, W. A. "Bill" Pinkerton, son of the founder and himself principal of the Pinkerton National Detective Agency, sued to have it removed from the subtitles. The judge threw the case out of court, *Variety*, March 17, 1922, p. 43. August Vollmer, chief of police, Berkeley, California, appeared in the serial *Officer 444* (1926). Courtesy of William K. Everson.

100. *Films in Review*, September 1965, p. 586.

101. Kalton Lahue, *Continued Next Week* (Norman: University of Oklahoma Press, 1954), p. 117.

102. *Moving Picture World*, August 2, 1924, advertisement section.

103. *The Bioscope*, November 13, 1924, p. 50.

104. *Moving Picture Magazine*, May 1926, p. 39.

105. *Philadelphia Record* quoted in *Moving Picture World*, June 8, 1912, p. 905.

106. Dr. D. P. Macmillan to Chicago Motion Picture Commission 1918, quoted in Short, *A Generation*, p. 37.

107. National Board of Censorship (Review), p. 294.

108. Reviewed in *The Survey*, April 15, 1926, quoted in Lynd and Lynd, *Middletown*, p. 268.

109. Jane Addams, *The Spirit of Youth and the City Streets* (New York: Macmillan, 1909), p. 75.

110. Addams, *The Spirit of Youth*, p. 92.

111. Addams, *The Spirit of Youth*, p. 93.

112. By Williams and Norgate, London. The Bishop of Birmingham was president of the commission, which included Lieutenant General Sir Robert Baden-Powell, founder of the Scout movement, the Rabbi Professor Gollancz, representing the Jewish community, T. P. O'Connor, the chief censor, a group of educational people and representatives of the industry, together with Dr. Marie Stopes, the advocate of birth control, *Report of the Cinema Commission*, p. xxi.

113. *Report of the Cinema Commission*, p. xlii.

114. *Report of the Cinema Commission*, p. xlv.

115. *Report of the Cinema Commission*, p. xliv.

116. *Report of the Cinema Commission*, p. 130.

117. *Report of the Cinema Commission*, p. 241.

118. *Christian Advocate*, July 16, 1925, p. 15, quoted in Jowett, *Film: The Democratic Art*, p. 145.

119. *Moving Picture World*, May 1915, p. 1290.

120. Lincoln Steffens, *Upbuilders* (New York: Doubleday, Page, 1909, reprinted by the University of Washington Press, Seattle, 1968), p. 96.

121. Ben Lindsey, "Problem of the Children," quoted in Steffens, *Upbuilders*, p. 100.

122. Quoted in Steffens, *Upbuilders*, p. 100.

123. Morris, *Postscript to Yesterday*, p. 308.

124. Lindsey and Borough, *The Dangerous Life*, p. 113.

125. Steffens, *Upbuilders*, p. 238.

126. Lindsey and Borough, p. 79.

127. Eric F. Goldman, *Rendezvous with Destiny* (New York: Vintage Books, 1955), p. 177.

128. This was something that astonished the authorities, who assumed that somehow Lindsey hypnotized the boys.

129. *Moving Picture World*, August 9, 1913, p. 680.

130. Ramsaye, *A Million and One Nights*, p. 611.

131. He returned in 1914 to run the Colorado Motion Picture Company.

132. *Moving Picture World*, August 9, 1913, p. 643.

133. Ibid.

134. *The Soul of Youth* survives at the Library of Congress in an excellent 35mm print.

135. *Moving Picture World*, April 4, 1914, p. 126.

136. *Moving Picture World*, August 15, 1914, p. 965.

137. King Vidor, *A Tree Is a Tree* (New York: Harcourt, Brace, 1953), p. 44.

138. Vidor, p. 46. Vidor's *Bud's Recruit* survives in the Library of Congress. See Brownlow, p. 134.

139. *AFI Catalogue*, 1921–1930, p. 93.

140. *Picture Play*, April 1925, p. 112.

141. *Variety*, January 21, 1924, p. 31: "Mrs. Wallace Reid in Person and New Picture Disappoint"—a report from Kansas City.

142. *Picture Play*, January 1925, p. 31.

143. *Variety*'s figures quoted in Norton Parker biography, p. 1. In the top 104 moneymakers of 1928, it was number 43, *Exhibitors Herald*, December 29, 1928, p. 34.

144. *AFI Catalogue,* 1921–1930, p. 659. The idea of a father about to attack his own daughter was also done in 1916 in *It May Be Your Daughter.*

145. *Photoplay,* May 1928, p. 114.

146. Ibid.

147. Such as Birmingham, Alabama, where an exhibitor took the matter to federal court and lost, de Grazia and Newman, *Banned Films,* p. 208.

148. Mrs. Norton S. Parker, letter to author, July 29, 1980. Grant Withers was later married to and divorced from Loretta Young.

149. Either censorship has struck and the climax to the strip poker scene has been removed, or it was never included in the final cut. I suspect the juvenile court people would have objected to any hint of nudity and the sequence would have been an early casualty.

150. Mrs. Norton S. Parker letter to author, July 29, 1980.

151. Letter to Cliff Broughton Productions, March 28, 1928, quoted in publicity.

152. Publicity material. Courtesy Mrs. Parker.

153. *The House of Correction* (1914) was a three-reeler released by Union Features about a reformatory run by a "philanthropic" magistrate where the boys are treated like animals. "Many of them lose their reason entirely, while others become so weak they can scarcely walk." The newspapers expose the scandal when a youth escapes and dies as a result of brutality by the warders, *Moving Picture World,* April 4, 1914, p. 126. The picture did not exaggerate the conditions of the worst of these places.

154. Eddie Quillan to author, Hollywood, June 1986.

155. *Motion Picture Magazine,* May 1928, p. 28.

156. George Duryea was later known as Tom Keene. He had starred on Broadway in the play *Abie's Irish Rose.*

157. *Motion Picture Magazine,* May 1928, p. 28.

158. Cecil B. DeMille, *The Autobiography of Cecil B. DeMille* (Englewood Cliffs, N.J.: Prentice-Hall, 1959), p. 263.

159. *Motion Picture Magazine,* May 1928, p. 28.

160. Eddie Quillan to author, Hollywood, June 1986.

161. Lina Basquette to author, Wheeling, West Virginia, June 1986.

162. *Photoplay,* July 1928, p. 54.

163. *Picture Play,* July 1929, pp. 92–94.

164. Schedule of costs and gross receipts of pictures personally directed by Cecil B. DeMille, 1913–1930, DeMille Estate. Courtesy Bob Birchard.

165. Lina Basquette to author, Wheeling, West Virginia, June 1986. See profile by Barry Paris in *The New Yorker,* February 13, 1989, p. 54–73.

166. John Hampton letter to author, July 1985.

167. DeMille, pp. 263–64.

168. *Variety,* April 3, 1929, p. 11.

169. Herbert Asbury, *The Gangs of New York* (New York: Knopf, 1927), p. 29.

170. Owen Kildare, *My Mamie Rose: The Story of My Regeneration* (New York: The Baker and Taylor Company, 1903), p. 78.

171. Asbury, p. 333.

172. Asbury, p. 342.

173. *The Biograph Bulletin,* October 31, 1912.

174. *The Biograph Bulletin* (Bowser), p. 452.

175. Carlos Clarens, *Crime Movies* (New York: Norton, 1980), p. 16.

176. Lillian Gish to author, London 1984. The actor, Adolph Lestina, was an expert with beards.

177. *Motion Picture News,* May 31, 1913, p. 7. Bald Jack Rose had promoted fights and vaudeville shows. He became president of the Humanology Motion Picture Company after *The Wages of Sin.*

178. *Moving Picture World,* June 21, 1913, p. 1250.

179. *Moving Picture World,* June 14, 1913, p. 1116.

180. Ibid.

181. *Moving Picture World,* June 14, 1913, p. 1158.

182. Also known as *The Gangsters.* Lauritzen and Lundquist in their *American Film Index, 1908–1915* (Stockholm: Film-Index, 1976) credit the direction of this to Christy Cabanne, but *Variety* (March 6, 1914) and other trade papers credit it to Kirkwood. Lauritzen and Lundquist also credit the story to Anita Loos, but she does not include it in her definitive list of credits in her book *Kiss Hollywood Good-by* (New York: Viking, 1974). *AFI Catalogue* credits Kirkwood with direction and suggests Kirkwood and Loos might have written it, p. 313.

183. *Moving Picture World,* February 21, 1914, p. 932.

184. *Variety,* March 13, 1914, p. 23.

185. *Variety,* March 13, 1914.

186. *New York Dramatic Mirror,* March 4, 1914, p. 42.

187. See Eugene Rosow, *Born to Lose* (New York: Oxford University Press, 1978), p. 80.

188. Published in 1903.

189. In 1911, Reliance had produced a very similar story as *The Gangfighter* (*Motion Picture News*, January 6, 1911, p. 29).

190. Herbert Asbury, *Gangs of New York*, p. 360.

191. *Variety*, August 20, 1915.

192. Raoul Walsh to author, Hollywood, 1967.

193. Raoul Walsh, *Each Man in His Time* (New York: Farrar, Straus and Giroux, 1974), p. 116.

194. Walsh, p. 116.

195. Walsh, p. 118.

196. Logan, *Against the Evidence*, p. 59.

197. Sinclair, *Upton Sinclair Presents William Fox*, pp. 188–89. Sheehan became vice president in charge of production at Fox and general manager of the studios.

198. The man who became chief attorney for Fox (and who represented Chaplin and many other film people), Nathan Burkan, was a Tammany district leader.

199. Walsh, p. 118.

200. Charles Chaplin, in a taped conversation with Richard Meryman in 1966, revealed an unexpected knowledge of Sheehan's life. He had been in New York at the time of the Rosenthal killing and became interested in the case. He got to know Sheehan during the war, when, together with Pickford and Fairbanks, the comedian brought the city of New York to a stop on the Third Liberty Bond drive. Sheehan, then with Fox, took him on a tour of the underworld and introduced him to many of the gangsters. "This little Irishman," said Chaplin, "made a fortune with the whorehouses. He'd take a rake-off . . . He was a dear friend of mine. He left [the police] right after that because he was part of this whole outfit . . . Very clever, very astute."

201. An event which occurred in 1904, when the excursion boat S.S. *General Slocum* caught fire on the Hudson while carrying 1,400 German-Americans from the Lower East Side on a picnic to Locust Grove on Long Island Sound. One thousand thirty died, and the disaster shattered the German community, many of whom moved uptown to Yorktown. The captain was found guilty of negligence and sentenced to ten years at Sing Sing, *People's Chronology*, p. 698. In the film, the sequence ends with the reassuring title "All the kiddies were saved"—but there is no indication of how many adults perished. The scene was shot on the Hudson River near Nyack, *AFI Catalogue, 1911–1920*, p. 765.

202. Walsh, p. 119.

203. Cooper, *Dark Lady of the Silents*, p. 114.

204. Anna Q. Nilsson appeared in a two-reeler also called *Regeneration* in 1914—it was the story of a young prostitute attracted to a mission by the singing of hymns, who is taken as companion by a wealthy man's wife. It was a blackmail story with many references to the underworld, *New York Dramatic Mirror*, May 6, 1914.

205. *Moving Picture World*, February 15, 1916, p. 363.

206. *Picture Play*, June 1924, p. 91.

207. *AFI Catalogue, 1921–1930*, p. 261.

208. *Picture Play*, May 1923, p. 58.

209. *Photoplay*, July 1921, p. 82.

210. *Photoplay*, February 1921, p. 66.

211. Ibid., and *Variety*, November 19, 1920; in the novel he was not shot, but married the girl and became a philanthropic force in the community. Robert G. Anderson, *Faces, Forms, Films* (New York: Castle Books, 1971), p. 66.

212. *Picture Play*, October 1920, p. 44.

213. *Motion Picture Classic*, February 1921, p. 96.

214. *Brooklyn Daily Eagle*, January 23, 1921, quoted in Short, *A Generation*, p. 169.

215. Short, *A Generation*, February 1924, p. 307.

216. *Photoplay*, February 1924, p. 27.

217. *Photoplay*, February 1924, p. 63 *Big Brother* was remade with Richard Dix as *Young Donovan's Kid* (1931).

218. Sponsored by prominent criminologists and humanitarians.

219. *Photoplay*, April 1924, p. 52.

220. *Variety*, December 27, 1923, p. 26.

221. Allan Dwan to author, "Hollywood" TV series, 1977.

222. *Variety*, December 27, 1923, p. 26.

223. The complete film no longer survives, but an abridged version was once available on 9.5mm under the title *The Bickel Affair*.

224. *Variety*, January 12, 1927, p. 18.

225. Ibid.

226. *Photoplay*, March 1927, p. 94.

227. In Ben Hecht's *A Thousand and One Afternoons in Chicago*, George Pratt letter to author, June 26, 1972.

228. Ben Hecht, *A Child of the Century* (New York: Simon and Schuster, 1954), quoted in Josef von Sternberg, *Fun in a Chinese Laundry* (New York: Macmillan, 1965), p. 215.

229. Von Sternberg, p. 215.

230. Hecht, *A Child of the Century*, p. 479.

231. Von Sternberg, p. 216.

232. *Moving Picture World*, August 28, 1927.

233. Josef von Sternberg to author, quoted in *The Parade's Gone By . . .* (New York: Knopf, 1968), p. 202.

234. John Gunther in *Harper's Monthly Magazine*, October 1929, p. 5.

235. *Variety*, December 7, 1927. Writing about *The City Gone Wild* is a painful experience for me. Part of a historian's job—at least, this historian—is to try and find the film as well as the facts. And in 1971, I thought I had found this one. David Shepard, then with the American Film Institute's archive program, had a list of 35mm nitrate prints held in a vault Paramount had forgotten it had. He asked me which title I would select, out of all of them, to look at right away. I said *The City Gone Wild*. He called Paramount to bring it out of the vaults for our collection that afternoon. The projectionist went to pick it up. "Oh, there was some powder on that," said the vault keeper. "We threw it away." The film had been unspooled into a tank of water (recommended procedure for decomposing nitrate). Shepard complained officially to Paramount, who promised it would not happen again. He tried to rescue it, even from its watery grave, but a salvage company had carted it off by the time he got there. Had we not been so eager, the film would have survived.

236. Katcher, p. 241.

237. Katcher, p. 234.

238. *AFI Catalogue*, 1921–1930, p. 252.

239. Harry Behn had collaborated on *The Big Parade*. Del Andrews was a friend of Milestone's from the Ince days, when both were in the cutting room together.

240. Luciano J. Iorizzo and Salvatore Mondello, *The Italian Americans* (Boston: Twayne, 1980), p. 186.

241. Short, *Crime Inc.*, p. 82.

242. Gerald M. Peary, *The Racket, a* "Lost" Gangster Classic, *Velvet Light Trap* 14 (Winter 75), Gerald Peary on gangster films, p. 7.

243. *Variety*, February 8, 1928, p. 45.

244. Peary, *Velvet Light Trap*, p. 7.

245. Short, *Crime Inc.*, p. 84.

246. *Variety* (July 11, 1928) considered his career had been obliterated by "junk stories," which was hard on some of the films, although their lack of box-office success cannot be denied.

247. *Variety*, July 11, 1928, p. 13.

248. Ibid.

249. *Picture Play*, December 1928, p. 32.

250. *Photoplay*, August 1928, p. 56.

251. *Motion Picture Classic*, December 1928, p. 63.

252. Ibid.

253. Ibid.

254. Ibid.

255. *Motion Picture Classic*, December 1928, p. 66.

256. *Motion Picture Classic*, December 1928, p. 63.

257. *Judge*, July 28, 1928, quoted in *Pare Lorentz on Film* (New York: Hopkinson and Blake, 1975), p. 16.

258. *Variety*, August 15, 1928, p. 24.

259. *Variety*, July 11, 1928, p. 13.

260. *Picture Play*, September 1929, p. 12. *The Racket* was remade in 1951 for Howard Hughes by director John Cromwell, who had played the police captain in the play. Hughes, Milestone, and Bartlett Cormack collaborated on another Chicago subject, *The Front Page*, in 1931, which attacked Big Bill Thompson even more strongly. Adapted from a play by Ben Hecht and Charles MacArthur, it portrayed him "as a buffoon, heavy and crook," Peary, p. 9.

CHAPTER SIX: POLITICAL CORRUPTION

1. *New York Dramatic Mirror*, June 24, 1914.

2. Alistair Cooke, *America*, BBC, 1973, p. 288.

3. Steffens, *Shame of the Cities*, p. 212.

4. *Moving Picture World*, April 4, 1914, p. 79.

5. It was on the Sullivan and Considine vaudeville circuit that Chaplin was playing when he was signed on for films. Sullivan ran it with Jim Considine.

6. *Moving Picture World*, April 4, 1914, p. 79.

7. Katcher, *The Big Bankroll*, p. 72.

8. *Moving Picture World*, April 4, 1914, p. 79.

9. Katcher, p. 27.

10. The trade press linked Rubinstein and "B. L. Thomas" to the film—the *AFI Catalogue*, 1911–1920 (p. 514) credits Benjamin R. Tolmas as copyright owner.

11. *Moving Picture World*, April 4, 1914, p. 79.

12. *Moving Picture World*, April 11, 1914, p. 275.

13. *Moving Picture World*, April 11, 1914, p. 222. The old East Side was also home territory to pugilist "Gentleman Jim" Corbett, the man who beat John L. Sullivan. Corbett starred in John Ford's *The Prince of Avenue A* (1920), Ford's first non-Western, a comedy romance with a political background. (*Variety* said "they'll yell for more," February 27, 1920), p. 47. An independent film called

That Old Gang of Mine, directed by May Tully, starred veteran stage actor Maclyn Arbuckle. Made in 1925 as a five-reeler, it was suggested by the song of the same title. The song brings together bitter political opponents who return to their old neighborhood "and recall for each other the joys and sorrows of a Manhattan childhood," *AFI Catalogue,* 1921–1930, p. 796.

14. Harold Wentworth and Stuart Berg Flexner, eds., *Dictionary of American Slang* (New York: Thomas Crowell, 1975), p. 226.

15. *Moving Picture World,* March 22, 1913, p. 1256.

16. *Moving Picture World,* May 17, 1913, pp. 712 and 740.

17. There are conflicts of opinion as to the exact number of authors; Kalton Lahue says fifteen, Lauritzen says sixteen, the trade papers list eighteen.

18. *Moving Picture World,* November 27, 1915, p. 1680.

19. Ibid.

20. *New York Dramatic Mirror,* February 4, 1914.

21. *Motion Picture Classic,* April 1921, p. 86.

22. *Variety,* January 26, 1921; *AFI Catalogue,* 1921–1930, p. 257.

23. *Photoplay,* April 1921, p. 78.

24. Steffens, p. 3.

25. *Motion Picture Story Magazine,* November 1911, p. 89. When franchise-grabbing corporations realize that an honest alderman is their only obstacle, they resort to blackmail in *John Sterling, Alderman* (1912), a one-reeler directed for Imp by King Baggot, who also played the lead. They investigate his past, discovering that as a youth in the slums he had turned to burglary. While robbing a house, he was caught by the owner, a humanitarian who helped him instead of turning him in. He became a good citizen, working his way up, and now faces ruin. His wife encourages him to turn the matter over to the district attorney; he does so and the D.A. brings the grafters to justice, *Moving Picture World,* October 26, 1912, p. 351.

26. Jacob Friedman, *The Impeachment of Governor William Sulzer* (New York: Columbia University Press, 1939), p. 15.

27. Friedman, p. 18.

28. Friedman, p. 30.

29. Friedman, p. 36.

30. Friedman, p. 238.

31. *Motion Picture News,* November 8, 1913, p. 665.

32. Ibid.

33. *Motion Picture News,* November 15, 1913, p. 30.

34. He was defeated by former district attorney Charles Whitman, who had held an inquiry into Sulzer's charges against Tammany. No disclosures of any note resulted, Friedman, p. 263.

35. *Photoplay,* August 1915, p. 77.

36. *Variety,* June 18, 1915, p. 17.

37. Ibid.

38. *Moving Picture World,* June 5, 1915, p. 1631.

39. Friedman, p. 266.

40. James Curtis, *Between Flops* (New York: Harcourt Brace Jovanovich, 1982), p. 91.

41. Friedman, p. 270. Another victim of "invisible government" was Charles E. Sebastian, Mayor of Los Angeles. His resignation in 1917 was attributed to ill health. Fred H. Solomon, a dance-hall proprietor, put up the money for *Downfall of a Mayor,* which was said to cost $50,000. The director was H. G. Stafford. It was subtitled "An Exposé of Chemically Pure Los Angeles," *Variety,* May 4, 1917 p. 22. Sebastian said it was an accurate account of the events which led to his resignation, and *Variety* thought it was the most sensational of any film, from a political exposé standpoint, *Variety,* April 27, 1917, p. 19. Sebastian played himself, and much of the footage was devoted to his heroism as a policeman, saving girls from white slave dens. See illustration on page 212.

CHAPTER SEVEN: WOMEN'S SUFFRAGE

1. *New York Dramatic Mirror,* January 15, 1916.

2. Eleanor Flexner, *A Century of Struggle* (Cambridge, Mass.: Harvard University Press, 1975), p. 258.

3. *Moving Picture World,* May 2, 1908, p. 401.

4. *Ladies' Home Journal,* April 1905, quoted in *People's Chronology,* p. 704.

5. The word "suffragette" was coined in 1906 by a writer on the London *Daily Mail* to describe Mrs. Emmeline Pankhurst and her daughters.

6. *Baltimore American,* April 15, 1912, quoted in Flexner, *A Century of Struggle,* p. 268.

7. *Moving Picture World,* May 18, 1912, p. 617.

8. Ibid.

9. *Moving Picture World,* June 1, 1912, p. 811.

10. *Moving Picture World.* May 18, 1912, p. 617.

11. *Moving Picture World.* June 1, 1912, p. 811.

12. Kay Sloan, "Sexual Warfare in the Silent Cinema," *American Quarterly* (Fall 1981), p. 426.

13. *Motion Picture News.* April 19, 1912, p. 11.

14. This was photographed in October 1913 at the Chelsea Studios on West Thirty-first Street, New York City, *Moving Picture World.* January 3, 1914, p. 34. There are gaps in the action where titles have been removed.

15. After Rheta Childe Dorr's book *What Eighty Million Women Want.* (Small, Maynard, 1910). The original title was *Eighty Million Women Want*—and was produced by an outfit calling itself Uneek Films (not Unique, as the trades would have it) in cooperation with the Women's Political Union.

16. Mrs. Ad Schulberg to author, London, 1965.

17. Sloan, p. 429.

18. *Motography.* November 29, 1913, p. 407.

19. *Moving Picture World.* November 15, 1913, p. 726.

20. *Moving Picture World.* January 3, 1914, p. 34.

21. Malwine Rennert, Rome, *Bild und Film* Heft 6 1913–1914, quoted Renate Seydel et al., in *Asta Nielsen* (Munich: Universitas Verlag, 1981).

22. *Moving Picture World.* January 17, 1914, p. 296.

23. Ibid.

24. *New York Dramatic Mirror.* May 27, 1914.

25. *Moving Picture World.* May 25, 1912. p. 714.

26. *Moving Picture World.* March 29, 1913, p. 1391; Flexner, p. 273.

27. *Moving Picture World.* September 26, 1914, p. 1782. Kay Sloan says the NAWSA

had another film in preparation which had to be canceled when they learned of Mrs. McCormick's work, Sloan, p. 431.

28. *Moving Picture World.* September 26, 1914, p. 1782.

29. *Moving Picture World.* November 7, 1914, p. 764.

30. *Moving Picture World.* November 7, 1914, p. 765.

31. *Moving Picture World.* November 7, 1914, p. 764.

32. *New York Dramatic Mirror.* December 30, 1914.

33. *Moving Picture World.* October 31, 1914, p. 621.

34. The picture attacked laws which would be changed once women had the vote: the lack of fire escape protection by greedy landlords and the right of a father to collect his children's earnings through the child labor law, *Moving Picture World.* October 31, 1914, p. 620.

35. Sloan, p. 434.

36. *Motion Picture News.* December 9, 1916, p. 3654.

37. *Moving Picture World.* October 27, 1917, p. 523. The Woman's Suffrage party and the National Woman's party suggested the film be cut from eight to five reels and Robards did so, *AFI Catalogue.* 1911–1920. p. 640. Victor Fleming's *A Woman's Place* (1921) had Constance Talmadge as a flapper who ends up running a political machine, putting women in the key jobs.

38. According to Jon Tuska, Nat Levine acquired the film as a 2,300-foot programmer and padded it to feature length with 2,600 feet of titles. This suggests that he received it already cut down from the original five reels (around 4,700 feet). He paid $10,000 for it, and the film evidently grossed nearly $40,000, Jon Tuska, *The Vanishing Legion: A History of Mascot Pictures. 1927–1935* (Jefferson, N.C.: McFarland & Company, 1982), pp. 8, 9.

39. The Reid-Robards studio was at Santa Cruz, California.

CHAPTER EIGHT: PRISONS

1. King and King, *Problems of Modern American Crime.* p. 271.

2. Program for *The Honor System.* February 17, 1917. Lyric Theatre, New York.

3. *Moving Picture World.* June 22, 1912, p. 1159.

4. Ibid.

5. *Moving Picture World.* December 27, 1913, p. 1587. Probably photographed by

Pliny Horne, it was filmed at Yuma, after it had closed.

6. *Moving Picture World.* December 27, 1913. p. 1587.

7. See *Moving Picture World.* August 17, 1912, p. 656.

8. *Moving Picture World.* Setember 7, 1912, p. 1000.

9. *Moving Picture World.* February 21, 1914, p. 932.

10. *Moving Picture World,* February 14, 1914, p. 811.

11. *Moving Picture World,* March 14, 1914, p. 1388.

12. Blake McKelvey, *American Prisons* (Montclair, N.J.: Paterson Smith, 1977), p. 262.

13. *Who Was Who in America* (Chicago: Marquis Who's Who Inc., 1981), p. 921.

14. John Drinkwater, *The Life and Adventures of Carl Laemmle* (London: Heinemann, 1931), p. 271.

15. *AFI Catalogue, 1921–1930,* p. 655. *The Gray Brother* did not appear until 1921 under the title *The Right Way.* It was reissued in 1927 by Standard Productions in a revised version with the title *Within Prison Walls* (the title of Osborne's book on his days in prison). It was also reviewed as *Making Good, AFI Catalogue, 1921–1930,* p. 655.

16. *Moving Picture World,* April 11, 1914, p. 214. The film was also known as *Joliet Prison, Joliet, Ill.*

17. *New York Dramatic Mirror,* April 1, 1914.

18. *Moving Picture World,* March 11, 1916, p. 1871.

19. *Moving Picture World,* March 22, 1919, p. 1688.

20. *Photoplay,* June 1921, pp. 56, 81, 86. Eytinge's opinion was shared by men in other prisons. One from Leavenworth referred to "the general moral uplift" of the movies which, Eytinge said, "is respectfully referred to our vexatious, vociferous and vixenish reformers"—who were objecting to spending tax money on showing movies to convicts.

21. *Pearson's Magazine,* December 1921, pp. 242–45.

22. Ibid.

23. *Motion Picture Classic,* December 1928, p. 66.

24. Peter Milne, *Motion Picture Direction* (New York: Falk, 1922), p. 232.

25. *Variety,* April 8, 1921, p. 40; *AFI Catalogue, 1921–1930,* p. 129.

26. *New York Herald,* April 4, 1921, The *New York Post* said that Meighan had not allowed them to cut his hair, but then he was a privileged prisoner. The story was remade as *Shadow of the Law* (1930) with William Powell.

27. *Motion Picture Magazine,* January 1924, p. 40; Jay Robert Nash, in *Murder, America,* p. 392.

28. *Moving Picture World,* August 9, 1919.

29. *Photoplay,* June 1921, p. 56. Meighan returned to Sing Sing for *The Man Who Found Himself* (1925).

30. *Photoplay,* June 1921, p. 86.

31. *Photoplay,* June 1921, p. 56.

32. *Motion Picture Magazine,* August 1923, p. 55.

33. *Moving Picture World,* June 22, 1912, p. 1136.

34. *Moving Picture World,* February 17, 1912, p. 563.

35. Ibid.

36. McKelvey, p. 251.

37. *Moving Picture World,* May 11, 1912, p. 516.

38. Ibid.

39. *Moving Picture World,* August 9, 1913, p. 642.

40. McKelvey, p. 257.

41. Lubin Bulletin, courtesy Linda Kowall and undated clipping, Sloman scrapbook.

42. *Moving Picture World,* May 16, 1914, p. 1011.

43. *Photoplay,* February 1924, p. 90.

44. *New York Times,* February 13, 1917, 9:4.

45. *Variety,* February 16, 1917, p. 24.

46. *New York Dramatic Mirror,* February 17, 1917, p. 32.

47. *Variety,* March 16, 1917, p. 33.

48. Marcus, who played in Walsh's *Regeneration* in 1915, was also an assistant director.

49. *Picture Play,* April 1917, pp. 200–212.

50. The synopsis is from the Brandon Collection, Museum of Modern Art, New York City. Governor Hunt appeared with Romaine Fielding in *A Western Governor's Humanity* (1915).

51. Interview with Jean-Louis Noames, "Entrétien avec Raoul Walsh," *Cahiers du Cinema,* April 1964, trans. by Walter Conley; see Walter Conley, *Silent Picture* (Winter 1970–1971), p. 6.

52. Walsh, *Each Man in His Time,* pp. 144–47. Walsh claims to have shot it in three and a half weeks, which, for a ten-reeler, beats even *Traffic in Souls.* It actually took twelve weeks.

53. Cooper, *Dark Lady of the Silents,* pp. 127, 134.

54. Raoul Walsh to author, Hollywood, 1967.

55. *The Honor System* program, Lyric Theatre, New York, February 17, 1917.

56. *New York Times,* February 13, 1917, 9:4.

57. *Variety,* February 16, 1917, p. 24.

58. The story in *Picture Play,* April 1917, pp. 200–212, retained the tragic ending.

59. Quoted in *Moving Picture World,* March 17, 1917, p. 1764.

60. *Photoplay,* July 1916, p. 99. The soloist was Henry I. MacMahan, *AFI Catalogue,* 1911–1921, p. 421.

61. *Picture Play,* January 1925, p. 25.

62. *Films in Review,* December 1971, p. 613.

63. Quoted in Cooper, p. 134.

64. Will Irwin, *The House That Shadows Built* (Garden City, N.Y.: Doubleday Doran, 1928), p. 126.

65. *Moving Picture World,* February 1, 1913, p. 440.

66. *Moving Picture World,* December 4, 1915, p. 1912.

67. *Variety,* March 13, 1914, p. 23.

68. *Moving Picture World,* April 25, 1914, p. 487.

69. *Moving Picture World,* December 5, 1914, p. 1396.

70. Karl Brown, *Adventures with D. W. Griffith* (New York: Farrar, Straus and Giroux, 1973), p. 117.

71. Brown, p. 118.

72. Brown, p. 120.

73. *Variety,* January 9, 1915, p. 24.

74. *Photoplay,* November 1916, pp. 27–40. The Stielow case had occurred too late for Griffith to use it in his film.

75. Richard Schickel, *D. W. Griffith* (London: Pavilion Books, 1984), p. 311.

76. *New York Times,* December 11, 1916, 7:3.

77. *New York Dramatic Mirror,* December 23, 1916.

78. *Variety,* December 15, 1916, p. 35.

79. *Moving Picture Weekly,* April 28, 1916, pp. 18–19, quoted in Sloan, *The Loud Silents,* p. 141.

80. *New York Dramatic Mirror,* April 14, 1915.

81. *Moving Picture World,* March 3, 1917, p. 1372.

82. *Motion Picture Studio Directory,* 1918, p. 220. She was given permission to visit the death house at Sing Sing to gather research, *New York Dramatic Mirror,* June 30, 1917. *AFI Catalogue,* 1911–1920, p. 1031, says Gilson Willets rewrote her original story.

83. *Moving Picture World,* December 22, 1917, p. 1800. A private presentation was given to members of the Chicago branch of the Anti-Capital Punishment Society of America, and among the audience was Clarence Darrow. Among the prominent people who endorsed it was Thomas Mott Osborne, *New York Dramatic Mirror,* September 8, 1917.

84. *Photoplay,* March 1923, p. 98. Other races to the rescue included *Night Patrol* (1926), a Richard Talmadge film, Fred Niblo's *Mother o' Mine* (1921), in which the race took place in a storm. *Bright Lights of Broadway* (1923) with Harrison Ford had two races going at the same time, the second being the villain trying to stop his confession being revealed (he is killed in a smash). Edward Sloman's *The Last Hour* was actually one example of anticapital punishment propaganda hiding under the camouflage of melodrama—the hanging mechanism fails, and the victim (Milton Sills) is given a last hour while the gallows are put in working order. During this hour, the real killer arrives by auto and confesses. Universal's *Legally Dead* (1923) had a race to the rescue arriving too late—the hero has been hanged. A scientist injects adrenalin, and life returns. This was a reflection of the publicity given to adrenalin and its miraculous effects. Miraculous or not, as Scott O'Dell pointed out, it was of little use with a broken neck. The hero was Milton Sills again. Scott O'Dell, *Representative Photoplays Analyzed* (Hollywood: Palmer Institute, 1924), p. 109.

85. Sam Jaffe, production manager, Preferred Studios, to Sue McConachy, "Hollywood" TV series, 1976.

86. Nash, p. 396. Clarence Darrow, *The Story of My Life.* (New York: Charles Scribner's Sons, 1932), p. 226. Darrow wrote that Leopold had a high intellect and that Loeb, strangely enough, was "kind," p. 231.

87. *AFI Catalogue,* 1921–1930, p. 110.

88. Budd Schulberg, *Moving Picture* (New York: Souvenir Press, 1981), p. 134.

89. *Motion Picture Classic,* April 1925, p. 49.

90. *Variety,* February 4, 1925, p. 33.

91. *Picture Play,* May 1925, p. 68.

92. *Picture Play,* April 1925, p. 33.

CHAPTER NINE: POVERTY

1. Sidney Lens, *Poverty, Yesterday and Today* (New York: Thomas Y. Crowell, 1973), p. 126.

2. Sanger, *An Autobiography,* p. 88.

3. One film record of slum conditions I have seen which shows even the vermin in close-up was filmed in the 1920s in Somers Town, London, for a Housing Trust. The 16mm footage was incorporated into a Thames TV documentary on Somers Town

made by Richard Broad in 1984 for Channel 4 and the footage donated to the National Film Archive.

4. Upton Sinclair, *The Jungle* (London: Penguin, 1982; originally published in 1906), p. 94.

5. *Motion Picture Story Magazine,* July 1911, p. 79.

6. Ibid.

7. *New York Dramatic Mirror,* January 20, 1915.

8. Ibid.

9. Ibid.

10. Ibid.

11. *Motion Picture News,* February 6, 1915, p. 47.

12. *Moving Picture World,* March 13, 1915, p. 1612.

13. *People's Chronology,* 1979, p. 582.

14. *Moving Picture World,* November 18, 1911, p. 535; *Edison Kinetogram,* December 15, 1910, pp. 3–4.

15. Martin S. Pernick, *Edison's Tuberculosis Films,* Hastings Center Report 8 (June 1978), pp. 21–27.

16. Tannura, the son of a shoemaker who made shoes for the actors at the Edison studio, played the role of a boy. A few years later, he became a cameraman.

17. *Moving Picture World,* December 2, 1911, p. 746.

18. Lauritzen and Lundquist list Charles France, but *Edison Kinetogram,* December 1, 1913, gives Ridgely.

19. *New York Dramatic Mirror,* June 24, 1914.

20. Pernick, pp. 21–27.

21. John Purroy Mitchel, a lawyer, served in Mayor George Brinton McClellan's second administration (1900–1910) as commissioner of accounts. His assistant, Raymond Fosdick, had been a resident of the Henry Street Settlement and had helped organize the campaign for the reelection of District Attorney William Travers Jerome. In 1913, Mitchel was elected mayor and, thanks to the advice of men like Fosdick, surrounded himself with a cabinet of settlement house and social workers. He appointed Katharine Bement Davis to the post of commissioner of correction, Allen F. Davis, *Spearheads for Reform* (New York: Oxford University Press, 1967), p. 186.

22. *Moving Picture World,* December 5, 1914, p. 1359.

23. Pernick, p. 23.

24. *Moving Picture World,* December 2, 1916, p. 1325.

25. *Moving Picture World,* May 22, 1915, p. 1275.

26. Bourne, among a variety of jobs, played the piano for the movies. Born in 1886, he died in the flu epidemic of 1918.

27. *The New Republic 3,* July 3, 1915, p. 233, quoted Carl Resek, ed., in *War and the Intellectuals* (New York: Harper, 1964), pp. 171–74.

28. *Motion Picture News,* March 18, 1916, p. 1165.

29. Ibid.

30. *Motion Picture News,* April 22, 1916, p. 2359.

31. *Variety,* April 14, 1916, p. 25.

32. *Motion Picture News,* April 22, 1916, p. 2359.

33. *New York Dramatic Mirror,* October 20, 1917, p. 18. Dick Rosson remade *The Escape* (1914) in 1928.

34. *Variety,* October 19, 1917, p. 32.

35. *Moving Picture World,* June 21, 1913, p. 1233; city government crusade: *Motion Picture News,* May 11, 1912, p. 15.

36. *Moving Picture World,* October 5, 1912, pp. 22–25.

37. *Moving Picture World,* June 21, 1913, p. 1233.

38. Ibid.

39. *Moving Picture World,* May 3, 1913, p. 489.

40. *Moving Picture World,* May 17, 1913, p. 713.

41. Leslie Wood, *Miracle of the Movies* (London: Burke Publishing Company, 1947), p. 201.

42. *Moving Picture World,* December 30, 1911, p. 1081.

43. Goldman, *Rendezvous with Destiny,* p. 198.

44. Bowser, ed., *The Biograph Bulletins,* p. 277.

45. *Moving Picture World,* September 18, 1909, p. 385.

46. *Moving Picture World,* December 14, 1912, p. 1108; *Moving Picture World,* December 21, 1912, pp. 1099–1200.

47. Lubin Bulletin, n.d. Courtesy Linda Kowall.

48. *Motion Picture News,* February 24, 1912, p. 9. Courtesy Q. David Bowers.

49. *Motion Picture Magazine,* July 1911, pp. 143–50. (These stories were elaborated for publication; some of the details may have been imposed upon the Edison original.) Perhaps the most bizarre plot for any film connected with poverty was *The Amazing Woman* (1920), about a girl so touched by the sufferings in the slums that she becomes a high-class prostitute, using the money for the relief of the poor, *Morals of the Movie* quoted in Gerald Mast, ed., *The Movies in Our Midst,* p. 200.

50. Blanche Sweet to author, "Hollywood" TV series, New York, 1977.

51. *Moving Picture World,* June 20, 1914, p. 47.

52. *Variety,* June 5, 1914, p. 19.

53. *Moving Picture World,* June 20, 1914, p. 47; *AFI Catalogue, 1911–1920,* p. 244.

54. *Variety,* June 5, 1914, p. 19.

55. *Moving Picture World,* June 20, 1914, p. 47.

56. *Variety,* June 5, 1914, p. 19.

57. *New York Dramatic Mirror,* June 10, 1914, p. 42.

58. Mast, p. 105. The Paul Armstrong play was remade as *The Escape,* directed by Richard Rosson, in 1928.

59. Adams, Jr., *The Age of Industrial Violence, 1910–1915,* p. 179.

60. Ibid.

61. *Variety,* May 28, 1915, p. 17.

62. By Charles Kenyon and Arthur Hornblow (Sr.)

63. *Photoplay,* December 1915, p. 100.

64. *Variety,* July 16, 1915, p. 17.

65. *New York Dramatic Mirror,* July 21, 1915, p. 24. DeMille shot the film in seventeen days. It was his first with Thomas Meighan, who became a DeMille stalwart. (It was Meighan's second film.) A film with a very similar plot was *The Child of the Tenements* (Solax, 1912).

66. Figures from DeMille Estate. Courtesy Bob Birchard.

67. *Photoplay,* March 1916, p. 69.

68. Howard Hickman married Bessie Barriscale.

69. *Photoplay,* July 1915, p. 120.

70. *New York Dramatic Mirror,* April 21, 1915, p. 26.

71. *New York Dramatic Mirror,* July 8, 1917, p. 15. Hoover appeared in a prologue.

72. *Variety,* June 29, 1917, p. 30.

73. *New York Dramatic Mirror,* July 8, 1917, p. 15.

74. *Variety,* June 29, 1917, p. 30.

75. Albert S. Parker is best known for his *The Black Pirate* (1926).

76. *New York Dramatic Mirror,* August 11, 1917, p. 19.

77. Ibid.

78. Ibid.

79. *Photoplay,* November 1917, p. 132.

80. *Variety,* August 10, 1917, p. 23.

81. *The Bioscope,* August 15, 1918, p. 31. *Cheating the Public,* directed by Richard Stanton from a Mary Murillo story, was shot in 1917 and released in 1918. This one was about a canning factory owner who cuts wages and his son who protects the heroine, a girl from the slums who is the sole support of her family. Mary's mother dies of malnutrition, and Mary leads the factory workers in a strike. They storm the house of the profiteer, and when the attack is beaten off and the workers jailed, she pulls out a revolver and, as in *Intolerance,* another bullet kills him. But Mary goes on trial and is given the death sentence. An eleventh-hour rescue, also as in *Intolerance,* saves her life, *Moving Picture World,* February 2, 1918, p. 684; *New York Dramatic Mirror,* January 26, 1918, p. 19.

82. Lens, p. 143.

83. *Picture Play,* April 1926, advertisement.

84. *People's Chronology,* p. 856.

85. *Photoplay,* November 1921, p. 113.

86. *Variety,* August 19, 1921, p. 35.

87. Anthony Slide, "The Blot," in Magill, ed., *Magill's Survey of Cinema,* vol. 1, p. 242.

88. Calhern was Julius Caesar in the Joseph Mankiewicz film.

89. *The Blot* appears to have had its influence. *The Woman's Home Companion* produced a two-reeler with a very similar story entitled *Under Paid;* it was about the poverty of a church minister and his sister, who is tempted to steal. She does not do so but her suspicious actions are spotted by a neighbor. The film was once available from the Kodascope libraries.

90. Vidor, *A Tree Is a Tree,* p. 99. According to Scott Simmon and Raymond Durgnat, Vidor's story, written with John V. A. Weaver in 1926, was called *The Clerk.* A treatment called *March of Life* followed the same year, *King Vidor, American* (Berkeley: University of California Press, 1988), p. 81.

91. Vidor, p. 99.

92. *Motion Picture Magazine,* January 1928, p. 95.

93. Murray's end was so tragic that Vidor wrote a script based on it. It came in New York one night in July 1936: "He had borrowed money and bought liquor, and he was clowning for a bunch of tourists on a pier on the Hudson. He pretended he was in makeup, waiting for the movie company to arrive. He was trying to entertain this group of tourists, dancing on the edge of the pier. He did a sort of false step and fell in and everybody laughed. They thought it was a gag. But he didn't come up. They went and looked over and he was floating face down, dead."

94. King Vidor to author, "Hollywood" TV series, 1976.

95. Vidor to author, 1976.

96. Charles Silver, Museum of Modern Art retrospective program, November 1972.

97. King Vidor to Nancy Dowd, AFI Oral History, 1971.

98. Vidor to Dowd, 1971.

99. Vidor to author, 1976.

100. Ibid.

101. Eleanor Boardman to author, "Hollywood" TV series, 1976.

102. Vidor to Dowd, 1971.

103. Boardman to author, 1976.

104. *The Film Spectator,* December 24, 1927, p. 7.

105. *Photoplay,* December 1927, p. 52.

106. *Variety,* February 22, 1928, p. 20.

107. Samuel Marx, *Mayer and Thalberg: The Make-Believe Saints* (New York: Random House, 1975), p. 255. Russell Merritt has sent me his investigation into the first-run behavior of the picture and found it the flop everyone said it was. "If a film didn't make money in the major cities," he wrote, "where did it make money?" He was astonished by the $69,000 profit figure, which comes from Eddie Mannix's records, MGM. Merritt to author, December 3, 1987.

CHAPTER TEN: THE FOREIGNERS

1. Maldwyn A. Jones, *Destination America* (London: Weidenfeld & Nicolson, 1976), p. 11.

2. Henry Pratt Fairchild, *Immigration* (New York: Macmillan, 1913 and 1925), p. 230.

3. *People's Chronology,* p. 632.

4. Edward A. Ross, "The Old World and the New" quoted in Richard Hofstadter, *The Age of Reform* (New York: Knopf, 1955), p. 180. Ross, a former Populist, was a leading spokesman for the Progressives.

5. Fairchild, p. 203.

6. Pitkin, *Keepers of the Gate,* p. 31.

7. Pitkin, p. 48.

8. Pitkin, p. 51.

9. Pitkin, p. 112.

10. Pitkin, p. 115.

11. *Moving Picture World,* December 7, 1912, p. 978.

12. Blaché, *Memoirs,* p. 56.

13. *Moving Picture World,* October 26, 1912, p. 353.

14. Ibid.

15. *Moving Picture World,* January 7, 1914, p. 340.

16. *New York Dramatic Mirror,* March 25, 1914.

17. Lars Lindstrom believes these are parents rather than hired hands. The films were discovered by the late Gardar Sahlberg.

18. Lars Lindstrom letter to author, December 25, 1984.

19. Anthony Slide, *Early American Cinema* (New York: A. S. Barnes, 1970), p. 51.

20. Despite her exotic name, Valeska Suratt came from Terre Haute, Indiana. She was a vaudeville headliner.

21. *Moving Picture World,* January 8, 1916, p. 236.

22. *New York Dramatic Mirror,* January 1, 1916, p. 28.

23. "Unknown Chaplin" was a TV series produced by David Gill and the author for Thames TV in 1983. It was first shown in the U.S. in 1986.

24. Carlyle Robinson, *La Verité sur Charlie Chaplin* (Paris: Société Parisienne d'Edition, 1935), p. 18. Chaplin used the old immigrant dream of finding the streets of America paved with gold when he finds a coin outside the café.

25. Pitkin, p. 14.

26. The Mexicans were equally despised, and it is all the more remarkable that a film was made about their plight called *The Land of Promise* (Imp 1912).

27. Pitkin, p. 15.

28. Pitkin, p. 26.

29. In 1889, in New Orleans, eleven Italians acquitted of murder were lynched.

30. Fairchild, p. 141.

31. Lens, *Poverty,* pp. 117, 118.

32. Jones, pp. 198–99.

33. Bowser, ed., *The Biograph Bulletins,* p. 341.

34. *Moving Picture World,* February 24, 1912, p. 698.

35. *Moving Picture World,* December 16, 1911, p. 5; *Moving Picture World,* January 13, 1912, p. 32; *Moving Picture World,* December 25, 1911, pp. 6, 22.

36. Hal Mohr to author, Hollywood, 1970.

37. Short, *Crime Inc.,* p. 30. *Moving Picture World,* January 21, 1911, p. 128, reported a little girl who saw a Black Hand film and a picture about a fire and wrote a note demanding five dollars, threatening to burn the house unless the money was left under the mat. She was caught.

38. Short, p. 77.

39. Short, p. 85.

40. Iorizzo and Mondello, *The Italian Americans,* p. 72.

41. Iorizzo and Mondello, p. 207.

42. *Variety,* October 16, 1909, p. 12.

43. *Moving Picture World,* January 30, 1909, p. 125.

44. Ibid.

45. Short, p. 32. *Motion Picture News,* March 22, 1913, p. 13, announced a film, directed by Sidney Goldin, about Petrosino—*Whispering Winds.* It was also known as *The Adventures of Lieutenant Petrosino* or *The Life and Death of Lieutenant Petrosino* (1912). It was made with the "special permission of Madame Petrosino." *AFI Catalogue,* 1911–1920, p. 6.

46. *Moving Picture World,* April 5, 1913, p. 49.

47. *Moving Picture World,* October 24, 1914, p. 540.

48. *Static Flashes,* February 20, 1915, p. 4. *AFI Catalogue,* 1911–1920, p. 12, lists Ned van Buren as cameraman.

49. *New York Dramatic Mirror,* February 3, 1917.

50. *New York Dramatic Mirror,* June 2, 1915, p. 28.

51. Ibid.

52. *Photoplay,* June 1915.

53. *Motion Picture Magazine,* April 1916, p. 141. Beban remade *The Alien* in 1922 as *The Sign of the Rose,* under the direction of Harry Garson, and he repeated the florist shop sketch on the stage. The personal appearance idea was dropped after a five-week run in New York—the public preferred the photoplay, *Photoplay,* September 1916, p. 131.

54. *Wid's,* March 7, 1918, p. 986.

55. Ibid. Camille Ankewich changed her name to Marcia Manon, *AFI Catalogue,* 1911–1920, p. 677.

56. *Wid's,* March 7, 1918, p. 986.

57. Ibid.

58. *Motion Picture Magazine,* June 1918, p. 105.

59. In *The Wop* Luigi and his small daughter suffer in a strike. Gathering coal at the railroad yard, Luigi is dragged to jail, leaving his daughter freezing and helpless. When he comes out he cannot find the girl. He determines to get even with the man who sentenced him; he breaks into his home and is about to stab the man's child when she awakes. It is his own daughter, *Moving Picture World,* July 5, 1913, pp. 82–84.

60. Ince's publicity said the company had gone to Venice, Italy (an unlikely journey in November 1914).

61. Perhaps it was cut when the film was reduced from six reels to five, synopsis and *Variety,* January 4, 1915, but that still does not justify the arrival of Annette as though she were returning from a cruise. (Beban made up for it with *One More American.*)

62. Beppo's letter is dated April 11, 1913; had it been 1914, Beppo would have only a few months before returning to Italy to enlist.

63. Locations were at the Plaza (the Mexican district) in Los Angeles and three small streets in the nearby Italian quarter. But there were no real slums in Los Angeles. Slum streets were shot in San Francisco, and the ward boss's home in Oakland, California. Harbor scenes were in San Francisco because P. J. Beban and Louis G. Beban, George's brothers, were working for the port authority, *Motion Picture News,* November 14, 1914, p. 36.

64. Ince publicity claimed this had been a real accident and that Beban had almost been killed. It was probably a way of drawing attention to the $25,000 insurance taken out by the company on Beban, *Moving Picture World,* November 21, 1914, p. 1060.

65. Anthony Slide and Edward Wagenknecht, *Fifty Great American Films* (New York: Dover, 1980), p. 25.

66. *Los Angeles Herald,* November 19, 1919.

67. Ibid.

68. Ibid.

69. Ibid.

70. Lindsey, *The Art of the Moving Picture,* p. 71.

71. William K. Everson to author, 1971.

72. Only one of Beban's films was shown in Italy (*One Man in a Million,* 1921). *Il gondoliere di Venezia* is said to be their title for *The Italian,* but this is an error. Courtesy Vittorio Martinelli.

73. William Peterson, "The Chinese and Japanese," *Essays and Data on American Ethnic Groups,* edited by Thomas Sowell (Harvard Urban Institute, 1978), p. 220.

74. *Moving Picture World,* February 10, 1917, p. 877.

75. *Wid's,* February 15, 1917, p. 103.

76. *Variety,* January 28, 1921, p. 2. The most astonishing re-creation of a tong war was staged for a comedy—Buster Keaton's *The Cameraman* (1928).

77. T. K. Peters's letter to author June 2, 1973. Peters was also a scientist and thanks to his knowledge of precision flight instruments, was appointed head of the Chinese Air Force college in Georgia by Sun Yat-sen, "the father of Modern China," as he was known; *American Cinematographer,* February 1974, p. 228. I can find no record of the release of this series.

78. *Moving Picture World,* June 27, 1914, p. 1842.

79. Geoffrey Bell, letter to author, July 2, 1985.

80. *Moving Picture World*, June 20, 1914, pp. 1705, 1738–39.

81. *Variety*, August 9, 1918, p. 33.

82. *Exhibitors Herald*, September 28, 1918, p. 27.

83. *Variety*, September 13, 1918, p. 41.

84. One story broker received calls from four producers asking him to dig out whatever Chinese stuff he had, purely as a result of the success of this play, *Variety*, January 24, 1919, p. 48. Sidney Franklin made the film for Joseph Schenck with Constance Talmadge. A San Franciscan, Franklin remained interested in the Chinese and directed what was probably the most sympathetic film on the subject ever made in America, *The Good Earth* (1937). *East Is West* has just been found in a collection in Holland.

85. *Motion Picture Magazine*, July 1919, p. 97.

86. *Motion Picture Magazine*, November 1932, p. 6.

87. Richard A. Oehling, "Hollywood and the Image of the Oriental," quoted in Richard L. Stromgren, "The Chinese Syndrome: The image of China and the Chinese in Silent Movies," unpublished ms., p. 19.

88. Frances Taylor Patterson, *Cinema Craftsmanship* (New York: Harcourt Brace, 1920), p. 164. Frances Patterson was a scenario writer herself. The film was not a commercial failure.

89. Richard Barthelmess letter to Barnet Bravermann, May 2, 1945, quoted by Arthur Lennig in *The Film Journal* (Fall-Winter 1972), p. 3. Dorothy Gish Productions was a Griffith subsidiary.

90. Barthelmess letter to Bravermann, May 2, 1945.

91. Lillian Gish to author, New York, May 1983. Richard Schickel says Griffith rehearsed Carol Dempster in this role (*D. W. Griffith*, p. 391).

92. Lillian Gish to author, London, October 1983.

93. In the twenties, female drug addicts were known to the police as Broken Blossoms, Norman Dash, *Yesterday's Los Angeles* (Miami, Fla.: E. A. Seemann Publishing, 1976), p. 134.

94. Lillian Gish, *The Movies, Mr. Griffith, and Me* (Englewood Cliffs, N.J.: Prentice-Hall, 1969), p. 220.

95. Gish, p. 221.

96. Tino Balio, *United Artists* (Madison: University of Wisconsin Press, 1971), p. 31.

97. Rex Ingram made a film about the Chinese in 1916 called *Broken Fetters*.

98. *Moving Picture World*, April 17, 1920, p. 388. I obtained the patent description from the U.S. Patent Office (it took eighteen months!), and it showed the "invention" limited to two rows of colored bulbs recessed in light trays, aimed at the screen at such an angle that the brilliance of projection would not be diminished.

99. Brown, *Adventures with D. W. Griffith*, p. 240. The lights around the auditorium would have been an additional effect by Clune's management.

100. Brown, pp. 241–42.

101. The trade press was upset by "anti-British prejudice." "There is a reference which almost amounts to a sneer, to the brutal prize-fighters' 'great country' and the episode in the police station, when a constable is made to remark that 'things are better today; only 40,000 casualties,' has no connection with the picture or the story, and it is difficult to see it as anything but a gratuitous jeer at the ghastly errors of the latter middle period of the war which cost us so much in treasured young life. America should remember that, even if she ultimately saved us, we had first saved her and all civilisation, though it drained our life-blood in the doing. It is anticipated that these subtitles will be eliminated, but it is to be regretted that a man of such wide artistic and spiritual perception as Griffith should have moments of parochial littleness of mind," *Kine Weekly*, January 20, 1920, p. 106.

102. *Moving Picture World*, September 20, 1919, p. 1800. *The First Born* was filmed in 1921 with Sessue Hayakawa, Helen Jerome Eddy, and a Chinese cast.

103. Brown, p. 242.

104. *American Cinematographer*, December 1921, p. 11. "Jimmy the Assistant" was a regular column written (anonymously) by Karl Brown in this publication.

105. *Picture Play*, July 1920, p. 31. The Chinese charged some Japanese actors with the willful misrepresentation of the Chinese for the benefit of Japan.

106. R. G. Burnett and E. D. Martell, *The Devil's Camera* (London: The Epworth Press, 1932), p. 6 on *The Thief of Bagdad*.

107. James B. Leong, Jr., to author, telephone interview and letter, May 1984.

108. *Picture Play*, January 1922, p. 84.

109. *Picture Play*, April 1922, p. 73.

110. *Picture Play*, February 1925, p. 47.

111. Edward Sakamoto, *Los Angeles Times*, July 12, 1987, p. 40.

112. "Anna May Wong and the Dragon-Lady syndrome," in ibid.

113. *Picture Play,* September 1926, pp. 83–86. Gubbins later worked on Harold Lloyd's *Welcome Danger* (1929), a parody of these serials, which nonetheless upset some Chinese. Lloyd later made up for it with his sympathetic portrayal of Chinese in *The Cat's Paw* (1934).

114. *Photoplay,* March 1924, p. 96; *Motion Picture Classic,* April 1924, p. 52.

115. *Moving Picture World,* January 5, 1918, p. 57.

116. Rowland V. Lee, "Adventures of a Film Director," unpublished autobiography, p. 184.

117. *Motion Picture Classic,* April 1922, p. 27.

118. Lee, unpublished autobiography, p. 185.

119. This was not a Hollywood invention. The only method of family limitation known to poor Chinese was infanticide of girl babies by suffocation or drowning; Sanger, *An Autobiography,* p. 344.

120. *AFI Catalogue 1921–1930,* p. 62.

121. From the Electric Theatre, Centralia, quoted in *Photoplay,* December 1923, p. 114.

122. Quoted by Carl Sandburg, *Carl Sandburg at the Movies: A Poet in the Silent Era, 1920–1927,* eds. Dale Featherling and Doug Featherling (Metuchen, N.J.: Scarecrow Press, 1985), p. 85.

123. Harry Perry, with Lieutenant Colonel Oscar Estes, Jr., "How We Filmed the Virginian and Shadows and Other Preferred Pictures," *Classic Film Collector,* no. 22, p. 32. Perry was shocked when he saw a bad 16mm dupe of the film in 1959 and was sad when he learned nothing better survived. A 35mm nitrate original, however, is in England, as yet uncopied.

124. *Picture Play,* May 1923, p. 83.

125. *Photoplay,* January 1923, p. 67.

126. *Photoplay,* January 1923, p. 96.

127. *Photoplay,* May 1924, p. 98.

128. Sherwood, ed., *Best Moving Pictures,* pp. 27–28.

129. Sherwood, ed., pp. 27–28.

130. It was a Japanese gardener suffering a mental breakdown who shot the pioneer director Francis Boggs.

131. T. Iyenaga and Kenoske Sato, *Japan and the California Problem* (New York: G. P. Putnam, 1921), p. 12.

132. *People's Chronology,* p. 832.

133. *Moving Picture World,* November 29, 1913, p. 995.

134. The same year, 1913, Eclair opened a studio in Tokyo, *Motion Picture News,* February 1, 1913, p. 29.

135. *Moving Picture World,* June 21, 1913, p. 1231.

136. Ibid.

137. Written by Eugene Mullins.

138. Written by James Young. Both films were directed by James Young, who later directed Sessue Hayakawa. The Vitagraph party was shown around a film studio, where the light was diffused through translucent paper, providing a softness "that has no equal elsewhere." (Americans used canvas or muslin.) The grounds, landscaped with ponds, gardens, and grottoes, were a picture makers' paradise. The Americans pointed out the difference between the two great Oriental nations— Japan was building studios, while the Chinese were still superstitious and camera shy, *Moving Picture World,* June 21, 1913, p. 1231.

139. *Moving Picture World,* May 26, 1917, p. 1266. Wallace Beery also tried to make pictures in Japan.

140. *Moving Picture World,* October 17, 1914, p. 314. Abbe's real name was Utaka Abe; he played Hayakawa's valet in *The Cheat.*

141. *Moving Picture World,* October 10, 1914, p. 199.

142. *Photoplay Journal,* May 1920, p. 20. Tsuru Aoki's real name was Kawakami.

143. *Moving Picture World,* January 31, 1914, p. 554.

144. *Photoplay,* December 1919, p. 51.

145. Dewitt Bodeen, "Sessue Hayakawa," *Films in Review,* April 1976, p. 193.

146. Ibid.

147. *Moving Picture World,* July 11, 1914, p. 156.

148. *Moving Picture World,* June 20, 1914, p. 1665.

149. Kotani—a native of Honolulu— was an actor and later cameraman who went to Japan and became a highly paid director. So did another actor in the film, Thomas Kurihara.

150. Lindsay, *The Art of the Moving Picture,* p. 80.

151. *Photoplay,* March 1916, p. 139.

152. Bodeen, p. 193.

153. *Moving Picture World,* December 25, 1915, p. 2384. The location of the Japanese garden was at the home of Dr. Sanss in Santa Monica, *Photoplay,* May 1916, p. 35. While filming Fannie Ward crossing a Japanese bridge, the wooden structure collapsed, depositing Miss Ward in the stream. This shot survives in DeMille's accident reel at the DeMille Estate.

154. Bodeen, p. 193.

155. *Variety,* December 17, 1915, p. 18.

156. *Moving Picture World,* February 19, 1916, p. 1114.

157. *Moving Picture World,* February 21, 1921, p. 1064. Libretto by Paul Milliet and André Lorde.

158. *Variety,* February 18, 1921, p. 2.

159. Colette, *Colette at the Movies,* Alain and Odette Virmaux eds. (New York: Frederick Ungar, 1980), pp. 19–20.

160. Colette, p. 18. *The Cheat* was remade, in Hollywood in 1923 (when the collector becomes a crook masquerading as an Indian prince!), and in France in 1937 with Hayakawa. In 1944, Hayakawa was able to produce his own version on the stage. *The Cheat* gave Hayakawa a career in British and French films. A stage version called *I.O.U.,* adapted by Turnbull and Willard Mack, opened on Broadway in 1918, but failed. A 1931 talkie starred Tallulah Bankhead and Irving Pichel.

161. *Motion Picture Magazine,* November 1924, pp. 21–27.

162. Ibid.

163. Karl Brown letter to author, March 4, 1985.

164. *Photoplay,* August 1916, p. 160. Yet in Lasky's *Forbidden Paths* (1917), which also starred Hayakawa, it is suggested that suicide and murder are preferable to miscegenation.

165. Fairchild, p. 461. Hayakawa had encountered "picture brides" on his voyage to the United States.

166. Florence Vidor to author, Santa Monica, California, 1969.

167. *Variety,* September 20, 1918, p. 45.

168. Bessie Love to author, London, 1984.

169. *Mon Ciné,* March 9, 1922, p. 22.

170. One could sense the end for Hayakawa some time before he left America. Audiences began kidding his film *Who Is Your Servant?* (1920) when the titles approximated the Japanese speaking broken English. *Variety* criticized the film, a spy story, for bad timing: "When an effort is being made by the entire world to sign a lasting peace, arousing prejudice by hinting at Japanese spies employed as servants in the households of naval officers is going a little too far. . . . The picture looks as if it has been on the market for some time. About the best thing they can do is to put a lot of crepe over the negative and then apply the match and forget it ever happened," *Variety,* February 27, 1920, p. 47.

171. *Motion Picture Magazine,* January 1929, pp. 33, 90–91. *La Bataille* broke box office records in France.

172. *Variety,* November 24, 1922, p. 38. Borzage, who had played with the Japanese at Inceville, directed other Japanese stories such as *Who Is to Blame?* (1918).

173. *Exhibitors Herald,* March 11, 1922.

174. Ibid.

175. Quoted in Kemp Niver, *The First Twenty Years* (Los Angeles: Locare Research Group, 1968), p. 91.

176. Fred Balshofer and Arthur Miller, *One Reel a Week* (Berkeley: University of California Press, 1967), p. 46.

177. Ibid.

178. *Variety,* July 25, 1908, p. 13.

179. *Variety,* October 23, 1909, p. 13.

180. *Variety,* January 29, 1910, p. 13.

181. *Variety,* July 25, 1908, p. 13.

182. Ibid.

183. *Moving Picture World,* April 1916, p. 458.

184. Brownlow, *The Parade's Gone By . . . ,* p. 18.

185. *Resurrection* was made by the Masko Film Company with mainly Russian actors.

186. *The Bioscope,* February 28, 1918, p. 6.

187. Jay Leyda, *Kino* (London: George Allen and Unwin, 1960), p. 91; Ramsaye, *A Million and One Nights,* p. 727; Brownlow, p. 18.

188. Leon Trotksy, *My Life* (London: Penguin, 1971), pp. 278, 289. *My Official Wife* was reissued on December 25, 1916.

189. Trotsky, p. 279.

190. Program, author's collection. The British, who cordially disliked the Imperial Russian government, but who were allied with it, changed the title to *The Spider and the Fly,* to avoid offense.

191. Rapid cutting appears in another Edison film, *The Unbeliever* (1918, Alan Crosland), so it may have been the work of a talented editor! Rapid cutting was perfected by Abel Gance in *La Roue* (1919–1922) before being adopted by the Soviets for "Russian montage." *The Cossack Whip* is now being restored by Paolo Cherchi Usai at Eastman House.

192. Viola Dana letter to author, May 2, 1984. Miss Dana was born in 1897.

193. It was copyrighted in September 1916.

194. *Wid's,* November 16, 1916, p. 1110.

195. *Variety,* November 17, 1916, p. 26.

196. Viola Dana to DeWitt Bodeen, *Films in Review,* March 1976, p. 147.

197. Its original title was *The Downfall of the Romanoffs.*

198. Alex de Jonge, *The Life and Times of Grigorii Rasputin* (New York: Coward, McCann and Geoghegan, 1982), p. 148.

199. De Jonge, p. 338.

200. If only it had survived!

201. Later Stalingrad, now Volgograd.

202. De Jonge, p. 204.

203. Ramsaye, *A Million and One Nights*, p. 766.

204. De Jonge, p. 319.

205. Synopsis from program for premiere, Ritz-Carlton ballroom, September 6, 1917: Theatre Arts Collection, Lincoln Center, New York City. Courtesy George Geltzer.

206. *New York Times*, September 7, 1917, 9:2.

207. Kyril Zinovieff letter to author, March 15, 1984. In 1921, cameraman Floyd Traynham made a film for the American Relief Administration called *America's Gift to Famine-Stricken Russia*. It includes shots of Iliodor "the Mad Monk" ruling a village in the hills called the Commune of Eternal Peace. The two-reel film is in the National Archives in Washington, D.C.

208. Letter from the Iliodor Corporation to Russian Art Film Corporation, September 6, 1917, Selznick archives, at Harry Ransom Library, University of Texas at Austin. Courtesy Raymond Daum.

209. Jay Leyda letter to author, November 9, 1984. Documents in the Selznick archives suggest Austin Strong may have ghost-written the book, but Brooks told Leyda that he did the work.

210. Adam Ulam, *Russia's Failed Revolutions* (London: Weidenfeld and Nicolson, 1981), p. 275.

211. At this period the Gregorian calendar was thirteen days ahead of the Julian calendar. We will remain with the Julian, otherwise the October Revolution will occur in November.

212. Leyda, p. 92.

213. Jacob Rubin, *Moscow Mirage* (London: Geoffrey Bles, 1935), p. 128. Published in U.S. as *I Live to Tell* (Indianapolis: Bobbs Merrill, 1934).

214. Arkatov, who had made a number of Jewish films in Russia, went to Hollywood and, calling himself Dr. Arkatov, claimed to be the true director of Robert Wiene's *The Cabinet of Dr. Caligari* (1919). Since he was in Russia at the time, any connection with it is highly unlikely, but he was desperate for a job. He was going to make *Studies in Wives* for J. G. Bachman, but nothing came of it. He opened a photographic salon in San Francisco in 1929 and in 1940 became a director of training films for the U.S. Army. After the war, in Hollywood, he formed an audio-visual company to make filmstrips teaching the

stories of the Bible. He died in 1961 at 72. (Jim Arkatov letter to Yuri Tsivian, February 18, 1982. Courtesy Yuri Tsivian.)

215. Rubin, p. 131.

216. Leyda, p. 144.

217. *Variety*, in a review of *Kerensky in the Russian Revolution of 1917*, said "it is very doubtful if the rank and file of the American public will have enough interest in the internal affairs of the new republic to make the pictures a financial success," *Variety*, August 14, 1917, p. 24. The U.S. government made unsuccessful efforts to send propaganda films to Russia. See Leyda, p. 123.

218. Gilbert Seldes to author, Philadelphia, March 1964.

219. N. P. Hiley, "Counter-Espionage and Security in Great Britain during the First World War," in the *English Historical Review*, July 1986, pp. 635–70. Among the papers of Sir Horace Rumbold (the minister in Warsaw) in the Bodleian Library, Oxford University, Nick Hiley discovered a letter from Lord Hardinge of Penshurst which said that Basil Thomson was sending a troupe of fifteen people to Poland for an anti-Bolshevik propaganda film under the direction of Harold Shaw: "They are starting for Warsaw, via Dantzig, on March 1st (1920). Their intention is said to be merely to photograph one or two streets and a few villages with peasants, etc. Thomson asks that they may be treated kindly if they get into any difficulty, and I should be very grateful if you would help them in case of need." The trip was presumably diverted when, in March 1920, Red Army divisions massed on the Berezina River, threatening to attack Poland.

220. Hiley, pp. 635–70.

221. Sidney Felstead, *In Search of Sensation* (London: Robert Hale, 1945), pp. 90–91.

222. *Daily Herald*, November 3, 1921, p. 2:4. Courtesy Nick Hiley.

223. *Variety*, June 18, 1920, p. 2.

224. Harold Shaw, born in Tennessee, was an actor and director at Edison. He came to England as chief stage director for the London Film Company, which operated out of Twickenham Studios, in 1913, the same year as George Loane Tucker and Bannister Merwin. Shaw married Edna Flugrath in 1917 and was killed in a car crash in 1926.

225. *Pictures and Picturegoer*, July 24, 1920, p. 107. Edna Flugrath was the sister of Viola Dana and Shirley Mason. In March 1920, a coup d'état was attempted by General Walther V. Lüttwitz, com-

mander of troops in the Berlin area, and Wolfgang Kapp, an East Prussian official. The so-called Kapp Putsch failed.

226. *Pictures and Picturegoer,* July 24, 1920, p. 107.

227. John M. East, *'Neath the Mask* (London: Allen & Unwin, 1967), pp. 315–21.

228. East, p. 317.

229. *The Kine Weekly,* July 8, 1920, p. 97.

230. *The Bioscope,* July 8, 1920, p. 43. Phyllis Bedella and Laurent Novikoff were the leading dancers of the Imperial Ballet.

231. *The Bioscope,* July 8, 1920, p. 43.

232. Quoted in *The Bioscope,* July 8, 1920, p. 18.

233. *The Kine Weekly,* July 8, 1920, p. 97.

234. Laurence Irving, unpublished memoirs, p. 413.

235. Robert Allen, "Motion Picture Exhibiton in Manhattan 1906–12," *Cinema Journal* 18, no. 2 (Spring 1979), p. 4.

236. Harold Hoadley letter to H. Lyman Broening, February 23, 1913. Courtesy Marc Wanamaker.

237. Edward Sloman to author, Hollywood, 1970.

238. Fairchild, p. 139.

239. Quoted in Thomas Cripps, "The Movie Jew," *Journal of Popular Film 3,* 1975, p. 201.

240. Friedman, *Hollywood's Image of the Jew,* p. 52.

241. *Moving Picture World,* October 25, 1913, p. 355.

242. Short, p. 135.

243. Short, pp. 135–37.

244. *Moving Picture World,* April 18, 1914, p. 337.

245. *The Jeffersonian,* quoted in John P. Roche, *The Quest for the Dream* (New York: Macmillan, 1963), p. 89.

246. Ibid.

247. *Variety,* July 30, 1915, p. 19.

248. Ibid.

249. *Moving Picture World,* March 27, 1915, p. 1952.

250. Roche, p. 89.

251. Roche, p. 90.

252. *Variety,* August 27, 1915, p. 15.

253. *Variety,* September 13, 1915, p. 18.

254. *Moving Picture World,* September 18, 1915, p. 2126. In 1920, Oscar Micheaux produced the Negro film *Within Our Gates,* based on the Frank case.

255. Steve Oney, "The Lynching of Leo Frank," in *Esquire,* September 1985, p. 90.

This article contains recent evidence exonerating Frank.

256. Keith Sward, *The Legend of Henry Ford* (New York: Rinehart & Company, 1948), p. 151.

257. Sward, p. 143.

258. One resourceful Jewish producer—William Fox—managed to keep a denigrating article out of the *Independent* by threatening to send cameramen to every crash involving a Ford car and including the footage in his twice-weekly newsreel, Sinclair, *Upton Sinclair Presents William Fox,* p. 216.

259. *Moving Picture World,* March 5, 1921, pp. 20–21.

260. David L. Lewis, "Pioneering the Business Film," in *Public Relations Journal,* June 1971, pp. 14–17. Ford's *Weekly* was replaced by the Ford Education Library, which circulated films to schools, churches, and other groups.

261. *Variety,* October 22, 1920, p. 47.

262. Joseph Goebbels, *The Goebbels Diaries, 1939–1941,* trans. and ed. by Fred Taylor (London: Sphere, 1983), p. 89.

263. Lloyd Morris, *Not So Long Ago* (New York: Random House, 1949), p. 305.

264. *Moving Picture World,* July 30, 1927, p. 305.

265. *The Jazz Singer,* scenario edited and with an introduction by Robert L. Carringer (Madison: Wisconsin Center for Film and Theater Research, University of Wisconsin Press, 1979), p. 24.

266. Randall Miller, ed., *Ethnic Images in American Film and Television* (Philadelphia: The Balch Institute, 1978), p. 23.

267. Friedman, p. 9.

268. H. Lyman Broening, oral history, 1982 by Marc Wanamaker.

269. *The Universal Weekly,* August 2, 1913, p. 32, quoted in Judith N. Goldberg, *Laughter Through Tears* (East Brunswick, N.J.: Associated University Presses, 1983), p. 35.

270. *Moving Picture World,* June 14, 1913, p. 1180.

271. Patricia Erens points out that persistent desertion of families by immigrant husbands was a great problem in *The Jew in American Cinema* (Bloomington: Indiana University Press, 1984), p. 44.

272. *Moving Picture World,* July 19, 1913, p. 300.

273. *The Universal Weekly,* September 6, 1913, p. 8, quoted in Goldberg, p. 122.

274. *New York Dramatic Mirror,* October 8, 1913, p. 30. Goldin collaborated with George K. Rolands on *Bleeding Hearts* and *Sorrows of Israel.*

275. Goldberg, p. 38.

276. *New York Times*, April 6, 1914, quoted in Goldberg, p. 39.

277. Ulam, *Russia's Failed Revolutions*, p. 187.

278. *People's Chronicle*, p. 703. Life for Jews had entered a horrific new phase on March 13, 1881, when Alexander II was assassinated. His son, Alexander III, decided that the Jews were the ideal scapegoats and declared he would kill a third, drive out another third, and convert the rest. The formula emanated from Pobedonostzev, procurator of the Synod, whose influence was equally strong on Nicholas II.

279. *Moving Picture World*, December 13, 1913, p. 1288.

280. Perhaps this was because a converted Jew, ostracized by his people, was shown giving evidence against Beilis.

. 281. *Variety*, December 5, 1913, p. 16. So familiar was the habit of film people of presenting topical events with the leading protagonist of that event playing himself that *Variety* expected to see the real Mendel Beilis on the screen. Beilis left Russia in 1914 and tried to settle in Palestine. In 1922 he came to America, where Boris Thomashefsky featured him in a play Thomashefsky had written—but even playing himself, Beilis was not a convincing actor. A 1915 Russian version of the story in six reels was directed by Josef Soifer in the actual Ukrainian locations. It suffered from the censorship that confiscated or cut every film that mentioned the Jews and did not see the light of day until the February revolution, Leyda, p. 83. In the light of the worldwide outcry that the Beilis case aroused, the Russians must have wished they had never embarked on it. A collaborator of Goldin, George K. Rolands, who also came from Odessa, had his own film corporation. *Terrors of Russia* (1913) was shot at Carmel, New Jersey, a Jewish colony. Five hundred immigrant Jews and Russians took part in the pogrom scenes. Yet another film, *The Mystery of the Beilis Case*, was released in the United States in April 1914. Although the advertisements promised that it had been photographed on the scene in Kiev, it had actually been made in Germany the previous year. The film was based on the account of the ex-Chief of Secret Police of Kiev, Nicolai Krasovsky, who wrote the script together with the journalist Brazul-Brushkovsky.

282. *Moving Picture World*, February 7, 1914, p. 660. The Chicago police seized the Goldin film in December 1913, Goldberg, p. 39–40.

283. *Moving Picture World*, May 9, 1914, p. 795.

284. *Moving Picture World*, July 11, 1914, p. 284

285. *Variety*, June 19, 1914, p. 21..

286. Molly Picon to author, New York City, November 1983.

287. *AFI Catalogue*, 1921–1930, p. 210.

288. Jim Hoberman, *Career of Sidney Goldin*, typescript, September 1986.

289. Frank Borzage to George Pratt, George Eastman House, oral history, 1958. "The first time I started looking for locations [in the ghetto]," said Borzage, "I was dressed just as I normally would and they looked at me and I heard one of the Jewish people say, 'There is a *goniff*,' which means a thief. So I decided that I would come down in old clothes. So this I did and I spent three or four weeks, just moving around and getting my locations. As a matter of fact, I hid a camera in the back of a truck with just the lens sticking out, and I had the cameraman in there and I'd be there myself. I'd say, 'Move down there. Get this.' And they'd move right over and get natural people trying on collars and hats and ties or whatever. And I got the opening of my picture with about 500 feet of just these wonderful shots of these great characters."

290. Frances Marion, *Off With Their Heads* (New York: Macmillan, 1972), p. 71.

291. *Motion Picture Classic*, February 1921, p. 59.

292. Gilbert Warrenton to author, Hemet, California, 1972.

293. *O. Henry Memorial Award: Prize Stories 1919* (Garden City, N.Y.: Doubleday, Page, 1921), chosen by the Society of Arts and Sciences. Introduction by Blanche Colton Williams, 1921, pp. 148–79.

294. Marion, p. 74.

295. Frances Marion to author, Hollywood, 1970.

296. *Variety*, June 4, 1920, p. 27.

297. *Picture Play*, July 1920, p. 70.

298. "I enjoyed two thirds of the way they handled my *Humoresque*," Fannie Hurst quoted in *Motion Picture Classic*, June 1924, p. 77.

299. Fannie Hurst to author, New York, 1964.

300. Marion, p. 74. Hearst must have been mollified by the personality *Photoplay* selected to receive the medal. It was William Randolph Hearst. "The Medal goes to the producer because no picture can be greater than its producer. It takes the producer's faith, foresightedness, money and appreciation to make a great picture. Mr.

Hearst believed in Fannie Hurst's great short story, which appeared in *Cosmopolitan* magazine. He believed in Frank Borzage. He brought these two together. The result has been seen, wept over and applauded by nearly everyone in the world," *Photoplay,* December 1921, p. 56.

301. Telegram from Samuel Goldwyn to Frank Godsol, January 11, 1921. These and other telegrams and memos are from MGM legal files.

302. Sam Goldwyn to Frank Godsol, January 11, 1921.

303. Sam Goldwyn to Abe Lehr, February 24, 1921.

304. Anzia Yezierska, *The Bread Givers,* introduction by Alice Kessler Harris (London: Women's Press, 1984). The child grew up to be an authoress herself, Louise Henriksen; see Anzia Yezierska, *A Writer's Life* (New Brunswick, N.J.: Rutgers University Press, 1988). Anzia was, in the United States, Hattie Mayer until she reverted to her original name.

305. Frank Crane, quoted in Anzia Yezierska, *Red Ribbon on a White Horse* (New York: Charles Scribner's Sons, 1950), p. 121.

306. Frank Godsol to Sam Goldwyn, January 15, 1921.

307. *Motion Picture Classic,* November 1922, p. 41.

308. Yezierska, *Red Ribbon on a White Horse,* p. 45.

309. Estimated cost $130,000–145,000, probable final cost $160,000.

310. Lee, unpublished autobiography, p. 363. Extract from letter written by Seymour Stern at Bern's death; "His deeds of decency affected all Hollywood. There was a legion of people on Vine Street or Hollywood Boulevard—actors, actresses, ex-directors, cameramen, prop men, 'extras' —whom Bern helped and saved from starvation . . . The time I came to Bern asking for $10,000 for a labor film, his refusal was so decent that I could not feel disappointed about it. He was in accord with the idea, but he explained (this was last winter [1931]) that so many people around town were dependent upon him for the winter that he couldn't risk their welfare by helping us!" Letters to Larchmont. Courtesy Ira Gallen.

311. Marx, *Mayer and Thalberg,* p. 46.

312. Sam Goldwyn to Abe Lehr, June 1, 1921.

313. *Picture Play,* January 1928, p. 72.

314. William Wellman to author, Brentwood, California, 1965.

315. *Motion Picture Classic,* November 1922, p. 41.

316. Yezierska, *Red Ribbon on a White Horse,* p. 49.

317. Abe Lehr to G. Hess, May 5, 1922.

318. Abe Lehr letter to Frank Godsol, April 17, 1922.

319. Her real name was Kaufman. She had played in Chet Withey's *New Moon.*

320. Sam Goldwyn to Abe Lehr, June 17, 1921.

321. Sam Goldwyn to Abe Lehr, June 21, 1921.

322. Abe Lehr to Sam Goldwyn, June 4, 1921.

323. Sam Goldwyn to Abe Lehr, September 9, 1921.

324. Sam Goldwyn to Abe Lehr, September 15, 1921.

325. Abe Lehr to Sam Goldwyn, September 15, 1921.

326. Abe Lehr to Sam Goldwyn, September 16, 1921.

327. Sam Goldwyn to Abe Lehr, September 17, 1921.

328. Abe Lehr to Sam Goldwyn, September 17, 1921.

329. Abe Lehr to Sam Goldwyn, September 20, 1921.

330. Abe Lehr to G. Hess, May 1, 1922.

331. Ibid.

332. Anzia Yezierska to Abe Lehr, May 10, 1921.

333. Abe Lehr to Sam Goldwyn, September 30, 1921.

334. Abe Lehr to Sam Goldwyn, October 3, 1921.

335. Helen Ferguson to author, Palm Springs, California, 1970.

336. *Motion Picture Classic,* April 1922, p. 79.

337. Helen Ferguson to author, Palm Springs, California, 1970.

338. The publicity department claimed that Hopper discovered Budin on the street and that Budin bought the store out of the money he earned on the picture. But photographs of his store show that it is anything but new.

339. Abe Lehr to Sam Goldwyn, October 6, 1921.

340. Ibid.

341. Sam Goldwyn to Abe Lehr, October 7, 1921.

342. Yezierska, Sam Goldwyn to Abe Lehr, November 1, 1921.

343. Yezierska, *The Bread Givers.* The short stories in *Hungry Hearts* were connected only by the fact that they dealt with ghetto people. The script had to be written more or less from scratch, with elements borrowed from other stories. The letter from America was condensed from "The

Miracle" and "How I Found America." The arrival in the dark tenement occurs in both "My Own People" and "How I Found America," with the same crack repeated in both: "It ain't so dark. It's only a little shady," pp. 224, 264.

344. Anzia Yezierska, *Hungry Hearts* (London: T. Fisher Unwin, 1922), p. 271.

345. Abe Lehr to HEE, December 19, 1921.

346. Abe Lehr to Sam Goldwyn, February 27, 1922.

347. Frank Godsol to Abe Lehr, May 2, 1922.

348. Ibid.

349. Frank Godsol to Abe Lehr, May 24, 1922. It was cut down to 6,538 from around 8700 feet.

350. *Motion Picture Classic*, April 1922, p. 79. Glass's title read: "Titled in part by Montague Glass."

351. *The American Hebrew*, September 8, 1922, p. 387. The magazine even liked Montague Glass's titles; *Variety*, December 1, 1922.

352. *The American Hebrew*, September 8, 1922.

353. Ibid.

354. *Motion Picture Classic*, June 1922, p. 46.

355. John Cannon, who was then running an arts association in East Anglia, England, found it by an extraordinary coincidence. A house in Peterborough was raided by vandals who left it in such a state that the local paper printed a photograph of the debris. Cannon noticed streams of film across the wreckage. He went at once to the house and discovered an eccentric gentleman who had filled the place with his birthday presents, carefully rewrapped, his mother's clothes, carefully preserved, and, not so carefully preserved, masses of nitrate film he had picked up from local projectionists. *Hungry Hearts* was one of the films.

356. Louise Henriksen letter to author, November 30, 1984. Anzia was paid $15,000.

357. Jetta Goudal's real name was Julie Henriette Goudeket; she was the daughter of a Jewish diamond cutter and was born in Holland, *Films in Review*, May 1986, p. 319. There was a scene of a tenement flat shared by three old ladies, played by inmates of the Home of Old Israel, 204 Henry Street, New York. One was Jennie Freeman, 108 years old, *Picture Show*, February 14, 1925. Courtesy Cliff Howe. The Yiddish newspaper scenes were peopled with New York motion picture trade paper editors, *Exhibitors Trade Review*, November 29, 1924, p. 45. Courtesy Richard Koszarski.

358. *Picture Show* Art Supplement, July 3, 1926, p. 11.

359. *Variety*, February 25, 1925, p. 31.

360. Louise Henriksen to author, London, May 1985.

361. *Variety*, February 25, 1925, p. 31.

362. *Photoplay*, December 1925, p. 132.

363. Edward Sloman, unpublished autobiographical fragment, pp. 18–19.

364. Ibid.

365. *Moving Picture World*, January 8, 1916, p. 257.

366. Ibid.

367. Edward Sloman to author, Hollywood, 1967.

368. Brownlow, p. 162.

369. Undated publication, Sloman scrapbook, author's collection.

370. Louella Parsons, Universal Service Syndicated, November 2, 1925.

371. Undated film paper, probably *Film Spectator*, scrapbook, n.d.

372. Alfred A. Cohn was a former Chicago newspaperman who had coedited *Photoplay* in its early days and written some of its best articles. He was to write the scripts for *The Cohens and the Kellys*, *The Jazz Singer*, *We Americans*, and *Abie's Irish Rose* and was thus a key figure in the production of films about the Jews. Charles Whittaker was born in Ireland, was also a journalist, and wrote such scenarios as *Woman* for Maurice Tourneur.

373. Sloman, autobiography, p. 20.

374. Undated Jewish paper (Los Angeles), Sloman scrapbook.

375. *The Bioscope*, p. 43. December 3, 1925, p. 43.

376. The Universal publicity department crammed all the sensational reactions into advertisements and then credited the direction to Harry Pollard!

377. To the small-town audiences, the ghetto sets and the New York subway scenes were so realistic that Universal put a title on the front pointing out that "every scene in the picture was taken at the Universal Coast Studios," in case they might think stock or location shots had been used.

378. Undated Jewish paper (Los Angeles), Sloman scrapbook. *His People* cost $107,396.80 and grossed $439,587.57—making a profit of $139,961.03—a healthy sum for Universal in those days, according to Richard Koszarski, but considerably less than I would have expected. Koszarski adds that these figures, which he copied from Laemmle's personal register,

were revenue, funds accruing back to Universal. "It is possible there was once a figure for box office gross, which would have been much higher, though Universal would not have seen that much money," letter of April 2, 1984.

379. Undated Jewish paper (Los Angeles), Sloman scrapbook.

380. Ibid.

381. The name "Stein" signals a Jew of German origin, from an earlier wave of immigration. These Jews had achieved a striking degree of social prominence and mostly kept themselves apart from the East Side Jews, although they did charitable work among them.

382. In Frank Capra's *The Younger Generation* (1929) (from a Fannie Hurst story), the young Jew denies his parents by introducing them as hired help. This picture featured Rosa Rosanova and was produced by Jack Cohn for Columbia. See page 420.

383. Joseph Schildkraut, *My Father and I* (New York: Viking, 1959), p. 24.

384. Brownlow, p. 163.

385. Undated Jewish paper (Los Angeles), Sloman scrapbook.

386. Edward Sloman letter to author, March 2, 1966. Edward G. Robinson had preceded Muni as the lead in *We Americans*. Muni Weisenfreund played the Jewish gangster in the stage version of *Four Walls*, but John Gilbert played him on the screen. Erens, *Jew in American Cinema*, p. 97.

387. Undated press cutting, Edward Sloman scrapbook.

388. Ibid.

389. Once the immigrant entered the glass-enclosed hall, his baggage was taken away to be examined and labeled with the tickets of the railroad or steamship company by which he was to travel next. The immigrant passed through a series of small rooms in which he received a medical examination, an intelligence test, and filled out a dossier with his date of birth, his occupation, and his destination. Then he went to the money-changing bureau and into the restaurant. "This," according to Inspector Baker, "is one of the most difficult things to provide for such a cosmopolitan clientele. A Scandinavian, for instance, doesn't care anything about spaghetti, and Italians would turn up their noses at Swedish bread. A glance into the food box which an immigrant can purchase for $1.50 is a keen insight into international dietetics," undated press cutting, Sloman scrapbook.

390. Undated press cutting, Sloman scrapbook.

391. Ibid.

392. *Motion Picture Magazine,* June 1928, p. 61.

393. Carringer, ed., p. 13.

394. Ibid.

395. *Moving Picture World,* June 4, 1927, p. 340.

396. Carringer, p. 18.

397. Title writer Jack Jarmuth may have been responsible for making the film less offensive to blacks than it might have been. Alfred Cohn's final shooting script gives Otto Lederer the title, when seeing Jolson in blackface for the first time, "It talks like Jakie, but it looks like a nigger." In the film, the title reads, "He talks like Jakie—but he looks like his shadow," J. B. Kaufman.

398. Warner Oland's singing voice was dubbed by Joseph Diskay, not Rosenblatt, courtesy Miles Kreuger.

399. Joseph Green to author, New York, 1983.

400. Columbia University oral history transcription, quoted in Carringer, ed., introduction, p. 21.

401. It was Goldfish in America. Goldwyn's name in Poland was Schmuel Gelbfisz. A. Scott Berg, *Goldwyn* (London: Hamish Hamilton, 1989), p. 5.

402. *Motion Picture Magazine,* July 1927, p. 36. "When Shakespeare wrote *Abie's Irish Rose,* he used different dialogue and called it *Romeo and Juliet,*" Preston Sturges, quoted in Curtis, *Between Flops,* p. 94.

403. *Motion Picture Classic,* March 1925, p. 21.

404. Patricia Erens says this echoes sentiments more Christian than Jewish, *The Jew in American Cinema,* p. 107.

405. The first wedding is at an Episcopal Church.

406. *The Film Spectator,* March 31, 1928, p. 5.

407. *Variety,* December 26, 1928, p. 27.

408. Jesse Lasky, *I Blow My Own Horn* (New York: Doubleday & Co., 1957), p. 223.

409. Anne Nichols sued the producers of *The Cohens and the Kellys* for plagiarism, *Motion Picture Magazine,* September 1928, p. 35. She lost. The court decided that while the underlying themes were similar, there was no infringement because the theme itself was trite and motivated many other plays, *Authors' League Bulletin,* May 1929, p. 20.

CHAPTER ELEVEN: INDUSTRY

1. Lindsey and Borough, *The Dangerous Life,* p. 94.

2. Steffens, *Upbuilders,* pp. 202–5.

3. Stephen B. Wood, *Constitutional Politics in the Progressive Era; Child Labor and the Law* (Chicago: University of Chicago Press, 1968), pp. 4–6.

4. *Moving Picture World,* March 13, 1915, p. 1622.

5. Apart from leading the campaigns that resulted in the State Widows' Pension Law, Loeb also worked for the New York motion picture law, which ensured that theatres were sanitary and fireproof. She was the first woman called in as mediator in an industrial dispute; in 1917 she settled a New York taxicab strike.

6. *Photoplay,* September 1920, p. 108.

7. Addams, *The Second Twenty Years at Hull-House,* p. 36.

8. *Image,* no. 51, May 1957, p. 114.

9. Marc Wanamaker, "Encyclopaedia of the Movie Studios," unpublished ms., p. 49. Paterson, New Jersey, was not known for employing child labor, which was presumably one reason why the Edison people selected it. Edison had touched on child labor in 1909 with *Suffer Little Children.*

10. Child labor was not only an American problem, nor did it die out. (In England, it has recently been established by a press survey that 2 million children are secretly employed.)

11. *Moving Picture World,* March 9, 1912, p. 866.

12. *Moving Picture World,* April 27, 1912, p. 305.

13. An act excluding the products of child labor from interstate commerce was passed in the first few months of the Woodrow Wilson administration. Goldman, *Rendezvous with Destiny* p. 169, but in 1918 another child labor law was declared unconstitutional by the Supreme Court as "an encroachment on states rights," *People's Chronology,* p. 786. When in 1922 Congress passed a new law levying a heavy tax on child labor products, the Supreme Court found it invalid.

14. *Moving Picture World,* May 11, 1912, p. 529.

15. "Mrs. Browning's poem has been to the particular evil it deals with what *Uncle Tom's Cabin* was to the slavery question," *Bioscope,* October 10, 1912. *Cry of the Children* was also the title of a 1908 book by Mrs. John van Voorst (New York: Moffet Yard) on child labor in the South. John Spargo published *The Bitter Cry of the Children* in 1906 with Macmillan, New York. Sloan, *The Loud Silents, p.* 70.

16. Nevertheless, Eline's performance was selected by *Moving Picture World* as "the very breath of poetry," May 11, 1912, p. 529. The role was not played by Helen Badgley, another Thanhouser kidlet, as has been stated, according to Q. David Bowers.

17. Possibly George Nichols; the cameraman was Carl L. Gregory, according to Q. David Bowers. He sometimes co-directed.

18. *Moving Picture World,* April 27, 1912, pp. 305–6.

19. "Anarchism looked as if it might rival the European successes of the 'Black International' until a bomb went off in Chicago's Haymarket Square . . . in 1886 and killed the movement by associating it with black bearded horror." Goldman, p. 35.

20. Steven J. Ross, "Cinema and Class Conflict: Labor, Capital, The State and American Silent Film," ms., pp. 16–17. This essay will appear in Robert Sklar and Charles Musser, eds., *Resisting Images: Radical Pespectives on Film and History* (Philadelphia: Temple University Press, 1990). *A Martyr to His Cause* was produced at the W. H. Seeley Studio, Ohio. Philip S. Foner has recently discovered the scenario for *A Martyr to His Cause*: See *Labor History* 24, pp. 103–111.

21. Ross, "Cinema and Class Conflict," pp. 16–17.

22. *Moving Picture World,* September 20, 1913, p. 1323.

23. *Moving Picture World,* September 13, 1913, p. 1185.

24. Compiled for unpublished ms., Thomas Brandon Collection, MoMA. Steven Ross feels that if Brandon had taken a broader view of politics, he would have greatly increased the number, letter to author, August 8, 1989.

25. Goldman, pp. 36–64.

26. Adams Jr., *The Age of Industrial Violence, 1910–1915,* p. 140.

27. *Moving Picture World,* May 31, 1913, pp. 903, 923.

28. *Moving Picture World,* June 14, 1913, p. 1138.

29. *Moving Picture World,* May 31, 1913, p. 923.

30. Ibid.

31. Hal Mohr was another cameraman, and he also edited the film. Maltin, *The Art of the Cinematographer,* p. 77. Keane began in pictures in 1895 or '96. He also made a

film about V.D., *The Spreading Evil* (1918), Martin Sopocy, letter to author, October 16, 1987. This is now in the National Film Archive, London.

32. *New York Dramatic Mirror,* February 10, 1915.

33. *Moving Picture World,* September 26, 1914, p. 1780.

34. *New York Dramatic Mirror,* February 10, 1915.

35. *Moving Picture World,* September 26, 1914, p. 1790.

36. Upton Sinclair letter to Nicolai Lebedev, May 4, 1923, Brandon Collection, MoMA/ Lilly Library, Indiana University.

37. Upton Sinclair letter to Nicolai Lebedev, May 4, 1923.

38. Herbert Blaché telegram to Upton Sinclair, November 25, 1916, Brandon Collection, MoMA/Lilly Library.

39. Upton Sinclair letter to Nicolai Lebedev, May 4, 1923. *The Moneychangers* was directed by Jack Conway. The story was credited to Benjamin B. Hampton and Sinclair.

40. Federal Photoplays letter to Upton Sinclair, March 3, 1921, Brandon Collection, MoMA.

41. Horsley was a socialist, which makes his failure as an early capitalist in Hollywood somewhat more understandable. Steven Ross, who has examined his papers (in the library of the Academy of Motion Picture Arts and Sciences, Los Angeles), concludes that while he was committed to radical politics, he saw the MMPC as a good way to sell his studio and make a great deal of money, letter to author, August 8, 1989.

42. Upton Sinclair letters, January 18, 1921, and May 4, 1923, Brandon Collection, MoMA.

43. A potentially splendid collaboration—between Sinclair and Douglas Fairbanks—never took place. Sinclair tried to interest Fairbanks in *The Millennium.* Fairbanks wrote to Sinclair on December 13, 1924: "Think maybe we were talking a bit at cross purposes Thursday. You know I have had the seed of an idea for a Utopian story in the back part of my mind for a number of years only waiting for a time to put it into execution. That time has never yet seemed ripe. What I meant to convey to you was that in case I should ever decide to go on with the idea there might be a possibility that we should like to collaborate on it. All that, however, is in the problematic future and would in no way interfere with your disposal of the play and picture rights to *The Millennium.*"

44. *New York Dramatic Mirror,* August 12, 1914.

45. *Moving Picture World,* December 12, 1914, p. 1498.

46. Bowser, ed., *The Biograph Bulletins,* p. 150. The speculator was played by Frank Powell, later a director of social films himself (and of the 1914 Theda Bara classic, *A Fool There Was*). The story was probably inspired by the case of Joseph Leiter, a Chicago millionaire, who had attempted to corner the wheat market in the late 1890s. He borrowed vast sums to buy all the wheat in America, forcing up the price so that when he sold it he made an immense profit. He was outwitted by a rival (who imported wheat from Canada) and ended up owing $9 million. Nicholas Mosley, *The Rules of the Game* (London: Secker & Warburg, 1983), p. 13.

47. *New York Dramatic Mirror,* quoted in George Pratt, *Spellbound in Darkness* (Greenwich, Conn.: New York · Graphic Society Ltd., 1966), pp. 67–68.

48. Schickel, *D. W. Griffith,* p. 144.

49. Tourneur and Carré would have a highly rewarding partnership spanning several years.

50. *New York Dramatic Mirror,* December 11, 1915.

51. *Variety,* November 29, 1918.

52. Ross, "Cinema and Class Conflict," p. 20.

53. *Photo-Play Journal,* January 1920, p. 5.

54. *Variety,* November 14, 1919, p. 65.

55. Leuchtenburg, *Perils of Prosperity,* p. 66.

56. Ibid., p. 78.

57. They landed in Finland and were given an official welcome by the Russians. But they arrived at a period of famine, blockade, and terror, and most were thoroughly miserable, Rubin, *Moscow Mirage,* p. 201.

58. Sinclair, *Autobiography of Upton Sinclair,* p. 139. Several colonists became well-known writers, including Sinclair Lewis.

59. According to Raymond Rohauer, the title was changed to *Shattered Dreams* in 1920 to lengthen its commercial life. But I can find no reference to this in print. The film's working title was *Red Republic;* alternate *Shattered Dreams* (AFI *Catalogue,* 1911–1920), p. 86

60. Russell Campbell in *Silent Picture* 19, p. 26, says the pamphlets are the work of Scott Nearing and John Spargo, together with a report by a writer on the left-wing *New York Call.*

61. The hotel in Florida used as a location was the Royal Poinciana Hotel, Palm Beach, owned by Henry Flagler, said to be the largest resort hotel in the world.

62. *Moving Picture World,* April 19, 1919, p. 424.

63. *Variety,* April 30, 1920, p. 48.

64. *Moving Picture World,* May 17, 1919, p. 1058.

65. Duncan Mansfield, who did such a brilliant job on *Tol'able David* (1921).

66. Donn Byrne was the pseudonym of an Irish-American, Brian Oswald Donn-Byrne, who was educated at University College, Dublin, and at Paris and Leipzig.

67. *Moving Picture World,* February 14, 1920, n.p.

68. *Moving Picture World,* April 10, 1920, p. 248.

69. Seldes said ten years, but a study of how the Russian Revolution was reported by the *New York Times* over a period of two years concluded that it was a disaster—"the net effect was almost always misleading," *The New Republic,* August 4, 1920, pp. 3, 10, quoted in Kaplan, *Lincoln Steffens,* p. 232. *New York Times* correspondent Walter Duranty (1921–1940) was a Soviet apologist, Tim La Haye, *Hidden Censors* (New York: Power Books, 1984), p. 53.

70. H. H. Van Loan, *How I Did It* (Los Angeles: Whittingham Press, 1922), p. 32.

71. Kaplan, p. 229.

72. Van Loan, p. 33.

73. *Variety,* May 16, 1919, p. 53. The cameraman was the Russian immigrant David Abel.

74. *Wid's,* May 17, 1919.

75. *Photoplay,* August 1919, p. 118.

76. Van Loan, p. 65.

77. *Picture Play,* January 1920, p. 66. The picture starred Robert Anderson; the future star Colleen Moore was a supporting player.

78. *Picture Play,* January 1920, p. 66.

79. *Variety,* October 17, 1919, p. 65.

80. *Variety,* January 3, 1924, p. 21.

81. The leading radical in the film is clearly intended to be Jewish. I can find no director credit, but the film was written by O. E. Goebel and Condé B. Pallen. Goebel was sent to prison for misappropriating Catholic diocese funds to back a talkie in 1929, Kay Thackrey, unpublished ms. p. 176B.

82. A full synopsis is in the Library of Congress, Washington, D.C.

83. *Variety,* August 15, 1919, p. 71.

84. *Wid's,* June 29, 1919.

85. *Variety,* September 5, 1919, p. 71.

86. *Photoplay,* November 1919, p. 13.

87. *Wid's,* August 24, 1919.

88. *Photoplay,* December 1919, p. 117.

89. *Variety,* November 21, 1919, p. 55.

90. *Variety,* June 4, 1920, p. 38.

91. *Wid's,* 1920 Year Book, p. 383.

92. *Variety,* January 9, 1920, p. 58.

93. *Variety,* June 4, 1920, p. 38.

94. *Moving Picture World,* February 7, 1920, p. 878. Franklin Lane wrote to Adolph Zukor, July 29, 1920, expressing his embarrassment that only one film had been produced on the Americanism theme. Courtesy Russell Merritt.

95. Letter from Bert Patenaude to author, January 26, 1988.

96. For information about Donald Thompson's activities in WWI, see Brownlow, *The War, the West and the Wilderness,* p. 8, and *American Newsfilm 1914-1919: The Underexposed War,* unpublished thesis by David Mould, University of Kansas, p. 100.

97. Memo regarding photographic account, April 7, 1920, Herbert Hoover Archives, Stanford University. Courtesy Bert Patenaude.

98. Invitation from George Barr Baker to Governor Gilbert, January 8, 1920, Herbert Hoover Archives.

99. *New York Times,* January 10, 1920, p. 9:2.

100. *Variety,* January 24, 1920, p. 61. Hoover and Baker agreed that the famine and misery in the film were the result of Bolshevism. At other times, especially in 1921–1922, when they dealt directly with Russia, Hoover and Baker insisted that people turned to Bolshevism *because* they were hungry. Bolshevism could be cured through food, Bert Patenaude.

101. *New York Times,* January 10, 1920, p. 9:2.

102. *Moving Picture World,* January 24, 1920, p. 635.

103. Invitation from George Barr Baker to Alexander J. Hemphill, January 8, 1920, Herbert Hoover Archives.

104. Bureau of Labor Statistics, quoted in *People's Chronology,* p. 792.

105. *Variety,* January 16, 1920, p. 61.

106. Letter from George Barr Baker to Herbert Hoover, January 13, 1920 (misdated 1919).

107. *Variety,* January 16, 1920, p. 61.

108. Letter from George Barr Baker to Fred B. Warren, July 24, 1920, Herbert Hoover Archives.

109. Letter from George Barr Baker to the New York State Income Tax Bureau, Albany, State of New York, January 25, 1923, Herbert Hoover Archives. He helped to stop an attempt by Zimmer to publish

a volume of stills through Alfred A. Knopf in 1929.

110. Letter from George Barr Baker to New York State Income Tax Bureau, Albany, April 19, 1923, Herbert Hoover Archives.

111. In 1919, Griffith's *Intolerance* had got through the blockade into Russia, where it had a profound effect on Soviet filmmakers. Lenin saw it and arranged to have it shown throughout Russia. He tried, through an intermediary, to persuade Griffith to come and take charge of the Soviet film industry, Leyda, *Kino,* p. 142. According to Leyda, of three stories, (the Christ episode was censored) The Modern Story had by far the strongest impact. "Russian audiences had never seen such a believable tragedy on American working class life—it must have given life to every slogan they had heard, about the sympathies of foreign workers with the revolution in Russia," Leyda, *Kino,* p. 143. The film ran for ten years.

112. *Author's League Bulletin* VII, no. 3, June 1924, pp. 5–7. MoMA/Lilly Library, Upton Sinclair Collection.

113. *Author's League Bulletin,* June 1924, pp. 5–7.

114. Ibid.

115. *Variety,* August 2, 1923, p. 3.

116. *American Film Institute Catalogue, 1921–1930,* p. 207.

117. *Daily Worker,* January 18, 1924, quoted in Brandon ms. Mussolini appears in a shot beside the king reviewing his troops entering Rome.

118. Balshofer and Miller, *One Reel a Week,* p. 166.

119. *Photoplay,* January 1924, p. 5.

120. Balshofer and Miller, p. 166.

121. Winifred Johnston, *Memo on the Movies* (Norman, Okla.: Cooperative Books, 1939), p. 46.

122. DeMille, *Autobiography,* p. 248.

123. Lenore Coffee, *Storyline* (London: Cassell, 1973), p. 140. The song, allegedly sung in the 1860s by the men hauling the boats along the Volga, was popularized by Feodor Chaliapin, the celebrated Russian bass.

124. *Photoplay,* November 1926, p. 112.

125. *Picture Play,* July 1926, p. 60.

126. Jan and Cora Gordon, *Stardust in Hollywood* (London: Harrap, 1930), p. 187. The general was probably Lodijenski. Another adviser was Vasili Kalmykoff.

127. *Motion Picture Magazine,* May 1934, p. 72.

128. *Picture Play,* July 1926, p. 60.

129. Sidney Lens, *The Labor Wars* (Garden City, N.Y.: Doubleday & Co., Inc., 1973), p. 6.

130. George Baer, president of the Reading Railroad in 1902, quoted in Lens, p. 141.

131. Lens, p. 7.

132. It was a Chinese who gave them their nickname when he had trouble pronouncing the Ws and referred to them as the "I Wobble Wobble." One film, J. Stuart Blackton's *Life's Greatest Problem* (1919), was the exception that proved the rule—it had the I.W.W. threaten to blow up a shipyard and mentioned them by name.

133. *Motion Picture News,* June 11, 1914, p. 82.

134. *Moving Picture World,* October 6, 1908, p. 266.

135. *Variety,* September 26, 1908, p. 12.

136. *Moving Picture World,* October 6, 1908, p. 266.

137. Lens, p. 11.

138. Lens, p. 10.

139. *Moving Picture World,* December 12, 1908, p. 485. Kalem produced so many films on Irish themes—some filmed on location in Ireland—its employees became known as the O'Kalems.

140. *Moving Picture World,* May 15, 1909, p. 634.

141. *Moving Picture World,* July 2, 1910, p. 1910.

142. Jacobs, *The Rise of the American Film,* p. 151.

143. *Moving Picture World,* April 2, 1910, p. 509.

144. *Moving Picture World,* June 24, 1911, p. 1424.

145. Ibid.

146. *Velvet Light Trap,* no. 17 (Winter 1977), p. 38. Solax, however, also produced the socialist *Child of the Tenements* the same year.

147. *New York Dramatic Mirror,* April 29, 1914. Muriel Ostriche played a loyal girl employee wounded by a bullet. A fictionalization appeared in *Photoplay,* June 1914, pp. 158–64. The location was Stamford, Connecticut, according to Q. David Bowers.

148. *New York Dramatic Mirror,* April 29, 1914.

149. *Moving Picture World,* May 3, 1913, p. 489.

150. Credits on the print at the National Archives, Washington D.C., and Steven J. Ross, letter to author, August 8, 1989. In *Motion Picture News,* February 14, 1914, p. 23, Charles Hite says the United States Steel Corporation came to him in 1913 and asked for a film to be made showing the human side of the company.

151. A close-up of the man filmed against a backcloth jars badly with the next shot, showing him at the Battery surrounded by people.

152. *Moving Picture World*, April 26, 1913, p. 418.

153. Ross, "Cinema and Class Conflict," p. 13.

154. Undated Chicago newspaper quoted in *Moving Picture World*, May 24, 1913, p. 81.

155. *Moving Picture World*, May 24, 1913, p. 81.

156. *Moving Picture World*, February 21, 1920, p. 1257; the use of cameramen in a strike was revealed in a murder trial.

157. *Moving Picture World*, August 7, 1915, p. 1039, and Ross, "Cinema and Class Conflict," p. 14.

158. *New York Dramatic Mirror*, September 22, 1915.

159. *Moving Picture World*, October 24, 1914, p. 538.

160. *Moving Picture World*, October 31, 1914, p. 658.

161. John Collier, in *The Survey*, August 7, 1915, p. 424.

162. Adapted by Richard Willis from a novel by Jacques Futrelle. The mob scene near the end was shot on the steps of the State Capitol at Sacramento, California. "One of the beauties of the offering is its convincing atmosphere . . . Among its specially interesting elements are the foundry scenes, taken in some big steel plants and showing, as backgrounds for the early life of its hero, the great machine tools at which he works, the pouring of molten metal and the flying sparks that in the dusky shop scatter from the whirling emory wheels biting into the steel," *Moving Picture World*, March 20, 1915, p. 1780. Favorite Players was Carlyle Blackwell's short-lived company.

163. *Moving Picture World*, March 20, 1915, p. 1780.

164. *Moving Picture World*, December 13, 1913, p. 1266.

165. *Moving Picture World*, April 24, 1914, p. 576.

166. Sinclair, *Autobiography*, p. 124.

167. *Poison* was made in collaboration with the Westfield Pure Food Movement to alert the public to the dangers of canned and bottled foods. Professor Lewis Allyn, the pure food expert, appeared in it.

168. Sinclair, *Autobiography*, p. 135.

169. Sinclair, *The Jungle*.

170. Upton Sinclair letter to Joseph Malkin, April 5, 1923, Lilly Library, Indiana University (as with all other Sinclair letters and documents).

171. Grau, *Theatre of Science*, p. 69. The All-Star Feature Corporation had organized in 1913, and its first production was Augustus Thomas's *Arizona*.

172. *New York Times*, August 13, 1934, pp. 1, 13, Augustus Thomas's obituary.

173. *Motography*, July 4, 1914, pp. 21–22.

174. William S. Hart, *My Life East and West* (Boston: Houghton Mifflin, 1929), p. 274.

175. Upton Sinclair letter to Joseph Cannon, August 21, 1920.

176. Upton Sinclair letter to Joseph Malkin, April 5, 1923, and to Nicolai Lebedev, May 4, 1923.

177. *Moving Picture World*, June 20, 1914, p. 1625.

178. Ibid. Upton Sinclair letter to Albert Rhys Williams, June 30, 1924.

179. Clement Wood, *The Appeal to Reason*, June 12, 1914, quoted Brandon ms. This proved to be Sinclair's favorite review.

180. Brandon ms./Philip S. Foner, "Upton Sinclair's The Jungle: The Movie," in *Upton Sinclair, Literature and Social Reform* (Frankfurt: Peter Lang, 1989), p. 156.

181. Brandon writes that this happened much later, when Sinclair tried to distribute it himself, i.e., 1927—but this reference is from a letter to Joseph Malkin, April 5, 1923, in a paragraph referring to the original run. Philip Foner considers the picture was kept off the screen by big business, frightened by the enthusiastic response of the working-class audiences, a campaign foreshadowing that which the industry conducted to keep Sinclair from becoming governor of California in 1934. Foner, op. cit., p. 156.

182. J. Johnson, Colorado Springs, letter to Upton Sinclair, February 3, 1916. The film was especially valued at Socialist party meetings.

183. Upton Sinclair letter to Joseph Cannon, August 21, 1920.

184. Joseph Cannon to Upton Sinclair, September 20, 1920. Cannon suggested Sinclair had made a mistake playing the orator at the end—"he weakened Sinclair and he weakened *The Jungle*. It is placing Sinclair in a field where he does not really function," letter, September 20, 1920.

185. Upton Sinclair to Joseph Cannon, September 27, 1920.

186. Joseph Cannon to Upton Sinclair, August 4, 1921.

187. Joseph Cannon to Upton Sinclair, August 4, 1921.

188. Joseph Cannon to Upton Sinclair, August 15, 1921.

189. Joseph Cannon to Upton Sinclair, November 18, 1921.

190. Upton Sinclair, to Augustus Thomas, October 22, 1921.

191. Sinclair, *Autobiography,* pp. 216–17. Augustus Thomas was completing his autobiography at this period; he makes mention of none of his films. But neither does he decry socialism. He comes out strongly for organized labor (see pp. 462–3) but opposes class warfare.

192. C. W. Pugsley letter to the Labor Film Service, November 1921.

193. Joseph Cannon to Upton Sinclair, November 29, 1921.

194. Upton Sinclair to Joseph Cannon, December 5, 1921.

195. Film Craft Laboratory to Joseph Cannon, May 18, 1922.

196. Joseph Cannon to *New York Call,* June 20, 1922.

197. It later became the theatre where foreign films and Workers Newsreels were shown in the thirties.

198. Joseph Cannon to Upton Sinclair, August 15, 1922.

199. Upton Sinclair to Nicolai Lebedev, May 4, 1923.

200. Upton Sinclair to Joseph Malkin, April 5, 1923.

201. Censors' report, October 29, 1927, quoted in Brandon ms.

202. Ibid.

203. Sinclair, *Autobiography,* pp. 216–17.

204. Addams, *The Second Twenty Years at Hull-House,* p. 36. For a full account of industrial safety films, see *Photoplay,* November 1918, p. 54.

205. Lens, p.148.

206. Ross, "Cinema and Class Conflict," p. 9.

207. *New York Dramatic Mirror,* October 21, 1914. It was produced by Broadway Star for Vitagraph.

208. *New York Dramatic Mirror,* October 21, 1914. The name was changed from Emanuel to Emanon ("no name" spelled backward) in the story in *Motion Picture Magazine* and probably in release prints.

209. *Moving Picture World,* November 20, 1915, p. 1469.

210. *New York Dramatic Mirror,* May 5, 1915.

211. Logan, *Against the Evidence,* p. 124.

212. Adams, Jr., p. 149.

213. In 1912–1913 alone, 151 people caught typhoid, Adams, Jr., p. 148.

214. Adams, Jr., p. 159.

215. Harry Perry with Colonel Oscar Estes, unpublished autobiograhy.

216. Ibid.

217. Victor Milner letter to author, October 28, 1972.

218. Quoted in *Moving Picture World,* December 6, 1913, p. 1155.

219. Victor Milner letter to author, October 1972.

220. *The Photographic Times,* June 1913, p. 236.

221. *New York Dramatic Mirror,* June 10, 1914.

222. Ibid.

223. Ibid.

224. Synopsis of *Graft,* episode 8, Library of Congress.

225. *Moving Picture World,* February 19, 1916, p. 1152.

226. *Variety,* February 18, 1916, p. 21.

227. *New York Dramatic Mirror,* February 27, 1916.

228. *Screenland,* June 1930, p. 38.

229. *New York Dramatic Mirror,* February 27, 1916.

230. *San Francisco Call and Post,* March 8, 1916.

231. Memorandum from FBI files, August 1922, Chaplin exhibition, David Robinson collection.

232. Griffith was also inspired by a Bayonne, New Jersey, industrialist "fervid in charity and zealous in ecclesiastical activities" whose guards killed nineteen strikers, Drew, *Intolerance,* p. 32.

233. Machine guns could not operate with blank cartridges at this period.

234. *Lubin Bulletin,* n.d. Courtesy Linda Kowall. A satire of Rockefeller was *The Subpoena Server* (1906 American Mutoscope & Biograph Co.) Rockefeller hired a public relations specialist after Ludlow. A 1,240-seat luxury theatre was built at his Pueblo, Colorado, steelworks in 1916. His Colorado Fuel and Iron Company sponsored programs of free films for their workers. "In industrial plants where films are shown," wrote Sir Gilbert Parker, "the men have remained more contented than they otherwise would be. Besides, the films took them away from Socialist and extreme radical meetings," Steven Ross ms. Ross also describes a five-reel film made by socialists in New York, *What Is to Be Done?* (1914), which depicted the Ludlow massacre.

235. *Photoplay,* February 1917, p. 26.

236. The story was by William Ritchey. Henry King recalled that he wrote the scripts himself, but Ritchey, who was responsible for other social films, should be credited with the original stories.

237. *Photoplay,* February 1917, p. 26.

238. *New York Dramatic Mirror,* September 2, 1916. Adapted by Douglas Bron-

ston from a story by Louis Tracy, the series was directed by W. A. Douglas and Harry Harvey. Other episode titles suggest their contents: *The Hypocrites, The Butterflies, Mammon and Moloch, Into the Pit, Humanity Triumphant.*

239. Von Sternberg, *Fun in a Chinese Laundry,* p. 41.

240. Born and trained in England, Warde went to America in 1874 and played with Edwin Booth. He was an authority on Shakespeare. The small boy was played by a girl—Helen Badgley.

241. *Variety,* June 8, 1917, p. 19. Jeanne Eagels's MGM film with John Gilbert, ten years later, started life with the same title— *Fires of Youth*—but was eventually called *Man, Woman and Sin.*

242. Quoted in *Motion Picture Magazine,* May 1918, p. 8.

243. *Wid's,* May 31, 1917, p. 341.

244. *Moving Picture World,* January 11, 1919, p. 202.

245. *Variety,* November 19, 1920, p. 30.

246. Ibid.

247. Ross, "Cinema and Class Conflict," p. 14.

248. Brandon ms. Besides Cannon, the Labor Film Service Board of directors included the president, Thomas D. Healy, of the Waterfront Federation; Darwin J. Meserole, publicist; I. M. Sackin, attorney; Dr. Isaac Grossman; and Herman Ross, business manager, *Labor Film Service Bulletin,* Upton Sinclair Collecton, MoMA/Lilly Library.

249. *New York Call,* August 12, 1920, quoted in Brandon ms.

250. Joseph Cannon to Upton Sinclair, August 23, 1920.

251. Joseph Cannon to Upton Sinclair, August 20, 1921; Ross, "Cinema and Class Conflict," p. 33.

252. *Variety,* February 24, 1922, p. 38.

253. Ibid.

254. *Variety,* September 20, 1923, p. 18.

255. *Cineaste* 6, no. 4, n.p. It was the coal strike which drove the last of the East Coast studios to California and all but emptied Fort Lee, *Variety,* September 1, 1922, p. 47.

256. *Wid's,* December 25, 1921.

257. Margaret Mann, the mother in John Ford's *Four Sons* (1928), had a role in *The New Disciple.*

258. *Photoplay,* March 1922, p. 116.

259. *Variety,* December 23, 1921, p. 35.

260. *Daily Worker,* March 18, 1924, quoted in Brandon ms.

261. Steven Ross letter to author, June 9, 1989; Ross, "Cinema and Class Conflict," p. 37.

262. *The New Majority,* October 17, 1925, quoted in Brandon ms.

263. *The New Majority,* October 17, 1925.

264. Ross, "Cinema and Class Conflict," p. 35.

265. *AFI Catalogue,* 1921–1930, p. 504.

266. *Motion Picture Magazine,* May 1926, p. 28.

267. Laurence A. Hughes, ed., *The Truth About the Movies* (Hollywood: Hollywood Publishers, 1924), p. 455.

268. *Picture Play,* June 1927, pp. 24–25.

269. Ibid.

270. *AFI Catalogue,* 1921–1930, p. 505.

271. *Picture Play,* June 1927, p. 25. Lionel Stander made his first film appearance in *Men of Steel,* although he appeared only in the studio scenes shot in New York. The only incident he could recall was that some structure fell on top of some extras— probably the water tower effect, Stander to author, Cannes, 1964. Stander was later in trouble with McCarthy for being a "radical."

272. *Picture Play,* June 1927, p. 25.

273. *Variety,* July 14, 1926, p. 14.

274. Ibid.

275. Ibid.

276. *Photoplay,* September 1926, p. 54.

277. *Motion Picture Magazine,* October 1926, p. 60.

278. *Picture Play,* February 1927, p. 10.

279. Mary Heaton Vorse wrote, "During that week (the fourth week of the strike) Margaret Larkin began her work as publicity director which meant that she worked all day and night, saw the newspaper men, ran to the court house, marched on the picket line, telephoned for speakers, got out daily statements and later got up concerts and worked on the moving picture," *The Passaic Textile Strike 1926–27* (General Relief Textile Strikers, 1927), quoted in Barry Sabath, "The Passaic Strike Comes to the Screen," unpublished ms., 1976, Brandon Collection, MoMA.

280. Letter from Albin Zwiazek to author, August 1983.

281. Ibid.

282. Gus Deak to author, Garfield, New Jersey, November 1983.

283. Sam Brody to author, letter and telephone interview, August 1986.

284. Martha Stone Asher to author, London, May 1988.

285. The facts for this section come from *Passaic, The Story of a Struggle,* told by Albert Weisbord, published by the Workers (Communist) Party, Daily Worker Publishing Company, 1926, reprinted by AIMS press in New York in 1976; Paul L. Murphy, with Kermit Hall and David

Klaassen, *The Passaic Textile Strike of* 1926 (Belmont, Calif.: Wadsworth, 1974).

286. When, in 1919, the school authorities introduced a new scheme for the teaching of English, the millowners put such pressure on them they abandoned it. This was attributed to the owners' fear of Bolshevism, although Bolshevism had flourished well enough in Russian and Hungarian.

287. Gus Deak to author, November 1983.

288. Ibid.

289. Ibid.

290. *New York Times,* March 4, 1926, quoted in Murphy, p. 12.

291. *New York Times,* March 5, 1926, quoted in Murphy, p. 15.

292. Albert Weisbord, questioned by Tom Brandon in 1976, declared that no film had been made of the strike, Weisbord letter to Brandon, January 6, 1976, Brandon Collection, MoMA.

293. *Daily Worker,* May 10, 1927, p. 2, Brandon Collection, MoMA.

294. *Daily Worker,* October 18, 1926, p. 6, Brandon Collection, MoMA.

295. *Daily Worker,* October 12, 1926, p. 5, Brandon Collection, MoMA.

296. *Daily Worker,* October 26, 1926, p. 4, quoted in Sabath, p. 9.

297. *Daily Worker,* December 1, 1926, p. 3, quoted in Sabath, p. 10.

298. *Daily Worker,* January 7, 1927, quoted in Sabath, p. 11.

299. *Passaic Daily News,* November 30, 1926, p. 2, quoted in Sabath, p. 11.

300. *Daily Worker,* March 4, 1927, p. 5.

301. Alfred Wagenknecht interview, *Daily Worker,* May 10, 1927, p. 2, Brandon Collection, MoMA.

302. *Daily Worker,* August 13, 1928, pp. 1, 3, Brandon Collection, MoMA. There is no record of this film being completed.

303. Gus Deak to author, November 1983. Albert Weisbord was expelled from the Communist party as a Trotskyite. According to Martha Asher, he devoted the years that followed to writing books and speaking wherever he could, "advancing the position of the Trotskyites in his never-ending attacks on the party." She recalled a New Jersey Historical Society meeting in the 1970s when he was invited to speak on the strike, and instead he spent two hours making it clear that he was not associated with the Communist party. "He was obsessed, and that was unfortunate because he never told his story."

304. Martha Asher to author, London, May 1988.

Selected Bibliography

A book by Edward Wagenknecht appeared in 1962 that described the American silent film and the author's long love affair with it—*The Movies in the Age of Innocence* (University of Oklahoma Press). The result was both informative and enchanting. I have echoed his title not just to cover the same epoch, but to deal with the kind of films young Wagenknecht would not, as a rule, have seen.

The long-awaited *American Film Institute Catalogue of Feature Films, 1911–1920* was published after I had written this manuscript, too late for me to take full advantage of its value. I have used it for checking the facts, but how many weeks of research it would have saved had it come out earlier! For besides listing casts, credits, and synopses, it provides references for reviews of the early films of four reels and over. No film historian can afford to be without it. Now we need a catalogue for films of three reels and under.

K. B.

Adams, Graham, Jr. *The Age of Industrial Violence, 1910–1915.* New York: Columbia University Press, 1966.

Addams, Jane. *The Second Twenty Years at Hull-House.* New York: Macmillan, 1930.

———. *The Spirit of Youth and the City Streets.* New York: Macmillan, 1909.

———. *Twenty Years at Hull-House.* New York: Macmillan, 1910.

Alexander, William. *Film on the Left.* Princeton University Press, 1981.

Alvarez, Max Joseph. *Index to Motion Pictures Reviewed by Variety, 1907–1980.* Metuchen, N. J.: Scarecrow Press, 1982.

Anderson, Clinton. *Beverly Hills Is My Beat.* London: W. H. Allen, 1960.

Anderson, Robert G. *Faces, Forms, Films.* New York: Castle Books, 1971.

Asbury, Herbert. *The French Quarter.* New York: Alfred A. Knopf, 1936.

———. *The Gangs of New York.* New York: Alfred A. Knopf, 1927.

Balio, Tino, ed. *The American Film Industry.* Madison: University of Wisconsin Press, 1976.

Bell, Geoffrey. *The Golden Gate and the Silver Screen.* East Brunswick, N.J.: Associated University Presses, 1984.

Bennett, Joan, and Lois Kibbee. *The Bennett Playbill.* New York: Holt, Rinehart and Winston, 1970.

Blaché, Roberta, and Simone Blaché, trans. *The Memoirs of Alice Guy Blaché.* Edited by Anthony Slide. Metuchen, N.J.: Scarecrow Press, 1986.

Blocker, Jack S., Jr. *Retreat from Reform.* Westport, Conn.: Greenwood Press, 1976.

Bowser, Eileen, ed. *Biograph Bulletins, 1908–1912.* New York: Octagon Books, 1973.

Brown, Karl. *Adventures with D. W. Griffith.* New York: Farrar, Straus and Giroux, 1973.

Brownlow, Kevin. *The War, The West, and the Wilderness.* New York: Alfred A. Knopf, 1978.

Buhle, Mari-Jo. *Women and American Socialism, 1870–1920.* Urbana, Ill.: University of Illinois Press, 1981.

Burnett, R. G. and E. D. Martell. *The Devil's Camera.* London: The Epworth Press, 1932.

Carringer, Robert L. *The Jazz Singer,* edited with an introduction by Robert L. Carringer. Madison: University of Wisconsin Press, 1979.

Case, Frank. *Do Not Disturb.* New York: Garden City Publishing, 1943.

The Cinema Report of the Cinema Commission of Enquiry. London: Williams and Norgate, 1917.

Clarens, Carlos. *Crime Movies.* New York: Norton, 1980.

Cooper, Miriam, with Bonnie Herndon. *Dark Lady of the Silents.* New York: Bobbs-Merrill, 1973.

Cripps, Thomas. *Slow Fade to Black.* New York; Oxford University Press, 1977.

Darrow, Clarence. *The Story of My Life.* New York: Charles Scribner's Sons, 1932.

Dash, Norman. *Yesterday's Los Angeles.* Miami, Fla.: E. A. Seemann Publishing, 1976.

Davis, Allen F. *Spearheads of Reform.* New York: Oxford University Press, 1967.

Dean, Joseph. *Hatred, Ridicule and Contempt, a Book of Libel Cases.* London: Constable, 1953.

De Jonge, Alex. *The Life and Times of Grigorii Rasputin.* New York: Coward, McCann and Geoghegan, 1982.

DeMille, Cecil B. *The Autobiography of Cecil B. DeMille.* Donald Hayne, ed. Englewood Cliffs, N.J.: Prentice Hall, 1959.

Doctorow, E. L. *Ragtime.* New York: Random House, 1975.

Drew, William M. *D. W. Griffith's Intolerance: Its Genesis and Its Vision.* Jefferson, N. C.: McFarland & Co., 1986.

Drinkwater, John. *The Life and Adventures of Carl Laemmle.* London: William Heinemann, 1931.

Dufty, William. *Sugar Blues.* New York: Warner Books, 1975.

Duster, Troy. *The Legislation of Morality.* New York: The Free Press, 1970.

Encyclopaedia Americana, International edition, Danbury, Conn.: Grolier, 1986.

Ernst, Morris, and Pare Lorentz. *Censored—The Private Life of the Movie.* New York: Jonathan Cape & Harrison Smith, 1930.

Everson, William K. *American Silent Film.* New York: Oxford University Press, 1978.

Fairchild, Henry Pratt. *Immigration.* New York: Macmillan 1913, 1925.

Featherling, Dale, and Doug Featherling, eds. *Carl Sandburg at the Movies: A Poet in the Silent Era, 1920–1927.* Metuchen, N.J.: Scarecrow Press, 1985.

Feldman, Charles. *National Board of Censorship (Review) of Motion Pictures.* New York: Arno Press, 1977.

The Film Index. New York: Museum of Modern Art Film Library and H. W. Wilson, 1941.

Flexner, Eleanor. *A Century of Struggle.* Cambridge, Mass.: Harvard University Press, 1975.

Freeman, Joseph. *An American Testament.* London: Victor Gollancz, 1938.

French, Philip. *The Movie Moguls.* London: Penguin, 1971.

Friedman, Jacob. *The Impeachment of Governor William Sulzer.* New York: Columbia University Press, 1939.

Friedman, Lester D. *Hollywood's Image of the Jew.* New York: Frederick Ungar, 1982.

Fülöp-Miller, René. *Rasputin, the Holy Devil.* New York: G. P. Putnam's Sons, 1928.

Gish, Lillian. *The Movies, Mr. Griffith, and Me.* Englewood Cliffs, N. J.: Prentice-Hall, 1969.

Goldberg, Judith N. *Laughter Through Tears.* East Brunswick, N.J.: Associated University Presses, 1973.

Goldman, Eric. A. "A World History of the Yiddish Cinema." Ph.D. dissertation for New York University Department of Cinema Studies, June 1979.

Goldman, Eric F. *Rendevous with Destiny.* New York: Vintage Books, 1955.

Grau, Robert. *Theatre of Science.* New York: Broadway Publishing, 1914.

Griffith, D. W. *The Rise and Fall of Free Speech in America.* Hollywood: Larry Edmunds Bookshop, reprinted 1967.

Guiles, Fred Laurence. *Marion Davies.* New York: McGraw-Hill, 1972.

Hampton, Benjamin B. *The History of the American Film Industry.* New York: Dover, 1970. (Originally *A History of the Movies,* New York: Covici-Friede, 1931.)

Hawkins, Hugh, ed. *Booker T. Washington and His Critics.* Lexington, Mass.: D. C. Heath, 1974.

Hayakawa, Sessue. *Zen Showed Me the Way.* Crosswell Brown, ed. London: Allen and Unwin, 1961.

Hecht, Ben. *A Child of the Century.* New York: Simon and Schuster, 1954.

Higham, Charles. *Cecil B. DeMille.* New York: Charles Scribner's Sons, 1973.

Hoover, Herbert. *The Memoirs of Herbert Hoover.* London: Hollis & Carter, 1952.

Inglis, Ruth A. *Freedom of the Movies.* Chicago: University of Chicago Press, 1947.

Iorizzo, Luciano J., and Salvatore Mondello. *The Italian Americans.* Boston: Twayne, 1980.

Iyenaga, T., and Kenoske Sato. *Japan and the California Problem.* New York: G. P. Putnam's Sons, 1921.

Jacobs, Lewis. *The Rise of the American Film.* New York: Columbia University Teachers College Press, 1968.

Johnston, Alva. *The Legendary Mizners.* New York: Farrar, Straus and Young, 1953.

Jones, Maldwyn A. *Destination America.* London: Weidenfeld and Nicolson, 1976.

Jowett, Garth, for the American Film Institute. *Film: The Democratic Art.* Boston: Little, Brown, 1976.

Kaplan, Justin. *Lincoln Steffens.* London: Jonathan Cape, 1975.

Katcher, Leo. *The Big Bankroll.* New York: Cardinal, 1961.

Katz, Ephraim. *The International Film Encyclopaedia.* London: Macmillan, 1979.

Lasky, Jesse with Don Weldon. *I Blow My Own Horn.* New York: Doubleday, 1957.

Lauritzen, Einar, and Gunnar Lundquist. *American Film Index, 1908–1915.* Stockholm, Sweden: Film-Index, 1976.

———. *American Film Index, 1916–1920.* Stockholm, Sweden: Film-Index, 1984.

Lawrence, Jerome. *Actor: The Life and Times of Paul Muni.* New York: G. P. Putnam's Sons, 1974.

Leab, Daniel J. *From Sambo to Superspade.* Boston: Houghton Mifflin, 1975.

Lens, Sidney. *The Labor Wars.* Garden City, N. Y.: Doubleday & Co., 1973.

———. *Poverty, Yesterday and Today.* New York: Thomas Y. Crowell, 1973.

Leuchtenburg, William E. *Perils of Prosperity.* Chicago: University of Chicago Press, 1958.

Leyda, Jay. *Kino.* London: George Allen and Unwin, 1960.

Lindsay, Vachel. *The Art of the Moving Picture.* New York: Liveright, reprinted 1970. (Originally published 1915.)

Lindsey, Judge Ben, and Rube Borough. *The Dangerous Life.* London: The Bodley Head, 1931.

Logan, Andy. *Against the Evidence.* London: Weidenfeld and Nicolson, 1970.

Lorentz, Pare. *Pare Lorentz on Film.* New York: Hopkinson and Blake, 1975.

Low, Rachel. *The History of the British Film.* London: George Allen and Unwin, 1950.

Luckett, Richard. *The White Generals.* London: Longman, 1971.

Lynd, Robert S., and Helen Merrell Lynd. *Middletown.* New York: Harcourt, Brace, 1929.

Maltin, Leonard. *The Art of the Cinematographer.* New York: Dover Publications, 1978.

Marston, William, Jr. *Motion Picture Problems.* New York: Avondale Press, 1929.

Marx, Sam, *Mayer and Thalberg.* London: W. H. Allen, 1976.

Mast, Gerald, ed. *The Movies in Our Midst.* Chicago: University of Chicago Press, 1982.

May, Lary. *Screening Out the Past.* New York: Oxford University Press, 1980.

McKelvey, Blake. *American Prisons.* Montclair, N.J.: Paterson Smith, 1977.

Merz, Charles. *The Dry Decade.* New York: Doubleday, 1930. (Reprinted 1969 by the University of Washington Press, Seattle.)

Morris, Lloyd. *Not So Long Ago.* New York: Random House, 1949.

———. *Postscript to Yesterday.* New York: Random House, 1947.

Mowry, George E. *The Twenties.* Englewood Cliffs, N.J.: Prentice-Hall, 1963.

Nash, Jay Robert. *Murder, America.* London: Harrap, 1981.

Nesbit, Evelyn. *The Untold Story.* London: John Long, 1934.

O'Neill, William. *Everyone Was Brave.* Chicago: Quadrangle Books, 1969.

Palmer, A. W. *A Dictionary of Modern History.* London: Penguin, 1964.

Petersen, William. *The Chinese and Japanese. Essays and Data on American Ethnic Groups.* Edited by Thomas Sowell. Harvard Urban Institute, 1978.

Pfau, Pamela, and Kenneth Marx. *The Times We Had. Marion Davies.* London: Angus and Robertson, 1976.

Pitkin, Thomas Monroe. *Keepers of the Gate: A History of Ellis Island.* New York: New York University Press, 1975.

Quigley, Martin. *Decency in Motion Pictures.* New York: Macmillan, 1937.

Ramsaye, Terry. *A Million and One Nights.* London: Frank Cass, reprinted 1964. (Originally published by Simon and Schuster, 1926.)

Randal, William Pierce. *The Ku Klux Klan: A Century of Infamy.* London: Hamish Hamilton, 1965.

Randall, Richard S. *Censorship of the Movies.* Madison: University of Wisconsin Press, 1968.

Reichenbach, Harry. *Phantom Fame.* New York: Simon and Schuster, 1931.

Riley, Veronica, and Paul Riley. *Problems of Modern American Crime.* London: Heath Cranton, 1926.

Roche, John P. *The Quest for the Dream.* New York: Macmillan, 1963.

Rosenberg, Bernard, and Harry Silverstein. *The Real Tinsel.* New York: Macmillan, 1970.

Rosow, Eugene. *Born to Lose.* New York: Oxford University Press, 1978.

Rubin, Jacob. *Moscow Mirage.* London: Geoffrey Bles, 1935.

Sanger, Margaret. *An Autobiography by Margaret Sanger.* New York: Dover, 1938. (Reprinted 1971.)

Schickel, Richard. *D. W. Griffith, An American Life.* London: Pavilion Books, 1984.

———. *His Picture in the Papers.* New York· Charterhouse, 1973.

———. *The Men Who Made the Movies.* New York: Atheneum, 1975.

Schulberg, Budd. *Moving Pictures.* New York: Souvenir Press, 1981.

Seabury, William Marston. *Motion Picture Problems.* New York: Avondale Press, 1929.

Sherwood, Robert, ed. *The Best Moving Pictures of 1922–1923.* Boston: Small, Maynard, 1923.

Short, Martin. *Crime Inc.* London: Thames-Methuen, 1984.

Short, William H. *A Generation of Moving Pictures.* New York: The National Committee for the Study of Social Values in Motion Pictures, 1928, reprinted by Garland Publishing, 1978.

Silva, Fred, ed. *Focus on The Birth of a Nation.* Englewood Cliffs, N.J.: Prentice-Hall, 1971.

Silver, Gary, ed. *The Dope Chronicles.* San Francisco: Harper & Row, 1979.

Sinclair, Upton. *Autobiography of Upton Sinclair.* London: W. H. Allen, 1960.

———. *The Jungle.* London: Penguin, 1982.

———. *Upton Sinclair Presents William Fox.* Los Angeles: published by the author, 1933.

Sklar, Robert. *Movie Made America.* New York: Random House, 1975.

Sleeper, Jim. *Great Movies Shot in Orange County.* Trabuco Canyon: California Classics, 1980.

Slide, Anthony. *Early American Cinema.* New York: A. S. Barnes, 1970.

———and Edward Wagenknecht. *Fifty Great American Films.* New York: Dover Publications, 1980.

———. *The Kindergarten of the Movies: A History of the Fine Arts Company.* Metuchen, N. J.: Scarecrow Press, 1980.

———. *Selected Film Criticism, 1896–1911.* Metuchen, N.J.: The Scarecrow Press, 1982.

Starks, Michael. *Cocaine Fiends and Reefer Madness.* East Brunswick, N.J.: Cornwall Books, 1982.

Steffens, Lincoln. *The Shame of the Cities.* Boston: McClure, Phillips, 1904. (Reprinted by Hill and Wang, 1957.)

———. *Upbuilders.* New York: Doubleday, Page, 1909. (Reprinted by the University of Washington Press, 1968.)

Stewart, Donald Ogden. *By a Stroke of Luck.* London: Paddington Press, 1975.

Thaw, Evelyn. *The Story of My Life.* London: John Long, 1914.

Theimer, Walter. *The Penguin Political Dictionary.* London: Penguin, 1939.

Thernstrom, Stephan, ed. *Harvard Encyclopedia of American Ethnic Groups.* Cambridge, Mass.: Harvard University Press, 1980.

Thomas, Augustus. *The Print of My Remembrance.* New York: Charles Scribner's Sons, 1922.

Thomas, Bob. *King Cohn.* New York: G. P. Putnam's Sons, 1967.

Ulam, Adam. *Russia's Failed Revolutions.* London: Weidenfeld and Nicolson, 1981.

Vidor, King. *On Film Making.* New York: David McKay, 1972.

———. *A Tree Is a Tree.* London: Longmans Green, 1954.

Walker, William O., III. *Drug Control in the Americas.* Albuquerque: University of New Mexico Press, 1981.

Walker, Alexander. *Rudolph Valentino*. London: Elm Tree Books, 1976.

———. *The Shattered Silents*. London: Elm Tree Books, 1978.

———. *Stardom, The Hollywood Phenomenon*. London: Michael Joseph, 1970.

Walsh, Raoul. *Each Man in His Time*. New York: Farrar, Straus and Giroux, 1974.

Warner, Jack L. *My First Hundred Years*. New York: Random House, 1964.

Wenden, D. C. *The Birth of the Movies*. New York: E. P. Dutton, 1975.

Wheeler, Keith. *The Railroaders*. New York: Time-Life Books, 1973.

Williams, Blanche Colton, ed. *O. Henry Memorial Award: Prize Stories, 1919*. Garden City, N.Y.: Society of Arts and Sciences, 1921.

Wood, Leslie. *Miracle of the Movies*. London: Burke Publishing Company, 1947.

Wood, Stephen B. *Constitutional Politics in the Progressive Era*. Chicago: University of Chicago Press, 1968.

Yezierska, Anzia. *Red Ribbon on a White Horse*. New York: Charles Scribner's Sons, 1950.

Index

A NOTE ABOUT THE AUTHOR

Kevin Brownlow, who lives in London, is a historian of silent
films, which he began collecting at the age of eleven. He has written
about them in *The Parade's Gone By . . . ; The War, the West and the Wilderness;
Hollywood: The Pioneers;* and *Napoleon: Abel Gance's Classic Film,* which recounted
his acclaimed reconstruction of that famous masterpiece. As a filmmaker,
he has made two features with Andrew Mollo—*It Happened Here* and
Winstanley—and several television documentaries with David Gill,
including the thirteen-part series *Hollywood,* first shown in
1980, and more recently *Unknown Chaplin, Buster Keaton:
A Hard Act to Follow,* and *Harold Lloyd:
The Third Genius.*

A NOTE ON THE TYPE

This book was set in a typeface called Garamond No. 3.
Jean Jannon has been identified as the designer of this face,
which is based on Garamond's original models but is much lighter
and more open. The italic is taken from a font of Granjon, which
appeared in the repertory of the Imprimerie Royale and was
probably cut in the middle of the sixteenth century.

Composed by Creative Graphics, Inc.,
Allentown, Pennsylvania
Printed and bound by Halliday Lithographers,
West Hanover, Massachusetts
Designed by Mia Vander Els